BLAKE'S POETRY

AUTHORITATIVE TEXTS

ILLUMINATIONS IN COLOR AND MONOCHROME

RELATED PROSE

CRITICISM

W. W. NORTON & COMPANY, INC.
also publishes

THE NORTON ANTHOLOGY OF AMERICAN LITERATURE
edited by Ronald Gottesman et al.

THE NORTON ANTHOLOGY OF ENGLISH LITERATURE
edited by M. H. Abrams et al.

THE NORTON ANTHOLOGY OF MODERN POETRY
edited by Richard Ellmann and Robert O'Clair

THE NORTON ANTHOLOGY OF POETRY
edited by Arthur M. Eastman et al.

THE NORTON ANTHOLOGY OF SHORT FICTION
edited by R. V. Cassill

THE NORTON ANTHOLOGY OF WORLD MASTERPIECES
edited by Maynard Mack et al.

THE NORTON FACSIMILE OF
THE FIRST FOLIO OF SHAKESPEARE
prepared by Charlton Hinman

THE NORTON INTRODUCTION TO LITERATURE
edited by Carl E. Bain, Jerome Beaty, and J. Paul Hunter

THE NORTON READER
edited by Arthur M. Eastman et al.

A NORTON CRITICAL EDITION

BLAKE'S POETRY AND DESIGNS

AUTHORITATIVE TEXTS
ILLUMINATIONS IN COLOR
AND MONOCHROME

RELATED PROSE

CRITICISM

Selected and Edited by

MARY LYNN JOHNSON
GEORGIA STATE UNIVERSITY

JOHN E. GRANT
THE UNIVERSITY OF IOWA

W · W · NORTON & COMPANY
New York *London*

ACKNOWLEDGMENTS

William Blake: excerpts and selected letters, collated as indicated with other editions, from *The Complete Writings of William Blake*, edited by Geoffrey Keynes (Oxford University Press, 1966).

Harold Bloom: from *The Visionary Company*. Copyright © 1961 by Harold Bloom. Copyright © 1971 by Cornell University. Reprinted by permission of Cornell University Press.

Samuel Taylor Coleridge: extract from letter of February 12, 1818, to C. A. Tulk, from *Collected Letters of Samuel Taylor Coleridge*, edited by Earl Leslie Griggs, Vol. IV (Oxford University Press, 1959).

T. S. Eliot: from "William Blake," in *Selected Essays*, New Edition. Copyright © 1932, 1936, 1950 Harcourt Brace Jovanovich, Inc.; copyright © 1960, 1964 T. S. Eliot. Reprinted by permission of Harcourt Brace Jovanovich, Inc., and Faber and Faber Ltd.

David V. Erdman: from "America: New Expanses," in *Blake's Visionary Forms Dramatic*, edited by David V. Erdman and John E. Grant. Copyright © 1970 Princeton University Press. Reprinted by permission of Princeton University Press.

Northrop Frye: "Blake's Treatment of the Archetype," from *English Institute Essays, 1950*, edited by Alan S. Downer (Columbia University Press, 1951). Reprinted by permission of the author and the publisher.

Robert F. Gleckner: "Point of View and Context in Blake's Songs," *Bulletin of the New York Public Library* 61 (1957). Reprinted by permission of the author and the publisher.

Jean H. Hagstrum: "Innocence and Experience," from *William Blake: Poet and Painter*, pp. 78–87. Copyright © 1964, University of Chicago Press. Reprinted by permission of the author and the publisher.

Charles Lamb: letter to Bernard Barton, May 15, 1824, in *Blake Records*, edited by G. E. Bentley, Jr. (Oxford University Press, 1969).

Martin K. Nurmi: from *Blake's Marriage of Heaven and Hell: A Critical Study*, Research Series III of the *Kent State University Bulletin*, 45, no. 4 (April, 1957), pp. 14–23, 28–29, 59–61. Reprinted by permission of the author and Haskell House Publishers.

Martin Price: from "The Standard of Energy," in *To the Palace of Wisdom: Studies in Order and Energy from Dryden to Blake* (Doubleday Anchor, 1965). Reprinted by permission of the author.

E. J. Rose: from "The Symbolism of the Opened Center and Poetic Theory in Blake's *Jerusalem*," *Studies in English Literature*, 5 (1965). Reprinted in abridged form by permission of the author.

Frederick Tatham: from "Life of Blake," in *Blake Records*, edited by G. E. Bentley (Oxford University Press, 1969). Reprinted by permission of Oxford University Press.

Irene Tayler: "The Woman Scaly," *Bulletin of the Midwest Modern Language Association*, 6 (Spring 1973). Reprinted by permission of the author and the Editor, *Bulletin of the Midwest MLA*.

Sources of pictorial reproductions are acknowledged in the "List of Illustrations"; published by permission of Auckland Public Library, Bodleian Library, Blake Trust, British Library, British Museum, Cincinnati Art Museum, Fitzwilliam Museum, Houghton Library, Library of Congress, Metropolitan Museum of Art, New York Public Library, Pierpont Morgan Library, Princeton University Library, and Mr. and Mrs. Paul Mellon.

Library of Congress Cataloging in Publication Data
Blake, William, 1757–1827.
Blake's poetry and designs.
(A Norton critical edition)
Bibliography: p.
Includes indexes.
I. Johnson, Mary Lynn. II. Grant, John Ernest. III. Title.
PR4141.5.J64 821'.1 78-20958
ISBN 0-393-04487-4
ISBN 0-393-09083-3 pbk.

Published simultaneously in Canada by George J. McLeod Limited, Toronto.
Printed in the United States of America.

FIRST EDITION

1 2 3 4 5 6 7 8 9 0

Contents

List of Illustrations xiii
Preface xxiii
Chronology xxviii
Map: Blake's Britain xxxix
Map: Blake's London, 1757–1827 xl
Map: The Holy Land xlii
A Note on the Texts xliii

The Texts of the Poems xlvii

List of Key Terms xlviii

Poems and Prophecies
From Poetical Sketches 1
To Spring 1
To Summer 2
To Autumn 2
To Winter 3
To the Evening Star 3
To Morning 4
Song: "How sweet I roam'd" 4
Song: "My silks and fine array" 4
Song: "Love and harmony combine" 5
Song: "I love the jocund dance" 5
Song: "Memory, hither come" 6
Mad Song 6
Song: "Fresh from the dewy hill" 7
Song: "When early morn walks forth" 8
To the Muses 8
Prologue: Intended for a Dramatic Piece of *King Edward IV* 9
Prologue to *King John* 9
A War Song to Englishmen 10
[Poems Written in a Copy of *Poetical Sketches*]
Song by a Shepherd 11
Song by an Old Shepherd 11

All Religions Are One (Illuminated Book) 12
There Is No Natural Religion (Illuminated Book) 14
Songs of Innocence and of Experience (Illuminated Book) 15
Songs of Innocence
Introduction 19
The Shepherd 20
The Ecchoing Green 20
The Lamb 21
The Little Black Boy 22
The Blossom 25
The Chimney Sweeper 25
The Little Boy Lost 26
The Little Boy Found 27
Laughing Song 27
A Cradle Song 28
The Divine Image 30
Holy Thursday 32
Night 33
Spring 34
Nurse's Song 35
Infant Joy 35
A Dream 36
On Another's Sorrow 36
Songs of Experience 40
Introduction 40
Earth's Answer 41
The Clod & the Pebble 42
Holy Thursday 42
The Little Girl Lost 43
The Little Girl Found 44
The Chimney Sweeper 46
Nurse's Song 47
The Sick Rose 47
The Fly 48
The Angel 49
The Tyger 49
My Pretty Rose Tree 50
Ah! Sun-Flower 51
The Lilly 51
The Garden of Love 51
The Little Vagabond 52
London 53
The Human Abstract 53
Infant Sorrow 54

A Poison Tree 55
A Little Boy Lost 56
A Little Girl Lost 57
To Tirzah 58
The School-Boy 59
The Voice of the Ancient Bard 60
A Divine Image 60
The Book of Thel (Illuminated Book) 60
Visions of the Daughters of Albion (Illuminated Book) 68
The Marriage of Heaven and Hell (Illuminated Book) 81
America: A Prophecy (Illuminated Book) 102
Europe: A Prophecy (Illuminated Book) 121
The Song of Los (Illuminated Book) 134
Africa 135
Asia 137
The Book of Urizen (Illuminated Book) 140
The Book of Ahania (Illuminated Book) 160
The Book of Los (Illuminated Book) 168
Poems from Blake's Notebook 175
I. Working Drafts
London (Drafts ca. 1792) 176
London (Printed version, 1794) 177
The Tyger (Drafts, ca. 1792) 178
The Tyger (Printed version, 1794) 179
Infant Sorrow (Drafts, of uncertain date) 180
Infant Sorrow (Printed version, 1794) 182
II. A Projected Plate
"O lapwing thou fliest around the heath" 182
An answer to the parson 182
[Experiment]: "Thou hast a lap full of seed" 182
Riches 183
"If you trap the moment before its ripe" 183
III. Vision
Eternity 183
"Since all the Riches of this World" 183
To God 183
To Nobodaddy 183
"If it is True What the Prophets write" 184
"The Hebrew Nation did not write it" 184
"Some Men created for destruction come" 184
"You dont believe I wont attempt to make ye" 184
"Mock on Mock on Voltaire Rousseau" 184
"I will tell you what Joseph of Arimathea" 185
Merlins prophecy 185

An ancient Proverb 185
"The sword sung on the barren heath" 185
"Why should I care for the men of thames" 185
"Who will exchange his own fire side" 186
"Let the Brothels of Paris be opened" 186
"Great Men & Fools do often me Inspire" 186
"Her whole Life is an Epigram . . ." 187
"The Errors of a Wise Man make your Rule" 187
Lacedemonian Instruction 187
Motto to the Songs of Innocence & of Experience 187
"Anger & Wrath my bosom rends" 187
"The Angel that presided oer my birth" 187
"I am no Homers Hero you all know" 187
"I heard an Angel singing" 187
"Terror in the house does roar" 188
"Great things are done when Men & Mountains meet" 188
"When Klopstock England defied" 188
Day 189
Morning 189

IV. Love: The Sexes

"What is it men in women do require" 189
"Abstinence sows sand all over" 189
"In a wife I would desire" 190
"When a Man has Married a Wife" 190
"A Woman Scaly & a Man all Hairy" 190
"Why was Cupid a Boy" 190
How to know Love from Deceit 190
"The look of love alarms" 191
"Soft deceit & Idleness" 191
"Silent Silent Night" 191
"Are not the joys of morning sweeter" 191

V. Love: Stories

The Fairy 191
"Never pain to tell thy love" 192
"I feard the fury of my wind" 192
"I saw a chapel all of gold" 192
"I laid me down upon a bank" 193
"I asked a thief to steal me a peach" 193
Soft Snow 193
"An old maid early eer I knew" 193
"Grown old in Love from Seven Times Seven" 194
The Washer Womans Song 194
A cradle song 194
To my Mirtle 194

"My Spectre around me night & day" 195
[Related stanzas] 196
The Birds 197
VI. Art and Artists
"Now Art has lost its mental Charms" 197
To the Queen 198
"The Caverns of the Grave Ive seen" 198
"I rose up in the dawn of day" 199
"You say their Pictures well Painted be" 199
Blakes apology for his Catalogue 199
English Encouragement of Art 200
"The only man that eer I knew" 200
"Madman I have been calld . . ." 200
The Pickering Manuscript 200
The Smile 201
The Golden Net 202
The Mental Traveller 202
The Land of Dreams 205
Mary 206
The Crystal Cabinet 207
The Grey Monk 208
Auguries of Innocence 209
Long John Brown & Little Mary Bell 212
William Bond 212
From The Four Zoas 214
Milton (Illuminated Book) 234
From Jerusalem (Illuminated Book) 308
The Ghost of Abel (Illuminated Book) 359
The Everlasting Gospel 364
"There is not one moral virtue . . ." 364
"If Moral Virtue was Christianity" 364
"What can this Gospel of Jesus be?" 365
"Was Jesus Born of a Virgin Pure" 366
"Was Jesus Humble . . ." 366
"Was Jesus gentle . . ." 368
"Was Jesus Chaste . . ." 369
"The Vision of Christ that thou dost see" 372
To the Accuser who is The God of This World 373

Related Prose
An Island in the Moon 374
Prospectus: To the Public 395
From A Descriptive Catalogue and [An Advertisement] 396
From A Vision of the Last Judgment 408

A Public Address to the Chalcographic Society 417
The Laocoön (Yah and His Two Sons) 425
On Homer's Poetry 428
On Virgil 428
Blake's Marginalia 429
On John Casper Lavater, *Aphorisms on Man* (ca. 1789) 430
On Emanuel Swedenborg, *The Wisdom of Angels, Concerning Divine Love and Divine Wisdom* (1788) 431
On R. Watson, Bishop of Llandoff, *An Apology for the Bible . . . addressed to Thomas Paine* (1797) 432
On Francis Bacon, *Essays Moral, Economical and Political* (1798) 437
On Henry Boyd, *A Translation of "The Inferno" in English Verse, with Historical Notes* (1785) 438
On *The Works of Sir Joshua Reynolds, Knight,* Edited by Edmund Malone (3 volumes) (1798) 438
On George Berkeley, *Siris: A Chain of Philosophical Reflections* (1744) 444
On William Wordsworth, Preface to *The Excursion, Being A Portion of the Recluse, A Poem* (1814) 445
On William Wordsworth, *Poems: Including Lyrical Ballads,* Vol. I (1815) 446
On Robert John Thornton, *The Lord's Prayer, Newly Translated* (1827) 446
Blake's Letters
To the Reverend Dr. John Trusler, August 23, 1799 448
To William Hayley, May 6, 1800 449
To George Cumberland, July 2, 1800 450
To John Flaxman, September 12, 1800 451
To William Hayley, September 16, 1800 452
To Thomas Butts, September 23, 1800 453
To Thomas Butts, October 2, 1800 454
To Thomas Butts, January 10, 1802 456
To Thomas Butts, November 22, 1802 459
To Thomas Butts, November 22, 1802 (second letter) 460
To James Blake, January 30, 1803 462
To Thomas Butts, April 25, 1803 465
To Thomas Butts, August 16, 1803 467

Blake's Memorandum, August 1803 470
To William Hayley, October 7, 1803 472
To William Hayley, October 23, 1804 473
To William Hayley, December 11, 1805 475
To Dawson Turner, June 9, 1818 476
To George Cumberland, April 12, 1827 477

Criticism

Comments by Contemporaries
Samuel Taylor Coleridge · Letter to C. A. Tulk, February 12, 1818 481
Charles Lamb · Letter to Bernard Barton, May 15, 1824 483
John Thomas Smith · *From* Nollekens and his Times (1828) 484
Frederick Tatham · *From* "Life of Blake" (1832?) 489
Henry Crabb Robinson · *From* Reminiscences (1852) 496
Samuel Palmer · Letter to Alexander Gilchrist, August 23, 1855 502

Twentieth-Century Criticism
T. S. Eliot · William Blake 507
Northrop Frye · Blake's Treatment of the Archetype 510
Jean H. Hagstrum · [On Innocence and Experience] 525
Robert F. Gleckner · Point of View and Context in Blake's Songs 533
Irene Tayler · The Woman Scaly 538
Martin K. Nurmi · [On *The Marriage of Heaven and Hell*] 553
Martin Price · The Standard of Energy 565
David V. Erdman · *America:* New Expanses 577
Harold Bloom · [On *Milton*] 588
E. J. Rose · The Symbolism of the Opened Center and Poetic Theory in Blake's *Jerusalem* 594

Bibliography 602

Index of Titles and First Lines 609

List of Illustrations

EXPLANATION OF PLATE NUMBERS AND COPY DESIGNATIONS

Because Blake was a professional engraver as well as a poet and painter, he was able to act as his own publisher by using an innovative process which he called "illuminated printing." To make a typical page in one of his illuminated books, Blake incorporated words and pictures into a total design which he etched on a copper plate, printed on fine paper, and then colored by hand. To refer to either a line of poetry or a design in one of these books, scholars cite the number of the plate from which the page was printed. Further, since *each* copy of each illuminated book is unique because of different inking and printing and variations of details touched up by hand, scholars refer to individual copies by letter designations when they wish to discuss specific details in a particular copy. Thus *Songs* 39, Copy Z, refers to "The Sick Rose," the poem and picture printed from plate 39 of *Songs of Innocence and of Experience*, in the version of this page which appears in Copy Z (which happens to be a particularly beautiful copy in the Lessing J. Rosenwald Collection of the Library of Congress).

Occasionally this numbering system may seem puzzling; for example, the captions for our color plates 3 and 4 refer to two versions of the second page of "The Little Black Boy" as plate 30 and plate 10 respectively. The reason for this difference in plate numbers is that our color plate 3 is taken from a copy of *Songs of Innocence* (1789), in which "The Little Black Boy" appears on plates 29 and 30, but our color plate 4 comes from a copy of the later work, *Songs of Innocence and of Experience* (1794), which has a different ordering of plates. The reader should understand, moreover, that this system is not of Blake's own invention, but merely a classification device for keeping track of the variety of his illuminated books, like the call numbers that distinguish printed editions of his writings in libraries. These conventional plate numbers and copy designations are used in this list and throughout this book, according to the usage of Blake scholars everywhere.

Our plate numbers (which immediately follow Blake's titles in this list) and our alphabetical reference system for the various copies of his books (A, B, C, etc.) are those of Geoffrey Keynes and Edwin Wolf II in *William Blake's Illuminated Books: A Census* (New York: Grolier Club, 1953). Blake's plates are numbered differently in different copies of his books, but the numeration adopted in the *Census* has become standardized; it is also followed, with modifications, by David V. Erdman in *The Illuminated Blake* (Garden City, N.Y.: Doubleday, 1970), and by G. E. Bentley, Jr. in *Blake Books* (Oxford: Clarendon, 1977).

We have made an exception in the case of *Milton* because the standardized reference system does not provide numbers for most of the full-page illustrations. In this list our plate numbers for *Milton* follow copy D, as in *The Illuminated Blake*, but references to the plate numbers of the *Census* and to plate numbers used in the standard editions are also provided in parentheses (see the headnote to *Milton*, p. 236). In the text itself, plate numbers correspond to the standard editions. We follow Keynes and Erdman in providing dual plate numbers for one section of *Jerusalem* (see the headnote to *Jerusalem*, p. 311).

"Blake Trust" refers to the series of hand-colored facsimiles produced and published under the supervision of Arnold Fawcus, by the Trianon Press, Paris and Jura, for the William Blake Trust, London; some of our reproductions are taken from this series.

The plate sizes listed are approximate measurements of the picture area, exclusive of ornamental framing lines or borders.

We are grateful to the libraries, museums, and private owners acknowledged in the following list for permission to reproduce photographs of plates from Blake's illuminated books in their collections.

COLOR PLATES

The relationship of these plates to Blake's poems is indicated by the insertion of footnotes at appropriate points in the text. Especially in *Urizen*, *Milton*, and *Jerusalem*, the reader should not expect to find a direct illustrative relationship between design and text. In all works, but most noticably in these, Blake's sequences of words and pictures are elaborately orchestrated: in some designs the pictures at least partly illustrate the accompanying text, but often the most closely related words and pictures appear on different plates. We have sought to include poems and pictures which are excellent in themselves as well as exemplary of Blake's major themes. Blake often rearranged his pages and placed full-page designs next to different texts to vary his effects; the reader should feel free, in imagination, to do the same and to look for correspondences between words and pictures in addition to those we have suggested in the captions to the color plates. (The plates follow page 304.)

1. *Songs of Innocence and of Experience* 1. General title page. Copy U. Princeton University Library, Department of Rare Books and Special Collections. 4 5/16″ by 2 11/16″.

2. *Songs* 2. Frontispiece to *Innocence*. Copy Z (Blake Trust). Lessing J. Rosenwald Collection, Library of Congress. 4 5/16″ by 2 11/16″.

3. *Songs* 10. "The Little Black Boy." Second page. *Innocence* 30, Copy B (Blake Trust). Lessing J. Rosenwald Collection, Library of Congress. 4 5/16″ by 2 3/4″.

4. *Songs* 10. "The Little Black Boy." Second page. Copy V. Thorne Collection, Pierpont Morgan Library. 4 5/16″ by 2 3/4″.

5. *Songs* 25. "Infant Joy." Copy Z (Blake Trust). Lessing J. Rosenwald Collection, Library of Congress. 4 3/8″ by 2 11/16″.

6. *Songs* 28. Frontispiece to *Experience*. Copy Z (Blake Trust). Lessing J. Rosenwald Collection, Library of Congress. 4 5/16″ by 2 3/4."

7. *Songs* 34. "The Little Girl Lost." Copy Z (Blake Trust). Lessing J. Rosenwald Collection, Library of Congress. 4 7/16″ by 2 9/16″.

8. *Songs* 39. "The Sick Rose." Copy Z (Blake Trust). Lessing J. Rosenwald Collection, Library of Congress. 4 3/8″ by 2 5/8″.

9. *The Book of Thel* ii. Title page. Copy N. Cincinnati Art Museum. Mr. and Mrs. John J. Emery, donors. 6 1/8″ by 4 3/16″.

10. *Visions of the Daughters of Albion* i. Frontispiece. Copy P. Fitzwilliam Museum, Cambridge. 6 3/4″ by 4 3/4″.

11. *Visions* ii. Title page. Copy P. Fitzwilliam Museum, Cambridge. 6 7/16″ by 5″.

12. *Visions* iii. "Argument." Copy P. Fitzwilliam Museum, Cambridge. 5 3/8″ by 4 1/8″

13. *The Marriage of Heaven and Hell* 1. Title page. Copy G. The Houghton Library, Harvard University. 5 7/8″ by 4″.

14. *Marriage* 3. Copy G. The Houghton Library, Harvard University. 5 7/8″ by 4 1/8″.

15. *America: A Prophecy* ii. Title page. Copy O. Fitzwilliam Museum, Cambridge. Reduced from 8 11/16″ by 6 15/16″.

16. *America* 7. Copy O. Fitzwilliam Museum, Cambridge. Reduced from 8 11/16″ by 6 7/16″.

17. *Europe: A Prophecy* i. Frontispece ("Ancient of Days"). Copy K. Fitzwilliam Museum, Cambridge. Reduced from 9 1/8″ by 6 11/16″.

18. *Europe* ii. Title page. Copy K. Fitzwilliam Museum, Cambridge. Reduced from 9″ by 6 1/2″.

19. *The Book of Urizen* 1. Title page. Copy G (Blake Trust). Lessing J. Rosenwald Collection, Library of Congress. 5 7/8″ by 4 1/16″.

20. *Urizen* 21. Copy G (Blake Trust). Lessing J. Rosenwald Collection, Library of Congress. 6 1/2″ by 4 1/16″.

21. *Urizen* 22. Copy G (Blake Trust). Lessing J. Rosenwald Collection, Library of Congress. 6 1/8″ by 4″.

22. *Milton: A Poem* 1. Title page. Copy C. Lenox Collection, Rare Book Division, New York Public Library. 6 5/16″ by 4 7/16″.

23. *Milton* 47 (43, *Census* 21). Copy C. Lenox Collection, Rare Book Division, New York Public Library. 6 5/16″ by 4 3/8″.

24. *Jerusalem: The Emanation of the Giant Albion* 1. Frontispiece. Copy E (Blake Trust). Collection of Mr. Paul Mellon. Reduced from 8 9/16″ by 6 1/4″.

25. *Jerusalem* 2. Title page. Copy E (Blake Trust). Collection of Mr. Paul Mellon. Reduced from 8 5/8″ by 6 1/4″.

26. *Jerusalem* 6. Copy E (Blake Trust). Collection of Mr. Paul Mellon. Reduced from 8 5/8″ by 6 5/16″.

27. *Jerusalem* 25. Copy E (Blake Trust). Collection of Mr. Paul Mellon. Reduced from 8 9/16″ by 6 5/16″.

28. *Jerusalem* 32 (46). Copy E (Blake Trust). Collection of Mr. Paul Mellon. Reduced from 8 5/8″ by 6 5/16″.

29. *Jerusalem* 46 (41). Copy E (Blake Trust). Collection of Mr. Paul Mellon. Reduced from 8 11/16″ by 6 5/16″.

30. *Jerusalem* 76. Copy E (Blake Trust). Collection of Mr. Paul Mellon. Reduced from 8 13/16″ by 6 7/16″.

31. *Jerusalem* 99. Copy E (Blake Trust). Collection of Mr. Paul Mellon. Reduced from 8 15/16″ by 6 1/16″.

32. *Jerusalem* 100. Tailpiece. Copy E (Blake Trust). Collection of Mr. Paul Mellon. Reduced from 8 3/4″ by 5 3/4″.

BLACK-AND-WHITE ILLUSTRATIONS

Each of Blake's illuminated books is meant to be seen as a whole. Although some designs appear without an accompanying text, scarcely any full-page text is altogether lacking in ornamentation. No reasonably priced edition can do full justice to Blake's unique form of publication, as may be appreciated from the thirty-two color plates in this book. To give some idea of Blake's intentions, however, we have embellished the text with monochrome reproductions and line cuts of closely related designs, with the size and placement of the designs adjusted to the pagination of this edition. For further study, readers will need to consult facsimiles and microfilms of the originals. (In the following list, the numbers on the right-hand side indicate the pages on which the illustrations fall.)

Songs of Innocence and of Experience 3. Title page for *Innocence*. Electrotype—exact duplicate of Blake's plate—from Alexander Gilchrist, *Life of William Blake*, 1863. 18

Songs 6. "The Ecchoing Green," first page. Gilchrist electrotype. 20

Songs 7. "The Ecchoing Green," second page. Copy Z. Lessing J. Rosenwald Collection, Library of Congress. 21

Songs 8. "The Lamb." Gilchrist electrotype. 22

Songs 9. "The Little Black Boy," first page. *Innocence*, Copy B. Lessing J. Rosenwald Collection, Library of Congress. 22

Songs 11. "The Blossom." *Innocence*, Copy B. Lessing J. Rosenwald Collection, Library of Congress. 24

Songs 12. "The Chimney Sweeper." Bottom detail. *Innocence*, Copy B. Lessing J. Rosenwald Collection, Library of Congress. 26

Songs 15. "Laughing Song." Top detail. Copy Z. Lessing J. Rosenwald Collection, Library of Congress. 27

Songs 17. "A Cradle Song," second page. Bottom detail. Copy Z. Lessing J. Rosenwald Collection, Library of Congress. 29

Songs 18. "The Divine Image." Gilchrist electrotype. 31

Songs 19. "Holy Thursday." Top detail: *Innocence* 23, Copy S. Beverly Chew Collection, Cincinnati Art Museum. Bottom detail: *Songs*, Copy S. Collection of Mr. and Mrs. John J. Emery, Cincinnati Art Museum. 32

Songs 24. "Nurse's Song," *Innocence*. Gilchrist electrotype. 35

Songs 29. Title page for *Experience*. Copy Z. Lessing J. Rosenwald Collection, Library of Congress. 38

Songs 30. "Introduction" to *Experience*. Copy Z. Lessing J. Rosenwald Collection, Library of Congress. 39

Songs 36. "The Little Girl Found," second page. Bottom detail. Gilchrist electrotype. 45

Songs 37. "The Chimney Sweeper," *Experience*. Bottom detail. Copy Z. Lessing J. Rosenwald Collection, Library of Congress. 46

Songs 38. "Nurse's Song," *Experience*. Bottom detail. Copy Z. Lessing J. Rosenwald Collection, Library of Congress. 47

Songs 40. "The Fly." Bottom detail. Copy Z. Lessing J. Rosenwald Collection, Library of Congress. 48

Songs 42. "The Tyger." Bottom detail. Copy Y. Metropolitan Museum of Art, New York City. 50

Songs 46. "London." Top detail. Gilchrist electrotype. 52

Songs 47. "The Human Abstract." Bottom detail. Gilchrist electrotype. 54

Songs 48. "Infant Sorrow." Bottom detail. Gilchrist electrotype. 55

Songs 52. "To Tirzah." Bottom detail. Unidentified copy, widely reproduced. 58

The Book of Thel 1. Top detail. Copy O. Lessing J. Rosenwald Collection, Library of Congress. 62

Thel 2. Bottom detail. Copy O. Lessing J. Rosenwald Collection, Library of Congress. 64

Thel 4. Top detail. Copy O. Lessing J. Rosenwald Collection, Library of Congress. 65

Thel 5. Bottom detail. Copy O. Lessing J. Rosenwald Collection, Library of Congress. 66

Thel 6. Bottom detail. Copy O. Lessing J. Rosenwald Collection, Library of Congress. 68

Visions of the Daughters of Albion 1. Top and bottom details. Copy J. Lessing J. Rosenwald Collection, Library of Congress. 71, 73

Visions 2. Middle detail. Copy J. Lessing J. Rosenwald Collection, Library of Congress. 73

Visions 3. Bottom detail. Copy J. Lessing J. Rosenwald Collection, Library of Congress. 74

Visions 4. Top detail. Copy J. Lessing J. Rosenwald Collection, Library of Congress. 75

Visions 6. Bottom detail. Copy J. Lessing J. Rosenwald Collection, Library of Congress. 78

Visions 7. Top detail. Copy J. Lessing J. Rosenwald Collection, Library of Congress. 79

Visions 8. Bottom detail. Copy J. Lessing J. Rosenwald Collection, Library of Congress. 80

The Marriage of Heaven and Hell 2. "The Argument." Copy B. Douce Collection, Bodleian Library, Oxford. 84

Marriage 10. Bottom detail. Copy B. Douce Collection, Bodleian Library, Oxford. 91

Marriage 11. Top detail. Copy I. Fitzwilliam Museum, Cambridge. 91

Marriage 16. Top detail. Copy B. Douce Collection, Bodleian Library, Oxford. 94

Marriage 20. Bottom detail. Copy B. Douce Collection, Bodleian Library, Oxford. 97

Marriage 21. Top detail. Copy B. Douce Collection, Bodleian Library, Oxford. 98

Marriage 24. Bottom detail. Copy I. Fitzwilliam Museum, Cambridge. 100

America: A Prophecy i. Frontispiece. Copy E. Lessing J. Rosenwald Collection, Library of Congress. 105

America 1. Copy E. Lessing J. Rosenwald Collection, Library of Congress. 106

America 2. Copy E. Lessing J. Rosenwald Collection, Library of Congress. 109

America 8. Top detail. Copy E. Lessing J. Rosenwald Collection, Library of Congress. 113

America 10. Bottom detail. Copy E. Lessing J. Rosenwald Collection, Library of Congress. 115

America 16. Copy E. Lessing J. Rosenwald Collection, Library of Congress. 120

Europe: A Prophecy 4. Bottom detail. Copy I. Sir George Grey Collection, Auckland Public Library, New Zealand. 126

Europe 9. Copy I. Sir George Grey Collection, Auckland Public Library, New Zealand. 129

The Book of Urizen 11. Copy B. Pierpont Morgan Library, New York City. 149

Urizen 24. Copy B. Pierpont Morgan Library, New York City. 157

The Four Zoas, p. 26 (infra-red photography). Department of Manuscripts, British Library (Additional Ms. 39764, p. 13v). 220

The Four Zoas, p. 86 (infra-red photography). Department of Manuscripts, British Library (Additional Ms. 39764, p. 43v). 225

The Four Zoas, p. 112 (infra-red photography). Department of Manuscripts, British Library (Additional Ms. 39764, p. 56v). 227

Milton: A Poem 4 (*Census* a, text 3). Bottom detail. Copy D. Lessing J. Rosenwald Collection, Library of Congress. 242

Milton 10 (*Census* 8). Copy A. Department of Prints and Drawings, British Museum. 249

Milton 16 (*Census* 13). Copy A. Department of Prints and Drawings, British Museum. 259

Milton 18 (*Census* 15; text 16). Copy A. Department of Print and Drawings, British Museum. 265

Milton 32 (*Census* 29). Copy A. Department of Prints and Drawings, British Museum. 285

Milton 36 (*Census* 32, text 33). Bottom detail. Unidentified copy, widely reproduced. 292

Milton 40 (*Census* 36, text 36). Bottom detail. Copy A. Department of Prints and Drawings, British Museum. 297

Milton 50 (*Census* 45, text 43). Copy D. Lessing J. Rosenwald Collection, Library of Congress. 307

Jerusalem: The Emanation of the Giant Albion 14. Bottom detail. Copy D. The Houghton Library, Harvard University. 318

Jerusalem: 28. Top detail. Copy D. The Houghton Library, Harvard University. Also Proof copy. Pierpont Morgan Library. 324

Jerusalem 35 (31). Copy E. Collection of Mr. Paul Mellon. 326

Jerusalem 37 (33). Copy E. Collection of Mr. Paul Mellon. 327

Jerusalem 41 (37). Bottom detail. Copy D. The Houghton Library, Harvard University. 329

Jerusalem 50. Bottom detail. Copy D. The Houghton Library, Harvard University. 330

Jerusalem 53. Top detail. Copy E. Collection of Mr. Paul Mellon. 333

Jerusalem 54. Middle detail. Unidentified copy, widely reproduced. 334

Jerusalem 57. Copy D. The Houghton Library, Harvard University. 335

Jerusalem 62. Copy D. The Houghton Library, Harvard University. 339

Jerusalem 70. Middle detail. Copy D. The Houghton Library, Harvard University. 344

Jerusalem 72. Middle detail. Unidentified copy, widely reproduced. 345

Jerusalem 78. Top detail. Copy D. The Houghton Library, Harvard University. 348

Jerusalem 81. Bottom detail. Unidentified copy, widely reproduced. 349

Jerusalem 93. Top detail. Unidentified copy, widely reproduced. 353

Jerusalem 97. Bottom detail. Copy D. The Houghton Library, Harvard University. 356

Gates of Paradise: For the Sexes 19: "To the Accuser. Copy G. Collection of Mr. and Mrs. Paul Mellon. 373

Preface

The life of William Blake was filled to overflowing—not with events but with works of art. He produced carefully crafted engravings for publishers of other writers' books, painted brilliant water colors and temperas on Biblical, literary, and historical subjects for a few faithful patrons, and wrote, etched, printed, and colored illuminated books for himself—and for the "Children of the future Age" he came to regard as his audience. From the evidence of sheer numbers—some 1,400 designs for commercial projects, over a thousand pictures for patrons, and almost 400 plates for his own illuminated books—it is obvious that Blake must have worked hard. He discovered when young that there is a "Moment in each Day that Satan cannot find"; this moment is any instant of present time which is filled with productive activity. His wife Catherine told a friend that she had never seen Blake with his hands idle, except when in conversation or reading. According to accounts of his life by those who knew him, he did his professional engraving during the day and woke up in the night to work on poems and designs for his own books, on his own time.

Blake was well prepared for his life's work as poet, printer, painter, and prophet, both by formal training in his craft and by self-education in the liberal arts. He came from a middle-class family of London shopkeepers: his father and one brother were hosiers; another brother was apprenticed to a gingerbread baker but ran away to become a soldier. When Blake was ten years old he went to drawing school; when he was fourteen he began his seven-year apprenticeship as an engraver; when he was twenty-one he was admitted, after a three-month probationary period, to the Royal Academy, with a ticket entitling him to draw in the galleries and to attend lectures and exhibitions for six years. He supplemented his formal training with a study of sixteenth-century prints, some from his own collection, which he began forming in his teens with money supplied by his father. During the same period, he showed an interest in poetry; his first book was made up of poems written between the ages of twelve and twenty. His friends were invariably impressed with the range of his reading. He studied the Bible and the major works of literature, especially Milton; he read widely in philosophy, theology, and art theory; he concerned himself deeply with the revolutionary events of his time, their causes and effects.

Like other great artists, he had a profound intuitive grasp of human psychology. More explicitly than any English writer before him, however, he pointed out the interrelationship of problems associated with cruelty, self-righteousness, sexual disturbance, social inequity, repression of energy by reason, and revolutionary violence. He identified all these ills as symptoms rather than causes: symptoms of the absence of love, the starvation of the spirit, and the fragmentation of both the individual personality and the human family.

For Blake, the fragmentation and emptiness of most people's lives can best be understood through a myth of the fall of man. The prophet sees all the misery and bewilderment resulting from the fall; his duty is both to identify the causes of evil and to dispel the illusion that it is inevitable: "The Nature of my Work is Visionary or Imaginative; it is an Endeavour to Restore what the Ancients calld the Golden Age." Blake dreamed dreams and saw visions not for escape but for change and renewal. The purpose of art, he insisted, is to enable all people to share in vision, to coordinate a prophetic insight into contemporary events with a visionary perception of how life might be different and better. Blake's images of alternatives are not primarily historical or utopian but apocalyptic. That is, they are based on a belief that significant change cannot occur through step-by-step improvements of the existing order or even by violent conversion to some new form of the present system. Rather, significant change can occur only through the radical regeneration of each person's own power to imagine. One must reject the insidious error of confusing vision with delusion; one must transform the processes of thinking and perceiving in order to restore to the rational mind the lost faculties of intuition, imagination, and feeling. When Blake's artist-hero Los, a blacksmith, finally achieves a clear vision of the human community that ought to be built, his work begins to make sense. Rejecting the conventional wisdom that art cannot change the world, Los ignores the voices of mockery and despair and keeps patiently at his useful tasks. Both in his own life and in his illuminated poems, Blake understood the value of steady, plodding, day-by-day work—and also the necessity of centering such work in the visionary powers. With him, a few of his contemporaries were able to recognize that artistic innovations, unlike debates in Parliament or battles in Europe, can unify and inspire a society to work for the New Age. They saw Blake's illuminated books, in particular, as agents and instruments—or friends and companions—in the enterprise of building Jerusalem in England's green and pleasant land.

This selection of Blake's work includes almost all of his published writings, most of his best shorter poetry that remained in manuscript, and much of his most energetic prose. His illuminated books are his major publications; these are the poems and prose works he considered important enough to etch on copper, with designs, to print on paper (usually with color added), to make into books, and to offer for sale. For these works we identify each page by plate number, a reference to the etched plate from which the text and design were printed. In another category are two of Blake's three works which were printed without designs in ordinary letterpress: these are *Poetical Sketches* (never sold) and *Descriptive Catalogue* (offered for sale at Blake's exhibition); *The French Revolution* (printed but not published) is not included. Some of his works were left untitled and are known by "editorial titles." Works in all these categories are intermixed in this edition to reveal the unfolding of Blake's vision through his long productive years. Of Blake's major epics, *Milton* is printed in full, in its longest version; *Jerusalem* has been abridged by two thirds, and *The Four Zoas* (which Blake left in manuscript) is represented by brief selections.

There is also a generous selection of reproductions—thirty-two in color, eighty in monochrome—of whole pages or details from Blake's illuminated books. Any presentation of Blake's illuminated texts in type alone creates an impression quite different from that made by the originals; therefore the gallery of reproductions in this edition will help to show what the printed texts alone cannot provide, while the printed texts will compensate for whatever legibility may be lost in pictorial reproduction.

After *Songs of Innocence and of Experience* (1794), Blake's major works become increasingly longer and more complex, more concerned with problems in theology and philosophy, more innovative in myth and form, and less immediately rewarding to the casual reader. Largely for these reasons, a tradition of effective annotation of Blake's texts has been both greatly needed and slow to develop. The first who tried were Edwin J. Ellis and W. B. Yeats (1893), but their work is now of interest primarily to Yeats scholars. Heroic efforts by S. Foster Damon (1924), D. J. Sloss and J.P.R. Wallis (1926), F. W. Bateson (1957), and Harold Bloom (1965) have advanced the general understanding of Blake, but their comments sometimes distract the reader by emphasizing details that seem to support a tenuous thesis while neglecting to bring out relevant facts and connections with other writings by Blake. The fullest and most satisfactory scholarly annotations appear in the Longman/Norton Annotated English Poets series, edited by W. H. Stevenson (1971). The concise notes and commentaries in the Rinehart edition by Hazard Adams (1970) and the Penguin edition by Alicia Ostriker (1977) are also helpful. In our headnotes, we have sought to maintain an unobtrusive editorial relationship both to Blake's writings and to the reader; yet this volume is frankly intended as a guided tour to Blake's work. We have occasionally suggested our own interpretations of difficult or controversial points, but where possible we have simply presented the current critical consensus on each work. For information particularly attributable to a single scholar, we provide a brief reference, but usually we do not attempt to give credit for material that appears in standard critical and reference works: S. Foster Damon's *A Blake Dictionary* (1965); W.H. Stevenson's annotations in *The Poems of William Blake* (1971); David V. Erdman's *Blake: Prophet Against Empire* (third edition, 1977), his *Concordance* (1967), or *The Illuminated Blake* (1974); Northrop Frye's *Fearful Symmetry* (1947); and Harold Bloom's *Blake's Apocalypse* (revised edition, 1970). For the sake of concision, we usually give only the last names of our sources; the Bibliography should be consulted to supplement the footnotes. The Chronology and Maps help to frame both the mundane and the visionary activities of Blake. The List of Key Terms, by directing the reader to the most important footnote on each major subject, serves as a brief glossary of Blakean motifs.

Our selection of criticism has been guided by a concern to present plain and direct discussions of some central issues in the study of Blake. The chronological arrangement of criticism by Blake's contemporaries is of special interest: though Blake's obscurity in his lifetime is now a part of his legend, it is important to understand that he was never entirely without an audience; he always attracted some who could understand and appreciate him. In our selection of recent criticism, our first consideration has been to provide essays that we have found helpful to students. We have not included essays merely for the sake of representing the various schools of Blake criticism: for example, the critics concerned with Blake's use of Neoplatonic and other esoteric sources are omitted because we consider most of them misleading, especially to beginners. T. S. Eliot's somewhat condescending essay, on the other hand, is included because of its enduring value, not only as a chapter in the history of Blake's reputation but as an appreciation of one of Blake's major virtues as an artist: his forthrightness. After a magisterial essay by Frye on Blake's symbolism, the rest of the selections follow our editorial arrangement of Blake's poems and prophecies, beginning with Jean Hagstrum and Robert F. Gleckner on the *Songs* and concluding with discussions of *Milton* and *Jerusalem* by Harold Bloom and E. J. Rose.

We are grateful to David V. Erdman for his unstinting encouragement, editorial advice, and generous assistance in making photographs available to us. The following friends provided help with photographs, critiques of various parts of the manuscript, and technical advice on bookmaking: Robert N. Essick, Everett C. Frost, and Joseph Anthony Wittreich, Jr. Cynthia Bathhurst-Rodgers and Linnea Aycock helped with errands; some of the typing was done by David Elliott and some of the research work by Byron van Buren and Caryl Bucksbaum, who also typed many preliminary drafts. We commend the technical skills of Art Loomis, who made color photographs of Blake Trust facsimiles, and of Karen McHaney, who drew the maps. Special thanks are due to Brenda Azurmendi for cheerfully and speedily producing finished copy from drafts that were sometimes nearly illegible; also to Lois Luckman and Sarah S. Johnson for work done out of sheer good nature. Funds and services provided by Georgia State University and The University of Iowa smoothed out small problems at all stages of our work. We are also particularly grateful to Professor M. H. Abrams and to Emily Garlin, John Francis, and the staff of W. W. Norton and Company for their perseverance and expert advice. The collectors and museums who have permitted us to publish reproductions of Blake's works in their possession are acknowledged in the List of Illustrations.

In appreciation for the interest in Blake and the encouragement of our efforts shown by our mothers, Sarah Stevenson Johnson and Christine Currier Grant Turner, we dedicate this book to them, to the vibrant memory of the former and the spirited presence of the latter—and to their grandson, William Josiah.

MARY LYNN JOHNSON (GRANT)
JOHN E. GRANT

Chronology of the Life and Times of William Blake

Life	Times
1757 (November 28) William, the second of five children, was born at 28 Broad Street, Carnaby Market, London (see map), to James Blake, a hosier, and his wife, Catherine.	
1761 At age four, Blake had a vision of God; later saw a tree full of angels in a field at Peckham Rye.	1762 Rousseau's *The Social Contract*.
	1765 Percy's *Reliques of Ancient English Poetry*.
1767 (August 4) Robert Blake, William's favorite brother, was born.	
1768 After being taught at home, Blake was sent to Henry Pars's Drawing School (see map), where he continued lessons until 1772.	
1769 Began to write lyrics later printed in *Poetical Sketches*.	1770 Chatterton a suicide (b. 1752).
1772 (August 4) Began seven-year apprenticeship to James Basire (see map), engraver to London Society of Antiquaries, who in 1774 sent Blake to make drawings at Westminster Abbey, where he acquired a taste for the Gothic style. Began to form a collection of prints.	

Life

1773 Engraved his earliest known picture, "Joseph of Arimathea" after a figure in Michelangelo's *The Crucifixion of St. Peter*.

1779 (October 8) Began study in the Royal Academy (see map) under G. M. Moser. Engraving of *Edward and Elinor* and watercolor of *The Penance of Jane Shore*; commercial engraving for Joseph Johnson, bookseller (see map), who later published Priestley, Paine, Godwin, and Wollstonecraft.

1780 Original drawing for the "Glad Day" engraving. First exhibit at Royal Academy. Caught up in the Gordon Riots of June 2–8 and witnessed burning of Newgate Prison. Met Flaxman, sculptor, Cumberland, amateur etcher, and Stothard, painter, (Sept. ?). Taken prisoner with fellow artists Ogleby and Stothard under mistaken suspicion of being a French spy, while on a sketching trip on the Medway river.

Times

1775 Battles of Lexington and Concord; Bunker Hill.

1776 Declaration of American Independence; war between England and America.

1781 Surrender at Yorktown.

Life	Times
1782 (August 18) Married Catherine Boucher (b. 1762), the illiterate daughter of a Battersea market-gardener. They lived at 23 Green Street, Leicester Fields, and then moved to 27 Broad Street (see map). Catherine learned to read, write, and make prints; they had no children.	1782 Fuseli's *The Nightmare* exhibited.
1783 *Poetical Sketches* printed at the expense of John Flaxman and the Reverend A. S. Mathew, but not sold. According to Mathew, Blake wrote all poems in the volume between ages twelve and twenty. In the Mathew salon, Blake sang his songs to tunes he composed himself, a practice he continued throughout his life.	1783 Barry's murals, *The Progress of Human Culture*, completed at the Society of Arts.
1784 Engravings for *Wit's Magazine*. Exhibited *War Unchained* and A *Breach in a City Wall* at Royal Academy. (July) Blake's father died. (October) Opened Parker and Blake print shop at 27 Broad Street. Wrote *An Island in the Moon*, containing earliest of *Songs of Innocence* (not published).	1784 (December) Death of Dr. Johnson.
1785 Print shop failed. Blakes moved to Poland Street (see map). Exhibited at Royal Academy: three drawings of Joseph from the Bible and *The Bard* from Gray.	
	1786 Burns's *Poems Chiefly in the Scottish Dialect*.
1787 (February) After Blake nursed his brother for two weeks without sleep, Robert Blake died of consumption at age nineteen; at the moment	

Life	Times
of death, Blake saw Robert's spirit ascending through the ceiling, clapping its hands for joy. Began using Robert's sketchbook as his all-purpose private Notebook of poetry, prose and drawings. Acquaintance with the painter J. H. Fuseli perhaps began.	
1788 Annotated Fuseli's translation of Lavater's *Aphorisms* and Swedenborg's *Wisdom of Angels Concerning Divine Love and Divine Wisdom*. Associated with Swedenborgian Society. Produced first works in illuminated printing: *All Religions Are One* and *There Is No Natural Religion*.	1788 Passage of law protecting chimney sweepers by setting minimum age of eight (not enforced).
1789 Wrote and illustrated (never published) *Tiriel*. Published illuminated books: *Songs of Innocence* and *The Book of Thel*.	1789 (June) Beginning of the French Revolution.
1790 Began *Marriage of Heaven and Hell* and annotated Swedenborg's *The Wisdom of Angels Concerning Divine Providence*. Moved across Thames to 13 Hercules Buildings, Lambeth (see map).	1790 (November 1) Burke's *Reflections on the Revolution in France*.
1791 Illustrated Wollstonecraft's *Original Stories from Real Life*. *The French Revolution* set in type but never published.	1791 (February) Paine, *The Rights of Man*, Part I. Debate on slave trade.
1792 Worked on engravings for Stedman's *Narrative, of a five years' expedition, against the Revolted Negroes of Surinam, in Guiana, on the Wild Coast of South America*. Completed *The Marriage of Heaven and Hell*. (April 3) Four plates for Stuart and Revett's *Antiquities of Athens*.	1792 (February 17) Paine, *The Rights of Man*, Part II. Wollstonecraft, *A Vindication of the Rights of Woman*. (April 23) Invasion of France halted at

Life	Times
	Valmy. (September 22) France proclaimed a Republic; Year One of revolutionary calendar. (December) Paine, indicted for seditious utterance, left England for France.
1793 Notebook entry: "I say I shan't live five years, and if I live one it will be a wonder." Illuminated books: *Visions of the Daughters of Albion, For Children: The Gates of Paradise,* and *America: A Prophecy.* (Oct. 10) Prospectus "To the Public" lists "works now published and on sale at Mr. Blake's." Probably became acquainted with his patron, Thomas Butts, a civil servant.	1793 (January 21) Execution of Louis XVI. Cult of Goddess of Reason; decimal system established. (February 1) Britain declared war on France. Wordsworth's *An Evening Walk.* William Godwin, *Political Justice.* (September) French Reign of Terror.
1794 Illuminated books: *Songs of Innocence and of Experience, Europe: A Prophecy,* and *The First Book of Urizen.*	1794 (July) Fall of Robespierre. Paine, *The Age of Reason,* Part I. Wollstonecraft, *A Historical and Moral View of the Origin and Progress of the French Revolution.* (November) Trials of Hardy and Horne Tooke.
1795 Series of twelve color prints, including "Newton" and "Nebuchadnezzar." Illuminated books: *The Song of Los, The Book of Los, The Book of Ahania.* (September) Was "mobbed and robbed."	1795 Year of famine in England
1796 Began 537 watercolor drawings, of which a selection of forty-three were engraved for an edition of Young's *Night Thoughts,* on atlas-sized	1796 Paine, *The Age of Reason,* Part II. Stedman's *Narrative of a Five Years'*

Life	Times
paper, published by Edwards in 1797. More than twenty deluxe copies with plates tinted in watercolors, most not by Blake, were issued.	*Expedition* [*in*] . . . *South America*, with engravings by Blake, published.
1797 Used paper from *Night Thoughts* project for text and sketches for *Vala*, his first long poem, revised over a ten-year period as *The Four Zoas*, and abandoned in manuscript.	1797 (April-June) Mutinies at Spithead and Nore in British Navy. Bank crisis.
1798 Annotations to Watson's *An Apology for the Bible . . . Addressed To Thomas Paine*. Began to annotate Reynolds's *Discourses*.	1798 (Summer) Wolf Tone Rebellion in Ireland, suppressed. (August) Battle of the Nile. *Lyrical Ballads*, by Wordsworth and Coleridge
1799 (May) Exhibited at Royal Academy: *The Last Supper*. Unemployed as an engraver, he was commissioned by Butts to execute temperas on Biblical and literary subjects, completed in 1800.	1799 Napoleon's *coup d'état* of 18th Brumaire.
1800–3 Moved to Felpham, on the English Channel near Chichester, and lived under the patronage of William Hayley, a minor poet. Painted *Heads of the Poets*. Perhaps wrote the "Pickering Manuscript" poems and worked on *The Four Zoas* by night while carrying out Hayley's artistic assignments by day. Studied Greek, Latin, and Hebrew.	1800 Act of Union with Ireland. Wordsworth, Preface to the second edition of *Lyrical Ballads*.
1802 Hayley's *A Series of Ballads*, with fourteen engravings by Blake.	1802 (March 27) Peace of Amiens, ending English-French hostilities for just over a year. Coleridge, *Dejection: An Ode*.

Life	Times
1803 (August 12) Blake evicted the drunken soldier Scofield from his garden and was accused by Scofield of uttering seditious threats against the King. (September) Returned to London, to new lodgings at 17 South Molton Street (see map).	1803 (May 10) War with France renewed.
1804 (January 11–12) Trial for sedition ended in acquittal at Chichester Quarter Sessions, to the cheers of the spectators. Dated title pages of *Milton* and *Jerusalem*. In London (October), visited Truchsessian Gallery of Pictures, where he "was again enlightened with the light I enjoyed in my youth."	1804 Napoleon crowned emperor, taking crown from the Pope and placing it on his own head.
1805 Designs for Blair's *Grave*, purchased cheaply by Cromek, who in violation of his agreement gave the lucrative engraving contract to the artist Schiavonetti. Designs for Hayley's *Ballads*, second set. Completed a series of over eighty Biblical watercolors for Butts (begun in 1800). Probably completed 116 watercolor illustrations for Gray's *Poems*.	1805 (October 21) Battle of Trafalgar, death of Nelson. 1805–6 Scott's *Lay of the Last Minstrel*. Moore's *Irish Melodies*. Byron's *Hours of Idleness*. Malkin's *Memoirs of His Child* (January 1806) contains a long account of Blake.
1806 Cromek stole the idea of Blake's *Canterbury Pilgrims* and gave it to Stothard for an engraving by Schiavonetti. (June) Blake's letter to *Bell's Weekly Messenger* defending Fuseli's art.	
1807 Notebook entry: "Tuesday Jan. 20, 1807, between Two & Seven in the Evening—Despair." (May) Stothard's *Canterbury Pilgrims* exhibited. Royal Academy exhibits Phillips's portrait of Blake (May). Petworth version of *The Last Judgment* commissioned.	1807 Wordsworth's *Poems in Two Volumes*. Abolition of the British slave trade.

Life	Times
1808 Publication of Cromek's edition of Robert Blair's *The Grave*, with portrait of Blake by Phillips, dedicatory poem to the Queen by Blake, and designs by Blake, engraved by Schiavonetti. (August 28) Blake's *Grave* designs mocked by Robert Hunt in *The Examiner*. Blake's frustrations vented in notebook epigrams. Watercolors *Jacob's Dream* and *Christ in the Sepulchre* exhibited at Royal Academy. Second series of watercolor drawings for *Paradise Lost*. Copies A and B of *Milton* probably completed.	1808–13 The Peninsular Campaign, commanded by Sir Arthur Wellesley, later Duke of Wellington.
1809–10 First and only one-man show, of sixteen paintings, which featured heroic-satiric allegories of Pitt and Nelson and a huge painting, *The Ancient Britons*. Held in his brother's shop, 28 Broad Street. For the show, Blake wrote *A Descriptive Catalogue*. It was ignored by critics and the public, except for a vicious review (September) by Robert Hunt and visits by H. C. Robinson. Drafted *Public Address* and *A Vision of the Last Judgment*, describing his seven-foot by five-foot tempera painting, now lost.	1809 Byron, *English Bards and Scotch Reviewers*.
1810 Notebook entry: "23 May 1810 found the Word Golden." (October 8) Engraving of *The Canterbury Pilgrims*. Perhaps painted the first set of watercolor drawings for *The Book of Job*, for Butts.	
1811 *An Allegory of the Spiritual Condition of Man*, Blake's largest surviving painting: five feet by four feet.	1811 George III declared incompetent; his son named Prince Regent.

Life	Times
1812 *Philoctetes and Neoptolemos on Lemnos,* an heroic watercolor. Three temperas and specimens of *Jerusalem* exhibited by the Associated Painters in Watercolors.	1812 War with United States (1814). Napoleonic invasion of Russia. Byron's *Childe Harold* I–II.
	1813 Shelley's *Queen Mab.*
	1814 (March) Fall of Paris. Napoleon exiled to Elba. Wordsworth's *The Excursion.*
1815 Engraved 185 figures of dishes on 18 plates for a catalogue of Josiah Wedgwood's pottery. Visited the Royal Academy to draw *The Laocoön.*	1815 Napoleon's Hundred Days: March 1–June 15. Waterloo; end of Napoleonic Wars; economic depression in England. Wordsworth, *Poems.*
1816 Designs for *L'Allegro* and *Il Penseroso.*	1816 Coleridge's *Christabel,* "Kubla Khan." Shelley's "Alastor."
1817 *The Judgment of Paris,* a watercolor.	1817 Flaxman's *Hesiod* designs, engraved by Blake. Byron's *Manfred.* Coleridge's *Biographia Literaria.* Elgin Marbles exhibited.
1818 *The Everlasting Gospel* drafted in his Notebook. Met John Linnell, a younger painter. *The Gates of Paradise* revised: "To the Sexes."	1818 Keats's *Endymion.* Hazlitt's *The English Poets, The English Comic Writers.* Byron's *Childe Harold,* IV.

Life	Times
1819 Drew "Visionary Heads" and "Ghost of a Flea" for the astrologer and occultist John Varley.	1819 (August) Peterloo Massacre. Byron's *Don Juan*, I–II.
1820 First copy of *Jerusalem* printed. Woodcuts for Thornton's *Virgil*. Issued *The Laocoön*, *On Homer's Poetry*, and *On Virgil*. Annotations to Berkeley's *Siris*.	1820 (January 29) Death of George III. Prince Regent becomes George IV (coronation June, 1821). Keats's last volume of poems. Shelley's *Prometheus Unbound*. Shelley's *Adonais*, Southey's *A Vision of Judgment*. Byron's *Cain*, *Don Juan* III–V.
1821 Sold collection of prints to raise money. Painted new series of *Job* watercolors for Linnell. Moved to small apartment at 3 Fountain Court, the Strand (see map).	1821 Death of Keats in Italy.
1822 *The Ghost of Abel*, Blake's final work in relief etching. Three watercolor drawings for a third set of designs for *Paradise Lost*. Received a donation of £25 from the Royal Academy.	1822 Byron's *The Vision of Judgment*. Death of Shelley in Italy.
1823 (March 25) Agreement with Linnell to engrave *Job* designs.	1823 Byron's *Don Juan* VI–XIV.
1824 *Pilgrim's Progress* designs. Acquainted with Samuel Palmer, the most distinguished painter in a group of young admirers. Began making 100 Dante drawings for Linnell, of which seven were engraved by 1827.	1824 Byron's *Don Juan*, XV–XVI. Death of Byron in Greece. Shelley, *Posthumous Poems*.
1825 (March 8) Tempera paintings: *The Black Madonna*, *The Characters of Spenser's Faerie Queene*, illustrations for *Paradise Regained*. *Job* engravings dated, but probably not completed until November.	1825 Hazlitt's *The Spirit of The Age*.

Life	Times
1826 (March) Publication of *Job* engravings (one copy colored). Severe bout with stomach illness. Annotations to Wordsworth's *Poems* (1815) and *The Excursion* (1814). *The Wise and Foolish Virgins* and *Queen Katherine's Dream* sold to Sir Thomas Lawrence.	
1827 Annotations to Thornton's *New Translation of the Lord's Prayer*. Worked on Dante engravings and made separate print of *Europe* frontispiece, "The Ancient of Days." Died, aged sixty-nine, at 6 P.M., August 12, singing about what he saw in heaven.	
1831 (October 18) Death of Catherine Blake, aged sixty-nine.	

CARTOGRAPHY BY KAREN McHANEY

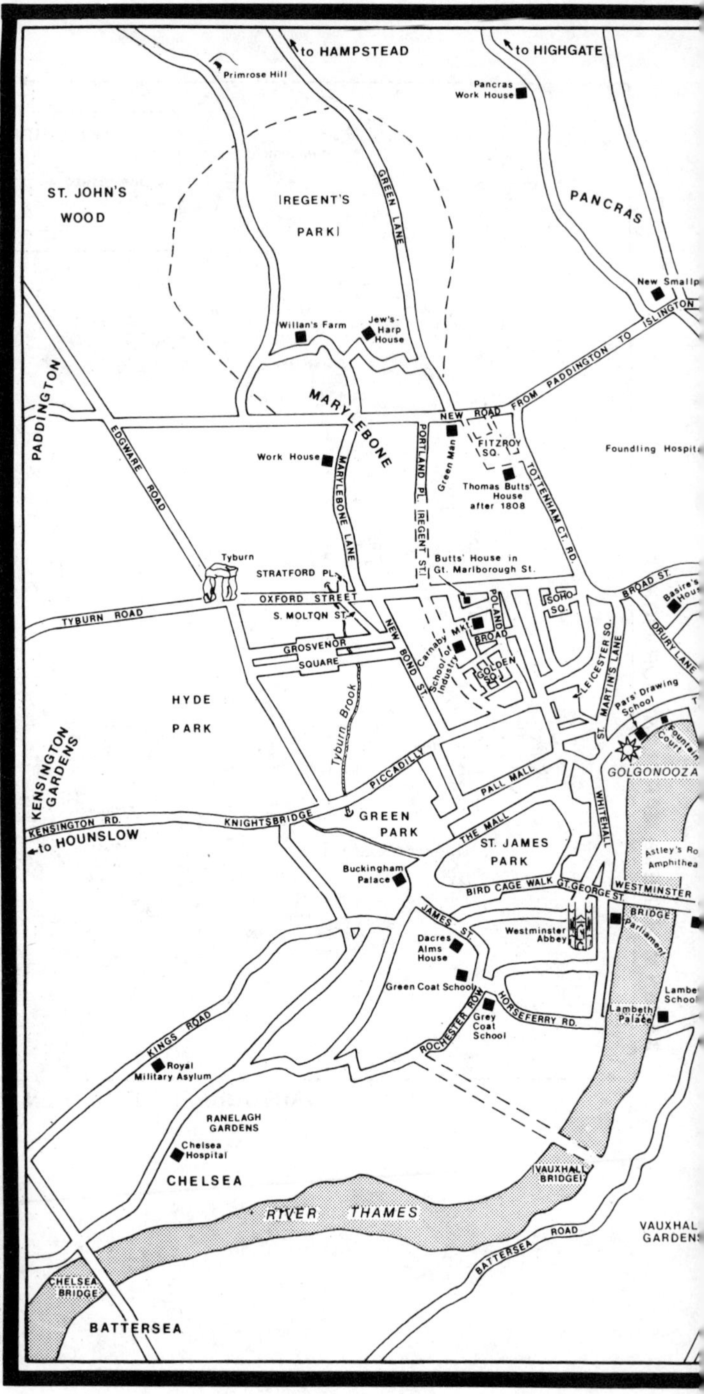
to HAMPSTEAD
to HIGHGATE
Primrose Hill
Pancras Work House
ST. JOHN'S WOOD
(REGENT'S PARK)
GREEN LANE
PANCRAS
New Smallp
ISLINGTON
Willan's Farm
Jew's-Harp House
PADDINGTON
MARYLEBONE
NEW ROAD FROM PADDINGTON TO ISLINGTON
Green Man
FITZROY SQ.
Foundling Hospit
EDGWARE ROAD
Work House
MARYLEBONE LANE
PORTLAND PL.
(REGENT ST.)
Thomas Butts' House after 1808
TOTTENHAM CT. RD.
Tyburn
STRATFORD PL.
Butts' House in Gt. Marlborough St.
BROAD ST.
Basire's Hous
TYBURN ROAD
OXFORD STREET
S. MOLTON ST.
POLAND
SOHO SQ.
DRURY LANE
GROSVENOR SQUARE
NEW BOND ST.
Carnaby Mkt.
School of Industry
BROAD
GOLDEN SQ.
LEICESTER SQ.
ST. MARTIN'S LANE
HYDE PARK
Tyburn Brook
Pars' Drawing School
Fountain Court
KENSINGTON GARDENS
GOLGONOOZA
PICCADILLY
PALL MALL
KENSINGTON RD.
KNIGHTSBRIDGE
GREEN PARK
to HOUNSLOW
THE MALL
ST. JAMES PARK
WHITEHALL
Astley's Ro Amphithea
Buckingham Palace
BIRD CAGE WALK
GT. GEORGE ST.
WESTMINSTER BRIDGE
JAMES ST.
Westminster Abbey
Parliament
Dacres Alms House
Green Coat School
ROCHESTER ROW
HORSEFERRY RD.
Grey Coat School
Lambeth Palace
Lambe School
KINGS ROAD
Royal Military Asylum
RANELAGH GARDENS
Chelsea Hospital
CHELSEA
(VAUXHALL BRIDGE)
RIVER THAMES
VAUXHAL GARDENS
BATTERSEA ROAD
CHELSEA BRIDGE
BATTERSEA

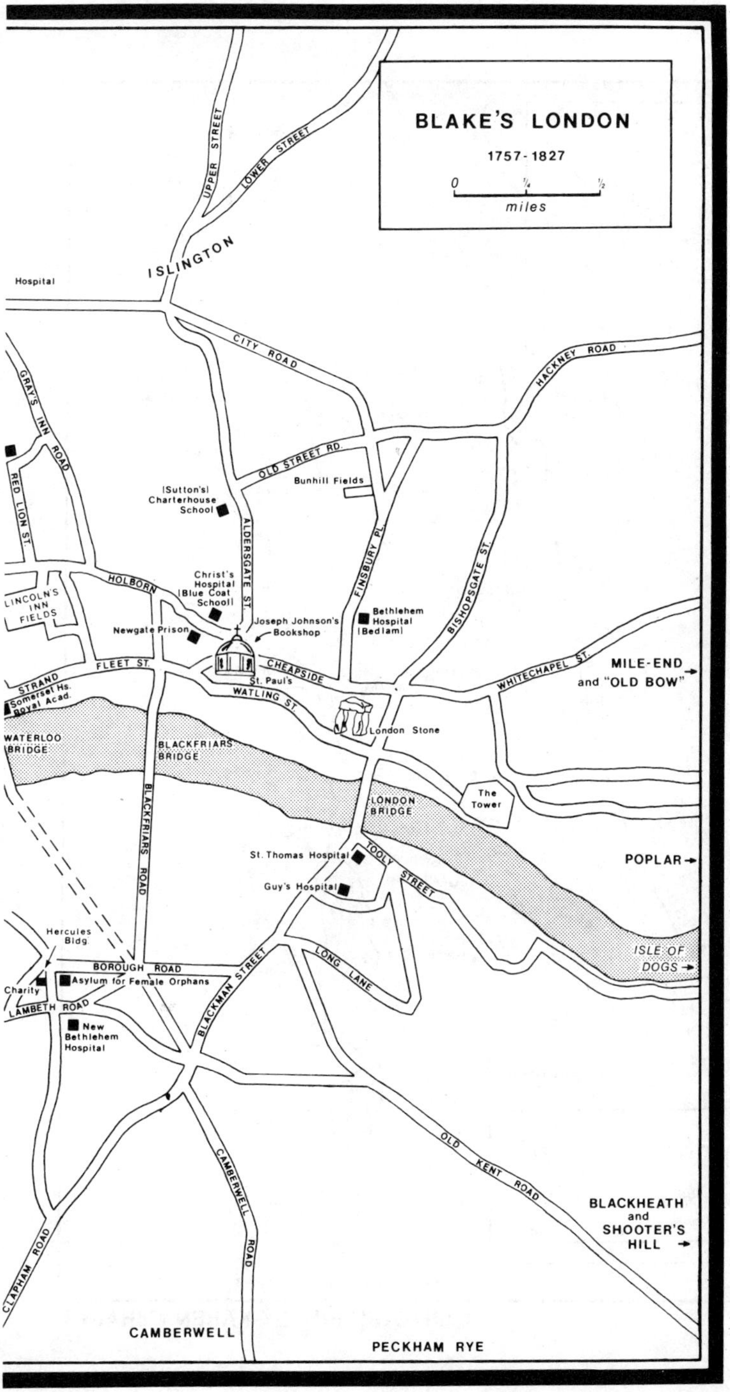

BLAKE'S LONDON
1757-1827
0
¼
½
miles
UPPER STREET
LOWER STREET
ISLINGTON
Hospital
CITY ROAD
HACKNEY ROAD
GRAY'S INN ROAD
OLD STREET RD.
Bunhill Fields
RED LION ST.
(Sutton's) Charterhouse School
ALDERSGATE ST.
FINSBURY PL.
BISHOPSGATE ST.
HOLBORN
Christ's Hospital (Blue Coat School)
Bethlehem Hospital (Bedlam)
LINCOLN'S INN FIELDS
Joseph Johnson's Bookshop
Newgate Prison
FLEET ST.
CHEAPSIDE
WHITECHAPEL ST.
MILE-END and "OLD BOW"
STRAND
St. Paul's
Somerset Hs. Royal Acad.
WATLING ST.
London Stone
WATERLOO BRIDGE
BLACKFRIARS BRIDGE
LONDON BRIDGE
The Tower
BLACKFRIARS ROAD
St. Thomas Hospital
TOOLY STREET
POPLAR
Guy's Hospital
Hercules Bldg.
LONG LANE
ISLE OF DOGS
BOROUGH ROAD
Asylum for Female Orphans
BLACKMAN STREET
Charity
LAMBETH ROAD
New Bethlehem Hospital
OLD KENT ROAD
CAMBERWELL ROAD
BLACKHEATH and SHOOTER'S HILL
CLAPHAM ROAD
CAMBERWELL
PECKHAM RYE

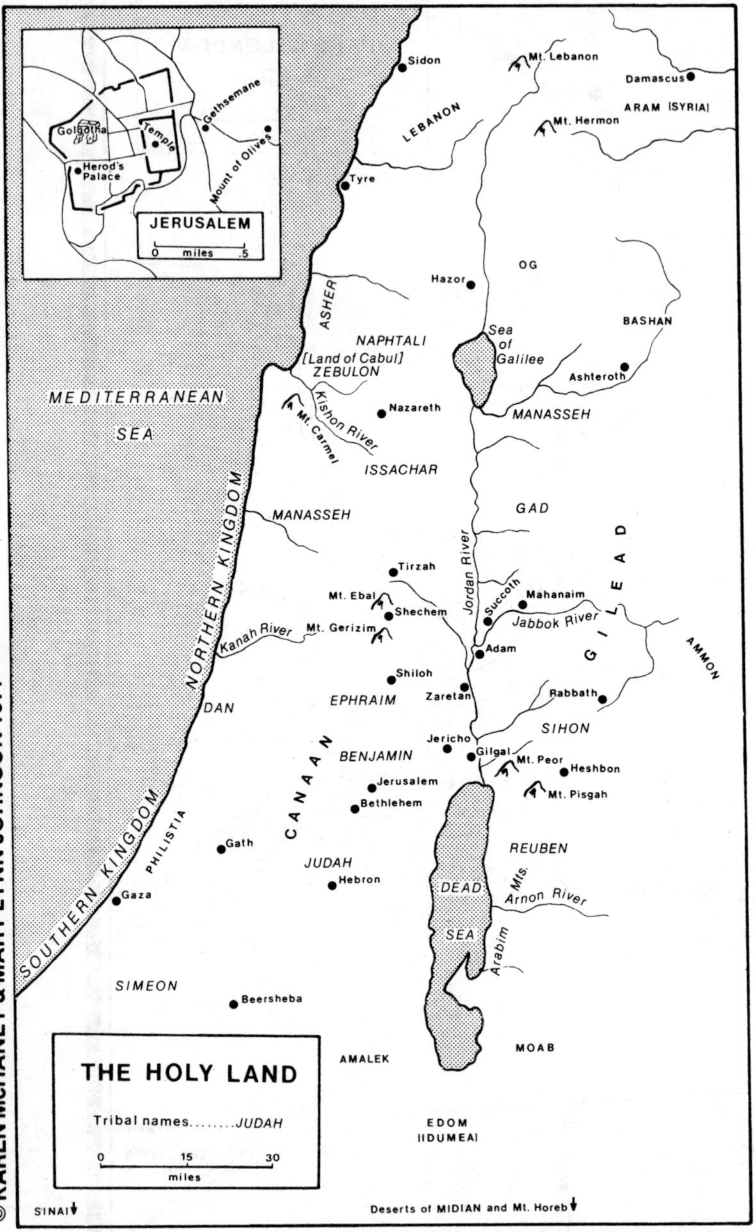

CARTOGRAPHY BY KAREN McHANEY

A Note on the Texts

Because Blake himself (or, more precisely, the team of William and Catherine Blake) etched, printed, and colored the texts and pictures of his illuminated books, it ought to be easier to edit Blake's basic writings than those of a poet whose works were conventionally printed. In this medium a misprint in the usual sense of the word is impossible, for Blake was his own editor and printer—though like anyone else he occasionally dropped out or repeated letters or words. Nonetheless, it is difficult to convert Blake's etched text into an accurate and readable printed text. One reason is that each copy Blake made is different from all the others; therefore, editors identify each copy of a given work by a letter designation (copy A, B, C, etc.) in order to refer to textual variations. Each page of the illuminated books is identified by a plate number, which refers to the copper plate from which the page was printed. With few exceptions, the original copper plates have been destroyed, and the text must be based on one or more of the printed copies. Furthermore, Blake's spelling, capitalization, and especially punctuation are loose and eccentric, even for a time when such matters were not perfectly standardized.

The principles adopted in the two great standard editions of Blake's writings illustrate the character of the editorial problem. In *The Writings of William Blake* (1925), revised over the years under different titles and now called *The Complete Writings of William Blake* (Oxford, 1966, with improved printings to 1974), Geoffrey Keynes took his texts from a single copy of each work, noted the variants, and modernized the punctuation. David V. Erdman, in editing *The Poetry and Prose of William Blake* (Doubleday, 1965, with improved printings to 1970), collated several copies of each work, followed what seems to be Blake's final or preferred text, supplied deleted passages in brackets, presented most drafts and variants in textual notes, and tried to duplicate Blake's punctuation. But there are no typographical equivalents for such Blakean marks as oblong periods and enlongated colons (or are they short exclamation points? lopped-off question marks?) And what of other exotic punctuation, such as the upper part of a question mark over a comma base? Or what is sometimes called his "breathing stop"—a dot raised above the line of the text and interrupting a grammatical unit? Or his birds, butterflies, squiggles, and plant tendrils? Even Erdman does not attempt to reproduce these wonderful creations. In the Clarendon edition of Blake's writings, edited by G. E. Bentley, Jr., which we received when this edition was in galley proofs (1979), Blake's unorthodox marks are represented by their closest equivalents in standard punctuation, superfluous periods are deleted, and essential supplementary punctuation is added. For scholars, nothing short of a study of the punctuation of each separate copy in scattered museums and private collections can settle a fine point of textual analysis or criticism. For most people, a readable text faithful to one of Blake's hand-made copies is not only sufficient but more desirable than a scholar's text.

We have settled on a compromise that preserves most of Blake's eccentricities while removing serious obstacles to understanding. For each illuminated book, we have based our text on a single copy—usually a copy that is readily available in facsimile so that readers can look at our source when in doubt about a passage—and we mention in headnotes which copies are used. The plate number is printed at the beginning of the text for each plate, and this plate number (followed by line number) is given in all references to text passages—e.g., "*Europe* 4:10–14," which means lines 10 through 14 of plate 4 in *Europe*. When variant texts involve a substantial change in meaning, we list them in footnotes. The reader will notice that copies chosen for color plates frequently differ from those used as copy texts. We have usually chosen highly colored copies for our illustrations and more simply printed copies for our texts.

We have imitated Blake's own spacings of passages and indentations of verse-paragraphs—useful guides to his meaning—more faithfully than is customary in other editions. In place of paragraphing, Blake often uses ornamental lines and flourishes, the most significant of which we have represented by lines across the text. The pause at the end of the poetic line often serves as an invisible mark of punctuation, since Blake's unit of thought ordinarily corresponds to the length of his line of verse. We have retained all of Blake's spellings, except for obvious slips, most of his capitalizations, and most of his odd punctuation. However, we have omitted punctuation marks which come in the middle of units of thought, have represented nonstandard marks by the closest possible standard equivalents, and have sparingly altered or added punctuation and capitalization elsewhere, without attempting to regulate or normalize the grammatical units. We have supplied apostrophes for nouns in the possessive case (though in the original the singular and plural forms of some words are indistinguishable); but where the meaning is not affected, we have not imposed a false consistency on a poet who did not wish to be consistent: for example, Blake wrote "gatherd," "gather'd," or "gathered" as the spirit moved him and we have let him have his way. Blake customarily omits quotation marks. In supplying them for the reader's convenience we have occasionally had to spoil certain special effects: the surprise of discovering at the end of an expository passage that it is a quotation (for example, in the first stanza of the preface to *Europe*) and the puzzlement of deciding which of two or even more speakers has delivered a speech of ambivalent attribution (as in *Europe* 4:10–14). (Incidentally, one of the best ways to study Blake is to make one's own penciled punctuation—particularly to consider where long speeches begin and to note in the margin who is speaking.) Most of our printed titles ignore Blake's irregular capitalization and punctuation.

Some of our editorial punctuation has broken up Blake's "swinging door" units of grammar: for example, a phrase that can be taken to modify the main clause of either the sentence before or the one after it, or a noun or noun-cluster that could be either an object in one sentence or a subject in the following sentence (as in *Jerusalem* 4:12).

Many times in removing Blake's medial periods or incorporating his apparent fragments into larger units, we have had to be heavy-handed where he was being precise and delicate: for example, Oothoon's new start in *Visions* 6:21 is emphasized by the preceding period, but since Blake did not capitalize the next word we did not print the new idea as a fragment. "But Oothoon is not so. a virgin fill'd with virgin fancies" is the punctuation of the original, which we have altered merely by changing the period to a semicolon. We hope that whenever readers become absorbed in a problem of interpretation, they will go to facsimiles of Blake's books and to the Keynes and Erdman editions for further study.

For Blake's writings that appeared in conventional typography and for those that remained in manuscript we have generally followed Keynes, with emendations from our own study of the originals, the facsimiles, or the proposals of other editors, especially Erdman's work on Blake's Notebook. Our selections from *Poetical Sketches* are left as printed, except where altered by Blake, and except where by modern expectations the older punctuation obscures his meaning. For the Notebook poems, we have accepted Erdman's deciphering of the words and have left them unpunctuated, as Blake wrote them, since the meaning of these short poems is clear without our intrusion. In some manuscript poems, we have restored a few of Blake's canceled words when his alterations (which we supply in footnotes) were incomplete or otherwise inferior to his earlier draft. For Blake's manuscript prose and his annotations of other writers, we have sought to combine accuracy with readability. Our paragraphing and punctuation bring out the sense of the passages more clearly than is possible in the scholarly editions, which also tend to bury Blake's corrected statements in a mass of deleted variants. Similarly, in presenting the contemporary accounts of Blake left in manuscript by Charles Lamb, Henry Crabb Robinson and Frederick Tatham, we have streamlined the texts of G. E. Bentley, Jr., in *Blake Records* (Oxford: Clarendon, 1969) by repunctuating, omitting variants, and silently correcting obvious slips of the pen.

Comments and queries from our students on these matters, as on all others, have helped us to understand what the ideal of readability may entail. One soon gets used to Blake's expressive idiosyncracies. We believe that the reader will find the textual difficulties less formidable in the actual use of this edition than in our description of them.

The Texts of The Poems

List of Key Terms

Ahania (Emanations) 161
Albion 214
Atlantis 114
Beulah (Four States) 239, 287
Covering Cherub 93, 298, 350
Druid 130
Eden (Four States) 293
Elect (Satan) 240, 255
Emanations (Four Zoas) 214
Enion (Emanations) 214, 218
Enitharmon (Emanations) 122
Eternity 235
Four States: Eden, Beulah, Generation, Ulro 293
Four Zoas (and Emanations): Urizen (Ahania), Urthona-Los (Enitharmon), Luvah-Orc (Vala), Tharmas (Enion) 215
Generation (Four States) 58
Golgonooza 271
Limits: Opacity, Contraction; Satan, Adam 255
Los (Urthona; Four Zoas) 310
Luvah (Orc; Four Zoas) 64, 223
Mills 238, 319
Mundane Shell 261
Non-entity 79
Orc (Luvah; Four Zoas) 103, 107
Polypus 258
Rahab (Tirzah) 261
Ratio 88
Redeemed (Palamabron) 240
Reprobate (Rintrah) 240, 248
Rintrah 85, 127
Satan 240, 257, 300
Selfhood 257
Seven Eyes 215, 254, 360
Shadowy Female (Vala) 107, 262
Sons of Albion 309, 315
Spectre (Emanation) 316
Spiritual Sun 174
States 289, 303, 331
Tharmas 215
Three Classes: Elect, Redeemed, Reprobate 240
Tirzah (Rahab) 58
Udan-Adan (Entuthon Benython) 269
Ulro (Four States) 292
Urizen (Four Zoas) 76, 140
Urthona (Los; Four Zoas) 101
Vala (Emanations) 214, 309
Vegetated 258
Vortex 258

Poems and Prophecies

From Poetical Sketches

In 1783, while Blake was associated with the literary salon of the Reverend A. S. Mathew and his wife, Harriet, his first volume of poems was privately printed at the expense of the Mathews and another friend, the sculptor John Flaxman. It appeared in letterpress, without illuminations, in a small edition; twenty-two copies are extant, a few corrected in Blake's hand. Apparently he never offered the book for sale.

The twenty-six poems in the *Sketches* range over most of the important genres and subjects of the late eighteenth-century Age of Sensibility, but they are boldly experimental in metrics and imagery. Among them are represented the verse drama, the ballad, the "Elizabethan" song, the "Ossianic" prose-poem (see headnote to *Visions of the Daughters of Albion*), and the poem on the cardinal seasons and the times of day, as well as the invocation to the classical Muses. In about 1787 Blake added three pastoral poems by hand in one copy, thus strengthening the representation of one of the important genres recognized in his day. According to a prefatory note, probably by Mathew, the *Sketches* were composed between Blake's twelfth and twentieth years (1769–77), a period roughly corresponding to his apprenticeship as an engraver. Although the note speaks condescendingly of "irregularities and defects in almost every page," most of the poems are excellent and none unworthy. Those selected for this edition anticipate some of Blake's later themes and techniques. The standard study of Blake's sources for this volume is Margaret Ruth Lowery, *Windows of the Morning* (New Haven and London: Yale University Press, 1940).

To Spring[1]

O thou, with dewy locks, who lookest down
Thro' the clear windows of the morning, turn
Thine angel eyes upon our western isle,
Which in full choir hails thy approach, O Spring!

The hills tell each other, and the list'ning
Vallies hear; all our longing eyes are turned
Up to thy bright pavillions: issue forth,
And let thy holy feet visit our clime.

1. Pope's first volume of poetry (*Pastorals*, 1709), written when he was sixteen, was organized according to the four seasons. The most famous eighteenth-century seasonal cycle was James Thomson's *The Seasons*. Blake's seasonal poems anticipate his later work in richness of Biblical and Miltonic allusions; "To Spring" echoes the Song of Solomon; *Lycidas,* line 163; *Comus,* line 744; *Samson Agonistes*, line 119; and Horace, *Odes*, I, v, 3–5.

Come o'er the eastern hills, and let our winds
Kiss thy perfumed garments;[2] let us taste
Thy morn and evening breath; scatter thy pearls
Upon our love-sick land that mourns for thee.

O deck her forth with thy fair fingers; pour
Thy soft kisses on her bosom; and put
Thy golden crown upon her languish'd head,
Whose modest tresses were bound up for thee!

To Summer

O thou, who passest thro' our vallies in
Thy strength, curb thy fierce steeds, allay the heat
That flames from their large nostrils! thou, O Summer,
Oft pitched'st here thy golden tent, and oft
Beneath our oaks hast slept, while we beheld
With joy, thy ruddy limbs and flourishing hair.

Beneath our thickest shades we oft have heard
Thy voice, when noon upon his fervid car
Rode o'er the deep of heaven; beside our springs
Sit down, and in our mossy vallies, on
Some bank beside a river clear, throw thy
Silk draperies off, and rush into the stream:
Our vallies love the Summer in his pride.

Our bards are fam'd who strike the silver wire:
Our youths are bolder than the southern swains:
Our maidens fairer in the sprightly dance:
We lack not songs, nor instruments of joy,
Nor echoes sweet, nor waters clear as heaven,
Nor laurel wreaths against the sultry heat.

To Autumn

O autumn, laden with fruit, and stained
With the blood of the grape, pass not, but sit
Beneath my shady roof; there thou may'st rest,
And tune thy jolly voice to my fresh pipe;
And all the daughters of the year shall dance!
Sing now the lusty song of fruits and flowers.

"The narrow bud opens her beauties to
The sun, and love runs in her thrilling veins;
Blossoms hang round the brows of morning, and
Flourish down the bright cheek of modest eve,
Till clust'ring Summer breaks forth into singing,
And feather'd clouds strew flowers round her head.

2. Worn by a Middle Eastern bridegroom; the "lovesick land" is the bride.

"The spirits of the air live on the smells
Of fruit; and joy, with pinions light, roves round
The gardens, or sits singing in the trees."
Thus sang the jolly Autumn as he sat;
Then rose, girded himself, and o'er the bleak
Hills fled from our sight; but left his golden load.

To Winter[3]

O Winter! bar thine adamantine doors:
The north is thine; there hast thou built thy dark
Deep-founded habitation. Shake not thy roofs,
Nor bend thy pillars with thine iron car.

He hears me not, but o'er the yawning deep
Rides heavy; his storms are unchain'd, sheathed
In ribbed steel; I dare not lift mine eyes;
For he hath rear'd his sceptre o'er the world.

Lo! now the direful monster, whose skin clings
To his strong bones, strides o'er the groaning rocks:
He withers all in silence, and his hand
Unclothes the earth, and freezes up frail life.

He takes his seat upon the cliffs; the mariner
Cries in vain. Poor little wretch! that deal'st
With storms; till heaven smiles, and the monster
Is driv'n yelling to his caves beneath mount Hecla.

To the Evening Star

Thou fair-hair'd angel of the evening,
Now, whilst the sun rests on the mountains, light
Thy bright torch of love; thy radiant crown
Put on, and smile upon our evening bed!
Smile on our loves; and, while thou drawest the
Blue curtains of the sky, scatter thy silver dew
On every flower that shuts its sweet eyes
In timely sleep. Let thy west wind sleep on
The lake; speak silence with thy glimmering eyes,
And wash the dusk with silver. Soon, full soon,
Dost thou withdraw; then the wolf rages wide,
And the lion glares thro' the dun forest:
The fleeces of our flocks are cover'd with
Thy sacred dew: protect them with thine influence.

3. The atmosphere in this poem recalls others in the sublime tradition: William Collins's *Ode to Fear* and *Ode to Evening*, as well as the vision of Winter's court in Thomson's *Winter*, the poem which made the Icelandic volcano Mount Hecla famous (Lowery, pp. 152–55). There is another Mount Hecla in the Outer Hebrides. All four of the seasonal personifications anticipate Blake's later forging of myths that unite human perception and natural phenomena.

To Morning[4]

O holy virgin! clad in purest white,
Unlock heav'n's golden gates, and issue forth;
Awake the dawn that sleeps in heaven; let light
Rise from the chambers of the east, and bring
The honied dew that cometh on waking day.
O radiant morning, salute the sun,
Rouz'd like a huntsman to the chace; and, with
Thy buskin'd feet, appear upon our hills.

Song[5]

How sweet I roam'd from field to field,
  And tasted all the summer's pride,
'Till I the prince of love beheld,
  Who in the sunny beams did glide!

He shew'd me lilies for my hair,
  And blushing roses for my brow;
He led me through his gardens fair,
  Where all his golden pleasures grow.

With sweet May dews my wings were wet,
  And Phœbus fir'd my vocal rage;
He caught me in his silken net,
  And shut me in his golden cage.[6]

He loves to sit and hear me sing,
  Then, laughing, sports and plays with me;
Then stretches out my golden wing,
  And mocks my loss of liberty.

Song

My silks and fine array,
  My smiles and languish'd air,
By love are driv'n away;
  And mournful lean Despair
Brings me yew to deck my grave:
Such end true lovers have.

4. Both this poem and "To the Evening Star" echo Spenser's *Epithalamion*, lines 285–95; cf. also Psalm 19.

5. Blake was said by his friend Malkin to have written this poem before he was fourteen years old.

6. Bloom, in *The Visionary Company* (1961), recalls Sir John Davies's *A Contention Betwixt a Wife, a Widow, and a Maid:* "Wives are as birds in golden cages kept" (line 77). Cf. also Quid's song, "Matrimony's Golden Cage," in *An Island in the Moon*, chapter 9.

His face is fair as heav'n,
  When springing buds unfold;
O why to him was't giv'n,
  Whose heart is wintry cold?
His breast is love's all worship'd tomb,
Where all love's pilgrims come.

Bring me an axe and spade,
  Bring me a winding sheet;
When I my grave have made,
  Let winds and tempests beat:
Then down I'll lie, as cold as clay.
True love doth pass away!

Song

Love and harmony combine,
And around our souls intwine,
While thy branches mix with mine,
And our roots together join.

Joys upon our branches sit,
Chirping loud, and singing sweet;
Like gentle streams beneath our feet
Innocence and virtue meet.

Thou the golden fruit dost bear,
I am clad in flowers fair;
Thy sweet boughs perfume the air,
And the turtle buildeth there.

There she sits and feeds her young,
Sweet I hear her mournful song;
And thy lovely leaves among,
There is love: I hear his[7] tongue.

There his charming nest doth lay,
There he sleeps the night away;
There he sports along the day,
And doth among our branches play.

Song

I love the jocund dance,
  The softly-breathing song,
Where innocent eyes do glance,
  And where lisps the maiden's tongue.

7. Printed as "her" but corrected by hand in one copy.

I love the laughing vale,
  I love the echoing hill,
Where mirth does never fail,
  And the jolly swain laughs his fill.

I love the pleasant cot,
  I love the innocent bow'r,
Where white and brown is our lot,
  Or fruit in the mid-day hour.

I love the oaken seat,
  Beneath the oaken tree,
Where all the old villagers meet,
  And laugh our sports to see.

I love our neighbors all,
  But, Kitty, I better love thee;
And love them I ever shall;
  But thou art all to me.

Song

Memory, hither come,
  And tune your merry notes;
And, while upon the wind
  Your music floats,
I'll pore upon the stream,
Where sighing lovers dream,
And fish for fancies as they pass
Within the watery glass.

I'll drink of the clear stream,
  And hear the linnet's song;
And there I'll lie and dream
  The day along:
And, when night comes, I'll go
  To places fit for woe;
Walking along the darken'd valley,
  With silent Melancholy.

Mad Song[8]

The wild winds weep,
  And the night is a-cold;
Come hither, Sleep,
  And my griefs infold:

8. Cf. the mad songs in *King Lear*, III. In line 4 "infold" is corrected by hand from "unfold"; "birds" in line 7 is corrected from "beds."

But lo! the morning peeps
  Over the eastern steeps,
And the rustling birds of dawn
The earth do scorn.

Lo! to the vault
  Of paved heaven,
With sorrow fraught
  My notes are driven:
They strike the ear of night,
  Make weep the eyes of day;
They make mad the roaring winds,
  And with tempests play.

Like a fiend in a cloud
  With howling woe,
After night I do croud,
  And with night will go;
I turn my back to the east,
From whence comforts have increas'd;
For light doth seize my brain
With frantic pain.

Song

Fresh from the dewy hill, the merry year
Smiles on my head, and mounts his flaming car;
Round my young brows the laurel wreathes a shade,
And rising glories beam around my head.

My feet are wing'd, while o'er the dewy lawn,
I meet my maiden, risen like the morn:
Oh bless those holy feet, like angels' feet;
Oh bless those limbs, beaming with heav'nly light!

Like as an angel glitt'ring in the sky,
In times of innocence and holy joy;
The joyful shepherd stops his grateful song,
To hear the music of an angel's tongue.

So when she speaks, the voice of Heaven I hear;
So when we walk, nothing impure comes near;
Each field seems Eden, and each calm retreat;
Each village seems the haunt of holy feet.

But that sweet village where my black-ey'd maid
Closes her eyes in sleep beneath night's shade:
Whene'er I enter, more than mortal fire
Burns in my soul, and does my song inspire.

Song

When early morn walks forth in sober grey,
Then to my black ey'd maid I haste away;
When evening sits beneath her dusky bow'r,
And gently sighs away the silent hour,
The village bell alarms, away I go;
And the vale darkens at my pensive woe.

To that sweet village, where my black ey'd maid
Doth drop a tear beneath the silent shade,
I turn my eyes; and, pensive as I go,
Curse my black stars, and bless my pleasing woe.

Oft when the summer sleeps among the trees,
Whisp'ring faint murmurs to the scanty breeze,
I walk the village round; if at her side
A youth doth walk in stolen joy and pride,
I curse my stars in bitter grief and woe,
That made my love so high, and me so low.

O should she e'er prove false, his limbs I'd tear,
And throw all pity on the burning air;
I'd curse bright fortune for my mixed lot,
And then I'd die in peace, and be forgot.

To the Muses

Whether on Ida's shady brow,[9]
  Or in the chambers of the East,
The chambers of the sun, that now
  From antient melody have ceas'd;[1]

Whether in Heav'n ye wander fair,
  Or the green corners of the earth,
Or the blue regions of the air,
  Where the melodious winds have birth;

Whether on chrystal rocks ye rove
  Beneath the bosom of the sea[2]
Wand'ring in many a coral grove,
  Fair Nine, forsaking Poetry!

9. Either Mount Ida near Troy, where the Judgment of Paris took place and the gods watched the Trojan War, or another Mount Ida in Crete, where Zeus was reared.

1. A favorite poetical theme, the Westering of Culture, is presented here; cf. especially Thomas Gray, *The Progress of Poetry* (1757).

2. The last of the four elements in the series beginning with fire ("Heav'n," line 3), which was originally located with the stars. See also comments by T. S. Eliot, p. 507, below.

How have you left the antient love
  That bards of old[3] enjoy'd in you!
The languid strings do scarcely move!
  The sound is forc'd, the notes are few!

Prologue

INTENDED FOR A DRAMATIC PIECE OF

King Edward the Fourth

O for a voice like thunder, and a tongue
To drown the throat of war!—When the senses
Are shaken, and the soul is driven to madness,
Who can stand? When the souls of the oppressed
Fight in the troubled air that rages, who can stand?
When the whirlwind of fury comes from the
Throne of God, when the frowns of his countenance
Drive the nations together, who can stand?
When Sin claps his broad wings over the battle,
And sails rejoicing in the flood of Death;
When souls are torn to everlasting fire,
And fiends of Hell rejoice upon the slain,
O who can stand? O who hath caused this?
O who can answer at the throne of God?
The Kings and Nobles of the Land have done it!
Hear it not, Heaven, thy Ministers have done it!

Prologue to *King John*

Justice hath heaved a sword to plunge in Albion's breast; for Albion's sins are crimson dy'd, and the red scourge follows her desolate sons! Then Patriot rose; full oft did Patriot rise, when Tyranny hath stain'd fair Albion's breast with her own children's gore. Round his majestic feet deep thunders roll; each heart does tremble, and each knee grows slack. The stars of heaven tremble: the roaring voice of war, the trumpet, calls to battle! Brother in brother's blood must bathe, rivers of death! O land, most hapless! O beauteous island, how forsaken! Weep from thy silver fountains; weep from thy gentle rivers! The angel of the island weeps! Thy widowed vir-

3. The Celtic and classical traditions of poetry are imagined to have been compatible in some primordial time, though they have suffered a split since. The Welsh bards (made famous in Gray's *The Bard* [1757], a poem later illustrated by Blake; see notes to *A Descriptive Catalogue*) had oracular powers and were often compared with the inspired Hebrew prophets. In "The Voice of the Ancient Bard," the "Introduction" to *Songs of Experience*, and later works, Blake's ideal poet is the British Bard rather than the Greek lyrist.

gins weep beneath thy shades! Thy aged fathers gird themselves for war! The sucking infant lives to die in battle; the weeping mother feeds him for the slaughter! The husbandman doth leave his bending harvest! Blood cries afar! The land doth sow itself! The glittering youth of courts must gleam in arms! The aged senators their ancient swords assume! The trembling sinews of old age must work the work of death against their progeny; for Tyranny hath stretch'd his purple arm, and "blood," he cries; "the chariots and the horses, the noise of shout, and dreadful thunder of the battle heard afar!" —Beware, O Proud! thou shalt be humbled; thy cruel brow, thine iron heart is smitten, though lingering Fate is slow. O yet may Albion smile again, and stretch her peaceful arms, and raise her golden head, exultingly! Her citizens shall throng about her gates, her mariners shall sing upon the sea, and myraids shall to her temples crowd! Her sons shall joy as in the morning! Her daughters sing as to the rising year!

A War Song to Englishmen

Prepare, prepare the iron helm of war,
Bring forth the lots, cast in the spacious orb;
Th' Angel of Fate turns them with mighty hands,
And casts them out upon the darken'd earth!
Prepare, prepare.

Prepare your hearts for Death's cold hand! prepare
Your souls for flight, your bodies for the earth!
Prepare your arms for glorious victory!
Prepare your eyes to meet a holy God!
Prepare, prepare.

Whose fatal scroll is that? Methinks 'tis mine!
Why sinks my heart, why faultereth my tongue?
Had I three lives, I'd die in such a cause,
And rise, with ghosts, over the well-fought field.
Prepare, prepare.

The arrows of Almighty God are drawn!
Angels of Death stand in the low'ring heavens!
Thousands of souls must seek the realms of light,
And walk together on the clouds of heaven!
Prepare, prepare.

Soldiers, prepare! Our cause is Heaven's cause;
Soldiers, prepare! Be worthy of our cause:
Prepare to meet our fathers in the sky:
Prepare, O troops, that are to fall to-day!
Prepare, prepare.

Alfred shall smile, and make his harp rejoice;
The Norman William, and the learned Clerk,
And Lion Heart, and black-brow'd Edward with
His loyal queen shall rise, and welcome us!
Prepare, prepare.

Poems Written in a Copy of *Poetical Sketches*

Composed about 1787

Song by a Shepherd

Welcome, stranger, to this place,
Where joy doth sit on every bough,
Paleness flies from every face;
We reap not what we do not sow.

Innocence doth like a rose
Bloom on every maiden's cheek;
Honour twines around her brows,
The jewel health adorns her neck.

Song by an Old Shepherd

When silver snow decks Sylvio's clothes
And jewel hangs at shepherd's nose,
We can abide life's pelting storm
That makes our limbs quake, if our hearts be warm.

Whilst Virtue is our walking-staff
And Truth a lantern to our path,
We can abide life's pelting storm
That makes our limbs quake, if our hearts be warm.

Blow, boisterous Wind, stern Winter frown,
Innocence is a winter's gown;
So clad, we'll abide life's pelting storm
That makes our limbs quake, if our hearts be warm.

All Religions Are One and There Is No Natural Religion

These explosive little tractates were printed from plates averaging less than five square inches, each of which contains a single proposition and an accompanying picture. Probably Blake made the first copies in 1788, a year before he printed *Songs of Innocence* and *The Book of Thel*. The concise aphorisms that make up the tractates presume the possibility of a direct assault on truth and of the liberation of the mind from venerated superstitions. Taken together, these two tractates exhibit two basic tendencies of Blake's imagination: affirmation and refutation. His pithy affirmations hit with the force of radical novelty, while his counterstatements vigorously challenge widely held assumptions.

Blake's name does not appear in *All Religions Are One*; instead, the echo of Isaiah and John the Baptist on the frontispiece suggests that this work is the utterance of a new prophet "crying in the Wilderness." To proclaim the identity of all religions was not unprecedented in scholarly speculation of the period, but as a doctrine it was both heretical and politically radical, for it challenged the unique authority of the established church. The Argument, the seven Principles, and the Conclusion are all concerned with defining the Poetic Genius, "the true faculty of knowing." As is also made clear in plate twelve of *The Marriage of Heaven and Hell*, Blake understands Poetic Genius or the human imagination to be the source of all perceptions of God and all conceptions of regenerate humanity. With this declaration, Blake begins his lifelong effort to demolish tyrannical conceptions of divinity and he lays the foundation for his claim that true divinity originates within human nature, as it awakens to its visionary capacity.

The title of *There Is No Natural Religion* announces an attack on the deistic and atheistic notion that "natural religion" is an Enlightened alternative to the "revealed religion" of ecclesiastical and scriptural authority. Series [*a*] begins with a resounding denial (matching the grand assertion of the other tractate) of the common eighteenth-century liberal idea that God can be approached through Nature. The educational propositions that follow are dedicated to overcoming the theory that humanity is or should be limited to what it perceives through the five senses (a theme treated at length in *The Marriage of Heaven and Hell*). This is merely the "ratio," or rational reflection upon accumulated sense-data. The revolutionary idea of the work, adumbrated in series [*a*] and made explicit in series [*b*], is that a human being's desires become unlimited as his senses expand but that desires once set free can never be satisfied by sensory gratification alone. It provides also a critique of Reason, a favorite eighteenth-century standard of judgment, and of "the bounded," probably intended to encompass the social evil of bondage as well as the intellectual fetters imposed by rigid philosophical systems. Although Blake seems at this point to associate the

Infinite with the unbounded, in his *Descriptive Catalogue* of 1809 he later adds the clarification that a "bounding line" in art and life is necessary to distinguish true vision from the "indefinite."

In these polemical tractates at the beginning of his career Blake presents basic ideas that inform all his later work. With prophetic certitude he sets himself in opposition to both the superstition and repressiveness of the established church and the rationalism and materialism of its critics, and he announces that the source of spiritual power and authority is the human imagination itself, nourished by the delights of the senses but not confined to the world they perceive.

The several known copies of *There Is No Natural Religion,* all incomplete, consist of loose pages which have become scrambled, with the result that one proposition in the second series seems to be lost. The work originally consisted of twenty-one plates: an Argument, followed by two sets of numbered Propositions, and rounded off by an Application, a Conclusion, and a corollary "Therefore." Our text follows the reconstruction proposed by Keynes in the Blake Trust facsimile, except that we have placed the Conclusion before the Application. Our text for *All Religions Are One* is also taken from the Blake Trust facsimile. Both Geoffrey Keynes and David V. Erdman have recently recognized that *All Religions Are One* was printed earlier than *There Is No Natural Religion*. This sequence is consistent with Blake's usual practice of introducing an affirmative work such as *Songs of Innocence* independently, before balancing it with a counterstatement such as *Songs of Experience.*

All Religions Are One

The Voice of one crying in the Wilderness

The Argument

As the true method of knowledge is experiment, the true faculty of knowing must be the faculty which experiences. This faculty I treat of.

Principle 1st

That the Poetic Genius is the true Man, and that the body or outward form of Man is derived from the Poetic Genius. Likewise that the forms of all things are derived from their Genius, which by the Ancients was call'd an Angel & Spirit & Demon.

Principle 2d

As all men are alike in outward form, So (and with the same infinite variety) all are alike in the Poetic Genius.

Principle 3d

No man can think write or speak from his heart, but he must intend truth. Thus all sects of Philosophy are from the Poetic Genius adapted to the weaknesses of every individual.

PRINCIPLE 4

As none by travelling over known lands can find out the unknown, So from already acquired knowledge Man could not acquire more; therefore an universal Poetic Genius exists.

PRINCIPLE 5

The Religions of all Nations are derived from each Nation's different reception of the Poetic Genius, which is every where call'd the Spirit of Prophecy.

PRINCIPLE 6

The Jewish & Christian Testaments are An original derivation from the Poetic Genius. This is necessary from the confined nature of bodily sensation.

PRINCIPLE 7th

As all men are alike (tho' infinitely various) So all Religions & as all similars have one source:

The true Man is the source, he being the Poetic Genius.

There is No Natural Religion

The Author & Printer W Blake

[a]

THE ARGUMENT

Man has no notion of moral fitness but from Education. Naturally he is only a natural organ subject to Sense.

I

Man cannot naturally Percieve but through his natural or bodily organs.

II

Man by his reasoning power can only compare & judge of what he has already perciev'd.

III

From a perception of only 3 senses or 3 elements none could deduce a fourth or fifth.

IV

None could have other than natural or organic thoughts if he had none but organic perceptions.

V

Man's desires are limited by his perceptions; none can desire what he has not perciev'd.

VI

The desires & perceptions of man untaught by any thing but organs of sense, must be limited to objects of sense.

[b]

I

Man's perceptions are not bounded by organs of perception. He percieves more than sense (tho' ever so acute) can discover.

II

Reason or the ratio of all we have already known is not the same that it shall be when we know more.

III[1]

IV

The bounded is loathed by its possessor. The same dull round even of a universe would soon become a mill with complicated wheels.

V

If the many become the same as the few when possess'd, More! More! is the cry of a mistaken soul; less than All cannot satisfy Man.

VI

If any could desire what he is incapable of possessing, despair must be his eternal lot.

VII

The desire of Man being Infinite, the possession is Infinite, & himself Infinite.

CONCLUSION

If it were not for the Poetic or Prophetic character the Philosophic & Experimental would soon be at the ratio of all things, & stand still, unable to do other than repeat the same dull round over again.

APPLICATION

He who sees the Infinite in all things sees God. He who sees the Ratio only sees himself only.

THEREFORE

God becomes as we are, that we may be as he is.

Songs of Innocence and of Experience (1789–94)

Blake's best-loved work, subtitled "Shewing the Two Contrary States of the Human Soul," is the only one of his books that during his lifetime attracted the admiration of his fellow writers—Wordsworth, Coleridge, and Lamb. The *Innocence* series was the first to be etched, in 1789 when Blake was thirty-two, though three of these songs appeared first in 1784 in the boisterous manuscript satire *An Island in the Moon*. At least twenty-two

1. This page, if it ever existed, is lost.

copies of the single volume *Songs of Innocence* and twenty-seven of the combined *Innocence and Experience* were printed; thus, these songs were by far the most widely circulated of Blake's works. "Holy Thursday" and "The Chimney Sweeper" of *Innocence* were reprinted in contemporary anthologies; "Introduction" and "Holy Thursday" of *Innocence*, and "The Tyger" and "The Garden of Love" (along with a poem from *Poetical Sketches*) were translated into German by Henry Crabb Robinson and published in 1811. Whatever literary reputation Blake had in his time, an age when Byron's first editions of 18,000 sold out overnight, rested on the *Songs*.

The relationship of Innocence and Experience, as contrary states of the soul and as cycles of songs, is not one of direct, static contrast but of shifting tensions. Blake's Innocence, with its central figures of child, lamb, flower, shepherd, and piper, should be considered the primary state, the norm by which Experience is evaluated, a clear vision of the way life ought to be and indeed can be for many children and for good-hearted adults like the Nurse and the Shepherd. Within the state of Innocence, however, there is the possibility of change and even of corruption: children must go indoors at nightfall because dangers may lurk about, shepherds are needed because there are wolves, and spring and summer die into winter. The state of Innocence is not a pastoral idyll in which the inhabitants are perfectly immune from menace. As Blake shows it, Innocence is a condition of mind and spirit, a freshness of perspective; yet to be innocent is not always to be ignorant of the facts that children get lost or punished, or have to live in orphanages, or are sold as slaves or chimney sweeps. In Innocence, even though children may be victimized by circumstances, they retain a spiritual resilience; with joy and contentment they love their enemies and dream of a better world.

Blake, the creator of these invincible innocents, was himself neither complacent nor naive nor did he expect his readers to be. The reader he addresses will neither deny the appearance and reality of happiness in Innocence nor attempt to explain away the evidences of woe that are also contained in the *Songs*. The child who inspires the first song of innocence (in the "Introduction" to *Innocence*) is an exemplary listener: he laughs on first hearing, then weeps, then weeps with joy. Similarly, the adult reader detects signs of external wretchedness that threaten the inner peace of characters in Innocence. Blake kept all these viewpoints before him. During the time he was printing, painting, and selling *Songs of Innocence*, *Thel*, *The Marriage of Heaven and Hell*, *Visions of the Daughters of Albion*, and *For Children: The Gates of Paradise*, he was also drafting and sketching the *Songs of Experience* in his Notebook. In 1793 he advertised the *Experience* volume for sale and published separate copies occasionally. The combined volume, *Songs of Innocence and of Experience*, is dated 1794 and was issued repeatedly over the years through 1826. *Songs of Innocence*, however, was not supplanted by *Experience* nor by the combined volume; Blake continued to produce it separately as late as 1808, as customers ordered it. He constantly reconsidered the interplay both *between* the two states of the soul and *among* the songs that convey these states: he transferred "The Little Girl Lost" and "The Little Girl Found," "The Schoolboy," and "The Voice of the Ancient Bard" from *Innocence* to *Experience*; he rearranged the order of the songs in most copies (until he standardized it in seven of the last eight issued); he added "To Tirzah" to *Experience* after 1805, while he was working on his major prophetic epics.

The voice that introduces—and in many copies also concludes—the *Experience* series is that of the Bard, who "Present, Past, & Future sees." He is aware that the fallen condition need not be permanent and his vision comprehends both Innocence and Experience, from the inside, as well as from without. But the notes of woe heard throughout Experience reecho "Earth's Answer," a fallen response to the Bard's "Introduction": the state of Experience is so dark and self-enclosed that there appears no way out. The dominant images are of prematurely blighted and embittered children, dark forests, sick flowers, wild beasts, the black and bloody city, and the poisonous dead Tree of Mystery that grows in the human brain. Adult figures who should be protective are hostile or indifferent, and parents in league with "God & his Priest & his King" run an evil system in which soldiers and harlots are as victimized as boys and girls. Yet here and there are glimmers of hope: a little vagabond singing of ultimate reconciliation, a lily freely offering herself in love, a flying and dancing boy and girl above the mournful scene on the title page of *Experience*.

In his later works Blake made a distinction between states and individuals: the individual is real and eternal, the state is a temporary condition of error or illusion through which the individual passes. In *The Marriage of Heaven and Hell* the point is made that "Without Contraries is no progression." And in a manuscript discussion of a painting of the Last Judgment Blake notes that "whenever any Individual Rejects Error & Embraces Truth a Last Judgment passes upon that Individual." Comments like these help the reader see that the fallen condition depicted on the general title page for *Innocence and Experience*—Adam and Eve in despair at the expulsion from Paradise—may be reversed at any time. The most important thing to keep in mind in reading each poem in the collection is that its presentation of the world is colored by the state the individual speaker is in. This point tends to be clearest in the contrasting poems which have identical titles, such as "Holy Thursday." It is a good exercise also to observe which speakers in *Innocence* seem destined shortly to move into *Experience*, and which speakers in *Experience* show signs of becoming able to awaken out of their erroneous perceptions. In the reader's mind the claims of Innocence and Experience should be weighed against each other; it is possible for the reader to share with the artist a vision that encompasses both and allows for the growth that comes out of a continual strife of contraries.

Our text follows Copy Z, the Blake Trust facsimile. Plate numbers are given in brackets to aid students in studying the facsimile, the microfilm of Copy AA available in most libraries, and the bibliographical information in Keynes and Wolf, *William Blake's Illuminated Books: A Census* (1953), and in scholarly essays. Color plates illustrating *Songs* are taken from Copy U (Princeton), Copy V (Pierpont Morgan Library), as well as Copy Z (Lessing J. Rosenwald Collection, Library of Congress). For comparison with the more simply colored early copies of the separate *Innocence* volume, see color plate 3, from Copy B of *Songs of Innocence*, Rosenwald collection, Library of Congress.

SONGS
of
Innocence
1789
The Author & Printer W Blake

Songs of Innocence and of Experience*

Shewing the Two Contrary States of the Human Soul

[PLATE 3]

SONGS OF INNOCENCE†
1789

The Author & Printer W Blake

[PLATE 4]

Introduction

Piping down the valleys wild
Piping songs of pleasant glee
On a cloud I saw a child,
And he laughing said to me:

"Pipe a song about a Lamb."[1]
So I piped with merry chear.
"Piper pipe that song again—"
So I piped, he wept to hear.

"Drop thy pipe thy happy pipe,
Sing thy songs of happy chear."
So I sung the same again
While he wept with joy to hear.

"Piper sit thee down and write
In a book that all may read—"
So he vanish'd from my sight.
And I pluck'd a hollow reed,

And I made a rural pen,
And I stain'd the water clear,
And I wrote my happy songs
Every child may joy to hear.

* See color plate 1 for general title page.
† See color plate 2 for frontispiece.
1. Piping is a conventional activity of pastoral poems; here perhaps it is related to the inappropriate piping in Luke 7:31–35. The song about a Lamb recalls the joy and sorrow associated with Jesus, Lamb of God (as presented in "The Lamb" and "Night").

[PLATE 5]

The Shepherd

How sweet is the Shepherd's sweet lot,
From the morn to the evening he strays:
He shall follow his sheep all the day
And his tongue shall be filled with praise.

For he hears the lambs' innocent call,
And he hears the ewes' tender reply,
He is watchful while they are in peace,
For they know when their Shepherd is nigh.

[PLATE 6]

The Ecchoing Green

The Sun does arise,
And make happy the skies.
The merry bells ring
To welcome the Spring.
The sky-lark and thrush,
The birds of the bush,
Sing louder around,
To the bells' chearful sound.
While our sports shall be seen
On the Ecchoing Green.

Old John with white hair
Does laugh away care,
Sitting under the oak,
Among the old folk.
[PLATE 7] They laugh at our play,
And soon they all say,
"Such, such were the joys,
When we all girls & boys,
In our youth-time were seen,
On the Ecchoing Green."

Till the little ones weary
No more can be merry.
The sun does descend,
And our sports have an end:
Round the laps of their mothers,
Many sisters and brothers,
Like birds in their nest,
Are ready for rest;
And sport no more seen,
On the darkening Green.

[PLATE 8]

The Lamb

Little Lamb who made thee?
Dost thou know who made thee?
Gave thee life & bid thee feed
By the stream & o'er the mead;
Gave thee clothing of delight,

Softest clothing wooly bright;
Gave thee such a tender voice,
Making all the vales rejoice:
  Little Lamb who made thee?
  Dost thou know who made thee?

  Little Lamb I'll tell thee,
  Little Lamb I'll tell thee:
He is called by thy name,
For he calls himself a Lamb:
He is meek & he is mild,
He became a little child:
I a child & thou a lamb,
We are called by his name.
  Little Lamb God bless thee.
  Little Lamb God bless thee.

[PLATE 9]

The Little Black Boy‡

My mother bore me in the southern wild,
And I am black, but O! my soul is white.
White as an angel is the English child:
But I am black as if bereav'd of light.

‡ See color plates 3 and 4 for two versions of the second page of this poem.

My mother taught me underneath a tree
And sitting down before the heat of day,
She took me on her lap and kissed me,
And pointing to the east began to say:

"Look on the rising sun: there God does live
And gives his light, and gives his heat away.
And flowers and trees and beasts and men recieve
Comfort in morning, joy in the noon day.

And we are put on earth a little space,
That we may learn to bear the beams of love,
And these black bodies and this sun-burnt face
Is but a cloud, and like a shady grove.

[PLATE 10]

For when our souls have learn'd the heat to bear
The cloud will vanish; we shall hear his voice,
Saying: 'Come out from the grove my love & care,
And round my golden tent like lambs rejoice.' "

Thus did my mother say and kissed me,
And thus I say to little English boy:
When I from black and he from white cloud free,
And round the tent of God like lambs we joy:

I'll shade him from the heat till he can bear
To lean in joy upon our father's knee.
And then I'll stand and stroke his silver hair,
And be like him and he will then love me.

The Blossom.
Merry Merry Sparrow
Under leaves so green
A happy Blossom
Sees you swift as arrow
Seek your cradle narrow
Near my Bosom.
Pretty Pretty Robin
Under leaves so green
A happy Blossom
Hears you sobbing sobbing
Pretty Pretty Robin
Near my Bosom.

[PLATE 11]

The Blossom

Merry Merry Sparrow
Under leaves so green
A happy Blossom
Sees you swift as arrow
Seek your cradle narrow
Near my Bosom.

Pretty Pretty Robin
Under leaves so green
A happy Blossom
Hears you sobbing sobbing
Pretty Pretty Robin
Near my Bosom.

[PLATE 12]

The Chimney Sweeper[2]

When my mother died I was very young,
And my father sold me while yet my tongue
Could scarcely cry weep weep weep weep.
So your chimneys I sweep & in soot I sleep.

2. Like other Songs, this poem presupposes some awareness of social institutions that no longer exist. Martin K. Nurmi, "Fact and Symbol in 'The Chimney Sweeper' . . .," (*Bulletin of the New York Public Library,* 1964; reprinted in Frye, *Blake: A Collection of Critical Essays*) describes the sweeps' misery: hazards of suffocation, permanently blackened skin, legs made crooked by the weight of heavy bags, and cancer of the scrotum; a law passed in 1788 to help the sweeps was never enforced. "Weep" in line 3 is an ironic rendering of the child's pronunciation of the street cry, "Sweep!"

There's little Tom Dacre, who cried when his head
That curl'd like a lamb's back, was shav'd, so I said,
"Hush Tom never mind it, for when your head's bare,
You know that the soot cannot spoil your white hair."

And so he was quiet, & that very night,
As Tom was a sleeping he had such a sight,
That thousands of sweepers Dick, Joe, Ned & Jack
Were all of them lock'd up in coffins of black.

And by came an Angel who had a bright key,
And he open'd the coffins & set them all free.
Then down a green plain leaping laughing they run
And wash in a river and shine in the Sun.

Then naked & white, all their bags left behind,
They rise upon clouds, and sport in the wind.
And the Angel told Tom if he'd be a good boy,
He'd have God for his father & never want joy.

And so Tom awoke and we rose in the dark
And got with our bags & our brushes to work.
Tho' the morning was cold, Tom was happy & warm,
So if all do their duty, they need not fear harm.

[PLATE 13]

The Little Boy Lost

"Father, father, where are you going
O do not walk so fast.
Speak father, speak to your little boy
Or else I shall be lost."

The night was dark, no father was there.
The child was wet with dew.
The mire was deep, & the child did weep
And away the vapour flew.

[PLATE 14]

The Little Boy Found

The little boy lost in the lonely fen,
Led by the wand'ring light,
Began to cry, but God ever nigh,
Appeard like his father in white.

He kissed the child & by the hand led
And to his mother brought,
Who in sorrow pale, thro' the lonely dale
Her little boy weeping sought.

[PLATE 15]

Laughing Song

When the green woods laugh with the voice of joy
And the dimpling stream runs laughing by,
When the air does laugh with our merry wit,
And the green hill laughs with the noise of it.

When the meadows laugh with lively green
And the grasshopper laughs in the merry scene,
When Mary and Susan and Emily,
With their sweet round mouths sing Ha, Ha, He.

When the painted birds laugh in the shade
Where our table with cherries and nuts is spread
Come live & be merry and join with me,
To sing the sweet chorus of Ha, Ha, He.

[PLATE 16]

A Cradle Song[3]

Sweet dreams form a shade,
O'er my lovely infant's head.
Sweet dreams of pleasant streams,
By happy silent moony beams.

Sweet sleep with soft down,
Weave thy brows an infant crown.
Sweet sleep Angel mild,
Hover o'er my happy child.

Sweet smiles in the night,
Hover over my delight.
Sweet smiles, Mother's smiles,
All the livelong night beguiles.

Sweet moans, dovelike sighs,
Chase not slumber from thy eyes.
Sweet moans, sweeter smiles,
All the dovelike moans beguiles.

Sleep sleep happy child.
All creation slept and smil'd.
Sleep sleep, happy sleep,
While o'er thee thy mother weep.

3. This poem is closely modeled on Watts's "Cradle Hymn," as explained by Vivian de Solo Pinto in *The Divine Vision* (1957) and Martha Winburn England, *Hymns Unbidden* (1966).

Sweet babe in thy face,
Holy image I can trace.
Sweet babe once like thee,
Thy maker lay and wept for me,

[PLATE 17]

Wept for me, for thee, for all,
When he was an infant small.
Thou his image ever see,
Heavenly face that smiles on thee;

Smiles on thee, on me, on all,
Who become an infant small,
Infant smiles are his own smiles,
Heaven & earth to peace beguiles.

[PLATE 18]

The Divine Image

To Mercy Pity Peace and Love,
All pray in their distress:
And to these virtues of delight
Return their thankfulness.

For Mercy Pity Peace and Love
Is God our father dear:
And Mercy Pity Peace and Love
Is Man his child and care.

For Mercy has a human heart
Pity, a human face:
And Love, the human form divine,
And Peace, the human dress.

Then every man of every clime,
That prays in his distress,
Prays to the human form divine
Love Mercy Pity Peace.

And all must love the human form,
In heathen, turk or jew.
Where Mercy, Love & Pity dwell
There God is dwelling too.

The Divine Image.

To Mercy Pity Peace and Love,
All pray in their distress:
And to these virtues of delight
Return their thankfulness.

For Mercy Pity Peace and Love,
Is God our father dear:
And Mercy Pity Peace and Love,
Is Man his child and care.

For Mercy has a human heart
Pity, a human face:
And Love, the human form divine,
And Peace, the human dress.

Then every man of every clime,
That prays in his distress,
Prays to the human form divine
Love Mercy Pity Peace.

And all must love the human form,
In heathen, turk or jew;
Where Mercy, Love & Pity dwell,
There God is dwelling too.

[PLATE 19]

Holy Thursday[4]

Twas on a Holy Thursday, their innocent faces clean,
The children walking two & two in red & blue & green;
Grey headed beadles walkd before with wands as white as snow,
Till into the high dome of Paul's they like Thames waters flow.

O what a multitude they seemed, these flowers of London town;
Seated in companies they sit with radiance all their own.
The hum of multitudes was there but multitudes of lambs,
Thousands of little boys & girls raising their innocent hands.

Now like a mighty wind they raise to heaven the voice of song
Or like harmonious thunderings the seats of heaven among.
Beneath them sit the aged men, wise guardians of the poor.
Then cherish pity, lest you drive an angel from your door.

4. Once a year as many as 6,000 destitute children were marched from their charity schools all over London to attend services held in Saint Paul's Cathedral beginning in 1782. This spectacle in honor of the patrons and founders of the schools took place on a Thursday during the Easter season, but *not* on Maundy Thursday (before Easter) or Ascension Day (forty days thereafter). See David V. Erdman, *Blake: Prophet Against Empire*; Robert Gleckner, *MLN* 71 (1956), 412–15; and T. E. Connolly, *Blake Studies 6* (1975), 179–187, for details. The last line of the poem echoes Hebrews 13:2.

[PLATE 20]

Night

The sun descending in the west
The evening star does shine.
The birds are silent in their nest,
And I must seek for mine.
The moon, like a flower,
In heaven's high bower,
With silent delight
Sits and smiles on the night.

Farewell green fields and happy groves,
Where flocks have took delight;
Where lambs have nibbled, silent moves
The feet of angels bright;
Unseen they pour blessing,
And joy without ceasing,
On each bud and blossom,
And each sleeping bosom.

They look in every thoughtless nest,
Where birds are covered warm;
They visit caves of every beast,
To keep them all from harm.
If they see any weeping,
That should have been sleeping,
They pour sleep on their head
And sit down by their bed.

[PLATE 21] When wolves and tygers howl for prey
They pitying stand and weep;
Seeking to drive their thirst away,
And keep them from the sheep.
But if they rush dreadful;
The angels most heedful,
Recieve each mild spirit,
New worlds to inherit.

And there the lion's ruddy eyes
Shall flow with tears of gold:
And pitying the tender cries,
And walking round the fold:
Saying: "Wrath by his meekness
And by his health, sickness,
Is driven away,
From our immortal day.

"And now beside thee bleating lamb,
I can lie down and sleep;[5]
Or think on him who bore thy name,
Grase after thee and weep.
For wash'd in life's river,[6]
My bright mane for ever
Shall shine like the gold,
As I guard o'er the fold."

[PLATE 22]

Spring

Sound the Flute!
Now it's mute.
Birds delight
Day and Night.
Nightingale
In the dale
Lark in Sky
Merrily
Merrily Merrily to welcome in the Year.

Little Boy
Full of joy.
[PLATE 23] Little Girl
Sweet and small,
Cock does crow
So do you.
Merry voice
Infant noise
Merrily Merrily to welcome in the Year.

Little Lamb
Here I am.
Come and lick
My white neck.
Let me pull
Your soft Wool.
Let me kiss
Your soft face.
Merrily Merrily we welcome in the Year.

5. The image of an idyllic state when the lion and lamb shall lie down together derives from Isaiah 11:6 and 65:25.

6. This image derives from Ezekiel 47:1–3 and Revelation 22:1–2.

[PLATE 24]

Nurse's Song

When the voices of children are heard on the green
And laughing is heard on the hill,
My heart is at rest within my breast
And every thing else is still

"Then come home my children, the sun is gone down
And the dews of night arise;
Come come leave off play, and let us away
Till the morning appears in the skies."

"No no let us play, for it is yet day
And we cannot go to sleep;
Besides in the sky, the little birds fly
And the hills are all covered with sheep."

"Well well go & play till the light fades away
And then go home to bed."
The little ones leaped & shouted & laugh'd
And all the hills ecchoed.

[PLATE 25]

Infant Joy†

"I have no name
I am but two days old.—"
"What shall I call thee?"
"I happy am
Joy is my name,—"
"Sweet Joy befall thee!

† See color plate 5.

"Pretty joy!
Sweet joy but two days old.
Sweet joy I call thee:
Thou dost smile.
I sing the while
Sweet joy befall thee."

[PLATE 26]

A Dream

Once a dream did weave a shade,
O'er my Angel-guarded bed,
That an Emmet lost its way
Where on grass methought I lay.

Troubled, wilderd, and folorn;
Dark, benighted, travel-worn,
Over many a tangled spray
All heart-broke I heard her say:

"O my children! do they cry,
Do they hear their father sigh?
Now they look abroad to see,
Now return and weep for me."

Pitying I drop'd a tear:
But I saw a glow-worm near:
Who replied: "What wailing wight
Calls the watchman of the night?

"I am set to light the ground,
While the beetle goes his round:
Follow now the beetle's hum,
Little wanderer, hie thee home."

[PLATE 27]

On Another's Sorrow

Can I see another's woe,
And not be in sorrow too?
Can I see another's grief,
And not seek for kind relief?

Can I see a falling tear,
And not feel my sorrow's share?
Can a father see his child
Weep, nor be with sorrow fill'd?

Can a mother sit and hear
An infant groan, an infant fear?
No no never can it be.
Never never can it be.

And can he who smiles on all
Hear the wren with sorrows small,
Hear the small bird's grief & care
Hear the woes that infants bear—

And not sit beside the nest
Pouring pity in their breast,
And not sit the cradle near
Weeping tear on infant's tear?

And not sit both night & day,
Wiping all our tears away?
O! no never can it be.
Never never can it be.

He doth give his joy to all.
He becomes an infant small.
He becomes a man of woe.
He doth feel the sorrow too.

Think not, thou canst sigh a sigh,
And thy maker is not by.
Think not, thou canst weep a tear,
And thy maker is not near.

O! he gives to us his joy,
That our grief he may destroy;
Till our grief is fled & gone
He doth sit by us and moan.

[PLATE 29]

SONGS OF EXPERIENCE‡

1794

The Author & Printer W Blake

‡ See color plate 6 for frontispiece, plate 28.

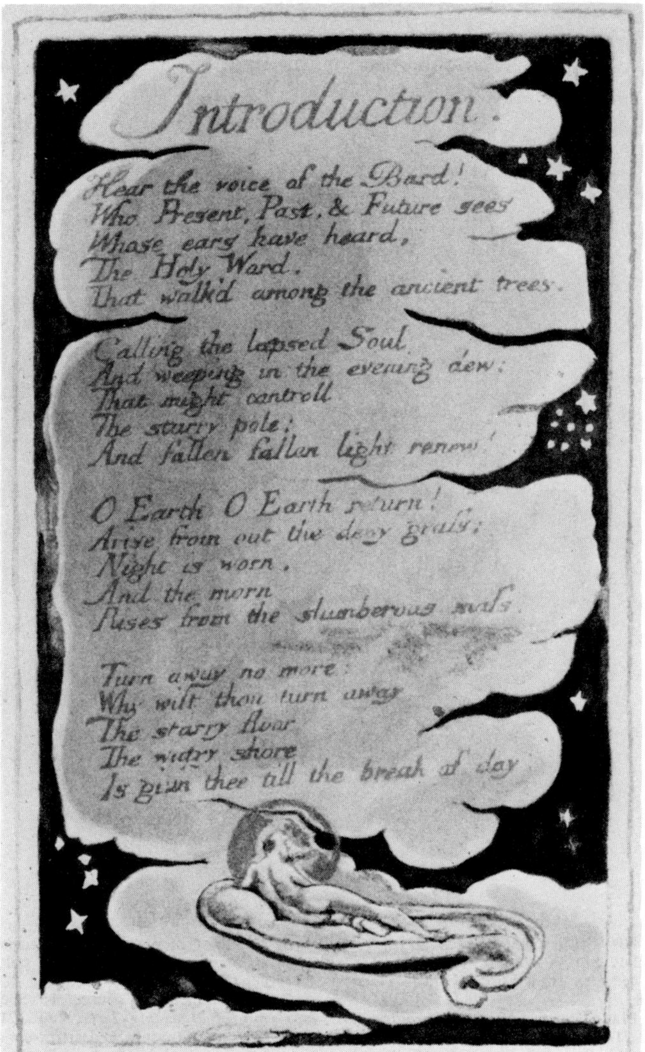
Introduction.
Hear the voice of the Bard!
Who Present, Past, & Future sees
Whose ears have heard,
The Holy Word,
That walk'd among the ancient trees.
Calling the lapsed Soul
And weeping in the evening dew;
That might controll
The starry pole;
And fallen fallen light renew!
O Earth O Earth return!
Arise from out the dewy grass;
Night is worn,
And the morn
Rises from the slumberous mass.
Turn away no more:
Why wilt thou turn away
The starry floor
The watry shore
Is giv'n thee till the break of day.

[PLATE 30]

Introduction

Hear the voice of the Bard![7]
Who Present, Past, & Future sees,
Whose ears have heard
The Holy Word,[8]
That walk'd among the ancient trees.

Calling the lapsed Soul[9]
And weeping in the evening dew:
That might controll
The starry pole:[1]
And fallen fallen light renew!

"O Earth O Earth return![2]
Arise from out the dewy grass;
Night is worn,
And the morn
Rises from the slumberous mass.

"Turn away no more:
Why wilt thou turn away?
The starry floor,
The watry shore
Is giv'n thee till the break of day."[3]

7. His vision comprehends all time and makes him a witness (line 3) of "the voice of the Lord God" (Genesis 3:8).

8. Blake follows Milton (*Paradise Lost*, X, 71–108) rather than Genesis in having the Son rather than the Father summon the lapsed Soul. See Frye, "Blake's Introduction to Experience," *Huntington Library Quarterly*, 21 (1957) 57–67; rpt. Frye, *Blake: A Collection of Critical Essays* (1966). In John 1:1 Jesus is identified as the "Word."

9. The adjective is probably dissyllabic.

1. The fallen world is benighted and the stars, though beautiful, are dim remnants of the light of eternity. In a regenerate state man would control the pole star rather than be whirled about it.

2. The immediate source is Spenser's *Hymn of Heavenly Love*, lines 218–25: "Then rouze thyself, O Earth, out of thy soil . . . And read through love [the Lord's] mercies manifold." Behind both is Jeremiah 22:29. "O Earth, earth, earth, hear the voice of the Lord." Cf. *Jerusalem* 4 :6–21.

3. In Job 38:10–11 the shore is a providential limit to the sea. The limiting "shore" and "floor" foreshadow the limits of opacity and contraction in *Milton* 13:20–21 and elsewhere.

[PLATE 31]

Earth's Answer

Earth rais'd up her head,
From the darkness dread & drear.
Her light fled:
Stony dread!
And her locks cover'd with grey despair.

"Prison'd on watry shore
Starry Jealousy does keep my den[4]
Cold and hoar
Weeping o'er
I hear the Father of the ancient men.

"Selfish father of men!
Cruel, jealous, selfish fear!
Can delight
Chain'd in night
The virgins of youth and morning bear?

"Does spring hide its joy
When buds and blossoms grow?
Does the sower?
Sow by night?
Or the plowman in darkness plow?

"Break this heavy chain,[5]
That does freeze my bones around
Selfish! vain!
Eternal bane!
That free Love with bondage bound."

4. Benighted Earth experiences her condition beneath the stars and beside the "watry shore" as bondage. In the "Introduction" the Son as "Word" and his prophet the "Bard" are the speakers; consequently, Earth's perception of the "father" indicates that she has not received the message as it is sent; cf. *Milton* 9:23. Some critics adopt Earth's perspective and condemn both Bard and Holy Word as hypocritical. Since fathers in Experience often appear as repressive figures, the distinction between Father and Son is crucial.

5. Earth demands to be liberated, rather than freeing herself.

[PLATE 32]

The Clod & the Pebble

"Love seeketh not Itself to please,
Nor for itself hath any care;
But for another gives its ease,
And builds a Heaven in Hell's despair."

So sang a little Clod of Clay,
Trodden with the cattle's feet:
But a Pebble of the brook,
Warbled out these metres meet:

"Love seeketh only Self to please,
To bind another to its delight;
Joys in another's loss of ease,
And builds a Hell in Heaven's despite."[6]

[PLATE 33]

Holy Thursday

Is this a holy thing to see,
In a rich and fruitful land,
Babes reduced to misery,
Fed with cold and usurous hand?

Is that trembling cry a song?
Can it be a song of joy?
And so many children poor?
It is a land of poverty!

And their sun does never shine.
And their fields are bleak & bare.
And their ways are fill'd with thorns.
It is eternal winter there.

For where-e'er the sun does shine,
And where-e'er the rain does fall:
Babe can never hunger there,
Nor poverty the mind appall.

6. The Clod's view recalls St. Paul's praise of charity in I Corinthians 13, whereas the Pebble's recalls Satan's defiant assertion in *Paradise Lost* I, 254–55: "The mind is its own place, and in itself / Can make a Heaven of Hell, a Hell of Heaven."

[PLATE 34]

The Little Girl Lost[7]*

In futurity
I prophetic see,[8]
That the earth from sleep,
(Grave[9] the sentence deep)

Shall arise and seek
For her maker meek:
And the desart wild
Become a garden mild.[1]

In the southern clime,
Where the summer's prime,
Never fades away,
Lovely Lyca[2] lay.

Seven summers old
Lovely Lyca told;
She had wanderd long,
Hearing wild birds' song.

"Sweet sleep come to me
Underneath this tree;
Do father, mother weep.—
'Where can Lyca sleep?'

"Lost in desart wild
Is your little child.
How can Lyca sleep,
If her mother weep?

"If her heart does ake,
Then let Lyca wake:
If my mother sleep,
Lyca shall not weep.

* See color plate 7.
7. This and the following work first appeared in *Innocence*.
8. The Bard, "Who Present, Past, & Future sees."
9. A serious pun on the severity of Earth's suffering, the solemnity of the bardic voice, and the engraving process.

1. Cf. Isaiah 35:1: "The desert shall rejoice and blossom as the rose."
2. A mythological name not used elsewhere in Blake's published writings, perhaps derived from Latin "wolf," since Lyca's story is similar to legends of children reared in the wild by wolves.

"Frowning frowning night,
O'er this desart bright,
Let thy moon arise,
While I close my eyes."

Sleeping Lyca lay:
While the beasts of prey,
Come from caverns deep,
View'd the maid asleep.

The kingly lion stood
And the virgin view'd,
Then he gambold round
O'er the hallowed ground:

[PLATE 35]

Leopards, tygers play,
Round her as she lay;
While the lion old,
Bow'd his mane of gold.

And her bosom lick,
And upon her neck,
From his eyes of flame,
Ruby tears there came:

While the lioness
Loos'd her slender dress,
And naked they convey'd
To caves the sleeping maid.

The Little Girl Found

All the night in woe
Lyca's parents go:
Over vallies deep,
While the desarts weep.

Tired and woe-begone,
Hoarse with making moan:
Arm in arm seven days,
They trac'd the desart ways.

Seven nights they sleep,
Among shadows deep:
And dream they see their child
Starv'd in desart wild.

Pale thro pathless ways
The fancied image strays,
[PLATE 36] Famish'd, weeping, weak
With hollow piteous shriek.

Rising from unrest,
The trembling woman prest
With feet of weary woe;
She could no further go.

In his arms he bore
Her arm'd with sorrow sore;
Till before their way,
A couching lion lay.

Turning back was vain,
Soon his heavy mane,
Bore them to the ground;
Then he stalk'd around,

Smelling to his prey.
But their fears allay,
When he licks their hands;
And silent by them stands.

They look upon his eyes
Fill'd with deep surprise:
And wondering behold,
A spirit arm'd in gold.

On his head a crown
On his shoulders down,
Flow'd his golden hair.
Gone was all their care.

"Follow me," he said,
"Weep not for the maid;
In my palace deep,
Lyca lies asleep."

Then they followed,
Where the vision led:
And saw their sleeping child,
Among tygers wild.

To this day they dwell
In a lonely dell
Nor fear the wolvish howl,
Nor the lions' growl.

[PLATE 37]

The Chimney Sweeper

A little black thing among the snow:
Crying weep, weep, in notes of woe!
"Where are thy father & mother? say?"
"They are both gone up to the church to pray.

"Because I was happy upon the heath,
And smil'd among the winter's snow:
They clothed me in the clothes of death,
And taught me to sing the notes of woe.

"And because I am happy, & dance & sing,
They think they have done me no injury:
And are gone to praise God & his Priest & King
Who make up a heaven of our misery."

[PLATE 38]

Nurse's Song

When the voices of children are heard on the green
And whisprings are in the dale:
The days of my youth rise fresh in my mind,
My face turns green and pale.

"Then come home my children, the sun is gone down
And the dews of night arise
Your spring & your day, are wasted in play
And your winter and night in disguise."

[PLATE 39]

The Sick Rose†

O Rose thou art sick.
The invisible worm
That flies in the night,
In the howling storm:

† See color plate 8.

Has found out thy bed
Of crimson joy:
And his dark secret love
Does thy life destroy.

[PLATE 40]

The Fly

Little Fly,
Thy summer's play
My thoughtless hand
Has brush'd away.

Am not I
A fly like thee?
Or art not thou
A man like me?

For I dance
And drink & sing;
Till some blind hand
Shall brush my wing.[3]

3. Cf. *King Lear* IV, i, 36–7: "As flies to wanton boys are we to the gods; / They kill us for ther sport."

If thought is life
And strength & breath:
And the want
Of thought is death;

Then am I
A happy fly,
If I live,
Or if I die.

[PLATE 41]

The Angel

I Dreamt a Dream! what can it mean?
And that I was a maiden Queen:
Guarded by an Angel mild;
Witless woe, was ne'er beguil'd!

And I wept both night and day
And he wip'd my tears away
And I wept both day and night
And hid from him my heart's delight.

So he took his wings and fled:
Then the morn blush'd rosy red:
I dried my tears & armd my fears
With ten thousand shields and spears.

Soon my Angel came again:
I was arm'd, he came in vain:
For the time of youth was fled
And grey hairs were on my head.

[PLATE 42]

The Tyger

Tyger, Tyger, burning bright,
In the forests of the night:[4]
What immortal hand or eye,
Could frame thy fearful symmetry?

In what distant deeps or skies
Burnt the fire of thine eyes?
On what wings dare he aspire?
What the hand dare sieze the fire?

4. Not merely *at* night; these forests *belong to* Night as an absolute principle, not just a time of darkness.

And what shoulder, & what art,
Could twist the sinews of thy heart?
And when thy heart began to beat,
What dread hand? & what dread feet?[5]

What the hammer? what the chain?
In what furnace was thy brain?
What the anvil? what dread grasp,
Dare its deadly terrors clasp?

When the stars threw down their spears
And water'd heaven with their tears:[6]
Did he smile his work to see?
Did he who made the Lamb[7] make thee?

Tyger, Tyger, burning bright,
In the forests of the night:
What immortal hand or eye,
Dare frame thy fearful symmetry?

[PLATE 43]

My Pretty Rose Tree

A flower was offerd to me;
Such a flower as May never bore.
But I said, "I've a Pretty Rose-tree."
And I passed the sweet flower o'er.

5. In one copy Blake altered "& what" to "Formd thy." In the letterpress text issued by his friend Malkin these words appeared as "forgd thy." Other minor variants also appear in Malkin's text.

6. Among the numerous echoes in Blake is Urizen's lament: "The stars threw down their spears and fled naked away / We fell" (*The Four Zoas,* V, 64:27–28), an allusion to the war in Heaven in *Paradise Lost* and Revelation.

7. This explicit reference to the counterpart poem in Innocence recalls the identification of Jesus as "The Lamb of God," as in John 1:29, 36; Revelation 5:6. On this highly controversial poem, see Adams and Grant, *Texas Studies in Literature and Language* (1961; rpt. Grant, ed., *Discussions*); also Winston Weathers, ed., *The Tyger* (1969).

Then I went to my Pretty Rose-tree
To tend her by day and by night.
But my Rose turnd away with jealousy:
And her thorns were my only delight.

Ah! Sun-Flower[8]

Ah Sun-flower! weary of time,
Who countest the steps of the Sun:
Seeking after that sweet golden clime
Where the traveller's journey is done.

Where the Youth pined away with desire,
And the pale Virgin shrouded in snow:
Arise from their graves and aspire,
Where my Sun-flower wishes to go.

The Lilly

The modest Rose puts forth a thorn:
The humble Sheep, a threatning horn:
While the Lilly white, shall in Love delight,
Nor a thorn nor a threat stain her beauty bright.

[PLATE 44]

The Garden of Love

I went to the Garden of Love,
And saw what I never had seen:
A Chapel was built in the midst,
Where I used to play on the green.

And the gates of this Chapel were shut,
And Thou shalt not writ over the door;[9]
So I turn'd to the Garden of Love,
That so many sweet flowers bore,

8. In Ovid, *Metamorphosis* IV, 192, Clytie, in love with Apollo, was spurned by the god and pined away till she became a heliotrope, a flower fabled always to face the sun. "My Pretty Rose-Tree," "Ah! Sun-Flower," and "The Lilly" are all printed on a single plate; this is the only three-poem sequence that of course was never varied when Blake rearranged the *Songs*.

9. Cf. the instructions in Deuteronomy 6:9 to write "Thou shalt Love the Lord thy God . . .," a positive commandment, "upon the posts of thy house and on thy gates"; also *Europe: A Prophecy* 12:28. As Mrs. [Sarah] Trimmer observed in *The Oeconomy of Charity* (1787; revised edition, 1801), "It will be of little use to persuade the poor to go to their proper places of worship if, when they do so, they either find the doors shut against their entrance, or no acommodation for them; . . . very few parish churches in the metropolis, whatever room there may be in the *locked-up pews,* furnish seats for the poor." (Rich people rented their pews.) The negative commandments pervade and corrupt all life.

And I saw it was filled with graves,
And tomb-stones where flowers should be:
And Priests in black gowns, were walking their rounds,
And binding with briars, my joys & desires.

[PLATE 45]

The Little Vagabond

Dear Mother, dear Mother, the Church is cold.
But the Ale-house is healthy & pleasant & warm;
Besides I can tell where I am use'd well.
Such usage in heaven will never do well.

But if at the Church they would give us some Ale,
And a pleasant fire, our souls to regale:
We'd sing and we'd pray, all the live-long day,
Nor ever once wish from the Church to stray;

Then the Parson might preach & drink & sing.
And we'd be as happy as birds in the spring:
And modest dame Lurch, who is always at Church,
Would not have bandy children nor fasting nor birch.

And God like a father rejoicing to see
His children as pleasant and happy as he:
Would have no more quarrel with the Devil or the Barrel,
But kiss him & give him both drink and apparel.

[PLATE 46]

London

I wander thro' each charter'd[1] street,
Near where the charter'd Thames does flow.
And mark in every face I meet
Marks of weakness, marks of woe.

In every cry of every Man,
In every Infant's cry of fear,
In every voice, in every ban,[2]
The mind-forg'd manacles[3] I hear:

How the Chimney-sweeper's cry
Every blackning Church appalls,
And the hapless Soldier's sigh,
Runs in blood down Palace walls.

But most thro' midnight streets I hear
How the youthful Harlot's curse
Blasts the new-born Infant's tear[4]
And blights with plagues the Marriage hearse.

[PLATE 47]

The Human Abstract[5]

Pity would be no more,
If we did not make somebody Poor:
And Mercy no more could be,
If all were as happy as we;

1. London holds ancient charters which grant certain liberties, but these are not extended to most of the inhabitants. The Magna Carta of 1215 is famous as a guarantee of liberty, hence the "chartered rights of Englishmen." To charter was also coming to mean "to limit" or "to hire." In drafting the poem Blake first tried the adjective "dirty." See working draft from the Notebook, p. 176 below.
2. A public prohibition or proclamation; also a curse.
3. Although manacles are objectively real, Blake's compound adjective emphasizes states of mind that give rise to the manacles—primarily the authorities of church and state, perhaps also the twisted minds of the compliant victims. In first drafting the poem Blake had tried "german forged," suggesting the tyranny of the German or Hanoverian King George III and also the German mercenaries employed by the crown.
4. The verbal curse becomes a metaphor for the plague of gonorrhea, which can cause blindness at birth.
5. Abstraction is the product of excessive rationality which generalizes rather than particularizes. In this context "human" means "all too human" or "mortal." "A Divine Image," p. 60, was etched earlier as a contrary poem for "The Divine Image" of *Innocence*.

And mutual fear brings peace;
Till the selfish loves increase.
Then Cruelty knits a snare,
And spreads his baits with care.

He sits down with holy fears,
And waters the ground with tears:
Then Humility takes its root
Underneath his foot.

Soon spreads the dismal shade
Of Mystery over his head;
And the Catterpiller and Fly,
Feed on the Mystery.

And it bears the fruit of Deceit,
Ruddy and sweet to eat;
And the Raven his nest has made
In its thickest shade.

The Gods of the earth and sea
Sought thro' Nature to find this Tree,[6]
But their search was all in vain:
There grows one in the Human Brain.

[PLATE 48]

Infant Sorrow

My mother groand! my father wept.
Into the dangerous world I leapt:
Helpless, naked, piping loud:
Like a fiend hid in a cloud.

6. The Tree of Mystery (line 13). Cf. "A Poison Tree" and *The Book of Ahania* 3:50, etc. This symbol derives from the tree of the knowledge of good and evil (Genesis 2:9) but probably resulted from Blake's reading about the poisonous upas tree of Java and the banyan tree, which grows by rerooting itself. Blake detested Mystery, which he understood to be the name of the Whore of Babylon (Revelation 17:5).

Struggling in my father's hands:
Striving against my swadling bands:
Bound and weary I thought best
To sulk upon my mother's breast.

[PLATE 49]

A Poison Tree[7]

I was angry with my friend:
I told my wrath, my wrath did end.
I was angry with my foe:
I told it not, my wrath did grow.

And I waterd it in fears,
Night & morning with my tears:
And I sunned it with smiles,
And with soft deceitful wiles.

And it grew both day and night.
Till it bore an apple bright.
And my foe beheld it shine,
And he knew that it was mine.

7. First entitled "Christian Forbearance."

And into my garden stole.
When the night had veild the pole;
In the morning glad I see
My foe outstretchd beneath the tree.

[PLATE 50]

A Little Boy Lost

"Nought loves another as itself
Nor venerates another so.
Nor is it possible to Thought
A greater than itself to know:[8]

"And Father, how can I love you,
Or any of my brothers more?
I love you like the little bird
That picks up crumbs around the door."

The Priest sat by and heard the child.
In trembling zeal he siez'd his hair:
He led him by his little coat:
And all admir'd the Priestly care.

And standing on the altar high,
"Lo what a fiend is here!" said he:
"One who sets reason up for judge
Of our most holy Mystery."

The weeping child could not be heard.
The weeping parents wept in vain:
They strip'd him to his little shirt,
And bound him in an iron chain.

And burn'd him in a holy place,
Where many had been burn'd before:
The weeping parents wept in vain.
Are such things done on Albions shore?[9]

8. According to St. Anselm, "God is the greatest thought it is possible to think."

9. Though people were no longer publicly burned for heresy, bonfires were made of subversive books like those of Tom Paine. In annotations to his 1971 edition of Blake's poems, W. H. Stevenson recalls Watts's hymn "On Obedience to Parents": "Have ye not heard what dreadful plagues / Are threatened by the Lord, / To him that breaks his father's law / Or mocks his mother's word? / What heavy guilt upon him lies, / How cursed is his name! / The ravens shall pick out his eyes, / And eagles eat the same."

[PLATE 51]

A Little Girl Lost

Children of the future Age,
Reading this indignant page:
Know that in a former time,
Love! sweet Love! was thought a crime.[1]

In the Age of Gold,[2]
Free from winter's cold:
Youth and maiden bright,
To the holy light,
Naked in the sunny beams delight.

Once[3] a youthful pair
Fill'd with softest care:
Met in garden bright,
Where the holy light,
Had just removed the curtains of the night.

There in rising day,
On the grass they play:
Parents were afar:
Strangers came not near:
And the maiden soon forgot her fear.

Tired with kisses sweet
They agree to meet,
When the silent sleep
Waves o'er heavens deep:
And the weary tired wanderers weep.

To her father white
Came the maiden bright:
But his loving look,
Like the holy book,
All her tender limbs with terror shook.

"Ona! pale and weak!
To thy father speak:
O the trembling fear!
O the dismal care!
That shakes the blossoms of my hoary hair."

1. The epigraph, in the voice of the Bard as a writer rather than a speaker, is directly addressed to us.
2. Traditionally a primordial time when all life was good, but the present tense of line 9 implies that it is or could be now. In *A Vision of the Last Judgment* Blake declared that all his work is "an Endeavour to Restore the Golden Age."
3. The adverb of time indicates a moment out of the timeless Age of Gold. Damon recalls *Paradise Lost* IV, 743, and Milton's reply to those who deplored free love.

[PLATE 52]

To Tirzah[4]

Whate'er is Born of Mortal Birth,
Must be consumed with the Earth
To rise from Generation[5] free;
Then what have I to do with thee?[6]

The Sexes[7] sprung from Shame & Pride
Blow'd in the morn: in evening died.
But Mercy changd Death into Sleep;
The Sexes rose to work & weep.

Thou Mother of my Mortal part
With cruelty didst mould my Heart,
And with false self-decieving tears,
Didst bind my Nostrils, Eyes & Ears.

4. This work was added to later copies of *Songs*—after mid-1805, according to Erdman's analysis of the style of lettering. The woman Tirzah is mentioned in Numbers 27:1–11, 36:3, Joshua 17:3–4, and Song of Solomon 6:4; the city Tirzah was the capital of the Hebrew Northern Kingdom, as opposed to Jerusalem in the South. In *The Four Zoas* VIII, *Milton* 17:11, and *Jerusalem* 67, 68, Tirzah and her cohort Rahab engage in sexual tortures of the male.

5. A name for Experience; in *Milton* 41:28 a time will come when "Generation is swallowed up in Regeneration," and in 7:65 "holy Generation" is declared to be an "Image of Regeneration."

6. Variations on this rebuke are suffered by both Elijah (I Kings 18:18) and Jesus himself (Matthew 12:46–50), but the crucial text is Jesus' rebuke to Mary just before conducting the miracle at Cana in his own way and time (John 2:4).

7. Adam and Eve. In Platonic myth, the change from a primordial androgynous state to one of sexual distinction is an aspect of the fall.

Didst close my Tongue in senseless clay,
And me to Mortal Life betray:
The Death of Jesus set me free;[8]
Then what have I to do with thee?

[PLATE 53]

The School-Boy[9]

I love to rise in a summer morn,
When the birds sing on every tree;
The distant huntsman winds his horn,
And the sky-lark sings with me.
O! what sweet company.

But to go to school in a summer morn,
O! it drives all joy away:
Under a cruel eye outworn,
The little ones spend the day,
In sighing and dismay.

Ah! then at times I drooping sit,
And spend many an anxious hour.
Nor in my book can I take delight,
Nor sit in learning's bower,
Worn thro' with the dreary shower.

How can the bird that is born for joy,
Sit in a cage and sing?
How can a child when fears annoy,
But droop his tender wing,
And forget his youthful spring?

O! father & mother, if buds are nip'd,
And blossoms blown away,
And if the tender plants are strip'd
Of their joy in the springing day,
By sorrow and care's dismay,

How shall the summer arise in joy?
Or the summer fruits appear?
Or how shall we gather what griefs destroy?
Or bless the mellowing year,
When the blasts of winter appear?

8. Cf. "The Everlasting Gospel." For Blake, Jesus sets us free not because he atoned for our sins but because he inspires us through his exemplary act of self-sacrifice. The inscription about the raising of the "spiritual body" is from I Corinthians 15:44. The whole passage, beginning at 15:35, was of the greatest interest to Blake and he makes use of it in many places; cf. also I Corinthians 12.

9. This poem was transferred from *Innocence* to *Experience* in late copies.

[PLATE 54]

The Voice of the Ancient Bard[1]

Youth of delight come hither,
And see the opening morn:
Image of truth new born.
Doubt is fled & clouds of reason,
Dark disputes & artful teazing.
Folly is an endless maze.
Tangled roots perplex her ways,
How many have fallen there!
They stumble all night over bones of the dead,[2]
And feel they know not what but care:
And wish to lead others when they should be led.

A Divine Image[3]

Cruelty has a Human Heart
And Jealousy a Human Face;
Terror, the Human Form Divine
And Secrecy, the Human Dress.

The Human Dress, is forged Iron
The Human Form, a fiery Forge.
The Human Face, a Furnace seal'd
The Human Heart, its hungry Gorge.

The Book of Thel

This early work, dated 1789 on the title page, consists of eight plates, two of which are hardly decorated in most copies. One of these nearly bare pages contains only "Thel's Motto," which appears last in two late copies but in most copies confronts the reader even before he sees the title page. This series of unanswered, starkly presented questions makes up the "Motto" of a person named "Thel" whom the reader knows nothing about. Whether this Motto appears as the first or last page of the book, it provides a riddling perspective for the main story.

The title page shows a young woman, presumably Thel, watching a sexual encounter between two human figures who have apparently sprung from two flowers. A nude young man launches himself at a lightly dressed,

1. This work was transferred from *Innocence* to *Experience* but continued to appear in some later copies of *Innocence* which were issued separately from *Experience*. This fact tends to refute the theory that the bardic voice is suited only to Experience.
2. Cf. John 11:9–10 and I John 2:10–11.
3. A draft for *Songs of Experience* that was engraved but then replaced by "The Human Abstract."

rather reluctant young woman. Smaller figures, active and contemplative, decorate the letters of the title. The story that is shown and narrated on succeeding plates implies concerns that are strongly though not exclusively sexual. Literally Thel is a young woman faced with the problems of coming to maturity. A shepherdess, dissatisfied with her easy life, she converses with nonhuman creatures who are depicted in human form—a Lilly (a virgin), a Cloud (a lover), and a Clod of Clay (a matron)—about how to live a meaningful life. At the end of the story she enters the land of the dead and hears a voice from her own grave lamenting that the senses are either too strong or too restrained. Terrified, she flees back to her former abode.

The pictures on plates 1 and 6 (pages 62 and 68 of this book) do not illustrate events actually narrated but imply some larger area of meaning than the story itself sets forth. These designs reinforce the sense of enigma communicated by the challenging questions of Thel's Motto and invite the reader to seek out an allegorical explanation of Thel and her adventures. The unfamiliar name of the heroine offers further grounds for speculation, since it may be derived from a Greek word meaning "wish" or "will," and Thel's shrieking and running away at the end of her adventures seem to be evidence of a deficiency in her will and desire. Yet the unanswered questions of her Motto and the final design that intervenes between her last action and "The End" of her story leave open the possibility that she at last knows something that she has found out for herself.

Our text is taken from Copy M, Berg Collection, New York Public Library; cf. the facsimile edited by Nancy Bogen (Providence, R.I.: Brown University Press; New York: New York Public Library, 1971). The color plate is from Copy N, Cincinnati Art Museum.

The Book of Thel*

The Author & Printer Willm Blake, 1789.

[PLATE i]

Thel's Motto[1]

Does the Eagle know what is in the pit?
Or wilt thou go ask the Mole:
Can Wisdom be put in a silver rod?
Or Love in a golden bowl?

* See color plate 9 for title page.

1. Proverbially, the eagle is sharp-sighted and the mole is blind, but in *Visions of the Daughters of Albion* 5:39–40, Oothoon implies that the mole is a more reliable witness. Ecclesiastes 12:5–6 prophesies a bad time in which desires will be overcome by fears of death: "Or ever the silver cord be loosed, or the golden bowl be broken." The substitution of "rod" for "cord" brings out masculine sexual implications; a rod is also a symbol of authority.

[PLATE 1]

Thel

I

The daughters of Mne Seraphim[2] led round their sunny flocks,
All but the youngest. She in paleness sought the secret air,
To fade away like morning beauty from her mortal day:
Down by the river of Adona[3] her soft voice is heard:
And thus her gentle lamentation falls like morning dew:

"O life of this our spring! why fades the lotus of the water?[4]
Why fade these children of the spring? born but to smile & fall.
Ah! Thel is like a watry bow, and like a parting cloud.
Like a reflection in a glass, like shadows in the water,
Like dreams of infants, like a smile upon an infant's face,
Like the dove's voice, like transient day, like music in the air:
Ah! gentle may I lay me down, and gentle rest my head,
And gentle sleep the sleep of death, and gentle hear the voice
Of him that walketh in the garden in the evening time."[5]

2. Seraphim are the highest order of angels; Mnemosyne is the Greek goddess of memory. According to the astrologer and alchemist Cornelius Agrippa (1486–1535), "Bne Seraphim" are the sons of the seraphim, intelligences of the planet Venus (*Occult Philosophy,* II, 22). Blake often made up strange names or used occult words for their odd sound, without reference to their original significance; he did not, however, ignore the context in his allusions to the Bible and English poetry. Though Thel and her sisters have an exalted lineage, their "flocks" indicate a pastoral world, an Arcadia where even the queen, as Thel is called, is a shepherdess.

3. The river Adonis in Lebanon is mentioned in *Paradise Lost* I, 450, in connection with amorous longings of women who mourn a dying god; Adonis is the name of the mortal beloved by Venus. In Spenser's *Faerie Queene* III, vi, the Gardens of Adonis are an earthly paradise, the seed ground of mortality.

4. The chief literary association is the fruit of oblivion eaten by the Lotos Eaters in *Odyssey* IX. The Egyptian lotus is an edible aquatic plant, sometimes called a water lily.

5. The allusion to Genesis 3:8, God's visit to the fallen Adam and Eve (cf. "the Holy Word" in the "Introduction" to *Experience*), is consistent with Thel's state of mind throughout the poem; in contrast, the Lilly says that God "smiles on all" and the Clod says that he "loves the lowly."

The Lilly of the valley[6] breathing in the humble grass
Answer'd the lovely maid and said: "I am a watry weed,
And I am very small, and love to dwell in lowly vales;
So weak, the gilded butterfly scarce perches on my head.
Yet I am visited from heaven and he that smiles on all
Walks in the valley, and each morn over me spreads his hand
Saying, 'Rejoice thou humble grass, thou new-born lilly flower,
Thou gentle maid of silent valleys, and of modest brooks:
For thou shalt be clothed in light, and fed with morning manna:
Till summer's heat melts thee beside the fountains and the springs
To flourish in eternal vales.' Then why should Thel complain,

[PLATE 2]

Why should the mistress of the vales of Har[7] utter a sigh?"

She ceasd & smild in tears, then sat down in her silver shrine.

Thel answered, "O thou little virgin of the peaceful valley,
Giving to those that cannot crave, the voiceless, the o'erfired.[8]
Thy breath doth nourish the innocent lamb; he smells thy milky garments,
He crops thy flowers while thou sittest smiling in his face,
Wiping his mild and meekin mouth from all contagious taints.
Thy wine doth purify the golden honey; thy perfume,
Which thou dost scatter on every little blade of grass that springs
Revives the milked cow, & tames the fire-breathing steed.
But Thel is like a faint cloud kindled at the rising sun:
I vanish from my pearly throne, and who shall find my place?"[9]

"Queen of the vales," the Lilly answered, "ask the tender cloud,
And it shall tell thee why it glitters in the morning sky,
And why it scatters its bright beauty thro' the humid air.
Descend O little cloud & hover before the eyes of Thel."

The Cloud descended, and the Lilly bowd her modest head:
And went to mind her numerous charge among the verdant grass.

6. Compare "The Lilly" in *Experience*. In Song of Solomon 2:1, the Bride is a "lily of the valleys," and the short-lived lilies of the field in the Sermon on the Mount are clothed by God more beautifully even than Solomon in all his glory (Matthew 6:28–30).

7. In the early manuscript *Tiriel,* not included in this edition, old Har and his wife Heva live idly in pleasant gardens, nursed by Mnetha; in *The Song of Los* 3:20 and 4:5, Har appears to be a ruler of a formerly paradisal state and the ancestor of a degenerate race. In *Thel* these vales retain their idyllic character but the heroine is discontented in them.

8. Usually emended to "o'ertired," but perhaps related to the Lilly's taming of the "fire-breathing" steed in 2:10. "Meekin" in 2:7 is probably a variant of "meek."

9. An echo of Job 7:9.

[PLATE 3]

II

"O little Cloud," the virgin said, "I charge thee tell to me,
Why thou complainest not when in one hour thou fade away:
Then we shall seek thee but not find; ah, Thel is like to thee:
I pass away, yet I complain, and no one hears my voice."

The Cloud then shew'd his golden head & his bright form emerg'd,
Hovering and glittering on the air before the face of Thel.

"O virgin know'st thou not our steeds drink of the golden springs
Where Luvah[1] doth renew his horses: look'st thou on my youth,
And fearest thou because I vanish and am seen no more
Nothing remains? O maid I tell thee, when I pass away,
It is to tenfold life, to love, to peace, and raptures holy.
Unseen descending, weigh my light wings upon balmy flowers:
And court the fair eyed dew, to take me to her shining tent;
The weeping virgin trembling kneels before the risen sun,
Till we arise link'd in a golden band, and never part;
But walk united, bearing food to all our tender flowers."

"Dost thou O little Cloud? I fear that I am not like thee;
For I walk through the vales of Har and smell the sweetest flowers,
But I feed not the little flowers: I hear the warbling birds,
But I feed not the warbling birds; they fly and seek their food.

1. In *Thel* this name connotes nothing more certain than an important personage, possibly a god. The sound of the name may suggest *lover* and thus recall the Prince of Love in "Song: How sweet I roam'd." In the major prophecies Luvah is one of the Zoas, the faculty of love, as in *The Four Zoas* I, 12:14.

But Thel delights in these no more because I fade away
And all shall say, 'Without a use this shining woman liv'd,
Or did she only live to be at death the food of worms?' "

The Cloud reclind upon his airy throne and answer'd thus:

"Then if thou art the food of worms, O virgin of the skies,
How great thy use, how great thy blessing; every thing that lives,
Lives not alone, nor for itself:[2] fear not and I will call
The weak worm from its lowly bed, and thou shalt hear its voice.
Come forth worm of the silent valley, to thy pensive queen."

The helpless worm arose, and sat upon the Lilly's leaf,
And the bright Cloud saild on, to find his partner in the vale.

[PLATE 4]

III

Then Thel astonish'd view'd the Worm upon its dewy bed.

"Art thou a Worm? image of weakness, art thou but a Worm?
I see thee like an infant wrapped in the Lilly's leaf:[3]
Ah weep not little voice, thou can'st not speak, but thou can'st weep.

2. A refrain repeated by the Clod, *Thel* 4:10, and affirmed by the Clod in "The Clod and the Pebble," *Songs of Experience*.
3. Reminiscent of the infant Jesus' swaddling clothes. A human-headed worm lying on an oak leaf in the frontispiece of *The Gates of Paradise*, not in this volume, is emblematic of the beginning of man's natural, "vegetative" life.

Is this a Worm? I see thee lay helpless & naked: weeping,
And none to answer, none to cherish thee with mother's smiles."

The Clod of Clay heard the Worm's voice, & raisd her pitying head;
She bow'd over the weeping infant and her life exhal'd
In milky fondness; then on Thel she fix'd her humble eyes.

"O beauty of the vales of Har, we live not for ourselves;
Thou seest me the meanest thing, and so I am indeed;
My bosom of itself is cold, and of itself is dark,

[PLATE 5]
But he that loves the lowly pours his oil upon my head,
And kisses me, and binds his nuptial bands around my breast,
And says: 'Thou mother of my children, I have loved thee.
And I have given thee a crown that none can take away.'[4]
But how this is sweet maid, I know not, and I cannot know.
I ponder, and I cannot ponder; yet I live and love."

The daughter of beauty wip'd her pitying tears with her white veil,
And said, "Alas! I knew not this, and therefore did I weep:
That God would love a Worm I knew, and punish the evil foot[5]

4. Like that given the faithful in I Peter 5:4 and Revelation 3:11.
5. God's sentence upon the serpent in Genesis 3:15 was that the offspring of woman "shall bruise thy head, and thou shalt bruise his heel."

That wilful bruis'd its helpless form: but that he cherish'd it
With milk and oil, I never knew; and therefore did I weep,
And I complained in the mild air, because I fade away,
And lay me down in thy cold bed, and leave my shining lot."

"Queen of the vales," the matron Clay answered; "I heard thy sighs.
And all thy moans flew o'er my roof, but I have call'd them down:
Wilt thou O Queen enter my house? 'Tis given thee to enter,
And to return;[6] fear nothing, enter with thy virgin feet."

[PLATE 6][7]

IV

The eternal gates' terrific porter lifted the northern bar;[8]
Thel enter'd in & saw the secrets of the land unknown:
She saw the couches of the dead, & where the fibrous roots
Of every heart on earth infixes deep its restless twists:
A land of sorrows & of tears where never smile was seen.

She wandered in the land of clouds thro' valleys dark, listning
Dolours & lamentations; waiting oft beside a dewy grave
She stood in silence, listning to the voices of the ground,
Till to her own grave plot[9] she came, & there she sat down,
And heard this voice of sorrow breathed from the hollow pit:

6. The return from a journey to the underworld is usually represented as being a dangerous and difficult exploit, as in *Aeneid* VI.

7. The printing style of this plate—and of the Motto—differs somewhat from that of the rest of the text and was probably etched no earlier than 1791, perhaps replacing an earlier conclusion for the poem.

8. The land of the dead is often imagined as cold, to the north. The guardian of the gates of death is usually formidable, as in *Paradise Lost* II, 645 ff., where Sin and Death together are the porters. Blake probably also drew on the images of gates and porter in *Faerie Queene* III, vi. 31–32. In *Milton* 26:13–22, Los, the Zoa of productive Imagination, is porter. In *Odyssey* XIII, 145 ff., the Cave of the Sea Nymphs has two gates: that to the south through which the gods descend, that to the north through which mortals descend. Neoplatonic interpreters, who must have been known to Blake by the notes to Pope's translation of the *Odyssey*—according to Rodney Baine, *Philological Quarterly*, 51 (1972), 957–61—had taken the northern door to be an allegory of the way the soul enters the body. There is no evidence, however, that Thel is disincarnate before her descent.

9. The voice from Thel's empty grave perhaps puts into words Thel's "sighs" and "moans" which the Clod "called down." Meditations on death as a way of evaluating human life filled works of the "Graveyard School" with images of worms and decay; Edward Young's *Night Thoughts*, Robert Blair's *The Grave* (1743), James Hervey's "Meditations Among the Tombs" (1746), and Thomas Gray's "Elegy Written in a Country Churchyard" (1751) were still widely read, and indeed Blake was to illustrate each of them. In "Fair Elenor," a poem in *Poetical Sketches* not included in this volume, Blake experimented with Gothic horror: after a nighttime visit to a castle crypt, Elenor "shriek'd aloud" like Thel; she then dies after unwrapping a napkin containing her husband's severed head. Blake's speaker in "The Garden of Love" of *Experience* laments the presence of "tombstones where flowers should be."

"Why cannot the Ear be closed to its own destruction?
Or the glistning Eye to the poison of a smile?
Why are Eyelids stord with arrows ready drawn,
Where a thousand fighting men in ambush lie?
Or an Eye of gifts & graces, show'ring fruits & coined gold?
Why a Tongue impress'd with honey from every wind?
Why an Ear a whirlpool fierce to draw creations in?
Why a Nostril wide inhaling terror, trembling, & affright?
Why a tender curb upon the youthful burning boy?
Why a little curtain of flesh on the bed of our desire?"[1]

The Virgin[2] started from her seat, & with a shriek
Fled back unhinderd till she came into the vales of Har.

The End

Visions of the Daughters of Albion

Albion is a traditional name for England, in honor of an ancestral giant who conquered the British isles (mentioned by Spenser in *The Faerie Queene* II, x, 11, and IV, xi, 16). "Daughters of Albion" is a mythologized way of saying "Englishwomen," not a puzzling name like "Daughters of Mne Seraphim" in *The Book of Thel*. Yet in many respects these two works about crises in the lives of young women are counterparts, related to one another almost like paired poems in *Songs of Innocence and of Experience*, showing "Two Contrary States of the Human Soul." *Visions*, dated 1793 on the title page, is more concerned than *Thel* with immediate social issues, especially the position of woman in a man's world. The

1. This crescendo of questions derives from Thel's terror at the increasing capacity and urgency of four of the senses; yet in *Thel* 6:19–20 Thel wishes ambivalently that the fifth sense, touch—physical desire—might be unrestrained. Lines 19–20 were deleted from two copies of *Thel*, perhaps at their owners' request.

2. The fact that Thel is called "virgin" five times in the poem and "maid" three times suggests that her stage of maturation is intimately related to her problem in understanding her "use" in life. Her "shriek" at the end of this line contrasts with the shriek of Ololon, a virgin who casts off fear in *Milton* 42:3.

refrain, "The Daughters of Albion hear her woes, & echo back her sighs" (2:20, 5:2, 8:13), indicates that the work is about the sufferings of a woman as perceived by other women, especially Englishwomen. Blake's name for his heroine seems to have been derived from "Oi-thona," a character in one of the prose poems which James Macpherson pretended were his translations from "Ossian," a Scottish Gaelic bard (1760–63). But Oothoon's character probably owes something to Blake's acquaintance with Mary Wollstonecraft, the first radical English feminist, author of the notoriously outspoken *A Vindication of the Rights of Woman* (1792). Oothoon is also identified as "the soft soul of America" (1:3), the spirit of the freedom, vulnerability, and extremism of the American Revolution. In Blake's time American revolutionary ideals had come to France and, despite authoritarian efforts to silence the word of freedom, they seemed certain to spread to England.

Although the chief emphasis of *Visions* is its critique of sexual customs, the work also denounces the enslavement of blacks and children and symbolically condemns exploitation of the new American land and its resources (and, by implication, its native people). Oppression is recognized as an interlocking system: all manner of exploitation and enslavement derives from the tyranny seen by the Chimney Sweeper of *Experience* as headed by "God & his Priest & King." Liberty, on the contrary, is absolute; there is no such thing as freedom for only certain people—like white men. The *Visions* as a whole is not a treatise on free love; only Oothoon's speeches constitute such a treatise, while thoughts of the two male characters drift elsewhere, mainly into philosophical questions of the problem of perception. At the end of the poem the Daughters of Albion, repeating their chorus, have not been changed by Oothoon's experience, but the motto or subtitle, "The Eye sees more than the Heart knows," implies that the consciousness of women and of all human beings would be raised if they could feel what they see.

The only remarkable event in *Visions* is a rape. It takes place quickly, in half a line (1:16), and the rest of the work is devoted to tracing its causes, consequences, and implications—for the victim, Oothoon, her fiancé, Theotormon, and the rapist, Bromion. The body of the work has three main parts, as Stevenson has pointed out: Part I (1:1–17) is a narrative in which the Daughters of Albion are introduced as a choral audience and the adventures of Oothoon are told. Narrative passages also tie the work together (as in 2:2–13) and conclude it (8:11–13) with the reminder that the Daughters of Albion are witnesses. Part II is made up of declamations by the principal characters: Bromion (1:18–2:2 and 4:12–24), Oothoon (2:14–16, 2:20–3:20), and Theotormon (3:22–4:11). Part III is a long, passionate oration by Oothoon (5:3–8:10). In the poem Oothoon never actually escapes from the two warped lovers she is bound to. The three appear locked in their situation in the full-page frontispiece (or tailpiece in one copy), plate i, in a sort of "No Exit" triangle, even though Oothoon has achieved psychological liberation and brings her message to the Daughters of Albion in the final design (see color plate 10 of this book). In their declamations the three characters constantly speak past one another, as though they were in hell, or in a twentieth-century absurdist play. As audience and chorus, the Daughters of Albion only passively sympathize with Oothoon, but the reader is left with the hope that the Daughters may feel in their hearts the meaning of their "Visions" and come to understand their own condition.

Our copy text is Erdman, *The Illuminated Blake* reproduction of Copy J, Rosenwald Collection, Library of Congress. Color plates are from Copy P, Fitzwilliam Museum, Cambridge.

Visions of the Daughters of Albion*

The Eye sees more than the Heart knows.

Printed by Will:^m Blake: 1793.

[PLATE iii]

The Argument†

I loved Theotormon
And I was not ashamed.
I trembled in my virgin fears
And I hid in Leutha's vale!

I plucked Leutha's flower,
And I rose up from the vale;
But the terrible thunders tore
My virgin mantle in twain.

* See color plates 10 and 11. The frontispiece (color plate 10) was placed after the title page in one copy and at the end of the book in another. It illustrates the plight of the three central characters in 2:5–7.

The title page (color plate 11) illustrates 1 : 14–15, with additional images associated with Urizen and the Daughters of Albion. The rainbow of promise painted across the sky is the alternative to the storm which dominates the design. Because the aphorism, "The Eye sees more than the Heart knows," is on the title page instead of being ascribed to the heroine as is Thel's Motto, there is an implication that Oothoon's perceptions are not perfectly coordinated with her feelings.

† See color plate 12. The design illustrates iii, 5 and 1:5–12 of *Visions*. Presumably "The Argument" is Oothoon's own summary of her state of mind up until the time of the rape. Her hiding, not mentioned in the main narrative, shows how far she has to come before her later advocacy of openness. "Leutha's vale" is not further identified in *Visions*, but a fascinating and sinister temptress named Leutha appears in several later works and in *Milton* 11:28 ff. she enacts the part of Sin in *Paradise Lost* II, 766–87. The question of sin underlies Oothoon's successive stages of fear, daring, guilt, and moral independence. Unlike Thel and the Lilly, Oothoon and the Marygold are nude.

[PLATE 1]

Visions[1]

ENSLAV'D,[2] the Daughters of Albion weep: a trembling lamentation
Upon their mountains, in their valleys, sighs toward America.

For the soft soul of America, OOTHOON,[3] wandered in woe,
Along the vales of Leutha seeking flowers to comfort her;
And thus she spoke to the bright Marygold of Leutha's vale:

"Art thou a flower! art thou a nymph! I see thee now a flower,[4]

1. Above the half-title "Visions" in Blake's design, one nude woman plays a serpent horn among the clouds while another rides a cloud and two nude men discharge bows; below the word "Visions" a draped figure holds out what appears to be a dripping paintbrush. On the rocks below, Bromion and Oothoon are stretched out exhausted after the rape (1 : 16–18); see p. 73.
2. This word on Blake's plate is formed with exceptionally large letters, not simply for decoration but as a way of emphasizing the central issue of freedom versus slavery. The cliché among the privileged classes, "free-born Englishmen," describes a system in which women and non-English people are everywhere in chains.
3. Oothoon is the mate of Theotormon in *Europe* and is scolded by her mother Enitharmon for giving up "woman's secrecy" (14:21–25); she serves as Leutha's "charming guard" during a love affair in *Milton* 13:44. In *Milton* 42:33 she weeps over her "Human Harvest," and in *Jerusalem* 41[37]:17 her "palace" is a "lovely heaven," though "Satan's Watch Fiends" call it Sin. These later roles of Oothoon are not implied by *Visions* but are not inconsistent with her character; at least they show that she will not remain in bondage. In view of the intensity of her indignation, "soft," "mild" (1:8) and "mildness" (2:28) may seem inappropriate, but this spirit of freedom is hardened into resistance only after her repression and abuse.
4. Both the human and vegetable forms of the Marygold, visible to Oothoon, are pictured on plate iii, in accordance with Blake's emphasis on imaginative perception, as in the verse epistle describing a "double vision": "With my inward Eye 'tis an old Man grey / With my outward, a Thistle across the way" (p. 461). Blake's spelling calls attention to the human name "Mary" and the "gold" of myths like that of the Golden Bough (*Aeneid* VI). Blake's indentation of the dialogue between Oothoon and the Marygold sets it apart from the rest of the story.

Now a nymph! I dare not pluck thee from thy dewy bed!"

The Golden nymph replied: "Pluck thou my flower, Oothoon the mild;
Another flower shall spring, because the soul of sweet delight
Can never pass away." She ceas'd & closd her golden shrine.

Then Oothoon pluck'd the flower[5] saying, "I pluck thee from thy bed
Sweet flower, and put thee here to glow between my breasts
And thus I turn my face to where my whole soul seeks."

Over the waves she went in wing'd exulting swift delight;
And over Theotormon's reign[6] took her impetuous course.

Bromion rent her with his thunders.[7] On his stormy bed
Lay the faint maid, and soon her woes appalld his thunders hoarse.

Bromion spoke: "Behold this harlot[8] here on Bromion's bed,
And let the jealous dolphins sport around the lovely maid;
Thy soft American plains are mine and mine thy north & south:
Stampt with my signet are the swarthy children of the sun:[9]
They are obedient, they resist not, they obey the scourge:
Their daughters worship terrors and obey the violent.[1]

5. Traditionally, the plucking of a flower signifies sexual experience; Oothoon is ready now for experience.

6. Etymologically, Theotormon's name suggests that he is tormented by God, or by his idea of God as the "Father of Jealousy" accused by Oothoon in 7 : 12. In one of Blake's later allusions to this character, he is author of a religion based on jealousy (*Milton* 22:38). Although most descriptions of his relationship to Oothoon in *Visions* indicate an engagement, Theotormon behaves like a wronged husband. His "reign" is the ocean, probably the Atlantic.

7. The name of this rapist suggests the Greek word for "roarer"; his attack is mythologized as "thunders." In the late prophecies he is identified as Theotormon's brother, one of the sons of Los who usually works for the liberation of man. His second speech in *Visions* hints that he, more than Theotormon, is capable of change.

8. The tendency to condemn and even blame the victimized woman is strong in traditional sexual morality, on the assumption that she must have been looking for trouble. Under this system, as Mary Wollstonecraft observes, "A woman who has lost her honour, imagines that she cannot fall lower, and as for recovering her former station, it is impossible; no exertion can wash this stain away. Losing thus every spur, and having no other means of support, prostitution becomes her only refuge" (*A Vindication of the Rights of Woman*, 1792, ed. Carol H. Poston [New York: Norton, 1975], pp. 71–72). Compare the fate of the heroine in "Mary," p. 206, and Blake's insistence "To the Accuser who is the God of This World" that "Every Harlot was a Virgin once / Nor canst thou ever change Kate into Nan."

9. The reference to the branding of slaves and the design on plate 2 are reminders that the assault on Oothoon, soul of America, includes the enslavement of black and red Americans.

1. Compliance as a result of intimidation, particularly in women, is taken as evidence that the victims actually desire violence. See Tayler, pp. 539–53 below; Diana Hume George, *Centennial Review* 23 (1979); Susan Fox, *Critical Inquiry* 3 (1977).

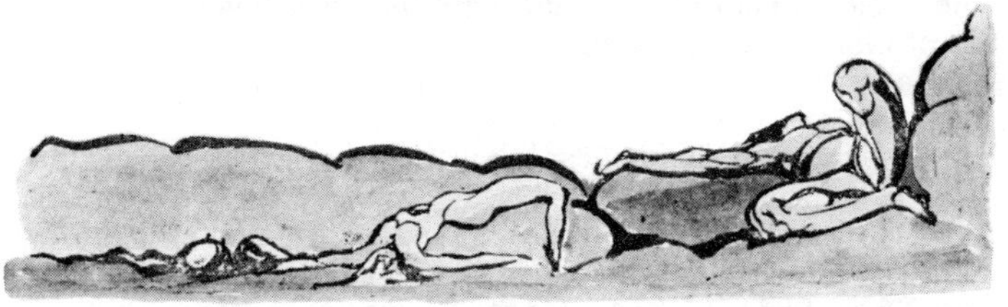

[PLATE 2]

Now thou maist marry Bromion's harlot, and protect the child
Of Bromion's rage, that Oothoon shall put forth in nine moons' time."[2]

Then storms rent Theotormon's limbs; he rolld his waves around
And folded his black jealous waters round the adulterate pair;
Bound back to back in Bromion's caves[3] terror & meekness dwell.

At entrance Theotormon sits wearing the threshold hard
With secret tears; beneath him sound, like waves on a desart shore,
The voice of slaves beneath the sun, and children bought with money,
That shiver in religious caves beneath the burning fires
Of lust, that belch incessant from the summits of the earth.[4]

Oothoon weeps not: she cannot weep! her tears are locked up;
But she can howl incessant, writhing her soft snowy limbs
And calling Theotormon's Eagles to prey upon her flesh.[5]

"I call with holy voice! kings of the sounding air,
Rend away this defiled bosom that I may reflect
The image of Theotormon on my pure transparent breast."

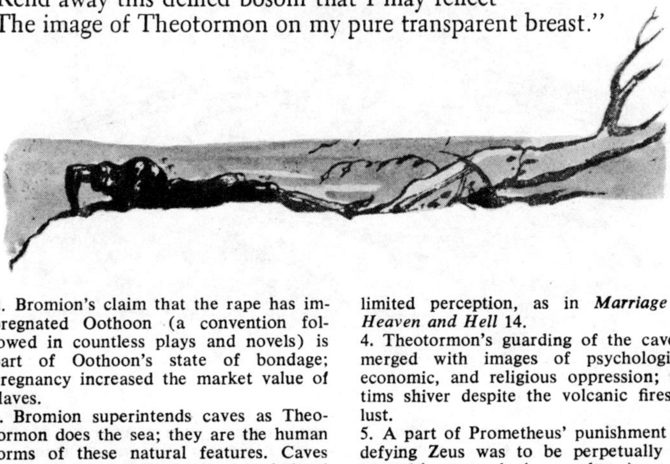

2. Bromion's claim that the rape has impregnated Oothoon (a convention followed in countless plays and novels) is part of Oothoon's state of bondage; pregnancy increased the market value of slaves.

3. Bromion superintends caves as Theotormon does the sea; they are the human forms of these natural features. Caves since the time of Plato have symbolized limited perception, as in *Marriage of Heaven and Hell* 14.

4. Theotormon's guarding of the cave is merged with images of psychological, economic, and religious oppression; victims shiver despite the volcanic fires of lust.

5. A part of Prometheus' punishment for defying Zeus was to be perpetually devoured by an eagle (or a vulture).

The Eagles at her call descend & rend their bleeding prey;
Theotormon severely smiles; her soul reflects the smile;
As the clear spring mudded with feet of beasts grows pure & smiles.

The Daughters of Albion hear her woes & eccho back her sighs.

"Why does my Theotormon sit weeping upon the threshold;
And Oothoon hovers by his side, perswading him in vain?
I cry, 'Arise O Theotormon, for the village dog
Barks at the breaking day; the nightingale has done lamenting;
The lark does rustle in the ripe corn, and the Eagle returns
From nightly prey, and lifts his golden beak to the pure east,
Shaking the dust from his immortal pinions to awake
The sun that sleeps too long. Arise, my Theotormon, I am pure:
Because the night is gone that clos'd me in its deadly black.
They told me that the night & day were all that I could see;
They told me that I had five senses to inclose me up.
And they inclos'd my infinite brain into a narrow circle,
And sunk my heart into the Abyss, a red round globe hot burning,
Till all from life I was obliterated and erased.[6]
Instead of morn arises a bright shadow, like an eye
In the eastern cloud: instead of night a sickly charnel house.'
That Theotormon hears me not! to him the night and morn
Are both alike: a night of sighs, a morning of fresh tears;

[PLATE 3]
And none but Bromion can hear my lamentations.

6. When Theotormon fails to acknowledge Oothoon's vision of a new day, the heroine explores the relationship of man's sensory perception to his conception of reality, a pervasive theme in Blake.

"With what sense is it that the chicken shuns the ravenous hawk?
With what sense does the tame pigeon measure out the expanse?
With what sense does the bee form cells? have not the mouse & frog
Eyes and ears and sense of touch? yet are their habitations
And their pursuits, as different as their forms and as their joys.
Ask the wild ass why he refuses burdens: and the meek camel
Why he loves man; is it because of eye ear mouth or skin
Or breathing nostrils? No, for these the wolf and tyger have.
Ask the blind worm the secrets of the grave, and why her spires
Love to curl round the bones of death; and ask the rav'nous snake
Where she gets poison: & the wing'd eagle why he loves the sun:
And then tell me the thoughts of man, that have been hid of old.

"Silent I hover all the night, and all day could be silent,
If Theotormon once would turn his loved eyes upon me.
How can I be defiled when I reflect thy image pure?
Sweetest the fruit that the worm feeds on & the soul prey'd on by woe,
The new wash'd lamb ting'd with the village smoke & the bright swan
By the red earth[7] of our immortal river: I bathe my wings,
And I am white and pure to hover round Theotormon's breast."

Then Theotormon broke his silence, and he answered:

"Tell me what is the night or day to one o'erflowd with woe?
Tell me what is a thought? & of what substance is it made?
Tell me what is a joy? & in what gardens do joys grow?
And in what rivers swim the sorrows? and upon what mountains

[PLATE 4]

7. As in *Marriage of Heaven and Hell* 13 and *Milton* 19:10, this is an allusion to the literal meaning of "Adam." The "immortal river" recalls the river in *Thel* 1:4; the four rivers of Eden become important in Blake's later symbolism.

Wave shadows of discontent? and in what houses dwell the wretched
Drunken with woe forgotten and shut up from cold despair?

"Tell me where dwell the thoughts forgotten till thou call them forth?
Tell me where dwell the joys of old? & where the ancient loves?
And when will they renew again & the night of oblivion past?
That I might traverse times & spaces far remote and bring
Comforts into a present sorrow and a night of pain!
Where goest thou O thought? to what remote land is thy flight?
If thou returnest to the present moment of affliction
Wilt thou bring comforts on thy wings and dews and honey and balm;
Or poison from the desart wilds, from the eyes of the envier?"[8]

Then Bromion said: and shook the cavern with his lamentation:

"Thou knowest that the ancient trees seen by thine eyes have fruit;
But knowest thou that trees and fruits flourish upon the earth
To gratify senses unknown? trees beasts and birds unknown:
Unknown, not unpercievd, spread in the infinite microscope,
In places yet unvisited by the voyager and in worlds
Over another kind of seas, and in atmospheres unknown?
Ah! are there other wars, beside the wars of sword and fire!
And are there other sorrows, beside the sorrows of poverty?
And are there other joys, beside the joys of riches and ease?
And is there not one law for both the lion and the ox?
And is there not eternal fire, and eternal chains?
To bind the phantoms of existence from eternal life?"[9]

Then Oothoon waited silent all the day and all the night,

[PLATE 5]
But when the morn arose, her lamentation renewd,
The Daughters of Albion hear her woes, & eccho back her sighs.

"O Urizen! Creator of men! mistaken Demon of heaven:[1]
Thy joys are tears! thy labour vain, to form men to thine image.
How can one joy absorb another? are not different joys

8. To Theotormon, thought is vague and shadowy; objects hardly exist for him.

9. To Bromion, the senses are powerful; ultimate reality is mysterious and threatening.

1. In this first reference in Blake's works to the character set forth in *Urizen*, the "Creator of men" is a jealous, infernal god who wants interchangeable creatures, all in his image. This "Mistaken" god is revealed as the fallen faculty of Reason in later works, mistakenly set up as deity over fallen humanity. Here Oothoon, in a situation anticipating that in Hardy's *Tess of the D'Urbervilles,* has given up on both of the impossible men in her life and now tries to address the sort of god who could have made them, and the system under which they all suffer.

Holy, eternal, infinite! and each joy is a Love.

"Does not the great mouth laugh at a gift? & the narrow eyelids mock
At the labour that is above payment? and wilt thou take the ape
For thy councellor? or the dog for a schoolmaster to thy children?
Does he who contemns poverty, and he who turns with abhorrence
From usury feel the same passion, or are they moved alike?
How can the giver of gifts experience the delights of the merchant?
How the industrious citizen the pains of the husbandman?
How different far that fat fed hireling with hollow drum,
Who buys whole corn fields into wastes, and sings upon the heath:
How different their eye and ear! how different the world to them!
With what sense does the parson claim the labour of the farmer?
What are his nets & gins & traps? & how does he surround him
With cold floods of abstraction, and with forests of solitude,
To build him castles and high spires, where kings & priests may dwell?
Till she who burns with youth and knows no fixed lot is bound
In spells of law to one she loaths: and must she drag the chain
Of life, in weary lust? must chilling murderous thoughts obscure
The clear heaven of her eternal spring? to bear the wintry rage
Of a harsh terror driv'n to madness! bound to hold a rod
Over her shrinking shoulders all the day! & all the night
To turn the wheel of false desire! and longings that wake her womb
To the abhorred birth of cherubs in the human form,
That live a pestilence & die a meteor & are no more!
Till the child dwell with one he hates, and do the deed he loaths,
And the impure scourge force his seed into its unripe birth,
E'er yet his eyelids can behold the arrows of the day![2]

"Does the whale worship at thy footsteps as the hungry dog?
Or does he scent the mountain prey, because his nostrils wide
Draw in the ocean? does his eye discern the flying cloud
As the raven's eye? or does he measure the expanse like the vulture?
Does the still spider view the cliffs where eagles hide their young?
Or does the fly rejoice because the harvest is brought in?
Does not the eagle scorn the earth & despise the treasures beneath?
But the mole knoweth what is there, & the worm shall tell it thee.

2. This great series of rhetorical questions attacks the evils of Urizen's system of intertwined injustices: the "hollow drum" of the recruiting officer, the "fat fed hireling" of the wealthy landowner, the tithes extracted from the laborer by the parson to build "castles and high spires" for the oppressors. Oothoon sees women as the ultimate victims of the system, oppressed by masculine authority (25), loveless love-making (27), continual pregnancy (28), infant mortality (29), alienation of the next generation (30), and stillbirth (31).

Does not the worm erect a pillar in the mouldering church yard?

[PLATE 6]
And a palace of eternity in the jaws of the hungry grave?
Over his porch these words are written: Take thy bliss O Man!
And sweet shall be thy taste & sweet thy infant joys renew!

"Infancy, fearless, lustful, happy![3] nestling for delight
In laps of pleasure; Innocence! honest, open, seeking
The vigorous joys of morning light; open to virgin bliss,
Who taught thee modesty, subtil modesty? Child of night & sleep
When thou awakest, wilt thou dissemble all thy secret joys?
Or wert thou not awake when all this mystery was disclos'd?
Then com'st thou forth a modest virgin knowing to dissemble
With nets found under thy night pillow, to catch virgin joy,
And brand it with the name of whore: & sell it in the night,
In silence, ev'n without a whisper, and in seeming sleep.
Religious dreams and holy vespers light thy smoky fires;
Once were thy fires lighted by the eyes of honest morn.
And does my Theotormon seek this hypocrite modesty!
This knowing, artful, secret, fearful, cautious, trembling hypocrite?
Then is Oothoon a whore indeed! and all the virgin joys
Of life are harlots: and Theotormon is a sick man's dream
And Oothoon is the crafty slave of selfish holiness.

"But Oothoon is not so; a virgin fill'd with virgin fancies
Open to joy and to delight where ever beauty appears.
If in the morning sun I find it: there my eyes are fix'd

3. Infantile sexuality is held up as an innocent ideal, in contrast to the dissimulating cult of virginity. The mother in the manuscript "Cradle Song" (p. 194) is appalled at infant lust.

[PLATE 7]

In happy copulation; if in evening mild, wearied with work,
Sit on a bank and draw the pleasures of this free born joy.

"The moment of desire! the moment of desire! The virgin
That pines for man shall awaken her womb to enormous joys
In the secret shadows of her chamber; the youth shut up from
The lustful joy shall forget to generate & create an amorous image
In the shadows of his curtains and in the folds of his silent pillow.
Are not these the places of religion? the rewards of continence?
The self enjoyings of self denial? Why dost thou seek religion?[4]
Is it because acts are not lovely, that thou seekest solitude,
Where the horrible darkness is impressed with reflections of desire?

"Father of Jealousy, be thou accursed from the earth!
Why hast thou taught my Theotormon this accursed thing?
Till beauty fades from off my shoulders, darken'd and cast out,
A solitary shadow wailing on the margin of non-entity.[5]

"I cry, Love! Love! Love! happy happy Love! free as the mountain wind!
Can that be Love, that drinks another as a sponge drinks water?
That clouds with jealousy his nights, with weepings all the day:
To spin a web of age around him, grey and hoary! dark!
Till his eyes sicken at the fruit that hangs before his sight.
Such is self-love that envies all! a creeping skeleton
With lamplike eyes watching around the frozen marriage bed.

4. Oothoon's address to Urizen has exceeded its occasion and has become a general discourse on love, with a question at this point to Theotormon on his commitment to sexual abstinence, followed by a renewed attack on Urizen for teaching a perverting religion to the man she loves.

5. An important Blakean concept, here first introduced: "non-entity" is the utter loss of one's identity and sense of reality; the "margin" where Oothoon wails is the limit of a shadowy, derivative life.

"But silken nets and traps of adamant will Oothoon spread,
And catch for thee girls of mild silver, or of furious gold;
I'll lie beside thee on a bank & view their wanton play
In lovely copulation bliss on bliss with Theotormon:
Red as the rosy morning, lustful as the first born beam,
Oothoon shall view his dear delight, nor e'er with jealous cloud
Come in the haven of generous love; nor selfish blightings bring.

"Does the sun walk in glorious raiment on the secret floor

[PLATE 8]
Where the cold miser spreads his gold? or does the bright cloud drop
On his stone threshold? does his eye behold the beam that brings
Expansion to the eye of pity? or will he bind himself
Beside the ox to thy hard furrow? does not that mild beam blot
The bat, the owl, the glowing tyger, and the king of night?
The sea fowl takes the wintry blast for a cov'ring to her limbs:
And the wild snake, the pestilence to adorn him with gems & gold.
And trees & birds & beasts & men behold their eternal joy.
Arise you little glancing wings, and sing your infant joy![6]
Arise and drink your bliss, for every thing that lives is holy!"

Thus every morning wails Oothoon, but Theotormon sits
Upon the margind ocean conversing with shadows dire.

The Daughters of Albion hear her woes, & eccho back her sighs.
The End

6. Cf. "Infant Joy" of *Innocence,* and with line 10 cf. "A Song of Liberty," coda, *Marriage of Heaven and Hell* 27; *America* 8:13; *Four Zoas* 34:80. In the concluding design, the woman flying with outspread arms, in flames, must be Oothoon in her role as agitator, now bringing the word to Englishwomen, rather than running away from a flaming sky god as on the title page. Similarly, Wollstonecraft invokes aid in modulating "the language of persuasive reason, till I rouse my sex from the flowery bed on which they supinely sleep life away!" (*Vindication,* p. 121). The rousing implication of the design counterbalances the pessimistic conclusion of the verbal narrative.

The Marriage of Heaven and Hell

The first thing a reader of this work notices is that it challenges established ideas of right and wrong; the second is that the attack is more oblique than it appears to be. Even a strait-laced reader can hardly help enjoying the wit and sarcasm of the devils' arguments. The devils are so much quicker, brighter, and more exciting than the angels that one may think Blake's point is that Evil is really Good. Yet few passages, closely examined, can be summoned to support such an interpretation. How should the reader cope with his bewilderment?

The most reliable guide to interpreting a puzzling work is a recognition of its form: with what other literary works does it have affinities? In the *Marriage* the parodies of the Bible and of the religious teachings of Emanual Swedenborg (1688–1772), as well as the assaults on popular images of heaven and hell, point to the genre of satire. On the other hand, the repeated announcements that a new age is at hand indicate that the work is a manifesto or a prophetic proclamation. The omission of the author's name from the title page is characteristic of both satire and manifesto. Much of the originality of the *Marriage* consists of encounters between ideas not customarily considered together. Formal precedent for such a mixture may be found in Swift's *Tale of a Tub* (1704), a satire in which allegory alternates with philosophical "digressions." Swedenborg's dead-serious religious books are also written in a mixed style: each doctrinal section is followed by a section of "Memorable Relations," solemn circumstantial accounts of conversations and adventures with angels and devils. Blake altered these models to accommodate his apocalyptic premises and added other dimensions through his use of illuminations. His free-wheeling medley of humor and seriousness, exposition and anecdote, prose and poetry, demands readers who are quick-witted and not too literal-minded, who do not assume that every word in a book is the straightforward opinion of its author. Though obviously such "angels" as these are in the wrong, some of the "devils' " remarks don't ring true either. Page by page it becomes more clear that the *Marriage* does not propose to abolish or simply invert conventional moral categories, but rather it undermines unimaginative, simplistic systems in which passive "good" is valued over active "evil."

The title page of the work proclaims a "Marriage" and depicts an embrace, yet disputations in the body of the work are all won by the devils or their disciple. Hell occupies center stage in the *Marriage* because after an Age of Reason, the claims of Energy need to be aired; after eighteen centuries during which Christianity had come to identify itself with the interests of the ruling class, it was now high time to recall the disruptive and revolutionary actions of Jesus. The theoretical ideal is neither a static balance nor a "dialectical" synthesis but the liberation of all human powers which at present are in bondage to the institutions of church and state. During the early years of the French Revolution, when the *Marriage* was written, English radicals as well as French revolutionaries believed that the destruction of the old order had brought mankind to the edge of the Millennium.

The immediate satirical target of the *Marriage* is the thought of Swedenborg, the Swedish engineer and mystic whose Church of the New Jerusalem had set up a congregation in London in 1787. In 1789 the Blakes attended the first session of a general conference and signed a document approving Swedenborg's doctrines as "genuine Truths revealed from Heaven." Blake soon realized, however, that Swedenborg was actually a force for conservatism and that in trying to abolish churches he had merely added a new one. Parts of the *Marriage* are implicit takeoffs on Swedenborg's *Treatise Concerning Heaven and Hell* (1784). Using the same sort of imagery, language, and rhythms, Blake ridicules Swendenborg's "Memorable Relations" in a series of "Memorable Fancies" (i.e., fantasies). Blake's stories, like Swedenborg's, recount experiences that have prepared the narrator to articulate the prophecies contained in the expository sections. Blake's narrator has had to pass out of this world in order to recognize the value of the misnamed "infernal" energies on which all creative life is based. He has learned on the best authority that "the voice of honest indignation is the voice of God" and has gained the confidence to speak forthrightly. The design of the title page confirms what the narrator has learned by exploring the underworld: the place to look for the confrontation of powerful contraries is beneath surface appearances (see color plate 13).

Although Blake's celebration of "Contraries" (plates 3–6) is in part a corrective to Swedenborg's principle of "equilibrium," the positive propositions from Hell are new and independent. Aside from the struggle of Contraries (plates 2–6), the chief idea in Blake's counter-system is the expansion of sense perception (plates 6–13). A vision of the infinity and energetic holiness of the world through expanded senses is the "good news" of Blake's Gospel of Hell; it owes nothing to Swedenborg (or even to other mystics like Paracelsus and Behmen named on plate 22) but is derived from imagination, as were the visions of the prophets Ezekiel, Isaiah, Diogenes, the North American tribes, and the poets Dante, Shakespeare, and Milton. The doctrines of the Contraries and of expanded sense perception are brought together on plates 14–24. These ideas and their implications for the structure of the *Marriage* are discussed by Nurmi in the Criticism section of this volume, pp. 553–65.

The only verse in the twenty-seven plates of the *Marriage* occurs in the free verse of the "Argument" at the beginning and the numbered Bible-like verses of "A Song of Liberty" at the end. As Plowman pointed out in his 1927 edition of this work, the main prose text is divided into six "chapters," which are usually set off from one another by major pictures rather than verbal headings. These "chapters" (plates 3–4, 5–10, 11–13, 14–15, 16–20, 21–24) typically consist of a passage of exposition followed by an illustrative story or "Memorable Fancy." Before this regular "chapter" organization is established, the section entitled "The Voice of the Devil" sets forth revolutionary ethical principles, and seventy "Proverbs of Hell" make up a subdivision of the Memorable Fancy in the second "chapter" grouping. In studying the *Marriage* readers may find it helpful to note in the margin the numbers proposed by Nurmi for each "Exposition" and "Memorable Fancy" (see pp. 562–65).

Nine copies of the *Marriage* are known to have been issued from about 1793 to 1825, but the ideal date of the work is 1790, as Blake indicated in one copy by inscribing this date above the words "a new heaven is begun" on plate 3. In the context of the French Revolution the affinity of the *Marriage* with the eternal desire for spiritual and political liberation is particularly evident. Belief that a new era should begin *now* was signalized by the adoption of the French Revolutionary Calendar in October 1793, which reckoned time from September 1792 and gave new names to all the months. During this period Blake may have been completing the plates of the *Marriage*, while realizing that he had antedated the New Age. The concluding "Song of Liberty" contains a more explicit political allegory in telling of the conflict between a "new-born terror," or revolution, and the aged forces of reaction. The concluding line, "For every thing that lives is Holy," is repeated in *Visions of the Daughters of Albion* and *America: A Prophecy*, two other works on the theme of freedom through expansion of consciousness.

Our copy text is the Dent facsimile (1927) of Copy I, Fitzwilliam Museum, Cambridge. The color plates are from Copy G, Houghton Library, Harvard.

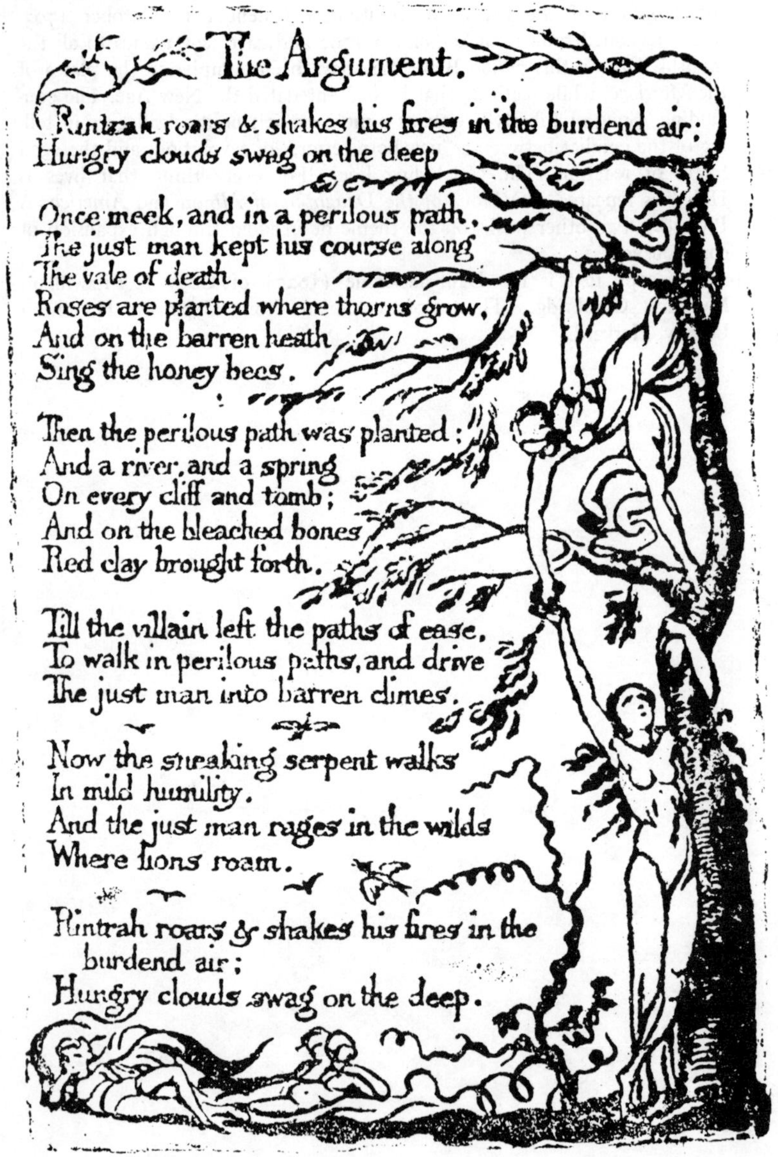

The Argument.

Rintrah roars & shakes his fires in the burdend air;
Hungry clouds swag on the deep

Once meek, and in a perilous path,
The just man kept his course along
The vale of death.
Roses are planted where thorns grow,
And on the barren heath
Sing the honey bees.

Then the perilous path was planted:
And a river, and a spring
On every cliff and tomb;
And on the bleached bones
Red clay brought forth.

Till the villain left the paths of ease,
To walk in perilous paths, and drive
The just man into barren climes.

Now the sneaking serpent walks
In mild humility.
And the just man rages in the wilds
Where lions roam.

Rintrah roars & shakes his fires in the
burdend air;
Hungry clouds swag on the deep.

The Marriage of Heaven and Hell*

[PLATE 2]

The Argument[1]

Rintrah[2] roars & shakes his fires in the burdend air;
Hungry clouds swag[3] on the deep.

Once meek,[4] and in a perilous path,
The just man[5] kept his course along
The vale of death.
Roses are planted where thorns grow.
And on the barren heath
Sing the honey bees.

Then the perilous path was planted:
And a river, and a spring[6]
On every cliff and tomb;
And on the bleached bones
Red clay brought forth.

Till the villain left the paths of ease,
To walk in perilous paths, and drive
The just man into barren climes.

Now the sneaking serpent walks
In mild humility.
And the just man rages in the wilds[7]
Where lions roam.

Rintrah roars & shakes his fires in the burdend air;
Hungry clouds swag on the deep.

* See color plate 13 for title page.

1. As an introduction to a larger work, this term usually refers to a prose summary of the action to be described in verse (like Milton's arguments to the separate books of *Paradise Lost*). In contrast, Blake's verse parable is an oblique enactment of principles to be set forth in the prose.

2. A proper name invented by Blake, characteristically introduced without explanation. In *Milton* Rintrah is a wrathful son of Los but here we are told only of his portentous roaring and brandishing his fires. The clouds are omens of a storm.

3. Sink down, lie heavy (Johnson's *Dictionary*).

4. The sequence of adverbs and verb tenses indicates that such transvaluations of meekness and rage occur repeatedly.

5. An allegory reminiscent of Bunyan's *Pilgrim's Progress* (which Blake later illustrated): The "just man," a pilgrim and a prophet, is dispossessed by the exploitative and ease-loving "villain," also identified with the serpent of Biblical tradition. This conflict foreshadows the one between Devils and Angels in the prose section.

6. An echo of Exodus 17:1–8. The regeneration of "Bleached bones" recalls Ezekiel's vision of resurrection in the Valley of Dry Bones (chapter 37). "Red clay" is the literal Hebrew meaning of Adam, who in plate 3 is said to return to Paradise.

7. As in the epigraph to *All Religions Are One*, "The Voice of one crying in the Wilderness" recalls Isaiah 40:3 and the prophets Elijah and John the Baptist.

[PLATE 3]

As a new heaven is begun,† and it is now thirty-three years since its advent, the Eternal Hell[8] revives. And lo! Swedenborg is the Angel[9] sitting at the tomb; his writings are the linen clothes folded up. Now is the dominion of Edom,[1] & the return of Adam into Paradise; see Isaiah XXXIV & XXXV Chap:[2]

Without Contraries is no progression. Attraction and Repulsion, Reason and Energy, Love and Hate, are necessary to Human existence.

From these contraries spring what the religious call Good & Evil. Good is the passive that obeys Reason. Evil is the active springing from Energy.

Good is Heaven. Evil is Hell.

† See color plate 14.

8. The implication that heavens are continually changing whereas Hell is one and eternal is intended to be outrageous. Thirty-three years before 1790 was 1757, the year of the Last Judgment, according to Swedenborg. Christ's age at his death and resurrection was thirty-three. For Blake, born in 1757, there was a further private significance in the date, but he drops no hint of this amusing coincidence.

9. If Swedenborg's writings are the grave clothing cast off by the resurrected Christ (John 20:4–13), the Swedenborgian New Heaven must already be out of date. The spirit of Christ now resurrected will appear Devil-like to the orthodox.

1. In Isaiah 63, a red man comes to take vengeance on Israel out of the land of Edom. This is a sequel to the prophecy in Isaiah 34 of Israel's dominion over Edom (Idumea). In Genesis 25:30 there was rivalry between Jacob, the smooth, devious man who became Israel, and his disinherited brother Esau, the hairy, crude man known as Edom (both Edom and Adam connote "red"); Isaac, their father, prophesies that one day Edom will "have dominion" (Genesis 27:40). Politically, "Edom" is the spirit of revolutionary France which threatens conservative England.

2. The references to Isaiah 34 (on the devastation of the wrath of God) and Isaiah 35 (on the redemption of the world) indicate that readers must be prepared to understand contemporary events in the light of Biblical stories. The idea that Adam, i.e., mankind, should one day return to paradise is a traditional Christian promise; what is revolutionary is to say that it must and does occur right now.

[PLATE 4]

The Voice of the Devil[3]

All Bibles or sacred codes have been the causes of the following Errors:

1. That Man has two real existing principles, Viz: a Body & a Soul.

2. That Energy, calld Evil, is alone from the Body; & that Reason, calld Good, is alone from the Soul.

3. That God will torment Man in Eternity for following his Energies.

But the following Contraries to these are:

1. Man has no Body distinct from his Soul, for that calld Body is a portion of Soul discernd by the five Senses, the chief inlets of Soul in this age.

2. Energy is the only life and is from the Body and Reason is the bound or outward circumference of Energy.

3. Energy is Eternal Delight.

[PLATE 5]

Those who restrain desire do so because theirs is weak enough to be restrained; and the restrainer or reason usurps its place & governs the unwilling.

And being restrained it by degrees becomes passive till it is only the shadow of desire.

The history of this is written in *Paradise Lost*,[4] & the Governor or Reason is call'd Messiah.

And the original Archangel, or possessor of the command of the heavenly host, is calld the Devil or Satan, and his children are call'd Sin & Death.

But in the Book of Job Milton's Messiah is call'd Satan.

For this history has been adopted by both parties.

It indeed appear'd to Reason as if Desire was cast out, but the Devil's account is, that the Messi-

3. Despite the infernal partisanship of the narrator throughout this work, the alert reader detects some "devilish" ideas that the author does not seem to endorse, such as the implication that energy comes exclusively from the body. To believe this overcorrection would be to perpetuate the false philosophic dualism that the *Marriage* aims to set right. In annotating Swedenborg's *Heaven and Hell* Blake cautioned against taking "Satan's blasphemies" as Milton's own opinons.

4. This diabolical interpretation of Milton's revered poem (like the re-interpretation of the Bible) is intended to be provocative, an overstatement of Blake's own reservations about the poet he admired most. In the Bible Satan is the accuser of Job; in *Paradise Lost* the Messiah is the accuser of mankind.

[PLATE 6]

ah fell & formed a heaven of what he stole from the Abyss.

This is shewn in the Gospel, where he prays to the Father to send the comforter[5] or Desire that Reason may have Ideas to build on, the Jehovah of the Bible being no other than he who dwells in flaming fire. Know that after Christ's death, he became Jehovah.

But in Milton, the Father is Destiny, the Son, a Ratio[6] of the five senses, & the Holy-ghost, Vacuum![7]

Note. The reason Milton wrote in fetters when he wrote of Angels & God, and at liberty when of Devils & Hell, is because he was a true Poet and of the Devil's party without knowing it.

A Memorable Fancy

As I was walking among the fires of hell, delighted with the enjoyment of Genius, which to Angels look like torment and insanity, I collected some of their Proverbs: thinking that as the sayings used in a nation mark its character, so the Proverbs of Hell shew the nature of Infernal wisdom better than any description of buildings or garments.

When I came home, on the abyss of the five senses, where a flat sided steep frowns over the present world, I saw a mighty Devil folded in black clouds, hovering on the sides of the rock, with cor-

[PLATE 7]

roding[8] fires he wrote the following sentence now percieved by the minds of men, & read by them on earth.

How do you know but ev'ry Bird that cuts the airy way
Is an immense world of delight, clos'd by your senses five?[9]

5. An interpretation of John 14:16–17.

6. Meaning both "reason" and "sum." Confinement by this "ratio" of sensory perception is the subject of *There Is No Natural Religion*, section b.

7. Milton was not a Trinitarian; thus the Holy Ghost rarely has a distinct presence in his work.

8. An allegorical allusion to the process of etching in which corrosive acid is used to burn away the surfaces of a metal plate.

9. Derived from *Bristowe Tragedie* by Thomas Chatterton (1752–70): "How dydd I knowe that eve'ry darte, / That cutte the Airie waie, / Myghte nott find passage toe my harte, / And close myne eyes for aie?" This allusion to the victimized poet (a suicide at seventeen) is perhaps another gesture of affiliation with the underdog.

Proverbs of Hell[1]

In seed time learn, in harvest teach, in winter enjoy.
Drive your cart and your plow over the bones of the dead.
The road of excess leads to the palace of wisdom.
Prudence is a rich ugly old maid courted by Incapacity.
He who desires but acts not, breeds pestilence.
The cut worm forgives the plow.
Dip him in the river who loves water.
A fool sees not the same tree that a wise man sees.
He whose face gives no light, shall never become a star.
Eternity is in love with the productions of time.
The busy bee has no time for sorrow.
The hours of folly are measur'd by the clock, but of wisdom: no clock can measure.
All wholsom food is caught without a net or a trap.
Bring out number, weight, & measure in a year of dearth.
No bird soars too high, if he soars with his own wings.
A dead body revenges not injuries.
The most sublime act is to set another before you.
If the fool would persist in his folly he would become wise.
Folly is the cloke of knavery.
Shame is Pride's cloke.

[PLATE 8]
Prisons are built with stones of Law, Brothels with bricks of Religion.
The pride of the peacock is the glory of God.
The lust of the goat is the bounty of God.
The wrath of the lion is the wisdom of God.
The nakedness of woman is the work of God.
Excess of sorrow laughs. Excess of joy weeps.
The roaring of lions, the howling of wolves, the raging of the stormy sea, and the destructive sword, are portions of eternity too great for the eye of man.
The fox condemns the trap, not himself.
Joys impregnate. Sorrows bring forth.
Let man wear the fell of the lion, woman the fleece of the sheep.
The bird a nest, the spider a web, man friendship.
The selfish smiling fool & the sullen frowning fool shall be both thought wise, that they may be a rod.
What is now proved was once only imagin'd.

1. These nuggets of infernal wisdom are the counterparts to the "heavenly" Book of Proverbs in the Old Testament. Collections of tamer aphorisms, such as La Rochefoucauld's *Maxims,* were popular at the time. Blake approvingly annotated his friend's Fuseli's translation of Lavater's *Aphorisms on Man* (1788); see p. 430.

The rat, the mouse, the fox, the rabbet watch the roots; the lion, the tyger, the horse, the elephant, watch the fruits.
The cistern contains; the fountain overflows.
One thought fills immensity.
Always be ready to speak your mind, and a base man will avoid you.
Every thing possible to be believ'd is an image of truth.
The eagle never lost so much time as when he submitted to learn of the crow.

[PLATE 9]
The fox provides for himself, but God provides for the lion.
Think in the morning, Act in the noon, Eat in the evening, Sleep in the night.
He who has sufferd you to impose on him knows you.
As the plow follows words, so God rewards prayers.
The tygers of wrath are wiser than the horses of instruction.
Expect poison from the standing water.
You never know what is enough unless you know what is more than enough.
Listen to the fool's reproach! it is a kingly title!
The eyes of fire, the nostrils of air, the mouth of water, the beard of earth.
The weak in courage is strong in cunning.
The apple tree never asks the beech how he shall grow, nor the lion the horse how he shall take his prey.
The thankful reciever bears a plentiful harvest.
If others had not been foolish, we should be so.
The soul of sweet delight can never be defil'd,
When thou seest an Eagle, thou seest a portion of Genius; lift up thy head!
As the catterpiller chooses the fairest leaves to lay her eggs on, so the priest lays his curse on the fairest joys.
To create a little flower is the labour of ages.
Damn braces: Bless relaxes.
The best wine is the oldest, the best water the newest.
Prayers plow not! Praises reap not!
Joys laugh not! Sorrows weep not!

[PLATE 10]
The head Sublime, the heart Pathos, the genitals Beauty, the hands & feet Proportion.
As the air to a bird or the sea to a fish, so is contempt to the contemptible.
The crow wish'd every thing was black, the owl, that every thing was white.
Exuberance is Beauty
If the lion was advise'd by the fox, he would be cunning.
Improvement makes strait roads, but the crooked roads without Improvement are roads of Genius.
Sooner murder an infant in its cradle than nurse unacted desires.

Where man is not nature is barren.
Truth can never be told so as to be understood, and not be believ'd.

Enough! or Too much

[PLATE 11]

The ancient Poets animated all sensible objects with Gods or Geniuses, calling them by the names and adorning them with the properties of woods, rivers, mountains, lakes, cities, nations, and whatever their enlarged & numerous senses could percieve.

And particularly they studied the genius of each city & country, placing it under its mental deity.

Till a system was formed, which some took advantage of & enslav'd the vulgar by attempting to realize or abstract the mental deities from their objects; thus began Priesthood.

Choosing forms of worship from poetic tales.

And at length they pronounced that the Gods had ordered such things.

Thus men forgot that All deities reside in the human breast.

[PLATE 12]

A Memorable Fancy[2]

The Prophets Isaiah and Ezekiel dined with me, and I asked them how they dared so roundly to assert that God spake to them; and whether they did not think at the time, that they would be misunderstood, & so be the cause of imposition.

Isaiah answer'd, "I saw no God, nor heard any, in a finite organical perception; but my senses discover'd the infinite in every thing, and as I was then perswaded, & remain confirm'd, that the voice of honest indignation is the voice of God, I cared not for consequences but wrote."

Then I asked: "Does a firm perswasion that a thing is so, make it so?"

He replied, "All poets believe that it does, & in ages of imagination this firm perswasion removed mountains; but many are not capable of a firm perswasion of any thing."

Then Ezekiel said, "The philosophy of the east taught the first principles of human perception. Some nations held one principle for the origin & some another; we of Israel taught that the Poetic Genius (as you now call it) was the first principle and all the others merely derivative, which was the cause of our despising the Priests & Philosophers of other countries, and prophecying that all Gods

[PLATE 13]

would at last be proved to originate in ours & to be the tributaries of the Poetic Genius. It was this that our great poet King David[3] desired so fervently & invokes so patheticly, saying by this he conquers enemies & governs kingdoms. And we so loved our God that we cursed in his name all the deities of surrounding nations, and asserted that they had rebelled. From these opinions the vulgar came to think that all nations would at last be subject to the Jews.

"This," said he, "like all firm perswasions, is come to pass, for all nations believe the Jews' code and worship the Jews' god, and what greater subjection can be?"[4]

I heard this with some wonder, & must confess my own conviction. After dinner I ask'd Isaiah to favour the world with his lost works: he said none of equal value was lost. Ezekiel said the same of his.

I also asked Isaiah what made him go naked and barefoot[5] three

2. This episode combines several conventional scenes: the philosophic dinner, as in Plato's *Symposium*, and the encounter with the famous dead, as in *Gulliver's Travels* III, vii-viii.

3. The psalmist David, though a murderer and an adulterer, was a man "after God's own heart" (I Samuel 13:14, Acts 13:22).

4. Christians have adopted what the prophet takes to be the most repressive laws of Judaism.

years. He answered, "The same that made our friend Diogenes the Grecian."

I then asked Ezekiel why he eat dung, & lay so long on his right & left side?[6] He answerd, "The desire of raising other men into a perception of the infinite. This the North American tribes practise,[7] & is he honest who resists his genius or conscience only for the sake of present ease or gratification?"

[PLATE 14]

The ancient tradition that the world will be consumed in fire at the end of six thousand years[8] is true, as I have heard from Hell.

For the cherub with his flaming sword is hereby commanded to leave his guard at tree of life,[9] and when he does, the whole creation will be consumed, and appear infinite and holy, whereas it now appears finite & corrupt.

This will come to pass by an improvement of sensual enjoyment.

But first the notion that man has a body distinct from his soul is to be expunged; this I shall do, by printing in the infernal method, by corrosives, which in Hell are salutary and medicinal, melting apparent surfaces away, and displaying the infinite which was hid.

If the doors of perception were cleansed every thing would appear to man as it is, infinite.

For man has closed himself up, till he sees all things thro' narrow chinks of his cavern.[1]

5. Isaiah 20:2. The Greek Diogenes the Cynic (ca. 412–323 B.C.), who cultivated austerity and lived in a barrel, is recognized as a fellow prophet. Isaiah and his friend Diogenes aren't the only prophets who were moved to go naked, as shown in the amusing story of Saul's brief experience as a prophet in I Kings 19:24.

6. In Ezekiel 4 the prophet is commanded to act out the siege of Jerusalem, and to lie 390 days on his left side to represent the years of Israel's iniquity and 40 days on his right side to represent the years of Judah's iniquity. When he is commanded to eat barley cakes "baked with" human dung, he prays to be spared and is then allowed to use cow's dung. Both Blake and Swedenborg apparently took this to mean that Ezekiel had to mix his barley cakes with the dung rather than just use it for fuel (cf. Swedenborg's *True Christian Religion*, [translated in 1781], section 130).

7. The disciplines the Native American medicine men subject themselves to are designed to produce visions for the enlightenment of the whole community; Blake's source book for this detail of Indian lore is unknown (cf. Blake's annotations to Watson in the Marginalia section of this book).

8. The traditional historical span of the creation, derived from texts in Revelation and II Peter 3:8, equated a thousand years with "one day" of God's time. History was supposed to last a "week" of thousand-year "days" corresponding to the six days of creation in Genesis.

9. In Genesis 3:24 God stationed cherubim and "a flaming sword which turned every way, to keep the way of the tree of life," but in Ezekiel 28:11–19 the prophet proclaims that the "Covering Cherub" will himself be burned up. This prohibiting angel is a major symbol in Blake's later writings; cf. *Milton* 37 and *Jerusalem* 89.

1. This variation on Plato's myth of the cave in the *Republic*, VII, also recalls the darkened chamber of the mind described by John Locke (1632–1704) in *Essay Concerning Human Understanding*, II, xi, 17: "a closet wholly shut from light, with only some little openings left to let in external visible resemblances or ideas of things without."

[PLATE 15]

A Memorable Fancy[2]

I was in a Printing house in Hell & saw the method in which knowledge is transmitted from generation to generation.

In the first chamber was a Dragon-Man, clearing away the rubbish from a cave's mouth; within, a number of Dragons were hollowing the cave.

In the second chamber was a Viper folding round the rock & the cave, and others adorning it with gold, silver, and precious stones.

In the third chamber was an Eagle with wings and feathers of air; he caused the inside of the cave to be infinite. Around were numbers of Eagle-like men, who built palaces in the immense cliffs.

In the fourth chamber were Lions of flaming fire raging around & melting the metals into living fluids.

In the fifth chamber were Unnam'd forms, which cast the metals into the expanse.

There they were reciev'd by Men who occupied the sixth chamber, and took the forms of books & were arranged in libraries.

[PLATE 16]

The Giants who formed this world into its sensual existence and now seem to live in it in chains are in truth the causes of its life & the sources of all activity. But the chains are the cunning of weak and tame minds which have power to resist energy, according to the proverb, "the weak in courage is strong in cunning."

2. This allegory on the transmission of knowledge refers to both the conceptual and productive aspects of creativity, to the cleansing of the senses, and to the processes of etching. Knowledge employs energies but the arrangement of books in "libraries" suggests that the terrific is finally tamed, perhaps even imprisoned.

Thus one portion of being, is the Prolific; the other, the Devouring: to the devourer it seems as if the producer was in his chains, but it is not so; he only takes portions of existence and fancies that the whole.

But the Prolific would cease to be Prolific unless the Devourer as a sea recieved the excess of his delights.[3]

Some will say, "Is not God alone the Prolific?" I answer, "God only Acts & Is, in existing beings or Men."

These two classes of men are always upon earth, & they should be enemies; whoever tries

[PLATE 17]

to reconcile them seeks to destroy existence.

Religion is an endeavour to reconcile the two.

Note. Jesus Christ did not wish to unite but to separate them, as in the Parable of sheep and goats! & he says, "I came not to send Peace but a Sword."[4]

Messiah or Satan or Tempter was formerly thought to be one of the Antediluvians who are our Energies.

A Memorable Fancy[5]

An Angel came to me and said, "O pitiable foolish young man! O horrible! O dreadful state! Consider the hot burning dungeon thou art preparing for thyself to all eternity, to which thou art going in such career."

I said, "Perhaps you will be willing to shew me my eternal lot & we will contemplate together upon it and see whether your lot or mine is most desirable."

So he took me thro' a stable & thro' a church & down into the church vault at the end of which was a mill: thro' the mill we went,

3. The contrary "Classes" of "prolific" and "Devourer" are formulated in an extreme fashion so as to make it clear that attempts to reconcile them would result in the destruction of the true character of one or both.

4. See Matthew 25:32–33, 10:34.

5. A comic descent into hell followed by a comic space flight; these are traditional story patterns. The succession of places on the road to hell constitutes an allegory of the devolution of Christianity. In the historical allegory, "to the east distant about three degrees" refers to the longitudinal distance between Paris and London. In the second episode of this Fancy the narrator plunges the Angel and himself into the sun, where the narrator dons the white clothing of a saint (Revelation 7:9). He shows the Angel his eternal lot in the void beyond Saturn, traditionally the outermost planet. On their re-entry to earth, dragged by the weight of Swedenborg's volumes, they pass through "seven houses of brick," (or "seven churches of Asia," Revelation 1:4) where theological disputation is satirized in an allegory of a monkey house. Aristotle's *Analytics*, treatises on logic, are symbolized as a skeleton because formal analysis disregards the vitality of prophetic vision, which enlivens "bleached bones" ("Argument," 2:12, and *Milton* 19:6–14.

and came to a cave. Down the winding cavern we groped our tedious way till a void boundless as a nether sky appeard beneath us, & we held by the roots of trees and hung over this immensity. But I said, "If you please, we will commit ourselves to this void, and see whether providence is here also. If you will not I will." But he answered, "Do not presume, O young-man, but as we here remain behold thy lot which will soon appear when the darkness passes away."

So I remaind with him sitting in the twisted

[PLATE 18]

root of an oak. He was suspended in a fungus which hung with the head downward into the deep.

By degrees we beheld the infinite Abyss, fiery as the smoke of a burning city. Beneath us at an immense distance was the sun, black but shining. Round it were fiery tracks on which revolv'd vast spiders, crawling after their prey, which flew or rather swum in the infinite deep, in the most terrific shapes of animals sprung from corruption; & the air was full of them, & seemd composed of them. These are Devils and are called Powers of the air. I now asked my companion which was my eternal lot? He said, "Between the black & white spiders."

But now, from between the black & white spiders a cloud and fire burst and rolled thro the deep, blackning all beneath, so that the nether deep grew black as a sea & rolled with a terrible noise. Beneath us was nothing now to be seen but a black tempest; till looking east between the clouds & the waves, we saw a cataract of blood mixed with fire and not many stones' throw from us appeard and sunk again the scaly fold of a monstrous serpent. At last to the east, distant about three degrees, appeard a fiery crest above the waves. Slowly it reared like a ridge of golden rocks till we discoverd two globes of crimson fire, from which the sea fled away in clouds of smoke. And now we saw, it was the head of Leviathan; his forehead was divided into streaks of green & purple like those on a tyger's forehead; soon we saw his mouth & red gills hang just above the raging foam tinging the black deep with beams of blood, advancing toward

[PLATE 19]

us with all the fury of a spiritual existence.

My friend the Angel climb'd up from his station into the mill. I remain'd alone, & then this appearance was no more; but I found myself sitting on a pleasant bank beside a river by moon light hearing a harper who sung to the harp, & his theme was, "The man who never alters his opinion is like standing water, & breeds reptiles of the mind."

But I arose, and sought for the mill, & there I found my Angel, who surprised asked me, how I escaped?

I answerd, "All that we saw was owing to your metaphysics: for when you ran away, I found myself on a bank by moonlight hearing a harper. But now we have seen my eternal lot, shall I shew you yours?" He laughd at my proposal; but I by force suddenly caught him in my arms, & flew westerly thro' the night, till we were elevated above the earth's shadow. Then I flung myself with him directly into the body of the sun. Here I clothed myself in white, & taking in my hand Swedenborg's volumes sunk from the glorious clime, and passed all the planets till we came to Saturn. Here I staid to rest & then leap'd into the void between Saturn & the fixed stars.

"Here," said I! "is your lot, in this space, if space it may be calld." Soon we saw the stable and the church, & I took him to the altar and open'd the Bible, and lo! it was a deep pit, into which I descended driving the Angel before me. Soon we saw seven houses of brick, one we entered; in it were a

[PLATE 20]

number of monkeys, baboons, & all of that species chaind by the middle, grinning and snatching at one another, but witheld by the shortness of their chains. However, I saw that they sometimes grew numerous; and then the weak were caught by the strong and with a grinning aspect, first coupled with & then devourd, by plucking off first one limb and then another till the body was left a helpless trunk. This after grinning & kissing it with seeming fondness they devourd too; and here & there I saw one savourily picking the flesh off of his own tail. As the stench terribly annoyd us both we went

into the mill, & I in my hand brought the skeleton of a body, which in the mill was Aristotle's Analytics.

So the Angel said: "Thy phantasy has imposed upon me & thou oughtest to be ashamed."

I answered: "We impose on one another, & it is but lost time to converse with you whose works are only Analytics."

Opposition is true Friendship.[6]

[PLATE 21]

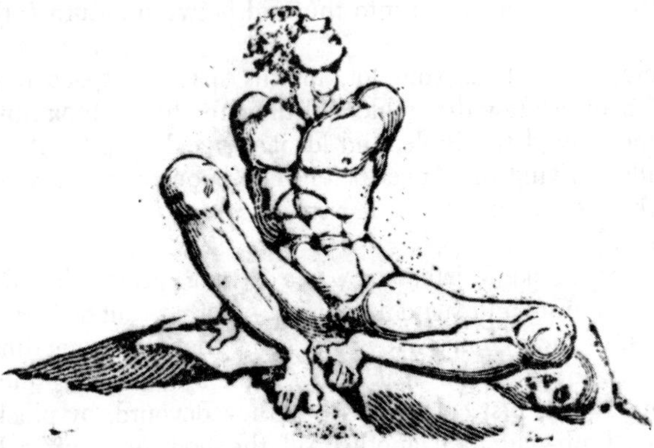

I have always found that Angels have the vanity to speak of themselves as the only wise; this they do with a confident insolence sprouting from systematic reasoning.

Thus Swedenborg boasts that what he writes is new, tho' it is only the Contents or Index of already publish'd books.

A man carried a monkey about for a shew, & because he was a little wiser than the monkey, grew vain, and conciev'd himself as much wiser than seven men. It is so with Swedenborg; he shews the folly of churches & exposes hypocrites, till he imagines that all are religious & himself the single

[PLATE 22]

one on earth that ever broke a net.

Now hear a plain fact: Swedenborg has not written one new truth. Now hear another: he has written all the old falshoods.

6. This motto was deleted in six of the nine copies of *The Marriage of Heaven and Hell.*

And now hear the reason: He conversed with Angels who are all religious, & conversed not with Devils who all hate religion, for he was incapable thro' his conceited notions.

Thus Swedenborg's writings are a recapitulation of all superficial opinions, and an analysis of the more sublime, but no further.

Have now another plain fact: Any man of mechanical talents may from the writings of Paracelsus or Jacob Behmen,[7] produce ten thousand volumes of equal value with Swedenborg's. And from those of Dante or Shakespear, an infinite number.

But when he has done this, let him not say that he knows better than his master, for he only holds a candle in sunshine.

A Memorable Fancy

Once I saw a Devil in a flame of fire, who arose before an Angel that sat on a cloud, and the Devil utterd these words:

"The worship of God is: Honouring his gifts in other men, each according to his genius, and loving the

[PLATE 23]

greatest men best. Those who envy or calumniate great men hate God, for there is no other God."

The Angel hearing this became almost blue, but mastering himself he grew yellow, & at last white, pink[8] & smiling, and then replied,

"Thou Idolater, is not God One? & is not he visible in Jesus Christ? and has not Jesus Christ given his sanction to the law of ten commandments and are not all other men fools, sinners, & nothings?"

7. Paracelsus (1493–1541) was the pen name of a Swiss alchemist, theorist of the occult, and medical pioneer. Jakob Boehme (1575–1624) was a German theosophist and shoemaker whose influential work was translated by William Law in 1761. Blake's letter-poem of Sept. 12, 1800 (p. 452) suggests that these two writers had much more influence on his thought than had Swedenborg. In addition to attacking Swedenborg in marginal annotations of his works, Blake has "Rintrah" describe him as "the Samson shorn by the Churches" (*Milton* 22:46). But the commentary on picture VII in the *Descriptive Catalogue*, "The Spiritual Preceptor," implies that Blake came to have a measure of respect for Swedenborg's teachings.

8. This scene recalls the embarrassment of the archangel Raphael in *Paradise Lost* VIII, 619, when asked by Adam how the angels make love. Such disputations in the spiritual world are common in Swedenborg's visions; in some cases Blake would probably have sided with the angels. For example, during a debate on the doctrine of the atonement as a sacrifice to an angry God, which takes place in a darkened, windowless temple, "The angel, on hearing this, was silent for a long time; then he broke the silence and said: 'Can the Christian world be so insane . . .?' " He explains at length that the crucifixion united Jesus' humanity with the divinity but was in no way a propitiation, and he appoints Swedenborg to give this news to the world, whereupon windows appear in the walls of the temple (*True Christian Religion*, section 134).

The Devil answer'd, Bray a fool in a morter with wheat,[9]" yet shall not his folly be beaten out of him. If Jesus Christ is the greatest man, you ought to love him in the greatest degree. Now hear how he has given his sanction to the law of ten commandments: did he not mock at the sabbath, and so mock the sabbath's God? murder those who were murderd because of him? turn away the law from the woman taken in adultery? steal the labor of others to support him? bear false witness when he omitted making a defence before Pilate? covet when he pray'd for his disciples, and when he bid them shake off the dust of their feet against such as refused to lodge them? I tell you, no virtue can exist without breaking these ten commandments. Jesus was all virtue, and acted from impulse

[PLATE 24]

not from rules."

When he had so spoken, I beheld the Angel, who stretched out

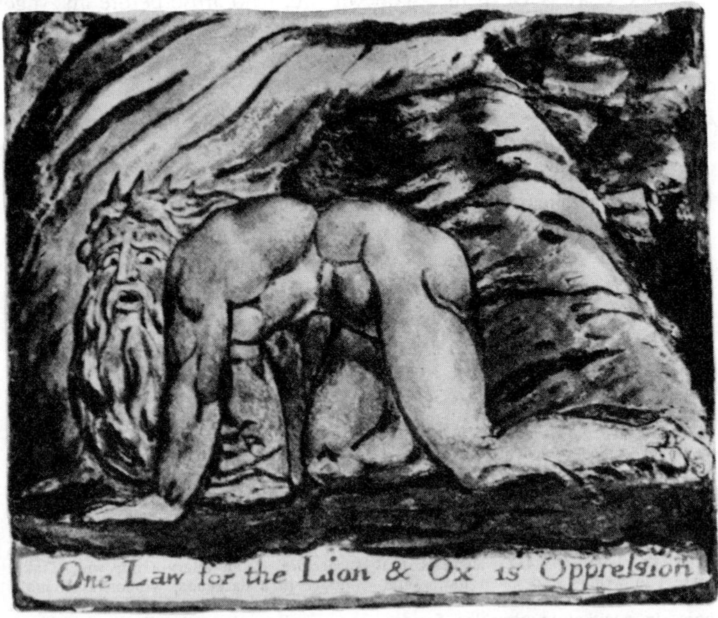
One Law for the Lion & Ox is Oppression

9. The devil's response paraphrases Proverbs 27:22; "bray" means to crush, as with a mortar and pestle. Christ as law-breaker is the subject of Blake's manuscript poem "The Everlasting Gospel" (c. 1818). The broken commandments are the fourth (Mark 12:2–13, sixth (Matthew 3:16–18), seventh (John 8:2–11), eighth (Luke 9:13; 22:8–14), ninth (Matthew 27:13–14), and tenth (Matthew 10:9–14).

his arms embracing the flame of fire, & he was consumed and arose as Elijah.[1]

Note. This Angel, who is now become a Devil, is my particular friend: we often read the Bible together in its infernal or diabolical sense, which the world shall have if they behave well.

I have also: The Bible of Hell,[2] which the world shall have whether they will or no.

One Law for the Lion & Ox is Oppression.[3]

[PLATE 25]

A Song of Liberty[4]

1. The Eternal Female groand! it was heard over all the Earth:
2. Albion's coast is sick, silent; the American meadows faint!
3. Shadows of Prophecy shiver along by the lakes and the rivers and mutter across the ocean. France, rend down thy dungeon;[5]
4. Golden Spain, burst the barriers of old Rome;
5. Cast thy keys,[6] O Rome, into the deep, down falling, even to eternity down falling,
6. And weep.
7. In her trembling hands she took the new born terror howling:
8. On those infinite mountains of light,[7] now barr'd out by the atlantic sea, the new born fire stood before the starry king![8]
9. Flag'd with grey brow'd snows and thunderous visages the jealous wings wav'd over the deep.
10. The speary hand burned aloft, unbuckled was the shield; forth went the hand of jealousy among the flaming hair, and

[PLATE 26]

hurl'd the new born wonder thro' the starry night.

11. The fire, the fire, is falling!
12. Look up! look up! O citizen of London, enlarge thy countenance! O Jew, leave counting gold! return to thy oil and wine. O African! black African! (go, winged thought, widen his forehead.)

1. The flame at the beginning of his dialogue contains the Devil. In II Kings 2:11 a chariot drawn by fiery horses appears and Elijah the prophet is swept to heaven in a whirlwind.
2. Refers to "A Song of Liberty" and presumably to other works of this period, the "Lambeth books" of *Urizen*, *Ahania*, and *Los*.
3. In *Visions of the Daughters of Albion* 4:22 Bromion believes that there must be such a law.
4. Added somehat later than most of the rest of the work, about 1792. Verses 2–6 and 10 emphasize the contemporary political and social dimension of the vision. The myth of the Eternal Female, verse 1, the newborn terror, verse 7, and the starry king, verse 8, is enacted in later works under the names of Enitharmon, Orc, and Urizen. "Urthona," in *The Four Zoas* the eternal name of the temporal redeemer, Los, is here introduced without explanation.
5. The Bastille, destroyed in 1789.
6. The keys of Saint Peter, traditional symbols of Papal authority.
7. Atlantis, referred to in *America* 10:6
8. Blake's stars are negative images when they are identified with the workings of an inhuman universe.

13. The fiery limbs, the flaming hair, shot like the sinking sun into the western sea.
14. Wak'd from his eternal sleep, the hoary element roaring fled away:[9]
15. Down rushd, beating his wings in vain, the jealous king; his grey brow'd councellors, thunderous warriors, curl'd veterans, among helms, and shields, and chariots, horses, elephants; banners, castles, slings and rocks:[1]
16. Falling, rushing, ruining! buried in the ruins, on Urthona's dens.
17. All night beneath the ruins; then, their sullen flames faded, emerge round the gloomy king.
18. With thunder and fire, leading his starry hosts thro' the waste wilderness,
[PLATE 27]
he promulgates his ten commands, glancing his beamy eyelids over the deep in dark dismay,
19. Where the son of fire in his eastern cloud, while the morning plumes her golden breast,
20. Spurning the clouds written with curses, stamps the stony law[2] to dust, loosing the eternal horses from the dens of night, crying "Empire is no more! and now the lion & wolf shall cease."[3]

Chorus

Let the Priests of the Raven of dawn,[4] no longer in deadly black, with hoarse note curse the sons of joy. Nor his accepted brethren whom, tyrant, he calls free; lay the bound or build the roof. Nor pale religious letchery call that virginity, that wishes but acts not!

For every thing that lives is Holy.[5]

America: A Prophecy

The phrase "in the year" on the title page of *America*, the first of Blake's works to be entitled "A Prophecy," calls attention to the date, 1793; only the date, without elaboration, appears on the title pages of other dated works. In 1793 Louis XVI was executed, Britain went to war against the French revolutionary government, Parliament passed harsh laws against sedi-

9. At the Apocalypse the sea disappears (Revelation 21:1).
1. The aged king of night, having cast out the rebellious youth (described as fire and sun), is himself brought to ruin; he recovers during the night by promulgating his commandments, but the fiery youth arises free in the east. This story recurs in *America* 8:14, *Europe* 10:1, and *Urizen* 28.
2. The ten commandments (see Exodus 31:18), as in *America* 8:5.
3. Blake used large lettering for this refrain, which is repeated in *America* 6:15.
4. Bloom points out that the raven was sacred to the Norse god Odin. The true bird of dawn is the lark, as in *Milton* 35:61–36:12.
5. Reiterated in *Visions* 8 and *America* 8:13.

tious publications, and the French Revolution was becoming so violent that English sympathizers like Blake found revolutionary activity increasingly difficult to justify. In *The Marriage of Heaven and Hell* and later in his annotations to Bishop Watson's *Apology for the Bible,* Blake enunciates principles of prophecy that seem especially relevant to the year 1793 and to the recent American history of 1776: for Blake, a prophet is a seer rather than a forecaster; he perceives the outlines of contemporary events and understands the implications of public issues; above all, he speaks out fearlessly to awaken his contemporaries. 1793 was a time to reflect on the imaginative origins of the contemporary revolution: why was it going wrong? Was the American Revolution more successful?

Blake's *The French Revolution,* an earlier work set in ordinary type but never published, either conventionally or in illuminated printing, is a visionary history following the revolution only up to 1791—well before the Terror. Blake had also designed a title page for a work to be entitled *The American War,* possibly a historical version of events in *America: A Prophecy.* Apparently neither scheme for a poetic history seemed imaginatively flexible enough to reveal the inner causes of political events. *America: A Prophecy* begins with a "Preludium" (plates 1–2) which envisions, in the form of myth, an outbreak of repressed energy: Orc breaks his chains and has violent intercourse with a nameless female principle. The specifically American and historical references come into prominence in the body of the work (plates 3–16). As Erdman has shown in his important essay on *America* in this volume, and elsewhere, Blake drew many details in this account from Joel Barlow's *Vision of Columbus* (1787). Although *America* is the most historically allusive of Blake's chief works, only a few details (apart from universally recognizable references to such heroes of the Revolution as Washington) require specific historical information in order to be intelligible. Historical figures are presented mainly as agents of the giant "spiritual forms," the antagonists of Orc and Urizen. The latter operates through the "guardian Prince of Albion" who resembles the repressive King George III but is not quite identical with him. Blake did not believe that individuals are unimportant, but he was committed to the idea that the major events of history can best be understood as they are expressed in the deeds of magnified human beings who possess a grandeur like that of the gods of earlier mythologies.

Although none of Blake's poems is named after Orc, *America* may be thought of as Orc's book; he precipitates most of the action. In the "Preludium" his first action is a *reaction* to his having been enchained during the first fourteen years of his life. The name Orc—whether it derives from "Orc" (sea monster), "Orcus" (hell, also a giant in Spenser), "cor" (heart), or "orchis" (testicle), or all of these—is used by Blake for a figure who struggles against political oppression, sexual repression, and all rational constrictions and restrictions on energy. In the myth of Orc, Blake establishes an identity between psychological and sociological expressions of rage and lust: Orc is the pent-up energy in human nature and human history that is at first held down but eventually erupts or explodes.

There are a number of verbal bridges between *America* and other texts in the canon that Blake hoped his ideal reader would recognize. Most of these are connected to "A Song of Liberty," notably the concluding words of the Chorus "For every thing that lives is Holy," (repeated by Orc in *America* 8:13, as well as by Oothoon in *Visions of the Daughters of Albion* 8:10). In addition, the last line of "Africa" in *The Song of Los* is repeated as the first line of "A Prophecy," *America* 3:1. The "Preludium" of *Europe* is a kind of sequel to the "Preludium" of *America*, and *America* 16:15 prophesies the French reception of Orc's furious light, confirmed in *Europe* 15:2. The same inflammatory influence is traced in "Asia" (*The Song of Los* 6:6), as if Blake foresaw in 1793 that the last of the continents would one day sing "The East is Red." A direct link between *Europe* and "Asia" is that the "howl" of reactionary forces in Europe (*Europe* 12:12, 14, 21) is heard by the kings of Asia (*Song of Los* 6:2).

For *America*, as for the other "continent" works, *Europe* and *The Song of Los*, Blake used copper plates measuring about nine by seven inches, to make books much larger than all other illuminated works except *Jerusalem*. The designs in *America* are beautifully woven into the text in a way more complicated than in earlier works; however, only four of the fifteen copies of *America* are colored. Earlier versions of four plates as well as some preliminary drawings are extant, showing that Blake changed his ideas about how best to render his material; minor pictorial and textual variants among the published copies indicate the care with which Blake considered and refined this work about the origins and fate of freedom in history.

Our text is taken from Copy E, Lessing J. Rosenwald Collection, Library of Congress; cf. *Blake Newsletter* facsimile of copy E (1975), which is misidentified as copy C. Color plates are from Copy O, Fitzwilliam Museum, Cambridge.

Preludium

The shadowy daughter of Urthona stood before red Orc.
When fourteen suns had faintly journey'd o'er his dark abode;
His food she brought in iron baskets, his drink in cups of iron;
Crown'd with a helmet & dark hair the namelefs female stood;
A quiver with its burning stores, a bow like that of night,
When pestilence is shot from heaven; no other arms she need:
Invulnerable tho' naked, save where clouds roll round her loins,
Their awful folds in the dark air; silent she stood as night;
For never from her iron tongue could voice or sound arise;
But dumb till that dread day when Orc afsay'd his fierce embrace.

Dark virgin; said the hairy youth, thy father stern abhorr'd;
Rivets my tenfold chains while still on high my spirit soars;
Sometimes an eagle screaming in the sky, sometimes a lion,
Stalking upon the mountains, & sometimes a whale I lash
The raging fathomlefs abyfs, anon a serpent folding
Around the pillars of Urthona, and round thy dark limbs,
On the Canadian wilds I fold, feeble my spirit folds.
For chaind beneath I rend these caverns; when thou bringest food
I howl my joy: and my red eyes seek to behold thy face
In vain! these clouds roll to & fro, & hide thee from my sight.

America
A Prophecy*

LAMBETH

Printed by William Blake in the year 1793.

[PLATE 1]

Preludium

The shadowy daughter of Urthona[1] stood before red Orc[2]
When fourteen suns had faintly journey'd o'er his dark abode;
His food she brought in iron baskets, his drink in cups of iron;
Crown'd with a helmet & dark hair the nameless female stood.
A quiver with its burning stores, a bow like that of night[3]
When pestilence is shot from heaven—no other arms she need:
Invulnerable tho' naked, save where clouds roll round her loins
Their awful folds in the dark air. Silent she stood as night:
For never from her iron tongue could voice or sound arise,
But dumb till that dread day, when Orc assay'd his fierce embrace.

"Dark virgin," said the hairy youth, "thy father[4] stern abhorr'd
Rivets my tenfold chains while still on high my spirit soars:

* See color plate 15 for title page.

1. The daughter is similar to the "Eternal Female," of "Song of Liberty," verse 1, *Marriage of Heaven and Hell;* her father is the unexplained Urthona, verse 16. In *Europe* 1:1–4 "the nameless shadowy female" is identified as the daughter of Enitharmon (who is the spouse of Los). Apparently, then, the shadowy female is the daughter of Enitharmon and Urthona (or Los). In *America*, her identity is incompletely specified because, as Nature, she is at first only potential, not yet actualized. In *The Four Zoas* she is named Vala and is a consort to Orc, who is called Luvah in Eternity.

2. In *Urizen,* VII:1 Orc is first named as son of Los and Enitharmon, though in "Song of Liberty" he has appeared as "the new born terror" and "the son of fire." He resembles Prometheus, both as rebel and as crucified victim. The fact that Orc is "hairy" (1:11; 2:2) as well as red emphasizes his relationship to Esau, the rebellious outcast also named Edom, whose "dominion" is mentioned in *Marriage of Heaven and Hell.*

3. A Diana figure (cf. "virgin" 1:10; 2:6); in wearing only a helmet, she also resembles the virginal goddess Athena, or a Valkyrie. The predominance of iron weapons and utensils suggests a primitive Iron Age.

4. It appears that Orc doesn't recognize Urthona as his father (called Los in *Urizen* 20 and *Four Zoas* I, 3:12); therefore he is unaware that this woman is his sister.

Sometimes an eagle screaming in the sky, sometimes a lion
Stalking upon the mountains, & sometimes a whale I lash
The raging fathomless abyss; anon a serpent[5] folding
Around the pillars of Urthona, and round thy dark limbs.
On the Canadian wilds[6] I fold, feeble my spirit folds,
For chaind beneath I rend these caverns. When thou bringest food
I howl my joy: and my red eyes seek to behold thy face——
In vain! these clouds roll to & fro, & hide thee from my sight."

[PLATE 2]
Silent as despairing love, and strong as jealousy,[7]
The hairy shoulders rend the links. Free are the wrists of fire;
Round the terrific loins he siez'd the panting struggling womb;
It joy'd: she put aside her clouds & smiled her first-born smile:
As when a black cloud shews its light'nings to the silent deep.

Soon as she saw the terrible boy, then burst the virgin cry:

"I know thee, I have found thee, & I will not let thee go:
Thou art the image of God who dwells in darkness of Africa.[8]
And thou art fall'n to give me life in regions of dark death.
On my American plains I feel the struggling afflictions
Endur'd by roots that writhe their arms into the nether deep:
I see a serpent in Canada, who courts me to his love;
In Mexico an Eagle, and a Lion in Peru;
I see a Whale in the South-sea, drinking my soul away.
O what limb rending pains I feel. Thy fire & my frost
Mingle in howling pains, in furrows by thy lightnings rent.
This is eternal death; and this the torment long foretold."

5. As a beast of fire, the serpent completes the representation of the four elements (with eagle, lion, and whale). The serpent is associated with both the phallus and the tempter in Eden; it also appeared as a symbol of defiance on the famous Revolutionary flag, "Don't Tread on Me." The same beasts are mentioned by the Female in 2: 12–14, but she identifies them as totem animals instead of exemplars of freedom.

6. Cf. 2:12. Perhaps this detail is ominous since Canada did not join the Revolution. Despite her "American plains" (2:10), this Female is not, like Oothoon, "the soft soul of America" (*Visions of the Daughters of Albion* 1:3).

7. In *Urizen* 20 (VII:4) and *Four Zoas* (60:22) Los binds Orc because he himself is bound by the "Chain of Jealousy."

8. Cf. "Africa," *Song of Los* 3:21 and *Visions of the Daughters of Albion* 1:21. In her idolatry of Orc the Female suggests that he is a fertility spirit and perhaps that she perceives him as a black man (though in the colored designs he is not black). Has Orc broken his chains only to enter a new state of enslavement?

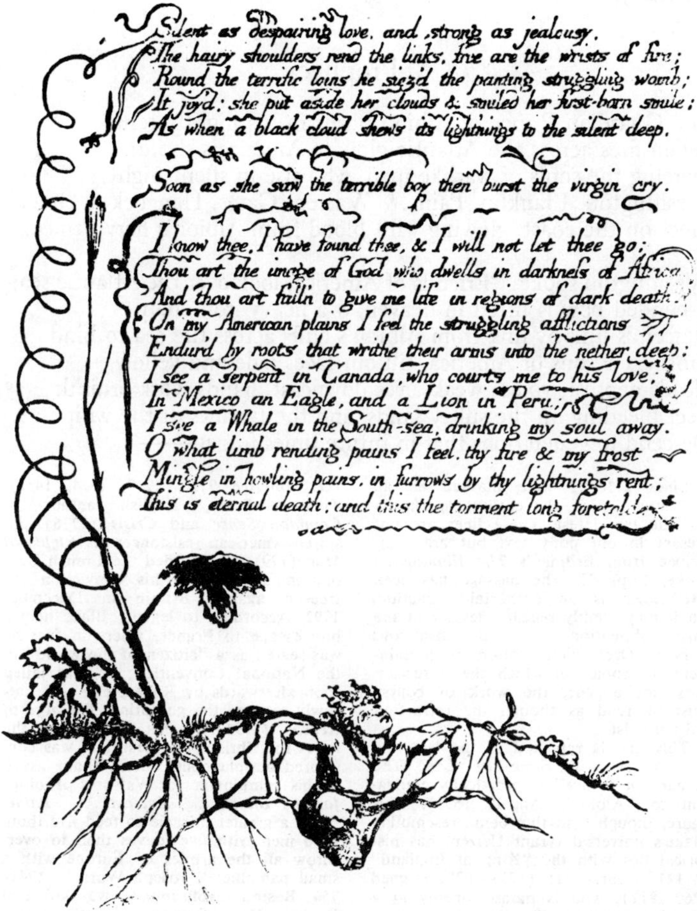

Silent as despairing love, and strong as jealousy,
The hairy shoulders rend the links, free are the wrists of fire;
Round the terrific loins he siez'd the panting struggling womb;
It joy'd: she put aside her clouds & smiled her first-born smile;
As when a black cloud shews its lightnings to the silent deep.

Soon as she saw the terrible boy then burst the virgin cry.

I know thee, I have found thee, & I will not let thee go;
Thou art the image of God who dwells in darkness of Africa;
And thou art fall'n to give me life in regions of dark death.
On my American plains I feel the struggling afflictions
Endur'd by roots that writhe their arms into the nether deep:
I see a serpent in Canada, who courts me to his love;
In Mexico an Eagle, and a Lion in Peru;
I see a Whale in the South-sea, drinking my soul away.
O what limb rending pains I feel. thy fire & my frost
Mingle in howling pains, in furrows by thy lightnings rent;
This is eternal death; and this the torment long foretold.

The stern Bard ceas'd, asham'd of his own song; enrag'd he swung
His harp aloft sounding, then dash'd its shining frame against
A ruin'd pillar in glittring fragments; silent he turn'd away,
And wander'd down the vales of Kent in sick & drear lamentings.[9]

[PLATE 3]

A Prophecy

The Guardian Prince of Albion burns in his nightly tent.[1]
Sullen fires across the Atlantic glow to America's shore:
Piercing the souls of warlike men, who rise in silent night.
Washington, Franklin, Paine & Warren, Gates, Hancock & Green[2]
Meet on the coast, glowing with blood from Albion's fiery Prince.

Washington spoke: "Friends of America, look over the Atlantic sea;
A bended bow is lifted in heaven, & a heavy iron chain
Descends link by link from Albion's cliffs across the sea to bind
Brothers & sons of America, till our faces pale and yellow,
Heads deprest, voices weak, eyes downcast, hands work-bruis'd,
Feet bleeding on the sultry sands, and the furrows of the whip
Descend to generations that in future times forget.——"

9. Lines 2:18–21 were masked on all but three copies, the earliest (perhaps) and the two latest. These lines are not present in our copy text but are transcribed from Erdman's *The Illuminated Blake,* Copy N. The passage has been interpreted as an authorial retraction, but it may simply register despair at the bardic obligation to tell the disastrous story of Orc's victimization or containment. In copies in which the retraction does not appear, the work of course must be read as though the retraction did not exist.

1. This line is repeated as the last line of "Africa" in *Song of Los.* The "Guardian Prince" is practically equivalent to "Albion's Angel" (5:1). This figure, though a mythic being resembling Blake's universal tyrant Urizen, has historical ties with the "King of England" (4:12), George III (1738–1820; reigned 1760–1811), who is named openly in a canceled passage. The fact that he is *burning* in his tent locates the initial source of fires and militancy on the political right. In line 2 the fires of Albion's Guardian inflame the rebellious Americans—possibly an allusion to the Boston Massacre (1770), as Damon suggests.

2. The speech of Washington (1732–99) is not based on any historical utterance (cf. *America* 9:10, 12:7, 13:4, 14:2). Thomas Paine, English author of *Common Sense* and *Crisis* (1776), inspired American resistance; his *Rights of Man* (1791–92) justified the French Revolution and led to his conviction for treason against Britain in December 1792. According to legend, Blake helped him escape to France, where in fact he was seated as a "citizen of the world" in the National Convention; he was jailed soon afterwards by Robespierre and narrowly escaped the guillotine. *The Age of Reason* (1794–96), his analysis of the bases for Christian superstition, was considered blasphemous, but as Blake asked in his marginalia to Watson's *Apology for the Bible . . . Against . . . Paine,* "Is it a greater miracle to feed five thousand men with five loaves than to overthrow all the armies of Europe with a small pamphlet?" Joseph Warren (1741–75), Boston revolutionary, was killed at Bunker Hill; General Horatio Gates (1728?–1806) received Burgoyne's surrender at Saratoga (1777) but was later defeated by Cornwallis at Camden (1780) and disgraced. John Hancock of Boston (1737–93) was the first signer of the Declaration of Independence. Nathaniel Greene (1742–86) was a general in the Continental Army.

The strong voice ceas'd; for a terrible blast swept over the heaving sea.
The eastern cloud rent: on his cliffs stood Albion's wrathful Prince.
A dragon form clashing his scales at midnight, he arose
And flam'd red meteors round the land of Albion beneath.
His voice, his locks, his awful shoulders, and his glowing eyes

[PLATE 4]
Appear to the Americans upon the cloudy night.

Solemn heave the Atlantic waves between the gloomy nations,
Swelling, belching from its deeps red clouds & raging Fires.
Albion is sick. America faints! enrag'd the Zenith grew,
As human blood shooting its veins all round the orbed heaven,
Red rose the clouds from the Atlantic in vast wheels of blood,
And in the red clouds rose a Wonder o'er the Atlantic sea.
Intense! naked! a Human fire fierce glowing, as the wedge
Of iron heated in the furnace: his terrible limbs were fire,
With myriads of cloudy terrors, banners dark, & towers
Surrounded; heat but not light went thro' the murky atmosphere.[3]

The King of England looking westward trembles at the vision.

[PLATE 5]
Albion's Angel stood beside the Stone of night,[4] and saw
The terror like a comet, or more like the planet red
That once inclos'd the terrible wandering comets in its sphere.
Then, Mars, thou wast our center, & the planets three flew round
Thy crimson disk; so e'er the Sun was rent from thy red sphere.
The Spectre glowed his horrid length, staining the temple long
With beams of blood, & thus a voice came forth and shook the temple:

[PLATE 6]
"The morning comes, the night decays, the watchmen leave their stations;
The grave is burst, the spices shed, the linen wrapped up;
The bones of death, the cov'ring clay, the sinews shrunk & dry'd,
Reviving shake, inspiring move, breathing! awakening!

3. The image of Orc the Rebel appears in response to Albion's dragon Prince; he represents a resurgence of American spirit after 4:4, full of violence without enlightenment.

4. Interpreting such texts as II Corinthians 3:3, Blake rejected both the authority of the stones of the Decalogue and (as a Protestant) the interpretation of Matthew 16:18 as an authorization for the Pope—or for the English King as Defender of the (Anglican) Faith. In the later writings stones are especially associated with Druidism. Cf. *Europe* 10:26.

Spring like redeemed captives when their bonds & bars are burst.
Let the slave grinding at the mill[5] run out into the field:
Let him look up into the heavens & laugh in the bright air;
Let the inchained soul shut up in darkness and in sighing,
Whose face has never seen a smile in thirty weary years,
Rise and look out; his chains are loose, his dungeon doors are open.
And let his wife and children return from the opressor's scourge.
They look behind at every step & believe it is a dream,
Singing, 'The Sun has left his blackness, & has found a fresher morning
And the fair Moon rejoices in the clear & cloudless night;
For Empire is no more, and now the Lion & Wolf shall cease.' "[6]

[PLATE 7]
In thunders ends the voice.† Then Albion's Angel wrathful burnt
Beside the Stone of Night; and like the Eternal Lion's howl
In famine & war, reply'd, "Art thou not Orc; who serpent-form'd
Stands at the gate of Enitharmon to devour her children?
Blasphemous Demon, Antichrist, hater of Dignities;
Lover of wild rebellion, and transgresser of God's Law,
Why dost thou come to Angels' eyes in this terrific form?"[7]

5. The design at the top of this plate reinforces the resurrection imagery of lines 1–4; it is a variation of the design for *Marriage* 21 (p. 98). The liberation imagery of lines 5–10 recalls the regeneration of Samson (see Judges 16:21; Milton's *Samson Agonistes* 41), who was made to grind "at the mill with slaves." Though factories were becoming widespread in England, Blake's frequent usage of "mill" seems generally to reflect the older technology of the grain mill. Cf. also Rousseau's slogan, "Man is born free and is everywhere in chains." In this speech the vision grows into an exhortation and projection of a just society; as Erdman has said, it is a poetic paraphrase of the claims of life, liberty, and the pursuit of happiness set forth in the Declaration of Independence.

6. Cf. "Song of Liberty" verse 20 (*Marriage of Heaven and Hell* 27).

† See color plate 16. The idyllic scene is an obvious contrast to the warlike words on this plate. The youth resting on the ram is probably Orc, and the other figure is probably his consort Vala (a new character who appears in *Vala*, retitled *The Four Zoas*).

7. To Albion's Angel, Orc recalls Chronos in Hesiod's *Theogony* and the dragon in Revelation 12:4, though described as a "serpent." "Antichrist" (I John 2:18, 4:3, II John 7) is the role enacted by Albion's Angel himself; cf. the climactic appearance of Antichrist in *Jerusalem* 89. The implicit answer to the concluding question of this Angel is given in *Marriage of Heaven and Hell* 20: "All that we saw was owing to your metaphysics."

[PLATE 8]

The terror answerd: "I am Orc, wreath'd round the accursed tree:
The times are ended; shadows pass, the morning 'gins to break;
The fiery joy, that Urizen perverted to ten commands,[8]
What night he led the starry hosts thro' the wide wilderness:
That stony law I stamp to dust:[9] and scatter religion abroad
To the four winds as a torn book, & none shall gather the leaves;
But they shall rot on desart sands, & consume in bottomless deeps,
To make the desarts blossom, & the deeps shrink to their fountains,
And to renew the fiery joy, and burst the stony roof,
That pale religious letchery, seeking Virginity,
May find it in a harlot, and in coarse-clad honesty
The undefil'd, tho' ravish'd in her cradle night and morn:
For every thing that lives is holy,[1] life delights in life;
Because the soul of sweet delight can never be defil'd.[2]
Fires inwrap the earthly globe, yet man is not consumed;
Amidst the lustful fires he walks: his feet become like brass,
His knees and thighs like silver, & his breast and head like gold."[3]

8. This recollection of *Marriage of Heaven and Hell* 23, "Song of Liberty" verse 18 (*Marriage of Heaven and Hell* 26–27) and *Urizen* 4 (II, 8) introduces Urizen into the poem; this tyrant is the ultimate proponent of royalism.

9. Cf. "Song of Liberty," verse 20 (*Marriage of Heaven and Hell* 27).

1. Cf. *Visions of the Daughters of Albion* 8:10 and the Chorus of "Song of Liberty" (*Marriage of Heaven and Hell* 27).

2. Cf. *Marriage of Heaven and Hell* 9:14.

3. Cf. Daniel 2:31–35, 3:25–27, where the prophets are impervious to fire. In 8:16–17, as Bloom points out, the transformed Orc is an improvement upon Nebuchadnezzar's dream-image (Daniel 2:31–35). The rising of Orc is depicted on plate 10, but Urizen's oppressive image accompanies the verbal description of Orc on plate 8.

[PLATE 9]

Sound! sound! my loud war-trumpets & alarm my Thirteen Angels!
Loud howls the eternal Wolf! the eternal Lion lashes his tail!
America is darkned; and my punishing Demons terrified
Crouch howling before their caverns deep, like skins dry'd in the wind.
They cannot smite the wheat, nor quench the fatness of the earth.
They cannot smite with sorrows, nor subdue the plow and spade.
They cannot wall the city, nor moat round the castle of princes.
They cannot bring the stubbed oak to overgrow the hills.
For terrible men stand on the shores, & in their robes I see
Children take shelter from the lightnings. There stands Washington
And Paine and Warren with their foreheads reard toward the east.
But clouds obscure my aged sight. A vision from afar!
Sound! sound! my loud war-trumpets & alarm my thirteen Angels!
Ah vision from afar! Ah rebel form that rent the ancient
Heavens, Eternal Viper self-renew'd, rolling in clouds:
I see thee in thick clouds and darkness on America's shore.
Writhing in pangs of abhorred birth. Red flames the crest rebellious
And eyes of death; the harlot womb oft opened in vain
Heaves in enormous circles. Now the times are return'd upon thee,
Devourer of thy parent,[4] now thy unutterable torment renews.
Sound! sound! my loud war trumpets & alarm my thirteen Angels!
Ah terrible birth! a young one bursting! where is the weeping mouth?
And where the mother's milk? Instead those ever-hissing jaws
And parched lips drop with fresh gore; now roll thou in the clouds.
Thy mother lays her length outstretch'd upon the shore beneath.
Sound! sound! my loud war-trumpets & alarm my thirteen Angels!
Loud howls the eternal Wolf! the eternal Lion lashes his tail!"

[PLATE 10]

Thus wept the Angel voice & as he wept the terrible blasts
Of trumpets blew a loud alarm across the Atlantic deep.
No trumpets answer; no reply of clarions or of fifes;
Silent the Colonies remain and refuse the loud alarm.

On those vast shady hills between America & Albion's shore,
Now barr'd out by the Atlantic sea, call'd Atlantean hills[5]
Because from their bright summits you may pass to the Golden world,

4. In 7:4 Albion's Angel had seen Orc, whom he addresses by name only once, as a devourer of children; here Orc is declared to be the devourer of his own parent, his mother country.

5. The mythical land of Atlantis, first mentioned by Plato in the *Timaeus,* is the land of the Golden Age (cf. 10:7) which has now sunk beneath the Atlantic, breaking the continental link between England and America; cf. "Song of Liberty" verse 8 (*Marriage of Heaven and Hell* 25).

An ancient palace, archetype of mighty Emperies,
Rears its immortal pinnacles, built in the forest of God
By Ariston the king of beauty for his stolen bride.[6]

Here on their magic seats the thirteen Angels sat perturb'd
For clouds from the Atlantic hover o'er the solemn roof.[7]

6. Mentioned in Herodotus' *History* 2:61 ff. as a King of Sparta who took the beautiful wife of his friend; similar to Plato's account in the *Critias* of the god Poseidon, King of Atlantis, who stole a mortal bride. Ariston is also mentioned in "Africa," *Song of Los* 3:4.
7. The leading spirits of the Colonies gather for a council which leads to their rebellion. After their conversion (12:1), Blake does not call them "devils," as he would have done in the *Marriage,* probably because that terminology would seem to accept the valuation of Albion's Angel. The rebel American "angels" recall the angelic insurgents who follow Satan in *Paradise Lost* V, 710 ff.

[PLATE 11]
Fiery the Angels rose, & as they rose deep thunder roll'd
Around their shores: indignant burning with the fires of Orc;
And Boston's Angel[8] cried aloud, as they flew thro' the dark night:

He cried: "Why trembles honesty and, like a murderer,
Why seeks he refuge from the frowns of his immortal station?
Must the generous tremble & leave his joy, to the idle: to the pestilence!
That mock him? Who commanded this? what God? what Angel!
To keep the gen'rous from experience till the ungenerous
Are unrestrained performers of the energies of nature,
Till pity is become a trade, and generosity a science
That men get rich by, & the sandy desart is giv'n to the strong!
What God is he writes laws of peace, & clothes him in a tempest?
What pitying Angel lusts for tears, and fans himself with sighs?
What crawling villain preaches abstinence & wraps himself
In fat of lambs? No more I follow, no more obedience pay!"

[PLATE 12]
So cried he, rending off his robe & throwing down his scepter
In sight of Albion's Guardian. And all the thirteen Angels
Rent off their robes to the hungry wind, & threw their golden scepters
Down on the land of America. Indignant they descended
Headlong from out their heav'nly heights, descending swift as fires
Over the land; naked & flaming are their lineaments seen
In the deep gloom. By Washington & Paine & Warren they stood,
And the flame folded, roaring fierce within the pitchy night
Before the Demon red, who burnt towards America
In black smoke, thunders, and loud winds, rejoicing in its terror,
Breaking in smoky wreaths from the wild deep, & gath'ring thick
In flames as of a furnace on the land from North to South

[PLATE 13]
What time the thirteen Governors that England sent convene
In Bernard's house;[9] the flames coverd the land. They rouze, they cry,
Shaking their mental chains;[1] they rush in fury to the sea

8. Since America's Angels are mythical colonial leaders or the guiding spirits of the colonies, rather than specific historical persons, they can be thought of as royal appointees while they wear their robes, but when they strip off these symbols of royal allegiance, they become American patriots. "Boston's Angel" is associated by Erdman with the Revolutionary activist Samuel Adams.

9. Though Sir Francis Bernard (1712–79), governor of Massachusetts (1760–69), was recalled before the Revolutionary War actually began, his name remained notorious as that of an English satrap.

1. Both the bonds of slavery and the self-limitations of the enslaved; the minds of the enslavers are likewise enchained by their prejudices (cf. "London": "mind-forg'd manacles"). Their rush to the sea recalls that of the swine possessed by cast-out devils in Matthew 8:28–34.

To quench their anguish; at the feet of Washington down fall'n
They grovel on the sand and writhing lie, while all
The British soldiers thro' the thirteen states sent up a howl
Of anguish: threw their swords & muskets to the earth & ran
From their encampments and dark castles seeking where to hide
From the grim flames; and from the visions of Orc; in sight
Of Albion's Angel; who, enrag'd, his secret clouds open'd
From north to south, and burnt outstretched on wings of wrath, cov'ring
The eastern sky, spreading his awful wings across the heavens.
Beneath him roll'd his num'rous hosts, all Albion's Angels camp'd,
Darkend the Atlantic mountains, & their trumpets shook the valleys,
Arm'd with diseases of the earth to cast upon the Abyss
Their numbers forty millions, must'ring in the eastern sky.[2]

[PLATE 14]
In the flames stood & view'd the armies drawn out in the sky
Washington, Franklin, Paine & Warren, Allen, Gates & Lee;[3]
And heard the voice of Albion's Angel give the thunderous command;
His plagues obedient to his voice flew forth out of their clouds,
Falling upon America, as a storm to cut them off
As a blight cuts the tender corn when it begins to appear.
Dark is the heaven above, & cold & hard the earth beneath;
And as a plague wind fill'd with insects cuts off man & beast;
And as a sea o'erwhelms a land in the day of an earthquake;

Fury! rage! madness! in a wind swept through America,
And the red flames of Orc that folded roaring fierce around
The angry shores, and the fierce rushing of th' inhabitants together:
The citizens of New York close their books & lock their chests;
The mariners of Boston drop their anchors and unlade;
The scribe of Pensylvania casts his pen upon the earth;
The builder of Virginia throws his hammer down in fear.[4]

2. Such biological warfare was not technologically possible in the eighteenth century, though Britain had suffered from plagues since the Middle Ages. Syphillis was popularly believed to have been brought to Europe from America by the crew of Columbus, as Voltaire notes in *Candide*, ch. IV. Blake mythologically transforms British oppression into a blood-dimmed tide (14:7) about to drown America as Atlantis had been deluged before. In the mythical mode of hyperbole far more soldiers are mentioned than the entire population of the British Isles.

3. Cf. 3:4. Two additional Revolutionary commanders are mentioned only here: General Ethan Allen (1748-89) was active on the Canadian front; "Light-Horse" Harry Lee (1756–89) fought on the Southern front.

4. "Scribe" and "builder" are suggestive of Franklin and Jefferson; historically, though, neither of these despaired, at least in public. The unlading in line 14 refers to the Boston Tea Party (1773).

Then had America been lost, o'erwhelm'd by the Atlantic,
And Earth had lost another portion of the infinite,[5]
But all rush together in the night in wrath and raging fire.
The red fires rag'd! the plagues recoil'd![6] then rolld they back with fury

[PLATE 15]
On Albion's Angels; then the Pestilence began in streaks of red
Across the limbs of Albion's Guardian, the spotted plague smote Bristol's
And the Leprosy London's Spirit, sickening all their bands.[7]
The millions sent up a howl of anguish and threw off their hammerd mail,
And cast their swords & spears to earth, & stood a naked multitude.
Albion's Guardian writhed in torment on the eastern sky.
Pale, quivring toward the brain his glimmering eyes, teeth chattering,
Howling & shuddering, his legs quivering, convuls'd each muscle & sinew,
Sick'ning, lay London's Guardian, and the ancient miter'd York:[8]
Their heads on snowy hills, their ensigns sick'ning in the sky.

The plagues creep on the burning winds, driven by flames of Orc,
And by the fierce Americans rushing together in the night;
Driven o'er the Guardians of Ireland and Scotland and Wales,
They, spotted with plagues, forsook the frontiers; & their banners seard
With fires of hell, deform their ancient heavens with shame & woe.
Hid in his caves, the Bard of Albion[9] felt the enormous plagues.
And a cowl of flesh grew o'er his head & scales on his back & ribs;
And rough with black scales all his Angels fright their ancient heavens.

5. Another reference to the myth of Atlantis; cf. 10:5–6.

6. As Erdman has pointed out, England suffered from a great plague in 1348 as a consequence of aggressive wars against France. The disorders in Britain during the American War, particularly the Gordon Riots of 1780, were not caused by disease but produced comparable disruption. Damon points out that a curse warded off is supposed to return against the curser; cf. "Mock on, mock on, Voltaire, Rousseau," lines 3–4.

7. Bristol was active in American trade; in Bristol and London domestic resistance to the war was particularly intense.

8. The actual men who served as Bishop of London and Archbishop of York are not distinctly delineated here. Damon argues that the former should be understood as the Archbishop of Canterbury, whose palace is in the London borough of Lambeth, though this guardian angel need not be represented by a religious authority.

9. William Whitehead (1715–85), poet laureate (1757–85), supported the American War. This lackey who justifies wars of oppression is the negation of the ideal of the Bard as liberator, the role unfulfilled by the Bard of 2:18–21.

The doors of marriage are open,[1] and the Priests in rustling scales
Rush into reptile coverts, hiding from the fires of Orc
That play around the golden roofs in wreaths of fierce desire,
Leaving the females naked and glowing with the lusts of youth.

For the female spirits of the dead, pining in bonds of religion,
Run from their fetters, reddening, & in long drawn arches sitting;
They feel the nerves of youth renew, and desires of ancient times
Over their pale limbs as a vine when the tender grape appears.

[PLATE 16]
Over the hills, the vales, the cities, rage the red flames fierce;
The Heavens melted from north to south; and Urizen who sat
Above all heavens in thunders wrap'd, emerg'd his leprous head
From out his holy shrine, his tears in deluge piteous
Falling into the deep sublime! Flag'd with grey-brow'd snows
And thunderous visages, his jealous wings wav'd over the deep;
Weeping in dismal howling woe he dark descended, howling
Around the smitten bands, clothed in tears & trembling, shudd'ring cold.
His stored snows he poured forth, and his icy magazines
He open'd on the deep, and on the Atlantic sea white shiv'ring.
Leprous his limbs, all over white, and hoary was his visage.
Weeping in dismal howlings before the stern Americans,
Hiding the Demon red with clouds & cold mists from the earth;
Till Angels & weak men twelve years should govern o'er the strong,[2]
And then their end should come, when France reciev'd the Demon's light.

1. This vision of British women freed from the sexual constraints devised by priests had little historical basis during the American War, but the ideal of liberated womanhood was strong in 1793 as a consequence and corollary of the French Revolution. Erdman suggests, in addition, that the furor in 1781 over the legality of certain chapel marriages was the first crack in the stony code of law. In that year a bill to secularize marriages was passed by the Commons but thrown out by the Lords.

2. Probably the period from the American victory at Yorktown in 1781 to the date of this Prophecy, during the French Revolution.

Over the hills, the vales, the cities, rage the red flames fierce;
The Heavens melted from north to south; and Urizen who sat
Above all heavens in thunders wrap'd, emerg'd his leprous head
From out his holy shrine, his tears in deluge piteous
Falling into the deep sublime! flag'd with grey-brow'd snows
And thunderous visages, his jealous wings wav'd over the deep;
Weeping in dismal howling woe he dark descended howling
Around the smitten bands, clothed in tears & trembling shudd'ring cold.
His stored snows he poured forth, and his icy magazines
He open'd on the deep, and on the Atlantic sea white shiv'ring.
Leprous his limbs, all over white, and hoary was his visage.
Weeping in dismal howlings before the stern Americans
Hiding the Demon red with clouds & cold mists from the earth;
Till Angels & weak men twelve years should govern o'er the strong;
And then their end should come, when France reciev'd the Demons light.

Stiff shudderings shook the heav'nly thrones! France Spain & Italy,
In terror view'd the bands of Albion, and the ancient Guardians
Fainting upon the elements, smitten with their own plagues
They slow advance to shut the five gates of their law-built heaven
Filled with blasting fancies and with mildews of despair
With fierce disease and lust, unable to stem the fires of Orc;
But the five gates were consum'd, & their bolts and hinges melted
And the fierce flames burnt round the heavens, & round the abodes of men

FINIS

Stiff shudderings shook the heav'nly thrones! France, Spain, & Italy,
In terror view'd the bands of Albion and the ancient Guardians,
Fainting upon the elements, smitten with their own plagues.
They slow advance to shut the five gates of their law-built heaven:[3]
Filled with blasting fancies and with mildews of despair,
With fierce disease and lust, unable to stem the fires of Orc.
But the five gates were consum'd, & their bolts and hinges melted,
And the fierce flames burnt round the heavens, & round the abodes of men.[4]

FINIS

Europe: A Prophecy

As *America* can be thought of as "The Book of Orc," so can its companion prophecy be considered "The Book of Enitharmon." The mother of Orc, Enitharmon, is everything that breeds revolution but simultaneously keeps it from developing. A spirit of queenly hauteur pervades the poem. The great Female triumphs over all; European civilization is at a standstill; Orc is silent and motionless. Shifting images form and disappear in Enitharmon's dreaming mind, during the dark night of eighteen Christian centuries. The language is oblique and compressed, in Blake's later style. *Europe* is a prophecy for a revolutionary era because it demonstrates how much

3. The portals of the five senses; cf. *Marriage of Heaven and Hell* 14, *Europe* iii. In *America*, Orc opens these gates permanently though he himself is temporarily obscured.

4. For further discussion see Erdman, pp. 577–87, below; Aileen Ward, *TriQuarterly*, 23–24 (1972), 204–27; and David E. Vames, *Studies in Romanticism*, 18 (1979), 235–52.

there is to rebel against, and how sorely this langorous, effeminate society is in need of a shakeup.

The poem opens slowly, with five preliminary plates before the main text. The first page is an impressive frontispiece, one of Blake's best-known and most successful designs: God the circumscriber and measurer, Urizen, popularly called Ancient of Days (see color plate 17). Then a title page depicts a coiled and upreared serpent, evidently a force too wily to come under the compasses of the left-handed God of the frontispiece; a part of his body writhes out of the boundaries of the printed plate (color plate 18). Another page, which occurs in only two of the twelve known copies, serves as an invocation to the muse: the author's encounter with the coolly insolent Fairy who dictates the poem. This invocation is followed by a two-page Preludium continuing the adventures of the "nameless shadowy female" who was raped by Orc in the Preludium to *America.* The true opening of the prophecy is delayed until the sixth page, plate 3. Each of the prefatory passages displays repressed and wasted energy, particularly sexual energy. The Fairy, a detached observer of the human scene, notes that "cavern'd Man" fails to use his five senses, particularly the sexual touch that liberates and unites the other senses. The Shadowy Female then complains that she continually breeds fiery terrors, Orc's offspring, but this progeny is continually rigidified and enslaved by the power of Enitharmon.

Who is this mighty Enitharmon? Where does her power come from? She is in a different role from her appearance in *Urizen* as merely the by-product of man's self-creation and self-enslavement, the personification of Pity and the practitioner of female wiles, center of the Oedipal conflict. Here in *Europe* from the heights of her "crystal house" she rules her husband and their numerous sons and daughters without lifting a finger, luxuriating in their attentions, languidly supervising their sports. Although she is Orc's mother, for her his birth is not the dawn of a new era but the beginning of a night when men yield up their power to women. During her sleep, time is collapsed so that to her the birth of Christ at the beginning of European civilization is the same event as the birth of revolution 1800 years later. She calls Orc to arise, but she really keeps him bound by sending her other sons Rintrah and Palamabron to disseminate her doctrine that woman's love is sin—and therefore irresistably desirable. Her curse on sex underlies Mariolatry, the chivalric code, and all devious efforts of women to wield power surreptitiously. Enitharmon's characterization as charming tyrant bears considerable resemblance to Wollstonecraft's portrait of Marie Antoinette in her *History of the French Revolution* (1793). The only one of Enitharmon's children who is not under her thumb is Oothoon, who has given up "woman's secrecy," as explained in her story in *Visions of the Daughters of Albion.* Other daughters personify chastity, jealousy, and seductiveness, and all the children display aspects of Enitharmon's dominance that have overspread Europe.

In the poem proper, nothing real ever happens. The first third of the poem prepares for Enitharmon's dream, the middle portion recounts the current history of Blake's time as a nightmare when revolution is blocked, and the final section describes Enitharmon's awakening. This circular narrative structure, like the compasses in the frontispiece and the coils of the serpent on the title page, are reminders—as Brian Wilkie has observed in an unpublished commentary—of the negative sense of the word "revolution," a re-turning of the cycle of tyrant and oppressed. The first and third sections are linked by the repeated command "Arise" as Enitharmon calls the roll of her children to enlist their aid in enslaving humanity. Orc is the first to be called but the last to respond, taking action only at the end of the 1800-year dream. This delay probably indicates that the birth of Jesus failed to result in revolutionary change but produced repressive religious and political institutions instead. Through mythological allusions, Orc is identified with Mars and Dionysus, violence and revelry. When Enitharmon awakens, Orc responds to her call, as dawn breaks, by shooting down from her heights and into "the vineyards of red France," leaving his mother to groan in dismay. The secular messiah may have come at last, but unfortunately in the closing lines of the poem there is an implication that Los the artist, who with his sons had played upon the harp at the opening of the poem, will become a warrior if that is the only way to make the new revolution succeed.

Our text is taken from Copy I, Auckland Public Library, New Zealand, as reproduced in Erdman, *The Illuminated Blake*. Color plates are from Copy K, Fitzwilliam Museum, Cambridge.

Europe
A Prophecy*

LAMBETH Printed by Will: Blake 1794

[PLATE iii][1]

"Five windows light the cavern'd Man:[2] thro' one he breathes the
air;
Thro' one, hears music of the spheres; thro' one, the eternal vine
Flourishes, that he may recieve the grapes; thro' one can look
And see small portions of the eternal world that ever groweth;
Thro' one, himself pass out what time he please, but he will not;
For stolen joys are sweet, & bread eaten in secret pleasant."[3]

* See color plates 17 (frontispiece) and 18 (title page).

1. The reason that this plate appears in only two of the twelve known copies, one made around 1800 and the other made after 1818, is unknown; one theory is that it was mislaid, another that it was inserted only for certain readers.

2. Locke's theory that the mind contains only what is imprinted on it by sense-impression, as in the "narrow chinks of the cavern" in *Marriage of Heaven and Hell* 14.

3. Proverbs 8:17.

So sang a Fairy mocking as he sat on a streak'd Tulip,[4]
Thinking none saw him: when he ceas'd I started from the trees:
And caught him in my hat as boys knock down a butterfly.
"How know you this," said I, "small Sir? where did you learn this
 song?"[5]
Seeing himself in my possession thus he answered me:
"My master, I am yours. Command me, for I must obey."

"Then tell me, what is the material world, and is it dead?"
He laughing answer'd: "I will write a book on leaves of flowers,
If you will feed me on love-thoughts, & give me now and then
A cup of sparkling poetic fancies, so when I am tipsie,
I'll sing to you to this soft lute; and shew you all alive
The world, when every particle of dust breathes forth its joy."

I took him home in my warm bosom: as we went along
Wild flowers I gatherd; & he shew'd me each eternal flower:
He laugh'd aloud to see them whimper because they were pluck'd.[6]
They hover'd round me like a cloud of incense: when I came
Into my parlour and sat down, and took my pen to write:
My Fairy sat upon the table, and dictated EUROPE.

[PLATE 1]

Preludium

The nameless shadowy female rose from out the breast of Orc:
Her snaky hair brandishing in the winds of Enitharmon
And thus her voice arose:

"O mother Enitharmon wilt thou bring forth other sons?
To cause my name to vanish, that my place may not be found?
For I am faint with travel![7]
Like the dark cloud disburdened in the day of dismal thunder.

4. In *Rasselas*, chapter X, Dr. Johnson's character Imlac the tutor advises the ideal poet not to "number the streaks of the tulip" but to remark "general properties and large appearances"; Blake's Fairly thinks he will be unnoticed down among the minute particulars, but the Bard of this prophecy is too sharp-sighted for him.

5. Similar to the question the Eternals ask the Bard in *Milton* 13:50: "Where hadst thou this terrible Song?"

6. The Fairy seems callous, but one should remember that Oothoon's Marygold insists on being plucked and that the eternal forms of the flowers linger on like incense; an animated world would have to feel pain as well as pleasure.

7. "Travel" = travail

My roots are brandish'd in the heavens, my fruits in earth beneath
Surge, foam, and labour into life, first born & first consum'd!
Consumed and consuming!
Then why shouldst thou, accursed mother, bring me into life?

I wrap my turban of thick clouds around my lab'ring head
And fold the sheety waters as a mantle round my limbs.
Yet the red sun and moon,
And all the overflowing stars rain down prolific pains.

[PLATE 2]
Unwilling I look up to heaven! unwilling count the stars!
Sitting in fathomless abyss of my immortal shrine.
I sieze their burning power
And bring forth howling terrors, all devouring fiery kings.

Devouring & devoured, roaming on dark and desolate mountains
In forests of eternal death, shrieking in hollow trees.
Ah mother Enitharmon!
Stamp not with solid form this vig'rous progeny of fires.

I bring forth from my teeming bosom myriads of flames.
And thou dost stamp them with a signet; then they roam abroad
And leave me void as death:
Ah! I am drown'd in shady woe, and visionary joy.

And who shall bind the infinite with an eternal band?
To compass it with swaddling bands? and who shall cherish it
With milk and honey?
I see it smile & I roll inward & my voice is past.

She ceast & rolld her shady clouds
Into the secret place.

[PLATE 3]

A Prophecy

The deep of winter came:
What time the secret child
Descended thro' the orient gates of the eternal day.
War ceas'd & all the troops like shadows fled to their abodes.[8]

8. An echo of Milton's "It was the winter wild, / While the Heaven-born child . . ." in "On the Morning of Christ's Nativity." Christ's birth should have overturned the old order, as Milton said it did; but there is need now for a new savior, a political revolutionary. The new government in France had proclaimed the Year One to be 1792, the end of the Christian era, and in *The Marriage of Heaven and Hell* Blake himself had dated the beginning of the New Age as 1790. For Enitharmon, the birth of Christ and the birth of Orc are the same event, and she plans to keep her power despite the birth of any Messiah.

Then Enitharmon saw her sons & daughters rise around.
Like pearly clouds they meet together in the crystal house:
And Los, possessor of the moon, joy'd in the peaceful night:
Thus speaking while his num'rous sons shook their bright fiery wings:

"Again the night is come[9]
That strong Urthona takes his rest,
And Urizen unloos'd from chains
Glows like a meteor in the distant north
Stretch forth your hands and strike the elemental strings!
Awake the thunders of the deep,

[PLATE 4]
"The shrill winds wake!
Till all the sons of Urizen look out and envy Los:
Sieze all the spirits of life and bind
Their warbling joys to our loud strings.
Bind all the nourishing sweets of earth
To give us bliss, that we may drink the sparkling wine of Los
And let us laugh at war,
Despising toil and care,
Because the days and nights of joy in lucky hours renew.

9. Blake uses no quotation marks; it is not clear who speaks lines 3:9–4:14. Possibly Los speaks lines 3:9–4:2, then Los's sons speak 4:3–9, and Enitharmon speaks 4:10–14; it would also be possible to read the whole passage as a speech of either Los or Enitharmon.

"Arise O Orc from thy deep den,
First born of Enitharmon rise!
And we will crown thy head with garlands of the ruddy vine;[1]
For now thou art bound;
And I may see thee in the hour of bliss, my eldest born."

The horrent Demon rose, surrounded with red stars of fire,
Whirling about in furious circles round the immortal fiend.

Then Enitharmon down descended into his red light.
And thus her voice rose to her children; the distant heavens reply:

[PLATE 5]
"Now comes the night of Enitharmon's joy![2]
Who shall I call? Who shall I send?
That Woman, lovely Woman! may have dominion?
Arise O Rintrah thee I call! & Palamabron thee![3]
Go! tell the Human race that Woman's love is Sin:
That an Eternal life awaits the worm of sixty winters
In an allegorical abode where existence hath never come;
Forbid all Joy, & from her childhood shall the little female
Spread nets in every secret path.

My weary eyelids draw towards the evening, my bliss is yet but new!

[PLATE 8]
"Arise O Rintrah eldest born: second to none but Orc:
O lion Rintrah raise thy fury from thy forests black;
Bring Palamabron, horned priest, skipping upon the mountains
And silent Elynittria the silver bowed queen:
Rintrah, where hast thou hid thy bride?
Weeps she in desart shades?
Alas, my Rintrah! bring the lovely jealous Ocalythron.

1. Orc resembles Dionysus and Mars rather than the Prince of Peace, but in the major prophecy of the Second Coming, Christ tramples the grapes of wrath and is himself imagined as a Dionysus-Mars figure (Revelation 19:11–15).

2. Immediately after Orc is summoned to arise, Enitharmon undoes the effect of this summons by calling up her other children, those under her dominion, with instructions to keep mankind in slavery. Plates 6 and 7 are full-page illustrations of Famine and Plague.

3. Rintrah was the roarer and shaker in *Marriage of Heaven and Hell;* here he is a furious king, not a prophet, and his brother Palamabron is a priest. Rintrah's bride Ocalythron personifies jealousy and Rintrah's queen Elynittria personifies chastity, two of the tricks of female domination. In *Milton*, Rintrah and Palamabron are loyal, hard-working sons of Los, helpers in his prophetic work, but here their sinister qualities have led Erdman in *Blake: Prophet Against Empire* to identify them historically with Pitt, the English prime minister, and Parliament, who formed a misalliance with the French counterrevolutionary forces.

Arise my son: bring all thy brethren, O thou king of fire.
Prince of the sun, I see thee with thy innumerable race:
Thick as the summer stars:
But each ramping his golden mane shakes,
And thine eyes rejoice because of strength, O Rintrah furious king!"

[PLATE 9]
Enitharmon slept,
Eighteen hundred years: Man was a Dream!
The night of Nature and their harps unstrung:[4]
She slept in middle of her nightly song
Eighteen hundred years, a female dream!

Shadows of men in fleeting bands upon the winds
Divide the heavens of Europe,
Till Albion's Angel smitten with his own plagues fled with his bands.[5]
The cloud bears hard on Albion's shore:
Fill'd with immortal demons of futurity:
In council gather the smitten Angels of Albion.
The cloud bears hard upon the council house; down rushing
On the heads of Albion's Angels.[6]

One hour they lay buried beneath the ruins of that hall;
But as the stars rise from the salt lake they arise in pain,
In troubled mists o'erclouded by the terrors of strugling times.

[PLATE 10]
In thoughts perturb'd, they rose from the bright ruins, silent following
The fiery King, who sought his ancient temple serpent-form'd
That stretches out its shady length along the Island white.
Round him roll'd his clouds of war; silent the Angel went,
Along the infinite shores of Thames to golden Verulam.
There stand the venerable porches that high-towering rear
Their oak-surrounded pillars, form'd of massy stones, uncut
With tool; stones precious; such eternal in the heavens,
Of colours twelve, few known on earth, give light in the opake,
Plac'd in the order of the stars, when the five senses whelm'd
In deluge o'er the earth-born man; then turn'd the fluxile eyes
Into two stationary orbs, concentrating all things.

4. During Enitharmon's sleep the harps played by Los and his sons (on plates 3 and 4) are unstrung.

5. When Enitharmon falls asleep, historical and geographical references enter the prophecy: the nightmare of current history is a sweet dream to her. As Erdman points out, the content of her dream is not the French Revolution itself but the British war against the Revolution. Cf. *America* 14:20–15:1.

6. According to Erdman, a reference to the collapse of Parliament, also alluded to in a cancelled plate of *America*.

Enitharmon slept,
Eighteen hundred years: Man was a Dream!
The night of Nature and their harps unstrung:
She slept in middle of her nightly song,
Eighteen hundred years, a female dream!
Shadows of men in fleeting bands upon the winds:
Divide the heavens of Europe:
Till Albions Angel smitten with his own plagues fled with his bands
The cloud bears hard on Albions shore:
Fill'd with immortal demons of futurity:
In council gather the smitten Angels of Albion
The cloud bears hard upon the council house; down rushing
On the heads of Albions Angels.
One hour they lay buried beneath the ruins of that hall;
But as the stars rise from the salt lake they arise in pain,
In troubled mists oerclouded by the terrors of struggling times.

The ever-varying spiral ascents to the heavens of heavens
Were bended downward; and the nostrils' golden gates shut,
Turn'd outward, barr'd and petrify'd against the infinite.

Thought chang'd the infinite to a serpent; that which pitieth
To a devouring flame; and man fled from its face and hid
In forests of night; then all the eternal forests were divided
Into earths rolling in circles of space, that like an ocean rush'd
And overwhelmed all except this finite wall of flesh.
Then was the serpent temple form'd, image of infinite
Shut up in finite revolutions, and man became an Angel;
Heaven a mighty circle turning; God a tyrant crown'd.[7]

Now arriv'd the ancient Guardian at the southern porch,
That, planted thick with trees of blackest leaf, & in a vale
Obscure, inclos'd the Stone of Night;[8] oblique it stood, o'erhung
With purple flowers and berries red: image of that sweet south,
Once open to the heavens and elevated on the human neck,
Now overgrown with hair and coverd with a stony roof,
Downward 'tis sunk beneath th' attractive north, that round the feet
A raging whirlpool draws the dizzy enquirer to his grave.

[PLATE 11]

Albion's Angel rose upon the Stone of Night.
He saw Urizen on the Atlantic;
And his brazen Book
That Kings & Priests had copied on Earth
Expanded from North to South.

7. This condensed passage, 10:1–23, is in Blake's later style, a rich compound of myth and metaphor. The "temple serpent-form'd" is Blake's earliest use of his Druid symbolism. Originally Biblical patriarchs, the Druids of Blake's myth became corrupted and practiced human sacrifice and natural religion; see Peter F. Fisher, "Blake and the Druids," *JEGP* 58 (1959), 589–612. The gate to the "Druidical" serpent-temple at Avebury is Bacon's home Verulam, because scientific rationalism and nature worship often go hand in hand in the sense that neither accepts the idea of any reality beyond the material world. The mechanical order of the heavens imitated by the Druid ruins is associated with the twelve signs of the zodiac and the twelve tribes of Israel. Blake envisions a huge serpent temple spread over all of Britain, in which human victims of war and oppression are sacrificed to the God of This World. To the degree that Christians interpret the Crucifixion as a blood-sacrifice and approve of wars and executions, they practice "Druidism" in Blake's sense of the word.

Because reason and energy are separated (10:16–23), thought is tyrannical and violent—as in the contrasting images depicted on the frontispiece and title page.

8. This central Druid stone, covered with poisonous nightshade, is identified with both London Stone, from which all distances in England are measured, and the stony human skull. Cf. *America* 5:1.

[PLATE 12]
And the clouds & fires pale rolld round in the night of Enitharmon,
Round Albion's cliffs & London's walls; still Enitharmon slept!
Rolling volumes of grey mist involve Churches, Palaces, Towers:
For Urizen unclaspd his Book! feeding his soul with pity.
The youth of England hid in gloom curse the paind heavens, compell'd
Into the deadly night to see the form of Albion's Angel.
Their parents brought them forth & aged ignorance preaches canting
On a vast rock, percieved by those senses that are clos'd from thought:
Bleak, dark, abrupt, it stands & overshadows London city.
They saw his boney feet on the rock, the flesh consum'd in flames:
They saw the Serpent temple lifted above, shadowing the Island white:
They heard the voice of Albion's Angel howling in flames of Orc,
Seeking the trump of the last doom.

Above the rest the howl was heard from Westminster louder & louder:
The Guardian of the secret codes forsook his ancient mansion,
Driven out by the flames of Orc; his furr'd robes & false locks
Adhered and grew one with his flesh, and nerves & veins shot thro' them
With dismal torment sick, hanging upon the wind: he fled
Groveling along Great George Street thro' the Park gate; all the soldiers
Fled from his sight: he drag'd his torments to the wilderness.

Thus was the howl thro Europe!
For Orc rejoic'd to hear the howling shadows.
But Palamabron shot his lightnings trenching down his wide back
And Rintrah hung with all his legions in the nether deep.

Enitharmon laugh'd in her sleep to see (O woman's triumph)
Every house a den, every man bound; the shadows are filld
With spectres, and the windows wove over with curses of iron:
Over the doors Thou shalt not; & over the chimneys Fear is written.
With bands of iron round their necks fasten'd into the walls,
The citizens; in leaden gyves the inhabitants of suburbs
Walk heavy; soft and bent are the bones of villagers.

Between the clouds of Urizen the flames of Orc roll heavy
Around the limbs of Albion's Guardian, his flesh consuming.
Howlings & hissings, shrieks & groans, & voices of despair
Arise around him in the cloudy
Heavens of Albion. Furious

[PLATE 13]
The red limb'd Angel siez'd, in horror and torment,
The Trump of the last doom; but he could not blow the iron tube!
Thrice he assay'd presumptuous to awake the dead to Judgment.

A mighty Spirit leap'd from the land of Albion,
Nam'd Newton; he siez'd the Trump, & blow'd the enormous blast![9]
Yellow as leaves of Autumn the myriads of Angelic hosts
Fell thro' the wintry skies seeking their graves;
Rattling their hollow bones in howling and lamentation.

Then Enitharmon woke, nor knew that she had slept.[1]
And eighteen hundred years were fled
As if they had not been.
She calld her sons & daughters
To the sports of night,
Within her crystal house;
And thus her song proceeds:

"Arise Ethinthus! tho' the earth-worm call;
Let him call in vain;
Till the night of holy shadows
And human solitude is past!

[PLATE 14]
"Ethinthus, queen of waters, how thou shinest in the sky:
My daughter, how do I rejoice! for thy children flock around
Like the gay fishes on the wave, when the cold moon drinks the dew.
Ethinthus! thou art sweet as comforts to my fainting soul:
For now thy waters warble round the feet of Enitharmon.

"Manathu-Vorcyon! I behold thee flaming in my halls,
Light of thy mother's soul! I see thy lovely eagles round;
Thy golden wings are my delight, & thy flames of soft delusion.

"Where is my lureing bird of Eden? Leutha, silent love!
Leutha, the many colourd bow delights upon thy wings:
Soft soul of flowers, Leutha!

9. Although the spirit of England is unable to bring about a Last Judgment, Newton succeeds because his science is the ultimate revelation of the purely material world. Further, despite Newton's commentary on the Biblical Revelation the angels are overcome by his law of gravitation (suggests Brian Wilkie in an unpublished commentary) and fall to earth. Instead of a resurrection of the dead, Newton initiates a killing off of the spiritual world.

1. On awakening, Enitharmon blandly continues holding court and calling upon her children to provide seductive entertainment for Orc; recognizing no difference between Orc and the Christ child, she believes she can sweeten and emasculate this new appearance of revolutionary change as she had begun to do eighteen hundred years ago.

Sweet smiling pestilence! I see thy blushing light:
Thy daughters many changing
Revolve like sweet perfumes ascending, O Leutha silken queen!

"Where is the youthful Antamon, prince of the pearly dew?
O Antamon, why wilt thou leave thy mother Enitharmon?
Alone I see thee, crystal form,
Floting upon the bosomd air:
With lineaments of gratified desire.
My Antamon, the seven churches of Leutha seek thy love.

"I hear the soft Oothoon in Enitharmon's tents:
Why wilt thou give up woman's secrecy, my melancholy child?
Between two moments bliss is ripe:
O Theotormon robb'd of joy, I see thy salt tears flow
Down the steps of my crystal house.

"Sotha & Thiralatha, secret dwellers of dreamful caves,
Arise and please the horrent fiend with your melodious songs.
Still all your thunders golden hoofd, & bind your horses black.
Orc! smile upon my children!
Smile, son of my afflictions.
Arise, O Orc, and give our mountains joy of thy red light."

She ceas'd, for All were forth at sport beneath the solemn moon,
Waking the stars of Urizen with their immortal songs,
That nature felt thro' all her pores the enormous revelry,
Till morning ope'd the eastern gate.
Then every one fled to his station, & Enitharmon wept.

But terrible Orc, when he beheld the morning in the east,

[PLATE 15]
Shot from the heights of Enitharmon;
And in the vineyards of red France appear'd the light of his fury.[2]

The sun glow'd fiery red!
The furious terrors flew around!
On golden chariots raging, with red wheels dropping with blood,
The Lions lash their wrathful tails!
The Tigers couch upon the prey & suck the ruddy tide:
And Enitharmon groans & cries in anguish and dismay.
Then Los arose; his head he reard, in snaky thunders clad:
And, with a cry that shook all nature to the utmost pole,
Call'd all his sons to the strife of blood.

FINIS

2. Enitharmon's power is broken and Orc appears in France in Dionysian and Martian fury. This is no optimistic conclusion, however, for "the strife of blood" is only beginning. See also Michael J. Tolley's essay in Erdman and Grant, eds., *Blake's Visionary Forms Dramatic* (1970).

The Song of Los

The cycle of poems on the continents which is set up in the prophecies *America* and *Europe* is completed in the songs "Africa" and "Asia." Instead of being aligned chronologically, the poems mesh through repeated phrases and images as described in the headnote to *America*. In the introductory stanza of *The Song of Los*, dated 1795, a presumably human singer presents to mortal listeners a song which Los sang to his fellow Eternals. Los is a creative force—a poet, a metal worker, and a prophet. The human voice conveying Los's song resembles the voice that invokes the Eternals to dictate their message at the beginning of *Urizen*. In *Europe* the songs of Los seem to have no influence on the power struggles of Urizen, Orc, and Enitharmon, and at the end of that prophecy Los prepares to become a warrior; in *The Song of Los*, however, the "Eternal Prophet" participates in world events as an artist, by singing of a relationship between the revolution and the two continents which have not yet been directly affected by the outbreak of Orc.

In the song proper the section on "Africa" recounts the progressive degeneration of the human race as a result of false doctrines received by religious and intellectual leaders from various members of the Blakean pantheon. Despite the title, Africa is present only in a reference to the traditional interpretation of the curse of perpetual servitude pronounced by Noah on his son Ham ("black grew the sunny African") and in the imagery of sterility describing the atheistic age that arises when, after the empiricism of Newton and Locke, there remain only "deceased Gods" of Asia in the Lebanese mountains and "Fallen Angels" in the "deserts of Africa." But since the last line of "Africa" is identical with the first line of *America*, the song implies that the tyranny of these corrupt and binding institutions has made inevitable a world-wide revolution in which the people of Africa will also be liberated. Africa is the appropriate setting for the general account of human degradation because of its long-standing association with slavery: not only was it the home of the contemporary traffic in black people but also, as Egypt, it was the Biblical place of bondage for the Jews.

Response to revolution rather than its causes is the subject of the "Asia" section of Los's song. The disturbance in Europe causes the Kings of Asia to recommend economic and political techniques for staving off social change. With its outpost in Ceylon and its influence over much of India, England itself in 1795 might be considered one of the reactionary rulers of Asia. Not until Byron took up the cause of Greek independence from Turkey in 1821 did a prominent Englishman identify himself with revolutionary forces in any part of the East.

The outcry of the Kings of Asia moves Urizen to return to Jerusalem, religious capital of the world, and as he returns his metal books of law begin to melt. Even so, humanity—in the form of Adam and Noah, who were the first to fall under Urizen's law in "Africa"—is merely a heap of bleached bones. But when Orc arises over Europe like the pillar of fire that guided the Israelites in the Exodus, a universal resurrection occurs in which imagery from Ezekiel's vision of the Valley of Dry Bones blends with a transfiguration of Mother Earth. The "nameless Female," the personification of Earth in the preludia to *America* and *Europe*, has been first a barren virgin and then a teeming but dissatisfied producer of Orc's abortive offspring—presumably failed revolutions. In the final stanza of "Asia," however, the insatiable Grave experiences a regenerative orgasm and becomes a fruitful womb. This stanza suggests that Orc will eventually fulfill the world's longings, and as the song of Los ends, "Urizen wept."

Our text is taken from Copy B, reproduced as a Blake Trust facsimile.

The Song of Los

LAMBETH Printed by W Blake 1795

[PLATE 3]

Africa

I will sing you a song of Los, the Eternal Prophet:
He sung it to four harps at the tables of Eternity.
In heart-formed Africa.
Urizen faded! Ariston[1] *shudderd!*
And thus the Song began:

ADAM stood in the garden of Eden:
And Noah on the mountains of Ararat;
They saw Urizen give his Laws to the Nations
By the hands of the children of Los.

Adam shuddered! Noah faded![2] black grew the sunny African

1. Greek *aristos* = "best"; cf. *America* 10:10. In this introduction to the main song two of Blake's invented characters have responded negatively to Los's song; in the song proper, figures from Biblical, classical, Hindu, Islamic, Norse, and English-French traditions show less and less reaction throughout history, as they receive progressively more erroneous doctrines from Blake's mythical beings.

2. Noah's cursed son Ham, condemned to servitude, is traditionally the ancestor of black people, according to legends of white people.

When Rintrah gave Abstract Philosophy to Brama[3] in the East:
(Night spoke to the Cloud!
"Lo these Human form'd spirits in smiling hipocrisy War
Against one another: so let them War on: slaves to the eternal Elements.")
Noah shrunk beneath the waters;
Abram fled in fires from Chaldea;
Moses beheld upon Mount Sinai forms of dark delusion:

To Trismegistus,[4] Palamabron gave an abstract Law:
To Pythagoras, Socrates, & Plato.

Times rolled on o'er all the sons of Har, time after time.
Orc on Mount Atlas howld, chain'd down with the Chain of Jealousy.
Then Oothoon hoverd over Judah & Jerusalem
And Jesus heard her voice (a man of sorrows); he recievd
A Gospel from wretched Theotormon.[5]

The human race began to wither, for the healthy built
Secluded places, fearing the joys of Love,
And the disease'd only propagated:
So Antamon call'd up Leutha from her valleys of delight:
And to Mahomet a loose Bible[6] gave.
But in the North, to Odin, Sotha gave a Code of War
Because of Diralada, thinking to reclaim his joy.

3. No causal connection between the Indian god Brahma's appearance and the blackness of the African need be inferred; Blake is asserting that Indian mythology is contemporaneous with the Biblical events immediately after the Flood. Blake knew Hindu myth through Charles Wilkins's translation of the *Bhagvat-Geeta* (1785), the subject of a painting—now lost—in Blake's exhibition of 1809 (*Descriptive Catalogue,* p. 406).

4. Hermes Trismegistus ("thrice greatest Hermes"), a legendary Egyptian philosopher-priest, was identified by Cicero with Thoth, god of speech and writing. He was supposed to be the author of secret sealed "Hermetic" books of ancient wisdom (actually written in the third century A.D.). His "Smaragdine Table," the basic alchemical text, is among the Spectre's works which Los smashes (*Jerusalem* 91:34). Pythagoras, born 582 B.C., was a philosopher, mathematician, and musician who was supposed to have learned secrets in Egypt and the East. His cult believed he had magical powers; he was also famous for his geometrical proofs and his mathematical theory of musical harmony. What the classical philosophers Sophocles and Plato have in common with mystics like Trismegistus and Pythagorus is that intentionally or not they were founders of quasi-religions; Greek philosophy has been "law" to Western civilization.

5. Apparently Jesus is sympathetic toward Oothoon, the victim of rape who is branded an adulteress in *Visions of the Daughters of Albion,* but his church takes the part of her "wronged," unforgiving spouse, and his monastic followers practice sexual abstinence.

6. One etymology for "Koran" is "a collection of loose sheets" (Stevenson).

[PLATE 4]

These were the Churches: Hospitals: Castles: Palaces:
Like nets & gins & traps to catch the joys of Eternity
And all the rest a desart;
Till like a dream Eternity was obliterated & erased.

Since that dread day when Har and Heva[7] fled,
Because their brethren & sisters liv'd in War & Lust;
And as they fled they shrunk
Into two narrow doleful forms:
Creeping in reptile flesh upon
The bosom of the ground:
And all the vast of Nature shrunk
Before their shrunken eyes.

Thus the terrible race of Los & Enitharmon gave
Laws & Religions to the sons of Har, binding them more
And more to Earth: closing and restraining:
Till a Philosophy of Five Senses was complete
Urizen wept & gave it into the hands of Newton & Locke.

Clouds roll heavy upon the Alps round Rousseau & Voltaire:[8]
And on the mountains of Lebanon round the deceased Gods
Of Asia; & on the desarts of Africa round the Fallen Angels.
The Guardian Prince of Albion burns in his nightly tent.

[PLATE 6]

Asia

THE KINGS of Asia heard
The howl rise up from Europe![9]
And each ran out from his Web,
From his ancient woven Den;
For the darkness of Asia was startled
At the thrick-flaming, thought-creating fires of Orc.

And the Kings of Asia stood
And cried in bitterness of soul:

7. Heva means "Eve"; these human ancestors, like Adam and Eve, are failures as parents in the manuscript poem *Tiriel* (not included in this edition).

8. With modern rationalists, man's spiritual degeneration has reached its limit, and even Urizen weeps, as in 7:66. The final line of "Africa" is identical to *America* 3:1.

9. Cf. *Europe* 11:21. Civilization was thought to have spread from east to west; revolution, having begun in America, is spreading from west to east.

Shall not the King call for Famine from the heath?[1]
Nor the Priest, for Pestilence from the fen?
To restrain! to dismay! to thin!
The inhabitants of mountain and plain;
In the day of full-feeding prosperity;
And the night of delicious songs.

"Shall not the Councellor throw his curb
Of Poverty on the laborious?
To fix the price of labour;
To invent allegoric riches:[2]

"And the privy admonishers of men
Call for fires in the City
For heaps of smoking ruins,
In the night of prosperity & wantonness[3]

"To turn man from his path,
To restrain the child from the womb,

[PLATE 7]

"To cut off the bread from the city,
That the remnant may learn to obey,

"That the pride of the heart may fail;
That the lust of the eyes, may be quench'd:[4]
That the delicate ear in its infancy
May be dull'd; and the nostrils clos'd up;

1. Although the Sultan of Mysore planted liberty trees and called himself "Citizen" (Erdman, *Blake: Prophet Against Empire,* 1977), there was little sign that the revolution would reach Asia. The cry of the Asian kings satirizes British economic policies as well as the contrast between the luxuries of the rulers and the desperate poverty of the workers. According to E. P. Thompson, in *The Making of the English Working Class* (1963), class antagonism inflamed by the French Revolution made it "a matter of public-spirited policy for the gentleman to remove cottagers from the commons, reduce his labourers to dependence, pare away at supplementary earnings, drive out the small-holder." In 1795 country people in fear of starvation blocked grain shipments, while city people blamed millers and middlemen for adulterating flour and holding it back to inflate prices, creating "an Artificall Famine in a Land of plenty."

2. Any form of invisible money—credit, stocks, interest—which is negotiable by the rich but unavailable to the poor; also the promise of riches in heaven that consoles the poor.

3. The Privy Council of London was occupied with the grain crisis from May to December, 1795. On "fires in the City," cf. *Milton* 5:40. Mobs of "Church and King" arsonists who attacked Jacobins were ignored, encouraged, or even hired by authorities in the early 1790s; the house of Joseph Priestley was burned in Birmingham in 1791.

4. An ironic use of I John 2:16; the senses are being narrowed as humanity accepts a religion of self-denial for the sake of the life hereafter.

To teach mortal worms the path
That leads from the gates of the Grave."

Urizen heard them cry!
And his shudd'ring waving wings
Went enormous above the red flames,
Drawing clouds of despair thro' the heavens
Of Europe as he went:
And his Books of brass, iron & gold
Melted over the land as he flew,
Heavy-waving, howling, weeping.

And he stood over Judea:
And stay'd in his ancient place:
And stretch'd his clouds over Jerusalem;

For Adam, a mouldering skeleton
Lay bleach'd on the garden of Eden;
And Noah as white as snow
On the mountains of Ararat.

Then the thunders of Urizen bellow'd aloud
From his woven darkness above.

Orc, raging in European darkness,
Arose like a pillar of fire above the Alps,
Like a serpent of fiery flame!

The sullen Earth
Shrunk!

Forth from the dead dust rattling bones to bones
Join: shaking, convuls'd, the shivring clay breathes[5]
And all flesh naked stands: Fathers and Friends;
Mothers & Infants; Kings & Warriors:

The Grave shrieks with delight, & shakes
Her hollow womb, & clasps the solid stem:
Her bosom swells with wild desire:
And milk & blood & glandous wine
In rivers rush & shout & dance,
On mountain, dale and plain.

The SONG of LOS is Ended.
Urizen Wept.

5. Cf. Ezekiel 37.

The Book of Urizen

The "Bible of Hell," which was announced on the last page of *The Marriage of Heaven and Hell,* is Blake's counter-myth to the myths of the Bible and classical antiquity. *The Book of Urizen, The Book of Ahania,* and *The Book of Los* were set up by Blake in double columns, with chapter and verse headings, to imitate the page design of the orthodox Bible. The original title for the first volume of Blake's "diabolical" Bible brings out its resemblance to the opening book of the "angelic" Bible, Genesis, which is known as "The First Book of Moses" because Moses was supposed to have written the first five books. Like Genesis, *Urizen* sets forth stories of origins, but most of the action in Blake's myth takes place on a superhuman level, before the creation of the physical universe. According to Blake's principle that "All Religions Are One," his counter-myth is derived not only from the Bible but also from Hesiod's *Theogony* (which he later helped to illustrate) and Ovid's *Metamorphoses;* other probable sources include stories from Norse mythology and speculative philosophers and occultists such as Jakob Boehme. Though these origins are sometimes recognizable by the learned reader, Blake's version of the creation story carries an authority of its own and challenges the authority even of the venerable Moses.

The Book of Urizen is *about* Urizen but not *by* him; the narrator is a visionary who speaks in the Preludium under the direction and inspiration of "Eternals." Urizen himself appears on the title page as a scribe blindly copying two accounts from the copybook of Nature on which he is seated (color plate 19). Behind him loom the dual tombstone-like tables of the Mosaic Law and above them is a bent tree whose branches re-enroot. The name Urizen probably derives from a Greek word meaning "limit," the root of "horizon." Since Urizen personifies the error of reducing all reality to what can be manipulated by cold, calculating rationality, his name has also been taken as Blake's pun on "Your Reason." Although the etymology and pronunciation of Blakean names must remain speculative, an accent on the first syllable of "Urizen" best suits Blake's metrical patterns. Both "Urizen" and "Urthona" (Los's eternal name) are probably meant to recall "Uranus," the primeval father of the Titans in Greek mythology, but the two are antagonists in the fallen world. Urizen is the "Eternal Priest" and Los is the "Eternal Prophet"; their opposition develops from that between priests and poets in *The Marriage of Heaven and Hell,* plate 11.

As usual in the "Lambeth books," the works issued during the time the Blakes lived on the south side of the Thames, 1794–1800, Blake identifies himself only as the printer (*The Marriage* is anonymous, and the noncontroversial *Thel* and *Songs* carry Blake's name as both author and printer). This reticence about responsibility for the heterodox stories contained in *The Book of Urizen* is consistent with the partially satirical purposes of the work, though both story and pictures are primarily awesome or "sublime," rather than satirical, in effect. *Urizen* contains a murky account of origins, in which the fall occurs at the same moment as the creation. This account competes with existing creation stories; its premise is that the world has gone wrong from the beginning and has remained so, down to its present condition of psychological, religious, and political disorganization.

The opening of the story of *Urizen* helps to liberate the reader from too absolute a sense of beginnings: to try to imagine a time before anything existed seemed impossible to Blake. The idea that a perfect being made a universe open to imperfection was unacceptable. In Blake's story there is no Prime Mover; the created world is not "something" made out of "nothing" but a finite and erroneous perception of the infinite fullness of being. The Fall occurs as the infinite divine mind chooses to limit itself. In chapter II Blake hastens into an account of Urizen's abstracting himself from the society of Eternals in order to secure a separate, unchanging identity. Urizen's primal separation of Self from Others, Mind from Matter, Finite from Infinite, and Subjective from Objective, precipitates a series of further separations: joy from pain, moral from immoral, time from eternity, human from animal, vegetable, and mineral. Also, matter is subdivided into the four elements. Urizen does not really create anything; all he "makes" is an inner void in which he separates himself from the full life of the myriads in Eternity, and thus in an act of anti-creation he generates the error of perceiving life as finite and corrupt, limited to the plane of physical existence.

A new character, Los, appears in chapter III; he is identified as the "Eternal Prophet" in chapter V, and in IV and V he is an artisan who—like Vulcan—works with a hammer, tongs, and bellows. Los the prophet (or imagination) is in pain because Urizen, the "primeval Priest" (or "eternal mind") has been "rent from his side" (III). After watching in vain for Eternity to do something about this separation, Los himself takes action, but his efforts to order Urizen's chaos result only in further separations and contractions: in chapter IV time is subdivided into hours, days, and years, and the human body is subdivided into the five senses and the separate organic functions. Los first reacts with horror and then with "Pity" at the product of his handiwork, becoming further self-divided. The personification of Los's Pity is his feminine aspect, Enitharmon, a projection of emotion onto the feminine half of humanity. This sexual division in chapter VI results in the still further separation between the generations in chapter VII as the child Orc arouses jealousy in his father. After this child is chained down by his parents, Urizen once more becomes active, exuding a web called the Net of Religion, under which his earthly children shrink and grow hard and opaque. Urizen's fiery son Fuzon calls together those who have escaped Urizen's net; they call the earth "Egypt" and, like the children of Israel, they leave it. The departure from Egypt is the subject of the Second Book of Moses in the Bible; Blake's version of Exodus appears in the sequel to *Urizen, The Book of Ahania.*

Urizen in its fullest version contains twenty-eight pages, ten of which are full-page designs without text. Of particular interest to scholars are the variations in Blake's arrangement of these pages, as well as his alterations of the text in the seven known copies of the work. Since Blake created a somewhat different work for each purchaser, no single arrangement of the plates can present the work with all the implications that Blake intended at one time or another. Moreover, some of this material was further recast for his later prophecy, *The Four Zoas.* Yet the reader who carefully studies any single copy will find that each is coherent in its own way. The first six copies were probably made between 1794 and 1800; the seventh was printed on paper watermarked 1815. A facsimile of this splendid seventh copy, G, was issued by the Blake Trust in 1958; we have used Copy G as our copy text, and our color plates are also from this copy. In the case of plate 4 we have followed Copy B, as in *The Illuminated Blake*. The standard plate-numbering system for *Urizen*, however, is based on Copy D, and this arrangement is followed in our text.

The Book of Urizen*

LAMBETH. Printed by Will Blake 1794

[PLATE 2]

Preludium to the Book of Urizen[1]

Of the primeval Priest's assum'd power,
When Eternals spurn'd back his religion:
And gave him a place in the north,
Obscure, shadowy, void, solitary.

Eternals, I hear your call gladly;
Dictate swift winged words, & fear not
To unfold your dark visions of torment.

[PLATE 3]

Chap: I

1. Lo, a shadow of horror is risen
In Eternity! Unknown, unprolific?
Self-closd, all-repelling: what Demon
Hath form'd this abominable void
This soul-shudd'ring vacuum?—Some said
"It is Urizen," But unknown, abstracted,
Brooding secret, the dark power hid.

* See color plate 19. "Book" is intensified in word and picture on this page, which serves both as title page and frontispiece: the old man sits on a copy book painting, engraving, or writing in the two volumes at either side, and two stone tablets behind him receive his ten commandments. The books and laws of Urizen are particularly mentioned in chapter II:6–8. The overarching, leafless tree, Urizen's Tree of Mystery, does not appear in words until the sequel, *Ahania* II:3, III:2ff. In the design there are evidences of Blake's satiric purpose: the text being copied is unintelligible, and the scribe is writing with both hands, his foot pointing to the text. For further discussion, see W. J. T. Mitchell, *Eighteenth-Century Studies* 3 (1969), 83–107. The original title of this poem was *The First Book of Urizen*.

1. The text of the Preludium, in epic formulation, summarizes the theme of the work and then invokes the "Eternals" to dictate stories "of torment." This mood is somewhat alleviated by the design (not shown) of a flying woman guiding a child, which Blake once printed separately with the caption, "Teach these souls to fly."

2. Times on times he divided, & measur'd[2]
Space by space in his ninefold darkness,
Unseen, unknown: changes appeard
In his desolate mountains rifted furious
By the black winds of perturbation,

3. For he strove in battles dire
In unseen conflictions with shapes
Bred from his forsaken wilderness,
Of beast, bird, fish, serpent & element,
Combustion, blast, vapour and cloud.

4. Dark revolving in silent activity:
Unseen in tormenting passions;
An activity unknown and horrible;
A self-contemplating shadow,
In enormous labours occupied.

5. But Eternals beheld his vast forests.
Age on ages he lay, clos'd, unknown,
Brooding shut up in the deep; all avoid
The petrific abominable chaos.

6. His cold horrors[3] silent, dark Urizen
Prepar'd: his ten thousands of thunders
Rang'd in gloom'd army stretch out across
The dread world, & the rolling of wheels,
As of swelling seas, sound in his clouds
In his hills of stor'd snows, in his mountains
Of hail & ice: voices of terror,
Are heard, like thunders of autumn,
When the cloud blazes over the harvests.

Chap: II

1. Earth was not; nor globes of attraction[4]
The will of the Immortal expanded
Or contracted his all flexible senses.
Death was not, but eternal life sprung.

2. This chapter might be called "Urizen divides Eternity and Infinity." Cf. a Proverb of Hell: "Bring out number, weight, and measure in a year of dearth."

3. Urizen, from his introduction in *Visions of the Daughters of Albion* 5:3, had been "cold" (*Visions* 5:19). His prototype is the uncreative spirit of "Winter" in *Poetical Sketches.*

4. The celestial mechanics of Newtonian space will obtain after the fall. Chapter II might be entitled "Urizen's Promulgation of His Laws," moral as well as physical laws. The epithet "Immortal" is repeated in chapters IV[a], IV[b], and V to emphasize states from which Urizen is falling. Immortals are characterized by their "flexible senses."

2. The sound of a trumpet the heavens
Awoke & vast clouds of blood roll'd
Round the dim rocks of Urizen, so nam'd
That solitary one in Immensity.

3. Shrill the trumpet: & myriads of Eternity
[PLATE 4] Muster around the bleak desarts:[5]
Now fill'd with clouds, darkness & waters
That roll'd perplex'd labring, & utter'd
Words articulate, bursting in thunders
That roll'd on the tops of his mountains.

4. "From the depths of dark solitude. From
The eternal abode in my holiness,
Hidden, set apart in my stern counsels
Reserv'd for the days of futurity,
I have sought for a joy without pain,
For a solid without fluctuation.
Why will you die O Eternals?
Why live in unquenchable burnings?

5. "First I fought with the fire;[6] consum'd
Inwards, into a deep world within:
A void immense, wild, dark & deep,
Where nothing was; Nature's wide womb
And self balanc'd, stretch'd o'er the void,
I alone, even I! the winds merciless
Bound; but condensing, in torrents
They fall & fall. Strong, I repell'd
The vast waves, & arose on the waters
A wide world of solid obstruction.

6. "Here alone I in books formd of metals
Have written the secrets of wisdom
The secrets of dark contemplation
By fightings and conflicts dire,
With terrible monsters Sin-bred:[7]
Which the bosoms of all inhabit:
Seven deadly Sins of the soul.

5. This page was omitted from four of the seven copies of *Urizen*. Since Urizen here combines characteristics of Milton's Satan and the Biblical Moses and Jehovah (Exodus 19:9), the page would have seemed offensive to many readers. But without this page the motives for the expulsion of Urizen are unclear.

6. Urizen's contentions turn inward the fire of vitality. His "deep world within" is a disorderly "void"; this word, mentioned eleven other times, is equivalent to "chaos" (I,5), the nether region between hell and the created universe through which Satan passes in *Paradise Lost*. When he has subdued three of the elements the massive earth arises, the solid objective world for which he has striven.

7. Urizen creates universal moral law out of his own psychological conflicts.

7. "Lo! I unfold my darkness: and on
This rock, place with strong hand the Book
Of eternal brass,[8] written in my solitude.

8. "Laws of peace, of love, of unity:
Of pity, compassion, forgiveness.
Let each chuse one habitation:
His ancient infinite mansion:
One command, one joy, one desire,
One curse, one weight, one measure
One King, one God, one Law."[9]

Chap: III

1. The voice ended. They saw his pale visage
Emerge from the darkness; his hand
On the rock of eternity unclasping
The Book of brass. Rage siez'd the strong.

2. Rage, fury, intense indignation
In cataracts of fire, blood, & gall,
In whirlwinds of sulphurous smoke:
And enormous forms of energy;
All the seven deadly sins of the soul
[PLATE 5] In living creations appear'd,[1]
In the flames of eternal fury.

3. Sund'ring, dark'ning, thund'ring!
Rent away with a terrible crash,
Eternity roll'd wide apart,
Wide asunder rolling
Mountainous all around
Departing: departing: departing:
Leaving ruinous fragments of life,
Hanging, frowning cliffs, & all between
An ocean of voidness unfathomable.

4. The roaring fires ran o'er the heav'ns
In whirlwinds & cataracts of blood
And o'er dark desarts of Urizen

8. Cf. *Europe* 11:2 and *Ahania* III, 4. This metal book is the counterpart to the stone tablets of the Law.

9. Cf. *Marriage of Heaven and Hell* 24: "One Law for the Lion & Ox is Oppression"; also *Visions of the Daughters of Albion* 4:22.

1. Law creates the sin it seeks to forbid, and Eternity is split apart from Urizen's world. Chapter III might be called "Urizen Cast out of Eternity."

Fires pour thro' the void on all sides
On Urizen's self-begotten armies.[2]

5. But no light from the fires. All was darkness
In the flames of Eternal fury.

6. In fierce anguish & quenchless flames
To the desarts and rocks he ran raging
To hide, but he could not: combining
He dug mountains & hills in vast strength,
He piled them in incessant labour,
In howlings & pangs & fierce madness
Long periods in burning fires labouring
Till hoary, and age-broke, and aged,
In despair and the shadows of death.

7. And a roof, vast petrific around,
On all sides he fram'd: like a womb;[3]
Where thousands of rivers in veins
Of blood pour down the mountains to cool
The eternal fires beating without
From Eternals; & like a black globe
View'd by sons of Eternity, standing
On the shore of the infinite ocean,
Like a human heart strugling & beating
The vast world of Urizen appear'd.

8. And Los round the dark globe of Urizen
Kept watch for Eternals to confine
The obscure separation alone;
For Eternity stood wide apart,
[PLATE 6] As the stars are apart from the earth.

9. Los wept howling around the dark Demon:
And cursing his lot; for in anguish,
Urizen was rent from his side;
And a fathomless void for his feet;
And intense fires for his dwelling.

10. But Urizen laid in a stony sleep
Unorganiz'd, rent from Eternity.

11. The Eternals said: "What is this? Death.
Urizen is a clod of clay."

2. In Eternity the Immortals, such as Urizen was, are both one and many. The pronouns in verse 6 were originally "they" rather than "he." In the fall Urizen becomes a multitude, and his fires of delight become the fires of torment, which give off no light. Line 15 was omitted in Copy A.

3. Urizen's tomb could become a place of rebirth.

[PLATE 7]

12. Los howld in a dismal stupor,
Groaning! gnashing! groaning!
Till the wrenching apart was healed.

13. But the wrenching of Urizen heal'd not
Cold, featureless, flesh or clay,
Rifted with direful changes,
He lay in a dreamless night

14. Till Los rouz'd his fires, affrighted
At the formless unmeasurable death.[4]

[PLATE 8]

Chap: IV [a]

1: Los, smitten with astonishment,
Frightend at the hurling bones

2: And at the surging sulphureous
Perturbed Immortal, mad raging

3: In whirlwinds & pitch & nitre
Round the furious limbs of Los;

4: And Los formed nets & gins
And threw the nets round about

5: He watch'd in shuddring fear
The dark changes & bound every change
With rivets of iron & brass;

6. And these were the changes of Urizen:

[PLATE 10]

Chap: IV [b]

1. Ages on ages roll'd over him!
In stony sleep ages roll'd over him!
Like a dark waste stretching chang'able
By earthquakes riv'n, belching sullen fires.
On ages roll'd ages in ghastly
Sick torment; around him, in whirlwinds
Of darkness, the eternal Prophet howl'd,

4. The motives of Los are admirable but his tactics are ineffectual; all he can do is to deepen Urizen's separation. In later poems, though, the human body—in head, heart, and loins—has gates to Paradise which can be opened; and time has moments which open to Eternity. Chapter IV could be called "The Attempts of Los to Control Urizen."

Beating still on his rivets of iron
Pouring sodor of iron; dividing
The horrible night into watches.

2. And Urizen (so his eternal name)
His prolific delight obscurd more & more
In dark secresy, hiding in surgeing
Sulphureous fluid his phantasies.
The Eternal Prophet heavd the dark bellows,
And turn'd restless the tongs; and the hammer
Incessant beat; forging chains new & new,
Numb'ring with links hours, days & years.

3. The eternal mind, bounded, began to roll
Eddies of wrath ceaseless round & round,
And the sulphureous foam surgeing thick
Settled, a lake, bright, & shining clear:
White as the snow on the mountains cold.

4. Forgetfulness, dumbness, necessity!
In chains of the mind locked up,
Like fetters of ice shrinking together,
Disorganiz'd, rent from Eternity.[5]
Los beat on his fetters of iron;
And heated his furnaces & pour'd
Iron sodor and sodor of brass.

5. Restless turnd the immortal, inchain'd
Heaving dolorous! anguish'd! unbearable,
Till a roof, shaggy, wild, inclos'd
In an orb, his fountain of thought.

6. In a horrible dreamful slumber,
Like the linked infernal chain:
A vast Spine writh'd in torment
Upon the winds; shooting pain'd
Ribs, like a bending cavern
And bones of solidness, froze
Over all his nerves of joy.
And a first Age passed over,
And a state of dismal woe.[6]

5. Cf. IV[a], verse 10. Los's effort to contain Urizen in the prison of the body and of the seven ages of history (verses 6–12) only produces greater disorder, the opposite of organization.

6. The construction of Urizen's body begins with the bones of his skull and skeleton and continues with the heart and circulatory system, the nervous system, the sensory organs, and in the "seventh age" instead of a period of rest there is a climactic torment as Urizen begins to move in his confining body.

Urizen . C:IV
From the caverns of his jointed Spine,
Down sunk with fright a red
Round globe hot burning deep
Deep down into the Abyss;
Panting: Conglobing, Trembling
Shooting out ten thousand branches
Around his solid bones.
And a second Age passed over;
And a state of dismal woe.
8. In harrowing fear rolling round;
His nervous brain shot branches
Round the branches of his heart
On high into two little orbs
And fixed in two little caves
Hiding carefully from the wind.
His Eyes beheld the deep.
And a third Age passed over;
And a state of dismal woe.
9. The pangs of hope began.
In heavy pain striving, struggling.
Two Ears in close volutions.
From beneath his orbs of vision
Shot spiring out, and petrified
As they grew. And a fourth Age pa
And a state of dismal woe.
10. In ghastly torment sick;
Hanging upon the wind;

[PLATE 11]

7. From the caverns of his jointed Spine,
Down sunk with fright a red
Round globe hot burning, deep
Deep down into the Abyss:
Panting: Conglobing, Trembling
Shooting out ten thousand branches
Around his solid bones.
And a second Age passed over,
And a state of dismal woe.

8. In harrowing fear rolling round:
His nervous brain shot branches
Round the branches of his heart
On high into two little orbs
And fixed in two little caves
Hiding carefully from the wind,
His Eyes beheld the deep,
And a third Age passed over:
And a state of dismal woe.

9. The pangs of hope began,
In heavy pain striving, struggling.
Two Ears in close volutions
From beneath his orbs of vision
Shot spiring out and petrified
As they grew. And a fourth Age passed
And a state of dismal woe.

10. In ghastly torment sick;
Hanging upon the wind;
[PLATE 13] Two Nostrils bent down to the deep.
And a fifth Age passed over;
And a state of dismal woe.

11. In ghastly torment sick;
Within his ribs bloated round,
A craving Hungry Cavern;
Thence arose his channeld Throat,
And like a red flame a Tongue
Of thirst & of hunger appeard.
And a sixth Age passed over:
And a state of dismal woe.

12. Enraged & stifled with torment
He threw his right Arm to the north
His left Arm to the south
Shooting out in anguish deep.

And his Feet stampd the nether Abyss
In trembling & howling & dismay.
And a seventh Age passed over:
And a state of dismal woe.

Chap: V

1. In terrors Los shrunk from his task:
His great hammer fell from his hand:
His fires beheld, and sickening,
Hid their strong limbs in smoke.
For with noises ruinous loud;
With hurtlings & clashings & groans
The Immortral endur'd his chains,
Tho' bound in a deadly sleep.

2. All the myriads of Eternity:
All the wisdom & joy of life:
Roll like a sea around him,
Except what his little orbs
Of sight by degrees unfold.

3. And now his eternal life
Like a dream was obliterated.

4. Shudd'ring, the Eternal Prophet smote
With a stroke, from his north to south region
The bellows & hammer are silent now.
A nerveless silence, his prophetic voice
Siez'd; a cold solitude & dark void
The Eternal Prophet & Urizen clos'd.[7]

5. Ages on ages rolld over them
Cut off from life & light, frozen
Into horrible forms of deformity.
Los suffer'd his fires to decay
Then he look'd back with anxious desire
But the space undivided by existence
Struck horror into his soul.

6. Los wept, obscur'd with mourning:
His bosom earthquak'd with sighs;
He saw Urizen deadly black,
In his chains bound, & Pity began,

7. In binding Urizen, Los himself becomes restrained. With the waning of his creative energy and the silencing of his prophetic voice, he enters Urizen's void.

7. In anguish dividing & dividing
(For pity divides the soul)[8]
In pangs eternity on eternity.
Life in cataracts pourd down his cliffs
The void shrunk the lymph into Nerves
Wand'ring wide on the bosom of night
And left a round globe of blood
Trembling upon the Void.

[PLATE 15] Thus the Eternal Prophet was divided
Before the death-image of Urizen
For in changeable clouds and darkness
In a winterly night beneath,
The Abyss of Los stretch'd immense:
And now seen, now obscur'd, to the eyes
Of Eternals the visions remote
Of the dark seperation appear'd.
As glasses discover Worlds
In the endless Abyss of space,
So the expanding eyes of Immortals
Beheld the dark visions of Los,
And the globe of life blood trembling.

[PLATE 18]
8. The globe of life blood trembled,
Branching out into roots;
Fibrous, writhing upon the winds:
Fibres of blood, milk and tears:
In pangs, eternity on eternity.
At length in tears & cries imbodied,
A female form trembling and pale
Waves before his deathy face.

9. All Eternity shudderd at sight
Of the first female now separate,[9]
Pale as a cloud of snow
Waving before the face of Los.

10. Wonder, awe, fear, astonishment,
Petrify the eternal myriads;
At the first female form now separate.
[PLATE 19] They call'd her Pity, and fled.

8. Love is fraternal, but pity implies condescension. Cf. "Pity would be no more / If we did not make somebody Poor" ("The Human Abstract"). Los also becomes separate from his own tender feelings, objectified as Enitharmon. Chapter V could be called "The Creation of Pity" or "The Separation of Woman from Humanity," since these are the same event. Plates 16 and 17 are full-page illustrations.

9. Blake's conception of this woman recalls the troublesome first woman Pandora in Hesiodic myth. In VI,3 the woman is called Enitharmon. When men and women play sexual roles, or lose sight of their common humanity, they torment one another; Los and Enitharmon see each other as sexual objects and play a courtship game of luring, chasing, repelling, and capturing.

11. "Spread a Tent, with strong curtains around them
Let cords & stakes bind in the Void
That Eternals may no more behold them."

12. They began to weave curtains of darkness.
They erected large pillars round the Void,
With golden hooks fastend in the pillars;
With infinite labour the Eternals
A woof wove, and called it Science.[1]

Chap: VI

1. But Los saw the Female & pitied.
He embrac'd her, she wept, she refus'd;
In perverse and cruel delight
She fled from his arms, yet he followed.

2. Eternity shudder'd when they saw
Man begetting his likeness
On his own divided image.

3. A time passed over; the Eternals
Began to erect the tent:
When Enitharmon, sick,
Felt a Worm within her womb.

4. Yet helpless it lay like a Worm
In the trembling womb
To be moulded into existence.

5. All day the worm lay on her bosom;
All night within her womb
The worm lay till it grew to a serpent
With dolorous hissings & poisons
Round Enitharmon's loins folding.

6. Coild within Enitharmon's womb
The serpent grew, casting its scales;
With sharp pangs the hissings began
To change to a grating cry.
Many sorrows and dismal throes
Many forms of fish, bird & beast,
Brought forth an Infant form
Where was a worm before.[2]

1. The spectacle of "love and jealousy" (*Four Zoas,* subtitle) is too painful for the Eternals to contemplate. Their Tent of Science is a new (and lower) ceiling over earthly life.

2. Blake's sources for this embryological recapitulation of evolutionary progress have been studied by Carmen S. Kreiter, *Studies in Romanticism* 4 (1965), 110–18. Chapter VI might be called "The Birth of Orc."

7. The Eternals, their tent finished,
Alarm'd with these gloomy visions
When Enitharmon groaning
Produc'd a man Child to the light.

8. A shriek ran thro' Eternity:
And a paralytic stroke:
At the birth of the Human shadow.

9. Delving earth in his resistless way:
Howling, the Child with fierce flames
Issu'd from Enitharmon.

10. The Eternals closed the tent:
They beat down the stakes, the cords
[PLATE 20] Stretch'd for a work of eternity;
No more Los beheld Eternity.

11. In his hands he siez'd the infant.
He bathed him in springs of sorrow
He gave him to Enitharmon.

Chap. VII

1. They named the child Orc; he grew
Fed with milk of Enitharmon.

2. Los awoke her: O sorrow & pain!
A tight'ning girdle grew
Around his bosom. In sobbings
He burst the girdle in twain,
But still another girdle
Oppressd his bosom. In sobbings
Again he burst it. Again
Another girdle succeeds.
The girdle was form'd by day;
By night was burst in twain.

3. These falling down on the rock
Into an iron Chain
In each other link by link lock'd.†

4. They took Orc to the top of a mountain.
O how Enitharmon wept!

† See color plate 20.

They chain'd his young limbs to the rock
With the Chain of Jealousy
Beneath Urizen's deathful shadow.

5. The dead heard the voice of the child
And began to awake from sleep.‡
All things heard the voice of the child
And began to awake to life.

6. And Urizen, craving with hunger,
Stung with the odours of Nature,
Explor'd his dens around.[3]

7. He form'd a line & a plummet
To divide the Abyss beneath.
He form'd a dividing rule:

8. He formed scales to weigh;
He formed massy weights;
He formed a brazen quadrant;
He formed golden compasses
And began to explore the Abyss
And he planted a garden of fruits.

9. But Los encircled Enitharmon
With fires of Prophecy
Form the sight of Urizen & Orc.

10. And she bore an enormous race.

Chap. VIII

1. Urizen explor'd his dens,
Mountain, moor, & wilderness,
With a globe of fire lighting his journey:
A fearful journey, annoy'd
By cruel enormities: forms
[PLATE 23] Of life on his forsaken mountains.

‡ See color plate 21, inserted after plate 20 in Copy D, but after plate 13 in Copies A and B, and after plate 8 in Copy G. Urizen has been bound by Los but is perhaps becoming awakened by Orc. Blake's varying arrangements of his plates in different copies suggest different interpretations of some of his more tantalizing and ambiguous designs.

3. Orc's protest animates "all things," including Urizen; in the system of contraries energy can awake reason as well as vice versa. The subject of Chapter VII is "The Sacrifice of Orc and the Awakening of Urizen." Urizen's explorations are really further measurings of the finite world. In chapter VIII, his globe of fire recalls the lamp of Diogenes the Cynic (*Marriage of Heaven and Hell* 13) but his compasses (see "The Ancient of Days," *Europe* 1) and other instruments receive more attention. His "garden of fruits" (verse 8) is an infernal garden, as in "The Poison Tree."

2. And his world teemd vast enormities:
Frightning; faithless; fawning
Portions of life; similitudes
Of a foot, or a hand, or a head
Or a heart, or an eye; they swam, mischevous
Dread terrors! delighting in blood.[4]

3. Most Urizen sicken'd to see
His eternal creations appear.
Sons & daughters of sorrow[5] on mountains.
Weeping! wailing! First Thiriel appear'd,
Astonish'd at his own existence
Like a man from a cloud born; & Utha
From the waters emerging, laments!
Grodna rent the deep earth, howling,
Amaz'd! his heavens immense cracks
Like the ground parch'd with heat; then Fuzon
Flam'd out! first begotten, last born.
All his eternal sons in like manner:
His daughters from green herbs & cattle
From monsters, & worms of the pit.

4. He, in darkness clos'd, view'd all his race
And his soul sicken'd! he curs'd
Both sons & daughters; for he saw
That no flesh nor spirit could keep
His iron laws one moment.

5. For he saw that life liv'd upon death;

[PLATE 25] The Ox in the slaughter house moans
The Dog at the wintry door,
And he wept, & he called it Pity,
And his tears flowed down on the winds.[6]

6. Cold he wander'd on high, over their cities
In weeping & pain & woe!
And where-ever he wanderd in sorrows
Upon the aged heavens
A cold shadow follow'd behind him
Like a spider's web, moist, cold, & dim,

4. Following the Platonic principle that this world is a poor copy of an ideal world, partial realities are accepted as sufficient unto the day. In Urizen's domain are chopped-off limbs like those on the battlefield and in Jack Tearguts's surgery (*Island in the Moon*). Chapter VIII could be named "Urizen's Suppression of his Progeny."

5. Their mother, Ahania, is not named until the sequel to *Urizen*. The children of Urizen are personifications of the four elements or the productions of subhuman nature (as in Hesiod's *Theogony*).

6. This alternating condemnation and hypocritical sympathy recall Los's behavior toward him in binding (IV[a],4) and pitying (V, 6).

Drawing out from his sorrowing soul
The dungeon-like heaven, dividing
Where ever the footsteps of Urizen
Walk'd over the cities in sorrow.

7. Till a Web dark & cold, throughout all
The tormented element, stretch'd
From the sorrows of Urizen's soul.
And the Web is a Female in embrio.
None could break the Web, no wings of fire,

8. So twisted the cords, & so knotted
The meshes: twisted like to the human brain.

9. And all calld it, The Net of Religion.[7]

Chap. IX

1. Then the Inhabitants of those Cities
Felt their Nerves change into Marrow[8]
And hardening Bones began
In swift diseases and torments,
In throbbings & shootings & grindings
Thro' all the coasts: till weaken'd
The Senses inward rush'd, shrinking
Beneath the dark net of infection.

2. Till the shrunken eyes, clouded over,
Discernd not the woven hipocrisy,
But the streaky slime in their heavens
Brought together by narrowing perceptions
Appeard transparent air; for their eyes
Grew small like the eyes of a man
And in reptile forms shrinking together
Of seven feet stature they remaind.[9]

3. Six days they shrunk up from existence
And on the seventh day they rested,[1]

7. The Web of Religion (verse 7) grows according to the pattern of the origin of priestcraft, (*Marriage of Heaven and Hell* 11) and Mystery ("The Human Abstract"). It is the counterpart of the Tent of Science (chapter V, 11–12; chapter VI, 3, 7, 10). Line 18 is deleted in Copy A.

8. As in the materialization of Urizen's body in chapter IV[b], 6, the process of the contraction of the Senses begins as the nerves harden, and "diseases" accompany the process of desensitizing. Chapter IX treats of "Degeneration and Rebellion."

9. In primeval times as explained in Genesis 6:4, "There were giants in the earth in those days." But "in reptile forms shrinking" recalls the fate of the devils in *Paradise Lost X*, 504–84, who were reduced to serpents.

1. This parody of Genesis 2:2–3 is one indication of Blake's counter-myth; here the ages of God's creativity become the ages of man's all-too-human fall.

And they bless'd the seventh day, in sick hope:
And forgot their eternal life.

4. And their thirty cities divided
In form of a human heart
No more could they rise at will
In the infinite void, but bound down
To earth by their narrowing perceptions,
[PLATE 28] They lived a period of years
Then left a noisom body
To the jaws of devouring darkness.

5. And their children wept, & built
Tombs in the desolate places,
And form'd laws of prudence, and call'd them
The eternal laws of God.

6. And the thirty cities remaind,
Surrounded by salt floods, now call'd
Africa: its name was then Egypt.[2]

7. The remaining sons of Urizen
Beheld their brethren shrink together
Beneath the Net of Urizen.
Perswasion was in vain;
For the ears of the inhabitants
Were wither'd & deafen'd & cold.
And their eyes could not discern
Their brethren of other cities.[3]

8. So Fuzon call'd all together
The remaining children of Urizen:
And they left the pendulous earth:
They called it Egypt, & left it.[4]

9. And the salt ocean rolled englob'd.

The End of the book of Urizen

2. See "heart-formed Africa" (*Song of Los*), the Egyptian phase of history, from which the Israelites issue in Exodus. The building of tombs (verse 5) seems the chief work of Egypt.

3. The constricted senses have cut them off from a sense of community with other men, as well as with Eternity.

4. "The pendulous earth" recalls *Paradise Lost IV*, 1000, "the pendulous round earth." The final word "englobed" (verse 9) emphasizes the roundness of the earth isolated in empty space, which Blake takes as characteristic of the fall. Similarly the "salt Ocean" recalls Noah's flood and the rolling of its waves recalls that of the Red Sea. Thus those who follow Fuzon, like the followers of Moses and Noah, are saved from destruction.

The Book of Ahania

Perhaps first planned as "The Second Book of Urizen," this sequel to the Genesis book of Blake's "Bible of Hell" is in some ways an Exodus. The dual role of the Biblical Moses is split between Urizen as lawgiver and his son Fuzon as rebel leader of an enslaved people. Though this work is named for Urizen's wife Ahania to suggest that *Ahania* is the mate or counterpart of *Urizen,* the plot is concerned for four chapters with Fuzon and only in the final chapter with Ahania, whose presence is expressed in her passionate lament. Having left the element of earth, renamed Egypt, under the control of Urizen, Fuzon and his band of the "remaining sons of Urizen" appear at the end of *Urizen* to be escaping from bondage, but at the beginning of *Ahania* Fuzon has already set himself up as a rival king who goes on to proclaim himself God as well. The action takes place in an imaginary no man's land, a mental space which recalls the desert between Egypt and the Promised Land.

In *The Book of Ahania* Urizen is reflected through his two opposites—the son who embodies all the fiery energy that he has suppressed in himself and others, and the wife who like soft wax retains an image of his unfallen nature. Blake frequently explores a primary character by means of his "sons," whose personalities and actions reveal contradictory elements within himself, as well as by means of his female counterpart, who embodies his softer or more devious aspects. Thus Fuzon is Urizen's pent-up lust and rage, and Ahania is the gentle and graceful side of reason, modeled in part on the goddess Athena and on Sophia, personification of divine wisdom.

Although the character of Fuzon bears an obvious resemblance to that of Orc, *The Book of Ahania* shows that Blake wishes to distinguish between two kinds of rebels. Fuzon's motivation is pure defiance, not the construction of a genuine new order of freedom; in contrast, Orc in *America* is a revolutionary with a vision of a better world that will appear when he has trampled Urizen's law to dust and scattered it abroad to make the desert bloom. Probably the reason Fuzon disappears from Blake's cast of characters after *Ahania* was that to deploy both Fuzon and Orc in a single work would have been redundant; also in the larger myth Blake wished to present sexual and revolutionary energy as powers for change originating in the imaginative faculty, not the rational one: Orc, son of Los, can change the world, whereas Fuzon, son of Urizen, can at most better himself.

Nevertheless, in his limited role as the fiery reaction unconsciously produced by cold rationality, Fuzon is superb. He has been developed far beyond his original scope early in *Urizen* as the personification of fire, one of the four elements internalized by Urizen in his struggle to master his environment. Fuzon's conflict with his father is largely moral and psychosexual rather than political. During a struggle for phallic supremacy, Fuzon castrates Urizen and separates him from his soul (or Emanation, to use

Blake's later term), his consort Ahania. In retaliation, Urizen slays Fuzon and nails his corpse on the Tree of Mystery. This Tree springs from Urizen's own brain, as in "The Human Abstract" of *Songs*, and upon it the corpse is reanimated. This dreadful tale blends and parodies elements of the father-son relationship between Zeus and Saturn, Absalom and David, and especially Jesus and Jehovah. The crucifixion story told here is one to which Blake repeatedly returned with refinements and reinterpretations, with Orc as the crucified one whose suffering is transformed into meaningful self-sacrifice by Jesus in the final epics. The weapons in the struggle between Urizen and Fuzon are fantastic ones drawn from the loins of the combatants: a globe that lengthens into a laserlike beam, a shieldlike disk with a cutting edge, a gigantic slingshot or bow made of a dead serpent's ribs, and a poisoned rock-projectile which falls to earth in the form of Mount Sinai.

The true victim of this terrible conflict is Ahania, bereft of both son and husband. She is a shadowy being, described first as a satellite of her husband, then as a mere voice in the void around Fuzon's tree. But in her lament the reader is given a glimpse into what the life of the mind ought to be and even could be, as she describes the unfallen relationship between Urizen and herself, or between true wisdom and intellectual grace, fertility, excitement, and delight. Ahania's song is filled with images of luxury and fecundity. She does not mourn Fuzon. She remembers Urizen as a virile and generous lover, father of many children, sower of seed in the human soul—not the austere, rocklike life-denier who has tyrannized over everything and everyone in *Urizen* and *Ahania*. But, as Ahania's wail ends, her voice is scarcely distinguishable from that of Earth in "Earth's Answer." As an outcast from Urizen's bosom, Ahania finds that her world now consists only of rocks and bones and the jealousy and fear of her beloved.

Like *The Book of Los*, this work—which exists in only one complete copy, dated 1795—stands somewhat apart from the other illuminated books: the double-columned text is set out in conventional intaglio etching, a less laborious process than Blake's distinctive relief etching. The fact that the textual areas of *Ahania* and *The Book of Los* are almost undecorated might also imply a merely trial status for these works. But the elaborately color-printed frontispieces, terminal designs, and carefully wrought title pages indicate that Blake wanted them to take their places in "The Bible of Hell." Unlike his friend Thomas Paine, who created a great stir by openly discussing apparent contradictions in the Holy Bible in *The Age of Reason* (1796), Blake did not think that alternate versions of important stories necessarily invalidate one another. Thus his counter-Bible could contain more than one account of what people do to damage themselves and each other. Eventually in his double epic, *Milton* and *Jerusalem*, begun in 1804, he set forth the fullest rendering of his comprehensive myth.

The Book of Ahania

LAMBETH Printed by W Blake 1795

[PLATE 2]

AHANIA

Chap: I[st]

1: Fuzon, on a chariot iron-wing'd
On spiked flames rose; his hot visage
Flam'd furious! sparkles his hair & beard
Shot down his wide bosom and shoulders.
On clouds of smoke rages his chariot
And his right hand burns red in its cloud—
Moulding into a vast globe, his wrath,
As the thunder-stone is moulded.
Son of Urizen's silent burnings.

2: "Shall we worship this Demon of smoke,"
Said Fuzon, "this abstract non-entity,
This cloudy God seated on waters
Now seen, now obscur'd; King of sorrow?"

3: So he spoke, in a fiery flame,
On Urizen frowning indignant.
The Globe of wrath shaking on high
Roaring with fury, he threw
The howling Globe: burning it flew
Lengthning into a hungry beam. Swiftly

4: Oppos'd to the exulting flam'd beam
The broad Disk of Urizen upheav'd
Across the Void many a mile.

5: It was forg'd in mills where the winter
Beats incessant; ten winters the disk
Unremitting endur'd the cold hammer.

6: But the strong arm that sent it, remember'd
The sounding beam;[1] laughing it tore through
That beaten mass, keeping its direction,
The cold loins of Urizen dividing.

1. The beam remembers the arm that sent it. History and personification of weapons are epic conventions.

7: Dire shriek'd his invisible Lust
Deep groan'd Urizen! stretching his awful hand.
Ahania (so name his parted soul)
He siez'd on his mountains of Jealousy,
He groand anguished & called her Sin,
Kissing her and weeping over her;
Then hid her in darkness, in silence;
Jealous tho' she was invisible.

8: She fell down, a faint shadow wandring
In chaos and circling dark Urizen,
As the moon anguishd circles the earth;
Hopeless! abhorrd! a death-shadow,
Unseen, unbodied, unknown,
The mother of Pestilence.

9: But the fiery beam of Fuzon
Was a pillar of fire to Egypt,
Five hundred years wandring on earth,
Till Los siezd it and beat in a mass
With the body of the sun.

[PLATE 3]

Chap: II[d]

1: But the forehead of Urizen gathering,
And his eyes pale with anguish, his lips
Blue & changing; in tears and bitter
Contrition he prepar'd his Bow,

2: Form'd of Ribs: that in his dark solitude
When obscur'd in his forests fell monsters
Arose. For his dire Contemplations
Rush'd down like floods from his mountains
In torrents of mud settling thick,
With Eggs of unnatural production
Forthwith hatching; some howl'd on his hills
Some in vales; some aloft flew in air.

3: Of these: an enormous dread Serpent
Scaled and poisonous horned
Approach'd Urizen even to his knees
As he sat on his dark rooted Oak.

4: With his horns he push'd furious.
Great the conflict & great the jealousy
In cold poisons: but Urizen smote him.

5: First he poison'd the rocks with his blood;
Then polish'd his ribs, and his sinews
Dried; laid them apart till winter;
Then a Bow black prepar'd: on this Bow,
A poisoned rock plac'd in silence:
He utter'd these words to the Bow:

6: "O Bow of the clouds of secresy!
O nerve of that lust form'd monster!
Send this rock swift, invisible thro'
The black clouds, on the bosom of Fuzon."

7: So saying, In torment of his wounds,
He bent the enormous ribs slowly;
A circle of darkness! then fixed
The sinew in its rest: then the Rock—
Poisonous source!—plac'd with art, lifting difficult
Its weighty bulk: silent the rock lay.

8: While Fuzon his tygers unloosing
Thought Urizen slain by his wrath.
"I am God," said he, "eldest of things!"

9: Sudden sings the rock, swift & invisible
On Fuzon flew, enter'd his bosom;
His beautiful visage, his tresses[2]
That gave light to the mornings of heaven
Were smitten with darkness, deform'd
And outstretch'd on the edge of the forest.

10: But the rock fell upon the Earth,
Mount Sinai, in Arabia.

Chap: III

1: The Globe shook; and Urizen seated
On black clouds his sore wound anointed
The ointment flow'd down on the void,
Mix'd with blood; here the snake gets her poison.

2: With difficulty & great pain, Urizen
Lifted on high the dead corse:
On his shoulders he bore it to where
A Tree hung over the Immensity.

3: For when Urizen shrunk away
From Eternals, he sat on a rock

2. Like Absalom's (II Samuel 14:25, 18:9); see Paley, *Energy and Imagination*, p. 83.

Barren; a rock which himself
From redounding fancies had petrified.
Many tears fell on the rock,
Many sparks of vegetation;
Soon shot the pained root
Of Mystery under his heel:
It grew a thick tree; he wrote
In silence his book of iron:
Till the horrid plant bending its boughs
Grew to roots when it felt the earth
And again sprung to many a tree.

4: Amaz'd started Urizen! when
He beheld himself compassed round
And high roofed over with trees.
He arose, but the stems stood so thick
He with difficulty and great pain
Brought his Books, all but the Book
[PLATE 4] Of iron, from the dismal shade.

5: The Tree still grows over the Void
Enrooting itself all around
An endless labyrinth of woe!

6: The corse of his first begotten
On the accursed Tree of *Mystery*:
On the topmost stem of this Tree
Urizen nail'd Fuzon's corse.

Chap: IV

1: Forth flew the arrows of pestilence[3]
Round the pale living Corse on the tree.

2: For in Urizen's slumbers of abstraction
In the infinite ages of Eternity,
When his Nerves of Joy melted & flow'd,
A white Lake on the dark blue air
In perturb'd pain and dismal torment
Now stretching out, now swift conglobing.

3: Effluvia vapor'd above
In noxious clouds; these hover'd thick
Over the disorganiz'd Immortal,
Till petrific pain scurfd o'er the Lakes
As the bones of man, solid & dark.

3. Recalling Saint Sebastian's martyrdom and Apollo's plague-carrying arrows in *Iliad* I, 47–61. Fuzon's rotting corpse both emits pestilential arrows and is tormented by them; the stymied revolution breeds diseases.

4: The clouds of disease hover'd wide
Around the Immortal in torment,
Perching around the hurtling bones,
Disease on disease, shape on shape,
Winged, screaming in blood & torment.

5: The Eternal Prophet beat on his anvils
Enrag'd in the desolate darkness
He forg'd nets of iron around
And Los threw them around the bones.

6: The shapes screaming flutter'd vain.
Some combin'd into muscles & glands,
Some organs for craving and lust;
Most remain'd on the tormented void:
Urizen's army of horrors.

7: Round the pale living Corse on the Tree
Forty years[4] flew the arrows of pestilence.

8: Wailing and terror and woe
Ran thro' all his dismal world;
Forty years all his sons & daughters
Felt their skulls harden; then Asia
Arose in the pendulous deep.

9: They reptilize upon the Earth.

10: Fuzon groand on the Tree.

Chap: V

1: The lamenting voice of Ahania
Weeping upon the void,
And round the Tree of Fuzon;
Distant in solitary night
Her voice was heard, but no form
Had she: but her tears from clouds
Eternal fell round the Tree.

2: And the voice cried: "Ah Urizen! Love!
Flower of morning! I weep on the verge
Of Non-entity; how wide the Abyss
Between Ahania and thee!

4. The length of time that the Israelites wandered in the wilderness on the way from Egypt to the promised land.

3: "I lie on the verge of the deep.
I see thy dark clouds ascend.
I see thy black forests and floods,
A horrible waste to my eyes!

4: "Weeping I walk over rocks,
Over dens & thro' valleys of death.
Why didst thou despise Ahania,
To cast me from thy bright presence
Into the World of Loneness?

5: "I cannot touch his hand:
Nor weep on his knees, nor hear
His voice & bow, nor see his eyes
And joy, nor hear his footsteps, and
My heart leap at the lovely sound!
I cannot kiss the place
Whereon his bright feet have trod,
[PLATE 5] But I wander on the rocks
With hard necessity.

6: "Where is my golden palace?[5]
Where my ivory bed?
Where the joys of my morning hour
Where the sons of eternity, singing

7: "To awake bright Urizen, my king?
To arise to the mountain sport,
To the bliss of eternal valleys:

8: "To awake my king in the morn!
To embrace Ahania's joy
On the bredth of his open bosom:
From my soft cloud of dew to fall
In showers of life on his harvests.

9: "When he gave my happy soul
To the sons of eternal joy:
When he took the daughters of life
Into my chambers of love:

10: "When I found babes of bliss on my bed
And bosoms of milk in my chambers
Fill'd with eternal seed,
O! eternal births sung round Ahania,
In interchange sweet of their joys.

5. Cf. Psalm 45, a song for the king's marriage; the figs and pomegranates in 5:26 recall the sexual imagery of the Song of Solomon.

11: "Swell'd with ripeness & fat with fatness,
Bursting on winds my odors,
My ripe figs and rich pomegranates
In infant joy at thy feet,
O Urizen, sported and sang;

12: "Then thou with thy lap full of seed
With thy hand full of generous fire
Walked forth from the clouds of morning
On the virgins of springing joy,
On the human soul to cast
The seed of eternal science.

13: "The sweat poured down thy temples.
To Ahania return'd in evening
The moisture awoke to birth
My mother's-joys sleeping in bliss.

14: "But now alone over rocks, mountains,
Cast out from thy lovely bosom:
Cruel jealousy! selfish fear!
Self-destroying: how can delight,
Renew in these chains of darkness
Where bones of beasts are strown
On the bleak and snowy mountains,
Where bones from the birth are buried
Before they see the light?"

FINIS

The Book of Los

The third work dealing with primordial events in Blake's "Bible of Hell" is closely tied to *Urizen* not as a sequel like *Ahania* but as an intersecting and overlapping version of the identical "Genesis" events from the point of view of Los, as introduced by a new character—Eno, "aged Mother." The Bible itself presents alternative versions of primeval relationship: in Genesis 2:4 begins a recapitulation of material in Genesis 1. In the fallen world, long after an obscurely cataclysmic event called "the day of thunders in old time," Eno remembers "Times remote," a period corresponding to "Eternity" in *Urizen* insofar as it is free from impurity and sin. As the first work in this trilogy makes clear, these evils are the conceptions of Urizen. Since "Times remote" are free of repression, the apparent vices of fallen time, Covet, Envy, Wrath, and Wantonness—which are *reactions* to deprivation—fulfill themselves without becoming pernicious. Fulfilled, they become their opposites, which might be called Generosity, Admiration, Gentleness, and Constancy.

A line drawn between stanzas 5 and 6 marks the conclusion of Eno's song; this opening section sets up an unfallen standard by which to judge the main events of the poem. No new narrator appears, but the perspective is omniscient and the style is the same as that of the seer who invokes the Eternals to reveal "dark visions of Torment" in the Preludium to *Urizen.* In the sixth stanza of the first chapter, Los comes to consciousness already in a fallen situation, in chains, watching the flames of desire and the shadow of Urizen—much as he is pictured on plate 11 of *Urizen.* Instead of consuming the flames inward as Urizen does, Los stamps out a space within them and flings off his chains. The imagery suggests another variation or parody of the creation story: instead of separating the waters above from the waters below to cause the firmament to appear, Los forms a void "between fire and fire." Within this void appears the "solid without fluctuation" which Urizen had tried to form in the book bearing his name.

In the rest of *The Book of Los* it becomes clear that when the story of the creation is told as Los experiences it, it is the Eternal Prophet rather than the Eternal Priest who is to blame for this fall from spirit into matter. In other words, the error of perceiving reality as brute matter results from a failure of imagination or creative energy (the attributes of Los). Stifled in the adamant, impenetrable solid, "black as marble of Egypt," Los breaks out of the Urizenic world into a boundless void of error. He is able to change the angle of this fall by elevating his thoughts and overcoming his wrath, but the fall is merely redirected, not arrested. The imagery for Los's works is biological, for his center of objective reality is the human body, specifically the Body he creates for Urizen, personification of Mind. Unlike Urizen, Los works with the fires of desire instead of suppressing them. It is evident in both *Urizen* and *Los* that the blacksmith Los is a skilled craftsman; he has built his own tools and knows how to use them. But he is not yet an artist as he is in *Jerusalem* or a true prophet as he is in *Milton;* the product of his imaginings in *Los* is only the "Human Illusion," a conception of mankind as mind contained and confined in flesh.

Like *The Book of Ahania,* this work in conventional intaglio etching exists in a unique copy, dated 1795. *Urizen, Ahania,* and *Los,* in irregular tetrameter and trimeter lines rather than the irregular heptameter used in most of Blake's prophecies, are set up in double columns to imitate the usual format of the Holy Bible.

The Book of Los

LAMBETH Printed by W Blake 1795

[PLATE 3]

LOS

Chap: I

1: Eno, aged Mother,
Who the chariot of Leutha guides,
Since the day of thunders in old time,

2: Sitting beneath the eternal Oak
Trembled and shook the stedfast Earth
And thus her speech broke forth:

3: "O Times remote!
When Love & Joy were adoration:
And none impure were deem'd.
Not Eyeless Covet
Nor Thin-lip'd Envy
Nor Bristled Wrath
Nor Curled Wantonness;

4: "But Covet was poured full:
Envy fed with fat of lambs:
Wrath with lions' gore:
Wantonness lulld to sleep
With the virgin's lute,
Or sated with her love.

5: "Till Covet broke his locks & bars,
And slept with open doors:
Envy sung at the rich man's feast:
Wrath was follow'd up and down
By a little ewe lamb
And Wantonness on his own true love
Begot a giant race."

6: Raging furious, the flames of desire
Ran thro' heaven & earth: living flames
Intelligent, organiz'd: arm'd
With destruction & plagues. In the midst
The Eternal Prophet, bound in a chain,
Compell'd to watch Urizen's shadow,

7: Rag'd with curses & sparkles of fury.
Round the flames roll as Los hurls his chains,
Mounting up from his fury, condens'd
Rolling round & round, mounting on high
Into vacuum: into non-entity.
Where nothing was! Dash'd wide apart
His feet stamp the eternal fierce-raging
Rivers of wide flame; they roll round
And round on all sides making their way
Into darkness and shadowy obscurity.

8: Wide apart stood the fires: Los remain'd
In the void between fire and fire.
In trembling and horror they beheld him
They stood wide apart, driv'n by his hands
And his feet which the nether abyss
Stamp'd in fury and hot indignation.

9: But no light from the fires. All was
[PLATE 4] Darkness round Los: heat was not; for bound up
Into fiery spheres from his fury
The gigantic flames trembled and hid.

10: Coldness, darkness, obstruction, a Solid
Without fluctuation, hard as adamant
Black as marble of Egypt; impenetrable,
Bound in the fierce raging Immortal.
And the seperated fires froze in
A vast solid without fluctuation,
Bound in his expanding clear senses.

Chap: II

1: The Immortal stood frozen amidst
The vast rock of eternity; times
And times; a night of vast durance:
Impatient, stifled, stiffend, hardned.

2: Till impatience no longer could bear
The hard bondage: rent, rent, the vast solid
With a crash from immense to immense

3: Crack'd across into numberless fragments.
The Prophetic wrath, strug'ling for vent
Hurls apart, stamping furious to dust
And crumbling with bursting sobs; heaves
The black marble on high into fragments.

4: Hurl'd apart on all sides, as a falling
Rock, the innumerable fragments away
Fell asunder; and horrible vacuum
Beneath him & on all sides round.

5: Falling, falling! Los fell & fell
Sunk precipitant, heavy, down, down,
Times on times, night on night, day on day.
Truth has bounds, Error none: falling, falling:
Years on years, and ages on ages,
Still he fell thro' the void, still a void
Found for falling day & night without end.
For tho' day or night was not; their spaces
Were measurd by his incessant whirls
In the horrid vacuity bottomless.[1]

6: The Immortal revolving, indignant,
First in wrath threw his limbs, like the babe
New born into our world: wrath subsided
And contemplative thoughts first arose.
Then aloft his head rear'd in the Abyss
And his downward-borne fall chang'd oblique;

7: Many ages of groans: till there grew
Branchy forms: organizing the Human
Into finite inflexible organs.

8: Till in process from falling he bore
Sidelong on the purple air, wafting
The weak breeze in efforts o'erwearied.

9: Incessant the falling Mind labour'd,
Organizing itself: till the Vacuum
Became element, pliant to rise,
Or to fall, or to swim, or to fly:
With ease searching the dire vacuity.[2]

Chap: III

1: The Lungs heave incessant, dull and heavy,
For as yet were all other parts formless,
Shiv'ring: clinging around like a cloud,
Dim & glutinous as the white Polypus
Driv'n by waves & englob'd on the tide.

1. In *Four Zoas, Milton*, and *Jerusalem* merciful limits are set to the fall (cf. the "starry floor" and "watry shore" of "Introduction" to *Experience*), but the three Lambeth books of the Bible of Hell are more pessimistic.

2. All reality is mental; Los is learning to live in chaos and becoming able to organize his perceptions of the newly fallen world. Blake's lines echo *Paradise Lost* II, 949–50, which describe Satan's progress through chaos.

2: And the unformed part crav'd repose.
Sleep began: the Lungs heave on the wave,
Weary overweigh'd; sinking beneath
In a stifling black fluid he woke.

3: He arose on the waters, but soon
Heavy, falling, his organs like roots
Shooting out from the seed, shot beneath,
And a vast world of waters around him
In furious torrents began.

4: Then he sunk, & around his spent Lungs
Began intricate pipes that drew in
The spawn of the waters. Outbranching,
[PLATE 5] An immense Fibrous form, stretching out
Thro' the bottoms of immensity, raging.

5: He rose on the floods: then he smote
The wild deep with his terrible wrath,
Seperating the heavy and thin.

6: Down the heavy sunk; cleaving around
To the fragments of solid: up rose
The thin, flowing round the fierce fires
That glow'd furious in the expanse.

Chap: IV

1: Then Light first began; from the fire's
Beams, conducted by fluid so pure,[3]
Flow'd around the Immense: Los beheld
Forthwith, writhing upon the dark void,
The Back bone of Urizen appear
Hurtling upon the wind
Like a serpent! like an iron chain
Whirling about in the Deep.

2: Upfolding his Fibres together
To a Form of impregnable strength,
Los, astonish'd and terrified, built
Furnaces; he formed an Anvil,
A Hammer of adamant; then began
The binding of Urizen. Day and night

3: Circling round the dark Demon, with howlings
Dismay & sharp blightings; the Prophet
Of Eternity beat on his iron links.

3. Ether, in medieval cosmologies the rarified element of the upper air, was adapted by Newton and others to explain how light waves can be transmitted in a vacuum. Blake believed Newton's mechanistic corpuscular theory of light was antivisionary (cf. "Mock on, Mock on, Voltaire, Rousseau," p. 184).

4: And first from those infinite fires
The light that flow'd down on the winds
He siez'd; beating incessant, condensing
The subtil particles in an Orb.

5: Roaring, indignant, the bright sparks
Endur'd the vast Hammer; but unwearied
Los beat on the Anvil; till glorious
An immense Orb of fire he fram'd.[4]

6: Oft he quench'd it beneath in the Deeps
Then survey'd the all-bright mass. Again
Siezing fires from the terrific Orbs
He heated the round Globe, then beat;
While roaring his Furnaces endur'd
The chaind Orb in their infinite wombs.

7: Nine ages completed their circles
When Los heated the glowing mass, casting
It down into the Deeps: the Deeps fled
Away in redounding smoke; the Sun
Stood self-balanc'd. And Los smild with joy.
He the vast Spine of Urizen siez'd
And bound down to the glowing illusion.

8: But no light, for the Deep fled away
On all sides, and left an unform'd
Dark vacuity: here Urizen lay
In fierce torments on his glowing bed

9: Till his Brain in a rock, & his Heart
In a fleshy slough formed four rivers[5]
Obscuring the immense Orb of fire
Flowing down into night: till a Form
Was completed, a Human Illusion
In darkness and deep clouds involvd.

The End of the
Book of LOS

4. Los is frequently depicted as the forger of the sun; his name is probably an anagram of Sol. From Swedenborg Blake derived a distinction between the material sun and the spiritual sun or human imagination (cf. *A Vision of the Last Judgment* p. 416). In the Lambeth books Los's sun appears to be the material sun, appropriate to Los's function as spirit of Time (*Milton* 24:68, 29:23), but when Blake defies Los in the form of the material sun he experiences "fourfold vision" (letter to Butts, November 22, 1802, p. 462). In the longer prophecies (see esp. *Milton* 22:5–14 and the designs for *Jerusalem* 1, 97, and 100) the light of Los is the visionary light of the spiritual sun.

5. There are four rivers in Eden, and also in hell. The description of the arteries as rivers prefigures Blake's myth of the giant man Albion who contains within himself the physical universe.

Poems from Blake's Notebook

Blake's Notebook, sometimes called "The Rossetti Manuscript" because Dante Gabriel Rossetti purchased it in 1847, is a remarkable workbook of poetry, prose, and drawings. Only by studying the superb facsimile edited by David V. Erdman and Donald K. Moore (1973; revised edition, 1977) can one appreciate its richness and variety. When Blake's brother and drawing pupil Robert died in 1787, Blake began using the blank pages in Robert's sketchbook as his own all-purpose private notebook, crowding in sketches and drafts until the book was almost completely filled up about 1818. The Notebook contains preliminary drafts for all but three of the *Songs of Experience* (1794), other never-published lyrics as good as Blake's best published work, angry epigrams, drafts of philosophic poetry such as *The Everlasting Gospel* (ca. 1818, printed separately by editors), miscellaneous verse never intended for publication, mingled with drafts of prose works such as the *Public Address* and *Vision of the Last Judgment* (to be discussed below), preliminary drawings for published works (primarily for *The Gates of Paradise*), as well as many hasty and tentative sketches. At times Blake simply used his Notebook as a diary to get something off his chest.

The Notebook is a fascinating resource for the study of Blake's process of composition. As examples of his working drafts, we have transcribed three poems in the process of extensive revision. "London" and "The Tyger" show inspired improvements in diction and organization. The incompletely revised long version of "Infant Sorrow" is interesting as a link between the short lyrics of *Experience* and the experimental symbolic ballads of The Pickering Manuscript. This version of "Infant Sorrow" tells a story of repression and rebellion similar to the one in "The Mental Traveller" (p. 202), except that its setting is more familiar, less dreamlike. Thematically, it belongs somewhere near "The Cradle Song" and "To My Mirtle." With minor simplifications and corrections, our transcriptions follow those in the Erdman and Moore edition. Blake's long diagonal and vertical cancellations do not always indicate deletions; they often show merely that a passage has reached a satisfactory stage of revision. Dividing lines and arabic numerals to indicate reordering are Blake's own markings. For the reader's convenience in comparing the drafts with finished poems, we have transcribed texts from Copy A of *Songs of Innocence and of Experience* (1794) because it was probably the first copy to be printed. No typographical setting, of course, can be identical with Blake's printed text, since his ornate embellishments often obliterate the arbitrary distinction between text and design.

Another purpose of the Notebook was to experiment with effective groupings of poems, such as the arrangement of related aphoristic verses under the general title "Several Questions Answered." We have followed Blake's directions for a grouping, marked to go "on 1 Plate"; this is a little miscellany of five short poems on various subjects which at one time were to be printed as a set.

In order to facilitate the reader's enjoyment of the poems as poems, we have arranged a selection of the better pieces in the Notebook under three chief headings: Vision, Love, and Art. In this selection of finished but unprinted poems, we have eliminated early drafts and, occasionally, what seem to be less inspired afterthoughts, so that what we present for each poem is the way it appeared at one effective stage of realization. Without the textual variants—interesting though they are—these poems can be appreciated as polished works of art. We have omitted most of the scurrilous and doggerel verses in which Blake complained about his friends, acquaintances, rivals, and pet antipathies, both because they have relatively little intrinsic merit and because they would require inordinate annotation. In the section on "Art and Artists" we have added the dedicatory poem, "To the Queen" which expresses some of Blake's most deeply held beliefs about the function of imaginative work. Though we have emphasized the aesthetic value of the Notebook above its biographical interest, we think our selections convey an accurate self-portrait of Blake the man. Despite the disputatious side that appears in the Notebook and in annotations of other people's books, the predominant impression of Blake that emerges from his private writings is of a happy and hard-working craftsman who often tempered his private outbursts of indignation with humor, fantasy, and gay irreverence.

To preserve the special character of the Notebook as the artist's workbook, intended for no eyes but his own, we have refrained from adding punctuation or capitalization of any kind. Poems are separated by ornamental rules.

I. WORKING DRAFTS

London

(Drafts, ca. 1792)

I wander thro each dirty street
Near where the dirty Thames does flow
mark
And ~~see~~ in every face I meet
Marks of weakness marks of woe

In every cry of every man
every infants cry of fear
In ~~every voice of every child~~
In every voice in every ban
mind manacles I hear
The ~~german~~ forgd ~~links I hear~~

How
~~But most~~ the chimney sweepers cry
Every blackning church appalls
~~Blackens oer the churches walls~~
And the hapless soldiers sigh
Runs in blood down palace walls

But most the midnight harlots curse
From every dismal street I hear
Weaves around the marriage hearse
And blasts the new born infants tear

thro wintry
But most ~~from every~~ streets I hear
How the midnight harlots curse
And blasts the new born infants tear
smites
And ~~hangs~~ with plagues the marriage hearse

But most the shrieks of youth I hear

But most thro midnight &c

How the youthful

London

(Printed version, 1794)

I wander thro' each charter'd street,
Near where the charter'd Thames does flow
And mark in every face I meet
Marks of weakness, marks of woe,

In every cry of every Man.
In every Infants cry of fear.
In every voice; in every ban.
The mind-forg'd manacles I hear

How the Chimney-sweepers cry
Every blackning Church appalls.
And the hapless Soldiers sigh
Runs in blood down Palace walls

But most thro' midnight streets I hear
How the youthful Harlots curse
Blasts the new born Infants tear
And blights with plagues the Marriage hearse

The Tyger

(Drafts, ca. 1792)

Tyger Tyger burning bright
In the forests of the night
What immortal hand or eye
~~Dare~~
~~Could~~ frame thy fearful symmetry

Burnt in
~~In what~~ distant deeps or skies
~~The cruel~~
~~Burnt the~~ fire of thine eyes
On what wings dare he aspire
What the hand dare sieze the fire

And what shoulder & what art
Could twist the sinews of thy heart
And when thy heart began to beat
What dread hand & what dread feet

~~Could fetch it from the furnace deep~~
~~And in thy horrid ribs dare steep~~
~~In the well of sanguine woe~~

~~In what clay & in what mould~~
~~Were thy eyes of fury rolld~~

Where **where**
~~What~~ the hammer ~~what~~ the chain
In what furnace was thy brain

dread grasp
What the anvil what ~~the arm arm grasp clasp~~
Dare
~~Could~~ its deadly terrors ~~clasp grasp~~ clasp

Tyger Tyger burning bright
In thee forests of the night
What immortal hand & eye
frame
Dare ~~form~~ thy fearful symmetry

(Trial Stanzas)

Burnt in distant deeps or skies
The cruel fire of thine eyes,
Could heart descend or wings aspire
What the hand dare sieze the fire

5 dare he ~~smile~~ ~~laugh~~
3 And ~~did he laugh~~ his work to see
~~ankle~~
~~What the shoulder what the knee~~
Dare
4 ~~Did~~ he who made the lamb make thee
1 When the stars drew down their spears
2 And waterd heaven with their tears

(Second Full Draft)

Tyger Tyger, burning bright.
In the forests of the night
What Immortal hand & eye
Dare frame thy fearful symmetry

And what shoulder & what art
Could twist the sinews of thy heart
And when thy heart began to beat
What dread hand & what dread feet

When the stars threw down their spears
And waterd heaven with their tears
Did he smile his work to see
Did he who made the lamb make thee

Tyger Tyger burning bright
In the forests of the night
What immortal hand & eye
Dare frame thy fearful symmetry

The Tyger

(Printed Version, 1794)

Tyger Tyger. burning bright.
In the forests of the night:
What immortal hand or eye.
Could frame thy fearful symmetry?

In what distant deeps or skies.
Burnt the fire of thine eyes?
On what wings dare he aspire?
What the hand, dare sieze the fire?

And what shoulder, & what art,
Could twist the sinews of thy heart?
And when thy heart began to beat.
What dread hand? & what dread feet?

What the hammer? what the chain,
In what furnace was thy brain?
What the anvil? what dread grasp.
Dare its deadly terrors clasp?

When the stars threw down their spears
And water'd heaven with their tears:
Did he smile his work to see?
Did he who made the Lamb make thee?

Tyger Tyger burning bright.
In the forests of the night:
What immortal hand or eye.
Dare frame thy fearful symmetry?

Infant Sorrow

(Drafts, of uncertain date)

My mother groand my father wept
Into the dangerous world I leapt
Helpless naked piping loud
Like a fiend hid in a cloud

Struggling in my fathers hands
Striving against my swaddling bands
Bound & weary I thought best
To sulk upon my mothers breast

soothd
~~smild~~
And I ~~grew~~ day after day
Till upon the ground I stray
smild
And I ~~grew~~ night after night
Seeking only for delight

~~But upon the nettly ground~~
~~No delight was to be found~~
And I saw before me shine
Clusters of the wandring vine
And many a lovely flower & tree
~~And beyond a mirtle tree~~
their
Stretchd ~~its~~ blossoms out to me

My father then
~~But many a~~
~~But a Priest~~ with holy look
their
In ~~his~~ hands a holy book
my
Pronounced curses on ~~his~~ head
And bound me in a mirtle shade
~~Who the fruit or blossoms shed~~
I beheld the Priests by night
They the blossoms
~~He embraced my mirtle bright~~
He
~~I beheld the Priests by day~~
Underneath the they
~~Where beneath my vines he lay~~
to
~~Like a serpents in the night~~
They blossoms
~~He embraced my mirtle bright~~
to holy men by
Like ~~a serpent in the~~ day
the they
Underneath ~~my~~ vines ~~he~~ lay

them their
So I smote ~~him~~ & ~~his~~ gore
Staind the roots my mirtle bore
But the time of youth is fled
And grey hairs are on my head

When I saw that rage was vain
lk
And to su~~ck~~ would nothing gain
Turning many a trick or wile
~~I began to so~~ ~~Seeking many an artful wile~~
I began to soothe & smile[1]

1. Blake indicates that this stanza is to be inserted after the stanza ending "To sulk upon my mother's breast" and before the stanza beginning "And I soothd day after day."

Infant Sorrow

(Printed version, 1794)

My mother groand! my father wept.
Into the dangerous world I leapt:
Helpless, naked. piping loud:
Like a fiend hid in a cloud.

Struggling in my fathers hands:
Striving against my swadling bands:
Bound and weary I thought best
To sulk upon my mothers breast.

II. A PROJECTED PLATE

O lapwing thou fliest around the heath
Nor seest the net that is spread beneath
Why dost thou not fly among the corn fields
They cannot spread nets where a harvest yields

An answer to the parson

Why of the sheep do you not learn peace
Because I dont want you to shear my fleece

[Experiment]

Thou hast a lap full of seed
And this is a fine country
Why dost thou not cast thy seed
And live in it merrily

Shall I cast it on the sand
And turn it into fruitful land
For on no other ground
Can I sow my seed
Without tearing up
Some stinking weed

Riches

The countless gold of a merry heart
The rubies & pearls of a loving eye
The indolent never can bring to the mart
Nor the secret hoard up in his treasury

If you trap the moment before its ripe
The tears of repentance youll certainly wipe
But if once you let the ripe moment go
You can never wipe off the tears of woe

III. VISION

Eternity

He who binds to himself a joy
Does the winged life destroy
But he who kisses the joy as it flies
Lives in eternity's sun rise

Since all the Riches of this World
May be gifts from the Devil & Earthly Kings
I should suspect that I worshipd the Devil
If I thankd my God for Worldly things

To God

If you have formed a Circle to go into
Go into it yourself & see how you would do

To Nobodaddy

Why art thou silent & invisible
Father of Jealousy
Why dost thou hide thyself in clouds
From every searching Eye

Why darkness & obscurity
In all thy words & laws
That none dare eat the fruit but from

The wily serpents jaws
Or is it because Secrecy
gains females loud applause

If it is True What the Prophets write
That the heathen Gods are all stocks & stones
Shall we for the sake of being Polite
Feed them with the juice of our marrow bones

And if Bezaleel & Aholiab drew
What the Finger of God pointed to their View
Shall we suffer the Roman & Grecian Rods
To compell us to worship them as Gods

They stole them from the Temple of the Lord
And Worshippd them that they might make Inspired
Art Abhorrd

The Wood & Stone were calld The Holy Things
And their Sublime Intent given to their Kings
All the Atonements of Jehovah spurnd
And Criminals to Sacrifices Turnd

The Hebrew Nation did not write it
Avarice & Chastity did shite it

Some Men created for destruction come
Into the World & make the World their home
Be they as Vile & Base as Eer they can
Theyll still be called The Worlds honest man

You dont believe I wont attempt to make ye
You are asleep I wont attempt to wake ye
Sleep on Sleep on while in your pleasant dreams
Of Reason you may drink of Lifes clear streams
Reason and Newton they are quite two things
For so the Swallow & the Sparrow sings
Reason says Miracle. Newton says Doubt
Aye thats the way to make all Nature out
Doubt Doubt & dont believe without experiment
That is the very thing that Jesus meant
When he said Only Believe Believe & Try
Try Try & never mind the Reason why

Mock on Mock on Voltaire Rousseau
Mock on Mock on tis all in vain
You throw the sand against the wind
And the wind blows it back again

And every sand becomes a Gem
Reflected in the beams divine

Blown back they blind the mocking Eye
But still in Israels paths they shine

The Atoms of Democritus
And Newtons Particles of light
And sands upon the Red sea shore
Where Israels tents do shine so bright

I will tell you what Joseph of Arimathea
Said to my Fairy was not it very queer
Pliny & Trajan what are You here
Come listen to Joseph of Arimathea
Listen patient & when Joseph has done
Twill make a fool laugh & a Fairy Fun
What can be done with such desperate Fools
Who follow after the Heathen Schools
I was standing by when Jesus died
What I calld Humility they calld Pride.[2]

Merlins prophecy

The harvest shall flourish in wintry weather
When two virginities meet together

The King & the Priest must be tied in a tether
Before two virginities can meet together

An ancient Proverb

Remove away that blackning church
Remove away that marriage hearse
Remove away that ——— of blood
Youll quite remove the ancient curse

The sword sung on the barren heath
The sickle in the fruitful field
The sword he sung a song of death
But could not make the sickle yield

Why should I care for the men of thames
Or the cheating waves of charterd streams
Or shrink at the little blasts of fear
That the hireling blows into my ear

2. Lines 7–10 have traditionally been included in *The Everlasting Gospel* as lines 21–24 of section "e."

Tho born on the cheating banks of Thames
Tho his waters bathed my infant limbs
The Ohio shall wash his stains from me
I was born a slave but I go to be free

Who will exchange his own fire side
For the stone of anothers door
Who will exchange his wheaten loaf
For the links of a dungeon floor

Fayette beheld the King & Queen
In curses & iron bound
But mute Fayette wept tear for tear
And guarded them around

O who would smile on the wintry seas
& Pity the stormy roar
Or who will exchange his new born child
For the dog at the wintry door

Let the Brothels of Paris be opened
With many an alluring dance
To awake the Physicians thro the city
Said the beautiful Queen of France

Then old Nobodaddy aloft
Farted & belchd & coughd
And said I love hanging & drawing & quartering
Every bit as well as war & slaughtering

Then he swore a great & solemn Oath
To kill the people I am loth
But If they rebel they must go to hell
They shall have a Priest & a passing bell

The King awoke on his couch of gold
As soon as he heard these tidings told
Arise & come both fife & drum
And the [*Famine*] shall eat both crust & crumb

The Queen of France just touched this Globe
And the Pestilence darted from her robe
But our good Queen quite grows to the ground
And a great many suckers grow all around

Great Men & Fools do often me Inspire
But the Greater Fool the Greater Liar

Her whole Life is an Epigram smack smooth & nobly pend
Platted quite neat to catch applause with a sliding noose at the end

---

The Errors of a Wise Man make your Rule
Rather than the Perfection of a Fool

Lacedemonian Instruction

Come hither my boy tell me what thou seest there
A fool tangled in a religious snare

Motto to the Songs of Innocence & of Experience

The Good are attracted by Mens perceptions
And think not for themselves
Till Experience teaches them to catch
And to cage the Fairies & Elves

And then the Knave begins to snarl
And the Hypocrite to howl
And all his good Friends shew their private ends
And the Eagle is known from the Owl

Anger & Wrath my bosom rends
I thought them the Errors of friends
But all my limbs with warmth glow
I find them the Errors of the foe

The Angel that presided oer my birth
Said Little creature formd of Joy & Mirth
Go love without the help of any Thing on Earth

I am no Homers Hero you all know
I profess not Generosity to a Foe
My Generosity is to my Friends
That for their Friendship I may make amends.
The Generous to Enemies promotes their Ends
And becomes the Enemy & Betrayer of his Friends

I heard an Angel singing
When the day was springing
Mercy Pity Peace
Is the worlds release

Thus he sung all day
Over the new mown hay
Till the sun went down
And haycocks looked brown

I heard a Devil curse
Over the heath & the furze
Mercy could be no more
If there was nobody poor

And pity no more could be
If all were as happy as we
At his curse the sun went down
And the heavens gave a frown

Down pourd the heavy rain
Over the new reapd grain
And Miseries increase
Is Mercy Pity Peace

Terror in the house does roar
But Pity stands before the door

Great things are done when Men & Mountains meet
This is not done by Jostling in the Street

When Klopstock England defied
Uprose terrible Blake in his pride
For old Nobodaddy aloft
Farted & Belched & coughd
Then swore a great oath that made heavn quake
And calld aloud to English Blake
Blake was giving his body ease
At Lambeth beneath the poplar trees
From his seat then started he
And turnd himself round three times three
The Moon at that sight blushd scarlet red
The stars threw down their cups & fled
And all the devils that were in hell
Answered with a ninefold yell
Klopstock felt the intripled turn
And all his bowels began to churn
And his bowels turned round three times three
And lockd in his soul with a ninefold key
That from his body it neer could be parted
Till to the last trumpet it was farted
Then again old Nobodaddy swore
He neer had seen such a thing before
Since Noah was shut in the ark
Since Eve first chose her hell fire spark

Since twas the fashion to go naked
Since the old anything was created
And so feeling he begd him to turn again
And ease poor Klopstock's nine fold pain
From pity then he redend round
And the Spell removed unwound
If Blake could do this when he rose up from shite
What might he not do if he sat down to write

Day

The Sun arises in the East
Clothd in robes of blood & gold
Swords & spears & wrath increast
All around his bosom rolld
Crownd with warlike fires & raging desires

Morning

To find the Western path
Right thro the Gates of Wrath
I urge my way
Sweet Mercy leads me on
With soft repentant moan
I see the break of day

The war of swords & spears
Melted by dewy tears
Exhales on high
The Sun is freed from fears
And with soft grateful tears
Ascends the sky

IV. LOVE: THE SEXES

What is it men in women do require
The lineaments of Gratified Desire
What is it women do in men require
The lineaments of Gratified Desire

Abstinence sows sand all over
The ruddy limbs & flaming hair
But Desire Gratified
Plants fruits of life & beauty there

In a wife I would desire
What in whores is always found
The lineaments of Gratified desire

When a Man has Married a Wife
he finds out whether
Her knees & elbows are only
glued together

A Woman Scaly & a Man all Hairy
Is such a Match as he who dares
Will find the Womans Scales scrape off the Mans Hairs

Why was Cupid a Boy
And why a boy was he
He should have been a Girl
For ought that I can see

For he shoots with his bow
And the Girl shoots with her Eye
And they both are merry & glad
And laugh when we do cry

And to make Cupid a Boy
Was the Cupid Girls mocking plan
For a boy cant interpret the thing
Till he is become a man

And then hes so piercd with care
And wounded with arrowy smarts
That the whole business of his life
Is to pick out the heads of the darts

Twas the Greeks love of war
Turnd Love into a Boy
And Woman into a Statue of Stone
And away fled every Joy

How to know Love from Deceit

Love to faults is always blind
Always is to joy inclind
Lawless wingd & unconfind
And breaks all chains from every mind

Deceit to secresy confind
Lawful cautious & refind
To every thing but interest blind
And forges fetters for the mind

The look of love alarms
Because tis filld with fire
But the look of soft deceit
Shall Win the lovers hire

Soft deceit & Idleness
These are Beautys sweetest dress

Silent Silent Night
Quench the holy light
Of thy torches bright

For possessd of Day
Thousand spirits stray
That sweet joys betray

Why should joys be sweet
Used with deceit
Nor with sorrows meet

But an honest joy
Does itself destroy
For a harlot coy

Are not the joys of morning sweeter
Than the joys of night
And are the vigrous joys of youth
Ashamed of the light

Let age & sickness silent rob
The vineyards in the night
But those who burn with vigrous youth
Pluck fruits before the light

V. LOVE: STORIES

The Fairy

Come hither my sparrows
My little arrows
If a tear or a smile
Will a man beguile
If an amorous delay
Clouds a sunshiny day
If the step of a foot
Smites the heart to its root
Tis the marriage ring
Makes each fairy a king

So a fairy sung
From the leaves I sprung
He leapd from the spray
To flee away
But in my hat caught
He soon shall be taught
Let him laugh let him cry
Hes my butterfly
For I've pulld out the Sting
Of the marriage ring

Never pain to tell thy love
Love that never told can be
For the gentle wind does move
Silently invisibly

I told my love I told my love
I told her all my heart
Trembling cold in ghastly fears
Ah she doth depart

Soon as she was gone from me
A traveller came by
Silently invisibly
O was no deny

I feard the fury of my wind
Would blight all blossoms fair & true
And my sun it shind & shind
And my wind it never blew

But a blossom fair or true
Was not found on any tree
For all blossoms grew & grew
Fruitless false tho fair to see

I saw a chapel all of gold
That none did dare to enter in
And many weeping stood without
Weeping mourning and worshipping

I saw a serpent rise between
The white pillars of the door
And he forcd & forcd & forcd
Down the golden hinges tore

And along the pavement sweet
Set with pearls & rubies bright
All his slimy length he drew
Till upon the altar white

Vomiting his poison out
On the bread & on the wine
So I turnd into a sty
And laid me down among the swine

I laid me down upon a bank
Where love lay sleeping
I heard among the rushes dank
Weeping Weeping

Then I went to the heath & the wild
To the thistles & thorns of the waste
And they told me how they were beguild
Driven out & compeld to be chaste

I asked a thief to steal me a peach
He turned up his eyes
I askd a lithe lady to lie her down
Holy & meek she cries

As soon as I went
An angel came.
He winkd at the thief
And smild at the dame—
And without one word spoke
Had a peach from the tree
And twixt earnest & joke
Enjoyd the lady.[3]

Soft Snow

I walked abroad in a snowy day
I askd the soft snow with me to play
She playd & she melted in all her prime
And the winter calld it a dreadful crime

An old maid early eer I knew
Ought but the love that on me grew
And now Im coverd oer & oer
And wish that I had been a Whore

O I cannot cannot find
The undaunted courage of a Virgin Mind
For Early I in love was crost
Before my flower of love was lost

---

3. Our text is from an earlier draft of this poem which we prefer on aesthetic grounds. Blake corrected "spoke" in line 9 to "said" and revised line 11 to read "And still as a maid." That he preferred this revised version is indicated by the fact that he transcribed it as a fair copy, signed "W Blake Lambeth 1796." In this version there is a stanza break between the last two quatrains.

Grown old in Love from Seven till Seven times Seven
I oft have wished for Hell for Ease from Heaven

The Washer Womans Song

I washd them out & washd them in
And they told me it was a great Sin

A cradle song

Sleep Sleep beauty bright
Dreaming oer the joys of night
Sleep Sleep: in thy sleep
Little sorrows sit & weep

Sweet Babe in thy face
Soft desires I can trace
Secret joys & secret smiles
Little pretty infant wiles

As thy softest limbs I feel
Smiles as of the morning steal
Oer thy cheek & oer thy breast
Where thy little heart does rest

O the cunning wiles that creep
In thy little heart asleep
When thy little heart does wake
Then the dreadful lightnings break

From thy cheek & from thy eye
Oer the youthful harvests nigh
Infant wiles & infant smiles
Heaven & Earth of peace beguiles

To my Mirtle

To a lovely mirtle bound
Blossoms showring all around
O how sick & weary I
Underneath my mirtle lie
Why should I be bound to thee
O my lovely mirtle tree

My Spectre around me night & day
Like a Wild beast guards my way
My Emanation far within
Weeps incessantly for my Sin

A Fathomless & boundless deep
There we wander there we weep
On the hungry craving wind
My Spectre follows thee behind

He scents thy footsteps in the snow
Wheresoever thou dost go
Thro the wintry hail & rain
When wilt thou return again

Dost thou not in Pride & Scorn
Fill with tempests all my morn
And with jealousies & fears
Fill my pleasant nights with tears

Seven of my sweet loves thy knife
Has bereaved of their life
Their marble tombs I built with tears
And with cold & shuddering fears

Seven more loves weep night & day
Round the tombs where my loves lay
And seven more loves attend each night
Around my couch with torches bright

And seven more Loves in my bed
Crown with wine my mournful head
Pitying & forgiving all
Thy transgressions great & small

When wilt thou return & view
My loves & them to life renew
When wilt thou return & live
When wilt thou pity as I forgive

Never Never I return
Still for Victory I burn
Living thee alone Ill have
And when dead Ill be thy Grave

Thro the Heaven & Earth & Hell
Thou shalt never never quell
I will fly & thou pursue
Night & Morn the flight renew

Till I turn from Female Love
And root up the Infernal Grove
I shall never worthy be
To Step into Eternity

And to end thy cruel mocks
Annihilate thee on the rocks
And another form create
To be subservient to my Fate

Let us agree to give up Love
And root up the infernal grove
Then shall we return & see
The worlds of happy Eternity

& Throughout all Eternity
I forgive you you forgive me
As our Dear Redeemer said
This the Wine & this the Bread

[Related Stanzas]

Oer my Sins Thou sit & moan
Hast thou no sins of thy own
Oer my Sins thou sit & weep
And lull thy own Sins fast asleep

What transgressions I commit
Are for thy Transgressions fit
They thy Harlots thou their Slave
And my Bed becomes their Grave

Poor pale pitiable form
That I follow in a Storm
Iron tears & groans of lead
Bind around my akeing head

And let us go to the highest downs
With many pleasing wiles
The Woman that does not love your Frowns
Will never embrace your smiles

The Birds

He. Where thou dwellest in what Grove
Tell me Fair one tell me love
Where thou thy charming Nest dost build
O thou pride of every field

She. Yonder stands a lonely tree
There I live & mourn for thee
Morning drinks my silent tear
And evening winds my sorrows bear

He. O thou Summers harmony
I have livd & mournd for thee
Each day I mourn along the wood
And night hath heard my sorrows loud

She. Dost thou truly long for me
And am I thus sweet to thee
Sorrow now is at an End
O my Lover & my Friend

He. Come on wings of joy well fly
To where my Bower hangs on high
Come & make thy calm retreat
Among green leaves & blossoms sweet

VI. ART AND ARTISTS

Now Art has lost its mental Charms
France shall subdue the World in Arms
So spoke an Angel at my birth
Then said Descend thou upon Earth
Renew the Arts on Britains Shore
And France shall fall down & adore
With works of Art their Armies meet
And War shall sink beneath thy feet
But if thy Nation Arts refuse
And if they scorn the immortal Muse
France shall the arts of Peace restore
And save thee from the Ungrateful shore

Spirit who lovst Brittannias Isle
Round which the Fiends of Commerce smile.[4]

---

4. This poem trails off, unfinished.

To the Queen[5]

The Door of Death is made of Gold,
That Mortal Eyes cannot behold;
But, when the Mortal Eyes are clos'd,
And cold and pale the Limbs repos'd,
The Soul awakes; and, wond'ring, sees
In her mild Hand the golden Key
The Grave is Heaven's golden Gate,
And rich and poor around it wait;
O Shepherdess of England's Fold,
Behold this Gate of Pearl and Gold!

To dedicate to England's Queen
The Visions that my Soul has seen,
And, by Her kind permission, bring
What I have borne on solemn Wing
From the vast regions of the Grave,
Before Her Throne my Wings I wave;
Bowing before my Sov'reign's Feet,
"The Grave produc'd these Blossoms sweet
In mild repose from Earthly strife;
The Blossoms of Eternal Life!"

The Caverns of the Grave Ive seen
And these I shewd to Englands Queen
But now the Caves of Hell I view
Who shall I dare to shew them to
What mighty Soul in Beautys form
Shall dauntless View the Infernal Storm
Egremonts Countess can controll
The flames of Hell that round me roll
If she refuse I still go on
Till the Heavens & Earth are gone
Still admird by Noble minds
Followd by Envy on the winds
Reengravd Time after Time
Ever in their youthful prime
My Designs unchangd remain
Time may rage but rage in vain
For above Times troubled Fountains
On the Great Atlantic Mountains
In my Golden House on high
There they Shine Eternally

---

5. Dedication to Blake's designs for Robert Blair's *The Grave* (1808); not in Notebook.

I rose up at the dawn of day
Get thee away get thee away
Prayst thou for Riches away away
This is the Throne of Mammon grey

Said I this sure is very odd
I took it to be the Throne of God
For every Thing besides I have
It is only for Riches that I can crave

I have Mental Joy & Mental Health
And Mental Friends & Mental wealth
Ive a Wife I love & that loves me
Ive all But Riches Bodily

I am in Gods presence night & day
And he never turns his face away
The accuser of sins by my side does stand
And he holds my money bag in his hand

For my worldly things God makes him pay
And hed pay for more if to him I would pray
And so you may do the worst you can do
Be assurd Mr Devil I wont pray to you

Then If for Riches I must not Pray
God knows I little of Prayers need say
So as a Church is known by its Steeple
If I pray it must be for other People

He says if I do not worship him for a God
I shall eat coarser food & go worse shod
So as I dont value such things as these
You must do Mr Devil just as God please

You say their Pictures well Painted be
And yet they are Blockheads you all agree
Thank God I never was sent to school
To be Flogd into following the Style of a Fool

Blakes apology for his Catalogue

Having given great offence by writing in Prose
Ill write in Verse as soft as Bartolloze
Some blush at what others can see no crime in
But nobody sees any harm in Rhyming
Dryden in Rhyme cries Milton only plannd
Every Fool shook his bells throughout the land

Tom Cooke cut Hogarth down with his clean graving
Thousands of Connoisseurs with joy ran raving
Thus Hayley on his Toilette seeing the sope
Cries Homer is very much improvd by Pope
Some say Ive given great Provision to my foes
And that now I lead my false friends by the nose
Flaxman & Stothard smelling a sweet savour
Cry Blakified drawing spoils painter & Engraver
While I looking up to my Umbrella
Resolvd to be a very contrary fellow
Cry looking quite from Skumference to Center
No one can finish so high as the original Inventor
Thus Poor Schiavonetti died of the Cromek
A thing thats tied around the Examiners neck
This is my sweet apology to my friends
That I may put them in mind of their latter Ends

English Encouragement of Art[1]

If you mean to Please Every body you will
Set to work both Ignorance & skill
For a great multitude are Ignorant
And skill to them seems raving & rant
Like putting oil & water into a lamp
Twill make a great splutter with smoke & damp
For there is no use as it seems to me
Of lighting a Lamp when you dont wish to see

The only Man that eer I knew
Who did not make me almost spew
Was Fuseli he was both Turk & Jew
And so dear Christian Friends how do you do

Madman I have been calld Fool they call thee
I wonder which they Envy Thee or Me

The Pickering Manuscript

This booklet of ten handwritten poems has no accompanying illustrations, and eight of the texts appear to be fair copies. Presumably the poems were written out in a form suitable to be read by some acquaintance, though there is no evidence that they were intended for publication in conventional printing. The manuscript is known by the name of its owner in 1866, B. M. Pickering. As fair copy, it has a different status from Blake's private Notebook, in which the texts are working drafts. Several of the Pickering

1. Blake's extensive revisions, emphasizing puns and word coinages, obsure the plain sense of this early draft.

ballads exist in other versions: there are working drafts of "The Golden Net" and "The Grey Monk" in the Notebook, and stanzas from the latter also occur in the prefatory poem in *Jerusalem* 52. The fact that lines 21–22 of "Mary" appeared in a different poem contained in a letter to Butts of August 16, 1803, has been taken as evidence of the date of the manuscript, but since lines 125–28 of "Auguries of Innocence" are also employed as lines 101–3 of section 4 of "The Everlasting Gospel" (p. 368 in this edition), probably a much later work, the basis for conjecture is not solid. Most authorities agree, however, that these poems were written between 1801 and 1805 and were transcribed by 1807.

As a group of poems that are mostly ballads, this collection invites comparison with the Wordsworth-Coleridge *Lyrical Ballads* (1798), though Blake's poems are more distinctly allegorical, even in comparison with his own earlier lyrics. According to Frye, the ballads are designed "to explore the relationship between innocence and experience instead of merely presenting their contrast as the two engraved sets do"; the longer poems, "Auguries of Innocence" and "The Mental Traveller" in particular, tend to bear out this theory. The fullest commentary on the entire collection is by Hazard Adams, *William Blake: A Reading of the Shorter Poems* (1963).

All but two of the poems are arranged in quatrains rhyming either in the second and fourth lines or in couplets; the couplets of "The Golden Net" and "Auguries of Innocence" also tend to fall into quatrains. The fact that Blake issued some nineteen copies of his *Songs* before he discovered an order that satisfied him may encourage an editor or reader to consider alternate arrangements of the Pickering poems. Thematic and formal affinities would be emphasized in the following reordering: "The Mental Traveller," "The Crystal Cabinet," "The Golden Net," "The Land of Dreams," "Mary," "Long John Brown & Little Mary Bell," "William Bond," "The Grey Monk," "The Smile," and "Auguries of Innocence." Two of Blake's major editors, John Sampson in 1905 and Erdman in 1965, have proposed alternate arrangements for the couplets of "Auguries of Innocence," though many readers will continue to prefer the impression of inspired heterogeneity made by the original order of both the collection as a whole and of "Auguries" in particular.

As a copy text we have consulted the facsimile of the manuscript published by the Pierpont Morgan Library, New York, with an introduction by Charles Ryskamp (1972).

The Smile

There is a Smile of Love,
And there is a Smile of Deceit,
And there is a Smile of Smiles
In which these two Smiles meet.

And there is a Frown of Hate,
And there is a Frown of disdain,
And there is a Frown of Frowns
Which you strive to forget in vain,

For it sticks in the Heart's deep Core
And it sticks in the deep Back bone;
And no Smile that ever was smild,
But only one Smile alone,

That betwixt the Cradle & Grave
It only once Smild can be;
But, when it once is Smild,
There's an end to all Misery.

The Golden Net

Three Virgins at the break of day:
"Whither, young Man, whither away?
Alas for woe! alas for woe!"
They cry, & tears for ever flow.
The one was Clothd in flames of fire,
The other Clothd in iron wire,
The other Clothd in tears & sighs
Dazling bright before my Eyes.
They bore a Net of golden twine
To hang upon the Branches fine.
Pitying I wept to see the woe
That Love & Beauty undergo,
To be consumd in burning Fires
And in ungratified desires,
And in tears clothd Night & day
Melted all my Soul away.
When they saw my Tears, a Smile
That did Heaven itself beguile,
Bore the Golden Net aloft
As on downy Pinions soft
Over the Morning of my day.
Underneath the Net I stray:
Now intreating Burning Fire,
Now intreating Iron Wire,
Now intreating Tears & Sighs.
O when will the morning rise?

The Mental Traveller

I traveld thro' a Land of Men,
A Land of Men & Women too,
And heard & saw such dreadful things
As cold Earth wanderers never knew.

For there the Babe is born in joy
That was begotten in dire woe;
Just as we Reap in joy the fruit
Which we in bitter tears did sow.

And if the Babe is born a Boy
He's given to a Woman Old,
Who nails him down upon a rock,
Catches his shrieks in cups of gold.[1]

She binds iron thorns around his head,
She pierces both his hands & feet,
She cuts his heart out at his side
To make it feel both cold & heat.

Her fingers number every Nerve,
Just as a Miser counts his gold;
She lives upon his shrieks & cries,
And she grows young as he grows old.

Till he becomes a bleeding youth,
And she becomes a Virgin bright;
Then he rends up his Manacles
And binds her down for his delight.

He plants himself in all her Nerves,
Just as a Husbandman his mould;
And she becomes his dwelling place
And Garden fruitful seventy fold.

An aged Shadow, soon he fades,
Wandring round an Earthly Cot,
Full filled all with gems & gold
Which he by industry had got.

And these are the gems of the Human Soul,
The rubies & pearls of a lovesick eye,
The countless gold of the akeing heart,
The martyr's groan & the lover's sigh.

They are his meat, they are his drink;
He feeds the Beggar & the Poor
And the wayfaring Traveller:
For ever open is his door.

His grief is their eternal joy;
They make the roofs & walls to ring;
Till from the fire on the hearth
A little Female Babe does spring.

1. In Revelation 17:4 the Whore of Babylon holds a golden cup full of abominations, the blood of saints and martyrs (17:6). In Norse mythology Loki is bound to a rock and a serpent drips poison on his head; his wife catches it in a cup but Loki suffers when she must empty it. As is the case with many motifs in this poem—for example, the cyclical age-changes—there are no exact parallels either in Blake or elsewhere. For commentaries, see John H. Sutherland, *ELH* 22 (1955), 136–47; Morton D. Paley, *Studies in Romanticism* 1 (1962), 97–104; Martin K. Nurmi, *Studies in Romanticism* 3 (1964), 109–17; Gerald E. Enscoe, *Papers on Language and Literature* 4 (1968), 400–413.

And she is all of solid fire
And gems & gold, that none his hand
Dares stretch to touch her Baby form,
Or wrap her in his swaddling-band.

But She comes to the Man she loves,
If young or old, or rich or poor;
They soon drive out the aged Host,
A Beggar at another's door.

He wanders weeping far away,
Untill some other take him in;
Oft blind & age-bent, sore distrest,
Untill he can a Maiden win.

And to allay his freezing Age
The Poor Man takes her in his arms;
The Cottage fades before his sight,
The Garden & its lovely Charms.

The Guests are scatterd thro' the land,
For the Eye altering alters all;
The Senses roll themselves in fear,
And the flat Earth[2] becomes a Ball.

The Stars, Sun, Moon, all shrink away:
A desart vast without a bound,
And nothing left to eat or drink,
And a dark desart all around.

The honey of her Infant lips,
The bread & wine of her sweet smile,
The wild game of her roving Eye,
Does him to Infancy beguile.

For as he eats & drinks he grows
Younger & younger every day;
And on the desart wild they both
Wander in terror & dismay.

Like the wild Stag she flees away,
Her fear plants many a thicket wild;
While he pursues her night & day,
By various arts of Love beguild,

2. In an important passage in *Milton* 15:21–35 Blake explains that the image of a globular earth, as opposed to an "infinite plane," is characteristic of the fall from Eternity.

By various arts of Love & Hate,
Till the wide desart planted o'er
With Labyrinths of wayward Love,
Where roam the Lion, Wolf & Boar;

Till he becomes a wayward Babe,
And she a weeping Woman Old.
Then many a Lover wanders here;
The Sun & Stars are nearer rolld.

The trees bring forth sweet Extacy
To all who in the desart roam;
Till many a City there is Built,
And many a pleasant Shepherd's home.

But when they find the frowning Babe,
Terror strikes thro' the region wide:
They cry "The Babe! the Babe is Born!"
And flee away on Every side.

For who dare touch the frowning form,
His arm is wither'd to its root;
Lions, Boars, Wolves, all howling flee,
And every Tree does shed its fruit.

And none can touch that frowning form,
Except it be a Woman Old;
She nails him down upon the Rock,
And all is done as I have told.

The Land of Dreams

"Awake, awake, my little Boy!
Thou wast thy Mother's only joy;
Why dost thou weep in thy gentle sleep?
Awake! thy Father does thee keep."

"O, what Land is the Land of Dreams?
What are its Mountains & what are its Streams?
O Father, I saw my Mother there,
Among the Lillies by waters fair.

"Among the Lambs, clothed in white,
She walk'd with her Thomas in sweet delight.
I wept for joy, like a dove I mourn;
O! when shall I again return?"

"Dear Child, I also by pleasant Streams
Have wander'd all Night in the Land of Dreams;
But tho calm & warm the waters wide,
I could not get to the other side."

"Father, O Father! what do we here
In this Land of unbelief & fear?
The Land of Dreams is better far,
Above the light of the Morning Star."

Mary

Sweet Mary, the first time she ever was there,
Came into the Ball room among the Fair;
The young Men & Maidens around her throng,
And these are the words upon every tongue:

"An Angel is here from the heavenly Climes,
Or again does return the Golden times.
Her eyes outshine every brilliant ray,
She opens her lips—'tis the Month of May."

Mary moves in soft beauty & conscious delight
To augment with sweet smiles all the joys of the Night,
Nor once blushes to own to the rest of the Fair
That sweet Love & Beauty are worthy our care.

In the Morning the Villagers rose with delight
And repeated with pleasure the joys of the night;
And Mary rose among Friends to be free,
But no Friend from henceforward thou, Mary, shalt see.

Some said she was proud, some calld her a whore,
And some when she passed by shut to the door;
A damp cold came o'er her, her blushes all fled;
Her lillies & roses are blighted & shed.

"O, why was I born with a different Face?
Why was I not born like this Envious Race?
Why did Heaven adorn me with bountiful hand,
And then set me down in an envious Land?

"To be weak as a Lamb & smooth as a dove,
And not to raise Envy, is calld Christian Love;
But if you raise Envy your Merit's to blame
For planting such spite in the weak & the tame.

"I will humble my Beauty, I will not dress fine,
I will keep from the Ball, & my Eyes shall not shine;
And if any Girl's Lover forsakes her for me,
I'll refuse him my hand & from Envy be free."

She went out in Morning attird plain & neat;
"Proud Mary's gone Mad," said the Child in the Street;
She went out in Morning in plain neat attire,
And came home in Evening bespatterd with mire.

She trembled & wept, sitting on the Bed side;
She forgot it was Night & she trembled & cried;
She forgot it was Night, she forgot it was Morn;
Her soft Memory imprinted with Faces of Scorn,

With Faces of Scorn & with Eyes of disdain
Like foul Fiends inhabiting Mary's mild Brain;
She remembers no Face like the Human Divine.
All Faces have Envy, sweet Mary, but thine:

And thine is a Face of sweet Love in despair,
And thine is a Face of mild sorrow & care,
And thine is a Face of wild terror & fear
That shall never be quiet till laid on its bier.

The Crystal Cabinet

The Maiden caught me in the Wild,
Where I was dancing merrily;
She put me into her Cabinet
And Lock'd me up with a golden Key.

This Cabinet is formd of Gold
And Pearl & crystal shining bright,
And within it opens into a World
And a little lovely Moony Night.

Another England there I saw,
Another London with its Tower,
Another Thames & other Hills,
And another pleasant Surrey Bower.

Another Maiden like herself,
Translucent, lovely, shining clear;
Threefold[3] each in the other closd—
O, what a pleasant trembling fear!

3. "Threefold," though associated pleasantly with "soft Beulah's night" in the epistolary poem to Butts of November 22, 1802 (p. 462), is here employed repeatedly in a sinister context.

O, what a smile! a threefold Smile
Filld me, that like a flame I burnd:
I bent to Kiss the lovely Maid,
And found a Threefold Kiss returnd.

I strove to sieze the inmost Form,
With ardor fierce & hands of flame,
But burst the Crystal Cabinet,
And like a Weeping Babe became—

A weeping Babe upon the wild,
And Weeping Woman pale reclind;
And in the outward air again
I filld with woes the passing Wind.

The Grey Monk

"I die, I die!" the Mother said,
"My Children die for lack of Bread.
What more has the merciless Tyrant said?"
The Monk sat down on the Stony Bed.

The blood red ran from the Grey Monk's side,
His hands & feet were wounded wide,
His Body bent, his arms & knees
Like to the roots of ancient trees.

His eye was dry, no tear could flow;
A hollow groan first spoke his woe.
He trembled & shudder'd upon the Bed;
At length with a feeble cry he said:

"When God commanded this hand to write
In the studious hours of deep midnight,
He told me the writing I wrote should prove
The Bane of all that on Earth I lovd.

"My Brother starvd between two Walls,
His Children's Cry my Soul appalls;
I mockd at the wrack & griding chain,
My bent body mocks their torturing pain.

"Thy Father drew his sword in the North,
With his thousands strong he marched forth;
Thy Brother has arm'd himself in Steel
To avenge the wrongs thy Children feel.

"But vain the Sword & vain the Bow,
They never can work War's overthrow.
The Hermit's Prayer & the Widow's tear
Alone can free the World from fear.

"For a Tear is an Intellectual Thing,
And a Sigh is the Sword of an Angel King,
And the bitter groan of the Martyr's woe
Is an Arrow from the Almightie's Bow.

"The hand of Vengeance found the Bed
To which the Purple Tyrant fled;
The iron hand crushd the Tyrant's head
And became a Tyrant in his Stead."

Auguries of Innocence

To see a World in a Grain of Sand
And a Heaven in a Wild Flower:
Hold Infinity in the palm of your hand
And Eternity in an hour.
A Robin Red breast in a Cage
Puts all Heaven in a Rage.
A dove house filld with doves & Pigeons
Shudders Hell thro all its regions.
A dog starvd at his Master's Gate
Predicts the ruin of the State.
A Horse misusd upon the Road
Calls to Heaven for Human blood.
Each outcry of the hunted Hare
A fibre from the Brain does tear.
A Skylark wounded in the wing,
A Cherubim does cease to sing.
The Game Cock clipd & armd for fight
Does the Rising Sun affright.
Every Wolf's & Lion's howl
Raises from Hell a Human Soul.
The wild deer wandring here & there
Keeps the Human Soul from Care.
The Lamb misusd breeds Public strife
And yet forgives the Butcher's Knife.
The Bat that flits at close of Eve
Has left the Brain that won't Believe.
The Owl that calls upon the Night
Speaks the Unbeliever's fright.

He who shall hurt the little Wren
Shall never be belovd by Men.
He who the Ox to wrath has movd
Shall never be by Woman lovd.
The wanton Boy that kills the Fly
Shall feel the Spider's enmity.
He who torments the Chafer's sprite
Weaves a Bower in endless Night.
The Catterpiller on the Leaf
Repeats to thee thy Mother's grief.
Kill not the Moth nor Butterfly,
For the Last Judgment draweth nigh.
He who shall train the Horse to War
Shall never pass the Polar Bar.
The Begger's Dog & Widow's Cat:
Feed them & thou wilt grow fat.
The Gnat that sings his Summer's song
Poison gets from Slander's tongue.
The poison of the Snake & Newt
Is the sweat of Envy's Foot.
The Poison of the Honey Bee
Is the Artist's Jealousy.
The Prince's Robes & Beggar's Rags
Are Toadstools on the Miser's Bags.
A truth that's told with bad intent
Beats all the Lies you can invent.
It is right it should be so:
Man was made for Joy & Woe,
And when this we rightly know
Thro the World we safely go.
Joy & Woe are woven fine,
A Clothing for the Soul divine;
Under every grief & pine
Runs a joy with silken twine.
The Babe is more than swadling Bands;
Throughout all these Human Lands.
Tools were made, & Born were hands,
Every Farmer Understands.
Every Tear from Every Eye
Becomes a Babe in Eternity;
This is caught by Females bright
And returnd to its own delight.
The Bleat, the Bark, Bellow & Roar,
Are Waves that Beat on Heaven's Shore.
The Babe that weeps the Rod beneath
Writes Revenge in realms of death.
The Beggar's Rags, fluttering in Air,
Does to Rags the Heavens tear.

The Soldier, armd with Sword & Gun,
Palsied strikes the Summer's Sun.
The poor Man's Farthing is worth more
Than all the Gold on Afric's Shore.
One Mite wrung from the Labrer's hands
Shall buy & sell the Miser's Lands,
Or if protected from on high
Does that whole Nation sell & buy.
He who mocks the Infant's Faith
Shall be mockd in Age & Death.
He who shall teach the Child to Doubt
The rotting Grave shall ne'er get out.
He who respects the Infant's faith
Triumphs over Hell & Death.
The Child's Toys & the Old Man's Reasons
Are the Fruits of the Two seasons.
The Questioner who sits so sly
Shall never know how to Reply;
He who replies to words of Doubt
Doth put the Light of Knowledge out.
The Strongest Poison ever known
Came from Caesar's Laurel Crown.
Nought can deform the Human Race
Like to the Armour's iron brace.
When Gold & Gems adorn the Plow
To peaceful Arts shall Envy Bow.
A Riddle or the Cricket's Cry
Is to Doubt a fit Reply.
The Emmet's Inch & Eagle's Mile
Make Lame Philosophy to smile.
He who Doubts from what he sees
Will ne'er Believe, do what you Please.
If the Sun & Moon should doubt,
They'd immediately Go out.
To be in a Passion you Good may do,
But no Good if a Passion is in you.
The Whore & Gambler, by the State
Licenc'd, build that Nation's Fate.
The Harlot's cry from Street to Street
Shall weave Old England's winding Sheet.
The Winner's Shout, the Loser's Curse,
Dance before dead England's Hearse.
Every Night & every Morn
Some to Misery are Born.
Every Morn & every Night
Some are Born to sweet delight.
Some are Born to sweet delight,
Some are Born to Endless Night.

We are led to Believe a Lie
When we see not Thro the Eye,
Which was Born in a Night to perish in a Night,[4]
When the Soul Slept in Beams of Light.
God Appears & God is Light
To those poor Souls who dwell in Night,
But does a Human Form Display
To those who Dwell in Realms of day.

Long John Brown & Little Mary Bell

Little Mary Bell had a Fairy in a Nut;
Long John Brown had the Devil in his Gut.
Long John Brown lovd Little Mary Bell,
And the Fairy drew the Devil into the Nut-shell.

Her Fairy Skipd out & her Fairy Skipd in;
He laughd at the Devil saying "Love is a Sin."
The Devil he raged & the Devil he was wroth,
And the Devil enterd into the Young Man's broth.

He was soon in the Gut of the loving Young Swain,
For John eat & drank to drive away Love's pain;
But all he could do he grew thinner & thinner,
Tho he eat & drank as much as ten Men for his dinner.

Some said he had a Wolf in his stomach day & night,
Some said he had the Devil & they guessd right;
The fairy skipd about in his Glory, Joy & Pride,
And he laughd at the Devil till poor John Brown died.

Then the Fairy skipd out of the old Nut shell,
And woe & alack for Pretty Mary Bell!
For the Devil crept in when the Fairy skipd out,
And there goes Miss Bell with her fusty old Nut.

William Bond

I wonder whether the Girls are mad,
And I wonder whether they mean to kill,
And I wonder if William Bond will die,
For assuredly he is very ill.

He went to Church in a May morning
Attended by Fairies, one, two & three;
But the Angels of Providence drove them away,
And he returnd home in Misery.

4. Cf. Jonah 4:10: "Thou hast had pity on the gourd . . . which came up in a night, and perished in a night."

He went not out to the Field nor Fold,
He went not out to the Village nor Town,
But he came home in a black, black cloud,
And took to his Bed & there lay down.

And an Angel of Providence at his Feet,
And an Angel of Providence at his Head,
And in the midst a Black, Black Cloud,
And in the midst the Sick Man on his Bed.

And on his Right hand was Mary Green,
And on his Left hand was his Sister Jane,
And their tears fell thro the black, black Cloud
To drive away the sick man's pain.

"O William, if thou dost another Love,
Dost another Love better than poor Mary,
Go & take that other to be thy Wife,
And Mary Green shall her Servant be."

"Yes, Mary, I do another Love,
Another I Love far better than thee,
And Another I will have for my Wife;
Then what have I to do with thee?

"For thou art Melancholy, Pale,
And on thy Head is the cold Moon's shine,
But she is ruddy & bright as day,
And the sun beams dazzle from her eyne."

Mary trembled & Mary chilld
And Mary fell down on the right hand floor,
That William Bond & his Sister Jane
Scarce could recover Mary more.

When Mary woke & found her Laid
On the Right hand of her William dear—
On the Right hand of his loved Bed,
And saw her William Bond so near—

The Fairies that fled from William Bond
Danced around her Shining Head;
They danced over the Pillow white,
And the Angels of Providence left the Bed.

I thought Love livd in the hot sun shine,
But O, he lives in the Moony light!
I thought to find Love in the heat of day,
But sweet Love is the Comforter of Night.

Seek Love in the Pity of others' Woe,
In the gentle relief of another's care,
In the darkness of night & the winter's snow,
In the naked & outcast, Seek Love there.

The Four Zoas

Blake's first work of epic proportions was entitled *Vala, Or The Death and Judgement of the Ancient Man, A Dream of Nine Nights* (1797). This work, which was probably intended to be presented as an illustrated manuscript rather than as a printed illuminated book, was by 1797 sufficiently polished for Blake to start making a final copy in elegant "copperplate" script. When later he decided to make drastic revisions, he used discarded proof sheets from his commercial project (1796–97) of engraving Edward Young's *Night Thoughts*. Along with the text, the pictures evolved in their own way, and the manuscript contains both developed drawings and crude sketches. Perhaps about 1805 this work, retitled *The Four Zoas: The Torments of Love & Jealousy in the Death and Judgement of Albion the Ancient Man*, had been substantially rewritten, and there is no indication that Blake ever considered it finished. Even an inexperienced reader who looks at the facsimile of the manuscript edited by G. E. Bentley, Jr., can appreciate both the difficulty of establishing an accurate and readable text and the fascination, beauty, and power of its myth and language. Some conception of the richness of this work is conveyed by the brief selections included in the present edition. Our text is based on our studies of the original manuscript, the Bentley facsimile, and transcriptions by Bentley, Keynes, and Erdman.

Though some material also appears in *Milton* and *Jerusalem*, the poem *Vala* or *The Four Zoas* is an independently conceived work of quite different scope and purpose. It is an attempt to coordinate and extend the separate stories told in Blake's earlier books into one grand story of mankind, from his origins to the end of time. As in the earlier prophecies, the action seems to take place simultaneously within the consciousness of the human race over the course of history and within the mind of each individual during his lifetime. Organized into nine "Nights" on the model of Young's *Night Thoughts*, it depicts the nightmare of a cosmic man, now fallen into disunity, who once embodied the divine and the human, male and female, subject and object, mind and nature. The cause of the fall is man's capitulation to his feminine portion, the deceptive goddess Vala, who represents Nature and the object of sexual desire. Her name and the veil she wears suggest the "veil" of material appearance that obscures spiritual reality. As the counterpart or object of man's sexual and emotional needs, Vala has an essential role in life, but as the controller of man's total personality, or as an obsession, she causes man's ruin. Like the Lambeth books, *Vala* presents an effective myth of the fall of mankind, but the myth of his regeneration seems to have been as elusive for Blake as for other poets.

In the process of revising *Vala* and renaming it *The Four Zoas*, Blake named The Man "Albion," the traditional ancestor of England, and attributed this fall to a war among his four primary attributes; at the same time he introduced the Christian theme of salvation as a possibility for Albion.

Cosmic man, lying unconscious in England, is dominated by his "Zoas," Blake's English plural for a word (already plural in Greek) which in the Authorized Version is translated "beasts" in Revelation 4:6, though the Hebrew equivalent is translated "living creatures" in Ezekiel 1:5, 19–23. Both of these Biblical passages describe the four beings who surround God's presence. From this hint, as suggested in postbiblical iconography, Blake developed a conception of man's fourfold nature. Humanity should be composed of wisdom, love, imagination, and strength, but in the fallen state it is torn apart by hypocritical morality, lust, rage, confused fantasy, and chaotic weakness. The personifications of cold reason, wild emotion, misguided imagination, and weakened instinct behave like Titans with fallible human personalities. Three of the four have been introduced, with their allegorical functions, in the minor prophecies; here for the first time we catch a glimpse of the unfallen natures and the proper interrelationship of the rational Urizen, the emotional Orc (named Luvah in Eternity), and the imaginative Los (formerly named Urthona). Tharmas, the fourth Zoa, is a vague, childlike, yet parental being who should be the unifying force of the personality (instinct) but has become an oceanic personification of shapelessness. Of the four, only Los is able to preserve a vestige of the Divine Vision through the Nights of Albion's sleep.

The fallen situation is further complicated by the fact that each of the Zoas has become separated from his "Emanation," or female counterpart, and therefore exists as a still further diminished relic of his original personality—so different, in the case of Los, that he splits off into a separate personality called the Spectre. Luvah and Vala, for example, were lovers in Eternity, but in the fallen state Luvah has become Orc and his alienation from Vala is both a symptom and a cause of his lust and rage. Ahania, as the pleasure which Urizen has banished, and Enitharmon, as the artist's inspiration which has become separated from Los, are familiar characters first introduced in the Lambeth books; the Emanation of Tharmas is the new character Enion—a primitive earth mother. In the apocalyptic ninth Night, the Zoas are reconciled with their Emanations as a part of the universal resurrection.

This resurrection is prophesied throughout *The Four Zoas* in intermittent accounts of the Eternity from which Albion has fallen. Eternity is a community of higher consciousness also called the Divine Humanity, and personified as Jesus. Eternity should not be thought of as preceding Time, although for the sake of the narrative Albion's unfallen condition is described as something that exists "before" and "after" his nightmare. In reality, Eternity is the fullness of any one moment in Time which is entered into and "opened" by man's consciousness. During Albion's sleep the possibility of this higher consciousness is represented by the loving concern and protectiveness of Jesus, who acts through a Council of God in seven "Eyes," which are historical phases in the development of man's image of God. These seven phases progress from a primitive conception of God as a baby-eating idol to God as a self-sacrificing Saviour. The way out of the horror of history is finally perceived in Night the Eighth. With the help of his own imagination, which is Los acting within him, Albion attains self-acceptance and a recognition of divinity within. In the ninth Night Albion is able to resume his life in Eternity; and once more the Zoas, with their Emanations, are subordinated to the total human personality and rejoin one another for the good of mankind as a whole.

For a study of the major pictures in *The Four Zoas,* see John E. Grant, "Visions in *Vala*" in *Blake's Sublime Allegory,*, eds. Stuart Curran and Joseph Anthony Wittreich, Jr. (Madison and London: University of Wisconsin Press, 1973); for a commentary on the poem, see Brian Wilkie and Mary Lynn Johnson, *Blake's Four Zoas: The Design of a Dream* (Cambridge: Harvard University Press, 1978).

From The Four Zoas

The torments of Love & Jealousy in
The Death and Judgement
of Albion the Ancient Man

by William Blake 1797

Rest before Labour

PAGE 3

Οτι ουκ εςτιν ημιν η παλη προς αιμα και ςαρκα, αλλα
προς τας αρχας, προς τας εξουςιας, προς τους
κοςμοκρατορας του ςκοτους του αιωνος τουτου, προς
τα πνευματικα της πονηριας εν τοις επουρανιοις.[1]

Εφες: VI κεφ. 12 ver.

VALA

Night the First

The Song of the Aged Mother which shook the heavens with wrath,
Hearing the march of long resounding strong heroic Verse
Marshalld in order for the day of Intellectual Battle:

Four Mighty Ones are in every Man: a Perfect Unity
Cannot Exist but from the Universal Brotherhood of Eden,
The Universal Man, to Whom be Glory Evermore, Amen.[2]

1. "For we wrestle not against flesh and blood, but against principalities, against powers, against the rulers of the darkness of this world, against spiritual wickedness in high places" (Ephesians 6:12): from Saint Paul's instructions on mental warfare. As a radical Protestant, Blake understands this as Biblical sanction to resist the established authority of church and state.

2. In the margin beside lines 4–6 Blake cites John 17:21–23 (Jesus' prayer that his disciples be as one, "as thou, Father, art in me, and I in thee, that they also may be as one in us") and John 1:14 ("And the Word was made flesh, and dwelt among us") and repeats part of the latter text in Greek. Both texts emphasize the unity of the divine and the human. The "Four Mighty Ones" are the Four Zoas, Urthona-Los (imagination), Urizen (intelligence), Luvah-Orc (passion), and Tharmas (instinct). Their Emanations or female counterparts are Enitharmon (inspiration), Ahania (pleasure), Vala (natural beauty), and Enion (maternal instinct). These are only approximate allegorical equivalents: the characters are in constant flux and have both fallen and unfallen identities.

What are the Natures of those Living Creatures the Heavenly Father only
Knoweth No Individual Knoweth nor Can know in all Eternity.

Los was the fourth immortal starry one, & in the Earth
Of a bright Universe Empery attended day & night,
Days & nights of revolving joy. Urthona was his name

PAGE 4

In Eden; in the Auricular Nerves of Human life,
Which is the Earth of Eden, he his Emanations propagated:
Fairies of Albion, afterwards Gods of the Heathen. Daughter of Beulah, Sing
His fall into Division & his Resurrection to Unity,
His fall into the Generation of Decay & Death & his Regeneration by the Resurrection from the dead.[3]

* * *

PAGE 18

* * *

Eternity groand and was troubled at the image of Eternal Death
Without the body of man, an Exudation from his sickning limbs.

Now Man was come to the Palm tree & to the Oak of Weeping
Which stand upon the Edge of Beulah & he sunk down
From the Supporting arms of the Eternal Saviour; who disposd
The pale limbs of his Eternal Individuality
Upon The Rock of Ages, Watching over him with Love & Care.[4]

3. Page numbers—not those supplied by Blake—follow the system of G. E. Bentley, ed., *Vala, or The Four Zoas: A Facsimile of the Manuscript, a Transcript of the Poem, and a Study of Its Growth and Significance* (Oxford: Clarendon, 1963). Roman numerals refer to the major sections or "Nights" of the poem. For the reader's convenience in locating the context of our selections, references to the Erdman and Keynes editions are supplied at the end of each excerpt. To compare this passage from pages 3 and 4 of the manuscript with the Erdman and Keynes editions, see David V. Erdman, ed., *The Poetry and Prose of William Blake* (Garden City, N. Y.: Doubleday, 1970), pp. 296–97; and Geoffrey Keynes, ed., *The Complete Writings of William Blake* (London and New York: Oxford University Press, 1974), pp. 263–64. The manuscript is illegible in places. This text is derived from notes on the original and a fresh collation of the Bentley, Keynes, and Erdman transcriptions; where there is disagreement that cannot be resolved by a study of the facsimile, Erdman's deciphering is preferred.

4. At this point Blake first wrote "End of the First Night," but editors agree that page 21 should follow page 18 and the Night should end three pages later, on page 20. The protective presence of the Divine Humanity is mentioned repeatedly, although Albion is unaware of this love and concern. The idea of a cosmic man comes from Cabalistic rabbinical Biblical commentaries that mention Adam Kadmon, a pre-Adamic divine giant who embodied God, man, and nature before the fall.

PAGE 21

Then those in Great Eternity met in the Council of God
As one Man for contracting their Exalted Senses
They behold Multitude or Expanding they behold as one,
As One Man all the Universal family & that one Man
They call Jesus the Christ & they in him & he in them
Live in Perfect harmony in Eden the land of life
Consulting as One Man above the Mountain of Snowdon Sublime[5]

Night II

PAGE 34

* * *

Thus Enion wails from the dark deep; the golden heavens tremble:[6]

PAGE 35

"I am made to sow the thistle for wheat, the nettle for a nourishing dainty;
I have planted a false oath in the earth, it has brought forth a poison tree;
I have chosen the serpent for a councellor & the dog
For a schoolmaster to my children;
I have blotted out from light & living the dove & nightingale,
And I have caused the earth worm to beg from door to door;
I have taught the thief a secret path into the house of the just;
I have taught pale artifice to spread his nets upon the morning;
My heavens are brass, my earth is iron, my moon a clod of clay,
My sun a pestilence burning at noon & a vapour of death in night.

"What is the price of Experience? do men buy it for a song?
Or wisdom for a dance in the street? No, it is bought with the price
Of all that a man hath: his house, his wife, his children.
Wisdom is sold in the desolate market where none come to buy,
And in the witherd field where the farmer plows for bread in vain.

"It is an easy thing to triumph in the summer's sun
And in the vintage & to sing on the waggon loaded with corn;
It is an easy thing to talk of patience to the afflicted,
To speak the laws of prudence to the houseless wanderer,

5. Cf. Erdman, p. 306, and Keynes, p. 277

6. Enion's song, written in Blake's fine copperplate hand, has apparently been carefully revised. Enion, the emanation of Tharmas, falls furthest into nonentity, and her fall draws Ahania away from Urizen. Enion's poignant laments are heard at the ends of Nights II, III, and VIII, the latter two in antiphony with Ahania. These female voices, drifting up from nonexistence, serve as choral commentary on the main action.

PAGE 36

"To listen to the hungry raven's cry in wintry season
When the red blood is filld with wine & with the marrow of lambs;
It is an easy thing to laugh at wrathful elements,
To hear the dog howl at the wintry door, the ox in the slaughter house moan,
To see a god on every wind & a blessing on every blast,
To hear sounds of love in the thunder that destroys our enemies' house,
To rejoice in the blight that covers his field, & the sickness that cuts off his children,
While our olive & vine sing & laugh round our door & our children bring fruits & flowers.

"Then the groan & the dolor are quite forgotten, & the slave grinding at the mill,
And the captive in chains, & the poor in the prison, & the soldier in the field
When the shatterd bone hath laid him groaning among the happier dead.

"It is an easy thing to rejoice in the tents of prosperity;
Thus could I sing & thus rejoice, but it is not so with me!"

Ahania heard the Lamentation & a swift Vibration
Spread thro her Golden frame. She rose up [ere] the dawn of day
When Urizen slept on his couch, drawn thro unbounded space
Onto the margin of Non Entity the bright Female came.
There she beheld the Spectrous form of Enion in the Void
And never from that moment could she rest upon her pillow.

End of the Second Night[7]

Night V

PAGE 60

* * *

But when fourteen summers & winters had revolved over
Their solemn habitation Los beheld the ruddy boy
Embracing his bright mother & beheld malignant fires
In his young eyes, discerning plain that Orc plotted his death.[8]

7. Cf. Erdman, pp. 318–19, and Keynes, pp. 290–91. "Ere" (line 15) = MS. "eer."

8. A fuller account of the Oedipal conflict described in *Urizen* 20 (VII) and depicted on *Urizen* 21 (see color plate 20).

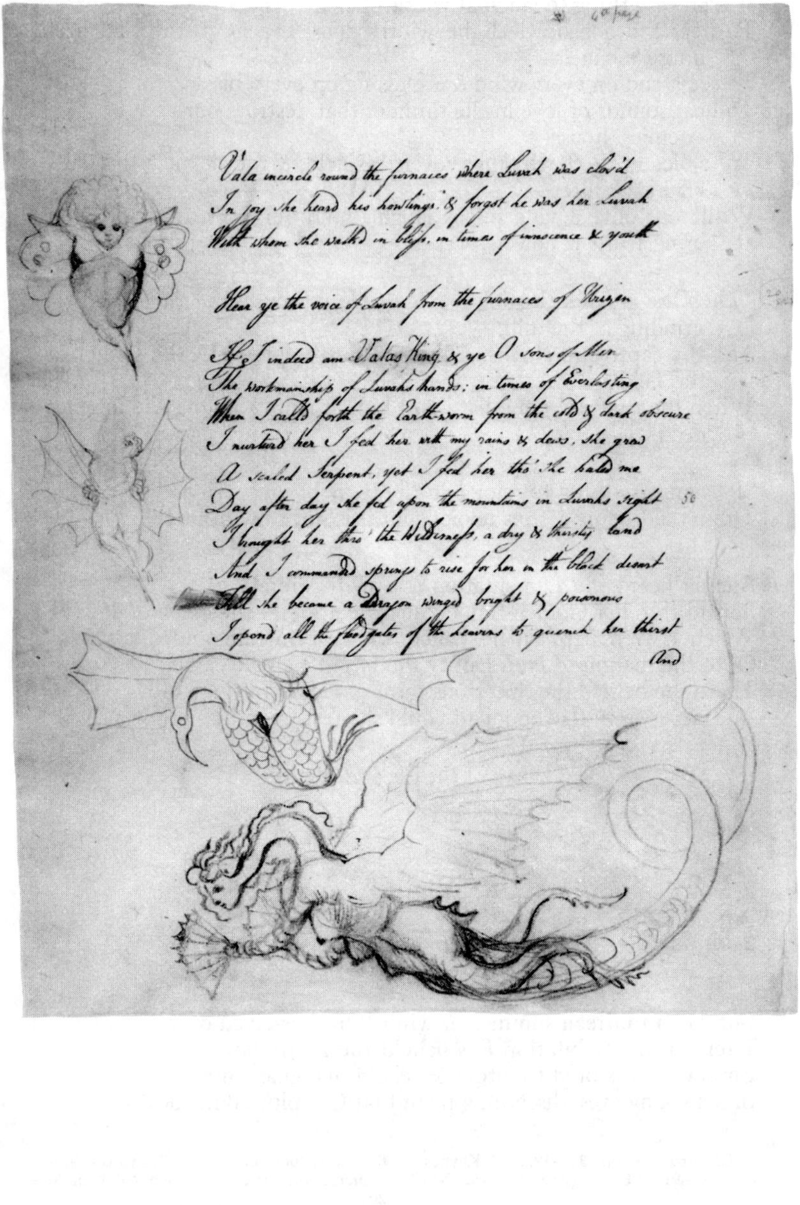
Vala incircle round the furnaces where Luvah was clos'd
In joy she heard his howlings, & forgot he was her Luvah
With whom she walkd in bliss, in times of innocence & youth

Hear ye the voice of Luvah from the furnaces of Urizen

If I indeed am Valas King & ye O sons of Men
The workmanship of Luvahs hands; in times of Everlasting
When I calld forth the Earth-worm from the cold & dark obscure
I nurturd her I fed her with my rains & dews, she grew
A scaled Serpent, yet I fed her tho' she hated me
Day after day she fed upon the mountains in Luvahs sight
I brought her thro' the Wilderness, a dry & thirsty land
And I commanded springs to rise for her in the black desart
Till she became a Dragon winged bright & poisonous
I opend all the floodgates of the heavens to quench her thirst
And

Grief rose upon his ruddy brows, a tightening girdle grew
Around his bosom like a bloody cord. In secret sobs
He burst it, but next morn another girdle succeeds
Around his bosom. Every day he viewd the fiery youth
With silent fear & his immortal cheeks grew deadly pale
Till many a morn & many a night passed over in dire woe
Forming a girdle in the day & bursting it at night.
The girdle was formd by day by night was burst in twain,
Falling down on the rock an iron chain link by link lockd.

Enitharmon beheld the bloody chain of nights & days
Depending from the bosom of Los & how with griding pain
He went each morning to his labours with the spectre dark;
Calld it the chain of Jealousy. Now Los began to speak
His woes aloud to Enitharmon, since he could not hide
His uncouth plague. He siezd the boy in his immortal hands
While Enitharmon followd him, weeping in dismal woe,
Up to the iron mountain's top & there the Jealous chain
Fell from his bosom on the mountain. The Spectre dark
Held the fierce boy; Los naild him down, binding around his limbs
The accursed chain. O how bright Enitharmon howld & cried
Over her son. Obdurate Los bound down her loved Joy.[9]

PAGE 62

* * *

But when returnd to Golgonooza Los & Enitharmon
Felt all the sorrow Parents feel. they wept toward one another
And Los repented that he had chaind Orc upon the mountain
And Enitharmon's tears prevaild; parental love returnd
Tho terrible his dread of that infernal chain They rose
At midnight hasting to their much beloved care
Nine days they traveld thro the Gloom of Entuthon Benithon
Los taking Enitharmon by the hand led her along
The dismal vales & up to the iron mountain's top where Orc
Howld in the furious wind he thought to give to Enitharmon
Her son in tenfold joy & to compensate for her tears
Even if his own death resulted so much pity him paind

But when they came to the dark rock & to the spectrous cave
Lo the young limbs had strucken root into the rock & strong
Fibres had from the Chain of Jealousy inwove themselves
In a swift vegetation round the rock & round the Cave
And over the immortal limbs of the terrible fiery boy
In vain they strove now to unchain. In vain with bitter tears
To melt the chain of Jealousy. Not Enitharmon's death
Nor the Consummation of Los could ever melt the chain
Nor unroot the infernal fibres from their rocky bed
Nor all Urthona's strength nor all the power of Luvah's Bulls
Tho they each morning drag the unwilling Sun out of the deep
Could uproot the infernal chain. for it had taken root

9. Cf. Erdman, p. 334, and Keynes, pp. 307–8. Also cf. *Urizen*, Chapter VII.

PAGE 63

Into the iron rock & grew a chain beneath the Earth,
Even to the Center, wrapping round the Center, &—the limbs
Of Orc entering with fibres—became one with him, a living Chain
Sustained by the Demon's life. Despair & Terror & Woe & Rage
Inwrap the Parents in cold clouds as they bend howling over
The terrible boy till fainting by his side the Parents fell.

Not long they lay. Urthona's spectre found herbs of the pit;
Rubbing their temples, he reviv'd them. All their lamentations
I write not here, but all their after life was lamentation.[1]

* * *

The Woes of Urizen shut up in the deep dens of Urthona:[2]

"Ah how shall Urizen the King submit to this dark mansion!
Ah how is this! Once on the heights I stretchd my throne
sublime;
The mountains of Urizen, once of silver, where the sons of wisdom
dwelt
And on whose tops the Virgins sang, are rocks of Desolation.

"My fountains, once the haunt of Swans, now breed the scaly
tortoise,
The houses of my helpers are become a haunt of crows,
The gardens of wisdom are become a field of horrid graves,
And on the bones I drop my tears & water them in vain.

PAGE 64

"Once how I walked from my palace in gardens of delight!
The sons of wisdom stood around, the harpers followd with harps,
Nine virgins clothd in light composd the song to their immortal
voices,
And at my banquets of new wine my head was crownd with joy.

"Then in my ivory pavilions I slumberd in the noon
And walked in the silent night among sweet smelling flowers
Till on my silver bed I slept & sweet dreams round me hoverd,
But now my land is darkend & my wise men are departed.

1. Cf. Erdman, pp. 335–36, and Keynes, p. 309.
2. The section with Urizen's lament is neatly written in Blake's ordinary letter-writing hand, perhaps indicating that it had been polished before being committed to paper. Urizen has been almost paralyzed and imprisoned by Los in the "dens" of the human body (cf. *Urizen* IV). Now awakening, he thinks of seeking a confrontation with Orc, who in his unfallen identity as Luvah was Urizen's ancient enemy and co-conspirator in the overthrow of Albion.

"My songs are turned to cries of Lamentation
Heard on my Mountains & deep sighs under my palace roofs
Because the Steeds of Urizen, once swifter than the light,
Were kept back from my Lord & from his chariot of mercies.[3]

"O did I keep the horses of the day in silver pastures!
O I refusd the Lord of day the horses of his prince!
O did I close my treasures with roofs of solid stone
And darken all my Palace walls with envyings & hate!

"O Fool to think that I could hide from his all piercing eyes
The gold & silver & costly stones, his holy workmanship!
O Fool could I forget the light that filled my bright spheres
Was a reflection of his face who calld me from the deep!

"I well remember, for I heard the mild & holy voice
Saying, 'O light spring up & shine,' & I sprang up from the deep.
He gave to me a silver scepter & crownd me with a golden crown
& said: 'Go forth & guide my Son who wanders on the ocean.'[4]

"I went not forth. I hid myself in black clouds of my wrath.
I calld the stars around my feet in the night of councils dark.
The stars threw down their spears & fled naked away.
We fell. I siezd thee, dark Urthona, in my left hand; falling,

"I siezd thee, beauteous Luvah. Thou art faded like a flower
And like a lilly is thy wife Vala, witherd by winds.
When thou didst bear the golden cup at the immortal tables[5]
Thy children smote their fiery wings crownd with the gold of
heaven;

3. The various Zoas give overlapping and sometimes contradictory accounts of the fall. Urizen's version is based on a combination of the myths of Lucifer and of Phaeton. "My Lord" is probably the Divine Humanity, Blake's true God; 4:22, recalls Genesis 1:3, "Let there be light." The excerpts in this edition emphasize the warfare among the Zoas, but the poem—especially in its earlier form called *Vala*—blames the fall equally on the seductiveness of the Emanations, as displayed in the design for page 86, and their refusal to cooperate with their counterparts as pictured in the design for page 112.

4. This passage recalls *Paradise Lost* V, 603–15, where the angels (including the unfallen Satan) are required to recognize their subordination to the Son, or Messiah. The Miltonic material has been modulated by Urizen into a divine command to lead Albion, mankind. Additionally, since Urizen is the light of the mind, "my Son" suggests a pun for the material *sun*, which needs direction. Like Satan, Urizen refuses to serve.

5. Resembling Ganymede, cupbearer for Zeus, Luvah is also associated with wine through his similarities with Dionysus and Christ; in a section of Night IX not excerpted here, when the crown of thorns drops from his head and he ceases to be a suffering god, he begins to harvest the "Human Grapes" and transform their blood to the wine of life. In this lament at the end of Night V, Urizen recalls his unfallen glory and regrets the confusion of functions between Urizen and Luvah which brought on the fall (cf. the confusion between duties of Satan and Palamabron in the Bard's song, *Milton* 7:10).

PAGE 65
"Thy pure feet stepd on the steps divine, too pure for other feet
And thy fair locks shadowd thine eyes from the divine effulgence;
Then thou didst keep with Strong Urthona the living gates of heaven,
But now thou art bound down with him even to the gates of hell,

"Because thou gavest Urizen the wine of the Almighty
For steeds of Light, that they might run in thy golden chariot of pride.
I gave to thee the Steeds. I pourd the stolen wine
And drunken with the immortal draught fell from my throne sublime.

"I will arise Explore these dens & find that deep pulsation
That shakes my caverns with strong shudders. Perhaps this is the night
Of Prophecy & Luvah hath burst his way from Enitharmon.
When Thought is closd in Caves, Then love shall shew its root in deepest Hell."[6]

End of the Fifth Night[7]

Night VII[*a*]

PAGE 80
And Urizen Read in his book of brass in sounding tones:[8]

"Listen O Daughters to my voice, Listen to the Words of Wisdom;
So shall you govern over all. Let Moral Duty tune your tongue,
But be your hearts harder than the nether millstone;

* * *

"Compell the poor to live upon a Crust of bread by soft mild arts;
Smile when they frown, frown when they smile, & when a man looks pale
With labour & abstinence say he looks healthy & happy,
And when his children sicken let them die. There are enough
Born, even too many, & our Earth will be overrun[9]

6. Cf. *Europe* 10:16–17. Urizen and Orc are locked in dynamic opposition, as the head and loins of fallen man. When intellect and feeling are separated and the mind is repressed, desire is driven underground and rejected as evil. The pulsations which Urizen feels are the stirrings of Orc as he reaches adolescence and struggles against the chains imposed on him by his father Los. Urizen's exploration of his dens is an assessment of life within the confines of the fall. Cf. *Urizen*, chapter VII, verse 6.
7. Cf. Erdman, pp. 336–37 and Keynes, pp. 310–11.
8. In this scene Urizen is reading to his daughters as a way of tormenting Orc, who is still in chains. The repressive techniques in Urizen's teachings are methods of stifling revolution.
9. Perhaps a reference to Thomas Malthus, *Essay on the Principles of Population* (1798), though this attitude toward the poor was current before Malthus.

Fly me & thou annihilate evaporate & be no more
For thou art but a form & organ of life & of thyself
Art nothing being Created continually by Mercy & Love divine
Los furious answerd. Spectre horrible thy words astound my Ear
With irresistible conviction I feel I am not one of those
Who when convincd can still persist. tho furious. controllable
By Reasons power. Even I already feel a World within
Opening its gates & in it all the real substances
Of which these in the outward World are shadows which pass away
Come then into my Bosom & in thy shadowy arms bring with thee
My lovely Enitharmon. I will quell my fury & teach
Peace to the soul of dark revenge & repentance to Cruelty
So spoke Los & Embracing Enitharmon & the Spectre
Clouds would have folded round in Extacy & Love uniting

Without these arts. If you would make the poor live with temper,
With pomp give every crust of bread you give, with gracious cunning
Magnify small gifts. Reduce the man to want a gift & then give with pomp.
Say he smiles if you hear him sigh, If pale say he is ruddy.
Preach temperance: say he is overgorgd & drowns his wit
In strong drink, tho you know that bread & water are all
He can afford. Flatter his wife, pity his children, till we can
Reduce all to our will, as spaniels are taught with art."[1]

* * *

PAGE 90

* * * Los, his hands divine inspired,[2] began
To modulate his fires; studious the loud roaring flames
He vanquishd; with the strength of Art bending their iron points
And drawing them forth delighted upon the winds of Golgonooza,
From out the ranks of Urizen's war & from the fiery lake
Of Orc; bending down as the binder of the Sheaves follows
The reaper, in both arms embracing the furious raging flames,
Los drew them forth out of the deeps, planting his right foot firm
Upon the Iron crag of Urizen, thence springing up aloft
Into the heavens of Enitharmon in a mighty circle.

And first he drew a line upon the walls of shining heaven
And Enitharmon tincturd it with beams of blushing love.
It remaind permanent, a lovely form inspird, divinely human.
Dividing into just proportions, Los unwearied labourd
The immortal lines upon the heavens, till with sighs of love
Sweet Enitharmon mild, Entrancd, breathd forth upon the wind
The spectrous dead. Weeping, the Spectres viewd the immortal works
Of Los, Assimilating to those forms, Embodied & Lovely
In youth & beauty, in the arms of Enitharmon mild reposing.[3]

1. Cf. Erdman, p. 348, and Keynes, pp. 322–23.
2. Abruptly in Night VII Los and his Spectre (see note to *Jerusalem* 10:18) are reconciled, and with the help of his emanation Enitharmon Los begins to do his first productive work. By creating beautiful forms, he attracts the dead specters—deadly thoughts—from the wars of Urizen and gives them life in the art palace of Golgonooza. This passage is usually interpreted as a mythic account of the cooperative artistic labors of William and Catherine Blake, since Catherine worked at Blake's side and sometimes colored the illuminated books.
3. Cf. Erdman, p. 356, and Keynes, pp. 331–32.

Night VII[*b*]

PAGE 92

* * *

Then left the Sons of Urizen the plow & harrow, the loom,[4]
The hammer & the Chisel, & the rule & compasses.
They forgd the sword, the chariot of war, the battle ax,
The trumpet fitted to the battle; & the flute of summer
And all the arts of life they changd into the arts of death:
The hour glass contemnd because its simple workmanship
Was as the workmanship of the plowman, & the water wheel
That raises water into Cisterns broken & burnd in fire
Because its workmanship was like the workmanship of the Shepherd.
And in their stead intricate wheels invented: Wheel without wheel
To preplex youth in their outgoings & to bind to labours
Of day & night the myriads of Eternity; that they might file
And polish brass & iron hour after hour, laborious workmanship,
Kept ignorant of the use; that they might spend the days of wisdom
In sorrowful drudgery to obtain a scanty pittance of bread,
In ignorance to view a small portion & think that All,
And call it Demonstration, blind to all the simple rules of life.[5]

Night VIII

PAGE 109

* * *

"Listen, I will tell thee what is done in the caverns of the grave:[6]

4. This passage on the rationalists' condemnation of simple machines, in what appears to be an earlier version of Night VII than the one labelled VII[a] above, presents the kind of problem Blake must have faced in revising: the loss of a beautiful section when its context no longer suited his plan. He may have intended somehow to combine the two versions; see *Blake: An Illustrated Quarterly*, 12:2 (Fall 1978).

5. Cf. Erdman, p. 396, and Keynes, p. 337.

6. At the end of a dialogue between Enion and Ahania on the subject of life and death, Enion recounts a debate between the grave and the plowed field. Imagery of the death and rebirth of nature conveys her theme of the death and rebirth of the human spirit, Albion. The narrative of Night VIII follows the Biblical accounts of the crucifixion; Enion expresses the state of the world during the last hours before the resurrection. Albion, who is man and nature, man and God, is on the verge of reuniting his scattered body, rehumanizing both nature and his alienated divinity.

PAGE 110

The Lamb of God has rent the Veil of Mystery, soon to return
In Clouds & Fires around the rock & the Mysterious tree.
As the seed waits Eagerly watching for its flower & fruit,
Anxious its little soul looks out into the clear expanse
To see if hungry winds are abroad with their invisible army,
So Man looks out in tree & herb & fish & bird & beast
Collecting up the scatterd portions of his immortal body
Into the Elemental forms of every thing that grows.
He tries the sullen north wind, riding on its angry furrows,
The sultry south when the sun rises & the angry east
When the sun sets, when the clods harden & the cattle stand
Drooping & the birds hide in their silent nests. He stores his thoughts
As in a store house in his memory; he regulates the forms
Of all beneath & all above & in the gentle West
Reposes where the Sun's heat dwells. He rises to the Sun
And to the Planets of the Night & to the stars that gild
The Zodiac & the stars that sullen stand to north & south.
He touches the remotest pole & in the Center weeps
That Man should Labour & sorrow & learn & forget & return
To the dark valley whence he came, to begin his labours anew.
In pain he sighs, in pain he labours in his universe,
Screaming in birds over the deep & howling in the Wolf
Over the slain & moaning in the cattle & in the winds
And weeping over Orc & Urizen in clouds & flaming fires;
And in the cries of birth & in the groans of death his voice
Is heard throughout the Universe: wherever a grass grows
Or a leaf buds, The Eternal Man is seen, is heard, is felt,
And all his Sorrows till he reassumes his ancient bliss."

Such are the words of Ahania & Enion. Los hears & weeps,
And Los & Enitharmon took the Body of the Lamb
Down from the Cross & placd it in a Sepulcher which Los had hewn
For himself in the Rock of Eternity, trembling & in despair.
Jerusalem wept over the Sepulcher two thousand Years,[7]

* * *

7. The Christian era, during which the spirit of humanity has been dead. Cf. Erdman, pp. 370–71, and Keynes, p. 355–56.

Night IX

* * *

PAGE 119

In the fierce flames the limbs of Mystery[8] lay consuming with howling
And deep despair. Rattling go up the flames around the Synagogue
Of Satan. Loud the Serpent Orc ragd thro his twenty Seven
Folds. The tree of Mystery went up in folding flames.
Blood issud out in mighty volumes, pouring in whirlpools fierce
From out the flood gates of the Sky. The Gates are burst, down pour
The torrents black upon the Earth, the blood pours down incessant.
Kings in their palaces lie drownd; Shepherds, their flocks, their tents,
Roll down the mountains in black torrents. Cities, Villages,
High spires & Castles drownd in the black deluge. Shoal on Shoal
Float the dead carcases of Men & Beasts driven to & fro on waves
Of foaming blood beneath the black incessant Sky, till all
Mystery's tyrants are cut off & not one left on Earth.

And when all Tyranny was cut off from the face of Earth,
Around the Dragon form of Urizen & round his stony form,
The flames rolling intense thro the wide Universe
Began to Enter the Holy City. Entring, the dismal clouds
In furrowd lightnings break their way, the wild flames whirring up
The Bloody Deluge, living flames winged with intellect
And Reason; round the Earth they march in order, flame by flame.
From the clotted gore & from the hollow den
Start forth the trembling millions into flames of mental fire
Bathing their Limbs in the bright visions of Eternity.[9]

* * *

PAGE 121

Urizen wept in the dark deep; anxious his Scaly form
To reassume the human, & he wept in the dark deep

8. Night IX is the Apocalypse, based closely on Revelation, but displaying Blake's unorthodox ideas. The destruction of Mystery, the Whore of Babylon (Revelation 17, 18) means the destruction of all mystifying doctrines of a remote divinity, including Christian doctrines. Likewise, the Synagogue of Satan (Revelation 2:9, 3:9) includes the Christian church with all other corrupt institutions. The mental flames that burn Mystery are purifying.

9. Cf. Erdman, p. 373, and Keynes, p. 359.

Saying, "O that I had never drank the wine nor eat the bread
Of dark mortality, nor cast my view into futurity, nor turnd
My back, darkning the present, clouding with a cloud,
And building arches high & cities, turrets, & towers, & domes
Whose smoke destroyd the pleasant garden & whose running
Kennels
Chokd the bright rivers, burdning with my Ships the angry deep;
Thro Chaos seeking for delight & in spaces remote
Seeking the Eternal which is always present to the wise;
Seeking for pleasure which unsought falls round the infant's path
And on the fleeces of mild flocks who neither care nor labour.
But I, the labourer of ages, whose unwearied hands
Are thus deformd with hardness, with the sword & with the spear
And with the Chisel & the mallet—I whose labours vast
Order the nations, separating family by family,
Alone enjoy not. I alone in misery supreme
Ungratified give all my joy unto this Luvah & Vala.
Then Go, O dark futurity; I will cast thee forth from these
Heavens of my brain, nor will I look upon futurity more!
I cast futurity away & turn my back upon that void
Which I have made, for lo futurity is in this moment!
Let Orc consume, let Tharmas rage, let dark Urthona give
All strength to Los & Enitharmon, & let Los self cursd
Rend down this fabric as a wall ruind & family extinct;
Rage, Orc! Rage, Tharmas! Urizen no longer curbs your rage!"

So Urizen spoke. He shook his snows from off his Shoulders & arose
As on a Pyramid of mist, his white robes scattering.
The fleecy white renewd, he shook his aged mantles off
Into the fires. Then glorious, bright, Exulting in his joy,
He sounding rose into the heavens in naked majesty
In radiant Youth.[1]

* * *

PAGE 122

* * *Rivn link from link the bursting Universe explodes.
All things reversd flew from their centers; rattling bones
To bones Join, shaking, convulsd, the shivering clay breathes.
Each speck of dust to the Earth's center nestles round & round
In pangs of an Eternal Birth, in torment & awe & fear.
All spirits deceasd let loose from reptile prisons come in shoals.

1. Cf. Erdman, pp. 375–76, and Keynes, pp. 361–62.

Wild furies from the tyger's brain & from the lion's Eyes
And from the ox & ass come moping terrors, from the Eagle
And raven, numerous as the leaves of autumn, every species
Flock to the trumpet muttring over the sides of the grave & crying
In the fierce wind round heaving rocks & mountains filld with groans.
On rifted rocks suspended in the air by inward fires
Many a woful company & many on clouds & waters,
Fathers & friends, Mothers & Infants, Kings & Warriors,
Priests & chaind Captives met together in a horrible fear,
And every one of the dead appears as he had livd before,

PAGE 123
And all the marks remain of the slave's scourge & tryant's Crown
And of the Priest's o'ergorged Abdomen & of the merchant's thin
Sinewy deception & of the warrior's outbraving & thoughtlessness
In lineaments too extended & in bones too strait & long.

They shew their wounds, they accuse, they sieze the opressor; howlings began
On the golden palace, Songs & joy on the desart. The Cold babe
Stands in the furious air, he cries; the children of six thousand years
Who died in infancy rage furious; a mighty multitude rage furious,
Naked & pale, standing on the expecting air to be deliverd,
Rend limb from limb the Warrior & the tyrant, reuniting in pain.
The furious wind still rends around, they flee in sluggish effort.

They beg, they intreat in vain now; they Listend not to intreaty.
They view the flames red rolling on thro the wide universe
From the dark jaws of death beneath & desolate shores remote,
These covering Vaults of heaven & these trembling globes of Earth.
One Planet calls to another & one star enquires of another:
"What flames are these coming from the South, what noise what dreadful rout
As of a battle in the heavens? Hark, heard you not the trumpet
As of fierce battle?" While they spoke the flames come on intense, roaring.

They see him whom they have piered; they wail because of him;
They magnify themselves no more against Jerusalem, Nor
Against her little ones. The innocent, accused before the Judges,
Shines with immortal Glory. Trembling, the Judge springs from his throne,
Hiding his face in the dust beneath the prisoner's feet & saying,
"Brother of Jesus, what have I done! Intreat thy lord for me,
Perhaps I may be forgiven." While he speaks the flames roll on.

And after the flames appears the Cloud of the Son of Man
Descending from Jerusalem with power and great Glory
All nations look up to the Cloud & behold him who was Crucified.[2]

* * *

PAGE 138

The Sun has left his blackness & has found a fresher morning,
And the mild moon rejoices in the clear & cloudless night,
And Man walks forth from midst of the fires; the evil is all consumd.
His eyes behold the Angelic spheres arising night & day,
The stars consumd like a lamp blown out & in their stead, behold
The Expanding Eyes of Man behold the depths of wondrous worlds.
One Earth, one sea beneath, nor Erring Globes wander, but Stars
Of fire rise up nightly from the Ocean & one Sun
Each morning like a New born Man issues with songs & Joy,
Calling the Plowman to his Labour & the Shepherd to his rest.
He walks upon the Eternal Mountains raising his heavenly voice,
Conversing with the Animal forms of wisdom night & day,
That risen from the Sea of fire renewd walk o'er the Earth.

For Tharmas brought his flocks upon the hills & in the Vales
Around the Eternal Man's bright tent the little Children play
Among the wooly flocks. The hammer of Urthona sounds
In the deep caves beneath, his limbs renewd.[3] His Lions roar
Around the Furnaces & in Evening sport upon the plains.
They raise their faces from the Earth conversing with the Man,

"How is it we have walkd thro fires & yet are not consumd?
How is it that all things are changd even as in ancient times?"

PAGE 139

The Sun arises from his dewy bed & the fresh airs
Play in his smiling beams, giving the seeds of life to grow,
And the fresh Earth beams forth ten thousand thousand springs of life.
Urthona is arisen in his strength, no longer now
Divided from Enitharmon, no longer the Spectre Los.
Where is the Spectre of Prophecy? where the delusive Phantom?

2. Cf. Erdman, pp. 377–78, and Keynes, pp. 363–64.

3. Urthona had been described as limping, like the blacksmith god Vulcan.

Departed; & Urthona rises from the ruinous walls
In all his ancient strength to form the golden armour of science
For intellectual War—The war of swords departed now,
The dark Religions are departed & sweet Science[4] reigns.

End of The Dream[5]

Milton

In this prophecy Blake reconsiders at length his epigrammatic criticism of Milton's theology and artistic psychology as set forth in *The Marriage of Heaven and Hell.* Among the ideas in the earlier critique is that Milton's image of God is too rationalistic, his vision of Hell contains all the energy, and his conception of the Holy Spirit is nonexistent. To understand Blake's strictures, we should recall what Milton meant to literate people during the century and more following his death in 1674. He was remembered not only as a poet who depicted eternal states—Heaven, Hell, Paradise—but also as a man who opposed tyranny, purified the Christianity of his time, and—despite his blindness—labored mightily in his poetic vocation. Milton's presentation of Christian mythology was perhaps more influential than that of the Bible itself, and his exemplary life strongly influenced ideals of behavior. Far more than any other writer, what Milton said and did were felt to be immediately relevant to the reader's own salvation and the salvation of the English people (as Wordsworth indicates in his sonnet of 1802, "Milton! thou shouldst be living at this hour").

Milton had served in an important position in the English revolutionary government of Cromwell, and had considered nationalistic subjects while planning his master work, but when his major poems appeared after the Restoration of the monarchy they were on Biblical subjects and touched on little that was specifically English. This neglect, whatever its cause, concerned Blake. Also, although the affliction of blindness is not mentioned in *Milton: A Poem,* one aspect of the poet's personal life that did seem important to Blake was his relationship with women. The fact that Milton had three wives and had stormy relations with the first, as well as with his three daughters, was part of his legend; moreover, Milton's belief in the preeminence of the male as head of the family and some of the emphasis in his characterizations of Eve and Dalila seemed antifeminist even by eighteenth-century standards. A further dimension to this area of his life was added by his having written in favor of divorce on the grounds of incompatibility, still a scandalous idea at the beginning of the nineteenth century. On the other hand, Milton's defense of unlicensed printing, contained in his treatise *Areopagitica,* had come to seem by Blake's time an admirable

4. Humane learning, the dispelling of Mystery. Blake's attacks on sterile, reductive, mechanistic systems should not be taken as repudiations of rationality; Urizen has an unfallen as well as a fallen identity, and in the unfallen state his emanation Ahania is Pleasure. Ideally, there is no conflict between "sweet Science" and the imaginative productivity directed by Urthona.

5. Cf. Erdman, pp. 391–92, and Keynes, p. 379.

formulation of liberal standards, even though the logic of his argument was still unacceptable to conservative forces. Strands from these aspects of the Milton legend are interwoven with themes, images, and stories from Blake's own life and mythological inventions, to make up the plot of the epic *Milton*. In addition to the illuminated poem, a full account of Blake's relationship to Milton would have to take into account several series of watercolor drawings (ca. 1801–22) which Blake made to illustrate five of Milton's major poems; these, with the designs in *Milton*, comprise more than a hundred separate pictures that celebrate various aspects of the Miltonic legacy.

Milton: A Poem is concerned with prophetic succession or how the role of a major poet is transmitted from the leading spirit of one age to the next, and how all people are influenced by the arts. The events that occur in the poem are few: in Book I Milton, unhappy in the heaven he had imagined in *Paradise Lost*, hears a Bard's song that inspires him to reenter the world of time and space in order to achieve self-redefinition through his influence on Blake. Milton falls through the bosom of Albion, the giant spirit of Britain, enters into Blake the artist, and wrestles in the Holy Land to reshape Urizen. Here Blake draws together what Milton had put asunder —Biblical myth and English history—and fuses them with a new psychological myth. The rest of Book I is taken up with a description of the works of Los, the spirit of Imagination. In Book II Milton's feminine counterpart, his sixfold emanation Ololon, follows Milton down into Blake's garden in Felpham and—despite the intervention of the Covering Cherub who always seeks to keep humanity from reclaiming Paradise—the lovers are reconciled. In this union Jesus is made manifest and as Albion stirs in his sleep the Last Judgment and Harvest are about to begin.

Though Blake is at pains in *Milton* to explain a number of his cosmological symbols, the poem can seem bewildering because customary expectations regarding the identities of characters and the sphere of their actions are not respected. A condition of Being outside time and space, called Eternity, is presupposed. Insofar as Eternity is superior to the mundane world and is the home of postmortal existence it is like traditional ideas of heaven, but insofar as it is a state of cosmic consciousness it is a total comprehension of mundane life. Time and space as well as Eternity are variously subdivided so that what are essentially the same events may be described in varied and apparently contradictory ways, and some events which are separated in ordinary space and time take place simultaneously in Eternity. Within Time and Space there can be no single adequate account of what happens; everything depends on the shifting perspectives of the observer, who also participates in the action.

Similarly, characters are not assigned a single invariable set of characteristics but are rather conceived as bundles of possibilities and perspectives expressed differently according to circumstances. Something analogous to Blake's *Milton* might be seen in a production of *Hamlet* if one group of actors performed the hero's role according to varied critical interpretations of the play and another group of actors performed the heroine's role (a composite of Ophelia and Gertrude) according to Hamlet's ambivalent responses to womankind. One actor in each group would also have to portray the male and female members of the audience and another pair would portray Shakespeare and the important women in his life. In *Milton* the two redemptive quests out of Eternity into time and space, undertaken by Milton and by Ololon, are described sequentially. But they are to be understood as occurring simultaneously, for all redemptive action takes place in a single "moment." The action occurs not only in Eternity but also in the three places where Blake the artist lived—Lambeth, Felpham, and South Molton Street. As Bloom has noted, the heroic quest of Milton is also a journey into the depths of the self. The new Milton at the end of the poem is Milton as Blake reimagined him, a reintegrated and regenerated person at one with his better self.

All four copies of this major prophecy have the date 1804 inscribed on the title page, but three are printed on paper watermarked 1808 and one on paper watermarked 1815. All are divided into two Books; the two earlier copies, A and B, consist of forty-five pages in all, including the Preface; the two later copies, C and D, omit the resounding Preface but add five or six pages and rearrange several others.

In this edition, the plate designations follow Erdman and (until 1974) Keynes by assigning the Preface a plate number and leaving off numbers for the seven full-page designs even though they are an integral part of the work. This convention does not correspond to any of Blake's own arrangements but is followed here for convenience of reference to other editions. Where the plate number of Copy D, our copy-text, differs from that of the standard editions, we supply the Copy D plate number in a footnote. The still different pagination of the Keynes and Wolf *Census* is noted only for full-page designs. We have printed the Preface from Copy A; it does not appear in Copy D. Color plates are from Copy C.

Milton

a Poem in 2 Books[1]

The Author & Printer W Blake 1804

To Justify the Ways of God to Men[2]

[PLATE 1]

Preface[3]

The Stolen and Perverted Writings of Homer & Ovid, of Plato & Cicero,[4] which all Men ought to contemn, are set up by artifice against the Sublime of the Bible. But when the New Age is at leisure to Pronounce, all will be set right: & those Grand Works of the more ancient & consciously & professedly Inspired Men will hold their proper rank, & the Daughters of Memory shall become the Daughters of Inspiration.[5] Shakespeare & Milton were both curbd by the general malady & infection from the silly Greek & Latin slaves of the Sword.[6]

Rouze up, O Young Men of the New Age! Set your foreheads

1. See color plate 22 for title page (plate 1 of Copy C).
When Blake etched the title page, dated 1804, he announced a twelve-book poem like *Paradise Lost.* Both the completed forty-five-page version (copies A and B) and the later forty-nine- and fifty-page versions (copies C and D) contain only two books, though the numeral 1 was incompletely altered and thus the title pages still seem to announce a twelve-book work.
2. Blake makes Milton's purpose (*Paradise Lost* I, 26) his own, but he rejects Milton's theology.
3. This contentious manifesto, containing some of Blake's most radical ideas on religion, politics, and art, as well as his most famous hymn, does not appear in the two last and longer versions of *Milton,* including our copy text, Copy D. It is reproduced here from Copy A.
4. This idea that the classics were plagiarized from the Bible, though shocking, had been articulated by Milton's Christ (*Paradise Regained* IV, 334 ff.).
5. In his preface to *The Reason of Church Government,* II, Milton rejects "Dame Memory and her Siren daughters" in favor of the Spirit who inspires prophecy and in *Paradise Lost* he invokes the heavenly muse Urania. According to Blake, however, Milton discovers after his death that he had nevertheless fallen under the sway of the wrong muses (*Milton* 14:29), an error Blake himself hopes to avoid.
6. In *On Homer's Poetry* and *On Virgil* Blake explains how the classical tradition glorifies militarism. Even though Milton rejects classical military heroism (*Paradise Lost* IX, 13–47), he had been ready to justify revolutionary warfare and thus failed to break cleanly from the militaristic bias of the classics.

against the ignorant Hirelings! For we have Hirelings in the Camp, the Court, & the University who would, if they could, for ever depress Mental & prolong Corporeal War.[7] Painters! on you I call! Sculptors! Architects! Suffer not the fashionable Fools to depress your powers by the prices they pretend to give for contemptible works or the expensive advertizing boasts that they make of such works; believe Christ & his Apostles that there is a Class of Men whose whole delight is in Destroying.[8] We do not want either Greek or Roman Models if we are just and true to our own Imaginations, those Worlds of Eternity in which we shall live for ever, in Jesus our Lord.

And did those feet in ancient time
Walk upon England's mountains green:
And was the holy Lamb of God,
On England's pleasant pastures seen!

And did the Countenance Divine,
Shine forth upon our clouded hills?
And was Jerusalem builded here,
Among these dark Satanic Mills?[9]

Bring me my Bow of burning gold:
Bring me my Arrows of desire:
Bring me my Spear: O clouds unfold!
Bring me my Chariot of fire!

I will not cease from Mental Fight,
Nor shall my Sword sleep in my hand:[1]
Till we have built Jerusalem,
In England's green & pleasant Land.[2]

7. In 1808 (the watermark date of the first three copies of *Milton*), the Napoleonic Wars had been going on for six years, with seven years yet to come before Waterloo; before the brief Peace of Amiens in 1802, England and France had been at war since 1793 (see chronology).

8. A development of the distinction between the Prolific and the Devouring in *Marriage of Heaven and Hell* 16.

9. Though there were as yet few factories with internal combustion engines in London, windmills, watermills, and treadmills were nothing new: Milton's Samson labors "Eyeless in Gaza at the Mill with slaves" (*Samson Agonistes*, line 41); cf. Blake's letter to Hayley, p. 474. Blake associated mills with mechanistic systems generally (*Public Address*, p. 421), such as involuted reductionist reasonings (*Four Zoas* IX, lines 818–20) and the orbits of the Newtonian universe (conclusion to *There is No Natural Religion* ⌊b⌋).

1. When Jerusalem was rebuilt after the captivity, only half the people worked while the other half stood guard with weapons, and "the builders, every one had his sword girded by his side, and so builded" (Nehemiah 4:18); for imagery of "Mental Fight," see Ephesians 6:10–20.

2. Cf. prefatory hymns to *Jerusalem*, II (p. 321) and IV (p. 348). On the *Milton* hymn as a whole see Nancy Goslee, *Studies in Romanticism* 13 (1974), 105–25.

Would to God that all the Lord's people were Prophets.
Numbers xi. ch. 29 v.[3]

[PLATE 2]

Milton

Book the First

Daughters of Beulah![4] Muses who inspire the Poet's Song
Record the journey of immortal Milton thro' your Realms
Of terror & mild moony lustre, in soft sexual delusions
Of varied beauty, to delight the wanderer and repose
His burning thirst & freezing hunger! Come into my hand
By your mild power; descending down the Nerves of my right arm
From out the Portals of my Brain, where by your ministry
The Eternal Great Humanity Divine planted his Paradise,[5]
And in it caus'd the Spectres of the Dead to take sweet forms
In likeness of himself. Tell also of the False Tongue! vegetated[6]
Beneath your land of shadows: of its sacrifices, and
Its offerings; even till Jesus, the image of the Invisible God,
Became its prey: a curse, an offering, and an atonement,[7]
For Death Eternal, in the heavens of Albion, & before the Gates
Of Jerusalem his Emanation, in the heavens beneath Beulah.

3. Blake cites Moses' prayer but alludes also to Milton's more optimistic echo in *Areopagitica*: "For now the time seems come, wherein Moses, the great prophet, may sit in heaven rejoicing to see that memorable and glorious wish of his fulfilled, when not only our seventy elders, but all the Lord's people, are become prophets."

4. In Isaiah 62:4 the happy married land; in *Pilgrim's Progress* the earthly paradise; cf. *Milton* 30:1. These "Muses" are the "Daughters of Inspiration" (*Milton* 1) within the poet's mind. Blake's invocation ("Say first . . . what cause") follows Milton's in *Paradise Lost* I, 26–33, but in *Milton,* as in *Paradise Regained,* the theme is redemption rather than the fall.

5. Literally a "garden"; the Garden of Eden is real not in remote history but in the mind of the true poet.

6. Psalm 120:2–4. The Satanic voice of the Accuser instigates the Crucifixion. The lying tongue is "beneath Beulah" because it inverts poetic truth. By metaphorical condensation the false tongue becomes identified with the flame that blocks the Western Gate of the Garden of Eden.

7. Although much of Milton's theology was radical—for example, he rejected the doctrine of the Trinity—his view of the atonement was the orthodox one that God demands man's death as punishment for sin, but accepts Jesus' sacrificial death as a substitute payment of man's debt (*Paradise Lost* III, 203–12, 236–41). To Blake, this view of the crucifixion was no different from "Druidical" sacrifice. According to H. C. Robinson, "Speaking of the Atonement in the ordinary Calvinistic sense, [Blake] said 'it is a horrible doctrine; if another pay your debt, I do not forgive it.' " On the relation of Blake's ideas of Classes and the Atonement see Mary Lynn Johnson, *Blake Studies* 6 (1973), 11–17.

Say first! what mov'd Milton, who walkd about in Eternity
One hundred years,[8] pondring the intricate mazes of Providence[9]
(Unhappy tho in heav'n, he obey'd, he murmur'd not, he was silent)
Viewing his Sixfold Emanation[1] scatter'd thro' the deep
In torment! To go into the deep her to redeem & himself perish?
What cause at length mov'd Milton to this unexampled deed?
A Bard's prophetic Song![2] for sitting at eternal tables,
Terrific among the Sons of Albion, in chorus solemn & loud,
A Bard broke forth! all sat attentive to the awful man:

Mark well my words! they are of your eternal salvation!

Three Classes[3] are Created by the Hammer of Los, & Woven

[PLATE 3]
By Enitharmon's Looms, when Albion was slain upon his Mountains
And in his Tent, thro envy of Living Form, even of the Divine Vision,
And of the sports of Wisdom in the Human Imagination,
Which is the Divine Body of the Lord Jesus, blessed for ever.
Mark well my words: they are of your eternal salvation!

Urizen lay in darkness & solitude, in chains of the mind lock'd up.[4]
Los siezd his Hammer & Tongs; he labourd at his resolute Anvil
Among indefinite Druid rocks & snows of doubt & reasoning.
Refusing all Definite Form, the Abstract Horror roofd, stony hard—
And a first Age passed over & a State of dismal woe!

8. Milton died in 1674.
9. Milton's own theology is as labyrinthine as that imagined by his fallen angels (*Paradise Lost* II, 561).
1. In corporeal form, his three wives and three daughters.
2. This song extends from 2:25 to 13:44.
3. They derive from Calvinist theology but are ironically inverted. The Elect are self-satisfied hypocrites, the Redeemed attempt to conform to the moral law, and the Reprobate are fiercely independent free-thinkers who—like the Devils in *Marriage of Heaven and Hell*—act from impulse and not from rules. In the agricultural terms of the Bard's song, the Reprobate plow new ground, the Redeemed harrow it for cultivation, and the Elect grind up the harvest in their mills. Satan is of the "Elect" because, like the Devil in *Paradise Regained*, he controls success in this world (cf. *Milton* 11:22, 25:36). He is not to be confused with "the Devil" in *Marriage of Heaven and Hell*. Satan is the essential evil of Negation, but "the Devil" personifies Energy and should be classed with the Reprobate rather than the Elect.
4. A reprise of *Urizen* 11:26.

Down sunk with fright a red round Globe hot burning; deep
Deep down into the Abyss: panting, conglobing, trembling—
And a second Age passed over & a State of dismal woe.

Rolling round into two little Orbs & closed in two little Caves
The Eyes beheld the Abyss: lest bones of solidness freeze over all—
And a third Age passed over & a State of dismal woe.

From beneath his Orbs of Vision, Two Ears in close volutions
Shot spiring out in the deep darkness & petrified as they grew—
And a fourth Age passed over & a State of dismal woe.

Hanging upon the wind, Two Nostrils bent down into the Deep—
And a fifth Age passed over & a State of dismal woe.

In ghastly torment sick, a Tongue of hunger & thirst flamed out—
And a sixth Age passed over & a State of dismal woe.

Enraged & stifled without & within: in terror & woe, he threw his
Right Arm to the north, his left Arm to the south, & his Feet
Stampd the nether Abyss in trembling & howling & dismay—
And a seventh Age passed over & a State of dismal woe.

Terrified Los stood in the Abyss & his immortal limbs
Grew deadly pale; he became what he beheld: for a red
Round Globe sunk down from his Bosom into the Deep. In pangs
He hoverd over it trembling & weeping: suspended it shook
The nether Abyss in tremblings. He wept over it, he cherish'd it
In deadly sickening pain: till [it] separated into a Female pale,
As the cloud that brings the snow: all the while from his Back
A blue fluid exuded in Sinews hardening in the Abyss
Till it separated into a Male Form howling in Jealousy.

Within labouring, beholding Without: from Particulars to Generals
Subduing his Spectre, they Builded the Looms of Generation.
They Builded Great Golgonooza Times on Times, Ages on Ages.
First Orc was Born, then the Shadowy Female, then All Los's Family.
At last Enitharmon brought forth Satan, Refusing Form in vain:
The Miller of Eternity made subservient to the Great Harvest,
That he may go to his own Place, Prince of the Starry Wheels.

[PLATE 4]
Beneath the Plow of Rintrah & the Harrow of the Almighty
In the hands of Palamabron, Where the Starry Mills of Satan
Are built beneath the Earth & Waters of the Mundane Shell:
Here the Three Classes of Men take their Sexual texture: Woven
The Sexual is Threefold: the Human is Fourfold.

"If you account it Wisdom when you are angry to be silent, and
Not to shew it: I do not account that Wisdom but Folly.
Every Man's Wisdom is peculiar to his own Individuality.
O Satan, my youngest born, art thou not Prince of the Starry Hosts
And of the Wheels of Heaven, to turn the Mills day & night?
Art thou not Newton's Pantocrator, weaving the Woof of Locke?
To Mortals thy Mills seem every thing & the Harrow of Shaddai
A scheme of Human conduct invisible & incomprehensible.
Get to thy Labours at the Mills & leave me to my wrath."

Satan was going to reply, but Los roll'd his loud thunders.

"Anger me not! thou canst not drive the Harrow in pity's paths.
Thy Work is Eternal Death, with Mills & Ovens & Cauldrons.
Trouble me no more: thou canst not have Eternal Life."

So Los spoke! Satan trembling obeyd, weeping along the way.
Mark well my words, they are of your eternal Salvation!

Between South Molton Street[5] & Stratford Place: Calvary's foot

5. Blake's home, 1803–21 (see map). This plate is a late addition to the poem, which in its shorter (forty-five-page) form refers to Blake's homes in Lambeth (1793–1800) and Felpham (1800–1803) (*Milton* 6:14; 36:21); Milton's presence in Blake's life, though described as a "moment" of revelation, extends over time and space. Tyburn's brook flowed underground near South Molton Street (see London map); Tyburn, the site of public executions (1196–1783), was to Blake a modern British Stonehenge or Calvary, a place of Druid sacrifice.

Where the Victims were preparing for Sacrifice, their Cherubim
Around their loins pourd forth their arrows & their bosoms beam
With all colours of precious stones, & their inmost palaces
Resounded with preparation of animals wild & tame,
(Mark well my words! Corporeal Friends are Spiritual Enemies)
Mocking Druidical Mathematical Proportion of Length, Bredth, Highth,
Displaying Naked Beauty! with Flute & Harp & Song.

[PLATE 5]
Palamabron with the fiery Harrow in morning returning
From breathing fields, Satan fainted beneath the artillery.[6]
Christ took on Sin in the Virgin's Womb, & put it off on the Cross.

All pitied the piteous & was wrath with the wrathful, & Los heard it.

And this is the manner of the Daughters of Albion in their beauty:
Every one is threefold in Head & Heart & Reins, & every one
Has three Gates into the Three Heavens of Beulah which shine
Translucent in their Foreheads & their Bosoms & their Loins,
Surrounded with fires unapproachable: but whom they please
They take up into their Heavens in intoxicating delight.
For the Elect cannot be Redeemd, but Created continually
By Offering & Atonement in the cruelties of Moral Law;
Hence the three Classes of Men take their fix'd destinations:
They are the Two Contraries & the Reasoning Negative.

While the Females prepare the Victims, the Males at Furnaces
And Anvils dance the dance of tears & pain: loud lightnings
Lash on their limbs as they turn the whirlwinds loose upon
The Furnaces, lamenting around the Anvils, & this their Song:

"Ah weak & wide astray! Ah shut in narrow doleful form,
Creeping in reptile flesh upon the bosom of the ground:
The Eye of Man, a little narrow orb closd up & dark,
Scarcely beholding the great light, conversing with the Void,
The Ear, a little shell in small volutions shutting out
All melodies & comprehending only Discord and Harmony;
The Tongue a little moisture fills, a little food it cloys,
A little sound it utters, & its cries are faintly heard,
Then brings forth Moral Virtue the cruel Virgin Babylon.

6. This story of how Satan took charge of the world "corrects" *Paradise Lost.* The biographical explanation that the Palamabron-Satan conflict represents Blake's quarrels at Felpham with his patron William Hayley from 1800 to 1803 does little to bring out its larger significance as an allegory of the way "mildness" becomes evil when it conceals rage and a desire for power (cf. "Argument," *Marriage of Heaven and Hell* 2). For another view of the "artillery" see *Milton* 5:43 and 12:38). For help with Blakean names not discussed here for lack of space, see S. Foster Damon, *A Blake Dictionary* (1967).

"Can such an Eye judge of the stars? & looking thro its tubes
Measure the sunny rays that point their spears on Udanadan?
Can such an Ear, filld with the vapours of the yawning pit,
Judge of the pure melodious harp struck by a hand divine?
Can such closed Nostrils feel a joy? or tell of autumn fruits
When grapes & figs burst their covering to the joyful air?
Can such a Tongue boast of the living waters? or take in
Ought but the Vegetable Ratio & loathe the faint delight?
Can such gross Lips percieve? Alas, folded within themselves
They touch not ought, but pallid turn & tremble at every wind."

Thus they sing, Creating the Three Classes among Druid Rocks.
Charles calls on Milton for Atonement. Cromwell is ready.
James calls for fires in Golgonooza, for heaps of smoking ruins
In the night of prosperity and wantonness which he himself Created,
Among the Daughters of Albion—among the Rocks of the Druids,
When Satan fainted beneath the arrows of Elynittria—
And Mathematic Proportion was subdued by Living Proportion.

[PLATE 6]
From Golgonooza, the spiritual Four-fold London eternal,
In immense labours & sorrows, ever building, ever falling.
Thro Albion's four Forests which overspread all the Earth;
From London Stone to Blackheath east: to Hounslow west:
To Finchley north: to Norwood south:[7] and the weights
Of Enitharmon's Loom play lulling cadences on the winds of Albion—
From Caithness in the north, to Lizard-point & Dover in the south.

Loud sounds the Hammer of Los, & loud his Bellows is heard
Before London to Hampstead's breadths & Highgate's heights, To
Stratford & old Bow: & across to the Gardens of Kensington
On Tyburn's Brook; loud groans Thames beneath the iron Forge
Of Rintrah & Palamabron, of Theotormon & Bromion, to forge the instruments
Of Harvest: the Plow & Harrow to pass over the Nations.

The Surrey hills glow like the clinkers of the furnace: Lambeth's Vale
(Where Jerusalem's foundations began; where they were laid in ruins,
Where they were laid in ruins from every Nation, & Oak Groves rooted)
Dark gleams before the Furnace-mouth, a heap of burning ashes.
When shall Jerusalem return & overspread all the Nations?
Return: return to Lambeth's Vale, O building of human souls!

7. These frequently mentioned suburbs (cf. *Milton* 26:19 and 35:13) are just outside the area covered by our map of London.

Thence stony Druid Temples overspread the Island white,
And thence from Jerusalem's ruins, from her walls of salvation
And praise: thro the whole Earth, where reard from Ireland
To Mexico & Peru west, & east to China & Japan; till Babel
The Spectre of Albion frownd over the Nations in glory & war.
All things begin & end in Albion's ancient Druid rocky shore,
But now the Starry Heavens are fled from the mighty limbs of Albion.

Loud sounds the Hammer of Los, loud turn the Wheels of Enitharmon.
Her Looms vibrate with soft affections, weaving the Web of Life
Out from the ashes of the Dead; Los lifts his iron Ladles
With molten ore: he heaves the iron cliffs in his rattling chains
From Hyde Park to the Alms-houses of Mile-end & old Bow.
Here the Three Classes of Mortal Men take their fixd destinations
And hence they overspread the Nations of the whole Earth & hence
The Web of Life is woven: & the tender sinews of life created
And the Three Classes of Men regulated by Los's Hammer:

[PLATE 7]
The first, The Elect from before the foundation of the World;
The second, The Redeem'd; The Third, The Reprobate & form'd
To destruction from the mother's womb: follow with me my plow![8]

Of the first class was Satan: with incomparable mildness,
His primitive tyrannical attempts on Los: with most endearing love
He soft intreated Los to give to him Palamabron's station;
For Palamabron returnd with labour wearied every evening
Palamabron oft refus'd; and as often Satan offer'd
His service till by repeated offers and repeated intreaties
Los gave to him the Harrow of the Almighty; alas blamable
Palamabron, fear'd to be angry lest Satan should accuse him of
Ingratitude, & Los believe the accusation thro Satan's extreme
Mildness. Satan labour'd all day (it was a thousand years);
In the evening returning terrified, overlabourd & astonish'd,
Embrac'd soft with a brother's tears Palamabron, who also wept.

Mark well my words! they are of your eternal salvation!

Next morning Palamabron rose: the horses of the Harrow
Were maddend with tormenting fury, & the servants of the Harrow,
The Gnomes, accus'd Satan, with indignation fury and fire.

8. This line is made up of two half-deleted lines; the equivalent of one line has been removed between "womb" and "follow." The original first line for this plate in Copies A and B was eradicated in C and D: "and woven (6:35) / By Enitharmon's Looms, & Spun beneath the Spindle of Tirzah" (7:1).

Then Palamabron, reddening like the Moon in an eclipse,
Spoke saying, "You know Satan's mildness and his self-imposition,
Seeming a brother, being a tyrant, even thinking himself a brother
While he is murdering the just: prophetic I behold
His future course thro' darkness and despair to eternal death.
But we must not be tyrants also! he hath assum'd my place
For one whole day, under pretence of pity and love to me:
My horses hath he maddend; and my fellow servants injur'd:
How should he, he, know the duties of another? O foolish
forbearance!
Would I had told Los all my heart! but patience O my friends,
All may be well: silent remain, while I call Los and Satan."

Loud as the wind of Beulah that unroots the rocks & hills
Palamabron call'd: and Los & Satan came before him
And Palamabron shew'd the horses & the servants, Satan wept,
And mildly cursing Palamabron, him accus'd of crimes
Himself had wrought. Los trembled; Satan's blandishments
almost
Perswaded the Prophet of Eternity that Palamabron
Was Satan's enemy, & that the Gnomes being Palamabron's friends
Were leagued together against Satan thro' ancient enmity.
What could Los do? how could he judge, when Satan's self
believ'd
That he had not oppres'd the horses of the Harrow, nor the
servants?

So Los said, "Henceforth Palamabron, let each his own station
Keep: nor in pity false, nor in officious brotherhood, where
None needs, be active." Mean time Palamabron's horses
Rag'd with thick flames redundant, & the Harrow maddend with
fury.
Trembling Palamabron stood, the strongest of Demons trembled:
Curbing his living creatures; many of the strongest Gnomes
They bit in their wild fury, who also madden'd like wildest beasts.

Mark well my words; they are of your eternal salvation!

[PLATE 8]
Mean while wept Satan before Los, accusing Palamabron;
Himself exculpating with mildest speech, for himself believ'd
That he had not opress'd nor injur'd the refractory servants.

But Satan returning to his Mills (for Palamabron had serv'd
The Mills of Satan as the easier task) found all confusion
And back return'd to Los, not fill'd with vengeance but with tears,
Himself convinc'd of Palamabron's turpitude. Los beheld
The servants of the Mills drunken with wine and dancing wild

With shouts and Palamabron's songs, rending the forests green

With ecchoing confusion, tho' the Sun was risen on high.

Then Los took off his left sandal, placing it on his head,[9]
Signal of solemn mourning: when the servants of the Mills
Beheld the signal they in silence stood, tho' drunk with wine.
Los wept! But Rintrah also came, and Enitharmon on
His arm lean'd tremblingly observing all these things.

And Los said, "Ye Genii of the Mills! the Sun is on high.
Your labours call you! Palamabron is also in sad dilemma.
His horses are mad! his Harrow confounded! his companions enrag'd.
Mine is the fault! I should have remember'd that pity divides the soul
And man, unmans: follow with me my Plow. This mournful day
Must be a blank in Nature: follow with me, and tomorrow again
Resume your labours, & this day shall be a mournful day."

Wildly they follow'd Los and Rintrah, & the Mills were silent.
They mourn'd all day, this mournful day of Satan & Palamabron:
And all the Elect & all the Redeem'd mourn'd one toward another
Upon the mountains of Albion among the cliffs of the Dead.

They Plow'd in tears! incessant pourd Jehovah's rain, & Molech's[1]
Thick fires contending with the rain thunder'd above, rolling
Terrible over their heads; Satan wept over Palamabron.
Theotormon & Bromion contended on the side of Satan
Pitying his youth and beauty; trembling at eternal death:
Michael contended against Satan in the rolling thunder
Thulloh[2] the friend of Satan also reprovd him; faint their reproof.

But Rintrah who is of the reprobate: of those form'd to destruction,
In indignation, for Satan's soft dissimulation of friendship,
Flam'd above all the plowed furrows, angry, red and furious.
Till Michael sat down in the furrow, weary dissolv'd in tears.
Satan, who drave the team beside him, stood angry & red;
He smote Thulloh & slew him, & he stood terrible over Michael
Urging him to arise: he wept! Enitharmon saw his tears.
But Los hid Thulloh from her sight, lest she should die of grief.
She wept: she trembled! she kissed Satan; she wept over Michael.
She form'd a Space for Satan & Michael & for the poor infected.
Trembling she wept over the Space, & clos'd it with a tender Moon.

9. A ludicrous gesture, as all mourning customs seem to be to those who do not share them. Blake may have heard of such a custom in the Indian *Mahabharata.*

1. A Miltonic devil based on a heathen idol who demanded the burning of children as sacrifices; cf. *Milton* 37:21.

2. A character invented to balance Michael, the traditional antagonist of Satan (Jude 9; Revelation 12:7; *Paradise Lost* VI).

Los secret buried Thulloh, weeping disconsolate over the moony
Space.

But Palamabron called down a Great Solemn Assembly,
That he who will not defend Truth may be compelled to
Defend a Lie, that he may be snared & caught & taken.

[PLATE 9]
And all Eden descended into Palamabron's tent
Among Albion's Druids & Bards, in the caves beneath Albion's
Death Couch, in the caverns of death, in the corner of the Atlantic.
And in the midst of the Great Assembly Palamabron pray'd:
"O God, protect me from my friends, that they have not power
over me;
Thou hast giv'n me power to protect myself from my bitterest
enemies."

Mark well my words, they are of your eternal salvation!

Then rose the Two Witnesses, Rintrah & Palamabron:
And Palamabron appeal'd to all Eden, and recievd
Judgment; and Lo! it fell on Rintrah and his rage:
Which now flam'd high & furious in Satan against Palamabron
Till it became a proverb in Eden: "Satan is among the Reprobate."[3]

Los in his wrath curs'd heaven & earth. He rent up Nations,
Standing on Albion's rocks among high-reard Druid temples
Which reach the stars of heaven & stretch from pole to pole.
He displacd continents, the oceans fled before his face.
He alter'd the poles of the world—east, west & north & south—
But he clos'd up Enitharmon from the sight of all these things.

For Satan flaming with Rintrah's fury hidden beneath his own
mildness
Accus'd Palamabron before the Assembly of ingratitude! of
malice:[4]

3. The mythology and allegory are perhaps excessively blended here. Satan, essentially a negative character, had seemed to have the "mildness" of Palamabron, but now he begins to "rage" as if he were Rintrah. Thus the issue becomes blurred so that the conflict between Palamabron and Satan is perceived as a question of who is to blame for this rage. A somewhat similar assumption of the role of Reprobate by a member of the Elect occurs in I Samuel 19:24, in which the prophetic power of Samuel so overcomes King Saul that he also strips naked and prophesies, causing people to ask, "Is Saul also among the prophets?"

4. By self-righteously claiming that he is being victimized, Satan becomes a usurping, repressive tyrant, a Jehovah. Cf. *Urizen* 4.

He created Seven deadly Sins, drawing out his infernal scroll
Of Moral laws and cruel punishments upon the clouds of Jehovah,
To pervert the Divine voice in its entrance to the earth,
With thunder of war & trumpet's sound, with armies of disease,
Punishments & deaths musterd & number'd; Saying, "I am God alone!
There is no other; let all obey my principles of moral individuality!
I have brought them from the uppermost innermost recesses
Of my Eternal Mind. Transgressors I will rend off for ever,
As now I rend this accursed Family from my covering."

Thus Satan rag'd amidst the Assembly! and his bosom grew
Opake against the Divine Vision; the paved terraces of
His bosom inwards shone with fires, but the stones becoming opake
Hid him from sight, in an extreme blackness and darkness.
And there a World of deeper Ulro was open'd, in the midst
Of the Assembly. In Satan's bosom a vast unfathomable Abyss.

Astonishment held the Assembly in an awful silence; and tears
Fell down as dews of night, & a loud solemn universal groan
Was utter'd from the east & from the west & from the south
And from the north; and Satan stood opake, immeasurable,
Covering the east with solid blackness, round his hidden heart,
With thunders utterd from his hidden wheels; accusing loud
The Divine Mercy, for protecting Palamabron in his tent.

Rintrah rear'd up walls of rocks and pourd rivers & moats
Of fire round the walls: columns of fire guard around
Between Satan and Palamabron in the terrible darkness.

And Satan not having the Science of Wrath, but only of Pity,
Rent them asunder, and wrath was left to wrath, & pity to pity.
He sunk down a dreadful Death, unlike the slumbers of Beulah.

The Separation was terrible: the Dead was repos'd on his Couch
Beneath the Couch of Albion, on the seven mountains of Rome
In the whole place of the Covering Cherub: Rome, Babylon, & Tyre.[5]
His Spectre raging furious descended into its Space.

5. This consolidation of error, derived from Ezekiel 28:16, reappears in formidable majesty in *Milton* 37:8 (see note). The traditional Protestant understanding of Revelation 17 is that the Church of Rome, perverter of the Word, is the Whore and Beast. The unscrambling of all such historical distortions—including Protestant ones—is the task of prophecy.

[PLATE 10]†
Then Los & Enitharmon knew that Satan is Urizen
Drawn down by Orc & the Shadowy Female into Generation.
Oft Enitharmon enterd weeping into the Space, there appearing
An aged Woman raving along the Streets (the Space is named
Canaan); then she returned to Los weary, frighted as from dreams.
The nature of a Female Space is this: it shrinks the Organs
Of Life till they become Finite & Itself seems Infinite.

And Satan vibrated in the immensity of the Space! Limited
To those without but Infinite to those within: it fell down and
Became Canaan: closing Los from Eternity in Albion's Cliffs
A mighty Fiend against the Divine Humanity mustring to War.

"Satan! Ah me! is gone to his own place," said Los! "Their God
I will not worship in their Churches, nor King in their Theatres.
Elynittria! whence is this Jealousy running along the mountains?
British Women were not Jealous when Greek & Roman were Jealous!
Everything in Eternity shines by its own Internal light: but thou
Darkenest every Internal light with the arrows of thy quiver
Bound up in the horns of Jealousy to a deadly fading Moon,
And Ocalythron binds the Sun into a Jealous Globe,
That every thing is fixd Opake without Internal light."

So Los lamented over Satan, who triumphant divided the Nations:

[PLATE 11]‡
He set his face against Jerusalem to destroy the Eon of Albion.

But Los hid Enitharmon from the sight of all these things,
Upon the Thames whose lulling harmony repos'd her soul:
Where Beulah lovely terminates in rocky Albion:
Terminating in Hyde Park, on Tyburn's awful brook.

And the Mills of Satan were separated into a moony Space
Among the rocks of Albion's Temples, and Satan's Druid sons
Offer the Human Victims throughout all the Earth, and Albion's
Dread Tomb immortal on his Rock, overshadowd the whole Earth:[6]

† Plate 11 in Copy D.
‡ Plate 12 in Copy D.
6. Satan's system of punishment, through Christian imperialism, "overshadowed the whole Earth" in the form of the British Empire.

Where Satan making to himself Laws from his own identity
Compell'd others to serve him in moral gratitude & submission,
Being call'd God: setting himself above all that is called God.
And all the Spectres of the Dead calling themselves Sons of God
In his Synagogues worship Satan under the Unutterable Name.

And it was enquir'd: "Why in a Great Solemn Assembly
The Innocent should be condemn'd for the Guilty?" Then an
    Eternal rose

Saying, "If the Guilty should be condemn'd, he must be an Eternal
    Death
And one must die for another throughout all Eternity.
Satan is fall'n from his station & never can be redeem'd
But must be new Created continually, moment by moment.
And therefore the Class of Satan shall be call'd the Elect, & those
Of Rintrah, the Reprobate, & those of Palamabron, the Redeem'd:
For he is redeem'd from Satan's Law, the wrath falling on Rintrah,
And therefore Palamabron dared not to call a solemn Assembly
Till Satan had assum'd Rintrah's wrath in the day of mourning
In a feminine delusion of false pride self-deciev'd."[7]

So spake the Eternal and confirm'd it with a thunderous oath.

But when Leutha[8] (a Daughter of Beulah) beheld Satan's
    condemnation
She down descended into the midst of the Great Solemn Assembly,
Offering herself a Ransom for Satan, taking on her, his Sin.

Mark well my words, they are of your eternal salvation!

And Leutha stood glowing with varying colours immortal,
    heart-piercing
And lovely: & her moth-like elegance shone over the Assembly.

At length, standing upon the golden floor of Palamabron
She spake: "I am the Author of this Sin! by my suggestion
My Parent power Satan has committed this transgression.
I loved Palamabron & I sought to approach his Tent,
But beautiful Elynittria with her silver arrows repelld me,

7. This hardly coherent justification for the suffering of the innocent is ascribed to "an Eternal." A theodicy, a justification of the ways of God to Man, must assert that somehow all evil works to a larger good. Blake is concerned with exposing the illogic in Christian systems that attribute both punishment and forgiveness to God. Free self-sacrifice breaks the cycle of sin and punishment, as will be seen in further redefinitions of the atonement.

8. This character, mentioned briefly in *Visions of the Daughters of Albion* 1, *Europe* 14, and *Book of Los* 3, becomes a Blakean version of Sin, the daughter and wife of Satan in *Paradise Lost,* II. Leutha's sudden appearance and offer of atonement introduces a feminine dimension and a new psychological element to the story of the Satan-Palambron conflict, a negative foreshadowing of the role Milton's own feminine counterpart is to play in his story.

[PLATE 12]§

For her light is terrible to me. I fade before her immortal beauty.
O wherefore doth a Dragon-form forth issue from my limbs
To sieze her new born son? Ah me! the wretched Leutha!
This to prevent, entering the doors of Satan's brain night after night[9]
Like sweet perfumes I stupified the masculine perceptions
And kept only the feminine awake. Hence rose his soft
Delusory love to Palamabron: admiration join'd with envy
Cupidity unconquerable! my fault, when at noon of day
The Horses of Palamabron call'd for rest and pleasant death:
I sprang out of the breast of Satan,[1] over the Harrow beaming
In all my beauty: that I might unloose the flaming steeds
As Elynittria use'd to do; but too well those living creatures
Knew that I was not Elynittria, and they brake the traces.
But me, the servants of the Harrow saw not: but as a bow
Of varying colours on the hills. Terribly rag'd the horses.
Satan astonishd, and with power above his own controll,
Compell'd the Gnomes to curb the horses, & to throw banks of sand
Around the fiery flaming Harrow in labyrinthine forms,
And brooks between to intersect the meadows in their course.
The Harrow cast thick flames: Jehovah thunderd above;
Chaos & ancient night fled from beneath the fiery Harrow:
The Harrow cast thick flames & orb'd us round in concave fires
A Hell of our own making. See, its flames still gird me round.
Jehovah thunder'd above! Satan in pride of heart
Drove the fierce Harrow among the constellations of Jehovah,
Drawing a third part[2] in the fires as stubble north & south
To devour Albion and Jerusalem the Emanation of Albion,
Driving the Harrow in Pity's paths. 'Twas then, with our dark fires
Which now gird round us (O eternal torment) I form'd the Serpent
Of precious stones & gold, turn'd poisons on the sultry wastes.
The Gnomes in all that day spar'd not: they curs'd Satan bitterly.

§ Plate 13 in Copy D.

9. As in *Paradise Lost* IV, 799, where Satan as a toad tempts Eve as she sleeps, and *Paradise Lost* IX, 187, where Satan enters the sleeping Serpent.

1. Cf. 12:38, "from the head of Satan." Derived from the Athena-like birth of Sin from the head of Satan in *Paradise Lost*, II, 758, based on James 1:15, "Then when lust hath conceived, it bringeth forth sin; and sin, when it is finished, bringeth forth death." Blake's transpositions of such symbols in Milton's work, which abound in this poem, are supposed (ideally) to be recognized by the reader, as well as by the character Milton as he listens to the Bard.

2. On the authority of Revelation 12:4 (cf. Daniel 8:10), in which the Dragon with his tail draws down "a third part of the stars of heaven," Milton describes the fallen angels as a third part of the heavenly host (*Paradise Lost* II, 692; V, 710).

To do unkind things in kindness! with power armd, to say
The most irritating things in the midst of tears and love:
These are the stings of the Serpent! thus did we by them; till thus
They in return retaliated, and the Living Creatures maddend.
The Gnomes labourd. I weeping hid in Satan's inmost brain;
But when the Gnomes refus'd to labour more, with blandishments
I came forth from the head of Satan! back the Gnomes recoil'd.
And call'd me Sin, and for a sign portentous held me.[3] Soon
Day sunk and Palamabron return'd; trembling I hid myself
In Satan's inmost Palace of his nervous fine wrought Brain:
For Elynittria met Satan with all her singing women.
Terrific in their joy & pouring wine of wildest power,
They gave Satan their wine: indignant at the burning wrath,
Wild with prophetic fury, his former life became like a dream.
Cloth'd in the Serpent's folds, in selfish holiness demanding purity,
Being most impure, self-condemn'd to eternal tears, he drove
Me from his inmost Brain & the doors clos'd with thunder's sound.
O Divine Vision who didst create the Female: to repose
The Sleepers of Beulah, pity the repentant Leutha. My

[PLATE 13]*
Sick Couch bears the dark shades of Eternal Death infolding
The Spectre of Satan. He furious refuses to repose in sleep.
I humbly bow in all my Sin before the Throne Divine;
Not so the Sick-one. Alas what shall be done him to restore?
Who calls the Individual Law, Holy: and despises the Saviour,
Glorying to involve Albion's Body in fires of eternal War—"

Now Leutha ceas'd: tears flow'd: but the Divine Pity supported her.

"All is my fault! We are the Spectre of Luvah the murderer
Of Albion: O Vala! O Luvah! O Albion! O lovely Jerusalem
The Sin was begun in Eternity, and will not rest to Eternity
Till two Eternitys meet together, Ah! lost! lost! for ever!"

So Leutha spoke. But when she saw that Enitharmon had
Created a New Space to protect Satan from punishment
She fled to Enitharmon's Tent & hid herself. Loud raging
Thundered the Assembly dark & clouded. And they ratify'd
The kind decision of Enitharmon & gave a Time to the Space,
Even Six Thousand years, and sent Lucifer for its Guard.[4]

3. Echoes *Paradise Lost* II, 760.
* Plate 14 in Copy D.
4. Lucifer ("light-bearer"), Isaiah 14:12, is the first of seven historical phases of the conception of God in the fallen world: the others are *Moloch* (a devourer of children), Leviticus 18:21, 20:2; *Elohim* ("gods"), Genesis 1; *Shaddai* ("God Almighty"), Exodus 6:3; *Pahad* ("Fear"), Genesis 31:42; *Jehovah* ("Lord God"), Genesis 2:4; *the Lamb* (i.e., Jesus), John 1:29. These are the "Seven Eyes of God" (*Jerusalem* 55:31).

But Lucifer refus'd to die & in pride he forsook his charge.
And they elected Molech, and when Molech was impatient
The Divine hand found the Two Limits: first of Opacity, then of Contraction:[5]
Opacity was named Satan, Contraction was named Adam.
Triple Elohim came: Elohim wearied fainted: they elected Shaddai.
Shaddai angry, Pahad descended: Pahad terrified, they sent Jehovah.
And Jehovah was leprous; loud he call'd, stretching his hand to Eternity,
For then the Body of Death was perfected in hypocritic holiness
Around the Lamb, a Female Tabernacle woven in Cathedron's Looms.[6]
He died as a Reprobate, he was Punish'd as a Transgressor!
Glory! Glory! Glory! to the Holy Lamb of God!
I touch the heavens as an instrument to glorify the Lord!

The Elect shall meet the Redeem'd, on Albion's rocks they shall meet
Astonish'd at the Transgressor, in him beholding the Saviour.[7]
And the Elect shall say to the Redeemd, "We behold it is of Divine
Mercy alone! of Free Gift and Election that we live.
Our Virtues & Cruel Goodnesses, have deserv'd Eternal Death."
Thus they weep upon the fatal Brook of Albion's River.

But Elynittria met Leutha in the place where she was hidden,
And threw aside her arrows, and laid down her sounding Bow.
She sooth'd her with soft words & brought her to Palamabron's bed
In moments new created for delusion, interwoven round about.
In dreams she bore the shadowy Spectre of Sleep, & namd him Death.
In dreams she bore Rahab the mother of Tirzah & her sisters
In Lambeth's vales: in Cambridge & in Oxford, places of Thought:
Intricate labyrinths of Times and Spaces unknown, that Leutha lived
In Palamabron's Tent and Oothoon was her charming guard.

5. The limits to the fall: the processes of becoming impervious to divine illumination (opacity) and of becoming confined within the body (contraction) are arrested just short of the point of no return. Donald Ault, *Blake's Visionary Physics* (1973), suggests that Blake was transforming Newton's conception of mathematical limits.

6. Cf. *Milton* 24:35, 26:36. In these looms Enitharmon weaves the merely physical body. The worship of the dead body of Christ as a "tabernacle" or shrine is the idolatry of Antichrist. The Bard recognizes that by identifying with the sinner Christ enacts forgiveness of sin.

7. A prophecy of mutual forgiveness and reconciliation through a recognition that Jesus was among the Reprobate. The "Elect" will no longer see themselves as a privileged elite immune from sin but will recognize that they also need Mercy because of their own evil of self-righteousness.

The Bard ceas'd. All consider'd and a loud resounding murmur
Continu'd round the Halls; and much they questiond the immortal
Loud voic'd Bard. And many condemn'd the high toned Song
Saying, "Pity and Love are too venerable for the imputation
Of Guilt." Others said, "If it is true! if the acts have been perform'd,
Let the Bard himself witness. Where hadst thou this terrible Song?"

The Bard replied, "I am Inspired! I know it is Truth! for I Sing

[PLATE 14]†
According to the inspiration of the Poetic Genius
Who is the eternal all-protecting Divine Humanity
To whom be Glory & Power & Dominion Evermore, Amen."

Then there was great murmuring in the Heavens of Albion
Concerning Generation & the Vegetative power & concerning
The Lamb, the Saviour: Albion trembled to Italy Greece & Egypt
To Tartary & Hindostan & China & to Great America
Shaking the roots & fast foundations of the Earth in doubtfulness.
The loud voic'd Bard terrify'd took refuge in Milton's bosom.[8]

Then Milton rose up from the heavens of Albion ardorous!
The whole Assembly wept prophetic, seeing in Milton's face
And in his lineaments divine the shades of Death & Ulro.
He took off the robe of the promise, & ungirded himself from the oath of God.[9]

And Milton said, "I go to Eternal Death! The Nations still
Follow after the detestable Gods of Priam;[1] in pomp
Of warlike selfhood, contradicting and blaspheming.

† Plate 15 in Copy D.

8. After his forthright declaration in *Milton* 13:51–14:3, which may be intended to recall Milton's *Areopagitica*, a treatise advocating freedom of the press, the Bard suddenly becomes intimidated and fugitive.

9. The afterlife Milton experiences in the Heavens of Albion is inauthentic because it is achieved only by the outer shell of his personality. His essential self, as well as the works he has created and the women he has loved, are left in an unresolved state of conflict in the world of time and space. Instead of waiting for his dead body to be resurrected, Milton is now imbued with the living Spirit and casts off his former self in preparation for reentering the "death" (cf. *Paradise Lost* I, 3) of the fallen world. By undergoing death as "self-annihilation," he will actually achieve new life, though it seems to him that he will be totally destroyed. This passage is illustrated on plate 16.

1. Cf. *Milton* 25:49. The chief gods of the Trojans were given the Roman names Venus and Mars after they came to Rome with Aeneas (cf. *On Virgil*); Milton's prophecies have not altered the war-loving nature of his readers.

When will the Resurrection come; to deliver the sleeping body
From corruptibility: O when Lord Jesus wilt thou come?
Tarry no longer; for my soul lies at the gates of death.
I will arise and look forth for the morning of the grave.
I will go down to the sepulcher to see if morning breaks!
I will go down to self annihilation and eternal death,
Lest the Last Judgment come & find me unannihilate
And I be siez'd & giv'n into the hands of my own Selfhood.
The Lamb of God is seen thro' mists & shadows, hov'ring
Over the sepulchers in clouds of Jehovah & winds of Elohim:
A disk of blood, distant; & heav'ns & earths roll dark between.
What do I here before the Judgment? without my Emanation?
With the daughters of memory, & not with the daughters of
inspiration?
I in my Selfhood am that Satan: I am that Evil One!
He is my Spectre! in my obedience to loose him from my Hells
To claim the Hells, my Furnaces, I go to Eternal Death."[2]

And Milton said, "I go to Eternal Death!" Eternity shudder'd
For he took the outside course, among the graves of the dead,
A mournful shade. Eternity shudderd at the image of eternal
death.

Then on the verge of Beulah he beheld his own Shadow:
A mournful form double: hermaphroditic:[3] male & female
In one wonderful body, and he enterd into it
In direful pain, for the dread shadow, twenty-seven-fold[4]
Reachd to the depths of dirast Hell, & thence to Albion's land:
Which is this earth of vegetation on which now I write.

The Seven Angels of the Presence[5] wept over Milton's Shadow.

2. Insofar as Milton's Satan represents Energy (*Marriage of Heaven and Hell* 4–5), he must be freed from the torment to which Milton had relegated him. Insofar as Milton, unable to recognize his own hypocrisy, has been imprisoned in his own Selfhood, he has been like Satan in the Bard's Song. Milton is changing his conception of Satan; no longer is the principle of evil embodied in a rebel angel; instead, it lies in one's own self-deception and self-righteousness.

3. Cf. *Milton* 19:33, 37:37. Embodying Milton's unresolved, unproductive, and self-contradictory views on sexuality, the nature of woman, and the women in his family.

4. Cf. *Milton* 17:24, 37:35. A number of incompletion (a multiple of three); when completed by one additional number, as in *Milton* 36:9, it becomes a multiple of the perfect number seven.

5. The eternal identities of the seven historically conceived images of God in *Milton* 13:17–27; guardian angels in *Milton* 39:3–13. In Eden (*Milton* 15:5), they join Milton himself to form a community of Eight. Biblically, the number seven represents perfection; it is used throughout Revelation and other visionary books; beyond this, eight is a transcendent or eternal number (cf. *Milton* 20:47).

[PLATE 15]‡
As when a man dreams, he reflects not that his body sleeps,
Else he would wake; so seem'd he entering his Shadow: but
With him the Spirits of the Seven Angels of the Presence
Entering, they gave him still perceptions of his Sleeping body,
Which now arose and walk'd with them in Eden, as an Eighth
Image Divine, tho' darken'd; and tho walking as one walks
In sleep; and the Seven comforted and supported him.

Like as a Polypus[6] that vegetates beneath the deep:
They saw his Shadow vegetated underneath the Couch
Of death: for when he enterd into his Shadow: Himself:
His real and immortal Self: was as appeard to those
Who dwell in immortality, as One sleeping on a couch
Of gold; and those in immortality gave forth their Emanations
Like Females of sweet beauty, to guard round him & to feed
His lips with food of Eden in his cold and dim repose!
But to himself he seemd a wanderer lost in dreary night.

Onwards his Shadow kept its course among the Spectres, call'd
Satan, but swift as lightning passing them. Startled the shades
Of Hell beheld him in a trail of light as of a comet
That travels into Chaos: so Milton went guarded within.[7]

The nature of infinity is this: That every thing has its
Own Vortex;[8] and when once a traveller thro' Eternity
Has passd that Vortex, he percieves it roll backward behind
His path, into a globe itself infolding; like a sun,
Or like a moon, or like a universe of starry majesty,
While he keeps onwards in his wondrous journey on the earth;
Or like a human form, a friend with whom he livd benevolent.

‡ Plate 17 in Copy D.

6. Here introduced as a simile, the Polypus becomes (in *Milton* 24:38, 29:31, 39:24, 34:31, 35:19, 36:13, and 38:2) a hideous symbol of the entrapping systems of Ulro, the lowest plane of existence; see Paul Miner, *Texas Studies in Literature and Language* 2 (1960), 198–205. The verb "vegetates" refers to Blake's idea that a nonspiritual materialistic existence is subhuman and formless; humanity is enmeshed in constricting vines (see *Milton* 24:34–43); these will be consumed in the apocalypse or "Last Harvest & Vintage."

7. Milton's journey recalls that of Satan, first to the Gate of Hell (*Paradise Lost,* II, 629) and then through Chaos (*Paradise Lost* II, 891). Milton's trail "as of a comet" (15:19) echoes *Paradise Lost* II, 708 (see design on p. 292); in Book II Ololon follows in Milton's track as Sin and Death follow in Satan's (*Milton* 21:7).

8. This passage contains Blake's most complete exposition of this cosmological symbol derived from Descartes. (See discussions in books by Frye, Adams, and Ault listed in the Bibliography.) Eternity is the temporal world turned inside out; these contrary planes of existence may be visualized as the two chambers of an hourglass if each chamber were thought of as a conical helix. The passage from one helix to the other would involve transformation at the connecting channel or point of intersection. See also Susan Fox, *Poetic Form in Blake's Milton* (1976).

As the eye of man views both the east & west encompassing
Its vortex; and the north & south, with all their starry host:
Also the rising sun & setting moon he views surrounding
His corn-fields and his valleys of five hundred acres square,
Thus is the earth one infinite plane, and not as apparent
To the weak traveller confin'd beneath the moony shade;
Thus is the heaven a vortex passd already, and the earth
A vortex not yet pass'd by the traveller thro' Eternity.

First Milton saw Albion upon the Rock of Ages,[9]
Deadly pale outstretchd and snowy cold, storm coverd:
A Giant form of perfect beauty outstretchd on the rock
In solemn death. The Sea of Time & Space thunderd aloud
Against the rock, which was inwrapped with the weeds of death.
Hovering over the cold bosom, in its vortex Milton bent down
To the bosom of death. What was underneath soon seemd above.
A cloudy heaven mingled with stormy seas in loudest ruin;
But as a wintry globe descends precipitant thro' Beulah bursting,
With thunders loud, and terrible: so Milton's shadow fell,
Precipitant loud thundring into the Sea of Time & Space.[1]

Then first I saw him in the Zenith as a falling star,[2]
Descending perpendicular, swift as the swallow or swift;
And on my left foot falling on the tarsus, enterd there;[3]
But from my left foot a black cloud redounding spread over Europe.

Then Milton knew that the Three Heavens of Beulah were beheld
By him on earth in his bright pilgrimage of sixty years

9. Britain in bondage is the eponymous ancestor laid out like a corpse. The "Rock of Ages" is derived from Biblical tradition rather than directly from the Bible.

1. As the Atlantic covers Atlantis, so the fallen world covers Eternity.

2. Cf. Mulciber's fall, *Paradise Lost* I, 745.

3. Like Los's gesture of putting his sandal on his head, this symbolism of the ankle bones of the left foot appears more whimsical or arbitrary than is usual in Blake. The foot is the lowest part of the body, and the left side—*gauche* or sinister—is traditionally considered the fallen side. In self-annihilation, Milton the starry soul is willing to fall down to Blake's foot to accomplish his purpose; when that foot is touched Blake is enabled to walk through Eternity (*Milton* 21:12–14). The connection between artists through the foot is perhaps associated with the lameness of Vulcan the blacksmith god (cf. *Four Zoas* IX, 138:8). Erdman, *The Illuminated Blake* (Garden City, N.Y.: Doubleday, 1974, p. 248) sees a pun alluding to the conversion experience on the Damascus Road which changed Saul of Tarsus into Paul the apostle (Acts 9:3). See illustration on p. 285.

[PLATE 17]§
In those three females whom his Wives, & those three whom his Daughters
Had represented and containd, that they might be resum'd
By giving up of Selfhood: & they distant view'd his journey
In their eternal spheres, now Human, tho' their Bodies remain clos'd
In the dark Ulro till the Judgment: also Milton knew they and
Himself was Human, tho' now wandering thro Death's Vale
In conflict with those Female forms, which in blood & jealousy
Surrounded him, dividing & uniting without end or number.

He saw the Cruelties of Ulro, and he wrote them down
In iron tablets: and his Wives' & Daughters' names were these:
Rahab and Tirzah, & Milcah & Malah & Noah & Hoglah.[4]
They sat rang'd round him as the rocks of Horeb round the land
Of Canaan: and they wrote in thunder, smoke, and fire
His dictate; and his body was the Rock Sinai: that body
Which was on earth born to corruption: & the six Females
Are Hor & Peor & Bashan & Abarim & Lebanon & Hermon,[5]
Seven rocky masses terrible in the Desarts of Midian.

But Milton's Human Shadow continu'd journeying above
The rocky masses of The Mundane Shell,[6] in the Lands
Of Edom & Aram & Moab & Midian & Amalek.[7]

§ Plate 19 in Copy D. Plate 16, which is plate 18 in Copy D, is the full-page design entitled "To Annihilate the Selfhood of Deceit & False Forgiveness," reproduced on p. 265.

4. Except for Rahab, these are the names of the five brotherless daughters of Zelophehad who established the right of female inheritance (Numbers 26:33). See also the note to "To Tirzah," p. 58. In Joshua 2:11 Rahab is a harlot of Jericho who harbored Hebrew spies before they captured the city. In traditional Christian commentaries, which justify Hebrew militarism, Rahab is glorified and set up as a type of the Church. Blake identifies her with the Whore of Babylon (Revelation 17).

5. Mountains and hills in adjacent lands hostile to the Jews (see map).

6. A major symbol of the material world mentioned on nine succeeding pages, depicted in *Milton* 33, and elaborately described in *Milton* 34:31–46. The conception of the universe as a primordial egg is of ancient origin, appearing in Plato's *Symposium*, and implied in Genesis and *Paradise Lost* I, 20–22. At first Milton is outside this egg and Ololon is within (*Milton* 21:30) but the shell between them is cracked by Milton's descent (*Milton* 34:40–42).

7. Tribes hostile to the Jews (see map).

The Mundane Shell is a vast Concave Earth: an immense
Hardend shadow of all things upon our Vegetated Earth
Enlarg'd into dimension & deform'd into indefinite space,
In Twenty-seven Heavens and all their Hells; with Chaos
And Ancient Night; & Purgatory. It is a cavernous Earth
Of labyrinthine intricacy, twenty-seven folds of opakeness
And finishes where the lark mounts; here Milton journeyed
In that Region call'd Midian, among the Rocks of Horeb.[8]
For travellers from Eternity pass outward to Satan's seat,
But travellers to Eternity pass inward to Golgonooza.

Los the Vehicular terror beheld him, & divine Enitharmon
Call'd all her daughters, Saying, "Surely to unloose my bond
Is this Man come! Satan shall be unloosd upon Albion!"[9]

Los heard in terror Enitharmon's words: in fibrous strength
His limbs shot forth like roots of trees against the forward path
Of Milton's journey. Urizen beheld the immortal Man,

[PLATE 18]*
And Tharmas Demon of the Waters, & Orc, who is Luvah.

The Shadowy Female[1] seeing Milton, howl'd in her lamentation
Over the Deeps, outstretching her Twenty seven Heavens over
    Albion.

And thus the Shadowy Female howls in articulate howlings:

"I will lament over Milton in the lamentations of the afflicted.
My Garments shall be woven of sighs & heart broken lamentations.
The misery of unhappy Families shall be drawn out into its border,
Wrought with the needle, with dire sufferings poverty pain & woe.
Along the rocky Island & thence throughout the whole Earth

8. Horeb, also called Sinai, is the holy mountain where Moses received the stone tablets of the law (Exodus 3:1); Midian is the land between Egypt and the Promised Land (Numbers 31:2). On one plane of action Milton is retracing Moses' journey, but in his Blakean incarnation he will move beyond the Law. As Milton moves inward toward his confrontation with selfhood, the true Satan, Blake moves outward with Los toward Golgonooza (22:26), the city of art, the "spiritual fourfold London" (represented on our London map by a star, since it is in another dimension from the physical city of London). A diagram of the intersecting journeys of Blake and Milton would look like a Vortex (*Milton* 15:22).

9. Milton the liberator wrote against tyranny and in favor of divorce. Enitharmon, though longing for her own freedom, fears the release of Satan (an identity claimed by Milton in 14:30). In Revelation 20:2–3, 7, Satan is both bound and freed by the same angel.

* Plate 20 in Copy D.

1. As the most indefinite manifestation of Vala, Orc's mate, she has been called the "Shadowy Daugher of Urthona" (*America* 1:1) and the "nameless shadowy female" (*Europe* 1:1).

There shall be the sick Father & his starving Family! there
The Prisoner in the stone Dungeon & the Slave at the Mill!
I will have Writings written all over it in Human Words
That every Infant that is born upon the Earth shall read
And get by rote as a hard task of a life of sixty years.
I will have Kings inwoven upon it & Councellors & Mighty Men.
The Famine shall clasp it together with buckles & Clasps,
And the Pestilence shall be its fringe & the War its girdle,
To divide into Rahab & Tirzah that Milton may come to our tents.
For I will put on the Human Form & take the Image of God,
Even Pity & Humanity, but my Clothing shall be Cruelty.
And I will put on Holiness as a breastplate & as a helmet
And all my ornaments shall be of the gold of broken hearts
And the precious stones of anxiety & care & desperation & death
And repentance for sin & sorrow & punishment & fear
To defend me from thy terrors O Orc! my only beloved!"

Orc answerd, "Take not the Human Form O loveliest. Take not
Terror upon thee! Behold how I am & tremble lest thou also
Consume in my Consummation; but thou maist take a Form
Female & lovely, that cannot consume in Man's consummation.
Wherefore dost thou Create & Weave this Satan for a Covering?
When thou attemptest to put on the Human Form, my wrath
Burns to the top of heaven against thee in Jealousy & Fear.
Then I rend thee asunder; then I howl over thy clay & ashes.
When wilt thou put on the Female Form as in times of old,
With a Garment of Pity & Compassion like the Garment of God?
His garments are long sufferings for the Children of Men;
Jerusalem is his Garment & not thy Covering Cherub, O lovely
Shadow of my delight who wanderest seeking for the prey."

So spoke Orc when Oothoon & Leutha hoverd over his Couch
Of fire in interchange of Beauty & Perfection, in the darkness
Opening interiorly into Jerusalem & Babylon, shining glorious
In the Shadowy Female's bosom. Jealous her darkness grew:
Howlings filld all the desolate places in accusations of Sin,
In Female beauty shining in the unformd void, & Orc in vain
Stretch'd out his hands of fire, & wooed: they triumph in his pain.

Thus darkend the Shadowy Female tenfold & Orc tenfold
Glowd on his rocky Couch against the darkness: loud thunders
Told of the enormous conflict. Earthquake beneath, around,
Rent the Immortal Females, limb from limb & joint from joint,
And moved the fast foundations of the Earth to wake the Dead.

Urizen emerged from his Rocky Form & from his Snows,

[PLATE 19]†

And he also darkend his brows: freezing dark rocks between
The footsteps and infixing deep the feet in marble beds:
That Milton labourd with his journey, & his feet bled sore
Upon the clay now changd to marble; also Urizen rose,
And met him on the shores of Armon; & by the streams of the brooks.

Silent they met, and silent strove among the streams of Arnon
Even to Mahanaim,[2] when with cold hand Urizen stoop'd down
And took up water from the river Jordan:[3] pouring on
To Milton's brain the icy fluid from his broad cold palm.
But Milton took of the red clay of Succoth,[4] moulding it with care
Between his palms; and filling up the furrows of many years
Beginning at the feet of Urizen, and on the bones
Creating new flesh on the Demon cold, and building him,
As with new clay, a Human form in the Valey of Beth Peor.[5]

Four Universes round the Mundane Egg remain Chaotic:
One to the North, named Urthona: One to the South, named Urizen:
One to the East, named Luvah: One to the West, named Tharmas.
They are the Four Zoas that stood around the Throne Divine!
But when Luvah assum'd the World of Urizen to the South
And Albion was slain upon his mountains, & in his tent;
All fell towards the Center in dire ruin, sinking down.
And in the South remains a burning fire; in the East a void;
In the West, a world of raging waters; in the North a solid,
Unfathomable! without end. But in the midst of these,
Is built eternally the Universe of Los and Enitharmon:
Towards which Milton went, but Urizen oppos'd his path.

† Plate 21 in Copy D.

2. Where angels met Jacob (Genesis 32:1–2) before he wrestled with the angel in Jabbok-Peniel (Genesis 32:22–30); also mentioned in *Paradise Lost* XI, 213–15.

3. The Arnon, flowing east into the Dead Sea and dividing Israelite and Amorite teritory, is geographically separate from the Jordan (see map) but the two rivers are brought together for their symbolic associations.

4. In the clay ground near Succoth, the cunning artisan Hiram cast brass utensils for Solomon's temple (I Kings 7:46). Red clay, the literal meaning of "Adam" (see *Marriage of Heaven and Hell* 2), was molded by God into human flesh (Genesis 2:7).

5. Where the Israelites rested (Deuteronomy 3:27–29) before entering the promised land, and where Moses was buried (Deuteronomy 34:6).

To Annihilate the Self-
hood of Deceit &
False Forgiveness

The Man and Demon strove many periods. Rahab beheld
Standing on Carmel;[6] Rahab and Tirzah trembled to behold
The enormous strife—one giving life, the other giving death
To his adversary—and they sent forth all their sons & daughters
In all their beauty to entice Milton across the river.[7]

The Twofold form Hermaphroditic: and the Double-sexed:
The Female-male & the Male-female, self-dividing stood
Before him in their beauty, & in cruelties of holiness:
Shining in darkness, glorious upon the deeps of Entuthon.[8]

Saying "Come thou to Ephraim! behold the Kings of Canaan!
The beautiful Amalekites;[9] behold the fires of Youth
Bound with the Chain of Jealousy by Los & Enitharmon;[1]
The banks of Cam:[2] cold learning's streams: London's
    dark-frowning towers:
Lament upon the winds of Europe in Rephaim's Vale[3]
Because Ahania, rent apart into a desolate night,
Laments! & Enion wanders like a weeping inarticulate voice,
And Vala labours for her bread & water among the Furnaces.
Therefore bright Tirzah triumphs; putting on all beauty.
And all perfection in her cruel sports among the Victims.
Come bring with thee Jerusalem with songs on the Grecian Lyre!
In Natural Religion! in experiments on Men,
Let her be Offerd up to Holiness! Tirzah numbers her:
She numbers with her fingers every fibre ere it grow;
Where is the Lamb of God? where is the promise of his coming?[4]

6. Removed from the scene of conflict, like Mount Ida in Homer's *Iliad*, from which the classical gods both witness and influence events. Mount Carmel is also the site of the contest between Elijah and Baal's prophets (I Kings 18:19).
7. The temptation for Milton is either to enter the promised land prematurely or to rule over the heathen lands surrounding Israel; to do either would be an error of worldly accommodation.
8. Cf. *Milton* 26:25. Entuthon Benython is the forest of error.
9. Antagonists of Joshua and Moses in battles near Horeb (Exodus 17:8–16).
1. In *Urizen* 20 and *Four Zoas* V (60:6–30) Orc is bound by his jealous father.
2. The river of Cambridge (*Milton* 13:42), where Milton had been a student.
3. Literally, "valley of the shades of the dead" where David repeatedly defeated the Philistines (II Samuel 5:18, 23:13); a place of scanty harvest (Isaiah 17:5).
4. The words of the scoffers in II Peter 3:4.

Her shadowy Sisters form the bones, even the bones of Horeb:
Around the marrow: and the orbed scull around the brain;
His Images are born for War! for Sacrifice to Tirzah!
To Natural Religion! to Tirzah the Daughter of Rahab the Holy!
She ties the knot of nervous fibres, into a white brain!
She ties the knot of bloody veins, into a red hot heart!
Within her bosom Albion lies embalmd, never to awake!
Hand is become a rock! Sinai & Horeb is Hyle & Coban;
Scofield is bound in iron armour before Reuben's Gate![5]
She ties the knot of milky seed into two lovely Heavens,[6]

[PLATE 20]‡
Two yet but one: each in the other sweet reflected! these
Are our Three Heavens beneath the shades of Beulah, land of rest!
Come then to Ephraim & Manasseh O beloved-one!
Come to my ivory palaces O beloved of thy mother!
And let us bind thee in the bands of War & be thou King
Of Canaan and reign in Hazor where the Twleve Tribes meet."

So spoke they as in one voice: Silent Milton stood before
The darkend Urizen; as the sculptor silent stands before
His forming image; he walks round it patient labouring.
Thus Milton stood forming bright Urizen, while his Mortal part
Sat frozen in the rock of Horeb: and his Redeemed portion
Thus form'd the Clay of Urizen; but within that portion,
His real Human walkd above in power and majesty,
Tho darkend; and the Seven Angels of the Presence attended him.

O how can I with my gross tongue that cleaveth to the dust,[7]
Tell of the Four-fold Man, in starry numbers fitly orderd?
Or how can I with my cold hand of clay! But thou O Lord
Do with me as thou wilt! for I am nothing, and vanity.
If thou chuse to elect a worm, it shall remove the mountains.
For that portion namd the Elect: the Spectrous body of Milton:
Redounding from my left foot into Los's Mundane space,
Brooded over his Body in Horeb against the Resurrection,
Preparing it for the Great Consummation; red the Cherub on Sinai
Glow'd; but in terrors folded round his clouds of blood.

5. Hand, Hyle, Coban, and Skofield are figures from Blake's trial who have prominent roles in *Jerusalem;* see p. 315.
6. The testes.

‡ Plate 22 in Copy D.
7. It is conventional for an epic poet to profess inability to do justice to his theme without divine aid.

Now Albion's sleeping Humanity began to turn upon his Couch:
Feeling the electric flame of Milton's awful precipitate descent.
Seest thou the little winged fly, smaller than a grain of sand?
It has a heart like thee: a brain open to heaven & hell,
Withinside wondrous & expansive; its gates are not clos'd;
I hope thine are not: hence it clothes itself in rich array;
Hence thou art cloth'd with human beauty, O thou mortal man.
Seek not thy heavenly father then beyond the skies:
There Chaos dwells & ancient Night & Og & Anak old:[8]
For every human heart has gates of brass & bars of adamant,
Which few dare unbar because dread Og & Anak guard the gates
Terrific! and each mortal brain is walld and moated round
Within: and Og & Anak watch here: here is the Seat
Of Satan in its Webs; for in brain and heart and loins
Gates open behind Satan's Seat to the City of Golgonooza
Which is the spiritual fourfold London, in the loins of Albion.

Thus Milton fell thro Albion's heart, travelling outside of
Humanity—
Beyond the Stars, in Chaos, in Caverns of the Mundane Shell.

But many of the Eternals rose up from eternal tables
Drunk with the Spirit; burning round the Couch of death they
stood
Looking down into Beulah: wrathful, fill'd with rage!
They rend the heavens round the Watchers in a fiery circle:
And round the Shadowy Eighth: the Eight close up the Couch
Into a tabernacle, and flee with cries down to the Deeps:
Where Los opens his three wide gates, surrounded by raging fires!
They soon find their own place & join the Watchers of the Ulro.[9]

Los saw them and a cold pale horror coverd o'er his limbs.
Pondering, he knew that Rintrah & Palamabron might depart:
Even as Reuben & as Gad; gave up himself to tears.
He sat down on his anvil-stock; and leand upon the trough.
Looking into the black water, mingling it with tears.

At last when desperation almost tore his heart in twain
He recollected an old Prophecy in Eden recorded,
And often sung to the loud harp at the immortal feasts,
That Milton of the Land of Albion should up ascend

8. Og, giant king of Bashan (Deuteronomy 3:11) and Anak, progenitor of giants (Numbers 13:33), are paired by Blake as enemies blocking the way to the promised land; in *Milton* 31:49 they guard the expanding center that opens into Eternity; see Rose's essay in the critical section of this edition.

9. The Eight are the seven spirits of the Presence plus Milton himself; the Watchers (cf. Daniel 4:13) turn out to be Ololon (*Milton* 21:16).

Forwards from Ulro, from the Vale of Felpham: and set free
Orc from his Chain of Jealousy. He started at the thought

[PLATE 21]§
And down descended into Udan-Adan;[1] it was night:
And Satan sat sleeping upon his Couch in Udan-Adan:
His Spectre slept, his Shadow woke: when one sleeps th'other wakes.

But Milton entering my Foot;[2] I saw in the nether
Regions of the Imagination; also all men on Earth,
And all in Heaven, saw in the nether regions of the Imagination
In Ulro beneath Beulah, the vast breach of Milton's descent.
But I knew not that it was Milton, for man cannot know
What passes in his members till periods of Space & Time
Reveal the secrets of Eternity: for more extensive
Than any other earthly things are Man's earthly lineaments.

And all this Vegetable World appeard on my left Foot,
As a bright sandal formd immortal of precious stones & gold:
I stooped down & bound it on to walk forward thro' Eternity.

There is in Eden a sweet River, of milk & liquid pearl.
Namd Ololon; on whose mild banks dwelt those who Milton drove
Down into Ulro: and they[3] wept in long resounding song
For seven days of eternity, and the river's living banks
The mountains wail'd! & every plant that grew, in solemn sighs lamented.

When Luvah's bulls each morning drag the sulphur Sun out of the Deep,
Harnessed with starry harness black & shining, kept by black slaves
That work all night at the starry harness, Strong and vigorous
They drag the unwilling Orb: at this time all the Family
Of Eden heard the lamentation, and Providence began.
But when the clarions of day sounded they drownd the lamentations
And when night came all was silent in Ololon: & all refusd to lament
In the still night fearing lest they should others molest.

§ Plate 23 in Copy D.

1. In *Milton* 23:60, 26:25, and 27:50 this is called a lake; in *Four Zoas* VIII (113:24) a "Lake not of Waters but of Spaces." Often paired with Entuthon Benython, a forest of error.

2. Reiterated in 15:49, 20:21. Such repetitions are points of orientation in a work without narrative progression; when the same event is described from different viewpoints and an instant of time is replayed, its various significances can be considered.

3. Ololon, at first identified as an Edenic river (cf. *Paradise Lost* III, 519; IV, 238), with increasing definiteness appears as multitudes, then as a twelve-year-old virgin Daughter of Beulah, and finally as Milton's own emanation.

Seven mornings Los heard them, as the poor bird within the shell
Hears its impatient parent bird; and Enitharmon heard them:
But saw them not, for the blue Mundane Shell inclos'd them in.

And they lamented that they had in wrath & fury & fire
Driven Milton into the Ulro; for now they knew too late
That it was Milton the Awakener: they had not heard the Bard,
Whose song calld Milton to the attempt; and Los heard these laments.
He heard them call in prayer all the Divine Family;
And he beheld the Cloud of Milton stretching over Europe.

But all the Family Divine collected as Four Suns
In the Four Points of heaven: East, West & North & South,
Enlarging and enlarging till their Disks approachd each other:
And when they touch'd closed together Southward in One Sun
Over Ololon: and as One Man, who weeps over his brother,
In a dark tomb, so all the Family Divine wept over Ololon.
Saying, "Milton goes to Eternal Death!" so saying, they groan'd in spirit
And were troubled! and again the Divine Family groaned in spirit!

And Ololon said, "Let us descend also, and let us give
Ourselves to death in Ulro among the Transgressors.
Is Virtue a Punisher? O no! how is this wondrous thing:
This World beneath, unseen before: this refuge from the wars
Of Great Eternity! unnatural refuge! unknown by us till now!
Or are these the pangs of repentance? let us enter into them!"

Then the Divine Family said, "Six Thousand Years are now
Accomplish'd in this World of Sorrow; Milton's Angel knew
The Universal Dictate; and you also feel this Dictate.
And now you know this World of Sorrow; and feel Pity. Obey
The Dictate! Watch over this World, and with your brooding wings;[4]
Renew it to Eternal Life! Lo! I am with you alway.
But you cannot renew Milton, he goes to Eternal Death."

So spake the Family Divine as One Man, even Jesus,
Uniting in One with Ololon & the appearance of One Man;
Jesus the Saviour appeard coming in the Clouds of Ololon:

[PLATE 22]*
Tho driven away with the Seven Starry Ones into the Ulro;
Yet the Divine Vision remains Every-where For-ever. Amen.

4. Cf. the Holy Spirit in *Paradise Lost* I, 19–22.

* Plate 24 in Copy D.

And Ololon lamented for Milton with a great lamentation.

While Los heard indistinct in fear, what time I bound my sandals
On, to walk forward thro' Eternity, Los descended to me: †
And Los behind me stood: a terrible flaming Sun: just close
Behind my back; I turned round in terror, and behold:
Los stood in that fierce glowing fire: & he also stoop'd down
And bound my sandals on in Udan-Adan. Trembling I stood
Exceedingly with fear & terror, standing in the Vale
Of Lambeth: but he kissed me, and wishd me health.
And I became One Man with him arising in my strength:
Twas too late now to recede. Los had enterd into my soul:
His terrors now posses'd me whole! I arose in fury & strength.[5]

"I am that Shadowy Prophet who Six Thousand Years ago
Fell from my station in the Eternal bosom. Six Thousand Years
Are finishd. I return! both Time & Space obey my will.
I in Six Thousand Years walk up and down: for not one Moment
Of Time is lost, nor one Event of Space unpermanent,
But all remain: every fabric of Six Thousand Years
Remains permanent: tho' on the Earth where Satan
Fell, and was cut off, all things vanish & are seen no more,
They vanish not from me & mine, we guard them first & last.
The generations of men run on in the tide of Time
But leave their destind lineaments permanent for ever & ever."

So spoke Los as we went along to his supreme abode.

Rintrah and Palamabron met us at the Gate of Golgonooza[6]
Clouded with discontent & brooding in their minds terrible things.

They said, "O Father most beloved! O merciful Parent!
Pitying and permitting evil, tho strong & mighty to destroy,
Whence is this Shadow terrible?[7] wherefore dost thou refuse

† See color plate 23.

5. The inspirational and historical relationships of poet and prophet have been established by the entrances of the Bard into Milton and of Milton into Blake the narrator. Here the union of Blake with Los unites the artist with the Eternal Prophet and the spirit of Time.

6. Golgonooza, which is explored for the rest of Book I, is like a great reservoir of artistic consciousness that contains a full range of models, past and potential, of human action.

7. In the eyes of Rintrah and Palambron, Blake is the incarnation of Milton. Los's sons view Milton as a threat to their civilizing work of building Golgonooza, city of art, on the ruins of London. They consider Milton as a political rebel who will loose the destructive forces of Orc and Satan upon civilization and as a Puritan who sides with the churches against the prophets. As lesser forms of Los, they have not experienced Los's illuminating moment of recalling the prophecy that Milton was to return through Blake ("from Felpham's vale") and break the Chain of Jealousy "from all its roots." Los sees that in the fullness of time Blake—inspired by Milton—will prophesy as Milton had truly intended, so that in politics there will not be an endless bloody cycle of tyrants and rebels, and in religion the Divine Humanity will be worshipped by creative acts instead of sacrifices.

To throw him into the Furnaces: knowest thou not that he
Will unchain Orc? & let loose Satan, Og, Sihon,[8] & Anak
Upon the Body of Albion? for this he is come; behold it written
Upon his fibrous left Foot black! most dismal to our eyes!
The Shadowy Female shudders thro' heaven in torment
inexpressible:
And all the Daughters of Los prophetic wail: yet in deceit,
They weave a new Religion from new Jealousy of Theotormon:
Milton's Religion is the cause: there is no end to destruction!
Seeing the Churches at their Period in terror & despair:
Rahab created Voltaire: Tirzah created Rousseau:[9]
Asserting the Self-righteousness against the Universal Saviour,
Mocking the Confessors & Martyrs, claiming Self-righteousness.
With cruel Virtue: making War upon the Lamb's Redeemed:
To perpetuate War & Glory, to perpetuate the Laws of Sin,
They perverted Swedenborg's Visions in Beulah & in Ulro;
To destroy Jerusalem as a Harlot & her Sons as Reprobates;
To raise up Mystery, the Virgin Harlot Mother of War,
Babylon the Great, the Abomination of Desolation!
O Swedenborg! strongest of men, the Samson shorn by the
Churches!
Shewing the Transgressors in Hell, the proud Warriors in Heaven:
Heaven as a Punisher & Hell as One under Punishment:
With Laws from Plato & his Greeks to renew the Trojan Gods,[1]
In Albion; & to deny the value of the Saviour's blood.
But then I rais'd up Whitefield, Palamabron raisd up Westley,[2]
And these are the cries of the Churches before the two Witnesses:
'Faith in God, the dear Saviour who took on the likeness of men:
Becoming obedient to death, even the death of the Cross,
The Witnesses lie dead in the Street of the Great City.
No Faith is in all the Earth: the Book of God is trodden under
Foot:
He sent his two Servants Whitefield & Wesley; were they Prophets
Or were they Idiots or Madmen? shew us Miracles!'[3]

8. Like Og and Anak (*Milton* 20:37), Sihon is a king hostile to the Jews but defeated by them (Joshua 2:10).

9. Cf. *Milton* 40:12; *Jerusalem* 66:12 (and headnote, p. 308), and "Mock on, Mock on, Voltaire, Rousseau" (p. 184).

1. The Gods of Priam (*Milton* 14:15; 25:49).

2. The great evangelists John Wesley (1703–71) and George Whitefield (1714–70) become the "two witnesses" of Revelation 11:3, with whom Rintrah and Palamabron identify themselves in *Milton* 23:11. (cf. Revelation 6:10 and 11:8).

3. In his Marginalia on Watson and elsewhere Blake insists that miracles are not magic and that to demand miracles is superstitious folly.

[PLATE 23]‡

Can you have greater Miracles than these? Men who devote
Their life's whole comfort to intire scorn & injury & death?
Awake thou sleeper on the Rock of Eternity! Albion awake!
The trumpet of Judgment hath twice sounded: all Nations are awake.
But thou art still heavy and dull: Awake Albion awake!
Lo Orc arises on the Atlantic! Lo his blood and fire
Glow on America's shore! Albion turns upon his Couch;
He listens to the sounds of War, astonished and confounded:
He weeps into the Atlantic deep, yet still in dismal dreams
Unwakend: and the Covering Cherub advances from the East;
How long shall we lay dead in the Street of the great City?[4]
How long beneath the Covering Cherub give our Emanations?
Milton will utterly consume us & thee our beloved Father.
He hath enterd into the Covering Cherub, becoming one with
Albion's dread Sons. Hand, Hyle & Coban surround him as
A girdle; Gwendolen & Conwenna as a garment woven
Of War & Religion. Let us descend & bring him chained[5]
To Bowlahoola, O father most beloved, O mild Parent!
Cruel in thy mildness, pitying and permitting evil
Tho strong and mighty to destroy, O Los our beloved Father!"

Like the black storm, coming out of Chaos, beyond the stars:
It issues thro the dark & intricate caves of the Mundane Shell,
Passing the planetary visions, & the well adorned Firmament;
The Sun rolls into Chaos & the stars into the Desarts;
And then the storms become visible, audible & terrible,
Covering the light of day, & rolling down upon the mountains,
Deluge all the country round. Such is a vision of Los;
When Rintrah & Palamabron spoke; and such his stormy face
Appeard, as does the face of heaven, when coverd with thick storms:
Pitying and loving, tho in frowns of terrible perturbation.

But Los dispersd the clouds even as the strong winds of Jehovah.
And Los thus spoke: "O noble Sons, be patient yet a little.
I have embracd the falling Death, he is become One with me.
O Sons we live not by wrath; by mercy alone we live!

‡ Plate 25 in Copy D.

4. This line is a combination of Revelation 6:10 and 11:8, expressing the impatience of martyrs and the fate of witnesses.

5. Gwendolen and Conwenna are the emanations of Hyle and Bowen, two major sons of Albion. See headnote to *Jerusalem*, p. 310.

I recollect an old Prophecy in Eden recorded in gold; and oft
Sung to the harp: That Milton of the land of Albion
Should up ascend forward from Felpham's Vale & break the Chain
Of Jealousy from all its roots; be patient therefore O my Sons
These lovely Females form sweet night and silence and secret
Obscurities to hide from Satan's Watch-Fiends[6] Human loves
And graces; lest they write them in their Books, & in the Scroll
Of mortal life, to condemn the accused: who at Satan's Bar
Tremble in Spectrous Bodies continually day and night,
While on the Earth they live in sorrowful Vegetations.
O when shall we tread our Wine-presses in heaven; and Reap
Our wheat with shoutings of joy, and leave the Earth in peace?
Remember how Calvin and Luther in fury premature
Sow'd War and stern division between Papists & Protestants?
Let it not be so now! O go not forth in Martyrdoms & Wars!
We were plac'd here by the Universal Brotherhood & Mercy
With powers fitted to circumscribe this dark Satanic death
And that the Seven Eyes of God may have space for Redemption.
But how this is as yet we know not, and we cannot know:
Till Albion is arisen: then patient wait a little while:
Six Thousand years are passd away; the end approaches fast.
This mighty one is come from Eden, he is of the Elect,
Who died from Earth & he is returnd before the Judgment. This thing
Was never known that one of the holy dead should willing return.
Then patient wait a little while till the Last Vintage is over:
Till we have quenched the Sun of Salah[7] in the Lake of Udan Adan.
O my dear Sons! leave not your Father, as your brethren left me.
Twelve Sons[8] successive fled away in that thousand years of sorrow

[PLATE 24]§
Of Palamabron's Harrow, & of Rintrah's wrath & fury;
Reuben & Manazzoth & Gad & Simeon & Levi,
And Ephraim & Judah were Generated, because
They left me, wandering with Tirzah: Enitharmon wept
One thousand years, and all the Earth was in a watry deluge.
We calld him Menassheh because of the Generations of Tirzah
Because of Satan: & the Seven Eyes of God continually

6. Cf. *Milton* 29:50; *Milton* 35:43. Satan means "accuser."
7. Salah was one of the descendants of Noah through Shem, ancestor of the Semitic people (Genesis 10:24); the quenching of his "Sun" would thus be the end of the ages after the Flood and the subsequent divisions of humanity into races and sects.
8. Six of the names in 24:2–3 are of Tribes of Israel; *Manazzoth* is a made-up Hebrew word (according to W. H. Stevenson's annotations in his 1971 edition of Blake), probably inserted to provide a lineage for Tirzah.
§ Plate 26 in Copy D.

Guard round them. But I the Fourth Zoa am also set
The Watchman of Eternity, the Three are not! & I am preserved!
Still my four mighty ones are left to me in Golgonooza,
Still Rintrah fierce, and Palamabron mild & piteous,
Theotormon filld with care, Bromion loving Science.
You O my Sons still guard round Los. O wander not & leave me!
Rintrah, thou well rememberest when Amalek & Canaan
Fled with their Sister Moab into that abhorred Void:
They became Nations in our sight beneath the hands of Tirzah.
And Palamabron, thou rememberest when Joseph, an infant,
Stolen from his nurse's cradle, wrapd in needle-work
Of emblematic texture, was sold to the Amalekite,
Who carried him down into Egypt where Ephraim & Menassheh
Gatherd my Sons together in the Sands of Midian.
And if you also flee away and leave your Father's side,
Following Milton into Ulro, altho your power is great,
Surely you also shall become poor mortal vegetations
Beneath the Moon of Ulro: pity then your Father's tears.
When Jesus raisd Lazarus from the Grave I stood & saw
Lazarus, who is the Vehicular Body of Albion the Redeemd,
Arise into the Covering Cherub, who is the Spectre of Albion,[9]
By martyrdoms to suffer, to watch over the Sleeping Body,
Upon his Rock beneath his Tomb. I saw the Covering Cherub
Divide Four-fold into Four Churches when Lazarus arose:
Paul, Constantine, Charlemaine, Luther; behold they stand
before us
Stretchd over Europe & Asia. Come O Sons, come, come away!
Arise O Sons, give all your strength against Eternal Death,
Lest we are vegetated, for Cathedron's Looms weave only Death,
A Web of Death: & were it not for Bowlahoola & Allamanda,
No Human Form but only a Fibrous Vegetation,
A Polypus of soft affections without Thought or Vision,
Must tremble in the Heavens & Earths thro all the Ulro space.
Throw all the Vegetated Mortals into Bowlahoola;
But as to this Elected Form who is returnd again,
He is the Signal that the Last Vintage now approaches,
Nor Vegetation may go on till all the Earth is reapd."

So Los spoke. Furious they descended to Bowlahoola & Allamanda[1]
Indignant, unconvinced by Los's arguments & thunders rolling.

9. The false Christian church is founded on the miracle of Lazarus' resurrection (John 11–12); its doctrines confuse reanimation of the physical body with renewal of the spirit. Lazarus has become part of the Covering Cherub, the problem rather than the solution.

1. Allegorical places not as clearly defined as Golgoonooza; Bowlahoola in Los's forge and the human bowels, is "Law" (*Milton* 24:48); Allamanda, cultivated land and perhaps the alimentary canal, is "Commerce" (*Milton* 27:42).

They saw that wrath now swayd and now pity absorbd him
As it was, so it remaind & no hope of an end.

Bowlahoola is namd Law by mortals: Tharmas founded it
Because of Satan, before Luban in the City of Golgonooza.
But Golgonooza is namd Art & Manufacture by mortal men.

In Bowlahoola Los's Anvils stand & his Furnaces rage:
Thundering the Hammers beat & the Bellows blow loud;
Living, self moving, mourning, lamenting & howling incessantly,
Bowlahoola thro all its porches feels, tho' too fast founded
Its pillars & porticoes to tremble at the force
Of mortal or immortal arm: and softly lilling flutes,
Accordant with the horrid labours, make sweet melody.
The Bellows are the Animal Lungs; the Hammers the Animal Heart;
The Furnaces the Stomach for digestion: terrible their fury.
Thousands & thousands labour; thousands play on instruments
Stringed or fluted to ameliorate the sorrows of slavery.
Loud sport the dancers in the dance of death, rejoicing in carnage.
The hard dentant Hammers are lulld by the flutes, lula lula;
The bellowing Furnaces' blare by the long sounding clarion;
The double drum drowns howls & groans; the shrill fife, shrieks & cries:
The crooked horn mellows the hoarse raving serpent[2] terrible but harmonious.
Bowlahoola is the Stomach in every individual man.

Los is by mortals nam'd Time; Enitharmon is nam'd Space.
But they depict him bald & aged who is in eternal youth
All powerful and his locks flourish like the brows of morning.
He is the Spirit of Prophecy, the ever apparent Elias.[3]
Time is the mercy of Eternity; without Time's swiftness—
Which is the swiftest of all things—all were eternal torment:
All the Gods of the Kingdoms of Earth labour in Los's Halls:
Every one is a fallen Son of the Spirit of Prophecy.
He is the Fourth Zoa that stood around the Throne Divine.

[PLATE 25]*

Loud shout the Sons of Luvah at the Wine-presses as Los descended
With Rintrah & Palamabron in his fires of resistless fury.

2. A spiral horn.
3. Elijah, eternal spirit of prophecy, identified with John the Baptist (Matthew 11:14).
* Plate 27 in Copy D.

The Wine-press on the Rhine[4] groans loud, but all its central beams
Act more terrific in the central Cities of the Nations,
Where Human Thought is crushed beneath the iron hand of Power.
There Los puts all into the Press, the Opressor & the Opressed
Together, ripe for the Harvest & Vintage & ready for the Loom.

They sang at the Vintage, "This is the Last Vintage! & Seed
Shall no more be sown upon Earth till all the Vintage is over,
And all gatherd in, till the Plow has passd over the Nations
And the Harrow & heavy thundering Roller upon the mountains!"

And loud the Souls howl round the Porches of Golgonooza
Crying, "O God deliver us to the Heavens or to the Earths,
That we may preach righteousness & punish the sinner with death."
But Los refused, till all the Vintage of Earth was gatherd in.

And Los stood & cried to the Labourers of the Vintage in voice of awe:

"Fellow Labourers! The Great Vintage & Harvest is now upon Earth;
The whole extent of the Globe is explored: Every scatterd Atom
Of Human Intellect now is flocking to the sound of the Trumpet.
All the Wisdom which was hidden in caves & dens, from ancient
Time, is now sought out from Animal & Vegetable & Mineral.
The Awakener is come, outstretched over Europe! the Vision of God is fulfilled.
The Ancient Man upon the Rock of Albion Awakes;
He listens to the sounds of War astonishd & ashamed:
He sees his Children mock at Faith and deny Providence:
Therefore you must bind the Sheaves not by Nations or Families.[5]
You shall bind them in Three Classes: according to their Classes
So shall you bind them, Separating What has been Mixed
Since Men began to be Wove into Nations by Rahab & Tirzah,
Since Albion's Death & Satan's Cutting-off from our awful Fields,
When under pretence to benevolence the Elect Subdud All
From the Foundation of the World. The Elect is one Class: You
Shall bind them separate: they cannot Believe in Eternal Life
Except by Miracle & a New Birth. The other two Classes:

4. This river between France and Germany has been the scene of warfare for centuries, though not in the early nineteenth century. The winepress as "the wrath of God," or warfare, derives from Isaiah 63:1–6 and Revelation 14:19–20.

5. A development and correction of the harvest imagery of Micah 4:12 and, generally, of Revelation 14:14–16, based on the parable of the wheat and the tares in Matthew 13:24–30.

The Reprobate who never cease to Believe, and the Redeemd
Who live in doubts & fears perpetually tormented by the Elect,
These you shall bind in a twin-bundle for the Consummation—
But the Elect must be saved [from] fires of Eternal Death,
To be formed into the Churches of Beulah that they destroy not the Earth.
For in every Nation & every Family the Three Classes are born,
And in every Species of Earth, Metal, Tree, Fish, Bird & Beast.
We form the Mundane Egg, that Spectres coming by fury or amity,
All is the same, & every one remains in his own energy.
Go forth Reapers with rejoicing. You sowed in tears,
But the time of your refreshing cometh. Only a little moment
Still abstain from pleasure & rest in the labours of eternity.
And you shall Reap the whole Earth from Pole to Pole! from Sea to Sea
Beginning at Jerusalem's Inner Court, Lambeth[6] ruin'd and given
To the detestable Gods of Priam: to Apollo, and at the Asylum
Given to Hercules: who labour in Tirzah's Looms for bread,
Who set Pleasure against Duty, who Create Olympic crowns
To make Learning a burden & the Work of the Holy Spirit: Strife.
The Thor & cruel Odin[7] who first reard the Polar Caves
Lambeth mourns, calling Jerusalem; she weeps & looks abroad
For the Lord's coming, that Jerusalem may overspread all Nations.
Crave not for the mortal & perishing delights, but leave them
To the weak, and pity the weak as your infant care; Break not
Forth in your wrath lest you also are vegetated by Tirzah.
Wait till the Judgment is past, till the Creation is consumed
And then rush forward with me into the glorious spiritual
Vegetation: the Supper of the Lamb & his Bride: and the
Awaking of Albion, our friend and ancient companion."

So Los spoke. But lightnings of discontent broke on all sides round
And murmurs of thunder rolling heavy long & loud over the mountains
While Los calld his Sons around him to the Harvest & the Vintage.

6. A southern section of London across the Thames (see map), where the Blakes lived (1791–1800), at number 13 Hercules Buildings. "Jerusalem's Inner Court" refers to Lambeth Palace, residence of the Archbishop of Canterbury; Apollo Gardens was a run-down amusement park; the Royal Asylum for Female Orphans kept the girls busy in textile work; "labour in Tirzah's looms" recalls Hercules' bondage to Omphale (see David V. Erdman, *Blake: Prophet Against Empire*.

7. The Norse gods are also "detestable gods of Priam" by other names. Blake knew Norse mythology through P. H. Mallet, *Northern Antiquities* (translated in 1770).

Thou seest the Constellations in the deep & wondrous Night.
They rise in order and continue their immortal courses
Upon the mountains & in vales with harp & heavenly song,
With flute & clarion, with cups & measures filled with foaming wine:
Glittring the streams reflect the Vision of beatitude,
And the calm Ocean joys beneath & smooths his awful waves!

[PLATE 26]†
These are the Sons of Los, & these the Labourers of the Vintage.
Thou seest the gorgeous clothed Flies that dance & sport in summer
Upon the sunny brooks & meadows: every one the dance
Knows in its intricate mazes of delight artful to weave:
Each one to sound his instruments of music in the dance:
To touch each other & recede: to cross & change & return.
These are the Children of Los. Thou seest the Trees on mountains:
The wind blows heavy, loud they thunder thro' the darksom sky,
Uttering prophecies & speaking instructive words to the sons
Of men: These are the Sons of Los! These the Visions of Eternity!
But we see only as it were the hem of their garments
When with our vegetable eyes we view these wond'rous Visions.

There are Two Gates thro which all Souls descend.[8] One Southward
From Dover Cliff to Lizard Point, the other toward the North:
Caithness & rocky Durness, Pentland & John Groat's House.[9]

The Souls descending to the Body, wail on the right hand
Of Los: & those delivered from the Body, on the left hand.
For Los against the east his force continually bends
Along the Valleys of Middlesex from Hounslow to Blackheath,
Lest those Three Heavens of Beulah should the Creation destroy
And lest they should descend before the north & south Gates.
Groaning with pity, he among the wailing Souls laments.

† Plate 28 in Copy D.

8. As Rodney M. Baine, *Philological Quarterly* 51 (1972), 957–61, has pointed out in connection with *Thel* 6:1, Blake probably became aware of this symbolism, derived from the Cave of the Nymphs in *Odyssey* XIII, 109–12, through the Neoplatonic commentary in Pope's translation.

9. Blake outlined these southern and northern limits of Albion on the plate; only the southern landmarks appear on the British map in this edition.

And these the Labours of the Sons of Los in Allamanda:
And in the City of Golgonooza: & in Luban: & around
The Lake of Udan-Adan, in the Forests of Entuthon Benython
Where Souls incessant wail; being piteous Passions & Desires
With neither lineament nor form, but like to watry clouds,
The Passions & Desires descend upon the hungry winds.
For such alone Sleepers remain, meer passion & appetite;
The Sons of Los clothe them & feed & provide houses & fields.

And every Generated Body in its inward form
Is a garden of delight & a building of magnificence,
Built by the Sons of Los in Bowlahoola & Allamanda
And the herbs & flowers & furniture & beds & chambers
Continually woven in the Looms of Enitharmon's Daughters
In bright Cathedron's golden Dome with care & love & tears.
For the various Classes of Men are all markd out determinate
In Bowlahoola; & as the Spectres choose their affinities
So they are born on Earth, & every Class is determinate
But not by Natural but by Spiritual power alone. Because
The Natural power continually seeks & tends to Destruction
Ending in Death: which would of itself be Eternal Death.
And all are Class'd by Spiritual, & not by Natural power.

And every Natural Effect has a Spiritual Cause, and Not
A Natural: for a Natural Cause only seems; it is a Delusion
Of Ulro: & a ratio of the perishing Vegetable Memory.

[PLATE 27]‡
But the Wine-press of Los is eastward of Golgonooza, before the Seat
Of Satan. Luvah laid the foundation & Urizen finish'd it in howling woe.
How red the sons & daughters of Luvah! here they tread the grapes.
Laughing & shouting, drunk with odours, many fall oerwearied.
Drownd in the wine is many a youth & maiden: those around
Lay them on skins of Tygers & of the spotted Leopard & the Wild Ass
Till they revive, or bury them in cool grots, making lamentation.

This Wine-press is call'd War on Earth, it is the Printing-Press
Of Los; and here he lays his words in order above the mortal brain,
As cogs are formd in a wheel to turn the cogs of the adverse wheel.

Timbrels & violins sport round the Wine-presses; the little Seed,
The sportive Root, the Earth-worm, the gold Beetle: the wise Emmet:

‡ Plate 29 in Copy D.

Dance round the Wine-presses of Luvah: the Centipede is there:
The ground Spider with many eyes, the Mole clothed in velvet,
The ambitious Spider in his sullen web (the lucky golden Spinner),
The Earwig armd, the tender Maggot (emblem of immortality),
The Flea: Louse: Bug: the Tape-Worm: all the Armies of Disease:
Visible or invisible to the slothful vegetating Man;
The slow Slug: the Grasshopper that sings & laughs & drinks:
Winter comes, he folds his slender bones without a murmur;
The cruel Scorpion is there: the Gnat: Wasp: Hornet & the Honey Bee:
The Toad & venomous Newt, the Serpent clothed in gems & gold:
They throw off their gorgeous raiment: they rejoice with loud jubilee
Around the Wine-presses of Luvah, naked & drunk with wine.

There is the Nettle that stings with soft down; and there
The indignant Thistle: whose bitterness is bred in his milk:
Who feeds on contempt of his neighbour: there all the idle Weeds
That creep around the obscure places, shew their various limbs.
Naked in all their beauty dancing round the Wine-presses.

But in the Wine-presses the Human grapes sing not, nor dance.
They howl & writhe in shoals of torment; in fierce flames consuming.
In chains of iron & in dungeons circled with ceaseless fires.
In pits & dens & shades of death: in shapes of torment & woe.
The plates & screws & wracks & saws & cords & fires & cisterns—
The cruel joys of Luvah's Daughters lacerating with knives
And whips their Victims, & the deadly sport of Luvah's Sons.
They dance around the dying, & they drink the howl & groan.
They catch the shrieks in cups of gold, they hand them to one another:
These are the sports of love, & these the sweet delights of amorous play—
Tears of the grape, the death sweat of the cluster, the last sigh
Of the mild youth who listens to the lureing songs of Luvah.

But Allamanda, calld on Earth Commerce, is the Cultivated land
Around the City of Golgonooza in the Forests of Entuthon:
Here the Sons of Los labour against Death Eternal; through all
The Twenty-seven Heavens of Beulah in Ulro, Seat of Satan,
Which is the False Tongue beneath Beulah: it is the Sense of Touch.
The Plow goes forth in tempests & lightnings & the Harrow cruel
In blights of the east; the heavy Roller follows in howlings of woe.

Urizen's sons here labour also: & here are seen the Mills
Of Theotormon, on the verge of the Lake of Udan-Adan:
These are the starry voids of night & the depths & caverns of earth.

These Mills are oceans, clouds, & waters ungovernable in their fury.
Here are the stars created & the seeds of all things planted,
And here the Sun & Moon recieve their fixed destinations.

But in Eternity the Four Arts—Poetry, Painting, Music,
And Architecture which is Science—are the Four Faces of Man.
Not so in Time & Space: there Three are shut out, and only
Science remains thro Mercy: & by means of Science, the Three
Become apparent in Time & Space, in the Three Professions.
[Poetry in Religion: Music, Law: Painting, in Physic & Surgery:][1]
That Man may live upon Earth till the time of his awaking,
And from these Three, Science derives every Occupation of Men.
And Science is divided into Bowlahoola & Allamanda.

[PLATE 28]§
Some Sons of Los surround the Passions with porches of iron & silver
Creating form & beauty around the dark regions of sorrow,
Giving to airy nothing a name and a habitation[2]
Delightful: with bounds to the Infinite putting off the Indefinite
Into most holy forms of Thought: (such is the power of inspiration).
They labour incessant: with many tears & afflictions:
Creating the beautiful House for the piteous sufferer.

Others: Cabinets richly fabricate of gold & ivory;
For Doubts & fears unform'd & wretched & melancholy.
The little weeping Spectre stands on the threshold of Death
Eternal; and sometimes two Spectres like lamps quivering,
And often malignant they combat (heart-breaking sorrowful & piteous).
Antamon[3] takes them into his beautiful flexible hands,
As the Sower takes the seed, or as the Artist his clay
Or fine wax, to mould artful a model for golden ornaments.
The soft hands of Antamon draw the indelible line,
Form immortal with golden pen, such as the Spectre admiring
Puts on the sweet form; then smiles Antamon bright thro his windows.
The Daughters of beauty look up from their Loom & prepare
The integument soft for its clothing with joy & delight.

But Theotormon & Sotha stand in the Gate of Luban anxious:

1. This line does not appear in Copy D.
§ Plate 30 in Copy D.
2. A variation on Theseus's formula for poetry in *Midsummer Night's Dream* V, i, 14–17 (cf. *Milton* 30:24, 29).
3. One of the artistic Sons of Los, along with Sotha (line 21), Ozoth (line 39), and others (line 44); not developed elsewhere in Blake's mythology.

Their numbers are seven million & seven thousand & seven hundred:
They contend with the weak Spectres, they fabricate soothing forms.
The Spectre refuses, he seeks cruelty. They create the crested Cock.
Terrified, the Spectre screams & rushes in fear into their Net
Of kindness & compassion & is born a weeping terror.
Or they create the Lion & Tyger in compassionate thunderings.
Howling the Spectres flee: they take refuge in Human lineaments.

The Sons of Ozoth within the Optic Nerve stand fiery glowing
And the number of his Sons is eight millions & eight.
They give delights to the man unknown; artificial riches
They give to scorn, & their posessors to trouble & sorrow & care,
Shutting the sun, & moon, & stars, & trees, & clouds, & waters,
And hills out from the Optic Nerve & hardening it into a bone
Opake, and like the black pebble on the enraged beach.
While the poor indigent is like the diamond which, tho cloth'd
In rugged covering in the mine, is open all within,
And in his hallowd center holds the heavens of bright eternity.
Ozoth here builds walls of rocks against the surging sea,
And timbers crampt with iron cramps bar in the joys of life
From fell destruction in the Spectrous cunning or rage. He Creates
The speckled Newt, the Spider & Beetle, the Rat & Mouse,
The Badger & Fox: they worship before his feet in trembling fear.

But others of the Sons of Los build Moments & Minutes & Hours
And Days & Months & Years & Ages & Periods: wondrous buildings.
And every Moment has a Couch of gold for soft repose,
(A Moment equals a pulsation of the artery)
And between every two Moments stands a Daughter of Beulah
To feed the Sleepers on their Couches with maternal care.
And every Minute has an azure Tent with silken Veils.
And every Hour has a bright golden Gate carved with skill.
And every Day & Night, has Walls of brass & Gates of adamant,
Shining like precious stones & ornamented with appropriate signs:
And every Month, a silver paved Terrace builded high:
And every Year, invulnerable Barriers with high Towers.
And every Age is Moated deep with Bridges of silver & gold:
And every Seven Ages is Incircled with a Flaming Fire.
Now Seven Ages is amounting to Two Hundred Years.
Each has its guard, each Moment Minute Hour Day Month & Year.
All are the work of Fairy hands of the Four Elements.
The Guard are Angels of Providence on duty evermore.
Every Time less than a pulsation of the artery
Is equal in its period & value to Six Thousand Years.

[PLATE 29]*
For in this Period the Poet's Work is Done: and all the Great
Events of Time start forth & are concievd in such a Period—
Within a Moment: a Pulsation of the Artery.

The Sky is an immortal Tent built by the Sons of Los
And every Space that a Man views around his dwelling-place,
Standing on his own roof, or in his garden on a mount
Of twenty-five cubits[4] in height, such space is his Universe.
And on its verge the Sun rises & sets; the Clouds bow
To meet the flat Earth[5] & the Sea in such an orderd Space;
The Starry heavens reach no further but here bend and set
On all sides & the two Poles turn on their valves of gold:
And if he move his dwelling-place, his heavens also move
Where'er he goes & all his neighbourhood bewail his loss:
Such are the Spaces called Earth & such its dimension:
As to the false appearance which appears to the reasoner,
As of a Globe rolling thro Voidness, it is a delusion of Ulro:
The Microscope knows not of this nor the Telescope. They alter
The ratio of the Spectator's Organs but leave Objects untouched.
For every Space larger than a red Globule of Man's blood
Is visionary: and is created by the Hammer of Los.
And every Space smaller than a Globule of Man's blood opens
Into Eternity of which this vegetable Earth is but a shadow.
The red Globule is the unwearied Sun by Los created
To measure Time and Space to mortal Men every morning.
Bowlahoola & Allamanda are placed on each side
Of that Pulsation & that Globule, terrible their power.

But Rintrah & Palamabron govern over Day & Night
In Allamanda & Entuthon Benython where Souls wail:
Where Orc incessant howls, burning in fires of Eternal Youth,
Within the vegetated mortal Nerves; for every Man born is joined
Within into One mighty Polypus, and this Polypus is Orc.

But in the Optic vegetative Nerves Sleep was transformed
To Death in old time by Satan the father of Sin & Death,
And Satan is the Spectre of Orc & Orc is the generate Luvah.[6]

* Plate 31 in Copy D.

4. This ancient unit of measurement is the length from the elbow to the tip of the middle finger. The basic units of creative thought are vital and human-centered: the time of an artery's pulsation and the space of a drop of blood.

5. In one's direct experience the earth is flat, although intellectually one is aware that it is round. The artist chooses models of the universe most useful to him, without respect to what is real or useful to an astronomer or a sailor. Milton had visited Galileo but adapted features of the Ptolemaic universe in *Paradise Lost* III, 482; X, 651–57.

6. Satan is Orc's spectre because of his false appearance of rebelliousness. Orc is not Satanic but is the fallen form of Luvah, or Love.

WILLIAM

But in the Nerves of the Nostrils—Accident being formed
Into Substance & Principle, by the cruelties of Demonstration—
It became Opake & Indefinite. But the Divine Saviour
Formed it into a Solid by Los's Mathematic power.
He named the Opake Satan: he named the Solid Adam.

And in the Nerves of the Ear, (for the Nerves of the Tongue are closed)
On Albion's Rock, Los stands creating the glorious Sun each morning.
And when unwearied in the evening he creates the Moon,
Death to delude, who all in terror at their splendor leaves
His prey, while Los appoints, & Rintrah & Palamabron guide
The Souls clear from the Rock of Death, that Death himself may wake
In his appointed season when the ends of heaven meet,
Then Los conducts the Spirits to be Vegetated into
Great Golgonooza, free from the four iron pillars of Satan's Throne
(Temperance, Prudence, Justice, Fortitude, the four pillars of tyranny)
That Satan's Watch-Fiends touch them not before they Vegetate.

But Enitharmon and her Daughters take the pleasant charge,
To give them to their lovely heavens till the Great Judgment Day,
Such is their lovely charge. But Rahab & Tirzah pervert
Their mild influences; therefore the Seven Eyes of God walk round
The Three Heavens of Ulro, where Tirzah & her Sisters
Weave the black Woof of Death upon Entuthon Benython
In the Vale of Surrey where Horeb terminates in Rephaim.
The stamping feet of Zelophehad's Daughters are coverd with Human gore
Upon the treddles of the Loom; they sing to the winged shuttle:
The River rises above his banks to wash the Woof:
He takes it in his arms: he passes it in strength thro his current.
The veil of human miseries is woven over the Ocean
From the Atlantic to the Great South Sea, the Erythrean.[7]

Such is the World of Los, the labour of six thousand years.
Thus Nature is a Vision of the Science of the Elohim.

End of the First Book

7. The Indian Ocean.

[PLATE 30]‡

Milton
Book the Second

There is a place where Contrarieties are equally True
This place is called Beulah.[8] It is a pleasant lovely Shadow
Where no dispute can come, Because of those who Sleep.
Into this place the Sons & Daughters of Ololon descended
With solemn mourning, into Beulah's moony shades & hills,
Weeping for Milton: mute wonder held the Daughters of Beulah
Enrapturd with affection sweet and mild benevolence.

Beulah is evermore Created around Eternity, appearing
To the Inhabitants of Eden around them on all sides.
But Beulah to its Inhabitants appears within each district
As the beloved infant in his mother's bosom round incircled
With arms of love & pity & sweet compassion. But to
The Sons of Eden the moony habitations of Beulah
Are from Great Eternity a mild & pleasant Rest.

And it is thus Created. Lo the Eternal Great Humanity—
To whom be Glory & Dominion Evermore Amen—
Walks among all his awful Family, seen in every face
As the breath of the Almighty. Such are the words of man to man
In the great Wars of Eternity, in fury of Poetic Inspiration,
To build the Universe stupendous: Mental forms Creating.

But the Emanations trembled exceedingly, nor could they
Live, because the life of Man was too exceeding unbounded.
His joy became terrible to them; they trembled & wept
Crying with one voice, "Give us a habitation & a place
In which we may be hidden under the shadow of wings;
For if we who are but for a time, & who pass away in winter,
Behold these wonders of Eternity, we shall consume.
But you O our Fathers & Brothers, remain in Eternity.
But grant us a Temporal Habitation. Do you speak
To us; we will obey your words as you obey Jesus
The Eternal who is blessed for ever & ever. Amen."

So spake the lovely Emanations; & there appeard a pleasant
Mild Shadow above: beneath: & on all sides round.

‡ Plate 33 in Copy D. The design for this plate (not shown) incorporates two mottoes in mirror writing: "How wide the Gulf & Unpassable between Simplicity & Insipidity" and "Contraries are Positives; A Negation is not a Contrary."

8. See note to 2:1. Blake's fullest description of this dreamy state of sexual fulfillment, emphasizing both its perfection in relation to fallen life and its passivity in relation to Eden, artistic creativity, the highest human activity.

[PLATE 31]§
Into this pleasant Shadow all the weak & weary
Like Women & Children were taken away as on wings
Of dovelike softness, & shadowy habitations prepared for them.
But every Man returnd & went still going forward thro'
The Bosom of the Father in Eternity on Eternity.
Neither did any lack or fall into Error without
A Shadow to repose in all the Days of happy Eternity.

Into this pleasant Shadow Beulah all Ololon descended.
And when the Daughters of Beulah heard the lamentation
All Beulah wept, for they saw the Lord coming in the Clouds.
And the Shadows of Beulah terminate in rocky Albion.

And all Nations wept in affliction, Family by Family:
Germany wept towards France & Italy: England wept & trembled
Towards America: India rose up from his golden bed:
As one awakend in the night: they saw the Lord coming
In the Clouds of Ololon with Power & Great Glory!

And all the Living Creatures of the Four Elements wail'd
With bitter wailing: these in the aggregate are named Satan
And Rahab: they know not of Regeneration, but only of Generation.
The Fairies, Nymphs, Gnomes & Genii of the Four Elements
Unforgiving & unalterable: these cannot be Regenerated
But must be Created, for they know only of Generation.
These are the Gods of the Kingdoms of the Earth: in contrarious
And cruel opposition: Element against Element, opposed in War
Not Mental, as the Wars of Eternity, but a Corporeal Strife
In Los's Halls, continual labouring in the Furnaces of Gologonooza.
Orc howls on the Atlantic: Enitharmon trembles: All Beulah weeps.

Thou hearest the Nightingale begin the Song of Spring;
The Lark sitting upon his earthy bed: just as the morn
Appears: listens silent; then springing from the waving Corn-field! loud
He leads the Choir of Day! trill, trill, trill, trill,
Mounting upon the wings of light into the Great Expanse:
Reecchoing against the lovely blue & shining heavenly Shell:
His little throat labours with inspiration; every feather
On throat & breast & wings vibrates with the effluence Divine;
All Nature listens silent to him & the awful Sun
Stands still upon the Mountain looking on this little Bird
With eyes of soft humility & wonder, love & awe.
Then loud from their green covert all the Birds begin their Song:

§ Plate 34 in Copy D.

The Thrush, the Linnet & the Goldfinch, Robin & the Wren
Awake the Sun from his sweet reverie upon the Mountain:
The Nightingale again assays his song, & thro the day,
And thro the night warbles luxuriant; every Bird of Song
Attending his loud harmony with admiration & love.
This is a Vision of the lamentation of Beulah over Ololon!

Thou percievest the Flowers put forth their precious Odours!
And none can tell how from so small a center comes such sweets,
Forgetting that within that Center Eternity expands
Its ever during doors,[9] that Og & Anak fiercely guard.
First, [ere] the morning breaks, joy opens in the flowery bosoms:
Joy even to tears, which the Sun rising dries. First the Wild Thyme
And Meadow-sweet downy & soft waving among the reeds,
Light springing on the air, lead the sweet Dance: they wake
The Honeysuckle sleeping on the Oak: the flaunting beauty
Revels along upon the wind; the White-thorn—lovely May—
Opens her many lovely eyes: listening the Rose still sleeps—
None dare to wake her; soon she bursts her crimson curtained bed
And comes forth in the majesty of beauty; every Flower:
The Pink, the Jessamine, the Wall-flower, the Carnation
The Jonquil, the mild Lilly opes her heavens! every Tree,
And Flower & Herb soon fill the air with an innumerable Dance,
Yet all in order sweet & lovely; Men are sick with Love!
Such is a Vision of the lamentation of Beulah over Ololon.

[PLATE 32]†
And Milton oft sat up on the Couch of Death & oft conversed
In vision & dream beatific with the Seven Angels of the Presence:

"I have turned my back upon these Heavens builded on cruelty.
My Spectre still wandering thro' them follows my Emanation.
He hunts her footsteps thro' the snow & the wintry hail & rain.
The idiot Reasoner laughs at the Man of Imagination
And from laughter proceeds to murder by undervaluing calumny."

Then Hillel who is Lucifer replied over the Couch of Death
And thus the Seven Angels instructed him & thus they converse:

"We are not Individuals but States:[1] Combinations of
Individuals.

9. Cf. *Paradise Lost* VII, 205–7: Heaven's "ever-during gates."

† Plate 35 in Copy D.

1. This distinction allows for universal salvation of individuals and gets rid of the most objectionable of uncharitable Christian doctrines, that of damnation. In Blake's pictures of the Last Judgment (see *A Vision of the Last Judgment,* p. 411) the figures going to hell are states, not individuals. "Hillel" is properly Helel the day-star, translated "Lucifer" (Isaiah 14:12).

We were Angels of the Divine Presence: & were Druids in Annandale,
Compelld to combine into Form by Satan, the Spectre of Albion,
Who made himself a God & destroyed the Human Form Divine.
But the Divine Humanity & Mercy gave us a Human Form
Because we were combind in Freedom & holy Brotherhood,[2]
While those combind by Satan's Tyranny—first in the blood of War
And Sacrifice & next in Chains of imprisonment—are Shapeless Rocks
Retaining only Satan's Mathematic Holiness: Length, Bredth, & Highth;
Calling the Human Imagination: which is the Divine Vision & Fruition
In which Man liveth eternally: madness & blasphemy, against
Its own Qualities, which are Servants of Humanity, not Gods or Lords.
Distinguish therefore States from Individuals in those States.
States Change: but Individual Identities never change nor cease:
You cannot go to Eternal Death in that which can never Die.
Satan & Adam are States Created into Twenty-seven Churches,
And thou O Milton art a State about to be Created
Called Eternal Annihilation that none but the Living shall
Dare to enter: & they shall enter triumphant over Death
And Hell & the Grave! States that are not, but ah! Seem to be.

Judge then of thy Own Self: thy Eternal Lineaments explore:
What is Eternal & what Changeable? & what Annihilable!
The Imagination is not a State: it is the Human Existence itself.
Affection or Love becomes a State, when divided from Imagination.
The Memory is a State always, & the Reason is a State
Created to be Annihilated & a new Ratio Created.
Whatever can be Created can be Annihilated. Forms cannot.
The Oak is cut down by the Ax. the Lamb falls by the Knife
But their Forms Eternal Exist For-ever. Amen, Hallelujah!"

Thus they converse with the Dead watching round the Couch of Death.
For God himself enters Death's Door always with those that enter
And lays down in the Grave with them, in Visions of Eternity,
Till they awake & see Jesus & the Linen Clothes lying
That the Females had Woven for them, & the Gates of their Father's House.

2. In the margin alongside lines 14–15, Blake inscribed Hebrew letters that may be transliterated as "Khrbm" (not a real word, but an error or perhaps an attempted pun on *cherubim* and *kerabim*, which means "multitudes"), followed by the phrases "as multitudes" and "Vox Populi," which means "voice of the people."

[PLATE 33]*
And the Divine Voice was heard in the Songs of Beulah Saying,

"When I first Married you, I gave you all my whole Soul.
I thought that you would love my loves & joy in my delights
Seeking for pleasures in my pleasures, O Daughter of Babylon.
Then thou wast lovely, mild & gentle; now thou art terrible
In jealousy & unlovely in my sight, because thou hast cruelly
Cut off my loves in fury till I have no love left for thee.
Thy love depends on him thou lovest & on his dear loves
Depend thy pleasures which thou hast cut off by jealousy.
Therefore I shew my Jealousy & set before you Death.
Behold Milton descended to Redeem the Female Shade
From Death Eternal; such your lot, to be continually Redeem'd
By death & misery of those you love & by Annihilation.
When the Sixfold Female percieves that Milton annihilates
Himself: that seeing all his loves by her cut off he leaves
Her also, intirely abstracting himself from Female loves,
She shall relent in fear of death. She shall begin to give
Her maidens to her husband, delighting in his delight;
And then & then alone begins the happy Female joy[3]
As it is done in Beulah; & thou O Virgin Babylon, Mother of
Whoredoms,
Shalt bring Jerusalem in thine arms in the night watches; and
No longer turning her a wandering Harlot in the streets
Shalt give her into the arms of God your Lord & Husband."

Such are the Songs of Beulah in the Lamentations of Ololon.

* Plate 36 in Copy D.

3. In Biblical stories such as Genesis 30, polygamy is held up as a model for marriage. In *Visions of the Daughters of Albion* 7:23 Oothoon espouses free love. Self-annihilation on the sexual plane (threefold Beulah) is enacted through Ololon's renunciation of jealousy, the Female Will; this corresponds to the risking of the total personality enacted on the fully human plane (fourfold Eden) by Milton: both involve surrender, self-liberation through rejection of selfishness. One of Blake's purposes was to have Milton reconsider his antifeminism; the question of whether Blake falls into the same error is discussed by Tayler, p. 539 in this edition.

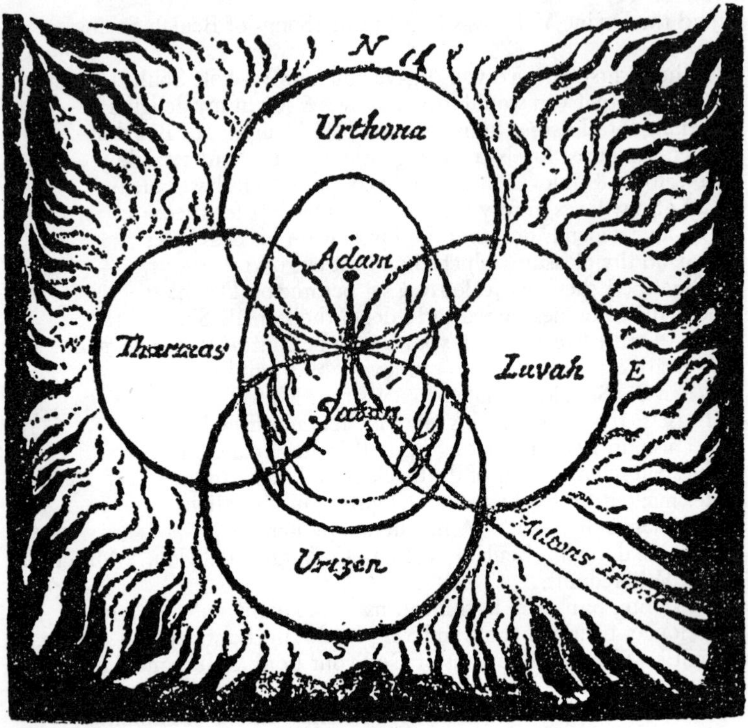

[PLATE 34]†

And all the Songs of Beulah sounded comfortable notes
To comfort Ololon's lamentation, for they said:
"Are you the Fiery Circle that late drove in fury & fire
The Eight Immortal Starry-Ones down into Ulro dark
Rending the Heavens of Beulah with your thunders & lightnings?
And can you thus lament & can you pity & forgive?[4]
Is terror changd to pity, O wonder of Eternity!"

And the Four States of Humanity in its Repose
Were shewed them: First of Beulah, a most pleasant Sleep
On Couches soft, with mild music, tended by Flowers of Beulah,
Sweet Female forms, winged, or floating in the air spontaneous;
The Second State is Alla & the third State Al-Ulro;

† Plate 38 in Copy D.

4. Apparently Ololon was part of the audience who rejected the Bard's song (*Milton* 13:47) without really hearing it (*Milton* 21:31–34), but her fury has now turned to pity.

But the Fourth State is dreadful: it is named Or-Ulro:[5]
The First State is in the Head, the Second is in the Heart:
The Third in the Loins & Seminal Vessels & the Fourth
In the Stomach & Intestines terrible, deadly, unutterable.
And he whose Gates are opend in those Regions of his Body
Can from those Gates view all these wondrous Imaginations.

But Ololon sought the Or-Ulro & its fiery Gates
And the Couches of the Martyrs: & many Daughters of Beulah
Accompany them down to the Ulro with soft melodious tears,
A long journey & dark thro Chaos, in the track of Milton's course
To where the Contraries of Beulah War beneath Negation's Banner.

Then view'd from Milton's Track they see the Ulro: a vast Polypus
Of living fibres down into the Sea of Time & Space growing,
A self-devouring monstrous Human Death Twenty-seven fold.
Within it sit Five Females & the nameless Shadowy Mother,
Spinning it from their bowels with songs of amorous delight
And melting cadences that lure the Sleepers of Beulah down
The River Storge[6] (which is Arnon) into the Dead Sea:
Around this Polypus Los continual builds the Mundane Shell.

Four Universes[7] round the Universe of Los remain Chaotic,
Four intersecting Globes, & the Egg form'd World of Los
In midst; stretching from Zenith to Nadir, in midst of Chaos.

5. These "four states" are not enumerated elsewhere by Blake; apparently Ololon descends to the lowest depths of Ulro (cf. Thel's more cautious descent). "Four States," in the sense of four worlds or visions of reality, are frequently referred to separately, but they are nowhere set forth in a schematic relationship to one another. Together Eden, Beulah, Generation, and Ulro constitute a fourfold paradigm of the possibilities of human action, ranging from communitarian freedom to solipsistic bondage: Eden is a fourfold state of creativity, Beulah a threefold sexual paradise, Generation is the twofold everyday world, Ulro the single vision of barren physicality or isolated subjectivity—though, as this passage suggests, Ulro too can be subdivided. Generation is a fallen reflection of "regeneration," or Eden (*Jerusalem* 7:65), Ulro a shattered Beulah (cf. "The Crystal Cabinet, p. 207). When the four States of Being are imagined simply as four rungs on a ladder, their interrelationship is not manifest; three concentric circles (with a fourth unbounded circle) offer a more adequate diagram of a four-dimensional mental universe, if the circles are thought of as interpenetrating spirals:

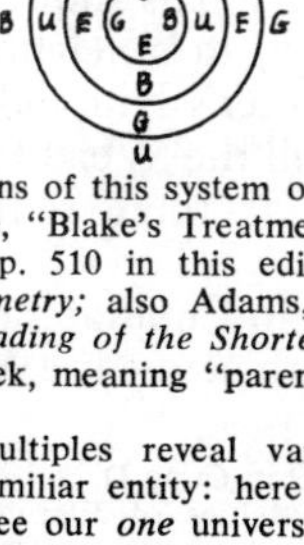

For discussions of this system of symbolism, see Frye, "Blake's Treatment of the Archetype," p. 510 in this edition, and *Fearful Symmetry;* also Adams, *William Blake: A Reading of the Shorter Poems.*
6. From Greek, meaning "parental affection."
7. Blake's multiples reveal various aspects of a familiar entity: here the *four* allow us to see our *one* universe in four new ways (see diagram on p. 292).

One of these Ruind Universes is to the North named Urthona;
One to the South: this was the glorious World of Urizen;
One to the East: of Luvah; One to the West: of Tharmas.
But when Luvah assumed the World of Urizen in the South
All fell towards the Center, sinking downward in dire Ruin.

Here in these Chaoses the Sons of Ololon took their abode,
In Chasms of the Mundane Shell which open on all sides round:
Southward & by the East within the Breach of Milton's descent
To watch the time, pitying & gentle, to awaken Urizen,
They stood in a dark land of death, of fiery corroding waters
Where lie in evil death the Four Immortals pale and cold,
And the Eternal Man, even Albion, upon the Rock of Ages.
Seeing Milton's Shadow, some Daughters of Beulah trembling
Returnd, but Ololon remaind before the Gates of the Dead.

And Ololon looked down into the Heavens of Ulro in fear.
They said, "How are the Wars of man which in Great Eternity
Appear around, in the External Spheres of Visionary Life,
Here renderd Deadly within the Life & Interior Vision?
How are the Beasts & Birds & Fishes, & Plants & Minerals
Here fixd into a frozen bulk subject to decay & death?
Those Visions of Human Life & Shadows of Wisdom & Knowledge

[PLATE 35]‡
Are here frozen to unexpansive deadly destroying terrors.
And War & Hunting:[8] the Two Fountains of the River of Life
Are become Fountains of bitter Death & of corroding Hell,
Till Brotherhood is changd into a Curse & a Flattery
By Differences between Ideas, that Ideas themselves (which are
The Divine Members) may be slain in offerings for sin.
O dreadful Loom of Death! O piteous Female forms compelled
To weave the Woof of Death! On Camberwell, Tirzah's Courts;
Malah's on Blackheath; Rahab & Noah dwell on Windsor's heights;
Where once the Cherubs of Jerusalem spread to Lambeth's Vale;
Milcah's Pillars shine from Harrow to Hampstead, where Hoglah
On Highgate's heights magnificent Weaves over trembling Thames
To Shooter's Hill and thence to Blackheath the dark Woof! Loud,
Loud roll the Weights & Spindles over the whole Earth, let down
On all sides round to the Four Quarters of the World,
    eastward on
Europe to Euphrates & Hindu, to Nile & back in Clouds
Of Death across the Atlantic to America North & South."

‡ Plate 39 in Copy D.
8. The activities of Eternity are mental; cf. Preface and *Jerusalem* 98.

So spake Ololon in reminiscence astonishd, but they
Could not behold Golgonooza without passing the Polypus,
A wondrous journey not passable by Immortal feet, & none
But the Divine Saviour can pass it without annihilation.
For Golgonooza cannot be seen till, having passd the Polypus,
It is viewed on all sides round by a Four-fold Vision,
Or till you become Mortal & Vegetable in Sexuality;
Then you behold its mighty Spires & Domes of ivory & gold.

And Ololon examined all the Couches of the Dead;
Even of Los & Enitharmon & all the Sons of Albion;
And his Four Zoas terrified & on the verge of Death.
In midst of these was Milton's Couch, & when they saw Eight
Immortal Starry-Ones, guarding the Couch in flaming fires,
They thunderous utterd all a universal groan, falling down
Prostrate before the Starry Eight, asking with tears forgiveness,
Confessing their crime with humiliation and sorrow.[9]

O how the Starry Eight rejoic'd to see Ololon descended!
And now that a wide road was open to Eternity,
By Ololon's descent thro Beulah to Los & Enitharmon!
For mighty were the multitudes of Ololon; vast the extent
Of their great sway, reaching from Ulro to Eternity,
Surrounding the Mundane Shell outside in its Caverns
And through Beulah; and all silent forbore to contend
With Ololon, for they saw the Lord in the Clouds of Ololon.

There is a Moment in each Day that Satan cannot find[1]
Nor can his Watch Fiends find it, but the Industrious find
This Moment & it multiply, & when it once is found
It renovates every Moment of the Day if rightly placed.
In this Moment Ololon descended to Los & Enitharmon
Unseen beyond the Mundane Shell, Southward in Milton's track.

Just in this Moment when the morning odours rise abroad,
And first from the Wild Thyme,[2] stands a Fountain in a rock

9. Modeled on Eve's prostration before Adam (*Paradise Lost* X, 911). The issue of male and female responsibility has been raised in Leutha's speech (*Milton* 11:35). In contrast to the thoroughfare between earth and Hell built in Satan's wake by Sin and Death (*Paradise Lost* X, 393), the multitude of Ololon opens a wide road to Eternity. The joyful welcome of the Starry Eight (which includes the highest form of Milton) suggests that Ololon's action has made possible a complete reconciliation between the sexes. The appearance of "the Lord in clouds," within Ololon, is a sign of the Second Coming.

1. Cf. the artist's moment in *Milton* 29:1.

2. Both the Wild Thyme and the Lark (line 61)—introduced in *Milton* 31:29, 51—have Shakespearean associations: the flower covering Titania's bower (*Midsummer Night's Dream*, II, i, 249), and the dawn-bird that sings "at heaven's gate" (Sonnet 29). As Los's messengers, they announce a new era. Milton's lark appears in the second of Blake's designs for "L'Allegro."

Of crystal flowing into two Streams: one flows thro Golgonooza
And thro Beulah to Eden beneath Los's western Wall;
The other flows thro the Aerial Void & all the Churches
Meeting again in Golgonooza beyond Satan's Seat.

The Wild Thyme is Los's Messenger to Eden, a mighty Demon,
Terrible deadly & poisonous his presence in Ulro dark;
Therefore he appears only a small Root creeping in grass,
Covering over the Rock of Odours, his bright purple mantle
Beside the Fount, above the Lark's nest in Golgonooza.
Luvah slept here in death & here is Luvah's empty Tomb;
Ololon sat beside this Fountain on the Rock of Odours.

Just at the place to where the Lark mounts, is a Crystal Gate:
It is the enterance of the First Heaven named Luther: for
The Lark is Los's Messenger thro the Twenty-seven Churches
That the Seven Eyes of God, who walk even to Satan's Seat
Thro all the Twenty-seven Heavens, may not slumber nor sleep.
But the Lark's Nest is at the Gate of Los, at the eastern
Gate of wide Golgonooza, & the Lark is Los's Messenger.

[PLATE 36]§
When on the highest lift of his light pinions he arrives
At that bright Gate, another Lark meets him & back to back
They touch their pinions tip tip; and each descend
To their respective Earths & there all night consult with Angels
Of Providence & with the Eyes of God all night in slumbers
Inspired: & at the dawn of day send out another Lark
Into another Heaven to carry news upon his wings:
Thus are the Messengers dispatchd till they reach the Earth again
In the East Gate of Golgonooza; & the Twenty-eighth bright
Lark met the Female Ololon descending into my Garden:
Thus it appears to Mortal eyes & those of the Ulro Heavens,
But not thus to Immortals; the Lark is a mighty Angel.

For Ololon step'd into the Polypus within the Mundane Shell;
They could not step into Vegetable Worlds without becoming
The enemies of Humanity, except in a Female Form.
And as One Female, Ololon and all its mighty Hosts,
Appear'd: a Virgin of twelve years;[3] nor time nor space was

§ Plate 40 in Copy D.

3. The youngest age a girl can be reasonably called a "virgin"; Ololon, neither hesitant like Thel nor a victim of rape like Oothoon, is shortly to give up her virginity (42:3), Male or female virginity on the sexual plane corresponds to Selfhood on the human plane.

To the perception of the Virgin Ololon, but as the
Flash of lightning—but more quick—the Virgin in my Garden
Before my Cottage stood; for the Satanic Space is delusion.

For when Los joind with me he took me in his firy whirlwind.
My Vegetated portion was hurried from Lambeth's shades.
He set me down in Felpham's Vale & prepard a beautiful
Cottage for me that in three years I might write all these Visions
To display Nature's cruel holiness: the deceits of Natural Religion.
Walking in my Cottage Garden, sudden I beheld
The Virgin Ololon & addres'd her as a Daughter of Beulah:

"Virgin of Providence, fear not to enter into my Cottage.
What is thy message to thy friend? What am I now to do?
Is it again to plunge into deeper affliction? behold me
Ready to obey, but pity thou my Shadow of Delight.
Enter my Cottage, comfort her, for she is sick with fatigue."

[PLATE 37]*
The Virgin answerd, "Knowest thou of Milton who descended
Driven from Eternity? Him I seek! terrified at my Act
In Great Eternity which thou knowest! I come him to seek!"

So Ololon utterd in words distinct the anxious thought.
Mild was the voice, but more distinct than any earthly,

* Plate 41 in Copy D.

That Milton's Shadow heard & condensing all his Fibres
Into a strength impregnable of majesty & beauty infinite,
I saw he was the Covering Cherub[4] & within him Satan
And Rahab, in an outside which is fallacious! within,
Beyond the outline of Identity, in the Selfhood deadly!
And he appeard the Wicker Man of Scandinavia in whom
Jerusalem's children consume in flames among the Stars.

Descending down into my Garden, a Human Wonder of God,
Reaching from heaven to earth, a Cloud & Human Form,
I beheld Milton with astonishment & in him beheld
The Monstrous Churches of Beulah, the Gods of Ulro dark—
Twelve monstrous dishumanizd terrors, Synagogues of Satan,
A Double Twelve & Thrice Nine: such their divisions.

And these their Names & their Places within the Mundane Shell:

In Tyre & Sidon I saw Baal & Ashtaroth; In Moab, Chemosh;
In Ammon, Molech: loud his Furnaces rage among the Wheels
Of Og, & pealing loud the cries of the Victims of Fire:
And pale his Priestresses infolded in Veils of Pestilence, border'd
With War; Woven in Looms of Tyre & Sidon by beautiful
Ashtaroth.
In Palestine, Dagon, Sea Monster! worshipd o'er the Sea.
Thammuz in Lebanon & Rimmon in Damascus curtaind;
Osiris: Isis: Orus: in Egypt; dark their Tabernacles on Nile
Floating with solemn songs, & on the Lakes of Egypt nightly
With pomp, even till morning break & Osiris appear in the sky.
But Belial of Sodom & Gomorrha, obscure Demon of Bribes
And secret Assasinations, not worshipd nor adord: but

4. Blake's symbol of ultimate evil, based on Ezekiel's condemnation of the Prince of Tyre (Ezekiel 28) as one who had claimed to be God. The prince is described as one perfect in wisdom and beauty: one who had been in Eden, who was covered with every precious stone, who had been upon the holy mountain (Horeb) and had walked up and down in the midst of the stones of fire. This imagery is strikingly similar to that associated with God (Exodus 19:8, Leviticus 10:2, Numbers 16:35, Deuteronomy 4:24, 9:3, Psalms 18:8, Hebrews 12:29). The Covering Cherub is to be destroyed by its own perfection, by a fire from within itself. Blake identified the Covering Cherub with the cherubim guarding Eden (Genesis 3 : 24) and probably with the gold-covered statues of cherubim covering the mercy seat in the Ark of the Covenant (Exodus 25:20) and guarding the Ark in the Holy of Holies of Solomon's temple (I Kings 6:23–28; Ezekiel 10). This image of holiness stands between fallen humanity and Divine Humanity and prevents man's return to Eden and his recognition of the divinity within, which is the Holy Spirit or human imagination. Previously, Milton had acknowledged his own selfhood as Satan; now he sees a larger evil which contains both Satan and Rahab, the Beast and the Whore of Revelation. Not only is the Covering Cherub a composite of various pagan idols (some of whom Milton had identified as devils in *Paradise Lost*), but it also contains the Jewish and Christian churches throughout their histories, from Adam through Luther (*Milton* 37:35–43). The Cherub turns out to be Milton's perception of God as he appeared to Moses on Sinai (or Horeb): a fiery jealous God, a projection from Milton's puritanical desire for holy perfection. Heroically, Milton is able to recognize this Satan-Rahab as his own false creation; by annihilating himself as a selfish member of the Elect, he annihilates the Covering Cherub as well, thus allowing his Divine Humanity to emerge.

With the fingers on the lips & the back turned to the light.
And Saturn, Jove, & Rhea of the Isles of the Sea remote.
These Twelve Gods are the Twelve Spectre Sons of the Druid Albion.

And these the names of the Twenty-seven Heavens & their Churches:
Adam, Seth, Enos, Cainan, Mahalaleel, Jared, Enoch,
Methuselah, Lamech: these are Giants mighty Hermaphroditic.
Noah, Shem, Arphaxad, Cainan the second, Salah, Heber,
Peleg, Reu, Serug, Nahor, Terah: these are the Female-Males,
A Male within a Female hid as in an Ark & Curtains.
Abraham, Moses, Solomon, Paul, Constantine, Charlemaine,
Luther: these seven are the Male-Females, the Dragon Forms,
Religion hid in War, a Dragon red & hidden Harlot.

All these are seen in Milton's Shadow who is the Covering Cherub,
The Spectre of Albion, in which the Spectre of Luvah inhabits;
In the Newtonian Voids between the Substances of Creation.

For the Chaotic Voids outside of the Stars are measured by
The Stars, which are the boundaries of Kingdoms, Provinces
And Empires of Chaos invisible to the Vegetable Man.
The Kingdom of Og is in Orion: Sihon is in Ophiucus;
Og has Twenty-seven Districts; Sihon's Districts Twenty-one.
From Star to Star, Mountains & Valleys, terrible dimension
Stretchd out, compose the Mundane Shell, a mighty Incrustation
Of Forty-eight deformed Human Wonders of the Almighty,
With Caverns whose remotest bottoms meet again beyond
The Mundane Shell in Golgonooza. But the Fires of Los rage
In the remotest bottoms of the Caves, that none can pass
Into Eternity that way, but all descend to Los—
To Bowlahoola & Allamanda & to Eututhon Benython.

The Heavens are the Cherub, the Twelve Gods are Satan,

[PLATE 38]†
And the Forty-eight Starry Regions are Cities of the Levites
The Heads of the Great Polypus, Four-fold twelve enormity
In mighty & mysterious comingling, enemy with enemy,
Woven by Urizen into Sexes from his mantle of years.
And Milton collecting all his fibres into impregnable strength
Descended down a Paved work of all kinds of precious stones
Out from the eastern sky; descending down into my Cottage
Garden: clothed in black, severe & silent he descended.[5]

† Plate 43 in Copy D.
5. Milton in Puritan dress, descending down a "Paved work of . . . precious stones" (cf. Exodus 24:10), appears to Blake as the Covering Cherub. This inhibiting figure symbolizes everything that impeded Milton in art and in love.

The Spectre of Satan stood upon the roaring sea & beheld
Milton within his sleeping Humanity! trembling & shuddring,
He stood upon the waves, a Twenty-seven-fold mighty Demon
Gorgeous & beautiful: loud roll his thunders against Milton.
Loud Satan thunderd, loud & dark upon mild Felpham shore;
Not daring to touch one fibre, he howld round upon the Sea.

I also stood in Satan's bosom & beheld its desolations!
A ruind Man: a ruind building of God not made with hands;[6]
Its plains of burning sand, its mountains of marble terrible:
Its pits & declivities flowing with molten ore & fountains
Of pitch & nitre: its ruind palaces & cities & mighty works;
Its furnaces of affliction in which his Angels & Emanations
Labour with blackend visages among its stupendous ruins:
Arches & pyramids & porches, colonades & domes,
In which dwells Mystery, Babylon. Here is her secret place;
From hence she comes forth on the Churches in delight.
Here is her Cup filld with its poisons, in these horrid vales,
And here her scarlet Veil woven in pestilence & war,
Here is Jerusalem bound in chains, in the Dens of Babylon.

In the Eastern porch of Satan's Universe Milton stood & said:

"Satan! my Spectre! I know my power thee to annihilate
And be a greater in thy place, & be thy Tabernacle,
A covering for thee to do thy will, till one greater comes
And smites me as I smote thee & becomes my covering.[7]
Such are the Laws of thy false Heavens! but Laws of Eternity
Are not such: know thou: I come to Self Annihilation;
Such are the Laws of Eternity that each shall mutually
Annihilate himself for others' good, as I for thee.
Thy purpose & the purpose of thy Priests & of thy Churches
Is to impress on men the fear of death; to teach
Trembling & fear, terror, constriction; abject selfishness.
Mine is to teach Men to despise death & to go on
In fearless majesty annihilating Self, laughing to scorn
Thy Laws & terrors, shaking down thy Synagogues as webs.
I come to discover before Heaven & Hell the Self righteousness
In all its Hypocritic turpitude, opening to every eye

6. Blake himself experiences the inner desolation of Satan; cf. the hell within of *Paradise Lost* III, 20. The "house not made with hands" (II Corinthians 5:1) should be the spiritual body.

7. If Milton should try to annihilate Satan as an external being, he would succeed only in becoming another layer of concealment over evil, a Miltonic church of "Milton's Religion" (*Milton* 22:39). Instead, Milton confronts his inmost "Self righteousness" and puts off in self-annihilation "all that is not of God alone" (all that is not true to his best sense of humanity). Satan's response is to try even harder to imitate the conventional image of God (*Milton* 39:23–28), but Milton can no longer be deceived. In annihilating Selfhood, Milton will annihilate Satan; the true Satan in each of us is our own selfishness.

These wonders of Satan's holiness, shewing to the Earth
The Idol Virtues of the Natural Heart, & Satan's Seat
Explore in all its Selfish Natural Virtue, & put off
In Self annihilation all that is not of God alone:
To put off Self & all I have ever & ever Amen."

Satan heard! Coming in a cloud, with trumpets & flaming fire,
Saying, "I am God the judge of all, the living & the dead.
Fall therefore down & worship me; submit thy supreme
Dictate to my eternal Will & to my dictate bow.
I hold the Balances of Right & Just & mine the Sword.
Seven Angels bear my Name & in those Seven I appear.
But I alone am God & I alone in Heaven & Earth
Of all that live dare utter this; others tremble & bow

[PLATE 39]‡
Till All Things become One Great Satan, in Holiness
Oppos'd to Mercy, and the Divine Delusion Jesus be no more."

Suddenly around Milton on my Path, the Starry Seven
Burnd terrible! my Path became a solid fire, as bright
As the clear Sun & Milton silent came down on my Path.
And there went forth from the Starry limbs of the Seven: Forms
Human, with Trumpets innumerable, sounding articulate
As the Seven spake; and they stood in a mighty Column of Fire
Surrounding Felpham's Vale, reaching to the Mundane Shell,
    Saying:

"Awake Albion awake! reclaim thy Reasoning Spectre. Subdue
Him to the Divine Mercy. Cast him down into the Lake
Of Los, that ever burneth with fire, ever & ever Amen!
Let the Four Zoas awake from Slumbers of Six Thousand Years."

Then loud the Furnaces of Los were heard! & seen as Seven
    Heavens
Stretching from south to north over the mountains of Albion.

Satan heard; trembling round his Body, he incircled it;
He trembled with exceeding great trembling & astonishment
Howling in his Spectre round his Body, hungring to devour
But fearing for the pain; for if he touches a Vital,
His torment is unendurable: therefore he cannot devour:
But howls round it as a lion round his prey continually.[8]
Loud Satan thunderd, loud & dark upon mild Felpham's Shore,

‡ Plate 44 in Copy D.
8. Cf. I Peter 5:8. Although Satan realizes that he is about to be annihilated, he cannot defend himself, because Milton's inmost selfishness which is threatening him is a part of himself.

Coming in a Cloud with Trumpets & with Fiery Flame,
An awful Form eastward from midst of a bright Paved-work
Of precious stones by Cherubim surrounded: so permitted
(Lest he should fall apart in his Eternal Death) to imitate
The Eternal Great Humanity Divine surrounded by
His Cherubim & Seraphim in ever happy Eternity.
Beneath sat Chaos: Sin on his right hand, Death on his left;
And Ancient Night spread over all the heaven his Mantle
of Laws.
He trembled with exceeding great trembling & astonishment.

Then Albion rose up[9] in the Night of Beulah on his Couch
Of dread repose seen by the visionary eye; his face is toward
The east, toward Jerusalem's Gates: groaning he sat above
His rocks. London & Bath & Legions & Edinburgh
Are the four pillars of his Throne; his left foot near London
Covers the shades of Tyburn: his instep from Windsor
To Primrose Hill, stretching to Highgate & Holloway.
London is between his knees: its basements fourfold.
His right foot stretches to the sea on Dover cliffs, his heel
On Canterbury's ruins; his right hand covers lofty Wales,
His left Scotland; his bosom girt with gold involves
York, Edinburgh, Durham & Carlisle & on the front
Bath, Oxford, Cambridge, Norwich; his right elbow
Leans on the Rocks of Erin's Land; Ireland, ancient nation.
His head bends over London: he sees his embodied Spectre
Trembling before him with exceeding great trembling & fear.
He views Jerusalem & Babylon, his tears flow down,
He movd his right foot to Cornwall, his left to the Rocks of
Bognor.
He strove to rise to walk into the Deep, but strength failing
Forbad, & down with dreadful groans he sunk upon his Couch
In moony Beulah. Los his strong Guard walks round beneath the
Moon.

Urizen faints in terror, striving among the Brooks of Arnon
With Milton's Spirit. As the Plowman or Artificer or Shepherd,
While in the labours of his Calling, sends his Thought abroad
To labour in the ocean or in the starry heaven, So Milton
Labourd in Chasms of the Mundane Shell, tho here before
My Cottage midst the Starry Seven, where the Virgin Ololon
Stood trembling in the Porch. Loud Satan thunder'd on the stormy
Sea
Circling Albion's Cliffs in which the Four-fold World resides,
Tho seen in fallacy outside: a fallacy of Satan's Churches.

9. Albion is awake but too weak to stand. "Legions" (line 35), named by the Romans, was an archbishopric in Glamorganshire (combined with Bath in *Jerusalem* 41:1). In *Jerusalem* 46:24 the four major cities are Edinburgh, York, London, and Verulam (see map).

[PLATE 40]§

Before Ololon Milton stood & percievd the Eternal Form
Of that mild Vision; wondrous were their acts by me unknown
Except remotely; and I heard Ololon say to Milton:

"I see thee strive upon the Brooks of Arnon; there a dread
And awful Man I see, o'ercoverd with the mantle of years.
I behold Los & Urizen; I behold Orc & Tharmas:
The Four Zoas of Albion, & thy Spirit with them striving,
In Self annihilation giving thy life to thy enemies.
Are those who contemn Religion & seek to annihilate it
Become in their Feminine portions the causes & promoters
Of these Religions? How is this thing? this Newtonian Phantasm?
This Voltaire & Rousseau: this Hume & Gibbon & Bolingbroke?
This Natural Religion! this impossible absurdity!
Is Ololon the cause of this? O where shall I hide my face?
These tears fall for the little-ones: the Children of Jerusalem,
Lest they be annihilated in thy annihilation."

No sooner she had spoke but Rahab Babylon appeard
Eastward upon the Paved work across Europe & Asia,
Glorious as the midday Sun, in Satan's bosom glowing:
A Female hidden in a Male, Religion hidden in War,
Namd Moral Virtue; cruel two-fold Monster shining bright,
A Dragon red & hidden Harlot which John in Patmos saw.

And all beneath the Nations innumerable of Ulro
Appeard: the Seven Kingdoms of Canaan & Five Baalim
Of Philistea, into Twelve divided, calld after the Names
Of Israel: as they are in Eden. Mountain, River & Plain,
City & sandy Desart, intermingled beyond mortal ken.

But turning toward Ololon in terrible majesty Milton
Replied, "Obey thou the Words of the Inspired Man!
All that can be annihilated must be annihilated,[1]
That the Children of Jerusalem may be saved from slavery.
There is a Negation, & there is a Contrary:
The Negation must be destroyed to redeem the Contraries.

§ Plate 46 in Copy D.

1. For Milton, selfhood is a State, a Negation, therefore annihilable, while individual humanity is eternal. When Ololon applies these principles in *Milton* 40:3, she finds that virginity is an annihilable state; when she is free of this Negation she can meet Milton as his Contrary. The nonentities "Virgin" and "Shadow" depart from Ololon and Milton and allow them to join as "One Man Jesus the Saviour" wrapped in a garment of suffering and war. This garment, the "Woof of Six Thousand Years," is the bloody covering of the fallen world (cf. the bloody Tent "Pinnd around from star to star" in (*Everlasting Gospel,* p. 366). The complete revelation of Divine Humanity has not occurred at this point. In Copy D the full-page design (color plate 23) showing Los's appearance to Blake (described in *Milton* 22, plate 24 in Copy D) follows this plate.

The Negation is the Spectre, the Reasoning Power in Man.
This is a false Body: an Incrustation over my Immortal
Spirit: a Selfhood, which must be put off & annihilated alway.
To cleanse the Face of my Spirit by Self-examination,

[PLATE 41]*
To bathe in the Waters of Life, to wash off the Not Human,
I come in Self-annihilation & the grandeur of Inspiration!
To cast off Rational Demonstration by Faith in the Saviour,
To cast off the rotten rags of Memory by Inspiration,
To cast off Bacon, Locke, & Newton from Albion's covering,
To take off his filthy garments, & clothe him with Imagination!
To cast aside from Poetry all that is not Inspiration,
That it no longer shall dare to mock with the aspersion of Madness
Cast on the Inspired, by the tame high finisher of paltry Blots,
Indefinite, or paltry Rhymes; or paltry Harmonies;
Who creeps into State Government like a catterpiller to destroy!
To cast off the idiot Questioner who is always questioning.
But never capable of answering; who sits with a sly grin
Silent plotting when to question, like a thief in a cave;
Who publishes doubt & calls it knowledge; whose Science is Despair,
Whose pretence to knowledge is Envy: whose whole Science is
To destroy the wisdom of ages to gratify ravenous Envy,
That rages round him like a Wolf day & night without rest.
He smiles with condescension; he talks of Benevolence & Virtue,
And those who act with Benevolence & Virtue, they murder time on time:
These are the destroyers of Jerusalem, these are the murderers
Of Jesus, who deny the Faith & mock at Eternal Life:
Who pretend to Poetry, that they may destroy Imagination:
By imitation of Nature's Images drawn from Remembrance.
These are the Sexual Garments, the Abomination of Desolation
Hiding the Human Lineaments as with an Ark & Curtains
Which Jesus rent: & now shall wholly purge away with Fire
Till Generation is swallowed up in Regeneration."

Then trembled the Virgin Ololon & replyd in clouds of despair:

"Is this our Feminine Portion, the Six-fold Miltonic Female?
Terribly this Portion trembles before thee, O awful Man!
Altho' our Human Power can sustain the severe contentions
Of Friendship, our Sexual cannot: but flies into the Ulro.
Hence arose all our terrors in Eternity! & now remembrance
Returns upon us! Are we Contraries O Milton, Thou & I?
O Immortal! how were we led to War the Wars of Death?
Is this the Void Outside of Existence, which if enter'd into

* **Plate 48 in Copy D.**

Color plate 1: Title page. *Songs of Innocence and of Experience* (1794), plate 1. Copy U, ca. 1815.

Color plate 2: Frontispiece to *Innocence. Songs of Innocence and of Experience* (1794), plate 2. Copy Z, 1826.

Piper, pipe that song again.

For when our souls have learn'd the heat to bear
The cloud will vanish we shall hear his voice.
Saying: come out from the grove my love & care
And round my golden tent like lambs rejoice.
Thus did my mother say and kissed me,
And thus I say to little English boy,
When I from black and he from white cloud free,
And round the tent of God like lambs we joy:
Ill shade him from the heat till he can bear,
To lean in joy upon our fathers knee.
And then Ill stand and stroke his silver hair,
And be like him and he will then love me.

Color plate 3: "The Little Black Boy." *Songs of Innocence* (1789), plate 30. Copy B, probably 1789.

I'll shade him from the heat till he can bear
To lean in joy upon our father's knee.

11
For when our souls have learn'd the heat to bear
The cloud will vanish we shall hear his voice.
Saying: come out from the grove my love & care,
And round my golden tent like lambs rejoice.
Thus did my mother say and kissed me,
And thus I say to little English boy.
When I from black and he from white cloud free,
And round the tent of God like lambs we joy:
Ill shade him from the heat till he can bear,
To lean in joy upon our fathers knee.
And then Ill stand and stroke his silver hair,
And be like him and he will then love me.

Color plate 4: "The Little Black Boy." *Songs of Innocence and of Experience* (1794), plate 10. Copy V, ca. 1818.

And then I'll stand and stroke his silver hair
And be like him, and he will then love me.

Color plate 5: "Infant Joy." *Songs of Innocence and of Experience* (1794), plate 25. Copy Z, 1826.

Sweet joy befall thee.

Color plate 6: Frontispiece to *Experience. Songs of Innocence and of Experience* (1794), plate 28. Copy Z, 1826.

Hear the voice of the Bard!

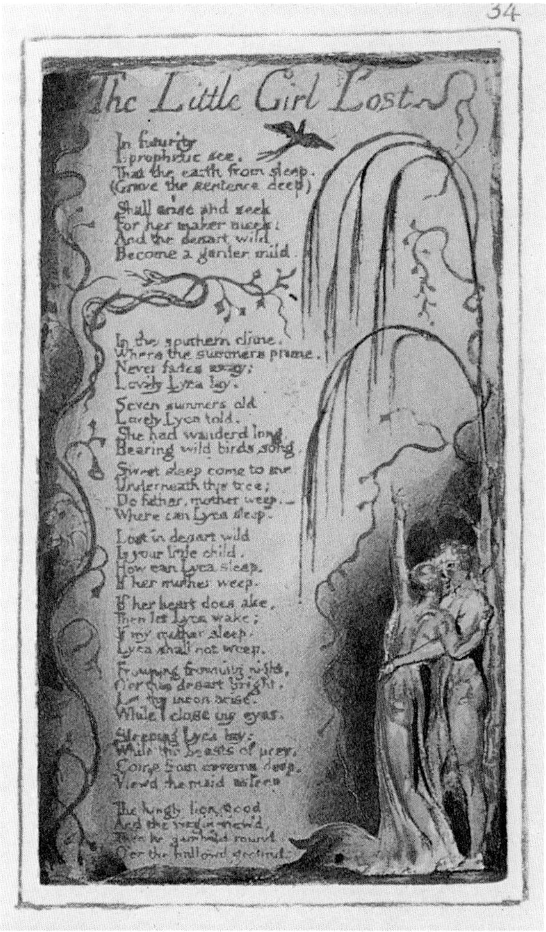

Color plate 7: "The Little Girl Lost," *Songs* (1794), plate 34. Copy Z, 1826.

And the desart wild
Become a garden mild.

Color plate 8: "The Sick Rose," *Songs* (1794), plate 39. Copy Z, 1826.

O Rose, thou art sick.

Color plate 9: Title page, *The Book of Thel* (1789), plate ii. Copy N, ca. 1815.

Why fade these children of the spring?

Color plate 10: Frontispiece, *Visions of the Daughters of Albion* (1794), plate i. Copy P, ca. 1815.

Bound back to back in Bromion's caves . . .

Color plate 11: Title page, *Visions of the Daughters of Albion* (1794), plate ii. Copy P, ca. 1815.

The Eye sees more than the Heart knows.

Color plate 12: "Argument," *Visions of the Daughters of Albion* (1794), plate iii. Copy P, ca. 1815.

I plucked Leutha's flower.

Color plate 13: Title page, *The Marriage of Heaven and Hell* (1790), plate 1. Copy G, ca. 1815.

Energy is Eternal Delight.

3
As a new heaven is begun, and it is now thir-
-ty-three years since its advent: the Eternal Hell
revives. And lo! Swedenborg is the Angel sitting
at the tomb: his writings are the linen clothes folded
up. Now is the dominion of Edom, & the return of
Adam into Paradise; see Isaiah XXXIV & XXXV Chap:
Without Contraries is no progreſsion. Attraction
and Repulsion, Reason and Energy, Love and
Hate, are neceſsary to Human existence.
From these contraries spring what the religious call
Good & Evil. Good is the paſsive that obeys Reason
Evil is the active springing from Energy.
Good is Heaven. Evil is Hell.

Color plate 14: *The Marriage of Heaven and Hell* (1790), plate 3. Copy G, ca. 1815.

Without Contraries is no progression.

Color plate 15: Title page, *America: A Prophecy* (1793), plate ii. Copy O, ca. 1822.

Albion is sick! America faints!

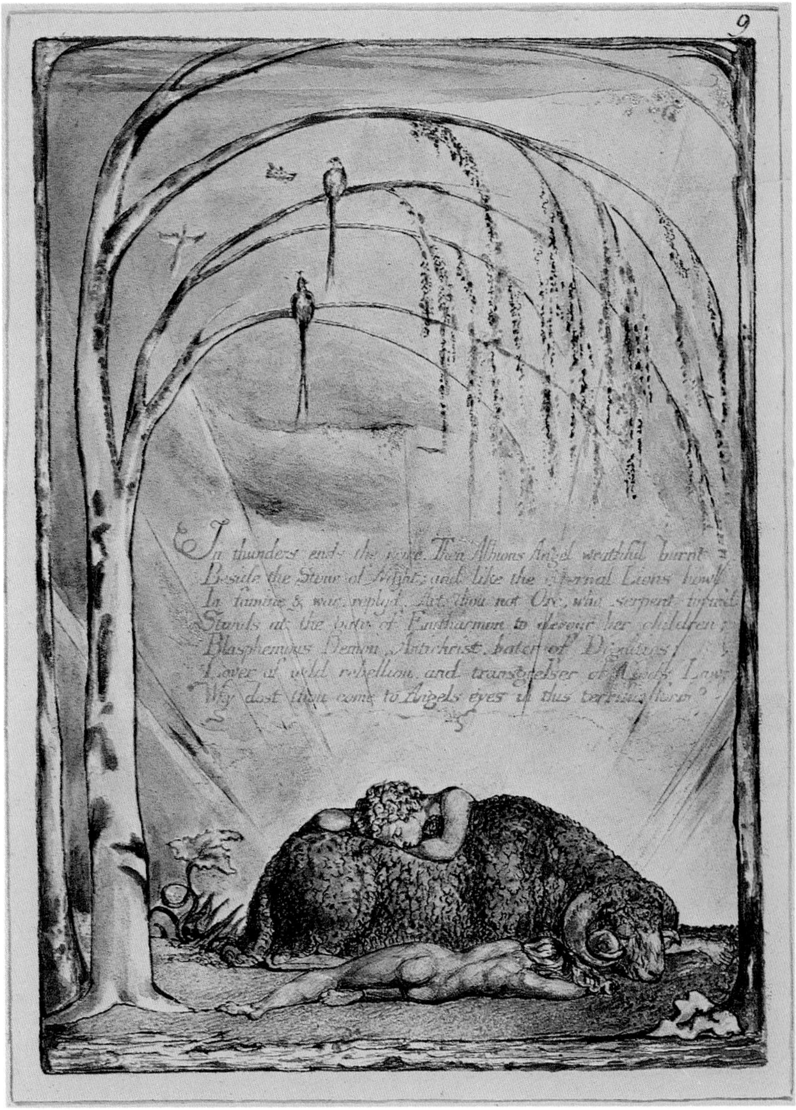

Color plate 16: **America** (1793), plate 7. Copy O, ca. 1822.

For every thing that lives is holy. . . .

Color plate 17: "The Ancient of Days," frontispiece, *Europe: A Prophecy* (1794), plate i. Copy K, ca. 1822.

Heaven a mighty circle turning . . .

Color plate 18: Title page, *Europe* (1794), plate ii. Copy K, ca. 1822.

Thought chang'd the infinite to a serpent.

Color plate 19: Title page, *The Book of Urizen* (1794), plate 1. Copy G, ca. 1815.

Here alone I in books formd of metals
Have written the secrets of wisdom.

Color plate 20: *Urizen* (1794), plate 21. Copy G, ca. 1815.

The Chain of Jealousy

Color plate 21: *Urizen* (1794), plate 22. Copy G, ca. 1815.

The Immortal endur'd his chains,
Tho' bound in a deadly sleep.

Color plate 22: Title page, *Milton: A Poem* (1804), plate 1. Copy C, ca. 1808.

I come to Self Annihilation.

Color plate 23: *Milton* (1804), plate 47; also numbered 43 or 21. Copy C, ca. 1808.

And Los behind me stood, a terrible flaming Sun.

Color plate 24: Frontispiece, *Jerusalem: The Emanation of the Giant Albion*(1804), plate 1. Copy E, ca. 1820.

Los took his globe of fire to search the interiors of Albion's Bosom. . . .

Color plate 25: Title page, *Jerusalem* (1804), plate 2. Copy E, ca. 1820.

Weeping was in all Beulah, and all the Daughters of Beulah
Wept for their Sister the Daughter of Albion, Jerusalem.

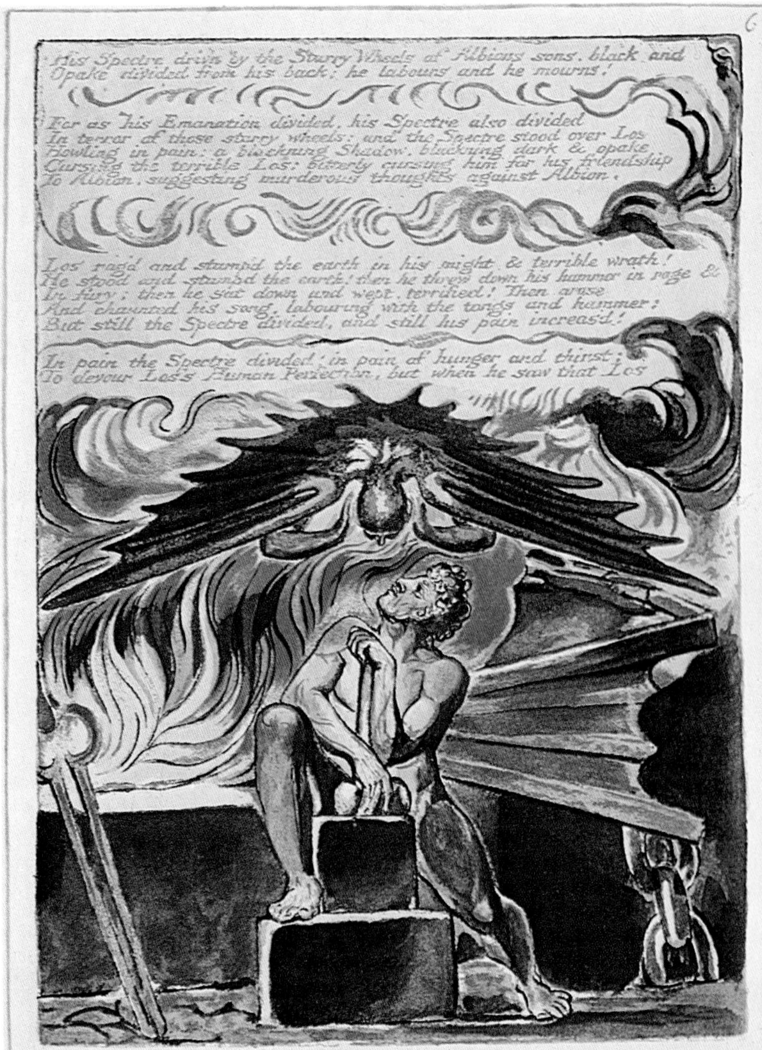

6
His Spectre driv'n by the Starry Wheels of Albions sons, black and
Opake divided from his back; he labours and he mourns!
For as his Emanation divided, his Spectre also divided
In terror of those starry wheels: and the Spectre stood over Los
Howling in pain: a blackning Shadow, blackning dark & opake
Cursing the terrible Los: bitterly cursing him for his friendship
To Albion, suggesting murderous thoughts against Albion.
Los rag'd and stamp'd the earth in his might & terrible wrath!
He stood and stamp'd the earth! then he threw down his hammer in rage &
In fury: then he sat down and wept, terrified! Then arose
And chaunted his song, labouring with the tongs and hammer:
But still the Spectre divided, and still his pain increas'd!
In pain the Spectre divided: in pain of hunger and thirst:
To devour Los's Human Perfection, but when he saw that Los

Color plate 26: *Jerusalem* (1804), plate 6. Copy E, ca. 1820.

Los answer'd unterrified to the opake blackening Fiend.

Color plate 27: *Jerusalem* (1804), plate 25. Copy E, ca. 1820.

Shriek not so, my only love!

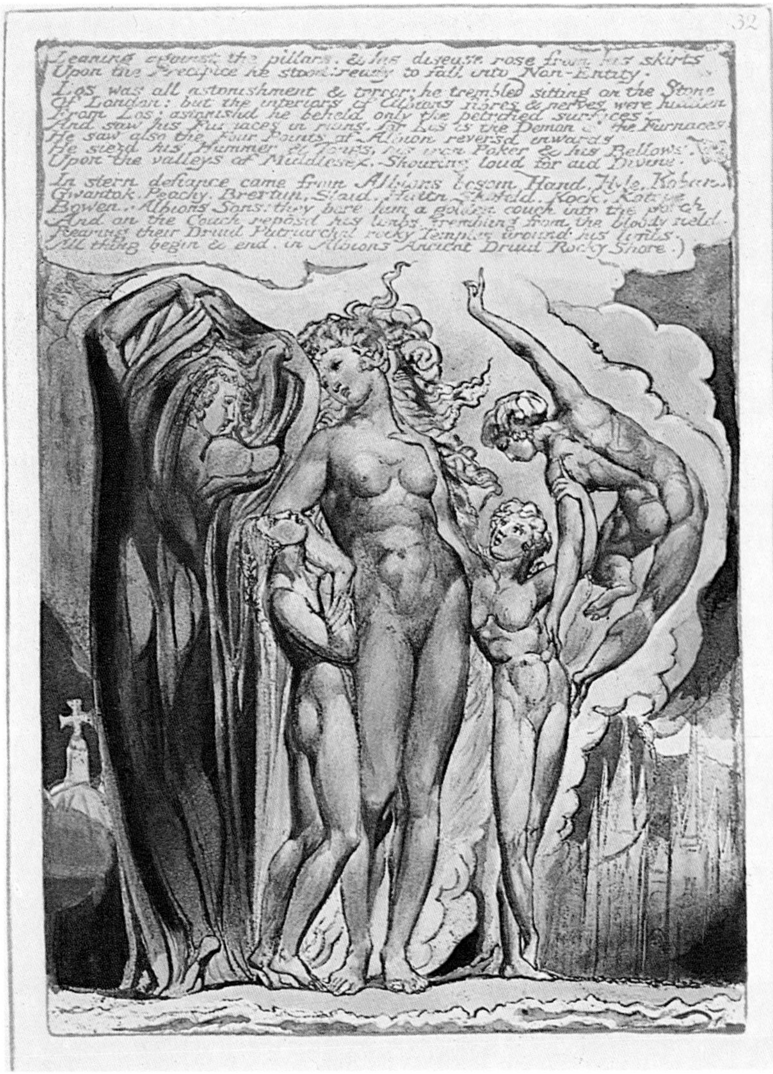

Color plate 28: ***Jerusalem*** (1804), plate 32; also numbered 46. Copy E, ca. 1820.

Jerusalem spoke, while Vala wove the veil of tears.

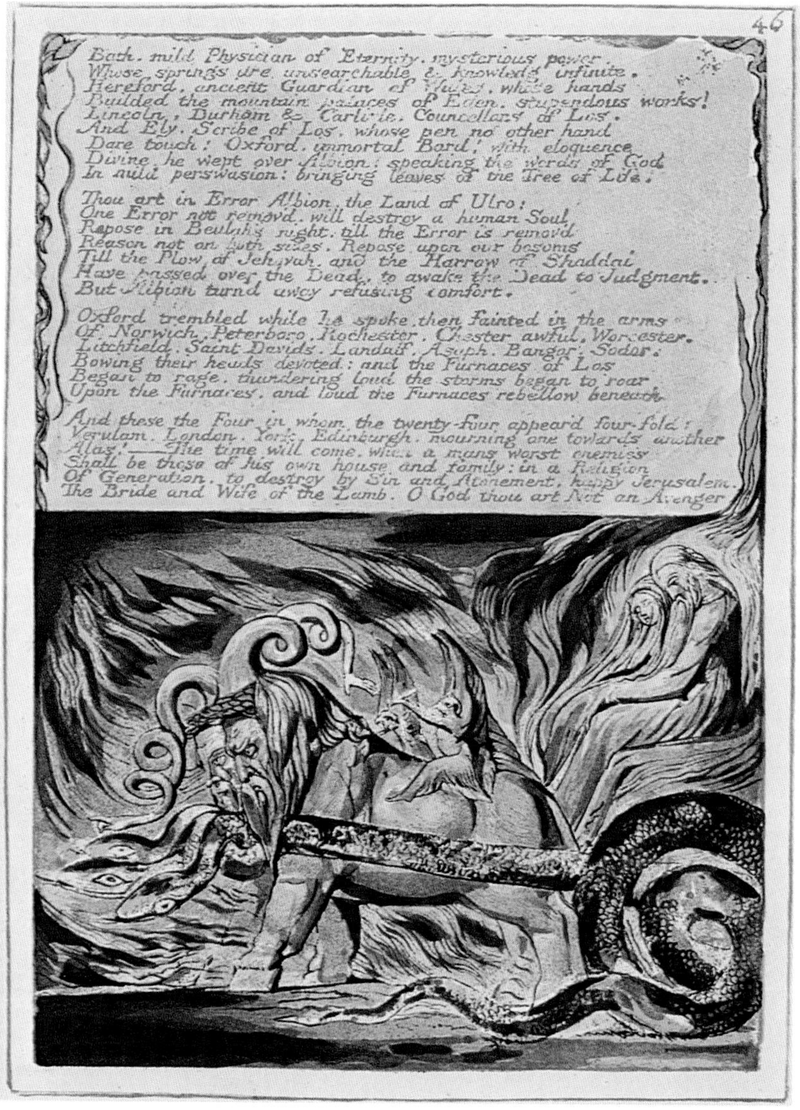

46

Bath, mild Physician of Eternity, mysterious power
Whose springs are unsearchable & knowledg infinite.
Hereford, ancient Guardian of Wales, whose hands
Builded the mountain palaces of Eden, stupendous works!
Lincoln, Durham & Carlisle, Councellors of Los.
And Ely, Scribe of Los, whose pen no other hand
Dare touch! Oxford, immortal Bard! with eloquence
Divine, he wept over Albion: speaking the words of God
In mild perswasion: bringing leaves of the Tree of Life.

Thou art in Error Albion, the Land of Ulro:
One Error not removd, will destroy a human Soul
Repose in Beulahs night, till the Error is removd
Reason not on both sides. Repose upon our bosoms
Till the Plow of Jehovah, and the Harrow of Shaddai
Have passed over the Dead, to awake the Dead to Judgment.
But Albion turnd away refusing comfort.

Oxford trembled while he spoke, then fainted in the arms
Of Norwich, Peterboro, Rochester, Chester awful, Worcester,
Litchfield, Saint Davids, Landaff, Asaph, Bangor, Sodor,
Bowing their heads devoted: and the Furnaces of Los
Began to rage, thundering loud the storms began to roar
Upon the Furnaces, and loud the Furnaces rebellow beneath

And these the Four in whom the twenty-four appeard four-fold:
Verulam, London, York, Edinburgh, mourning one towards another
Alas!—The time will come, when a mans worst enemies
Shall be those of his own house and family: in a Religion
Of Generation, to destroy by Sin and Atonement, happy Jerusalem,
The Bride and Wife of the Lamb. O God thou art Not an Avenger

Color plate 29: *Jerusalem* (1804), plate 46; also numbered 41.

. . . the Plow of Jehovah and the Harrow of Shaddai.

Color plate 30: *Jerusalem* (1804), plate 76. Copy E, ca. 1820.

Self was lost in the contemplation of faith. . . .

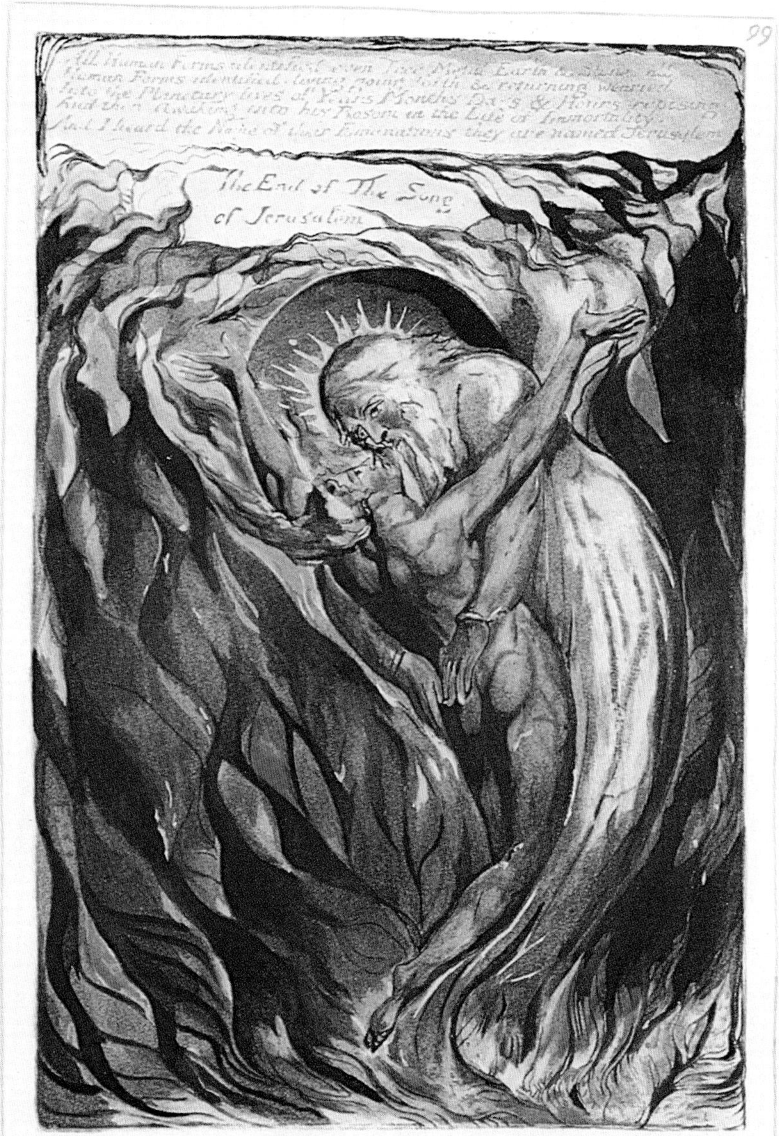

Color plate 31: *Jerusalem* (1804), plate 99. Copy E, ca. 1820.

Awakening into his Bosom in the Life of Immortality

Color plate 32: *Jerusalem* (1804), plate 100. Copy E, ca. 1820.

The blow of his Hammer is Justice, the swing of his Hammer, Mercy.

[PLATE 42]†
Becomes a Womb? & is this the Death Couch of Albion?
Thou goest to Eternal Death & all must go with thee!"

So saying, the Virgin divided Six-fold, & with a shriek
Dolorous that ran thro all Creation, a Double Six-fold Wonder:
Away from Ololon she divided & fled into the depths
Of Milton's Shadow as a Dove upon the stormy Sea.

Then as a Moony Ark Ololon descended to Felpham's Vale
In clouds of blood, in streams of gore, with dreadful thunderings
Into the Fires of Intellect that rejoic'd in Felpham's Vale
Around the Starry Eight. With one accord the Starry Eight
    became
One Man, Jesus the Saviour, wonderful! Round his limbs
The Clouds of Ololon folded as a Garment dipped in blood
Written within & without in woven letters: & the Writing
Is the Divine Revelation in the Litteral expression:
A Garment of War. I heard it namd the Woof of Six Thousand
    Years.

And I beheld the Twenty-four Cities of Albion
Arise upon their Thrones to Judge the Nations of the Earth,
And the Immortal Four in whom the Twenty-four appear Fourfold
Arose around Albion's body. Jesus wept & walked forth
From Felpham's Vale clothed in Clouds of blood, to enter into
Albion's Bosom, the bosom of death, & the Four surrounded him
In the Column of Fire in Felpham's Vale. Then to their mouths
    the Four
Applied their Four Trumpets & them sounded to the Four winds.

Terror struck in the Vale. I stood at that immortal sound;
My bones trembled. I fell outstretched upon the path
A moment, & my Soul returnd into its mortal state
To Resurrection & Judgment in the Vegetable Body.
And my sweet Shadow of Delight stood trembling by my side.[2]

Immediately the Lark mounted with a loud trill from Felpham's
    Vale
And the Wild Thyme from Wimbleton's green & impurpled
    Hills;
And Los & Enitharmon rose over the Hills of Surrey.

† Plate 49 in Copy D.

2. At the end of Blake's vision the apocalypse has not occurred, but the poem ends on a note of hope as the Great Harvest (interrupted by events in the Bard's song) begins. For a discussion of the concluding design, see John E. Grant in *Milton Reconsidered*, ed. John Karl Franson, Salzburg: Universitat Salzburg, 1976, pp. 97–99. The "Shadow of Delight" (36:31, 47:28) seems to be Catherine Blake; also Orc's name for Vala, the Shadowy Female (18:38).

Their clouds roll over London with a south wind; soft Oothoon
Pants in the Vales of Lambeth, weeping o'er her Human Harvest.
Los listens to the Cry of the Poor Man: his Cloud
Over London in volume terrific, low bended in anger.

Rintrah & Palamabron view the Human Harvest beneath.
Their Wine-presses & Barns stand open; the Ovens are prepar'd.
The Waggons ready: terrific Lions & Tygers sport & play,
All Animals upon the Earth are prepard in all their strength

[PLATE 43]‡
To go forth to the Great Harvest & Vintage of the Nations.

FINIS

‡ Plate 50 in Copy D.

To go forth to the Great Harvest & Vintage of the Nations
Finis

Jerusalem: The Emanation of the Giant Albion

Each of the four chapters in Blake's longest illuminated book begins with a prose and verse preface to a special audience: To the Public, To the Jews, To the Deists, and To the Christians. A consideration of the meaning and relationship of the central figures Jerusalem and Albion, along with their story of the fall, history, and redemption of mankind, may be postponed until these four prefaces have been studied, for in them Blake approaches his readers in unexpected ways that bring out his major themes.

In the first preface, the audience is not the "reading public" whose favor the author solicits; rather, it is a congregation of "Sheep" and "Goats" at the Judgment who must be lectured on the need for forgiveness and the importance of artistic freedom in a free state. In the second preface, Jews are addressed not as sinister devotees of a mistaken faith but as fellow believers in one religion, now divided, who need to be instructed in the connection between Jewish tradition and primordial Christianity as it developed mythically among the ancient Britons. To this audience Blake proposes that their own Cabalistic myth of cosmic man ought to be understood as applying to Albion, the traditional ancestral personification of England. Though Blake urges the Jews to "follow Jesus," he is not seeking to convert them to the established church; rather, he is recognizing that they are already fellow Christians in the sense that they share such virtues as humility, and he is inviting them to join in the British enterprise of building the new Jerusalem—a homeland in their place of exile. The conversion of the Jews had been prophesied as a sign of the Second Coming. Blake is saying that the conversion has already taken place and needs only to be acknowledged.

The exhortation to the Deists against natural morality and natural religion in the third preface charges that despite their libertarian principles and their disapproval of religious superstition, these rationalists have a false religion of their own: a devotion to things as they are, or the God of this World. In rejecting Christianity the Deists have rejected its cental tenet of the forgiveness of sins and have cut themselves off from the source of spiritual rebirth. They have explained away the problem of evil by redefining natural man as good. Thus when Rousseau rationalized his own shortcomings and Voltaire flattered Frederick the Great they repeated the errors of the Pharisees, the self-righteous attitude of mind responsible for the condemnation of Jesus and the persistence of corporeal warfare throughout the Christian era. These thinkers of the Enlightenment have something to learn from the religious extremism of the monks and Methodists whom they hold in contempt. Finally, the Christian audience—with whom most of Blake's potential readers would want to identify themselves—is urged to practice its faith by laboring in art and science to build up Jerusalem, the new Jerusalem promised in Revelation. Christian virtue should consist of activity or mental warfare rather than restraint, the development of mental gifts rather than the accusation of sin in others. The rest of the fourth preface is made up of a poem that characterizes Jesus as antireligious and a hymn on the union of Jerusalem and England which proclaims the return of the Lamb of God to "England's green & pleasant bowers" (echoing the introductory "Jerusalem hymn" in the early copies of *Milton*). With reference to specific communities of believers, Blake directs each of the four prefaces toward a definition of true Christianity as the spirit of forgiveness which releases the energies of a society into constructive activity, the building of Jerusalem.

Though Blake was so little a patriot, in some senses of the word, that he was tried for sedition—an experience which contributed to the bitter symbolism of the "Sons of Albion" in *Jerusalem*—he made his country the hero, the scene of action, and the focus of concern in his master work. Blake seeks to reunite England with its spiritual center, Jerusalem, and to awaken the English people to their Christian heritage, which has been polluted by the religious establishment. To this end he employs a rich complex of Anglo-centric "histories" that had been developed by eighteenth-century speculative mythologers, at times so persuasively that he appears actually to endorse theories that early man was an ancient Briton and that the Biblical patriarchs were Druids. At the beginning of the nineteenth century it was not a chauvinistic folly to think that what the British did affected the lives of people throughout the world: "All things begin and end in Albion's ancient Druid Rocky shore." A spiritual awakening of the most powerful industrial and military country in the world might easily be imagined as the apocalyptic event that would reunify the warring nations and shake humanity out of its crippling self-limitations.

In contemporary life the sleep in despair of the Giant Man Albion takes the form of war, empire, and exploitation. These miseries result from Albion's estrangement from his consort Jerusalem, spirit of freedom, "a City yet a Woman." He has been seduced and enslaved by the world of appearances, the beautiful but destructive nature-force called Vala or Babylon. His eyes have clouded over so that he no longer sees the Divine Vision, the spiritual presence within every human breast; he thinks of God as remote, jealous, inhuman. This condition of error is represented geographically by the separation between Biblical and English place names for what should be one landscape in the mind. In self-defense against his alienated God, Albion turns inward and his body of earth and stars is scattered away from him as he lapses into nightmare. The chief suspense in the poem is whether and by what means he can awaken, recognize his divine nature, and be reunited with his soul mate, Jerusalem.

Through a process of self-division Albion engenders a legion of negative characters who, in various alliances and rivalries, act out the symptoms of their father's illness. The twelve Sons of Albion, sometimes interwoven with the twelve tribes of Israel, are named after Blake's artistic and political enemies, though the evils they embody are much more significant than the deeds of their real-life counterparts. For example, to depict the triple-headed monster Hand, based on the coeditors John, Robert, and Leigh Hunt (whose journal *The Examiner* attacked Blake's one-man show of paintings in 1809), Blake builds upon Leigh Hunt's graphic signature: a printer's hand with a pointing finger, an image anticipated in the title of

Hunt's earlier journal *The Indicator*. But Blake's character Hand, the ogre derived from Hunt, cannot be reduced to a figment of Blake's personal pique: he epitomizes a universal Accuser. Other manifestations of this evil are the characters based on the soldiers who accused Blake of seditious utterance and the judges who presided over his trial. The point is not so much to vindicate Blake personally as to expand into myth specific instances of the kind of thing that happens over and over when a country falls ill, breaks apart, loses its soul, and rejects its spirit of liberty and forgiveness.

Just as the Sons of Albion show what is wrong with Englishmen, so the Daughters of Albion—offspring or subdivisions of Vala—show what is wrong with Englishwomen. These beauties are not oppressed victims like the silent chorus in *Visions of the Daughters of Albion*; almost all of them bear names of royal women in British legend, and they torture and dominate men and defame their rival Jerusalem. In contrast, the benevolent Erin, or Ireland, and the merciful Daughters of Beulah open time and space to eternity and protect the outcast Jerusalem. Blake's assignment of a redemptive role to the spirit of Ireland is in itself an act of vision penetrating the blindnesses of English policy. Other right-minded characters, the masculine Friends of Albion—who are personifications of the cathedral cities of England—try without success to bear up their fallen comrade. A fearsome amalgamation of male and female characteristics looms up in the form of the Covering Cherub as the poem draws to a conclusion; until this absolute negation is revealed and exorcized no real progress can be made in freeing Jerusalem from bondage and Albion from self-deluded idolatry.

The major character in *Jerusalem* retaining his power of action is Los, the creative blacksmith whose work preserves some basis of civility during the chaotic eons of Albion's sleep. Despite the antiartistic cynicism of his Spectre or alter ego and the domestic distractions of his consort Enitharmon, Los works with them both to build up the model city of Golgonooza (represented by a star on our London map) upon and within the continually disintegrating physical city of London. The Los plot depicts the efforts of the self-disciplined artist to redeem society and the attempts of the imagination to reawaken vision in mankind. Los not only imagines a better world but also encourages the faith of others and works patiently with them to bring the new world into reality. In Los's self-sacrifice Albion comes to recognize the spirit of Jesus and to break free of his self-centered fantasies.

Like Los, Blake himself labored over the years to give form to his *Jerusalem*. Of the five known complete copies, only one was colored and none was finished before 1820, though the title page is dated 1804. Blake deployed all the techniques perfected in earlier illuminated books to produce his climactic and comprehensive masterpiece. The 100 plates of *Jerusalem,* among Blake's largest—practically the same size as those in *America, Europe,* and *The Song of Los*—are crowded with powerful designs, except for fourteen relatively undecorated pages. *Jerusalem* is physically as well as thematically related to *Milton*; not only does it fulfill the promise of Apocalypse with which *Milton* ends, but each page is twice the size of those in the companion piece, also dated 1804 on the title page, and *Jerusalem* contains twice as many pages as *Milton*. In *Jerusalem,* above all other illuminated books, typographical presentation alone cannot do justice to

Blake's magnificent execution of the whole. The reproductions in our color plates 24–32, from Copy E, in the collection of Mr. Paul Mellon, suggest what may be seen in the full-sized, hand-colored Blake Trust facsimile of this copy owned by many college libraries.

Except for the preface to chapter 1, we have taken our text from Copy E, the only complete hand-colored copy. Perhaps as a sample for customers, Blake also colored the first twenty-five plates of *Jerusalem* in a more subdued way, and this incomplete copy, Copy B, has also been reproduced in facsimile in the Blake Trust series. In chapter 2 Blake varied the ordering of pages. We follow the sequence of Copies D and E, used also in the Keynes edition; the alternate pagination of Copies A, C, and F, used in the Erdman edition, is given in footnotes.

From Jerusalem

The Emanation of The Giant Albion*

1804 Printed by W. Blake Sth Molton S^{t}.[1]

[Plate 3][2]

Sheep — Goats

To the Public

After my three years' slumber[3] on the banks of the Ocean, I again display my Giant forms to the Public: My former Giants & Fairies having reciev'd the highest reward possible: the love and

* See color plate 24 for the frontispiece and color plate 25 for the title page.

1. Blake etched and dated the title pages of both *Milton* and *Jerusalem* in 1804, when he lived on this street, but he did not complete a satisfactory etched text of *Jerusalem* until about 1820. On a proof copy of the frontispiece, the doorway which Los enters is decorated with three inscriptions: (1) "There is a void outside of Existence, which if enterd into / Englobes itself & becomes a Womb; such was Albion's Couch / A pleasant Shadow of Repose calld Albion's lovely land. / His Sublime & Pathos become Two Rocks fixd in the Earth; / His Reason, his Spectrous Power, covers them above; / Jerusalem his Emanation is a Stone laying beneath. / O behold the Vision of Albion!" (2) " 'Half Friendship is the bitterest Enmity,' said Los / As he enterd the Door of Death for Albion's sake Inspired. / The long sufferings of God are not for ever; there is a Judgment," and (3) in reversed writing on the left side, "Every Thing has its Vermin, O Spectre of the Sleeping Dead!" These inscriptions are obliterated in the finished copies (see color plate 24), and Blake altered and rearranged other plates as well.

2. We depart from Copy E, our copy text, for the preface to chapter 1, following the heading "To the Public." This preface was savagely mutilated by Blake, probably in despair. For it (plate 3) we follow the text reconstructed by Erdman, *Studies in Bibliography* 17 (1964), 1–54, and 18 (1965), 281–82.

If the Goats on the right side of the page are to have their proper place on the left side of God (Matthew 25:33), the reader must stand in the position of those facing judgment: according to the way the reader judges *Jerusalem* he identifies himself with the Sheep or the Goats. Most of the mutilations of this preface obliterate conciliatory words to the reader. Perhaps Blake felt that he had already been judged by his readers and there was no longer any point in letting them know in what spirit he wished to be read.

3. Residence in Felpham, 1800–1803.

friendship of those with whom to be connected, is to be blessed, I cannot doubt that this more consolidated & extendéd Work will be as kindly recieved.

The Enthusiasm of the following Poem, the Author hopes no Reader will think presumptuousness or arrogance when he is reminded that the Ancients entrusted their love to their Writing, to the full as Enthusiastically as I have who Acknowledge mine for my Saviour and Lord,[4] for they were wholly absorb'd in their Gods. I also hope the Reader will be with me, wholly One in Jesus our Lord, who is the God of Fire and Lord of Love to whom the Ancients look'd and saw his day afar off, with trembling & amazement.

The Spirit of Jesus is continual forgiveness of Sin: he who waits to be righteous before he enters into the Saviour's kingdom, the Divine Body, will never enter there. I am perhaps the most sinful of men![5] I pretend not to holiness! yet I pretend to love, to see, to converse with daily, as man with man, & the more to have an interest in the Friend of Sinners. Therefore Dear Reader, forgive what you do not approve, & love me for this energetic exertion of my talent.

Reader! lover of books! lover of heaven,
And of that God from whom all books are given,
Who in mysterious Sinai's awful cave
To Man the wond'rous art of writing gave,[6]
Again he speaks in thunder and in fire!
Thunder of Thought, & flames of fierce desire:
Even from the depths of Hell his voice I hear,
Within the unfathomd caverns of my Ear.
Therefore I print; nor vain my types[7] shall be:
Heaven, Earth & Hell, henceforth shall live in harmony.

Of the Measure,[8] in which
the following Poem is written

We who dwell on Earth can do nothing of ourselves: every thing is conducted by Spirits, no less than Digestion or Sleep. To Note the last words of Jesus, Εδοθη μοι πασα εξουσια εν ουρανῳ και επι γης.[9]

4. Blake's somewhat garbled defense of enthusiasm in this mutilated passage is consistent with his belief that the Holy Spirit is the human imagination.
5. Saint Paul claimed to be chief of sinners (I Timothy 1:15).
6. The true gift of the Holy Spirit is art, not law (cf. Exodus 24).
7. Archetypes for myth and stereotypes for printing.
8. Cf. Milton's justification for his use of blank verse, in the prefatory note on "the Verse" for *Paradise Lost*.
9. Not the last words before his death but before his ascension: "All power is given unto me in heaven and in earth" (Matthew 28:18).

When this Verse was first dictated to me I consider'd a Monotonous Cadence like that used by Milton & Shakespeare & all writers of English Blank Verse, derived from the modern bondage of Rhyming, to be a necessary and indispensible part of Verse. But I soon found that in the mouth of a true Orator such monotony was not only awkward, but as much a bondage as rhyme itself. I therefore have produced a variety in every line, both of cadences & number of syllables. Every word and every letter is studied and put into its fit place: the terrific numbers are reserved for the terrific parts—the mild & gentle, for the mild & gentle parts, and the prosaic, for inferior parts: all are necessary to each other. Poetry Fetter'd, Fetters the Human Race! Nations are Destroy'd, or Flourish, in proportion as Their Poetry Painting and Music, are Destroy'd or Flourish! The Primeval State of Man, was Wisdom, Art, and Science.

[PLATE 4]

Μονος ὁ Ιεσους[1]

Jerusalem

Chap: 1

Of the Sleep of Ulro! and of the passage through
Eternal Death! and of the awaking to Eternal Life.

This theme calls me in sleep night after night,[2] & ev'ry morn
Awakes me at sun-rise, then I see the Saviour over me
Spreading his beams of love, & dictating the words of this mild song.

"Awake! awake O sleeper of the land of shadows, wake! expand![3]
I am in you and you in me, mutual in love divine:
Fibres of love from man to man thro Albion's pleasant land.
In all the dark Atlantic vale down from the hills of Surrey
A black water accumulates; return Albion! return!
Thy brethren call thee, and thy fathers, and thy sons,
Thy nurses and thy mothers, thy sisters and thy daughters
Weep at thy soul's disease, and the Divine Vision is darkend:

1. "Jesus alone" (John 8:9).
2. Cf. the "nightly visitation" by Milton's muse, *Paradise Lost* IX, 21–24.
3. The speech of the Divine Vision applies equally to the poet and to Albion, who is mankind as a whole.

Thy Emanation that was wont to play before thy face,
Beaming forth with her daughters into the Divine bosom:
Where hast thou hidden thy Emanation lovely Jerusalem
From the vision and fruition of the Holy-one?
I am not a God afar off, I am a brother and friend;
Within your bosoms I reside, and you reside in me:
Lo! we are One; forgiving all Evil; Not seeking recompense!
Ye are my members O ye sleepers of Beulah, land of shades!"

But the perturbed Man away turns down the valleys dark:[4]

"Phantom of the over heated brain! shadow of immortality!
Seeking to keep my soul a victim to thy Love! which binds
Man the enemy of man into deceitful friendships:
Jerusalem is not! her daughters are indefinite:
By demonstration, man alone can live, and not by faith.
My mountains are my own, and I will keep them to myself:
The Malvern and the Cheviot, the Wolds, Plinlimmon & Snowdon
Are mine. Here will I build my Laws of Moral Virtue!
Humanity shall be no more: but war & princedom & victory!"

So spoke Albion in jealous fears, hiding his Emanation
Upon the Thames and Medway, rivers of Beulah: dissembling
His jealousy before the throne divine, darkening, cold!

[PLATE 5]
The banks of the Thames are clouded! the ancient porches of Albion are
Darken'd! they are drawn thro' unbounded space, scatter'd upon
The Void in incoherent despair! Cambridge & Oxford & London,
Are driven among the starry Wheels, rent away and dissipated,
In Chasms & Abysses of sorrow, enlarg'd without dimension, terrible.
Albion's mountains run with blood, the cries of war & of tumult
Resound into the unbounded night, every Human perfection
Of mountain & river & city, are small & wither'd & darken'd.
Cam is a little stream! Ely is almost swallowd up!
Lincoln & Norwich stand trembling on the brink of Udan-Adan!
Wales and Scotland shrink themselves to the west and to the north!
Mourning for fear of the warriors in the Vale of Entuthon-Benython[5]
Jerusalem is scatterd abroad like a cloud of smoke thro' non-entity:
Moab & Ammon & Amalek & Canaan & Egypt & Aram[6]
Recieve her little-ones for sacrifices and the delights of cruelty.

4. Blake obliterated line 23: "Saying, 'We are not One: we are Many, thou most simulative.' "

5. Forest of Error; Udan-Adan in line 10 is a lake of spaces (see note to *Milton* 21:1).

6. Heathen territories surrounding the Promised Land (see Biblical map).

Trembling I sit day and night, my friends are astonish'd at me.
Yet they forgive my wanderings; I rest not from my great task!
To open the Eternal Worlds, to open the immortal Eyes
Of man inwards into the Worlds of Thought: into Eternity
Ever expanding in the Bosom of God, the Human Imagination.
O Saviour pour upon me thy Spirit of meekness & love:
Annihilate the Selfhood in me, be thou all my life!
Guide thou my hand which trembles exceedingly upon the rock of
    ages,
While I write of the building of Golgonooza, & of the terrors of
    Entuthon:
Of Hand & Hyle & Coban, of Kwantok, Peachey, Brereton, Slayd
    & Hutton:
Of the terrible sons & daughters of Albion. and their Generations.
Scofield! Kox, Kotope and Bowen, revolve most mightily upon
    The Furnace of Los.[7]

* * *

* * * Jerusalem & Vala weeping in the Cloud
Wander away into the Chaotic Void, lamenting with her Shadow
Among the Daughters of Albion, among the Starry Wheels;
Lamenting for her children, for the sons & daughters of Albion.

Los heard her lamentations in the deeps afar! his tears fall
Incessant before the Furnaces, and his Emanation divided in pain,
Eastward toward the Starry Wheels. But Westward, a black Horror,

[PLATE 6]
His spectre driv'n by the Starry Wheels of Albion's sons, black and
Opake, divided from his back; he labours and he mourns!

For as his Emanation divided, his Spectre also divided
In terror of those starry wheels: and the Spectre stood over Los†
Howling in pain: a blackning Shadow, blackning dark & opake
Cursing the terrible Los: bitterly cursing him for his friendship
To Albion, suggesting murderous thoughts against Albion.

7. The twelve "sons of Albion" are based on participants in Blake's trial (see Memorandum, p. 470): Hand is the editorial staff of John, Robert, and Leigh Hunt; Hyle is Hayley, also the Greek word for matter; Coban may be Bacon (which would be inconsistent with the fact that the other "sons" are Blake's contemporaries) or perhaps Hayley's publisher Colburn (according to John Adlard, cited by David V. Erdman in *Blake: Prophet Against Empire,* p. 459); Quantock, Peachey, Brereton are judges at Blake's trial; Schofield and Cock are the soldiers who accused Blake of sedition; Bowen is a lawyer in the area who may have been connected with the trial; Kotope, Slayd, and Hutton are unidentified but probably were involved with the trial. These characters are at times mingled with the twelve sons of Israel, heads of the twelve tribes; their Emanations are based on legendary women in British history. The whole villainous crew exhibits what has happened and is happening during the death and corruption of Albion.

† See color plate 26.

Los rag'd and stamp'd the earth in his might & terrible wrath!
He stood and stampd the earth! then he threw down his hammer in rage &
In fury: then he sat down and wept, terrified! Then arose
And chaunted his song, labouring with the tongs and hammer:
But still the Spectre divided, and still his pain increas'd!

* * *

[PLATE 10]

* * *

And this is the manner of the Sons of Albion in their strength:
They take the Two Contraries which are calld Qualities, with which
Every Substance is clothed; they name them Good & Evil.
From them they make an Abstract, which is a Negation
Not only of the Substance from which it is derived,
A murderer of its own Body: but also a murderer
Of every Divine Member: it is the Reasoning Power
An Abstract objecting power, that Negatives every thing.
This is the Spectre[8] of Man: the Holy Reasoning Power
And in its Holiness is closed the Abomination of Desolation.[9]

Therefore Los stands in London building Golgonooza,
Compelling his Spectre to labours mighty; trembling in fear
The Spectre weeps, but Los unmovd by tears or threats remains.

"I must Create a System, or be enslav'd by another Man's.
I will not Reason & Compare: my business is to Create."

So Los, in fury & strength: in indignation & burning wrath.
Shuddring the Spectre howls, his howlings terrify the night.
He stamps around the Anvil, beating blows of stern despair
He curses Heaven & Earth, Day & Night & Sun & Moon
He curses Forest Spring & River, Desart & sandy Waste
Cities & Nations, Families & Peoples, Tongues & Laws,
Driven to desperation by Los's terrors & threatning fears.

* * *

8. A Spectre is the hardened outer shell of one's personality that appears when one becomes divided from one's Emanation, or gentler self. Usually the Emanation emerges from the bosom and the Spectre emerges from the back. Specifically, Los's Spectre is that aspect of himself which blocks his creative labor by inhibiting or discouraging him. In *The Four Zoas,* Los accepts his Spectre as another self and is reunited with him. In *Jerusalem,* however, Los masters his Spectre and forces him to help build Golgonooza. Perhaps Blake's point is that things have become so desperate that the artist cannot allow himself the luxury of inner doubts but even in a state of conflict must do his duty and get on with the job at hand. The conflict is pictured in color plate 26.

9. The ultimate evil, a portent of the end in Daniel 9:27, 11:31, and 12:11; it is something unspeakably foul set up in the place of holiness. According to the Blakean principle that "everything that lives is holy," the idea of an especially set-aside holy place is itself abominable. The symbolism is intensified by Jesus in Matthew 24:15–16 and is associated with false Christs in Matthew 24:24; cf. Mark 13:14, 22.

* * * Los compelld the invisible Spectre
[PLATE 11]
To labours mighty, with vast strength, with his mighty chains,
In pulsations of time, & extensions of space, like Urns of Beulah
With great labour upon his anvils; & in his ladles the Ore
He lifted, pouring it into the clay ground prepar'd with art;
Striving with Systems to deliver Individuals from those Systems;
That whenever any Spectre began to devour the Dead,
He might feel the pain as if a man gnawd his own tender nerves.

* * *

[PLATE 12]

* * *

And they builded Golgonooza: terrible eternal labour!

What are those golden builders[1] doing? where was the
burying-place
Of soft Ethinthus? near Tyburn's fatal Tree?[2] is that
Mild Zion's hill's most ancient promontory; near mournful
Ever weeping Paddington? is that Calvary and Golgotha?
Becoming a building of pity and compassion? Lo!
The stones are pity, and the bricks, well wrought affections:
Enameld with love & kindness, & the tiles engraven gold,
Labour of merciful hands: the beams & rafters are forgiveness:
The mortar & cement of the work, tears of honesty: the nails,
And the screws & iron braces, are well wrought blandishments,
And well contrived words, firm fixing, never forgotten,
Always comforting the remembrance: the floors, humility,
The cielings, devotion: the hearths, thanksgiving:
Prepare the furniture O Lambeth in thy pitying looms!
The curtains, woven tears & sighs, wrought into lovely forms
For comfort. There the secret furniture of Jerusalem's chamber
Is wrought: Lambeth! the Bride the Lamb's Wife loveth thee:
Thou art one with her & knowest not of self in thy supreme joy.
Go on, builders in hope: tho Jerusalem wanders far away,
Without the gate of Los: among the dark Satanic wheels.

1. The renovation of London directed by city planner John Nash, 1813–23, which laid out Regent Street and Regent's Park and did away with slums in Paddington (see map), becomes Blake's metaphor for the building of Jerusalem (the soul) and Golgonooza (art). During the decade of Nash's project, demolition was more obvious than rebuilding. Jerusalem, "a City yet a Woman," is the Bride of the Lamb (Revelation 21:9), the holy city (Revelation 21:10–27) and the embodiment of Liberty (*Jerusalem* 26).

2. The gallows where criminals were publicly executed from about 1200 until 1783. The last person to be hanged there was the forger W. W. Ryland, whom Blake had rejected as engraving master because of a "hanging look." According to Peter Linebaugh in *Albion's Fatal Tree* (1975), the horror of being executed was deepened by the dread of being dissected afterwards by medical students, who fought with relatives over the bodies at Tyburn, sometimes before they were completely dead. After Tyburn, the place of execution was Newgate, inside the prison walls.

Fourfold the Sons of Los in their divisions: and fourfold,
The great City of Golgonooza: fourfold toward the north
And toward the south fourfold, & fourfold toward the east & west
Each within other toward the four points: that toward
Eden, and that toward the World of Generation,
And that toward Beulah, and that toward Ulro:
Ulro is the space of the terrible starry wheels of Albion's sons:
But that toward Eden is walled up, till time of renovation:
Yet it is perfect in its building, ornaments & perfection.

[PLATE 13]

* * *

The Vegetative Universe opens like a flower from the Earth's center:
In which is Eternity. It expands in Stars to the Mundane Shell
And there it meets Eternity again, both within and without,
And the abstract Voids between the Stars are the Satanic Wheels.

* * *

[PLATE 15]

* * *

I see the Four-fold Man.[3] The Humanity in deadly sleep
And its fallen Emanation. The Spectre & its cruel Shadow.
I see the Past, Present & Future, existing all at once
Before me; O Divine Spirit sustain me on thy wings!
That I may awake Albion from his long & cold repose.
For Bacon & Newton sheathd in dismal steel, their terrors hang
Like iron scourges over Albion; Reasonings like vast Serpents
Infold around my limbs, bruising my minute articulations.

3. Cf. headnote to *The Four Zoas*. Here the fourfold division seems to be Humanity, Emanation, Spectre, and Shadow. The "I" is the poet, who like Los has the responsibility of awakening Albion.

I turn my eyes to the Schools & Universities of Europe
And there behold the Loom of Locke whose Woof rages dire
Washd by the Water-wheels of Newton. Black the cloth
In heavy wreathes folds over every Nation.[4] Cruel Works
Of many Wheels I view, wheel without wheel, with cogs tyrannic
Moving by compulsion each other: not as those in Eden: which
Wheel within Wheel[5] in freedom revolve, in harmony & peace.

* * *

[PLATE 16]

* * *

All things acted on Earth are seen in the bright Sculptures of
Los's Halls[6] & every Age renews its powers from these Works,
With every pathetic story possible to happen from Hate or
Wayward Love, & every sorrow & distress is carved here:
Every Affinity of Parents, Marriages & Friendships are here
In all their various combinations wrought with wondrous Art,
All that can happen to Man in his pilgrimage of seventy years:
Such is the Divine Written Law of Horeb & Sinai:
And such the Holy Gospel of Mount Olivet & Calvary.

[PLATE 18]

* * *

Soon Hand mightily devour'd & absorb'd Albion's Twelve Sons.
Out from his bosom a mighty Polypus, vegetating in darkness,
And Hyle & Coban were his two chosen ones, for Emissaries
In War: forth from his bosom they went and return'd.[7]
Like Wheels from a great Wheel reflected in the Deep.
Hoarse turn'd the Starry Wheels, rending a way in Albion's Loins
Beyond the Night of Beulah. In a dark & unknown Night,
Outstretch'd his Giant beauty on the ground in pain & tears:

[PLATE 19]
His Children exil'd from his breast pass to and fro before him
His birds are silent on his hills, flocks die beneath his branches
His tents are fall'n! his trumpets, and the sweet sound of his harp
Are silent on his clouded hills, that belch forth storms & fire.
His milk of Cows, & honey of Bees, & fruit of golden harvest
Is gather'd in the scorching heat, & in the driving rain:

4. Lockean psychology and Newtonian physics shroud the earth.
5. Vision (Ezekiel 1:16) is opposed to Mechanism; Ezekiel's vision of angelic wheels is contrasted with the cogs and dustrial machinery. Other versions of the wheels within wheels are shown in *Jerusalem* 75 (not reproduced), in the *Night Thoughts* designs, and in a watercolor in the Boston Museum of Fine Arts.
6. The prototypes of all material reality, including the Law and the Gospel, are in the human imagination.
7. See the design for *Jerusalem* 50 and the text of *Jerusalem* 70.

Where once he sat he weary walks in misery and pain:
His Giant beauty and perfection fallen into dust:
Till from within his witherd breast grown narrow with his woes,
The corn is turn'd to thistles & the apples into poison:
The birds of song to murderous crows, his joys to bitter groans!
The voices of children in his tents, to cries of helpless infants!
And self-exiled from the face of light & shine of morning,
In the dark world a narrow house! he wanders up and down,
Seeking for rest and finding none! and hidden far within,
His Eon weeping in the cold and desolated Earth.

All his Affections now appear withoutside: all his Sons,
Hand, Hyle & Coban, Guantok, Peachey, Brereton, Slayd & Hutton,
Scofeld, Kox, Kotope & Bowen; his Twelve Sons: Satanic Mill!
Who are the Spectres of the Twentyfour, each Double-form'd:
Revolve upon his mountains groaning in pain: beneath
The dark incessant sky, seeking for rest and finding none:
Raging against their Human natures, ravning to gormandize
The Human majesty and beauty of the Twentyfour.

* * *

Albion's Circumference was clos'd: his Center began darkning
Into the Night of Beulah, and the Moon of Beulah rose
Clouded with storms: Los his strong Guard walkd round beneath the Moon
And Albion fled inward among the currents of his rivers.‡

* * *

[PLATE 26]

* * *

SUCH VISIONS HAVE APPEARED TO ME
AS I MY ORDERD RACE HAVE RUN
JERUSALEM IS NAMED LIBERTY
AMONG THE SONS OF ALBION

[PLATE 27]

To the Jews

Jerusalem the Emanation of the Giant Albion! Can it be? Is it a Truth that the Learned have explored? Was Britain the Primitive Seat of the Patriarchal Religion? If it is true: my title-page is also True, that Jerusalem was & is the Emanation of the Giant Albion. It is True, and cannot be controverted. Ye are united, O ye Inhabitants of Earth, in One Religion, The Religion of Jesus: the most Ancient, the Eternal: & the Everlasting Gospel[8]—The Wicked will

‡ See color plate 27, the final design for chapter 1, which depicts Albion's torture at the hands of his female enemies.

8. See note to "The Everlasting Gospel," p. 364. On p. 321 Blake quotes and explicates his own work: *Milton* 6: 25–26 (p. 245).

turn it to Wickedness, the Righteous to Righteousness. Amen! Huzza! Selah!

"All things Begin & End in Albion's Ancient Druid Rocky Shore."

Your Ancestors derived their origin from Abraham, Heber, Shem, and Noah, who were Druids: as the Druid Temples (which are the Patriarchal Pillars & Oak Groves) over the whole Earth witness to this day.

You have a tradition, that Man anciently containd in his mighty limbs all things in Heaven & Earth: this you recieved from the Druids.

"But now the Starry Heavens are fled from the mighty limbs of Albion."

Albion was the Parent of the Druids; & in his Chaotic State of Sleep, Satan & Adam & the whole World was Created by the Elohim.

The fields from Islington to Marybone,
To Primrose Hill and Saint John's Wood:[9]
Were builded over with pillars of gold,
And there Jerusalem's pillars stood.

Her Little-ones ran on the fields
The Lamb of God among them seen
And fair Jerusalem his Bride:
Among the little meadows green.

Pancrass & Kentish-town repose
Among her golden pillars high:
Among her golden arches which
Shine upon the starry sky.

The Jews-harp-house & the Green Man,
The Ponds where Boys to bathe delight,
The fields of Cows by Willan's farm:
Shine in Jerusalem's pleasant sight.

She walks upon our meadows green:
The Lamb of God walks by her side:
And every English Child is seen,
Children of Jesus & his Bride,

9. Throughout this song, the place-names refer to Nash's urban development; see London map and note to *Jerusalem* 12:25. The Jews-harp-house and Green Man were country inns north of London. In the early years of their marriage, the Blakes used to take thirty-mile walks, during which they would dine at an inn and return home the same day; this entire area was absorbed by Regent's Park and taken into the city. Regent Street was colonnaded from Carleton House to Picadilly Circus, as if in "pillars of gold," and houses facing the entire length were uniformly covered in gleaming cream-colored stucco.

Forgiving trespasses and sins
Lest Babylon with cruel Og,[1]
With Moral & Self-righteous Law
Should Crucify in Satan's Synagogue!

What are those golden Builders doing
Near mournful ever-weeping Paddington
Standing above that mighty Ruin
Where Satan the first victory won,

Where Albion slept beneath the Fatal Tree
And the Druids' golden Knife,
Rioted in human gore,
In Offerings of Human Life?

They groan'd aloud on London Stone
They groan'd aloud on Tyburn's Brook[2]
Albion gave his deadly groan,
And all the Atlantic Mountains shook.

Albion's Spectre from his Loins
Tore forth in all the pomp of War!
Satan his name: in flames of fire
He stretch'd his Druid Pillars far.

Jerusalem fell from Lambeth's Vale,
Down thro Poplar & Old Bow;
Thro Malden & acros the Sea,
In War & howling death & woe.

The Rhine was red with human blood:
The Danube rolld a purple tide:
On the Euphrates Satan stood:
And over Asia stretch'd his pride.

He witherd up sweet Zion's Hill
From every Nation of the Earth:
He witherd up Jerusalem's Gates,
And in a dark Land gave her birth.

1. Babylon the Whore is Jerusalem's opposite; the giant Og, king of Bashan, was an enemy of the Hebrews (*Milton* 20:33).

2. The ancient stone in the east central part of London and the site of public execution in the western part together form a London Stonehenge, a place of Druid sacrifice where Albion is tortured (see map). As British Druidism spreads, places of spiritual significance associated with Jerusalem wither. The brook Tyburn, which no longer exists, once flowed near the gallows site, crossed Oxford Street, and went underground at the intersection of South Molton and Stratford Place (see map). The upper tributary waters of Tyburn were diverted into ornamental ponds in Regent's Park; the whole brook was eventually paved over.

He witherd up the Human Form,
By laws of sacrifice for sin:
Till it became a Mortal Worm:
But O! translucent all within.

The Divine Vision still was seen
Still was the Human Form, Divine
Weeping in weak & mortal clay
O Jesus still the Form was thine.

And thine the Human Face & thine
The Human Hands & Feet & Breath
Entering thro' the Gates of Birth
And passing thro' the Gates of Death.

And O thou Lamb of God, whom I
Slew in my dark self-righteous pride:
Art thou return'd to Albion's Land?
And is Jerusalem thy Bride?

Come to my arms & never more
Depart; but dwell for ever here:
Create my Spirit to thy Love:
Subdue my Spectre to thy Fear.

Spectre of Albion! warlike Fiend!
In clouds of blood & ruin roll'd:
I here reclaim[3] thee as my own
My Selfhood! Satan! armd in gold.

Is this thy soft Family-Love
Thy cruel Patriarchal pride
Planting thy Family alone,
Destroying all the World beside?[4]

A man's worst enemies are those
Of his own house & family;
And he who makes his law a curse,
By his own law shall surely die.

In my Exchanges[5] every Land
Shall walk, & mine in every Land,
Mutual shall build Jerusalem:
Both heart in heart & hand in hand.

3. Meaning both "acknowledge" and "recover"; cf. Milton's words to his own Satan in *Milton* 14:30; 38:29–49.
4. A critique of the Jews' claim that they are an exclusively chosen people.
5. Currencies of countries all over the world flowed through the British commercial system. Money-lending and money-changing, traditionally Jewish occupations, are fallen metaphors of spiritual interchange. Cf. *Marriage of Heaven and Hell,* "Song of Liberty," verse 12).

If Humility is Christianity, you O Jews are the true Christians; If your tradition that Man contained in his Limbs, all Animals, is True & they were separated from him by cruel Sacrifices; and when compulsory cruel Sacrifices had brought Humanity into a Feminine Tabernacle, in the loins of Abraham & David:[6] the Lamb of God, the Saviour became apparent on Earth as the Prophets had foretold? The Return of Israel is a Return to Mental Sacrifice & War. Take up the Cross O Israel & follow Jesus.

6. Blake attacks the Jewish emphasis on genealogy, perpetuated in the Christian claims that Jesus was descended from David (Matthew 1).

[PLATE 28]

Jerusalem
Chap. 2

* * *

[PLATE 31]*

Fearing that Albion should turn his back against the Divine Vision
Los took his globe of fire to search the interiors of Albion's
Bosom, in all the terrors of friendship, entering the caves
Of despair & death, to search the tempters out, walking among
Albion's rocks & precipices! caves of solitude & dark despair,
And saw every Minute Particular of Albion degraded & murderd
But saw not by whom; they were hidden within in the minute particulars
Of which they had possessd themselves; and there they take up
The articulations of a man's soul, and laughing throw it down
Into the frame, then knock it out upon the plank, & souls are bak'd
In bricks to build the pyramids of Heber & Terah.[7] But Los
Searchd in vain: closd from the minutia he walkd, difficult.
He came down from Highgate thro Hackney & Holloway towards London
Till he came to old Stratford & thence to Stepney & the Isle
Of Leutha's Dogs,[8] thence thro the narrows of the River's side
And saw every minute particular, the jewels of Albion, running down
The kennels of the streets & lanes as if they were abhorrd.
Every Universal Form, was become barren mountains of Moral
Virtue: and every Minute Particular hardend into grains of sand:
And all the tendernesses of the soul cast forth as filth & mire,
Among the winding places of deep contemplation intricate
To where the Tower of London frownd dreadful over Jerusalem.†

* * *

[PLATE 38]‡

* * *

Turning from Universal Love petrific as he went,[9]
His cold against the warmth of Eden rag'd with loud
Thunders of deadly war (the fever of the human soul)

* Plate 45 in Blake's alternate numbering system (see headnote). This passage is illustrated in the frontispiece, color plate 24.

7. Cf. Hebrew slavery, Exodus 1:14, 5:17.

8. Los comes through the northern and eastern suburbs, past the Isle of Dogs (too far north and east to be shown on map). "Kennels" in line 18 are open sewers.

† See color plate 28 for a design illustrating the confrontation between Vala and Jerusalem, which takes place soon after this scene and is one of the horrors of Albion's inner life which Los observes in a passage not selected for this edition.

‡ Plate 34 in the alternate arrangement.

9. In this passage Albion has just hardened his heart against Los and against his own Emanation.

Then the Divine hand found the Two Limits, Satan and Adam,
In Albions bosom: for in every Human bosom those Limits stand.
And the Divine voice came from the Furnaces, as multitudes without
Number! the voices of the innumerable multitudes of Eternity.
And the appearance of a Man was seen in the Furnaces;
Saving those who have sinned from the punishment of the Law,
(In pity of the punisher whose state is eternal death,)
And keeping them from Sin by the mild counsels of his love.
Albion goes to Eternal Death: In Me all Eternity.
Must pass thro' condemnation, and awake beyond the Grave;
No individual can keep these Laws, for they are death
To every energy of man, and forbid the springs of life;
Albion hath enterd the State Satan! Be permanent O State!
And be thou for ever accursed! that Albion may arise again:
And be thou created into a State! I go forth to Create
States: to deliver Individuals evermore! Amen.
So spoke the voice from the Furnaces, descending into Non-

And One stood forth from
I feel my Spectre rising upon me! Albion! arouze
Why dost thou thunder with frozen Spectrous wrath against us
The Spectre is, in Giant Man; insane. and most deform'd
Thou wilt certainly provoke my Spectre against thine in fury
He has a Sepulcher hewn out of a Rock ready for thee:
And a Death of Eight thousand years forg'd by thyself, upon
The point of his Spear! if thou persistest to forbid with Laws
Our Emanations, and to attack our secret supreme delights
So Los spoke: But when he saw blue death in Albions feet,
Again he join'd the Divine Body, following merciful;
While Albion fled more indignant! revengeful covering

Fires and clouds of rolling smoke! but mild the Saviour follow'd him,
Displaying the Eternal Vision! the Divine Similitude!
In loves and tears of brothers, sisters, sons, fathers, and friends
Which if Man ceases to behold, he ceases to exist:

Saying: "Albion! Our wars are wars of life, & wounds of love,
With intellectual spears, & long winged arrows of thought:
Mutual in one another's love and wrath, all renewing
We live as One Man; for contracting our infinite senses
We behold multitude; or expanding: we behold as one,
As One Man all the Universal Family; and that One Man
We call Jesus the Christ: and he in us, and we in him,
Live in perfect harmony in Eden the land of life,
Giving, recieving, and forgiving each other's trespasses.
He is the Good shepherd, he is the Lord and master:
He is the Shepherd of Albion, he is all in all,
In Eden: in the garden of God: and in heavenly Jerusalem.
If we have offended, forgive us, take not vengeance against us."

Thus speaking: the Divine Family follow Albion:
I see them in the vision of God upon my pleasant valleys.

I behold London; a Human awful wonder of God!
He says: "Return, Albion, return! I give myself for thee:
My Streets are my Ideas of Imagination.
Awake Albion, awake! and let us awake up together.
My Houses are Thoughts: my Inhabitants; Affections,
The children of my thoughts, walking within my blood-vessels,
Shut from my nervous form which sleeps upon the verge of Beulah
In dreams of darkness, while my vegetating blood in veiny pipes,
Rolls dreadful thro' the Furnaces of Los, and the Mills of Satan.
For Albion's sake, and for Jerusalem thy Emanation
I give myself, and these my brethren give themselves for Albion."

So spoke London, immortal Guardian! I heard in Lambeth's shades:
In Felpham I heard and saw the Vision of Albion
I write in South Molton Street, what I both see and hear
In regions of Humanity, in London's opening streets.

* * *

[PLATE 41]§

* * *

There is a Grain of Sand in Lambeth that Satan cannot find
Nor can his Watch Fiends find it: tis translucent & has many Angles

§ Plate 37 in the alternate arrangement. Following this passage, see color plate 29 for a mysterious design which accompanies a text not selected for this edition, plate 46 (41 in the alternate arrangement).

But he who finds it will find Oothoon's palace, for within
Opening into Beulah every angle is a lovely heaven
But should the Watch Fiends find it, they would call it Sin
And lay its Heavens & their inhabitants in blood of punishment.

* * *

[PLATE 48]

* * *

And this the manner of the terrible Separation:
The Emanations of the grievously afflicted Friends of Albion
Concenter in one Female form, an Aged pensive Woman.[1]
Astonish'd! lovely! embracing the sublime shade, the Daughters of Beulah
Beheld her with wonder! With awful hands she took
A Moment of Time, drawing it out with many tears & afflictions
And many sorrows—oblique across the Atlantic Vale
Which is the Vale of Rephaim[2] dreadful from East to West,
Where the Human Harvest waves abundant in the beams of Eden—
Into a Rainbow of jewels and gold, a mild Reflection from
Albion's dread Tomb, Eight thousand and five hundred years
In its extension. Every two hundred years has a door to Eden.
She also took an Atom of Space, with dire pain opening it a Center
Into Beulah: trembling the Daughters of Beulah dried

1. Erin, personification of Ireland, location of another struggle for freedom. For a discussion of opening the center see the article by E. J. Rose, p. 594 in the critical section of this edition.
2. "Valley of the shades of the dead," II Samuel 23; cf. *Milton* 19:40.

Her tears; she ardent embrac'd her sorrows, occupied in labours
Of sublime mercy in Rephaim's Vale. Perusing Albion's Tomb
She sat: she walk'd among the ornaments solemn mourning.
The Daughters attended her shudderings, wiping the death sweat.
Los also saw her in his seventh Furnace, he also terrified
Saw the finger of God go forth upon his seventh Furnace,
Away from the Starry Wheels, to prepare Jerusalem a place.
When with a dreadful groan the Emanation mild of Albion
Burst from his bosom[3] in the Tomb like a pale snowy cloud,
Female and lovely, struggling to put off the Human form
Writhing in pain. The Daughters of Beulah in kind arms
    reciev'd
Jerusalem: weeping over her among the Spaces of Erin,
In the Ends of Beulah, where the Dead wail night & day.

* * *

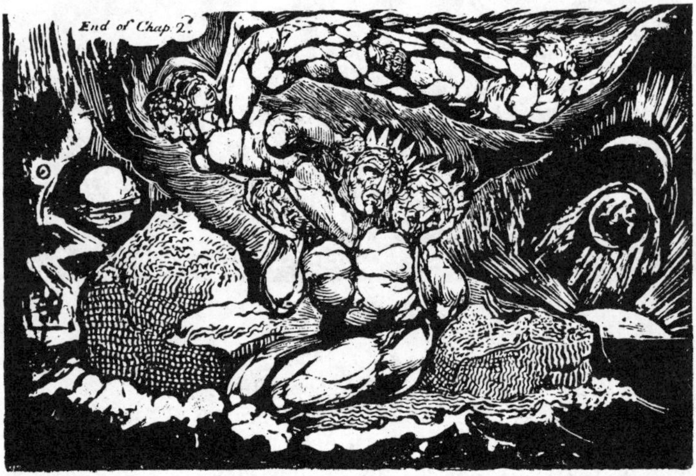

3. Jerusalem is usually described as the soul of Albion, a lovely woman who should be bride of the Lamb, except that Albion has hidden her in his heart. If Albion could recognize his unity with Jesus, he would not feel possessive and fight to keep his Emanation to himself. Here Jerusalem bursts forth as a sort of daughter to Albion, rather than a consort.

[PLATE 52]*

To the Deists

Rahab is an Eternal State[4]

The Spiritual States of the Soul are all Eternal Distinguish between the Man, & his present State

He never can be a Friend to the Human Race who is the Preacher of Natural Morality or Natural Religion.[5] He is a flatterer who means to betray, to perpetuate Tyrant Pride & the Laws of that Babylon which he forsees shall shortly be destroyed, with the Spiritual and not the Natural Sword: He is in the State named Rahab: which State must be put off before he can be the Friend of Man.

You O Deists profess yourselves the Enemies of Christianity: and you are so: you are also the Enemies of the Human Race & of Universal Nature. Man is born a Spectre or Satan & is altogether an Evil, & requires a New Selfhood continually & must continually be changed into his direct Contrary. But your Greek Philosophy (which is a remnant of Druidism) teaches that Man is Righteous in his Vegetated Spectre: an Opinion of fatal & accursed consequence to Man, as the Ancients saw plainly by Revelation to the intire abrogation of Experimental Theory; and many believed what they saw, and Prophecied of Jesus.

Man must & will have Some Religion; if he has not the Religion of Jesus, he will have the Religion of Satan, & will erect the Synagogue of Satan, calling the Prince of this World, God; and destroying all who do not worship Satan under the Name of God. Will any one say: Where are those who worship Satan under the Name of God! Where are they? Listen! Every Religion that Preaches Vengeance for Sin is the Religion of the Enemy & Avenger; and not of the Forgiver of Sin, and their God is Satan, Named by the Divine Name. Your Religion O Deists: Deism, is the Worship of the God of this World by the means of what you call Natural Religion and Natural Philosophy, and of Natural Morality or Self-Righteousness, the Selfish Virtues of the Natural Heart. This was the Religion of the Pharisees who murderd Jesus. Deism is the same & ends in the same.

Voltaire, Rousseau, Gibbon, Hume[6] charge the Spiritually Reli-

* Plate 52 is the preface to chapter 3.

4. States are fixed so that the individual can pass through them without being destroyed. Usually states are considered "annihilable" (*Milton* 32:10–38); Rahab seems to be particularly dangerous, as an eternal state.

5. The Deists taught that God can be known through his works. For Blake, the only God who can be derived from Nature is a bloodthirsty, unforgiving tyrant. Blake opposes church-taught superstition but considers "enlightened" Deism another form of superstition.

6. Representing various shades of eighteenth-century rationalism. See *Milton* 40:12.

gious with Hypocrisy! but how a Monk or a Methodist either, can be a Hypocrite: I cannot concieve. We are Men of like passions with others & pretend not to be holier than others: therefore, when a Religious Man falls into Sin, he ought not to be calld a Hypocrite: this title is more properly to be given to a Player who falls into Sin; whose profession is Virtue & Morality & the making Men Self-Righteous. Foote[7] in calling Whitefield, Hypocrite; was himself one: for Whitefield pretended not to be holier than others: but confessed his Sins before all the World. Voltaire! Rousseau! You cannot escape my charge that you are Pharisees & Hypocrites, for you are constantly talking of the Virtues of the Human Heart, and particularly of your own, that you may accuse others & especially the Religious, whose errors you by this display of pretended Virtue chiefly design to expose. Rousseau thought Men Good by Nature; he found them Evil & found no friend. Friendship cannot exist without Forgiveness of Sins continually. The Book written by Rousseau calld his Confessions is an apology & cloke for his sin & not a confession.

But you also charge the poor Monks & Religious with being the causes of War: while you acquit & flatter the Alexanders & Caesars, the Lewis's & Fredericks:[8] who alone are its causes & its actors. But the Religion of Jesus, Forgiveness of Sin, can never be the cause of a War nor of a single Martyrdom.

Those who Martyr others or who cause War are Deists, but never can be Forgivers of Sin. The Glory of Christianity is, To Conquer by Forgiveness. All the Destruction therefore, in Christian Europe has arisen from Deism, which is Natural Religion.

I saw a Monk of Charlemaine
Arise before my sight;
I talkd with the Grey Monk as we stood
In beams of infernal light.

Gibbon arose with a lash of steel
And Voltaire with a wracking wheel;
The Schools in clouds of learning rolld
Arose with War in iron & gold.

"Thou lazy Monk," they sound afar,
"In vain condemning glorious War;
And in your Cell you shall ever dwell.
Rise War & bind him in his Cell."

7. The actor-playwright Samuel Foote satirized Methodists in *The Minor* (1760).

8. Modern tyrants equivalent to the Caesars: Louis XIV and Frederick the Great.

The blood red ran from the Grey Monk's side
His hands & feet were wounded wide
His body bent, his arms & knees
Like to the roots of ancient trees.

When Satan first the black bow bent
And the Moral Law from the Gospel rent[9]
He forgd the Law into a Sword
And spilld the blood of mercy's Lord.

Titus! Constantine! Charlemaine![1]
O Voltaire! Rousseau! Gibbon! Vain
Your Grecian Mocks & Roman Sword
Against this image of his Lord!

For a Tear is an Intellectual thing;
And a Sigh is the Sword of an Angel King
And the bitter groan of a Martyr's woe
Is an Arrow from the Almightie's Bow!

9. The separation of Law and Gospel is Satanic.

1. Leaders in the progression from the Roman empire into the "Christian" Holy Roman Empire: Titus destroyed Jerusalem in A.D. 70; Constantine, by converting to Christianity, made Rome Christian without making it any less an empire (A.D. 274–337); Charlemagne was a militaristic emperor of western Europe (742-814). In "The Gray Monk," p. 208, the oppressor is simply the "Tyrant."

[PLATE 53]

Jerusalem
Chap: 3

* * *

[PLATE 54]

In Great Eternity, every particular Form gives forth or Emanates
Its own peculiar Light, & the Form is the Divine Vision
And the Light is his Garment. This is Jerusalem in every Man:
A Tent & Tabernacle of Mutual Forgiveness, Male & Female Clothings.
And Jerusalem is called Liberty among the Children of Albion.

* * *

[PLATE 55]

* * *

Silence remaind & every one resumd his Human Majesty
And many conversed on these things as they labourd at the furrow
Saying: "It is better to prevent misery, than to release from misery
It is better to prevent error, than to forgive the criminal:
Labour well the Minute Particulars, attend to the Little-ones:
And those who are in misery cannot remain so long
If we do but our duty: labour well the teeming Earth."

They Plow'd in tears, the trumpets sounded before the golden Plow
And the voices of the Living Creatures were heard in the clouds of heaven
Crying: "Compell the Reasoner to Demonstrate with unhewn Demonstrations;
Let the Indefinite be explored, and let every Man be Judged
By his own Works, Let all Indefinites be thrown into Demonstrations
To be pounded to dust & melted in the Furnace of Affliction:
He who would do good to another, must do it in Minute Particulars
General Good is the plea of the scoundrel hypocrite & flatterer:

York
London
And the voices of Bath & Canterbury & York & Edinburgh Cry
Over the Plow of Nations in the strong hand of Albion thundering along
Among the Fires of the Druid & the deep black rethundering Waters
Of the Atlantic which poured in impetuous loud loud. louder & louder.
And the Great Voice of the Atlantic howled over the Druid Altars:
Weeping over his Children in Stone-henge in Malden & Colchester.
Round the Rocky Peak of Derbyshire London Stone & Rosamonds Bower
What is a Wife & what is a Harlot? What is a Church? & What
Is a Theatre? are they Two & not One? can they Exist Separate?
Are not Religion & Politics the Same Thing? Brotherhood is Religion
O Demonstrations of Reason Dividing Families in Cruelty & Pride!
But Albion fled from the Divine Vision, with the Plow of Nations enflaming
The Living Creatures maddend and Albion fell into the Furrow and
The Plow went over him & the Living was Plowed in among the Dead
But his Spectre rose over the starry Plow. Albion fled beneath the Plow
Till he came to the Rock of Ages. & he took his Seat upon the Rock.
Wonder siezd all in Eternity! to behold the Divine Vision. open
The Center into an Expanse, & the Center rolled out into an Expanse.
Jerusalem

For Art & Science cannot exist but in minutely organized
Particulars
And not in generalizing Demonstrations of the Rational Power.
The Infinite alone resides in Definite & Determinate Identity
Establishment of Truth depends on destruction of Falshood
continually
On Circumcision: not on Virginity,[2] O Reasoners of Albion."
So cried they at the Plow. * * *

[PLATE 60]

* * *

But the Divine Lamb stood beside Jerusalem. Oft she saw
The lineaments Divine & oft the Voice heard, & oft she said:

"O Lord & Saviour, have the Gods of the Heathen pierced thee?
Or hast thou been pierced in the House of thy Friends?
Art thou alive! & livest thou for-evermore? or art thou
Not: but a delusive shadow, a thought that liveth not.
Babel mocks, saying, 'There is no God nor Son of God'—
That thou, O Human Imagination, O Divine Body, art all
A delusion. But I know thee O Lord when thou arisest upon
My weary eyes even in this dungeon & this iron mill.
The Stars of Albion cruel rise; thou bindest to sweet influences:
For thou also sufferest with me altho I behold thee not;
And altho I sin & blaspheme thy holy name, thou pitiest me;
Because thou knowest I am deluded by the turning mills.
And by these visions of pity & love because of Albion's death."

Thus spake Jerusalem, & thus the Divine Voice replied:

"Mild Shade of Man, pitiest thou these Visions of terror & woe!
Give forth thy pity & love. Fear not! lo I am with thee always.
Only believe in me that I have power to raise from death
Thy brother who Sleepeth in Albion: fear not trembling Shade.

[PLATE 61]

Behold: in the Visions of Elohim Jehovah, behold Joseph & Mary[3]
And be comforted O Jerusalem in the Visions of Jehovah Elohim."

2. The foreskin and the hymen are symbolically equivalent as veils of flesh. In Blake's symbolism circumcision is not a means of setting apart a clan but a form of self-sacrifice, of cutting away the surface to reveal what is hidden; see E. J. Rose, *Studies in Romanticism* 8 (1968), 16–25. Virginity, on the other hand, is a means of enshrining Mystery through secrecy. When Jesus rends the veil in the temple he also rends the fleshly veil of Mystery.

3. In Blake's beautiful retelling of this story (Matthew 1:18–24)—a relatively late addition to the poem—the Holy Spirit is Joseph's willingness to forgive Mary. Blake rejects the doctrine of the Virgin Birth because it implies that sexual reproduction is not holy (cf. "Everlasting Gospel"); Mary shares some of the insights of Oothoon (*Visions*), and her pregnancy becomes an occasion for the couple to experience mutual forgiveness, the spirit of Christ. Blake's version of the Christian doctrine of forgiveness emphasizes *mutual* forgiveness, "Perpetual Mutual Sacrifice," for "There is none that liveth & Sinneth not!"

She looked & saw Joseph the Carpenter in Nazareth & Mary
His espoused Wife. And Mary said, "If thou put me away from thee
Dost thou not murder me?" Joseph spoke in anger & fury.
"Should I
Marry a Harlot & an Adulteress?" Mary answered, "Art thou more pure
Than thy Maker who forgiveth Sins & calls again Her that is Lost?
Tho She hates, he calls her again in love. I love my dear Joseph
But he driveth me away from his presence, yet I hear the voice of God
In the voice of my Husband. Tho he is angry for a moment, he will not
Utterly cast me away. If I were pure, never could I taste the sweets
Of the Forgiveness of Sins! if I were holy! I never could behold the tears
Of love! of him who loves me in the midst of his anger in furnace of fire."

"Ah my Mary," said Joseph: weeping over & embracing her closely in
His arms: "Doth he forgive Jerusalem & not exact Purity from her who is
Polluted? I heard his voice in my sleep & his Angel in my dream:

Saying, 'Doth Jehovah Forgive a Debt only on condition that it shall
Be Payed? Doth he Forgive Pollution only on conditions of Purity?
That Debt is not Forgiven! That Pollution is not Forgiven!
Such is the Forgiveness of the Gods, the Moral Virtues of the
Heathen, whose tender Mercies are Cruelty. But Jehovah's Salvation
Is without Mercy & without Price, in the Continual Forgiveness of Sins,
In the Perpetual Mutual Sacrifice in Great Eternity! for behold!
There is none that liveth & Sinneth not! And this is the Covenant
Of Jehovah: If you Forgive one-another, so shall Jehovah Forgive You:
That He Himself may Dwell among You. Fear not then to take
To thee Mary thy Wife, for she is with Child by the Holy Ghost.' "

Then Mary burst forth into a Song! she flowed like a River of
Many Streams in the arms of Joseph & gave forth her tears of joy
Like many waters, and Emanating into gardens & palaces upon
Euphrates & to forests & floods & animals wild & tame from
Gihon to Hiddekel, & to corn fields & villages & inhabitants
Upon Pison[4] & Arnon & Jordan. And I heard the voice among

4. Euphrates, Gihon, Hiddekel, and Pison are the four rivers of Eden (Genesis 2:10–14); the Arnon and Jordan are in the Promised Land (see map).

The Reapers Saying, "Am I Jerusalem the lost Adulteress? or am I
Babylon come up to Jerusalem?" And another voice answered Saying:

"Does the voice of my Lord call me again? am I pure thro his Mercy
And Pity. Am I become lovely as a Virgin in his sight who am
Indeed a Harlot drunken with the Sacrifice of Idols? Does he
Call her pure as he did in the days of her Infancy when She
Was cast out to the loathing of her person?[5] The Chaldean took
Me from my Cradle. The Amalekite stole me away upon his Camels
Before I had ever beheld with love the Face of Jehovah; or known
That there was a God of Mercy: O Mercy O Divine Humanity!
O Forgiveness & Pity & Compassion! If I were Pure I should never
Have known Thee: If I were Unpolluted I should never have
Glorified thy Holiness, or rejoiced in thy great Salvation."

Mary leaned her side against Jerusalem, Jerusalem recieved
The infant into her hands in the Visions of Jehovah. Times passed on;
Jerusalem fainted over the Cross & Sepulcher. She heard the voice:
"Wilt thou make Rome thy Patriarch Druid & the Kings of Europe his
Horsemen? Man in the Resurrection changes his Sexual Garments at Will.
Every Harlot was once a Virgin: every Criminal an Infant Love!

[PLATE 62]
Repose on me till the morning of the Grave. I am thy life."

Jerusalem replied. "I am an outcast: Albion is dead!
I am left to the trampling foot & the spurning heel!
A Harlot I am calld. I am sold from street to street!
I am defaced with blows & with the dirt of the Prison!
And wilt thou become my Husband O my Lord & Saviour?
Shall Vala bring thee forth! shall the Chaste be ashamed also?
I see the Maternal Line,[6] I behold the Seed of the Woman:
Cainah, & Ada & Zillah & Naamah Wife of Noah.
Shuah's daughter & Tamar & Rahab the Canaanites:
Ruth the Moabite & Bathsheba of the daughters of Heth,
Naamah the Ammonite, Zibeah the Philistine, & Mary:

5. Cf. the prophets' descriptions of Jerusalem as a harlot beloved by God (Ezekiel 16, 23; Hosea 2).

6. From Matthew 1—in which the only women in Jesus' lineage (Tamar, Rahab, Ruth the Moabite, Bathsheba, and Mary) are women of questionable reputation or actions—Blake got the idea of a roll call of adulteresses and heathens as the ancestresses of Jesus; of cf. "Mother of my Mortal part" ("To Tirzah").

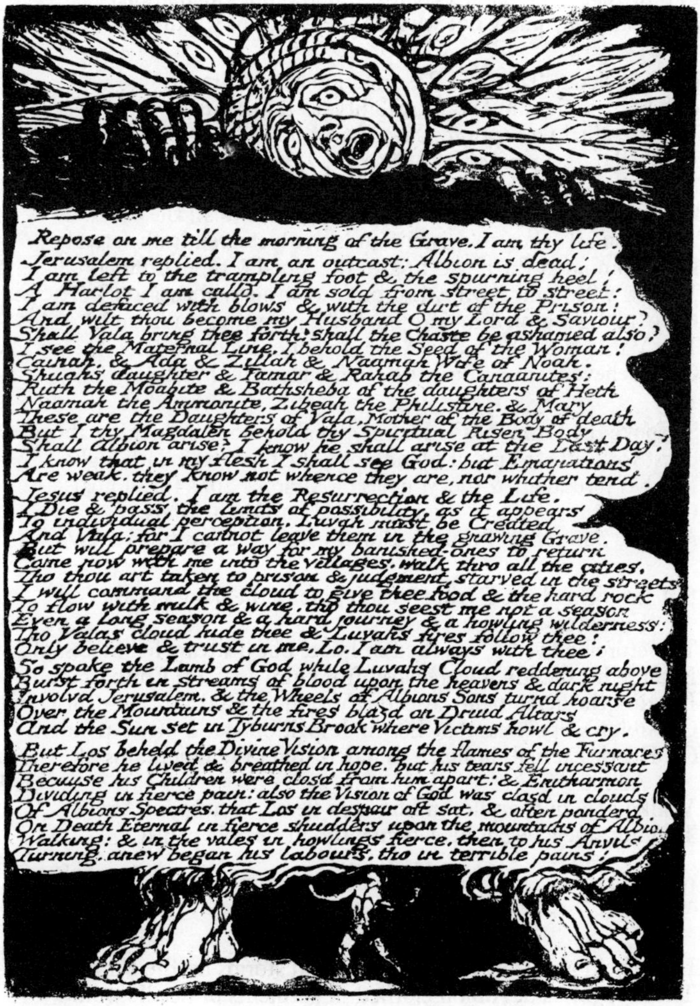

Repose on me till the morning of the Grave. I am thy life.
Jerusalem replied. I am an outcast: Albion is dead!
I am left to the trampling foot & the spurning heel!
A Harlot I am calld. I am sold from street to street!
I am defaced with blows & with the dirt of the Prison!
And wilt thou become my Husband O my Lord & Saviour?
Shall Vala bring thee forth! shall the Chaste be ashamed also?
I see the Maternal Line, I behold the Seed of the Woman!
Cainah, & Ada & Zillah & Naamah Wife of Noah.
Shuahs daughter & Tamar & Rahab the Canaanites:
Ruth the Moabite & Bathsheba of the daughters of Heth
Naamah the Ammonite, Zibeah the Philistine, & Mary
These are the Daughters of Vala, Mother of the Body of death
But I thy Magdalen behold thy Spiritual Risen Body
Shall Albion arise? I know he shall arise at the Last Day!
I know that in my flesh I shall see God: but Emanations
Are weak. they know not whence they are, nor whither tend.
Jesus replied. I am the Resurrection & the Life.
I Die & pass the limits of possibility, as it appears
To individual perception. Luvah must be Created
And Vala; for I cannot leave them in the gnawing Grave.
But will prepare a way for my banished-ones to return
Come now with me into the villages. walk thro all the cities.
Tho thou art taken to prison & judgment, starved in the streets
I will command the cloud to give thee food & the hard rock
To flow with milk & wine. tho thou seest me not a season
Even a long season & a hard journey & a howling wilderness:
Tho Valas cloud hide thee & Luvahs fires follow thee:
Only believe & trust in me, Lo. I am always with thee;
So spake the Lamb of God while Luvahs Cloud reddening above
Burst forth in streams of blood upon the heavens & dark night
Involvd Jerusalem. & the Wheels of Albions Sons turnd hoarse
Over the Mountains & the fires blazd on Druid Altars
And the Sun set in Tyburns Brook where Victims howl & cry.
But Los beheld the Divine Vision among the flames of the Furnaces
Therefore he lived & breathed in hope. but his tears fell incessant
Because his Children were closd from him apart: & Enitharmon
Dividing in fierce pain: also the Vision of God was closd in clouds
Of Albions Spectres, that Los in despair oft sat, & often ponderd
On Death Eternal in fierce shudders upon the mountains of Albio
Walking: & in the vales in howlings fierce, then to his Anvils
Turning, anew began his labours, tho in terrible pains;

These are the Daughters of Vala, Mother of the Body of death.
But I thy Magdalen behold thy Spiritual Risen Body.
Shall Albion arise? I know he shall arise at the Last Day!
I know that in my flesh I shall see God:[7] but Emanations
Are weak. they know not whence they are, nor whither tend."

Jesus replied: "I am the Resurrection & the Life.
I Die & pass the limits of possibility, as it appears
To individual perception. Luvah must be Created
And Vala; for I cannot leave them in the gnawing Grave,
But will prepare a way for my banished-ones to return.
Come now with me into the villages; walk thro all the cities.
Tho thou art taken to prison & judgment, starved in the streets
I will command the cloud to give thee food & the hard rock
To flow with milk & wine, tho thou seest me not a season—
Even a long season & a hard journey & a howling wilderness!
Tho Vala's cloud hide thee & Luvah's fires follow thee!
Only believe & trust in me, Lo. I am always with thee!"

So spoke the Lamb of God while Luvah's Cloud reddening above
Burst forth in streams of blood upon the heavens & dark night
Involvd Jerusalem, & the Wheels of Albion's Sons turnd hoarse
Over the Mountains & the fires blaz'd on Druid Altars
And the Sun set in Tyburn's Brook where Victims howl & cry.

But Los beheld the Divine Vision among the flames of the Furnaces.
Therefore he lived & breathed in hope, but his tears fell incessant
Because his Children were closd from him apart: & Enitharmon
Dividing in fierce pain: also the Vision of God was closd in clouds
Of Albion's Spectres, that Los in despair oft sat, & often ponderd
On Death Eternal, in fierce shudders upon the mountains of Albion
Walking: & in the vales in howlings fierce, then to his Anvils
Turning, anew began his labours, tho in terrible pains!

[PLATE 66]

* * *

Los beheld in terror: he pour'd his loud storms on the Furnaces:
The Daughters of Albion clothed in garments of needle work
Strip them off from their shoulders and bosoms; they lay aside
Their garments; they sit naked upon the Stone of trial.
The Knife of flint passes over the howling Victim: his blood
Gushes & stains the fair side of the fair Daughters of Albion.

7. Perhaps the most impressive of many Biblical allusions in this passage is this echo of Job 19:25–26.

They put aside his curls; they divide his seven locks upon
His forehead: they bind his forehead with thorns of iron
They put into his hand a reed, they mock: Saying: "Behold
The King of Canaan whose are seven hundred chariots of iron!"
They take off his vesture whole with their Knives of flint:
But they cut asunder his inner garments: searching with
Their cruel fingers for his heart, & there they enter in pomp,
In many tears; & there they erect a temple & an altar:
They pour cold water on his brain in front, to cause
Lids to grow over his eyes in veils of tears: and caverns
To freeze over his nostrils, while they feed his tongue from cups
And dishes of painted clay. Glowing with beauty & cruelty,
They obscure the sun & the moon; no eye can look upon them.

* * *

[PLATE 67]

* * *

Tirzah sits weeping to hear the shrieks of the dying: her Knife
Of flint is in her hand: she passes it over the howling Victim.
The Daughters Weave their Work in loud cries over the Rock
Of Horeb! still eyeing Albion's Cliffs, eagerly siezing & twisting
The threads of Vala & Jerusalem, running from mountain to mountain
Over the whole Earth: loud the Warriors rage in Beth Peor[8]
Beneath the iron whips of their Captains & consecrated banners.
Loud the Sun & Moon rage in the conflict: loud the Stars
Shout in the night of battle & their spears grow to their hands
With blood, weaving the deaths of the Mighty into a Tabernacle
For Rahab & Tirzah; till the Great Polypus of Generation covered the Earth.

In Verulam the Polypus's Head, winding around his bulk
Thro Rochester, and Chichester, & Exeter & Salisbury,
To Bristol: & his Heart beat strong on Salisbûry Plain
Shooting out Fibres round the Earth, thro Gaul & Italy
And Greece, & along the Sea of Rephaim into Judea
To Sodom & Gomorrha: thence to India, China & Japan.

The Twelve Daughters in Rahab & Tirzah have circumscribd the Brain
Beneath & pierced it thro the midst with a golden pin.
Blood hath staind her fair side beneath her bosom.

8. Moses' burial place. For English and Biblical place names, see maps; also notes to *Milton* 17, 19. Verulam (St. Albans) is associated with Bacon, who was Baron Verulam and Viscount St. Albans.

"O thou poor Human Form! said she. O thou poor child of woe!
Why wilt thou wander away from Tirzah: why me compel to bind thee?
If thou dost go away from me I shall consume upon these Rocks.
These fibres of thine eyes that used to beam in distant heavens
Away from me: I have bound down with a hot iron.
These nostrils that expanded with delight in morning skies
I have bent downward with lead melted in my roaring furnaces
Of affliction; of love; of sweet despair; of torment unendurable.
My soul is seven furnaces, incessant roars the bellows
Upon my terribly flaming heart, the molten metal runs
In channels thro my fiery limbs: O love! O pity! O fear!
O pain! O the pangs, the bitter pangs of love forsaken!
Ephraim was a wilderness of joy where all my wild beasts ran
The River Kanah[9] wanderd by my sweet Manasseh's side
To see the boy spring into heavens sounding from my sight!
Go, Noah[1] fetch the girdle of strong brass, heat it red-hot:
Press it around the loins of this ever expanding cruelty
Shriek not so my only love! I refuse thy joys: I drink
Thy shrieks because Hand & Hyle are cruel & obdurate to me.

[PLATE 68]
O Skofield why art thou cruel? Lo Joseph is thine! to make
You One: to weave you both in the same mantle of skin
Bind him down Sisters bind him down on Ebal, Mount of cursing:[2]
Malah come forth from Lebanon: & Hoglah from Mount Sinai:
Come circumscribe this tongue of sweets & with a screw of iron
Fasten this ear into the rock; Milcah the task is thine.
Weep not so Sisters! weep not so! our life depends on this
Or mercy & truth are fled away from Shechem & Mount Gilead
Unless my beloved is bound upon the Stems of Vegetation."

And thus the Warriors cry, in the hot day of Victory, in Songs:

"Look; the beautiful Daughter of Albion sits naked upon the Stone,
Her panting Victim beside her: her heart is drunk with blood,
Tho her brain is not drunk with wine: she goes forth from Albion
In pride of beauty: in cruelty of holiness: in the brightness
Of her tabernacle, & her ark & secret place, the beautiful Daughter
Of Albion, delights the eyes of the Kings. Their hearts & the

9. Border between the territories of Ephraim and Manasseh (Joshua 16:9), the half tribes who descended from Joseph's Egyptian wife (see map).

1. Not the patriarch but one of the brotherless daughters of Zelophead who inherited land in the half tribe of Manasseh (Joshua 17:3).

2. As opposed to Gerizim, mount of blessing (see map); also the mountain where sacrifices were offered and the law was plastered on great stones (Deuteronomy 27, Joshua 8:30).

Hearts of their Warriors glow hot before Thor & Friga. O Molech!
O Chemosh![3] O Bacchus! O Venus! O Double God of Generation!
The Heavens are cut like a mantle around from the Cliffs of Albion
Across Europe; across Africa; in howling & deadly War
A sheet & veil & curtain of blood is let down from Heaven
Across the hills of Ephraim & down Mount Olivet to
The Valley of the Jebusite: Molech rejoices in heaven
He sees the Twelve Daughters naked upon the Twelve Stones
Themselves condensing to rocks & into the Ribs of a Man.
Lo they shoot forth in tender Nerves across Europe & Asia.
Lo they rest upon the Tribes, where their panting Victims lie.
Molech rushes into the Kings in love to the beautiful Daughters
But they frown & delight in cruelty, refusing all other joy.
Bring your Offerings, your first begotten: pamperd with milk & blood
Your first born of seven years old: be they Males or Females:
To the beautiful Daughters of Albion! they sport before the Kings
Clothed in the skin of the Victim! blood! human blood! is the life
And delightful food of the Warrior: the well fed Warrior's flesh
Of him who is slain in War: fills the Valleys of Ephraim with
Breeding Women walking in pride & bringing forth under green trees
With pleasure, without pain, for their food is blood of the Captive.
Molech rejoices thro the Land from Havilah to Shur:[4] he rejoices
In moral law & its severe penalties: loud Shaddai & Jehovah
Thunder above: when they see the Twelve panting Victims
On the Twelve Stones[5] of Power, & the beautiful Daughters of Albion.
If you dare rend their Veil with your Spear; you are healed of Love!
From the Hills of Camberwell & Wimbledon: from the Valleys
Of Walton & Esher: from Stone-henge & from Malden's Cove
Jerusalem's Pillars fall in the rendings of fierce War
Over France & Germany: upon the Rhine & Danube
Reuben & Benjamin flee; they hide in the Valley of Rephaim.
Why trembles the Warrior's limbs when he beholds thy beauty
Spotted with Victims' blood? By the fires of thy secret tabernacle
And thy dark & holy place: at thy frowns, at thy dire revenge
Smitten as Uzzah[6] of old, his armour is softend; his spear
And sword faint in his hand, from Albion across Great Tartary.
O beautiful Daughter of Albion: cruelty is thy delight.
O Virgin of terrible eyes, who dwellest by Valleys of springs

3. Like Molech, one of the gods that Solomon's 700 wives persuaded him to worship (I Kings 11:7).
4. Land of the Ishmaelites, the outcast desert people descended from Abraham's concubine Hagar (Genesis 25:12–18).
5. One stone for each tribe, to commemorate the safe passage of the ark over Jordan (Joshua 4); here they are places of sacrifice.
6. Struck dead for touching the ark to keep it from falling (II Samuel 6:3–7). The holy of holies is identified with the women's untouchable "secret place" (68:15).

Beneath the Mountains of Lebanon, in the City of Rehob in Hamath
Taught to touch the harp: to dance in the Circle of Warriors
Before the Kings of Canaan: to cut the flesh from the Victim
To roast the flesh in fire: to examine the Infant's limbs
In cruelties of holiness: to refuse the joys of love: to bring
The Spies from Egypt, to raise jealousy in the bosoms of the Twelve
Kings of Canaan: then to let the Spies depart to Meribah Kadesh[7]
To the place of the Amalekite; I am drunk with unsatiated love
I must rush again to War: for the Virgin has frownd & refusd.[8]
Sometimes I curse & sometimes bless thy fascinating beauty.
Once Man was occupied in intellectual pleasures & energies
But now my soul is harrowd with grief & fear & love & desire
And now I hate & now I love & Intellect is no more:
There is no time for any thing but the torments of love & desire."
The Feminine & Masculine Shadows soft, mild & ever varying
In beauty: are Shadows now no more, but Rocks in Horeb.

7. Where Moses caused water, named "Strife," to flow out of a rock (Numbers 20); the "Spies" are based on the twelve spies sent to Canaan (Deuteronomy 13) and the two spies who lodged with the harlot Rahab in Jericho (Joshua 2).

8. An explicit account of the relationship between violence and frustrated desire, implied in the myth of Orc and Vala; here it is extended to the relationship between religious fanaticism and sadomasochism.

[PLATE 69]
Then all the Males combined into One Male & every one
Became a ravening eating Cancer growing in the Female
A Polypus of Roots of Reasoning Doubt Despair & Death.
Going forth & returning from Albion's Rocks to Canaan:
Devouring Jerusalem from every Nation of the Earth.

* * *

[PLATE 70]
And this the form of mighty Hand, sitting on Albion's cliffs
Before the face of Albion, a mighty threatning Form:

His bosom wide & shoulders huge overspreading wondrous
Bear Three strong sinewy Necks & Three awful & terrible Heads,
Three Brains in contradictory council brooding incessantly—
Neither daring to put in act its councils, fearing each-other,
Therefore rejecting Ideas as nothing & holding all Wisdom
To consist in the agreements & disagreements of Ideas,
Plotting to devour Albion's Body of Humanity & Love.

[PLATE 77]†

To the Christians

Devils are
False Religions
"Saul, Saul"
"Why persecutest thou me?"[9]

I give you the end of a golden string,
Only wind it into a ball:
It will lead you in at Heaven's gate,
Built in Jerusalem's wall.

We are told to abstain from fleshly desires that we may lose no time from the Work of the Lord. Every moment lost, is a moment that cannot be redeemed. Every pleasure that intermingles with the

† Plate 77 is the preface to chapter 4. Immediately preceding this plate is the full-page design (see color plate 30) which serves as a frontispiece to this final chapter.

9. What Jesus said in the vision on the Damascus Road which converted the Pharisee Saul into the apostle Paul (Acts 9:4). These quotation marks are supplied by Blake himself.

duty of our station is a folly unredeemable & is planted like the seed of a wild flower among our wheat. All the tortures of repentance are tortures of self-reproach on account of our leaving the Divine Harvest to the Enemy, the struggles of intanglement with incoherent roots.[1] I know of no other Christianity and of no other Gospel than the liberty both of body & mind to exercise the Divine Arts of Imagination: Imagination the real & eternal World of which this Vegetable Universe is but a faint shadow & which we shall live in our Eternal or Imaginative Bodies, when these Vegetable Mortal Bodies are no more. The Apostles knew of no other Gospel. What were all their spiritual gifts? What is the Divine Spirit? is the Holy Ghost any other than an Intellectual Fountain? What is the Harvest of the Gospel & its Labours? What is that Talent which it is a curse to hide? What are the Treasures of Heaven which we are to lay up for ourselves, are they any other than Mental Studies & Performances? What are all the Gifts of the Gospel; are they not all Mental Gifts? Is God a Spirit who must be worshipped in Spirit & in Truth and are not the Gifts of the Spirit Every-thing to Man? O ye Religious, discountenance every one among you who shall pretend to despise Art & Science! I call upon you in the Name of Jesus! What is the Life of Man but Art & Science? is it Meat & Drink? is not the Body more than Raiment? What is Mortality but the things relating to the Body, which Dies? What is Immortality but the things relating to the Spirit, which Lives Eternally? What is the Joy of Heaven but Improvement in the things of the Spirit? What are the Pains of Hell but Ignorance, Bodily Lust, Idleness, & devastation of the things of the Spirit? Answer this to yourselves, & expel from among you those who pretend to despise the labours of Art & Science, which alone are the labours of the Gospel: Is not this plain & manifest to the thought? Can you think at all & not pronounce heartily that to Labour in Knowledge is to Build up Jerusalem and to Despise Knowledge is to Despise Jerusalem & her Builders? And remember: He who despises & mocks a Mental Gift in another, calling it pride & selfishness & sin, mocks Jesus the giver of every Mental Gift, which always appear to the ignorance-loving Hypocrite, as Sins. But that which is a Sin in the sight of cruel Man, is not so in the sight of our kind God.

Let every Christian as much as in him lies engage himself openly

1. Cf. the parable of wheat and tares (Matthew 13:24–30). More than half the references to the New Testament in this passage are drawn from the Sermon on the Mount (Matthew 5).

& publicly before all the World in some Mental pursuit for the Building up of Jerusalem:

I stood among my valleys of the south
And saw a flame of fire, even as a Wheel
Of fire surrounding all the heavens: it went
From west to east against the current of
Creation and devourd all things in its loud
Fury & thundering course round heaven & earth.
By it the Sun was rolld into an orb:
By it the Moon faded into a globe,
Travelling thro the night: for from its dire
And restless fury, Man himself shrunk up
Into a little root a fathom long.
And I asked a Watcher & a Holy-One[2]
Its Name? He answerd, "It is the Wheel of Religion."
I wept & said, "Is this the law of Jesus,
This terrible devouring sword turning every way?"
He answered, "Jesus died because he strove
Against the current of this Wheel: its Name
Is Caiaphas, the dark Preacher of Death,
Of sin, of sorrow, & of punishment;
Opposing Nature! It is Natural Religion.
But Jesus is the bright Preacher of Life
Creating Nature from this fiery Law,
By self-denial & forgiveness of Sin.
Go therefore, cast out devils in Christ's name.
Heal thou the sick of spiritual disease.
Pity the evil, for thou art not sent
To smite with terror & with punishments
Those that are sick, like to the Pharisees
Crucifying & encompassing sea & land
For proselytes to tyranny & wrath.
But to the Publicans & Harlots go!
Teach them True Happiness, but let no curse
Go forth out of thy mouth to blight their peace;
For Hell is open'd to Heaven: thine eyes beheld
The dungeons burst & the Prisoners set free."

2. Daniel 4:13. Both the preface to chapter 4 and this poem seek to persuade Christians to disassociate themselves from the religious establishment, release the creative imagination, and practice the gospel of forgiveness. The sword in line 15 is that of the Covering Cherub who blocks the gate to Eden in Genesis 3:24; see *The Marriage of Heaven and Hell* 14 and note to *Milton* 37:8.

England! awake! awake! awake![3]
   Jerusalem thy Sister calls!
Why wilt thou sleep the sleep of death,
   And close her from thy ancient walls?

The hills & valleys felt her feet
   Gently upon their bosoms move:
Thy gates beheld sweet Zion's ways:
   Then was a time of joy and love.

And now the time returns again:
   Our souls exult & London's towers.
Recieve the Lamb of God to dwell
   In England's green & pleasant bowers!

[PLATE 78]

Jerusalem
Chap: 4

[PLATE 80]

* * *

"O sister Cambel," said Gwendolen, as their long beaming light
Mingled above the Mountain, "What shall we do to keep
Those awful forms in our soft bands?

* * *

3. This poem balances the prefatory hymn to *Milton*, which refers to a lost golden age when Jerusalem and England were together; now the promised new age has returned, and the Lamb of God is about to be restored to England. The last two lines have not usually been recognized as an imperative.

[PLATE 82]
"I have heard Jerusalem's groans; from Vala's cries & lamentations
I gather our eternal fate: Outcasts from life and love:
Unless we find a way to bind these awful Forms to our
Embrace we shall perish annihilate, discoverd our Delusions.
Look, I have wrought without delusion: Look! I have wept!
And given soft milk mingled together with the spirits of flocks
Of lambs and doves, mingled together in cups and dishes
Of painted clay. The mighty Hyle is become a weeping infant;
Soon shall the Spectres of the Dead follow my weaving threads."

The Twelve Daughters of Albion attentive listen in secret shades
On Cambridge and Oxford, beaming, soft uniting with Rahab's cloud
While Gwendolen spoke to Cambel, turning soft the spinning reel;
Or throwing the wingd shuttle; or drawing the cords with softest songs.
The golden cords of the Looms animate beneath their touches soft,
Along the Island white, among the Druid Temples, while Gwendolen
Spoke to the Daughters of Albion standing on Skiddaw's top.

So saying she took a Falshood & hid it in her left hand:
To entice her Sisters away to Babylon on Euphrates.
And thus she closed her left hand and utterd her Falshood:
Forgetting that Falshood is prophetic, she hid her hand behind
her,
Upon her back behind her loins & thus utterd her Deceit.

* * *

[PLATE 89]
Tho divided by the Cross & Nails & Thorns & Spear
In cruelties of Rahab & Tirzah, permanent endure
A terrible indefinite Hermaphroditic form:[4]
A Wine-press of Love & Wrath, double Hermaphroditic,
Twelvefold in Allegoric pomp, in selfish holiness—
The Pharisaion, the Grammateis, the Presbuterion,
The Archiereus, the Iereus, the Saddusaion[5]—double
Each withoutside of the other, covering eastern heaven.

Thus was the Covering Cherub reveald, majestic image
Of Selfhood, Body put off, the Antichrist accursed
Coverd with precious stones, a Human Dragon terrible
And bright, stretchd over Europe & Asia gorgeous.
In three nights he devourd the rejected corse of death.[6]

His Head dark, deadly, in its Brain incloses a reflexion
Of Eden all perverted: Egypt on the Gihon many tongued
And many mouthd: Ethiopia, Lybia, the Sea of Rephaim.
Minute Particulars in slavery I behold among the brick-kilns
Disorganiz'd, & there is Pharoh in his iron Court:
And the Dragon of the River & the Furnaces of iron.
Outwoven from Thames & Tweed & Severn, awful streams,
Twelve ridges of Stone frown over all the Earth in tyrant pride;
Frown over each River stupendous Works of Albion's Druid Sons.
And Albion's Forests of Oaks coverd the Earth from Pole to Pole.

His Bosom wide reflects Moab & Ammon; on the River
Pison, since calld Arnon, there is Heshbon beautiful,

4. Blake's fullest evocation of absolute evil, the Antichrist (I John 2:18, 4:3, II John 7) or Covering Cherub, cf. *Milton* 37. When this Abomination of Desolation appears, the Apocalypse is imminent (Matthew 24:15). There are too many proper names to annotate here; most of the Biblical names have been identified in other contexts. As in its appearance to Milton in Blake's companion epic, the Covering Cherub is an image of selfhood, of humanity's self-engendered barriers to Paradise—the false ideal of unapproachable holiness. This is the consolidation of error; Los's labors have finally forced error to take shape so that it can be recognized and rejected.

5. Classes of religious leaders with whom Jesus had to struggle, and who still rule churches today: Pharisees, Scribes, Elders, the High Priest, Priests and Sadducees.

6. Referring to the time Jesus was dead; cf. "The Everlasting Gospel," p. 371. Inside the mind of Antichrist the landscape of Eden becomes the wilderness both of the heathens and of industrial Britain.

The Rocks of Rabbath on the Arnon, & the Fish-pools of Heshbon
Whose currents flow into the Dead Sea by Sodom & Gomorra.
Above his Head high arching Wings, black, filld with Eyes,
Spring upon iron sinews from the Scapulae & Os Humeri.[7]
There Israel in bondage to his Generalizing Gods
Molech & Chemosh; & in his left breast is Philistea
In Druid Temples over the whole Earth with Victims' Sacrifice,
From Gaza to Damascus, Tyre & Sidon, & the Gods
Of Javan thro the Isles of Grecia, & all Europe's Kings,
Where Hiddekel pursues his course among the rocks.
Two Wings spring from his ribs of brass, starry, black as night
But transluscent their blackness as the dazling of gems.

His Loins inclose Babylon on Euphrates beautiful
And Rome in sweet Hesperia; there Israel scatterd abroad
In martyrdoms & slavery I behold: ah vision of sorrow!
Inclosed by eyeless Wings, glowing with fire as the iron
Heated in the Smith's forge, but cold the wind of their dread fury.

But in the midst of a devouring Stomach, Jerusalem
Hidden within the Covering Cherub as in a Tabernacle
Of threefold workmanship in allegoric delusion & woe.
There the Seven Kings of Canaan & Five Baalim of Philistea,
Sihon & Og, the Anakim & Emim, Nephilim & Gibborim,
From Babylon to Rome; & the Wings spread from Japan
Where the Red Sea terminates: the World of Generation & Death,
To Ireland's farthest rocks where Giants builded their Causeway[8]
Into the Sea of Rephaim, but the Sea oerwhelmd them all.

A Double Female now appeard within the Tabernacle:
Religion hid in War, a Dragon red & hidden Harlot
Each within other, but without a Warlike Mighty-one
Of dreadful power, sitting upon Horeb, pondering dire
And mighty preparations, mustering multitudes innumerable
Of warlike sons among the sands of Midian & Aram.
For multitudes of those who sleep in Alla descend,
Lured by his warlike symphonies of tabret, pipe & harp,
Burst the bottoms of the Graves & Funeral Arks of Beulah;
Wandering in that unknown Night beyond the silent Grave,
They become One with the Antichrist & are absorbed in him.

[PLATE 90]

* * *

But still the thunder of Los peals & thus the thunder's cry:
"These beautiful Witchcrafts of Albion are gratifyd by Cruelty:

7. Shoulder blades and upper arm bones where the Covering Cherub's wings are attached; such specificity is a source of the grotesque effect.

8. Giant's Causeway: vast basalt plinths, remnants of a natural bridge between Scotland and Ireland. The names in line 51 refers to giant enemies of the Israelites.

[PLATE 91]

"It is easier to forgive an Enemy than to forgive a Friend.
The man who permits you to injure him, deserves your vengeance:
He also will recieve it. Go Spectre! obey my most secret desire,
Which thou knowest without my speaking: Go to these Fiends of Righteousness
Tell them to obey their Humanities, & not pretend Holiness
When they are murderers. As far as my Hammer & Anvil permit
Go, tell them that the Worship of God, is honouring his gifts
In other men: & loving the greatest men best, each according
To his Genius: which is the Holy Ghost in Man. There is no other
God, than that God who is the intellectual fountain of Humanity;
He who envies or calumniates, which is murder & cruelty,
Murders the Holy-one. Go tell them this & overthrow their cup,
Their bread, their altar-table, their incense & their oath,
Their marriage & their baptism, their burial & consecration.
I have tried to make friends by corporeal gifts but have only
Made enemies: I never made friends but by spiritual gifts,
By severe contentions of friendship & the burning fire of thought.
He who would see the Divinity must see him in his Children.
One first, in friendship & love; then a Divine Family, & in the midst
Jesus will appear. So he who wishes to see a Vision, a perfect Whole,
Must see it in its Minute Particulars, Organized & not as thou
O Fiend of Righteousness pretendest. Thine is a Disorganized
And snowy cloud, brooder of tempests & destructive War.
You smile with pomp & rigor: you talk of benevolence & virtue!
I act with benevolence & Virtue & get murderd time after time.
You accumulate Particulars, & murder by analyzing, that you
May take the aggregate; & you call the aggregate Moral Law;
And you call that Swelld & bloated Form, a Minute Particular.
But General Forms have their vitality in Particulars: & every
Particular is a Man, a Divine Member of the Divine Jesus."

So Los cried at his Anvil in the horrible darkness weeping.

* * *

[PLATE 94]

* * *

Time was Finished! The Breath Divine Breathed over Albion
Beneath the Furnaces & starry Wheels and in the Immortal Tomb,
And England who is Brittannia awoke from Death on Albion's bosom.
She awoke pale & cold; she fainted seven times on the Body of Albion.[9]

9. Jerusalem has been referred to as Albion's soul, his beloved, or his daughter, bride of Christ; Brittania is here suddenly introduced as Albion's wife, who has been dead along with him.

"O pitious Sleep, O pitious Dream! O God, O God, awake! I have slain
In Dreams of Chastity & Moral Law, I have Murdered Albion! Ah!
In Stone-henge & on London Stone & in the Oak Groves of Malden
I have Slain him in my Sleep with the Knife of the Druid. O England!
O all ye Nations of the Earth! behold ye the Jealous Wife:
The Eagle & the Wolf & Monkey & Owl & the King & Priest were there."

[PLATE 95]
Her voice pierc'd Albion's clay cold ear. He moved upon the Rock.
The Breath Divine went forth upon the morning hills, Albion mov'd
Upon the Rock, he opend his eyelids in pain; in pain he mov'd
His stony members, he saw England. Ah! shall the Dead live again!

The Breath Divine went forth over the morning hills. Albion rose
In anger: the wrath of God breaking bright, flaming on all sides around
His awful limbs. Into the Heavens he walked, clothed in flames,
Loud thundring, with broad flashes of flaming lightning & pillars
Of fire, speaking the Words of Eternity in Human Forms, in direful
Revolutions of Action & Passion, thro the Four Elements on all sides
Surrounding his awful Members. Thou seest the Sun in heavy clouds
Struggling to rise above the Mountains. In his burning hand
He takes his Bow, then chooses out his arrows of flaming gold.
Murmuring, the Bowstring breathes with ardor! clouds roll round the
Horns of the wide Bow, loud sounding winds sport on the mountain brows!

Compelling Urizen to his Furrow; & Tharmas to his Sheepfold;
And Luvah to his Loom: Urthona he beheld mighty labouring at
His Anvil, in the Great Spectre Los unwearied labouring & weeping.
Therefore the Sons of Eden praise Urthona's Spectre in songs
Because he kept the Divine Vision in time of trouble.

* * *

[PLATE 96]
As the Sun & Moon lead forward the Visions of Heaven & Earth,
England who is Brittannia entered Albion's bosom rejoicing.

Then Jesus appeared, standing by Albion as the Good Shepherd
By the lost Sheep that he hath found, & Albion knew that it
Was the Lord, the Universal Humanity, & Albion saw his Form
A Man, & they conversed as Man with Man, in Ages of Eternity.
And the Divine Appearance was the likeness & similitude of Los.[1]

Albion said, "O Lord what can I do! my Selfhood cruel
Marches against thee, deceitful, from Sinai & from Edom
Into the Wilderness of Judah, to meet thee in his pride.
I behold the Visions of my deadly Sleep of Six Thousand Years
Dazling around thy skirts like a Serpent of precious stones & gold.
I know it is my Self: O my Divine Creator & Redeemer."

Jesus replied, "Fear not, Albion; unless I die thou canst not live.
But if I die I shall arise again & thou with me.
This is Friendship & Brotherhood; without it Man Is Not."

So Jesus spoke; the Covering Cherub coming on in darkness
Overshadowd them, & Jesus said, "Thus do Men in Eternity
One for another to put off by forgiveness, every sin."

Albion replyd, "Cannot Man exist without Mysterious
Offering of Self for Another; is this Friendship & Brotherhood?[2]
I see thee in the likeness & similitude of Los my Friend."

Jesus said, "Wouldest thou love one who never died
For thee or ever die for one who had not died for thee?
And if God dieth not for Man & giveth not himself
Eternally for Man, Man could not exist! for Man is Love:
As God is Love. Every kindness to another is a little Death
In the Divine Image, nor can Man exist but by Brotherhood."
So saying the Cloud overshadowing divided them asunder.

1. Jesus looks like Los because Los is the human imagination.
2. The reason Jesus died on the Cross was not to institute a mystery religion but to offer an example of the death of selfhood. See color plate 30.

Albion stood in terror; not for himself but for his Friend
Divine, & Self was lost in the contemplation of faith
And wonder at the Divine Mercy & at Los's sublime honour.

"Do I sleep amidst danger to Friends! O my Cities & Counties
Do you sleep! Rouze up, rouze up, Eternal Death is abroad!"

So Albion spoke & threw himself into the Furnaces of affliction.
All was a Vision, all a Dream; the Furnaces became
Fountains of Living Waters flowing from the Humanity Divine,
And all the Cities of Albion rose from their Slumbers, and All
The Sons & Daughters of Albion on soft clouds Waking from Sleep.
Soon all around remote the Heavens burnt with flaming fires,
And Urizen & Luvah & Tharmas & Urthona arose into
Albion's Bosom. Then Albion stood before Jesus in the Clouds
Of Heaven Fourfold among the Visions of God in Eternity.

[PLATE 97]
"Awake! Awake Jerusalem! O lovely Emanation of Albion,
Awake and overspread all Nations as in Ancient Time.
For lo! the Night of Death is past and the Eternal Day
Appears upon our Hills; Awake Jerusalem, and come away!"

So spake the Vision of Albion & in him so spake in my hearing
The Universal Father. Then Albion stretchd his hand into Infinitude.
And took his Bow. Fourfold the Vision, for bright beaming Urizen
Layd his hand on the South & took a breathing Bow of carved Gold;
Luvah his hand stretch'd to the East & bore a Silver Bow bright shining;
Tharmas Westward a Bow of Brass pure flaming richly wrought;
Urthona Northward in thick storms a Bow of Iron terrible thundering.

And the Bow is a Male & Female & the Quiver of the Arrows of Love
Are the Children of this Bow, a Bow of Mercy & Loving-kindness; laying
Open the hidden Heart in Wars of mutual Benevolence, Wars of Love.
And the Hand of Man grasps firm between the Male & Female Loves.
And he Clothed himself in Bow & Arrows in awful state Fourfold
In the midst of his Twenty-eight Cities, each with his Bow breathing.

[PLATE 98]
Then each an Arrow flaming from his Quiver fitted carefully
They drew fourfold the unreprovable String, bending thro the wide Heavens
The horned Bow Fourfold; loud sounding flew the flaming Arrow fourfold.

Murmuring, the Bow-string breathes with ardor. Clouds roll round the horns
Of the wide Bow; loud sounding Winds sport on the Mountain's brows.
The Druid Spectre was Annihilate; loud thundering, rejoicing, terrific vanishing
Fourfold Annihilation, & at the clangor of the Arrows of Intellect
The innumerable Chariots of the Almighty appeard in Heaven
And Bacon & Newton & Locke,[3] & Milton & Shakspear & Chaucer,
A Sun of blood red wrath surrounding heaven on all sides around,
Glorious incomprehensible by Mortal Man, & each Chariot was Sexual Threefold,

3. Even these Blakean anathemas find their proper place in the redemptive experience.

And every Man stood Fourfold. Each Four Faces had: One to the West,
One toward the East, One to the South, One to the North, the Horses Fourfold.
And the dim Chaos brightend beneath, above, around! Eyed as the Peacock,
According to the Human Nerves of Sensation, the Four Rivers of the Water of Life:

South stood the Nerves of the Eye; East in Rivers of bliss the Nerves of the
Expansive Nostrils; West, flowd the Parent Sense the Tongue; North stood
The labyrinthine Ear. Circumscribing & Circumcising the excrementitious
Husk & Covering, into Vacuum evaporating, revealing the lineaments of Man,
Driving outward the Body of Death, in an Eternal Death & Resurrection,
Awaking it to Life among the Flowers of Beulah, rejoicing in Unity:
In the Four Senses, in the Outline, the Circumference & Form, for ever,
In Forgiveness of Sins which is Self Annihilation; it is the Covenant of Jehovah.

The Four Living Creatures, Chariots of Humanity Divine Incomprehensible,
In beautiful Paradises expand. These are the four Rivers of Paradise
And the Four Faces of Humanity fronting the Four Cardinal Points
Of Heaven going forward, forward, irresistible from Eternity to Eternity.

And they conversed together in Visionary forms dramatic which bright
Redounded from their Tongues in thunderous majesty, in Visions,
In new Expanses, creating exemplars of Memory and of Intellect;
Creating Space, Creating Time, according to the wonders Divine
Of Human Imagination, throughout all the Three Regions immense
Of Childhood, Manhood & Old Age; & the all tremendous unfathomable Non Ens
Of Death was seen in regenerations terrific or complacent, varying
According to the subject of discourse; & every Word & Every Character
Was Human according to the Expansion or Contraction, the Translucence or
Opakeness of Nervous fibres. Such was the variation of Time & Space

Which vary according as the Organs of Perception vary; & they walked
To & fro in Eternity as One Man, reflecting each in each & clearly seen
And seeing: according to fitness & order. And I heard Jehovah speak
Terrific from his Holy Place & saw the Words of the Mutual Covenant Divine
On Chariots of gold & jewels, with Living Creatures starry & flaming
With every Colour, Lion, Tyger, Horse, Elephant, Eagle, Dove, Fly, Worm,
And the all wondrous Serpent clothed in gems & rich array Humanize
In the Forgiveness of Sins according to the Covenant of Jehovah. They Cry:
"Where is the Covenant of Priam, the Moral Virtues of the Heathen?
Where is the Tree of Good & Evil that rooted beneath the cruel heel
Of Albion's Spectre, the Patriarch Druid? where are all his Human Sacrifices
For Sin in War & in the Druid Temples of the Accuser of Sin; beneath
The Oak Groves of Albion that covered the whole Earth beneath his Spectre?
Where are the Kingdoms of the World & all their glory that grew on Desolation?
The Fruit of Albion's Poverty Tree when the Triple Headed Gog-Magog, Giant
Of Albion, Taxed the Nations into Desolation & then gave the Spectrous Oath?"

Such is the Cry from all the Earth, from the Living Creatures of the Earth,
And from the great City of Golgonooza in the Shadowy Generation,
And from the Thirty-two Nations of the Earth among the Living Creatures.

[PLATE 99]

All Human Forms identified, even Tree, Metal, Earth & Stone. All
Human Forms identified, living, going forth & returning[4] wearied
Into the Planetary lives of Years, Months, Days, & Hours; reposing
And then Awaking into his Bosom in the Life of Immortality.‡

4. Possibly Blake envisions an eternal cycle of life and death.

‡ See color plate 31.

And I heard the Name of their Emanations; they are named Jerusalem.

The End of The Song
of Jerusalem§

The Ghost of Abel

Blake's last work in illuminated printing is a little drama on two pages. The dedication to Lord Byron and the date of 1822 show that the work is a response to Byron's unorthodox drama *Cain: A Mystery*, published in 1821. Like most of Blake's writings, but more explicitly than most, *The Ghost of Abel* is thus designed as a counterstatement to another work. In Byron's hands, Cain is a sympathetic figure, the first person born outside Paradise, and his murder of his brother is a deliberate act of rebellion against an unjust God. To Blake, although Cain's rebellion may be understandable, any attempt to justify either murder or revenge is a Satanic self-deception, even if practiced by a daring and perceptive artist. To correct Byron he had to reinterpret the character of the Divinity in Genesis, separating the vengeful Elohim from the forgiving Jehovah. In none of his other writings does Blake take such explicit responsibility for his visions, or claim for them so high an authority, as he does in the subtitle to this work.

Yet Byron is specifically recognized as a fellow prophet: he is "in the Wilderness" like the just man in the Argument to *The Marriage of Heaven and Hell* and like John the Baptist, quoted on the title page of Blake's first work, *All Religions Are One* (a work which is also recalled in the colophon: "Blake's Original Stereotype Was 1788"). The prototype for John the Baptist was Elijah, who "comprehends all the Prophetic Characters" (*A Vision of the Last Judgment*) the question Blake directs to Byron as Elijah was asked of Elijah by an angel and then by God himself (I Kings 19:9, 13) as an injunction to restore the office of prophecy. It is noteworthy that Blake never printed a correction of anyone whom he regarded as antithetical to the spirit of prophecy: such intellectual enemies as Reynolds and Bacon are recipients of Blake's blistering marginalia but do not inspire separate works of counterstatement.

Our copy text is Copy B as reproduced in Geoffrey Keynes, ed., *William Blake's Laocoön: A Last Testament* (London: The Trianon Press for the William Blake Trust, 1976).

§ See color plate 32 for the tailpiece, depicting the Spectre (carrying the sun), Los (with hammer and tongs), and Enitharmon (weaving moonbeams), all working together in harmony.

PLATE 1

The Ghost of Abel

A Revelation In the Visions of Jehovah

Seen by William Blake

To LORD BYRON in the Wilderness
What doest thou here, Elijah?

Can a Poet doubt the Visions of Jehovah? Nature has no Outline: but Imagination has. Nature has no Tune: but Imagination has! Nature has no Supernatural & dissolves: Imagination is Eternity.

Scene. A rocky Country. Eve fainted over the dead body of Abel which lays near a Grave. Adam kneels by her. Jehovah stands above

Jehovah— Adam!

Adam— I will not hear thee more, thou Spiritual Voice!
Is this Death?

Jehovah— Adam!

Adam— It is in vain: I will not hear thee
Henceforth! Is this thy Promise that the Woman's Seed
Should bruise the Serpent's head: Is this the Serpent?
Ah!
Seven times, O Eve, thou hast fainted over the Dead.
Ah! Ah!

Eve revives

Eve— Is this the Promise of Jehovah! O it is all a vain delusion
This Death & this Life & this Jehovah!

Jehovah— Woman: lift thine eyes.

A Voice is heard coming on

Voice— O Earth cover not thou my Blood! cover not thou my
Blood!

Enter the Ghost of Abel

Eve— Thou Visionary Phantasm, thou art not the real Abel.

Abel— Among the Elohim[1] a Human Victim I wander. I am their House,
Prince of the Air,[2] & our dimensions compass Zenith & Nadir.
Vain is thy Covenant, O Jehovah, I am the Accuser & Avenger
Of Blood. O Earth, Cover not thou the Blood of Abel!

Jehovah— What Vengeance dost thou require?

Abel— Life for Life! Life for Life!

Jehovah— He who shall take Cain's life must also Die, O Abel.
And who is he? Adam wilt you, or Eve thou do this?[3]

Adam— It is all a Vain delusion of the all creative Imagination.
Eve, come away & let us not believe these vain delusions.
Abel is dead & Cain slew him! We shall also Die a Death
And then! what then? Be as poor Abel a Thought: or as
This! O what shall I call thee, Form Divine? Father of Mercies
That appearest to my Spiritual Vision? Eve, seest thou also?

Eve— I see him plainly with my Mind's Eye. I see also Abel living:

1. Blake distinguished between the conceptions of God represented by "Elohim" and "Jehovah," the names of God in two separate accounts of the creation which appear sequentially in Genesis 1 and 2. In the Seven Eyes or historical phases of man's conception of God, Elohim is third, superior only to the fallen angel Lucifer and the pagan idol Moloch (see *Milton* 13:19–29), but Jehovah the father-god is sixth, inferior only to Jesus the Divine Humanity. In contrast to Jesus, Jehovah is usually treated as a repressor by Blake. In this work, however, Jehovah wants to forgive; it is the Elohim (a plural word in Hebrew) who demand punishment for sin. They speak through the dead Abel, whose blood cries out from the ground (Genesis 4:10).

2. This phrase and the word "accuser" in line 12 are titles for Satan. Abel's refrain (lines 8, 13) consists of the words of Job 16:18 under the influence of Satan. His frantic demand in line 14 repeats the atrocious law of Exodus 21:23.

3. Jehovah points out that there is no end to a system of justice that demands blood for blood, life for life (cf. Blake's parable of the atonement, *Milton* 11:1–18). In the Biblical account, the only way to slow down the killing was to escalate the punishment: a mark on Cain warned that his death would be avenged sevenfold; yet only four generations later, Lamech required vengeance of "seventy and sevenfold" (Genesis 4:24).

Tho terribly afflicted as We also are, yet Jehovah sees him
[PLATE 2] Alive & not Dead. Were it not better to believe Vision
With all our might & strength tho we are fallen & lost?

Adam— Eve thou hast spoken truly; let us kneel before his feet.

They Kneel before Jehovah.

Abel— Are these the Sacrifices of Eternity, O Jehovah, a Broken Spirit
And a Contrite Heart?[4] O I cannot Forgive! the Accuser hath
Entered into Me as into his House & I loathe thy Tabernacles.
As thou hast said, so is it come to pass: My desire is unto Cain
And He doth rule over Me: therefore My Soul in fumes of Blood
Cries for Vengeance: Sacrifice on Sacrifice, Blood on Blood.

Jehovah— Lo I have given you a Lamb for an Atonement instead
Of the Transgresor, or no Flesh or Spirit could ever Live.

Abel— Compelld I cry, "O Earth cover not the Blood of Abel!"

Abel sinks down into the Grave from which arises Satan Armed in glittering scales with a Crown & a Spear.

Satan— I will have Human Blood & not the blood of Bulls or Goats,[5]
And no Atonement! O Jehovah the Elohim live on Sacrifice
Of Men; hence I am God of Men: Thou Human, O Jehovah.
By the Rock & Oak of the Druid, creeping Mistletoe & Thorn,

4. These are the only sacrifices required by the true God (Psalms 51:17).
5. Only Satan, Accuser rather than forgiver of sin, demands blood-sacrifice: his words are a distortion of Psalms 50:13 and Hebrews 9:12, 10:4.

Cain's City built with Human Blood, not Blood
of Bulls & Goats,
Thou shalt Thyself be Sacrified to Me, thy God on
Calvary;[6]

Jehovah— Such is My Will: *Thunders*
that Thou Thyself go to Eternal Death
In Self Annihilation, even till Satan Self-subdud
Put off Satan[7]
Into the Bottomless Abyss whose torment arises for
ever & ever.

On each side a Chorus of Angels entering Sing the following:

The Elohim of the Heathen Swore Vengeance for Sin! Then
Thou stoodst
Forth O Elohim Jehovah![8] in the midst of the darkness of the
Oath! All Clothed
In Thy Covenant of the Forgiveness of Sins: Death, O Holy!
Is this Brotherhood?
The Elohim saw their Oath Eternal Fire; they rolled apart
trembling over The
Mercy Seat: each in his station fixt in the Firmament by Peace,
Brotherhood, and Love.

The Curtain falls

The Voice of Abel's Blood

1822 W Blake's Original Stereotype was 1788

6. To Blake, a God who demands blood (cf. *Paradise Lost* III, 210–12) must be Satan; Jehovah's answer, "Such is my will," introduces the only means of overcoming the accuser: self-sacrifice, as practiced by Milton (*Milton* 38:29–49) and Albion (*Jerusalem* 96).

7. Although other passages may be interpreted, with some effort, as exaggerated restatements of orthodox Christian themes, this assertion is radically heterodox; cf. Altizer, *The New Apocalypse* (1967). Jehovah wills that the accuser have no one to accuse but Accusation itself.

8. When "Elohim" is used in combination with "Jehovah" it does not function as a proper name but means only "gods"; cf. *Jerusalem* 61:1. With the annihilation of Satan, the bloodthirsty "Elohim of the Heathen" who have been blocking the Mercy Seat (cf. notes on the Covering Cherub, *Milton* 37, *Jerusalem* 89) roll apart and are fixed in the firmament where they will do no further harm. This change in the nature of the divinity is the result of Adam's and Eve's decision to believe Vision rather than follow their natural instinct for revenge (1:22, 2:1).

This drama is a revelation of the point at which history could have been redeemed at its outset. Having rejected the vicious circles of sin and punishment, violence and vengeance, Adam and Eve with Cain would have returned to Paradise. But after the curtain falls the final design shows the Ghost of Abel pointing to the words "The Voice of Abel's Blood," written against the sky.

The Everlasting Gospel[1]

There is not one Moral Virtue that Jesus Inculcated but Plato & Cicero did Inculcate before him. What then did Christ Inculcate? Forgiveness of Sins. This alone is the Gospel & this is the Life & Immortality brought to light by Jesus. Even the Covenant of Jehovah, which is This: If you forgive one another your Trespasses so shall Jehovah forgive you, That he himself may dwell among you, but if you Avenge you Murder the Divine Image & he cannot dwell among you because you Murder him. He arises Again & you deny that he is Arisen & are blind to Spirit.[2]

[1]

If Moral Virtue was Christianity
Christ's Pretensions were all Vanity
And Caiphas[3] & Pilate Men
Praise Worthy, & the Lion's Den
And not the Sheepfold Allegories
Of God & Heaven & their Glories.
The Moral Christian is the Cause
Of the Unbeliever & his Laws;
The Roman Virtues, Warlike Fame,
Take Jesus & Jehovah's Name,

1. Blake's title refers to a term in Revelation 14:6 which was taken by some religious sects to be the name for the religion of Eternity, a dispensation which would supplant the New Testament as that gospel had supplanted the law of the Old Testament. It would reunite all nations in a post-moral creed that would make the New Testament seem legalistic by contrast. Members of apocalyptic groups believed that they were already experiencing the Everlasting Gospel and were free from the restrictions imposed by Christian churches (see A. L. Morton, *The Everlasting Gospel,* 1958). Blake mentioned the Everlasting Gospel several times in his earlier writings, notably in his annotations to Watson's *Apology for the Bible* (p. 436), before inserting it as the title over a section of the late draft poem in his Notebook. It seems an appropriate title for this whole fragmentary work. The present text is an editorial arrangement that presents a coherent reading text of the most important passages; it is based neither on the probable order of composition nor on Blake's probable intentions. References to the Keynes and Erdman texts are provided in following notes. For a discussion of textual problems, see Keynes, pp. 920–22; Erdman, pp. 791–96; Erdman in *From Sensibility to Romanticism,* eds. F. W. Hilles and H. Bloom (1965), pp 331–56; and Erdman and Moore in *The Notebook of William Blake* (revised edition, 1977). Where Blake adheres closely to familiar Gospel accounts, Biblical annotation is not provided.

2. Cf. *The Complete Writings of William Blake,* ed. Geoffrey Keynes (London and New York: Oxford, 1974), p. 757; and *The Poetry and Prose of William Blake,* ed. David V. Erdman (Garden City, N.Y.: Doubleday, 1970), p. 792.

3. Caiaphas, high priest who with his father-in-law Annas judged Jesus guilty by Jewish law and sent him to Pilate to be condemned to death by Roman law (John 18).

For what is Antichrist[4] but those
Who against Sinners Heaven close
With Iron bars in Virtuous State
And Rhadamanthus[5] at the Gate?[6]

[2]

What can this Gospel of Jesus be?
What Life & Immortality?
What was it that he brought to Light
That Plato & Cicero did not write?
The Heathen Deities wrote them all:
These Moral Virtues great & small.
What is the Accusation of Sin
But Moral Virtue's deadly Gin?
The Moral Virtues in their Pride
Did o'er the World triumphant ride
In Wars & Sacrifice for Sin,
And Souls to Hell ran trooping in.
The Accuser, Holy God of All
This Pharisaic Worldy Ball,[7]
Amidst them in his Glory Beams
Upon the Rivers & the Streams.
Then Jesus rose & said to Me,
"Thy Sins are all forgiven thee."
Loud Pilate Howld, loud Caiphas Yelld
When they the Gospel Light beheld.
It was when Jesus said to Me,
"Thy Sins are all forgiven thee."
The Christian trumpets loud proclaim
Thro all the World in Jesus' name
Mutual forgiveness of each Vice
And oped the Gates of Paradise.
The Mortal Virtues in Great fear
Formed the Cross & Nails & Spear,
And the Accuser standing by
Cried out, "Crucify, Crucify!"
Our Mortal Virtues ne'er can be
Nor Warlike Pomp & Majesty,
For Moral Virtues all begin
In the Accusations of Sin.[8]

* * *

4. Throughout the poem the contest is between Christ and Antichrist (see notes to *Jerusalem* 89); Blake is trying to extricate the true Jesus from both the historical Jesus and the Jesus worshipped in the churches. The true Jesus embodies imaginative forgiveness; all else—moral accusation and solitary holiness—is of the Antichrist, who is seen most clearly as the devourer of the dead body of Christ at the end of the "Chastity" section.

5. Judge and punisher in Hades (*Aenead* VI, 566).

6. Cf. Keynes, p. 758, and Erdman, p. 793.

7. Literally, Satan means "Accuser"; another of his names is "the God of this World."

8. Cf. Keynes, pp. 758–59, and Erdman, pp. 792–93.

[3]

Was Jesus Born of a Virgin Pure
With narrow Soul & looks demure?
If he intended to take on Sin
The Mother should an Harlot been,
Just such a one as Magdalen
With seven devils in her Pen,[9]
Or were Jew Virgins still more Curst
And more suckling devils nurst?
Or what was it which he took on
That he might bring Salvation?
A Body subject to be Tempted,
From neither pain nor grief Exempted,
Or such a body as might not feel
The passions that with Sinners deal?
Yes, but they say he never fell—
Ask Caiaphas, for he can tell:
"He mockd the Sabbath & he mockd
The Sabbath's God & he unlockd
The Evil spirits from their shrines
And turned Fishermen to Divines,
O'erturned the Tent of Secret Sins
& its Golden Cords & Pins."
'Tis the Bloody Shrine of War
Pinnd around from Star to Star,[1]
Halls of Justice hating Vice,
Where the Devil Combs his Lice.[2]

* * *

[4]

Was Jesus Humble or did he
Give any Proofs of Humility?
Boast of high Things with Humble tone
And give with Charity a Stone?
When but a Child he ran away
And left his Parents in dismay;

9. Mary Magdalen was possessed by seven devils (Mark 16:9), which Blake treats as psychosexual sicknesses; cf. "Long John Brown & Little Mary Bell," p. 212. His question about the mother of Jesus is whether a harlot or a virgin is possessed by more devils; "curst" also means "ill-tempered."

1. The "Tent" knocked over by Jesus is called the Mundane Shell in other works; it is the worldly order of things, material appearances. The Tent corresponds to the elaborately curtained tabernacle containing the ark, which was placed in the Holy of Holies in the temple (Exodus 25, I Kings 6:16–28, II Chron. 3:14; Rev. 11:19, 21:3, 22). Another word Blake sometimes used is "veil," the veil of flesh and matter which Jesus "rent" when the veil in the temple was rent at his crucifixion (Matthew 27:51, Hebrews 9:3, 10:20, recalling also the veil over Moses' face, II Corinthians 3:14). His destruction of the old moral order is equated with the rolling back of the heavens which reveals a new heaven and a new earth (Revelation 6:14, 21:1). It is quite possible that Caiaphas's speech continues through ". . . Combs his Lice," line 26.

2. Cf. Keynes, pp. 756–57, and Erdman, p. 794.

When they had wanderd three days long
These were the words upon his tongue:
"No Earthly Parents I confess
I am doing my Father's business."

* * *

What was he doing all that time
From twelve years old to manly prime?
Was he then Idle or the Less
About his Father's business,
Or was his wisdom held in scorn
Before his wrath began to burn
In Miracles throughout the Land
That quite unnervd Caiaphas' hand?
If he had been Antichrist, Creeping Jesus,
He'd have done any thing to please us:
Gone sneaking into Synagogues
And not usd the Elders & Priests like dogs,
But Humble as a Lamb or Ass
Obeyd himself to Caiaphas.
God wants not Man to Humble himself;
This is the trick of the ancient Elf.
This is the Race that Jesus ran:
Humble to God, Haughty to Man,
Cursing the Rulers before the People
Even to the temple's highest Steeple;
And when he Humbled himself to God
Then descended the Cruel Rod:
"If thou humblest thyself, thou humblest me;
Thou also dwellst in Eternity.
Thou art a Man, God is no more;
Thy own humanity learn to adore,
For that is my Sprit of Life.
Awake, arise to Spiritual Strife
And thy Revenge abroad display
In terrors at the Last Judgment day;
God's Mercy & Long Suffering
Is but the Sinner to Judgment to bring;
Thou on the Cross for them shalt pray
And take Revenge at the Last Day."[3]
Jesus replied & thunders hurld,
"I never will Pray for the World!
Once [I] did so when I prayd in the Garden;
I wishd to take with me a Bodily Pardon.
Can that which was of Woman born
In the absence of the Morn

3. The first part of Jehovah's speech expresses Blake's major theme of the unity of man and God, emphasized in *All Religions Are One, The Marriage of Heaven and Hell,* and throughout his major prophecies. However, in the last six lines of this speech, the voice of God infuriates Jesus by advocating revenge and punishment, a concept antithetical to Blake's understanding of divinity.

When the Soul fell into Sleep—[4]
And Archangels round it weep—
Shooting out against the Light
Fibres of a deadly night,
Reasoning upon its own dark Fiction
In doubt which is Self Contradiction?
Humility is only doubt.
And does the Sun & Moon blot out,
Rooting over with thorns & stems
The buried Soul & all its Gems.
This Life's dim Windows of the Soul
Distorts the Heavens from Pole to Pole
And leads you to Believe a Lie
When you see with, not thro, the Eye
That was born in a night to perish in a night
When the Soul slept in the beams of Light."
I'm sure This Jesus will not do
Either for Englishman or Jew.[5]

[5]

Was Jesus gentle or did he
Give any marks of Gentility?

* * *

John from the Wilderness loud cried,
Satan gloried in his Pride.
"Come," said Satan, "Come away—
I'll soon see if you'll obey.
John for disobedience bled,
But you can turn the stones to bread.
God's high king & God's high Priest
Shall Plant their Glories in your breast
If Caiaphas you will obey,
If Herod you with bloody Prey
Feed with the Sacrifice & be
Obedient. Fall down and worship me!"
Thunders & lightnings broke around
And Jesus' voice in thunders sound:
"Thus I seize the Spiritual Prey!
Ye smiters with disease, make way!
I come Your King & God to seize!
Is God a Smiter with disease?"
The God of this World raged in vain.

4. The night of the fallen world, an aspect of which is the division into sexes. The soul is self-benighted, self-blocked from Eternity. This unfinished question—lacking a verb—would have required more work before publication if Blake had gone on with this poem. Possibly Jesus' speech ends with ". . . Bodily Pardon," line 88, and the remainder of the "Humble" section is an authorial comment.

5. Cf. Keynes, pp. 751–53, and Erdman, pp. 510–12; for the final couplet of this section, see Keynes, p. 756, and Erdman, p. 796. Lines 103–6 are practically identical with "Auguries of Innocence," ll. 125–28 (p. 212).

He bound Old Satan in his Chain
And bursting forth his furious ire
Became a Chariot of fire.
Throughout the land he took his course
And traced Diseases to their Source;
He cursd the Scribe & Pharisee,
Trampling down Hipocricy
Where e'er his Chariot took its way;
There Gates of Death let in the day,
Broke down from every Chain & Bar.
And Satan in his Spiritual War
Dragd at his Chariot wheels; loud howld
The God of this World; louder rolld[6]
The Chariot Wheels; & louder still
His voice was heard from Zion's hill.
And in his hand the Scourge shone bright;
He scourgd the Merchant Canaanite
From out the Temple of his Mind,[7]
And in his Body tight does bind
Satan & all his Hellish Crew,
And thus with wrath he did subdue
The Serpent Bulk of Nature's dross
Till he had naild it to the Cross.
He took on Sin in the Virgin's Womb
And put it off on the Cross & Tomb
To be Worshipd[8] by the Church of Rome.[9]

[6]

Was Jesus Chaste or did he
Give any Lessons of Chastity?
The morning blushd fiery red;
Mary was found in Adulterous bed.[1]
Earth groand beneath & Heavens above
Trembled at discovery of Love.

6. In "Mental Fight," filled with purifying indignation, Jesus drags Satan (or the God of this World) behind his chariot. Since Blake did not supply punctuation, the antecedents for "his" are confusing.
7. An extrapolation from passages identifying the temple with the body (John 2:19, I Corinthians 6:19); this makes Jesus' scourging of moneylenders from the temple a form of clearing his own mind.
8. Although Blake condemns the Church of Rome for being preoccupied with the image of the Crucified Christ, he differs from most radical Protestants in that he is equally severe against other branches of Christendom for other errors—Swedenborgian as well as Anglican, Lutheran, and Calvinistic (e.g. in *Milton* 22:50, 23:47, 24:32). In this passage, based on Colossians 2:14, Romans 6:6, 7:24, Jesus subdues Satan by containing him and then sacrificing himself; for these difficult matters, see Thomas J. J. Altizer, *The New Apocalypse* (1967).
9. Cf. Keynes, pp. 748–49 and Erdman, pp. 514–15.
1. A merging of references to Mary Magdalen (Mark 16:9) and the woman taken in adultery (John 8:1–11), with implications for the character of the Virgin Mary. Cf. Jerusalem's vision of the conversation between Mary and Joseph (*Jerusalem* 61).

Jesus was sitting in Moses' Chair;
They brought the trembling Woman There.
Moses commands she be stoned to death;
What was the sound of Jesus' breath?
He laid His hand on Moses' Law;
The Ancient Heavens in Silent Awe,
Writ with Curses from Pole to Pole,
All away began to roll.[2]
The Earth trembling & Naked lay
In secret bed of Mortal Clay,[3]
On Sinai felt the hand Divine
Putting back the bloody shrine,
And she heard the breath of God,
As she heard by Eden's flood:
"Good & Evil are no more!
Sinai's trumpets cease to roar!
Cease, finger of God, to write!
The Heavens are not clean in thy Sight!
Thou art Good & thou Alone,
Nor may the sinner cast one stone.
To be Good only is to be
A Devil or else a Pharisee.
Thou Angel of the Presence Divine
That didst create this Body of Mine,
Wherefore has thou writ these Laws
And Created Hell's dark jaws?
My Presence I will take from thee;
A Cold Leper thou shalt be.[4]
Tho thou wast so pure & bright
That Heaven was Impure in thy Sight,
Tho thy Oath turnd Heaven Pale,
Tho thy Covenant built Hell's Jail,
Tho thou didst all to Chaos roll,
With the Serpent for its soul,
Still the breath Divine does move
And the breath Divine is Love."
"Mary, Fear Not, Let me see[5]
The Seven Devils that torment thee;
Hide not from my Sight thy Sin
That forgiveness thou maist win.

2. Once more, the old heavens are rolled back to reveal the new heaven and the new earth; the consequences of the fall are reversed.

3. Cf. "Earth's Answer," *Songs of Experience*.

4. When divinity is clearly seen in the human form of Jesus, the holy Jehovah enshrined by the churches is cast off as Nobodaddy; cf. Notebook poem, p. 183, and the "leprous" Jehovah in *Milton* 13:24. Here Jesus, the Seventh Eye of God, parts company with his predecessor, the sixth Eye (or sixth Angel of the Divine Presence). In turning aside the Mosaic law from the adulteress, Jesus rejects its author as well.

5. Even with the addition of punctuation not supplied by Blake, it is difficult to follow abrupt shifts; Jesus is still speaking, but he turns his attention now to Mary, and a few lines on he addresses her seven devils directly.

Has no Man Condemned thee?"
"No Man, Lord!" "Then what is he
Who shall Accuse thee?—Come Ye forth,
Fallen Fiends of Heavnly birth
That have forgot your Ancient love
And driven away my trembling Dove!
You shall bow before her feet;
You shall lick the dust for Meat;
And tho you cannot Love but Hate
Shall be beggars at Love's Gate.—
What was thy love? Let me see it:
Was it love or Dark Deceit?"
"Love too long from Me has fled.
Twas dark deceit to Earn my bread;
Twas Covet, or twas Custom, or
Some trifle not worth caring for,
That they may call a shame & Sin
Love's Temple that God dwelleth in,
And hide in secret hidden Shrine
The Naked Human form divine,
And render that a Lawless thing
On which the Soul Expands its wing.
But this, O Lord, this was my Sin:
When first I let these Devils in,
In dark pretence to Chastity,
Blaspheming Love, blaspheming thee.
Thence Rose Secret Adulteries
And thence did Covet also rise.
My sin thou hast forgiven me,
Canst thou forgive my Blasphemy?
Canst thou return to this dark Hell
And in my burning bosom dwell?
And canst thou die that I may live,
And canst thou Pity & forgive?"
Then Rolld the shadowy Man away[6]
From the Limbs of Jesus to make them his prey—
An Ever devouring appetite,
Glittering with festering Venoms bright—
Crying, "Crucify this cause of distress
Who don't keep the secrets of Holiness!
All Mental Powers by Diseases we bind,
But he heals the Deaf & the Dumb & the Blind.
Whom God has afflicted for Secret Ends
He comforts & Heals & calls them Friends."
But when Jesus was Crucified
Then was perfected his glittring pride;
In three Nights he devourd his prey,
And still he devours the Body of Clay,

6. The Spectre, Satan (or Antichrist); cf. *Milton* 39:16–31.

For dust & Clay is the Serpent's meat
Which never was made for Man to Eat.
Seeing this False Christ, In fury & Passion
I made my Voice heard all over the Nation.[7]

[7]

The Vision of Christ that thou dost see
Is my Vision's Greatest Enemy.
Thine has a great hook nose like thine;
Mine has a snub nose like to mine.
Thine is the friend of All Mankind;
Mine speaks in parables to the Blind.
Thine loves the same world that mine hates;
Thy Heaven doors are my Hell Gates.
Socrates taught what Melitus[8]
Loathd as a Nation's bitterest Curse;
And Caiphas was in his own Mind
A benefactor to Mankind.
Both read the Bible day & night,
But thou readst black where I read white.[9]

7. Cf. Keynes, pp. 253–55 and Erdman, pp. 512–14, for the final couplet in this section, see Keynes, p. 756, and Erdman, p. 795.

8. One of Socrates' three accusers; cf. design for *Jerusalem* 93, p. 353.

9. Cf. Keynes, p. 748, and Erdman, p. 516.

To The Accuser who is
The God of This World
Truly My Satan thou art but a Dunce
And dost not know the Garment from the Man
Every Harlot was a Virgin once
Nor canst thou ever change Kate into Nan
Tho thou art Worshipd by the Names Divine
Of Jesus & Jehovah: thou art still
The Son of Morn in weary Nights decline
The lost Travellers Dream under the Hill

This poem and design make up the concluding plate in *For the Sexes: The Gates of Paradise* (1818), a revised edition of an emblem book first published as *For Children: The Gates of Paradise* (1793).

Related Prose

An Island in the Moon

Blake's only extended work of prose fiction survives in a unique draft lacking a title (we use the traditional editorial title) and also missing one or more leaves of chapter 11. When the work was first published as a whole in 1907, its most important features seemed to be the three poems later included in *Songs of Innocence* and the discussion of illuminated printing; its significance as satire was first emphasized in Frye's *Fearful Symmetry* (1947). Like most satire, this work has a strongly topical flavor and a number of the fifteen characters who appear in it have been conjecturally related to various people in Blake's circle. Of these only Blake himself as Quid the Cynic and his brother Robert as Suction the Epicurean seem fairly certain identifications, though like their friends these "philosophers" are caricatures rather than lifelike portraits. The Islanders, like most characters in satire, are probably composites. Our notes on conjectured prototypes are meant as examples of the kinds of personalities among Blake's contemporaries who displayed the absurdities and whimsies held up to ridicule, but Blake's satiric target is foolishness rather than specific fools.

Though the major characters are fictional, such historical personages as the great surgeon John Hunter and the critic Samuel Johnson appear in the work as topics of conversation. There is also much talk of current fads: as Erdman notes, the reference to "Balloon hats" (chapter 8), which were in style for only a short time following Vincent Lunardi's balloon ascent in London in September 1784, helps establish the date of composition. A date of late 1784 is further corroborated by the reference to Dr. Johnson's experience in the afterlife: Johnson died in December 1784.

The alternation of spirited dialogue and songs has suggestive affinities with theatrical pieces, as Martha W. England has noted in her account of Samuel Foote's long-running vaudeville matinee, "Tea in the Haymarket," which opened in 1747 (see *Blake's Visionary Forms Dramatic,* ed. David V. Erdman and John E. Grant, Princeton, 1970). One can imagine *An Island in the Moon* as an entertainment for Blake's friends, perhaps along the lines of Everett Frost's production of Blake's piece as a radio play for Pacifica Radio in 1976—though Blake's manuscript is set up as narrative rather than drama. The closest literary affinities of *An Island in the Moon* are with short satirical "novels" such as Thomas Love Peacock's *Nightmare Abbey* (1818).

Underneath the preoccupations with fashionable literature, philosophy, religion, and mythology, one senses the emptiness of this salon style of life —the constant drifting from house to house in search of diversion, the isolation amid continual chit-chat, the pseudointellectual arguments that go nowhere. Perhaps Sipsop's response to Quid's song about "Old Corruption" indicates that satire can be effective even in the absence of moral norms. Sipsop doesn't know who is in the right, but he drops his own game and allows himself a moment of utter revulsion to the pain caused by his surgical operations. This is practically the only genuine expression of feeling in the story.

Written when Blake was twenty-seven, *An Island in the Moon* refutes the common supposition that the poet was naive at the age of thirty-two when he published *Songs of Innocence*. Yet it also affirms the power of innocence in a society permeated by boredom, frustration, and complacency—for example, in the hush that falls over the group after Obtuse Angle's performance of "Holy Thursday." The work, though difficult to read in its unpunctuated state, lacks nothing it needs except the missing pages. The gap in the manuscript at the point describing a technique of illuminated printing, though tantalizing, is probably not an indication of lost secrets. There is no evidence that Blake had worked out his distinctive process before 1788; his Prospectus of 1793 is the first reliable account of his special methods. Our text for *Island* is based on a collation of the Keynes and Erdman texts.

An Island in the Moon

Chap. 1

In the Moon is a certain Island near by a mighty continent, which small island seems to have some affinity to England, &, what is more extraordinary, the people are so much alike, & their language so much the same, that you would think you was among your friends. In this Island dwells three Philosophers—Suction the Epicurean, Quid the Cynic, & Sipsop the Pythagorean. I call them by the names of these sects, tho the sects are not ever mentiond there, as being quite out of date; however, the things still remain, and the vanities are the same.[1]

The three Philosophers sat together thinking of nothing. In comes Etruscan Column the Antiquarian,[2] & after an abundance of Enquiries to no purpose, sat himself down & described something that nobody listend to. So they were employd when Mrs. Gimblet came in, tipsy. The corners of her mouth seem'd—I don't know how, but very odd, as if she hoped you had not an ill opinion of

1. In the *Descriptive Catalogue*, the Canterbury Pilgrims are described as "the characters which compose all ages and nations. . . . We see the same characters repeated again and again. . . ." Above all, the Islanders shun anything that is "quite out of date."

2. G. M. Harper, in *The Neoplatonism of William Blake* (1961), suggests the Reverend John Brand (1744–1806), appointed secretary to the Society of Antiquaries in 1784, author of *Observations on Popular Antiquities* (1777).

her. To be sure, we are all poor creatures. Well, she seated [herself] & seemd to listen with great attention while the Antiquarian seemd to be talking of virtuous cats.[3] But it was not so; she was thinking of the shape of her eyes & mouth, & he was thinking of his eternal fame. The three Philosophers at this time were each endeavouring to conceal his laughter, not at them, but at his own imaginations.

This was the situation of this improving company when, in a great hurry, Inflammable Gass the Wind-finder[4] enterd. They seemd to rise & salute each other. Etruscan Column & Inflammable Gass fixd their eyes on each other; their tongues went in question & answer, but their thoughts were otherwise employd. "I don't like his eyes," said Etruscan Column. "He's a foolish puppy," said Inflammable Gass, smiling on him. The three Philosophers—the Cynic smiling, the Epicurean seeming studying the flame of the candle, & the Pythagorean playing with the cat—listend with open mouths to the edifying discourses.

"Sir," said the Antiquarian, "I have seen these works,[5] & I do affirm that they are no such thing. They seem to me to be the most wretched, paltry, flimsy stuff that ever—"

"What d'ye say? What d'ye say?" said Inflammable Gass. "Why—why, I wish I could see you write so."

"Sir," said the Antiquarian, "according to my opinion the author is an errant blockhead."

"Your reason—Your reason?" said Inflammable Gass. "Why—why, I think it very abominable to call a man a blockhead that you know nothing of."

"Reason, Sir?" said the Antiquarian. "I'll give you an example for your reason. As I was walking along the street I saw a vast number of swallows on the rails of an old Gothic square. They seemd to be going on their passage, as Pliny[6] says. As I was looking up, a little *outré* fellow, pulling me by the sleeve, cries, 'Pray, Sir, who do all they belong to?' I turnd myself about with great contempt. Said I,

3. According to Martha W. England, in *Blake's Visionary Forms Dramatic,* ed. David V. Erdman and John E. Grant (Princeton, 1970), one of Foote's comic routines spoofed a discussion by the Society of Antiquaries on the virtues of Dick Whittington's (1358?–1423) cat, who supposedly saved London from a plague of rats.

4. William Nicolson (1753–1815), author of *An Introduction to Natural Philosophy* (1782), according to Rodney M. and Mary R. Baine, *Blake Newsletter* number 38, 10 (1976), 51–52; or perhaps Gustavus Katterfelto, who performed three scientific stage shows daily (1783–84), or Dr. George Fordyce, who supplied hydrogen for Lunardi's balloon. Earlier scholars suggested Joseph Priestley (1733–1804), radical Dissenter and discoverer of oxygen. See Erdman, *Blake: Prophet Against Empire,* revised 1969, pp. 90–113.

5. Revealed later in this conversation to be the works of Voltaire. The Antiquarian rejects all modern writers; Inflammable Gass values only natural science, and Obtuse Angle, who joins the debate, appreciates only mathematical work.

6. The antiquarian's scientific authority is Pliny the Elder (A.D. 23–79), author of *Natural History,* who died while studying the eruption of Mount Vesuvius.

'Go along, you fool!' 'Fool!' said he, 'who do you call fool? I only ask'd you a civil question.' I had a great mind to have thrashd the fellow, only he was bigger than I." Here Etruscan Column left off—

Inflammable Gass, recollecting himself: "Indeed, I do not think the man was a fool, for he seems to me to have been desirous of enquiring into the works of nature!"

"Ha! Ha! Ha!" said the Pythagorean.

It was re-echo'd by Inflammable Gass to overthrow the argument.

Etruscan Column then, starting up & clenching both his fists, was prepared to give a formal answer to the company. But Obtuse Angle entering the room, having made a gentle bow, proceeded to empty his pockets of a vast number of papers, turned about & sat down, wiped his face with his pocket handkerchief, & shutting his eyes, began to scratch his head.

"Well, gentlemen," said he, "what is the cause of strife?"

The Cynic answer'd, "They are only quarreling about Voltaire."

"Yes," said the Epicurean, "& having a bit of fun with him."

"And," said the Pythagorean, "endeavoring to incorporate their souls with their bodies."

Obtuse Angle, giving a grin, said, "Voltaire understood nothing of the Mathematics, and a man must be a fool, i'faith, not to understand the Mathematics."

Inflammable Gass, turning round hastily in his chair, said, "Mathematics! He found out a number of Queries in Philosophy."

Obtuse Angle, shutting his eyes & saying that he always understood better when he shut his eyes: "In the first place, it is of no use for a man to make Queries, but to solve them; for a man may be a fool & make Queries, but a man must have a good sound sense to solve them. A query & an answer are as different as a strait line & a crooked one. Secondly—"

"I—I—I—aye! Secondly, Voltaire's a fool," sayd the Epicurean.

"Pooh!" says the Mathematician, scratching his head with double violence, "It is not worth Quarreling about."

The Antiquarian here got up &, hemming twice to shew the strength of his Lungs, said, "But, my Good Sir, Voltaire was immersed in matter, & seems to have understood very little but what he saw before his eyes, like the Animal upon the Pythagorean's lap, always playing with its own tail."

"Ha! Ha! Ha!" said Inflammable Gass. "He was the Glory of France. I have got a bottle of air that would spread a Plague."[7]

Here the Antiquarian shruggd up his shoulders, & was silent while Inflammable Gass talkd for half an hour.

7. "Flogiston" (phlogiston) was theoretically the inflammable principle of fire; in chapter 10 it is revealed to be gas from a privy.

When Steelyard the lawgiver coming in stalking, with an act of Parliament in his hand, said that it was a shameful thing that acts of Parliament should be in a free state, it had so engrossed his mind that he did not salute the company.

Mrs. Gimblet drew her mouth downwards.

Chap. 2

Tilly Lally, the Siptippidist, Aradobo, the Dean of Morocco, Miss Gittipin, Mrs. Nannicantipot, Mrs. Sigtagatist, Gibble Gabble, the wife of Inflammable Gass, & Little Scopprell enter'd the room.

(If I have not presented you with every character in the piece, call me Ass.)

Chap. 3

In the Moon, as Phebus stood over his oriental Gardening—"O ay, come, I'll sing you a song," said the Cynic.

"The trumpeter shit in his hat," said the Epicurean.

"—& clapt it on his head," said the Pythagorean.

"I'll begin again," said the Cynic.

Little Phebus came strutting in
With his fat belly & his round chin,
What is it you would please to have?
Ho! Ho!
I won't let it go at only so & so.

Mrs. Gimblet lookd as if they meant her. Tilly Lally laught like a cherry clapper. Aradobo askd, "Who was Phebus, Sir?"

Obtuse Angle answerd quickly, "He was the God of Physic, Painting, Perspective, Geometry, Geography, Astronomy, Cookery, Chymistry, Mechanics, Tactics, Pathology, Phraseology, Theology, Mythology, Astrology, Osteology, Somatology—in short, every art & science adornd him as beads round his neck."[8]

Here Aradobo look'd Astonishd & askd if he understood Engraving.

Obtuse Angle answerd, "Indeed he did."

"Well," said the other, "he was as great as Chatterton."

Tilly Lally turnd round to Obtuse Angle & askd who it was that was as great as Chatterton.

"Hay! How should I know?" answerd Obtuse Angle. "Who was It, Aradobo?"

"Why sir," said he, "the Gentleman that the song was about."

"Ah," said Tilly Lally, "I did not hear it. What was it, Obtuse Angle?"

8. These accomplishments of Phoebus Apollo, as Erdman points out, are the ones that a well-known *Theory of Painting* prescribes for painters.

"Pooh," said he. "Nonsense!"

"Mhm," said Tilly Lally.

"It was Phebus," said the Epicurean.

"Ah, that was the Gentleman," said Aradobo.

"Pray, Sir," said Tilly Lally, "who was Phebus?"

Obtuse Angle answer'd, "The heathens in the old ages usd to have Gods that they worshipd, & they usd to sacrifice to them. You have read about that in the Bible."

"Ah," said Aradobo, "I thought I had read of Phebus in the Bible."

"Aradobo, you should always think before you speak," said Obtuse Angle.

"Ha! Ha! Ha! He means Pharaoh," said Tilly Lally.

"I am ashamd of you,—making use of the names in the Bible," said Mrs. Sigtagatist.

"I'll tell you what, Mrs. Sinagain.[9] I don't think there's any harm in it," said Tilly Lally.

"No," said Inflammable Gass. "I have got a camera obscura[1] at home—What was it you was talking about?"

"Law!" said Tilly Lally. "What has that to do with Pharaoh?"

"Pho! nonsense! hang Pharoh & all his host," said the Pythagorean. "Sing away, Quid."

Then the Cynic sung—

> Honour & Genius is all I ask
> And I ask the Gods no more.[2]

No more, No more, } the three Philosophers
No more, No more. } bear Chorus.

Here Aradobo suckd his under lip.

Chap. 4

"Hang names!" said the Pythagorean, "What's Pharaoh better than Phebus, or Phebus than Pharoh?"

"Hang them both," said the Cynic.

"Don't be prophane," said Mrs. Sigtagatist.

"Why," said Mrs. Nannicantipot, "I don't think its prophane to say 'Hang Pharoh.' "

"Ah," said Mrs. Sinagain. "I'm sure you ought to hold your

9. Alternate name for Mrs. Sigtagatist.

1. A darkened chamber into which images of objects enter through an aperture and are projected on a surface. Everett Frost, in notes to his production for Pacifica radio, 1976, remarks that this device is used to view eclipses of the sun; perhaps this is the connection with Apollo.

2. Said by W. H. Stevenson, in annotations to *The Poems of William Blake* (1971), to be a parody of a song in James Harris's *Daphnis and Amaryllis* (1762).

tongue, for you never say any thing about the scriptures, & you hinder your husband from going to church."

"Ha, ha!" said Inflammable Gass. "What! don't you like to go to church?"

"No," said Mrs. Nannicantipot. "I think a person may be as good at home."

"If I had not a place of profit that forces me to go to church," said Inflammable Gass, "I'd see the parsons all hangd,—a parcel of lying—"

"O!" said Mrs. Sigtagatist. "If it was not for churches & chapels I should not have livd so long. There was I, up in a Morning at four o'clock, when I was a Girl. I would run like the dickins till I was all in a heat. I would stand till I was ready to sink into the earth. Ah, Mr. Huffcap[3] would kick the bottom of the Pulpit out with Passion, would tear off the sleeve of his Gown & set his wig on fire & throw it at the people. He'd cry & stamp & kick & sweat—and all for the good of their souls."

"I'm sure he must be a wicked villain," said Mrs. Nannicantipot, "a passionate wretch. If I was a man I'd wait at the bottom of the pulpit stairs & knock him down & run away!"

"You would, you Ignorant jade? I wish I could see you hit any of the ministers! You deserve to have your ears boxed, you do."

"I'm sure this is not religion," answers the other.

Then Mr. Inflammable Gass ran & shovd his head into the fire & set his hair all in a flame, & ran about the room,—No, no, he did not; I was only making a fool of you.

Chap. 5

Obtuse Angle, Scopprell, Aradobo, & Tilly Lally are all met in Obtuse Angle's study.

"Pray," said Aradobo, "is Chatterton a Mathematician?"

"No," said Obtuse Angle. "How can you be so foolish as to think he was?"

"Oh, I did not think he was—I only ask'd," said Aradobo.

"How could you think he was not, & ask if he was?" said Obtuse Angle.

"Oh no, Sir. I did not think he was, before you told me, but afterwards I thought he was not."

Obtuse Angle said, "In the first place you thought he was, & then afterwards when I said he was not, you thought he was not. Why, I know that—"

3. According to Erdman, a satire on George Whitefield (1714–70), the Methodist evangelist. His enthusiasm was also satirized by Foote in *The Minor* (1760) and by Hogarth in *Credulity, Superstition and Fanaticism* (1762). Whitefield is presented sympathetically in *Jerusalem* 72:51.

"Oh, no, sir, I thought that he was not, but I askd to know whether he was."

"How can that be?" said Obtuse Angle. "How could you ask & think that he was not?"

"Why," said he, "it came into my head that he was not."

"Why then," said Obtuse Angle, "you said that he was."

"Did I say so! Law! I did not think I said that."

"Did not he?" said Obtuse Angle.

"Yes," said Scopprell.

"But I meant—" said Aradobo, "I—I—I can't think. Law! Sir, I wish you'd tell me how it is."

Then Obtuse Angle put his chin in his hand & said, "Whenever you think, you must always think for yourself."

"How, sir?" said Aradobo. "Whenever I think, I must think myself? I think I do. In the first place—" said he with a grin.

"Poo! Poo!" said Obtuse Angle. "Don't be a fool."

Then Tilly Lally took up a Quadrant & askd, "Is not this a sun-dial?"

"Yes," said Scopprell, "but it's broke."

At this moment the three Philosophers enterd, and lowring darkness hover'd o'er the assembly.

"Come," said the Epicurean, "let's have some rum & water, & hang the mathematics! Come, Aradobo! Say something."

Then Aradobo began: "In the first place I think . . . I think in the first place that Chatterton was clever at Fissic, Follogy, Pistinology, Aridology, Arography, Transmography, Phizography, Hogamy, Hatomy, & hall that, but, in the first place, he eat wery little, wickly —that is, he slept very little, which he brought into a consumsion; & what was that that he took? Fissic or somethink—& so died!"[4]

So all the people in the book enterd into the room, & they could not talk any more to the present purpose.

Chap. 6

Then all went home & left the Philosophers. Then Suction Askd if Pindar was not a better Poet than Ghiotto was a Painter.

"Plutarch has not the Life of Ghiotto," said Sipsop.

"No," said Quid, "to be sure, he was an Italian."

"Well," said Suction, "that is not any proof."

"Plutarch was a nasty ignorant puppy," said Quid. "I hate your sneaking rascals. There's Aradobo in ten or twelve years will be a far superior genius."

4. On August 24, 1770, Thomas Chatterton, a seventeen-year-old poet from Bristol, poisoned himself after questions were raised about the authenticity of his poems, which purported to be translations of medieval verse. Unlike Quid in *Island*, Blake himself declared in 1825 that he believed Chatterton's claim.

"Ah!" said Pythagorean, "Aradobo will make a very clever fellow."

"Why," said Quid, "I think that any natural fool would make a clever fellow, if he was properly brought up."

"Ah, hang your reasoning!" said the Epicurean. "I hate reasoning. I do everything by my feelings."

"Ah!" said Sipsop, "I only wish Jack Tearguts[5] had had the cutting of Plutarch. He understands Anatomy better than any of the Ancients. He'll plunge his knife up to the hilt in a single drive and thrust his fist in, and all in the space of a Quarter of an hour. He does not mind their crying, tho they cry ever so. He'll swear at them & keep them down with his fist, & tell them that he'll scrape their bones if they don't lay still & be quiet. What the devil should the people in the hospital that have it done for nothing make such a piece of work for?"

"Hang that," said Suction; "let us have a Song."

Then the Cynic sang—

1

When Old Corruption[6] first begun,
   Adornd in yellow vest,
He committed on Flesh a whoredom—
   O, what a wicked beast!

2

From them a callow babe did spring,
   And Old Corruption smild
To think his race should never end,
   For now he had a child.

3

He call'd him Surgery, & fed
   The babe with his own milk,
For Flesh & he could ne'er agree,
   She would not let him suck.

4

And this he always kept in mind,
   And formd a crooked knife,
And ran about with bloody hands
   To seek his mother's life.

5

And as he ran to seek his mother
   He met with a dead woman,
He fell in love & married her,
   A deed which is not common.

6

She soon grew pregnant & brought forth
   Scurvy & Spott'd Fever.

5. Blake first wrote "Hunter" for the surname, thus making explicit reference to the father of modern surgery (1728–93).

6. Radical slang for the governmental establishment.

The father grind & skipt about,
And said, "I'm made for ever!

7

"For now I have procurd these imps
I'll try experiments."
With that he tied poor Scurvy down
& stopt up all its vents.

8

And when the child began to swell,
He shouted out aloud,
"I've found the dropsy out, & soon
Shall do the world more good."

9

He took up Fever by the neck
And cut out all its spots,
And thro the holes which he had made
He first discover'd guts.

"Ah," said Sipsop, "you think we are rascals—& we think you are rascals. I do as I chuse. What is it to any body what I do? I am always unhappy too. When I think of Surgery—I don't know.—I do it because I like it. My father does what he likes & so do I. I think, somehow, I'll leave it off. There was a woman having her cancer cut, & she shriekd so that I was quite sick."

Chap. 7

"Good-night," said Sipsop.

"Good-night," said the other two.

Then Quid & Suction were left alone. Then said Quid: "I think that Homer is bombast, & Shakespeare is too wild, & Milton has no feelings: they might be easily outdone. Chatterton never writ those poems! A parcel of fools, going to Bristol! If I was to go, I'd find it out in a minute, but I've found it out already."

"If I don't knock them all up next year in the Exhibition,[7] I'll be hangd," said Suction. "Hang Philosophy! I would not give a farthing for it! Do all by your feelings, and never think at all about it. I'm hangd if I don't get up to-morrow morning by four o'clock & work Sir Joshua."[8]

"Before ten years are at an end," said Quid, "how I will work those poor milksop devils,—an ignorant pack of wretches!"

So they went to bed.

Chap. 8

Steelyard the Lawgiver, sitting at his table, taking extracts from

7. The annual spring exhibition at the Royal Academy of Art; in 1784 Blake displayed two drawings, in 1785 four.

8. In 1798–1808 Blake attacked Sir Joshua Reynolds (1723–93), portrait painter and first president of the Royal Academy, in his annotations to *Discourses on Art* (p. 438).

Hervey's *Meditations Among the Tombs* & Young's *Night Thoughts*:[9]

"He is not able to hurt me," said he, "more than making me Constable or taking away the parish business. Hah!

'My crop of corn is but a field of tares.'[1]

Says Jerome:[2] 'Happiness is not for us poor crawling reptiles of the earth.' Talk of happiness & happiness! It's no such thing. Every person has a something.

Hear then the pride & knowledge of a Sailor,
His spirit sail, fore sail, main sail, & his mizen.
A poor frail man! God wot, I know none frailer.
I know no greater sinner than John Taylor.[3]

If I had only myself to care for I'd soon make Double Elephant look foolish, & Filligreework.[4] I hope I shall live to see—

'The wreck of matter & the crush of worlds',

as Young says."

Obtuse Angle enter'd the Room.

"What news, Mr. Steelyard?"

"I am reading *Theron & Aspasio*,"[5] said he.

Obtuse Angle took up the books one by one.

"I don't find it here," said he.

"O no," said the other, "it was the *Meditations*!"

Obtuse Angle took up the book & read till the other was quite tir'd out.

Then Scopprell & Miss Gittipin coming in, Scopprell took up a book & read the following passage:—

9. Perhaps about 1820 Blake painted an "epitome" of the *Meditations* (1746) with affinities to his paintings of the Last Judgment and Jacob's Ladder. James Hervey (1714–1758) was an early Methodist; in *Jerusalem* 72:51 he is, with Whitefield, presented sympathetically as a guard of the Gate toward Beulah and a guide to the "great Winepress of Love." Edward Young's *Night Thoughts* (1745) contains lugubrious "thoughts on Life, Death, and Immortality." This work was the subject of Blake's largest commercial project; he painted 537 watercolor illustrations and engraved 43, which were published in 1797.

1. From Chidiock Tichborne's "On the Eve of His Execution" (1586), written in the Tower of London at the age of eighteen.

2. Saint Jerome (A.D. 340?–420) lived six years as a desert hermit and renounced secular learning to translate the Bible into Latin (the Vulgate).

3. Either the dissenting clergyman and Hebraist (1694–1761) who wrote *The Scripture Doctrine of Original Sin* (1740); or a poet, pamphleteer, satirist, and sailor (1580–1653).

4. The largest size of art paper and tiny ornamental wirework; refers to huge and tiny books and evidently to specific artists who did such work. Miss Gittipin's quite different characterization of these names, her dislike of books, and Steelyard's reactions to her speeches suggest a long-standing disagreement between an incompatible couple. Flaxman resembled the Lawgiver in that at this time he held a petty bureaucratic job and was fond of religious literature; he later became a Swedenborgian.

5. Another work by Hervey (1775). The quotation attributed to Young is actually in Addison's *Cato,* V, i, 28 (produced 1713).

"*An Easy of Huming Understanding,*[6] by John Lookye Gent."

"John Locke," said Obtuse Angle.

"O, ay—Lock," said Scopprell.

"Now here," said Miss Gittipin,—"I never saw such company in my life. You are always talking of your books. I like to be where we talk. You had better take a walk, that we may have some pleasure. I am sure I never see any pleasure. There's Double Elephant's Girls, they have their own way; & there's Miss Filligreework, she goes out in her coaches, & her footman & her maids, & Stormonts & Balloon hats, & a pair of Gloves every day, & the Sorrows of Werter, & Robinsons, & the Queen of France's Puss colour,[7] & my Cousin Gibble Gabble says that I am like nobody else. I might as well be in a nunnery. There they go in Postchaises & Stages to Vauxhall & Ranelagh.[8] And I hardly know what a coach is, except when I go to Mr. Jacko's.[9] He knows what riding is, & his wife is the most agreeable woman—you hardly know she has a tongue in her head. And he is the funniest fellow, & I do believe he'll go in partnership with his master, & they have black servants lodge at their house. I never saw such a place in my life! He says he has six & twenty rooms in his house, and I believe it, & he is not such a liar as Quid thinks he is."

"Poo! Poo! Hold your tongue," said the Lawgiver.

This quite provokd Miss Gittipin, to interrupt her in her favourite topic, & she proceeded to use every Provoking speech that ever she could, & he bore it more like a Saint than a Lawgiver, and with great solemnity he address'd the company in these words:

"They call women the weakest vessel, but I think they are the strongest. A girl has always more tongue than a boy. I have seen a little brat no higher than a nettle, & she had as much tongue as a city clark; but a boy would be such a fool, not have any thing to say, and if anybody askd him a question he would put his head into a hole & hide it. I am sure I take but little pleasure. You have as much pleasure as I have. There I stand & bear every fool's insult. If I had only myself to care for, I'd wring off their noses."

To this Scopprell answer'd, "I think the Ladies' discourses, Mr.

6. *An Essay on Human Understanding* (1690) by John Locke (1632–1704). Scopprell blunders into a pun on David Hume (1711–76), another rationalist and empiricist philosopher. Blake detested both for their denunciation of "enthusiasm" and regarded Locke's name as poetic justice.

7. "Sorrows of Werther" was a hat style named after Goethe's novel of 1774. Mrs. Mary ("Perdita") Robinson, an actress, poetess, and former mistress of the Prince of Wales, set the fashions until she was crippled at the end of 1784. "Puss color" was Marie Antoinette's favorite *puce* ("flea") color.

8. Fashionable public gardens and amusement parks (see map).

9. Famous Parisian monkey that performed at Astley's Royal Amphitheatre in the summer of 1784; here probably the name for Richard Cosway (1740–1821), a rich miniature painter and dandy who in 1781 married Maria, an Italian beauty, and entertained celebrities in Schomberg House, where he moved in 1784. Cosway's "master" would be his patron, the Prince of Wales.

Steelyard, are some of them more improving than any book. That is the way I have got some of my knowledge."

"Then," said Miss Gittipin, "Mr. Scopprell, do you know the song of *Phebe and Jellicoe?*"[1]

"No, Miss," said Scopprell.

Then she repeated these verses, while Steelyard walkd about the room:

Phebe, dresst like beautie's Queen,
Jellicoe in faint pea green,
Sitting all beneath a grot
Where the little lambkins trot;

Maidens dancing, loves a-sporting,
All the country folks a-courting,
Susan, Johnny, Bet, & Joe
Lightly tripping on a row.

Happy people, who can be
In happiness compard with ye?
The Pilgrim with his crook & hat
Sees your happiness compleat.

"A charming song, indeed, Miss," said Scopprell. Here they receivd a summons for a merry making at the Philosophers' house.

Chap. 9

"I say, this evening we'll all get drunk. I say—dash!—an Anthem, an Anthem!" said Suction.

Lo the Bat with Leathern wing,[2]
Winking & blinking,
Winking & blinking,
Winking & blinking,
Like Doctor Johnson.

Quid: "Oho," said Dr. Johnson
To Scipio Africanus,[3]
"If you don't own me a Philosopher,
I'll kick your Roman Anus."

1. Partly a parody of a poem "On Miss C——" by Ambrose Philips (1674–1749), nicknamed "Namby-pamby" because of his insipid verses. This poem had been held up for derision in Pope's *Peri Bathos* or *The Art of Sinking in Poetry* (1727) under the category of "The Infantine."

2. "Ode to Evening" (lines 9–10) by William Collins (1721–59). The conservative man of letters, Dr. Samuel Johnson (1709–84), whose eyesight was bad, has just died on December 13 and is having an encounter in the underworld.

3. The father (237?–183 B.C.) defeated Hannibal; the son (185–129 B.C.) destroyed Carthage.

Suction: "Aha," to Dr. Johnson
Said Scipio Africanus,
"Lift up my Roman Petticoat
And kiss my Roman Anus."

And the Cellar goes down with a step.
(Grand Chorus).

"Ho, Ho, Ho, Ho, Ho, Ho, Ho, Hooooo, my poooooor siiides! I, I should die if I was to live here!" said Scopprell. "Ho, Ho, Ho, Ho, Ho!"

1st Vo. "Want Matches?"[4]
2nd Vo. "Yes, yes, yes."
1st Vo. "Want Matches?"
2nd Vo. "No—"

1st Vo. "Want Matches?"
2nd Vo. "Yes, yes, yes."
1st Vo. "Want Matches?"
2nd Vo. "No—"

Here was great confusion & disorder. Aradobo said that the boys in the street sing something very pretty & funny about London—O no, about Matches. Then Mrs. Nannicantipot sung:

I cry my matches as far as Guild hall;
God bless the duke & his aldermen all!

Then sung Scopprell:

I ask the Gods no more,—
no more, no more.

Then said Suction, "Come, Mr. Lawgiver, your song"; and the Lawgiver sung:

As I walkd forth one May morning
To see the fields so pleasant & so gay,
O there did I spy a young maiden sweet,
Among the Violets that smell so sweet,
Smell so sweet,
Smell so sweet,
Among the Violets that smell so sweet.

"Hang your Violets! Here's your Rum & water! O ay," said Tilly Lally, "Joe Bradley & I was going along one day in the Sugar-house.

4. In view of chapter 2 one expects this street cry to be sung by some of the merrymakers, but probably it comes from poor people outside whose voices faintly penetrate the party. Mrs. Nannicantipot's song, which blesses authorities, is the voice of the beneficiaries of the system; it is complemented by Scopprell's complacence.

Joe Bradley saw—for he had but one eye—saw a treacle Jar. So he goes of his blind side & dips his hand up to the shoulder in treacle. 'Here, lick, lick, lick!' said he. Ha! Ha! Ha! Ha! For he had but one eye. Ha! Ha! Ha! Ho!"

Then sung Scopprell:

And I ask the Gods no more,—
no more, no more,
no more, no more.

"Miss Gittipin," said he, "you sing like a harpsichord. Let your bounty descend to our fair ears and favour us with a fine song."

Then she sung:

This frog he would a-wooing ride,[5]
Kitty alone—Kitty alone—
This frog he would a-wooing ride:
Kitty alone & I.
Sing cock, I cary Kitty alone:
Kitty alone—Kitty alone—
Cock, I cary Kitty alone:
Kitty alone & I.'

"Charming! Truly elegant!" said Scopprell.
"And I ask the gods no more!"

"Hang your serious songs!" said Sipsop, & he sung as follows:

Fa ra so bo ro
Fa ra bo ra
Sa ba ra ra ba rare roro
Sa ra ra ra bo ro ro ro
Radara
Sarapodo no flo ro.

"Hang Italian songs! Let's have English!" said Quid. "English genius for ever! Here I go":

Hail Matrimony, made of Love,
To thy wide gates how great a drove
On purpose to be yok'd do come!
Widows & maids & Youths also,
That lightly trip on beauty's toe,
Or sit on beauty's bum.

Hail, finger-footed lovely Creatures!
The females of our human Natures,
Formed to suckle all Mankind.
'Tis you that come in time of need;

5. A traditional nursery rhyme.

Without you we should never Breed,
  Or any Comfort find.

For if a Damsel's blind or lame,
Or Nature's hand has crooked her frame,
  Or if she's deaf, or is wall eyed,
Yet if her heart is well inclined,
Some tender lover she shall find
  That panteth for a Bride.

The universal Poultice this,
To cure whatever is amiss
  In Damsel or in Widow gay.
It makes them smile, it makes them skip,
Like Birds just cured of the pip,
  They chirp, & hop away.

Then come ye Maidens, come ye Swains,
Come & be cured of all your pains
  In Matrimony's Golden cage.[6]

"Go & be hanged!" said Scopprell. "How can you have the face to make game of Matrimony?"

["What, you skipping flea, how dare ye? I'll dash you through your chair;" says the Cynic.

"This Quid," cries out Miss Gittipin, "always spoils good company in this manner & it's a shame."][7]

Then Quid call'd upon Obtuse Angle for a Song, & he, wiping his face & looking on the corner of the ceiling, sang:

To be, or not to be
Of great capacity,
  Like Sir Isaac Newton,
Or Locke, or Doctor South,
Or Sherlock upon death?
  I'd rather be Sutton.[8]

For he did build a house
For aged men & youth,
  With walls of brick & stone.
He furnish'd it within
With whatever he could win,
  And all his own.

6. Cf. "How sweet I roam'd," line 12.
7. This and the preceding paragraph were deleted from this manuscript by Blake.
8. In *Animadversions* (1690) Robert South (1634–1715), a celebrated Anglican preacher, attacked Dr. William Sherlock (164?–1707), dean of St. Paul's and author of *Practical Discourse Concerning Death* (1689). Thomas Sutton (1532–1611), a philanthropic coal mine owner, founded the Charterhouse ("Sutton's Hospital," 1611), a charity home and school for boys (see map).

He drew out of the Stocks
His money in a box,
  And sent his servant
To Green the Bricklayer
And to the Carpenter:
  He was so fervent.

The chimneys were three score,
The windows many more,
  And for convenience
He sinks & gutters made
And all the way he pav'd
  To hinder pestilence.

Was not this a good man,
Whose life was but a span,
  Whose name was Sutton,—
As Locke, or Doctor South,
Or Sherlock upon Death,
  Or Sir Isaac Newton?

The Lawgiver was very attentive & beg'd to have it sung over again & again, till the company were tired & insisted on the Lawgiver singing a song himself, which he readily complied with:

This city & this country has brought forth many mayors,
To sit in state & give forth laws out of their old oak chairs,
With face as brown as any nut, with drinking of strong ale;
Good English hospitality, O then it did not fail!

With scarlet gowns & broad gold lace would make a yeoman sweat,
With stockings rolld about their knees & shoes as black as jet,
With eating beef & drinking beer, O they were stout & hale!
Good English hospitality, O then it did not fail!

Thus sitting at the table wide, the Mayor & Aldermen
Were fit to give law to the city; each eat as much as ten.
The hungry poor enter'd the hall, to eat good beef & ale.
Good English hospitality, O then it did not fail![9]

Here they gave a shout, & the company broke up.

Chap. 10

Thus these happy Islanders spent their time. But felicity does not last long, for being met at the house of Inflammable Gass the windfinder, the following affairs happen'd.

9. In spirit this song recalls Fielding's "The Roast Beef of Old England" from the *Grub Street Opera.* In plate VIII of Hogarth's *Industry and Idleness* (1747) the poor are excluded from the feast, but in Hogarth's *Beer Street* (1750–51) all are jolly on good English beer.

"Come, Flammable," said Gibble Gabble, "& let's enjoy ourselves. Bring the Puppets."

"Hay,—Hay," said he, "you—sho—why—ya, ya. How can you be so foolish? Ha! Ha! Ha! She calls the experiments puppets!"

Then he went up stairs & loaded the maid with glasses, & brass tubes, & magic pictures.

"Here, ladies & gentlemen," said he, "I'll shew you a louse, or a flea, or a butterfly, or a cockchafer, the blade bone of a tittleback. No, no. Here's a bottle of wind that I took up in the boghouse, and —O dear, O dear, the water's got into the sliders! Look here, Gibble Gabble! Lend me your handkerchief, Tilly Lally."

Tilly Lally took out his handkerchief, which smeard the glass worse than ever. Then he screwd it on. Then he took the sliders, & then he set up the glasses for the Ladies to view the pictures. Thus he was employd, & quite out of breath. While Tilly Lally & Scopprell were pumping at the air-pump, "Smack" went the glass.

"Hang!" said Tilly Lally.

Inflammable Gass turnd short round & threw down the table & Glasses, & Pictures, & broke the bottles of wind, & let out the Pestilence. He saw the Pestilence fly out of the bottle, & cried out, while he ran out of the room:

"Come out! Come out! We are putrified! We are corrupted! Our lungs are destroyd with the Flogiston.[1] This will spread a plague all thro the Island!"

He was downstairs the very first. On the back of him came all the others in a heap.

So they need not bidding [to] go.

Chap. 11

Another merry meeting at the house of Steelyard the Lawgiver.

After supper, Steelyard & Obtuse Angle had pumpd Inflammable Gass quite dry. They playd at Forfeits, & tryd every method to get good humour.

Said Miss Gittipin: "Pray, Mr. Obtuse Angle, sing us a song."

Then he sung:

Upon a holy Thursday, their innocent faces clean,
The children walking two & two in grey & blue & green,
Grey headed beadles walk'd before, with wands as white as snow,
Till into the high dome of Paul's they like Thames' waters flow.

O what a multitude they seemd, these flowers of London town!
Seated in companies, they sit with radiance all their own.

1. Phlogiston, the hypothetical principle of fire as a material substance, was also supposed to cause plagues. Inflammable Gas has discovered methane gas in the privy.

The hum of multitudes were there, but multitudes of lambs,
Thousands of little girls & boys raising their innocent hands.

Then, like a mighty wind, they raise to heavn the voice of song,
Or like harmonious thunderings the seats of heavn among.
Beneath them sit the revrend men, the guardians of the poor;
Then cherish pity lest you drive an angel from your door.

After this they all sat silent for a quarter of an hour, & Mrs. Nannicantipot said, "It puts me in Mind of my mother's song:

When the tongues of children are heard on the green,
And laughing is heard on the hill,
My heart is at rest within my breast,
And every thing else is still.

"Then come home, my children, the sun is gone down,
And the dews of night arise;
Come, Come, leave off play, & let us away
Till the morning appears in the skies."

"No, No, let us play, for it is yet day,
And we cannot go to sleep:
Besides in the Sky the little birds fly,
And the meadows are cover'd with Sheep."

"Well, Well, go & play till the light fades away,
And then go home to bed."
The little ones leaped, & shouted, & laugh'd,
And all the hills ecchoed.

Then sung Quid:

"O father, father, where are you going?
O do not walk so fast;
O, speak, father, speak to your little boy,
Or else I shall be lost."

The night it was dark & no father was there,
And the child was wet with dew.
The mire was deep, & the child did weep,
And away the vapour flew.

Here nobody could sing any longer, till Tilly Lally pluckd up a spirit & he sung:

O I say you Joe,
Throw us the ball.
I've a good mind to go,
And leave you all.

I never saw such a bowler,
To bowl the ball in a turd,[2]
And to clean it with my hankercher,
Without saying a word.

That Bill's a foolish fellow,
He has given me a black eye.
He does not know how to handle a bat
Any more than a dog or a cat.
He has knockd down the wicket
And broke the stumps,
And runs without shoes to save his pumps.

Here a laugh began, and Miss Gittipin sung:

Leave, O leave me to my sorrows,
Here I'll sit & fade away,
Till I'm nothing but a spirit
And I lose this form of clay.

Then if chance along this forest
Any walk in pathless ways,
Thro the gloom he'll see my shadow,
Hear my voice upon the Breeze.

The Lawgiver all the while sat delighted to see them in such a serious humour. "Mr. Scopprell," said he, "you must be acquainted with a great many songs."

"Oh, dear sir! Ho, Ho, Ho, I am no singer. I must beg of one of these tender-hearted ladies to sing for me."

They all declined, & he was forced to sing himself:

There's Dr. Clash
And signior Falalasole:
O they sweep in the cash
Into their purse hole.
        Fa me la sol, La me fa sol.

Great A, little A,
Bouncing B.[3]
Play away, Play away,
You're out of the key.
        Fa me la sol, La me fa sol.

Musicians should have
A pair of very good ears,

2. Blake replaced this word with the euphemism "tansey," a yellow flower used in yellow puddings or cakes, but he neglected to change the rhyme.

3. A Mother Goose alphabet rhyme.

And Long fingers & thumbs,
And not like clumsy bears.
Fa me la sol, La me fa sol.

Gentlemen, Gentlemen!
Rap, rap, rap,
Fiddle, Fiddle, Fiddle,
Clap, Clap, Clap.
Fa me la sol, La me fa sol.

"Hm," said the Lawgiver, "Funny enough. Let's have Handel's water piece."[4] Then Sipsop sung:

A crowned king,
On a white horse sitting,
With his trumpets sounding,
And Banners flying,
Thro the clouds of smoke he makes his way.
And the shout of his thousands fills his heart with rejoicing & victory.
And the shout of his thousands fills his heart with rejoicing & victory.
Victory! Victory! 'twas William, the prince of Orange,—[5]

"—them, Illuminating the Manuscript."[6]

"Ay," said she, "that would be excellent."

"Then," said he, "I would have all the writing Engraved instead of Printed, & at every other leaf a high finishd print—all in three Volumes folio—& sell them a hundred pounds apiece. They would print off two thousand."

"Then," said she, "whoever will not have them will be ignorant fools, & will not deserve to live."

"Don't you think I have something of the Goat's face?" says he.

"Very like a Goat's face," she answer'd.

"I think your face," said he, "is like that noble beast the Tyger. Oh, I was at Mrs. Sicknacken's, & I was speaking of my abilities, but their nasty hearts, poor devils, are eat up with envy. They envy me my abilities, & all the Women envy your abilities."

"My dear, they hate people who are of higher abilities than their nasty, filthy Selves. But do you outface them, & then strangers will

4. The "Water Music" of Handel (1685–1759) was doubtless performed in London in the Handel festival of 1784.

5. William of Orange (1650–1702) led troops from Holland on November 5, 1688, to depose Catholic King James II in the Glorious Revolution which established the joint Protestant throne of William and Mary (sister of James II).

6. A leaf, or more, of the manuscript is missing just preceding this line. Damon suggests that the missing material was destroyed to keep secret Blake's method of printing, but an accident seems more probable. Quid's extravagant plans for mass production are not the same as those followed in the time-consuming process supposedly revealed to Blake by the spirit of his brother Robert in 1787–88. The woman Quid is speaking to is either Mrs. Nannicantipot or, less likely, Miss Gittipin.

see that you have an opinion—Now I think we should do as much good as we can when we are at Mr. Femality's.[7] Do you snap, & take me up, and I will fall into such a passion. I'll hollow and stamp, & frighten all the People there, & show them what truth is."

At this Instant Obtuse Angle came in.

"Oh, I am glad you are come," said Quid.

Prospectus†

TO THE PUBLIC

October 10, 1793

The Labours of the Artist, the Poet, the Musician, have been proverbially attended by poverty and obscurity; this was never the fault of the Public, but was owing to a neglect of means to propagate such works as have wholly absorbed the Man of Genius. Even Milton and Shakespeare could not publish their own works.

This difficulty has been obviated by the Author of the following productions now presented to the Public; who has invented a method of Printing both Letter-press and Engraving in a style more ornamental, uniform, and grand, than any before discovered, while it produces works at less than one fourth of the expense.

If a method of Printing which combines the Painter and the Poet is a phenomenon worthy of public attention, provided that it exceeds in elegance all former methods, the Author is sure of his reward.

Mr. Blake's powers of invention very early engaged the attention of many persons of eminence and fortune; by whose means he has been regularly enabled to bring before the Public works (he is not afraid to say) of equal magnitude and consequence with the productions of any age or country: among which are two large highly finished engravings (and two more are nearly ready) which will

7. In her unpublished study of underground religious groups from Blake to Yeats, Keith Schuchard suggests that this person is the Chevalier D'Eon, a French transvestite spy and member of British occultist circles in 1785 and later. Quid may resume speaking after the dash.

† This etched announcement was Blake's first attempt to advertise his unique works in illuminated printing. He also listed, as items one and two, examples of his work in ordinary engraving; item nine is now lost. *The Gates of Paradise,* item ten, is a little emblem book issued in 1793 with the heading *For Children*; it was revised to include verse and reissued about 1818 with the heading *For the Sexes.*

Our text is from the transcript in Alexander Gilchrist, *Life of William Blake, 'Pictor Ignotus,'* London and Cambridge: Macmillan, 1863), II, 263–64; Blake's original is now lost.

commence a Series of subjects from the Bible, and another from the History of England.

The following are the Subjects of the several Works now published on Sale at Mr. Blake's, No. 13, Hercules Buildings, Lambeth.

1. Job, a Historical Engraving. Size 1 ft. 7½ in. by 1 ft. 2 in.: price 12*s.*
2. Edward and Elinor, a Historical Engraving. Size 1 ft. 6½ in. by 1 ft.: price 10*s.* 6*d.*
3. America, a Prophecy, in Illuminated Printing. Folio, with 18 designs: price 10*s.* 6*d.*
4. Visions of the Daughters of Albion, in Illuminated Printing. Folio, with 8 designs, price 7*s.* 6*d.*
5. The Book of Thel, a Poem in Illuminated Printing. Quarto, with 6 designs, price 3*s.*
6. The Marriage of Heaven and Hell, in Illuminated Printing. Quarto, with 14 designs, price 7*s.* 6*d.*
7. Songs of Innocence, in Illuminated Printing. Octavo, with 25 designs, price 5*s.*
8. Songs of Experience, in Illuminated Printing. Octavo, with 25 designs, price 5*s.*
9. The History of England, a small book of Engravings. Price 3*s.*
10. The Gates of Paradise, a small book of Engravings. Price 3*s.*

The Illuminated Books are Printed in Colours, and on the most beautiful wove paper that could be procured.

No Subscriptions for the numerous great works now in hand are asked, for none are wanted; but the Author will produce his works, and offer them to sale at a fair price.

A *Descriptive Catalogue* and "An Advertisement"

The "Advertisement" and *Descriptive Catalogue* of Blake's single exhibition, held in 1809 in his brother's house, represent Blake's only attempt to explain his ideas in conventional printing. Due in part to the contemptuous notice of his designs for Robert Blair's *The Grave* in *The Examiner* of 1808, Blake chose in his *Catalogue* to put forward his opinions in an uncompromising manner that seemed provoking to those who held differing opinions. The one published review, by Robert Hunt, in *The Examiner* of September 17, 1809, was exceedingly hostile, dismissing Blake as a lunatic. While in the aggregate Blake's theories of art, philosophy, and mythological history were idiosyncratic, some aspects of his thought were shared by one or another of his contemporaries—for example, Henry Fuseli. At least two viewers met Blake's Miltonic standard: "Fit audience find tho' few." Charles Lamb attended the exhibition in June 1810 and was much impressed both by what he read and what he saw but unfortunately never published his opinions, though according to a letter of March 15, 1824, he vividly recalled some of the major pictures. Henry Crabb Robinson not only attended the show but purchased six copies of the *Catalogue* to give to friends and praised certain pictures and catalogue descriptions in his essay, "William Blake, Kunstler, Dichter and religiöser Schwärmer," *Vaterlandisches Museum*, January 1811.

Of the sixteen pictures exhibited, there is no evidence that any were purchased; however, since five have disappeared, it is not possible to be certain. Seven of the pictures already belonged to Blake's patron Thomas Butts and were lent for the occasion. The grandest and most controversial painting, now lost, was *The Ancient Britons*, which was intensely colored and measured some ten by fourteen feet. The primary purpose of the exhibition seems to have been to establish the validity of Blake's new method of "portable fresco" painting; pictures VI–IX are expressly referred to as "experiment pictures" and the comments on pictures I and II are chiefly about the medium employed. In part this emphasis on media was probably an attempt to avoid having to comment too explicitly on the anti-Establishmentarian implications of the pictorial allegory. But Blake did have something new and—as it proved—controversial to expound concerning his new (or rediscovered) medium. He was confident that he had perfected a way of painting in tempera—that is, watercolor—on a gesso ground applied to canvas, wood, or metal, so that pictures glowing with hard, enamellike color could be temporarily displayed on public buildings and then moved to accommodate new work. Durability, portability, and depth of color were regarded as the indubitable merits of oil painting, the most prestigious of all media. Blake wanted to combine the color values of the early Italian frescoes with the portability of oil paintings, but he detested oil as a medium. He was forced to concede in his *Catalogue*, however, that not all his frescoes were in good condition even in 1809. Nevertheless, his theories have been at least partially vindicated by the fact that some of his later frescoes are in nearly perfect condition, while many of the oil paintings by his contemporaries, including some famous ones by Reynolds, have cracked and faded badly.

One of the highlights of the *Descriptive Catalogue* is a figure-by-figure exposition of Blake's *Canterbury Pilgrims*, combined with what Lamb appreciated as a "most spirited criticism on Chaucer"; it is omitted from this edition because the brilliance of the particular observations can be appreciated only when one has available a reproduction of the picture large enough to permit detailed study (see Geoffrey Keynes, *Engravings by William Blake: The Separate Plates*, 1956, pp. 45–49 and pls. 27–33). Similarly, Blake presupposes a familiarity both with the contemporary British artistic scene and also with the work of earlier artists such as only a scholar can have nowadays; the issues have changed and the point of many of Blake's arguments would elude the reader who is not provided with more extensive editorial commentary than would be appropriate for this edition. We have featured Blake's aesthetic, ethical, and theological ideas, while retaining something of the flavor of his polemic.

An Advertisement

Exhibition of *Paintings in Fresco,*
Poetical and Historical Inventions,
By Wm. BLAKE

* * *

No. 28, Corner of BROAD STREET, Golden-Square.

"Fit audience find tho' few" MILTON.

THE INVENTION OF A PORTABLE FRESCO

A Wall [of] Canvas or Wood, or any other portable thing, of dimensions ever so large, or ever so small, which may be removed with the same convenience as so many easel Pictures; is worthy the consideration of the Rich and those who have the direction of public Works. If the Frescos of APELLES, of PROTOGENES, of RAPHAEL, or MICHAEL ANGELO could have been removed, we might, perhaps, have them now in England. I could divide Westminster Hall, or the walls of any other great Building, into compartments and ornament them with Frescos, which would be removable at pleasure.

Oil will not drink or absorb Colour enough to stand the test of very little Time and of the Air; it grows yellow, and at length brown. It was never generally used till after VANDYKE's time. All the little old Pictures, called cabinet Pictures, are in Fresco, and not in Oil.

Fresco Painting is properly Miniature, or Enamel Painting; every thing in Fresco is as high finished as Miniature or Enamel, although in Works larger than Life. The Art has been lost: I have recovered it. How this was done, will be told, together with the whole Process, in a Work on Art, now in the Press. The ignorant Insults of Individuals will not hinder me from doing my duty to my Art. Fresco Painting, as it is now practised, is like most other things, the contrary of what it pretends to be.

The execution of my Designs, being all in Water-colours, (that is in Fresco) are regularly refused to be exhibited by the *Royal Academy,* and the *British Institution* has, this year, followed its example, and has effectually excluded me by this Resolution;[1] I therefore invite those Noblemen and Gentlemen, who are its Subscribers, to

1. Blake had previously exhibited regularly at the Royal Academy (see Chronology), but the Selection Committee was not interested in his experimental temperas, and the new British Institution, which opened its first exhibition in 1806, apparently rejected watercolors altogether.

inspect what they have excluded: and those who have been told that my Works are but an unscientific and irregular Eccentricity, a Madman's Scrawls, I demand of them to do me the justice to examine before they decide.

There cannot be more than two or three great Painters or Poets in any Age or Country; and these, in a corrupt state of Society, are easily excluded, but not so easily obstructed. They have excluded Water-colours; it is therefore become necessary that I should exhibit to the Public, in an Exhibition of my own, my Designs, Painted in Water-colours. If Italy is enriched and made great by RAPHAEL, if MICHAEL ANGELO is its supreme glory, if Art is the glory of a Nation, if Genius and Inspiration are the great Origin and Bond of Society, the distinction my Works have obtained from those who best understand such things, calls for my Exhibition as the greatest of Duties to my Country.

[May 15, 1809] WILLIAM BLAKE

From A Descriptive Catalogue of Pictures

Poetical and Historical Inventions,

PAINTED BY William Blake in Water Colours, BEING THE ANCIENT METHOD OF *Fresco Painting Restored:* AND *Drawings, for Public Inspection,* AND FOR Sale by Private Contract.

CONDITIONS OF SALE

I. *One third of the price to be paid at the time of Purchase, and the remainder on Delivery.*

II. *The Pictures and Drawings to remain in the Exhibition till its close, which will be on the* 29th *of September* 1809; *and the Picture of the Canterbury Pilgrims, which is to be engraved, will be Sold only on condition of its remaining in the Artist's hands twelve months, when it will be delivered to the Buyer.*

PREFACE

The eye that can prefer the Colouring of Titian and Rubens to that of Michael Angelo and Rafael, ought to be modest and to doubt its own powers. Connoisseurs talk as if Rafael and Michael Angelo had never seen the colouring of Titian or Correggio: They ought to know that Correggio was born two years before Michael Angelo, and Titian but four years after. Both Rafael and Michael Angelo knew the Venetian, and contemned and rejected all he did with the utmost disdain, as that which is fabricated for the purpose to destroy art.

Mr. B. appeals to the Public, from the judgment of those narrow blinking eyes, that have too long governed art in a dark corner. The eyes of stupid cunning never will be pleased with the work any more than with the look of self-devoting genius. The quarrel of the Florentine with the Venetian is not because he does not understand Drawing, but because he does not understand Colouring. How should he? he who does not know how to draw a hand or a foot, know how to colour it?

Colouring does not depend on where the Colours are put, but on where the lights and darks are put, and all depends on Form or Outline, on where that is put; where that is wrong, the Colouring never can be right; and it is always wrong in Titian and Correggio, Rubens and Rembrandt. Till we get rid of Titian and Correggio, Rubens and Rembrandt, We never shall equal Rafael and Albert Dürer, Michael Angelo, and Julio Romano.

NUMBER I

The spiritual form of Nelson guiding Leviathan, in whose wreathings are infolded the Nations of the Earth.

* * *

NUMBER II, ITS COMPANION[2]

The spiritual form of Pitt, guiding Behemoth; he is that Angel who, pleased to perform the Almighty's orders, rides on the whirlwind, directing the storms of war: He is ordering the Reaper to reap the Vine of the Earth, and the Plowman to plow up the Cities and Towers.

* * *

The two pictures of Nelson and Pitt are compositions of a mythological cast, similar to those Apotheoses of Persian, Hindoo, and Egyptian Antiquity, which are still preserved on rude monuments, being copies from some stupendous originals now lost or perhaps buried till some happier age. The Artist having been taken in

2. Number I and number II are temperas now in the Tate Gallery, London. Despite Blake's panegyrical tone in the *Catalogue*, in the pictures themselves he reveals a satirical attitude toward Nelson and Pitt, as explained by David V. Erdman, *Blake: Prophet Against Empire* (Princeton: Princeton University Press, 1969), pp. 448–55.

vision into the ancient republics, monarchies, and patriarchates of Asia, has seen those wonderful originals called in the Sacred Scriptures the Cherubim, which were sculptured and painted on walls of Temples, Towers, Cities, Palaces, and erected in the highly cultivated states of Egypt, Moab, Edom, Aram, among the Rivers of Paradise, being originals from which the Greeks and Hetrurians copied Hercules Farnese, Venus of Medicis, Apollo Belvidere, and all the grand works of ancient art. They were executed in a very superior style to those justly admired copies, being with their accompaniments terrific and grand in the highest degree. The Artist has endeavoured to emulate the grandeur of those seen in his vision, and to apply it to modern Heroes, on a smaller scale.

No man can believe that either Homer's Mythology, or Ovid's, were the production of Greece or of Latium; neither will any one believe, that the Greek statues, as they are called, were the invention of Greek Artists; perhaps the Torso is the only original work remaining; all the rest are evidently copies, though fine ones, from greater works of the Asiatic Patriarchs. The Greek Muses are daughters of Mnemosyne, or Memory, and not of Inspiration or Imagination, therefore not authors of such sublime conceptions. Those wonderful originals seen in my visions, were some of them one hundred feet in height; some were painted as pictures, and some carved as basso relievos, and some as groupes of statues, all containing mythological and recondite meaning, where more is meant than meets the eye. The Artist wishes it was now the fashion to make such monuments, and then he should not doubt of having a national commission to execute these two Pictures on a scale that is suitable to the grandeur of the nation, who is the parent of his heroes, in high finished fresco, where the colours would be as pure and as permanent as precious stones, though the figures were one hundred feet in height.

* * *

NUMBER III[3]

Sir Jeffery Chaucer and the nine and twenty Pilgrims on their journey to Canterbury.

* * *

The characters of Chaucer's Pilgrims are the characters which compose all ages and nations: as one age falls, another rises, different to mortal sight, but to immortals only the same; for we see the same characters repeated again and again, in animals, vegetables, minerals, and in men; nothing new occurs in identical existence; Accident ever varies, Substance can never suffer change nor decay.

Of Chaucer's characters, as described in his Canterbury Tales,

3. A tempera now in Pollok House, The Glasgow Museums and Art Galleries.

some of the names or titles are altered by time, but the characters themselves for ever remain unaltered, and consequently they are the physiognomies or lineaments of universal human life, beyond which Nature never steps. Names alter, things never alter. I have known multitudes of those who would have been monks in the age of monkery, who in this deistical age are deists. As Newton numbered the stars, and as Linneus numbered the plants, so Chaucer numbered the classes of men.

* * *

Visions of these eternal principles or characters of human life appear to poets, in all ages; the Grecian gods were the ancient Cherubim of Phoenicia; but the Greeks, and since them the Moderns, have neglected to subdue the gods of Priam. These gods are visions of the eternal attributes, or divine names, which, when erected into gods, become destructive to humanity. They ought to be the servants, and not the masters of man, or of society. They ought to be made to sacrifice to Man, and not man compelled to sacrifice to them; for when separated from man or humanity, who is Jesus the Saviour, the vine of eternity, they are thieves and rebels, they are destroyers.

* * *

NUMBER IV[4]

The Bard, from Gray.

* * *

The connoisseurs and artists who have made objections to Mr. B.'s mode of representing spirits with real bodies, would do well to consider that the Venus, the Minerva, the Jupiter, the Apollo, which they admire in Greek statues are all of them representations of spiritual existences, of Gods immortal, to the mortal perishing organ of sight; and yet they are embodied and organized in solid marble. Mr. B. requires the same latitude, and all is well. The Prophets describe what they saw in Vision as real and existing men, whom they saw with their imaginative and immortal organs; the Apostles the same; the clearer the organ the more distinct the object. A Spirit and a Vision are not, as the modern philosophy supposes, a cloudy vapour, or a nothing: they are organized and minutely articulated beyond all that the mortal and perishing nature can produce. He who does not imagine in stronger and better lineaments, and in stronger and better light than his perishing and

4. A tempera now in the Tate Gallery. By 1805 Blake had completed fourteen large watercolor illustrations for Gray's *The Bard* as part of a series of 116 designs for Gray; see Irene Tayler, *Blake's Illustrations to the Poems of Gray* (1971), and Sir Geoffrey Keynes, *William Blake's Water-Colour Designs for the Poems of Thomas Gray* (1971).

mortal eye can see, does not imagine at all. The painter of this work asserts that all his imaginations appear to him infinitely more perfect and more minutely organized than any thing seen by his mortal eye. Spirits are organized men. Moderns wish to draw figures without lines, and with great and heavy shadows; are not shadows more unmeaning than lines, and more heavy? O who can doubt this!

* * *

NUMBER V[5]

The Ancient Britons

In the last Battle of King Arthur, only Three Britons escaped; these were the Strongest Man, the Beautifullest Man, and the Ugliest Man; these three marched through the field unsubdued, as Gods, and the Sun of Britain set, but shall arise again with tenfold splendor when Arthur shall awake from sleep, and resume his dominion over earth and ocean.

The three general classes of men who are represented by the most Beautiful, the most Strong, and the most Ugly, could not be represented by any historical facts but those of our own country, the Ancient Britons, without violating costume. The Britons (say historians) were naked civilized men, learned, studious, abstruse in thought and contemplation; naked, simple, plain in their acts and manners; wiser than after-ages. They were overwhelmed by brutal arms, all but a small remnant; Strength, Beauty, and Ugliness escaped the wreck, and remain for ever unsubdued, age after age.

The British Antiquities are now in the Artists's hands; all his visionary contemplations, relating to his own country and its ancient glory, when it was, as it again shall be, the source of learning and inspiration. Arthur was a name for the constellation Arcturus, or Boötes, the keeper of the North Pole. And all the fables of Arthur and his round table; of the warlike naked Britons; of Merlin; of Arthur's conquest of the whole world; of his death, or sleep, and promise to return again; of the Druid monuments or temples; of the pavement of Watling-street; of London stone; of the caverns in Cornwall, Wales, Derbyshire, and Scotland; of the Giants of Ireland and Britain; of the elemental beings called by us by the general name of fairies; and of these three who escaped, namely Beauty, Strength, and Ugliness. Mr. B. has in his hands poems of

5. This tempera has been lost. In the view of Robert Hunt, "the colouring of the flesh is exactly like hung beef" (The *Examiner*, September 17, 1809).

Also, number VI, *A Spirit Vaulting From a Cloud,* another tempera, is now lost, but a similar watercolor is in the British Museum Print Room. Number VII, *The Goats,* and number VIII, *The Spiritual Preceptor*, on a "subject taken from the visions of Emanuel Swedenborg, *Universal Theology*, No. 623," are also temperas, now lost.

the highest antiquity. Adam was a Druid, and Noah; also Abraham was called to succeed the Druidical age, which began to turn allegoric and mental signification into corporeal command, whereby human sacrifice would have depopulated the earth. All these things are written in Eden. The artist is an inhabitant of that happy country; and if every thing goes on as it has begun, the world of vegetation and generation may expect to be opened again to Heaven, through Eden, as it was in the beginning.

The Strong Man represents the human sublime. The Beautiful Man represents the human pathetic, which was in the wars of Eden divided into male and female. The Ugly Man represents the human reason. They were originally one man, who was fourfold; he was self-divided, and his real humanity slain on the stems of generation, and the form of the fourth was like the Son of God. How he became divided is a subject of great sublimity and pathos. The Artist has written it under inspiration, and will, if God please, publish it; it is voluminous, and contains the ancient history of Britain, and the world of Satan and of Adam.

In the mean time he has painted this Picture, which supposes that in the reign of that British Prince, who lived in the fifth century, there were remains of those naked Heroes in the Welch Mountains; they are there now, Gray saw them in the person of his bard on Snowdon; there they dwell in naked simplicity; happy is he who can see and converse with them above the shadows of generation and death. The giant Albion, was Patriarch of the Atlantic; he is the Atlas of the Greeks, one of those the Greeks called Titans. The stories of Arthur are the acts of Albion, applied to a Prince of the fifth century, who conquered Europe, and held the Empire of the world in the dark age, which the Romans never again recovered. In this Picture, believing with Milton the ancient British History, Mr. B. has done as all the ancients did, and as all the moderns who are worthy of fame, given the historical fact in its poetical vigour so as it always happens, and not in that dull way that some Historians pretend, who, being weakly organized themselves, cannot see either miracle or prodigy; all is to them a dull round of probabilities and possibilities; but the history of all times and places is nothing else but improbabilities and impossibilities; what we should say was impossible if we did not see it always before our eyes.

The antiquities of every Nation under Heaven, is no less sacred than that of the Jews. They are the same thing, as Jacob Bryant and all antiquaries have proved. How other antiquities came to be neglected and disbelieved, while those of the Jews are collected and arranged, is an enquiry worthy both of the Antiquarian and the Divine. All had originally one language, and one religion: this was the religion of Jesus, the everlasting Gospel. Antiquity preaches the Gospel of Jesus. The reasoning historian, turner and twister of causes and consequences, such as Hume, Gibbon, and Voltaire, cannot with all their artifice turn or twist one fact or disarrange self evident action and reality. Reasons and opinions concerning acts are not history. Acts themselves alone are history, and these are neither the exclusive property of Hume, Gibbon, nor Voltaire, Echard, Rapin, Plutarch, nor Herodotus. Tell me the Acts, O historian, and leave me to reason upon them as I please; away with your reasoning and your rubbish! All that is not action is not worth reading. Tell me the What; I do not want you to tell me the Why, and the How; I can find that out myself, as well as you can, and I will not be fooled by you into opinions, that you please to impose, to disbelieve what you think improbable or impossible. His opinions, who does not see spiritual agency, is not worth any man's reading; he who rejects a fact because it is improbable, must reject all History and retain doubts only.

It has been said to the Artist, "take the Apollo for the model of your beautiful Man, and the Hercules for your strong Man, and the Dancing Fawn for your Ugly Man." Now he comes to his trial. He knows that what he does is not inferior to the grandest Antiques. Superior they cannot be, for human power cannot go beyond either what he does, or what they have done; it is the gift of God, it is inspiration and vision. He had resolved to emulate those precious remains of antiquity; he has done so and the result you behold. * * *

* * *

It will be necessary for the Painter to say something concerning his ideas of Beauty, Strength and Ugliness.

The Beauty that is annexed and appended to folly, is a lamentable accident and error of the mortal and perishing life; it does but seldom happen; but with this unnatural mixture the sublime Artist can have nothing to do; it is fit for the burlesque. The Beauty proper for sublime art is lineaments, or forms and features that are capable of being the receptacles of intellect; accordingly the Painter has given in his beautiful man, his own idea of intellectual Beauty. The face and limbs that deviates or alters least, from infancy to old age, is the face and limbs of greatest Beauty and perfection.

The Ugly, likewise, when accompanied and annexed to imbecility and disease, is a subject for burlesque and not for historical grandeur; the Artist has imagined his Ugly man, one approaching to the beast in features and form, his forehead small, without frontals; his jaws large; his nose high on the ridge, and narrow; his chest, and the stamina of his make, comparatively little, and his joints and his extremities large; his eyes, with scarce any whites, narrow and cunning, and every thing tending toward what is truly Ugly, the incapability of intellect.

The Artist has considered his strong Man as a receptacle of

Wisdom, a sublime energizer; his features and limbs do not spindle out into length without strength, nor are they too large and unwieldy for his brain and bosom. Strength consists in accumulation of power to the principal seat, and from thence a regular gradation and subordination; strength is compactness, not extent nor bulk.

The strong Man acts from conscious superiority, and marches on in fearless dependence on the divine decrees, raging with the inspirations of a prophetic mind. The Beautiful Man acts from duty and anxious solicitude for the fates of those for whom he combats. The Ugly Man acts from love of carnage, and delight in the savage barbarities of war, rushing with sportive precipitation into the very teeth of the affrighted enemy.

* * *

The flush of health in flesh exposed to the open air, nourished by the spirits of forests and floods in that ancient happy period, which history has recorded, cannot be like the sickly daubs of Titian or Rubens. Where will the copier of nature, as it now is, find a civilized man, who has been accustomed to go naked? Imagination only can furnish us with colouring appropriate, such as is found in the Frescos of Rafael and Michael Angelo: the disposition of forms always directs colouring in works of true art. As to a modern Man, stripped from his load of cloathing, he is like a dead corpse. Hence Rubens, Titian, Correggio and all of that class, are like leather and chalk; their men are like leather, and their women like chalk, for the disposition of their forms will not admit of grand colouring; in Mr. B.'s Britons the blood is seen to circulate in their limbs; he defies competition in colouring.

* * *

NUMBER IX[6]

Satan calling up his Legions from Milton's Paradise Lost; a composition for a more perfect Picture afterward executed for a Lady of high rank. An experiment Picture.

6. This tempera, now in the Victoria and Albert Museum, London, is in poor condition; the other version (alluded to in the title) was made for the Countess of Egremont and is still at Petworth House, Sussex.

Numbers V–VIII and X–XIV, listed by title with little or no comment, are omitted here. Number VI, *A Spirit vaulting from a cloud*, was a "fresco," now lost. Numbers VII, *The Goats*, and VIII, *The Spiritual Preceptor*, a subject from "Swedenborg, Universal Theology, No. 623," were "experiment" pictures, now lost. Number X, *The Bramins*, depicting "Mr. Wilkins translating the Geeta," was a watercolor, now lost. Number XI, *The Body of Abel Found by Adam and Eve*, is a watercolor now in the Fogg Museum, Harvard. Number XII, *Soldiers Casting Lots for Christ's Garment*, is a watercolor now in the Fitzwilliam Museum, Cambridge. Number XIII, *Jacob's Ladder*, is a watercolor now in the British Museum Print Room. Number XIV, *Angels Hovering Over the Body of Jesus*, is a watercolor now in the Victoria and Albert Museum.

This Picture was likewise painted at intervals, for experiment on colours without any oil vehicle; it may be worthy of attention, not only on account of its composition, but of the great labour which has been bestowed on it, that is, three or four times as much as would have finished a more perfect Picture; the labour has destroyed the lineaments; it was with difficulty brought back again to a certain effect, which it had at first, when all the lineaments were perfect.

These Pictures, among numerous others painted for experiment, were the result of temptations and perturbations, labouring to destroy Imaginative power, by means of that infernal machine called Chiaro Oscuro, in the hands of Venetian and Flemish Demons, whose enmity to the Painter himself, and to all Artists who study in the Florentine and Roman Schools, may be removed by an exhibition and exposure of their vile tricks. They cause that every thing in art shall become a Machine. They cause that the execution shall be all blocked up with brown shadows. They put the original Artist in fear and doubt of his own original conception. The spirit of Titian was particularly active in raising doubts concerning the possibility of executing without a model, and when once he had raised the doubt, it became easy for him to snatch away the vision time after time, for, when the Artist took his pencil to execute his ideas, his power of imagination weakened so much and darkened, that memory of nature, and of Pictures of the various schools possessed his mind, instead of appropriate execution resulting from the inventions; like walking in another man's style, or speaking, or looking in another man's style and manner, unappropriate and repugnant to your own individual character; tormenting the true Artist, till he leaves the Florentine, and adopts the Venetian practice, or does as Mr. B. has done, has the courage to suffer poverty and disgrace, till he ultimately conquers.

* * *

NUMBER XV[7]

Ruth.—A Drawing.

* * *

The great and golden rule of art, as well as of life, is this: That the more distinct, sharp, and wirey the bounding line, the more perfect the work of art; and the less keen and sharp, the greater is the evidence of weak imitation, plagiarism, and bungling. Great inventors, in all ages, knew this: Protogenes and Apelles knew each other by this line. Rafael and Michael Angelo and Albert Dürer are

7. A watercolor now in the Southampton Art Gallery.

known by this and this alone. The want of this determinate and bounding form evidences the want of idea in the artist's mind, and the pretence of the plagiary in all its branches. How do we distinguish the oak from the beech, the horse from the ox, but by the bounding outline? How do we distinguish one face or countenance from another, but by the bounding line and its infinite inflexions and movements? What is it that builds a house and plants a garden, but the definite and determinate? What is it that distinguishes honesty from knavery, but the hard and wirey line of rectitude and certainty in the actions and intentions? Leave out this line, and you leave out life itself; all is chaos again, and the line of the almighty must be drawn out upon it before man or beast can exist. Talk no more then of Correggio, or Rembrandt, or any other of those plagiaries of Venice or Flanders. They were but the lame imitators of lines drawn by their predecessors, and their works prove themselves contemptible, disarranged imitations, and blundering, misapplied copies.

NUMBER XVI[8]

The Penance of Jane Shore in St. Paul's Church.—A Drawing.

This Drawing was done above Thirty Years ago, and proves to the Author, and he thinks will prove to any discerning eye, that the productions of our youth and of our maturer age are equal in all essential points. If a man is master of his profession, he cannot be ignorant that he is so; and if he is not employed by those who pretend to encourage art, he will employ himself, and laugh in secret at the pretences of the ignorant, while he has every night dropped into his shoe, as soon as he puts it off, and puts out the candle, and gets into bed, a reward for the labours of the day, such as the world cannot give, and patience and time await to give him all that the world can give.

FINIS

A Vision of the Last Judgment

Intermingled with the drafts for A *Public Address* in Blake's Notebook is an exposition of his masterwork as a painter, A *Vision of the Last Judgment*. This work, measuring seven by five feet and containing more than a thousand figures, was probably intended for an 1810 exhibition, but after the discouraging 1809 show, Blake ceased exhibiting his work publicly. Though the picture itself has been lost since the nineteenth century, several preliminary smaller versions are extant. The most finished of these, painted

8. A watercolor now in the Tate Gallery.

for the Countess of Egremont in 1808, is still displayed at Petworth House, Sussex; Blake's brief exposition of this picture is not included here. There is also a finely finished pencil and ink drawing in the Rosenwald Collection which closely resembles the lost masterwork (described by J. T. Smith, p. 487).

Blake's insistence that he knew exactly what each detail in his *Last Judgment* represents has encouraged Blakists to apply his claim that there is no "Insignificant Blur or Mark" to the study of his other works as well. Despite his Romantic-sounding dismissal of "Allegory," his discussions of particular figures in the painting are nothing if not "allegorical" in some senses of the word. According to an 1803 letter to Butts, Blake aspired to one form of allegory: "Allegory Address'd to the intellectual powers, while it is altogether hidden from the Corporeal Understanding, is My Definition of the Most Sublime Poetry" (July 6). Since the *Vision of the Last Judgment* is now lost, most of Blake's detailed exposition of the picture is omitted from this edition; the following selections make sense alone but should be studied further in the Keynes or Erdman editions (for which page references are supplied in footnotes). We have restored a few deleted passages to provide continuity. See S. Foster Damon's *A Blake Dictionary* (1967) for a reproduction and coded exposition of the Rosenwald drawing; also discussed by A. S. Roe (in Robert N. Essick, ed., *The Visionary Hand*, 1973) and W.J.T. Mitchell (special supplement to *Blake Newsletter*, 1975).

From A Vision of the Last Judgment

For the Year 1810

Additions to Blake's Catalogue of Pictures &c

The Last Judgment: when all those are Cast away who trouble Religion with Questions concerning Good & Evil or Eating of the Tree of those Knowledges or Reasonings which hinder the Vision of God, turning all into a Consuming Fire. When Imagination, Art & Science & all Intellectual Gifts, all the Gifts of the Holy Ghost, are lookd upon as of no use & only Contention remains to Man, then the Last Judgment begins, & its Vision is seen by Every one according to the situation he holds.

The Last Judgment is not Fable or Allegory, but Vision. Fable or Allegory are a totally distinct & inferior kind of Poetry. Vision or Imagination is a Representation of what Eternally Exists, Really & Unchangeably. Fable or Allegory is Formd by the daughters of Memory. Imagination is surrounded by the daughters of Inspiration, who in the aggregate are calld Jerusalem. Fable is Allegory, but what Critics call The Fable is Vision itself. The Hebrew Bible

& the Gospel of Jesus are not Allegory, but Eternal Vision or Imagination of All that Exists. Note here that Fable,or Allegory is seldom without some Vision. *Pilgrim's Progress* is full of it, the Greek Poets the same; but Allegory & Vision ought to be known as Two Distinct Things, & so calld for the Sake of Eternal Life. Plato has made Socrates say that Poets & Prophets do not know or Understand what they write or Utter; this is a most Pernicious Falshood. If they do not, pray is an inferior kind to be call'd Knowing? Plato confutes himself.[1]

The Last Judgment is one of these Stupendous Visions. I have represented it as I saw it; to different People it appears differently as everything else does; for tho on Earth things seem Permanent, they are less permanent than a Shadow, as we all know too well.

The Nature of Visionary Fancy, or Imagination, is very little Known, & the Eternal nature & permanence of its ever Existent Images is considerd as less permanent than the things of Vegetative & Generative Nature; yet the Oak dies as well as the Lettuce, but Its Eternal Image & Individuality never dies, but renews by its seed; just so the Imaginative Image returns by the seed of Contemplative Thought. The Writings of the Prophets illustrate these conceptions of the Visionary Fancy by their various sublime & Divine Images as seen in the Worlds of Vision.[2]

* * *

Let it here be Noted that Greek Fables originated in Spiritual Mystery & Real Visions, which are lost & clouded in Fable & Allegory, while the Hebrew Bible & the Greek Gospel are Genuine, Preservd by the Saviour's Mercy. The Nature of my Work is Visionary or Imaginative; it is an Endeavour to Restore what the Ancients calld the Golden Age.

This world of Imagination is the world of Eternity; it is the divine bosom into which we shall all go after the death of the Vegetated body. This World of Imagination is Infinite & Eternal, whereas the world of Generation, or Vegetation, is Finite & Temporal. There Exist in that Eternal World the Permanent Realities of Every Thing which we see reflected in this Vegetable Glass of Nature. All Things are comprehended in their Eternal Forms in the divine body of the Saviour, the True Vine of Eternity, The Human Imagination, who appeard to Me as Coming to Judgment among his Saints & throwing off the Temporal that the Eternal might be

1. Cf. *The Complete Writings of William Blake*, ed. Geoffrey Keynes (London and New York: Oxford, 1974), pp. 604–5; and *The Poetry and Prose of William Blake*, ed. David V. Erdman (Garden City, N.Y.: Doubleday, 1970), p. 544.

2. Cf. Keynes, p. 605, and Erdman, p. 544.

Establishd; around him were seen the Images of Existences according to a certain order Suited to my Imaginative Eye.[3]

* * *

* * * These States Exist now. Man Passes on, but States remain for Ever; he passes thro them like a traveller who may as well suppose that the places he has passed thro exist no more, as a Man may suppose that the States he has pass'd thro Exist no more. Every Thing is Eternal.

In Eternity one Thing never Changes into another Thing. Each Identity is Eternal; consequently Apuleius's Golden Ass & Ovid's Metamorphosis & others of the like kind are Fable, yet they contain Vision in a sublime degree, being derived from real Vision in More ancient Writings. Lot's Wife being Changed into [a] Pillar of Salt alludes to the Mortal Body being rendered a Permanent Statue, but not Changed or Transformed into Another Identity while it retains its own Individuality. A Man can never become Ass nor Horse; some are born with shapes of Men, who may be both, but Eternal Identity is one thing & Corporeal Vegetation is another thing. Changing Water into Wine by Jesus & into Blood by Moses relates to Vegetable Nature also.

* * * On the left, beneath the falling figure of Cain, is Moses casting his tables of stone into the deeps. It ought to be understood that the Persons, Moses & Abraham, are not here meant, but the States Signified by those Names, the Individuals being representatives or Visions of those States as they were reveald to Mortal Man in the Series of Divine Revelations as they are written in the Bible; these various States I have seen in my Imagination. When distant they appear as One Man, but as you approach they appear Multitudes of Nations. * * *[4]

The Ladies will be pleasd to see that I have represented the Furies by Three Men & not by three Women. It is not because I think the Ancients wrong, but they will be pleasd to remember that mine is Vision & not Fable. The Spectator may suppose them Clergymen in the Pulpit, scourging Sin instead of Forgiving it.[5]

* * * On the Right a Youthful couple are awaked by their Children; an Aged patriarch is awakd by his aged wife—He is Albion, our Ancestor, patriarch of the Atlantic Continent, whose History Preceded that of the Hebrews & in whose Sleep, or Chaos, Creation began; his Emanation or Wife is Jerusalem, who is about to be

3. Cf. Keynes, pp. 605–6, and Erdman, p. 545.
4. Cf. Keynes, pp. 606–7, and Erdman, p. 546.
5. Cf. Keynes, p. 608, and Erdman, p. 547.

recievd like the Bride of the [Lamb]; at their head the Aged Woman is Brittanica, the Wife of Albion: Jerusalem is their daughter. Little Infants creep out of the flowery mould into the Green fields of the blessed who in various joyful companies embrace & ascend to meet Eternity.

The Persons who ascend to Meet the Lord, coming in the Clouds with power & great Glory, are representations of those States described in the Bible under the Names of the Fathers before & after the Flood. Noah is seen in the Midst of these, Canopied by a Rainbow, on his right hand Shem & on his Left Japhet; these three Persons represent Poetry, Painting & Music, the three Powers in Man of conversing with Paradise, which the flood did not Sweep away * * *[6]

If the Spectator could Enter into these Images in his Imagination, approaching them on the Fiery Chariot of his Contemplative Thought, if he could Enter into Noah's Rainbow or into his bosom, or could make a Friend & Companion of one of these Images of wonder, which always intreats him to leave mortal things (as he must know), then would he arise from his Grave, then would he meet the Lord in the Air, & then he would be happy.

General Knowledge is Remote Knowledge; it is in Particulars that Wisdom consists & Happiness too. Both in Art & in Life, General Masses are as Much Art as a Pasteboard Man is Human. Every Man has Eyes, Nose & Mouth; this Every Idiot knows, but he who enters into & discriminates most minutely the Manners & Intentions, the Characters in all their branches, is the alone Wise or Sensible Man, & on this discrimination All Art is founded. I intreat, then, that the Spectator will attend to the Hands & Feet, to the Lineaments of the Countenances; they are all descriptive of Character, & not a line is drawn without intention, & that most discriminate & particular. As Poetry admits not a Letter that is Insignificant, so Painting admits not a Grain of Sand or a Blade of Grass Insignificant—much less an Insignificant Blur or Mark.[7]

* * *

A Last Judgment is Necessary because Fools flourish. Nations Flourish under Wise Rulers & are depressd under foolish Rulers. It is the same with Individuals as Nations: works of Art can only be produc'd in Perfection where the Man is either in Affluence or is Above the Care of it. Poverty is the Fool's Rod, which at last is turn'd on his own back.

6. Cf. Keynes, p. 609, and Erdman, p. 548. The statement that Jerusalem is Albion's "Emanation or Wife," Bride of the Lamb, was deleted by Blake.

7. Cf. Keynes, p. 611, and Erdman, p. 550.

This is A Last Judgment—when Men of Real Art Govern & Pretenders Fall. Some People & not a few Artists have asserted that the Painter of this Picture would not have done so well if he had been properly Encouragd. Let those who think so, reflect on the State of Nations under Poverty & their incapability of Art; tho Art is Above Either, the Argument is better for Affluence than Poverty; & tho he would not have been a greater Artist, yet he would have producd Greater works of Art in proportion to his means. A Last Judgment is not for the purpose of making Bad Men better, but for the Purpose of hindering them from opressing the Good with Poverty & Pain by means of Such Vile Arguments & Insinuations.

Around the Throne Heaven is opend & the Nature of Eternal Things Displayd, All Springing from the Divine Humanity. All beams from him Because as he himself has said, All dwells in him. He is the Bread & the Wine; he is the Water of Life. Accordingly on Each Side of the opening Heaven appears an Apostle: that on the Right Represents Baptism; that on the Left Represents the Lord's Supper.

All Life consists of these Two: Throwing off Error & Knaves from our company continually, & Recieving Truth or Wise Men into our Company continually. He who is out of the Church & opposes it is no less an Agent of Religion than he who is in it: to be an Error & to be Cast out is a part of God's design. No man can Embrace True Art till he has Explord & cast out False Art (such is the Nature of Mortal Things), or he will be himself Cast out by those who have Already Embraced True Art. Thus My Picture is a History of Art & Science, the Foundation of Society, Which is Humanity itself.

What are all the Gifts of the Spirit but Mental Gifts? Whenever any Individual Rejects Error & Embraces Truth, a Last Judgment passes upon that Individual.[8]

* * *

Many suppose that before the Creation All was Solitude & Chaos. This is the most pernicious Idea that can enter the Mind, as it takes away all sublimity from the Bible & Limits All Existence to Creation & to Chaos, To the Time & Space fixed by the Corporeal Vegetative Eye, & leaves the Man who entertains such an Idea the habitation of Unbelieving demons. Eternity Exists, and All things in Eternity, Independent of Creation, which was an act of Mercy.

I have represented those who are in Eternity by some in a Cloud within the Rainbow that Surrounds the Throne; they merely appear as in a Cloud when any thing of Creation, Redemption or Judgment are the Subjects of Contemplation, tho their Whole Contem-

8. Cf. Keynes, pp. 612–13, and Erdman, p. 551.

plation is concerning these things. The Reason they so appear is The Humiliation of the Reasoning & doubting Self-hood, & the Giving all up to Inspiration. By this it will be seen that I do not consider either the Just or the Wicked to be in a Supreme State, but to be every one of them States of the Sleep which the Soul may fall into in its deadly dreams of Good & Evil when it leaves Paradise following the Serpent.

The Greeks represent Chronos or Time as a very Aged Man; this is Fable, but the Real Vision of Time is in Eternal Youth. I have, however, somewhat accomodated my Figure of Time to the common opinion, as I myself an also infected with it & my Visions also infected, & I see Time Aged—alas, too much so.

Allegories are things that Relate to Moral Virtues. Moral Virtues do not Exist; they are Allegories & dissimulations. But Time & Space are Real Beings, a Male & a Female: Time is a Man, Space is a Woman, & her Masculine Portion is Death.

The Combats of Good & Evil is Eating of the Tree of Knowledge. The Combats of Truth & Error is Eating of the Tree of Life. These are not only Universal, but Particular. Each are Personified. There is not an Error but it has a Man for its Agent; that is, it is a Man. There is not a Truth but it has also a Man. Good & Evil are Qualities in Every Man, whether a Good or Evil Man. These are Enemies & destroy one another by every Means in their power, both of deceit & of open Violence. The Deist & the Christian are but the Results of these Opposing Natures. Many are Deists who would in certain Circumstances have been Christians in outward appearance. Voltaire was one of this number; he was as intolerant as an Inquisitor. Manners make the Man, not Habits. It is the same in Art: by their Works ye shall know them; the Knave who is Converted to Deism & the Knave who is Converted to Christianity is still a Knave, but he himself will not know it, tho Every body else does. Christ comes, as he came at first, to deliver those who were bound under the Knave, not to deliver the Knave. He Comes to deliver Man, the Accused, & not Satan, the Accuser. We do not find anywhere that Satan is Accused of Sin; he is only accused of Unbelief & thereby drawing Man into Sin that he may accuse him. Such is the Last Judgment—a deliverance from Satan's Accusation. Satan thinks that Sin is displeasing to God; he ought to know that Nothing is displeasing to God but Unbelief & Eating of the Tree of Knowledge of Good & Evil.

Men are admitted into Heaven not because they have curbed & governd their Passions, or have No Passions, but because they have Cultivated their Understandings. The Treasures of Heaven are not Negations of Passion, but Realities of Intellect, from which All the

9. Cf. Keynes, p. 614, and Erdman, pp. 552–53.

Passions Emanate Uncurbed in their Eternal Glory. The Fool shall not enter into Heaven let him be ever so Holy. Holiness is not The Price of Entrance into Heaven. Those who are cast out are All Those who, having no Passions of their own because No Intellect, Have spent their lives in Curbing & Governing other People's by the Various arts of Poverty & Cruelty of all kinds. Wo, Wo, Wo to you Hypocrites! Even Murder, the Courts of Justice, more merciful than the Church, are compelld to allow, is not done in Passion, but in Cool Blooded design & Intention.

The Modern Church Crucifies Christ with the Head Downwards.

Many Persons, such as Paine & Voltaire, with some of the Ancient Greeks, say: "We will not converse concerning Good & Evil; we will live in Paradise & Liberty." You may do so in Spirit, but not in the Mortal Body as you pretend, till after the Last Judgment; for in Paradise they have no Corporeal & Mortal Body—that originated with the Fall & was calld Death & cannot be removed but by a Last Judgment. While we are in the world of Mortality we Must Suffer. The Whole Creation Groans to be deliverd. There will always be as many Hypocrites born as Honest Men, & they will always have superior Power in Mortal Things. You cannot have Liberty in this World without what you call Moral Virtue, & you cannot have Moral Virtue without the Slavery of that half of the Human Race who hate what you call Moral Virtue.

The Nature of Hatred & Envy & of All the Mischiefs in the World are here depicted. No one Envies or Hates one of his Own Party; even the devils love one another in their Way; they torment one another for other reasons than Hate or Envy; these are only employd against the Just. Neither can Seth Envy Noah, or Elijah Envy Abraham, but they may both of them Envy the Success of Satan or of Og or Molech. The Horse never Envies the Peacock, nor the Sheep the Goat, but they Envy a Rival in Life & Existence whose ways & means exceed their own, let him be of what Class of Animals he will; a dog will envy a Cat who is pamperd at the expense of his comfort, as I have often seen. The Bible never tells us that devils torment one another thro Envy; it is thro this that they torment the Just—but for what do they torment one another? I answer: For the Coercive Laws of Hell, Moral Hypocrisy. They torment a Hypocrite when he is discoverd; they punish a Failure in the tormentor who has sufferd the Subject of his torture to Escape.

In Hell all is Self Righteousness; there is no such thing there as Forgiveness of Sin; he who does Forgive Sin is Crucified as an Abettor of Criminals, & he who performs Works of Mercy in Any shape whatever is punishd &, if possible, destroyd, not thro envy or Hatred or Malice, but thro Self Righteousness that thinks it does God service, which God is Satan. They do not Envy one another: They contemn & despise one another.

Forgiveness of Sin is only at the Judgment Seat of Jesus the Saviour, where the Accuser is cast out, not because he Sins, but because he torments the Just & makes them do what he condemns as Sin & what he knows is opposite to their own Identity.

It is not because Angels are Holier than Men or Devils that makes them Angels, but because they do not Expect Holiness from one another, but from God only.

The Player is a liar when he says: "Angels are happier than Men because they are better." Angels are happier than Men & Devils because they are not always Prying after Good & Evil in one another & eating the Tree of Knowledge for Satan's Gratification.

Thinking as I do that the Creator of this World is a very Cruel Being, & being a Worshipper of Christ, I cannot help saying: "The Son, O how unlike the Father!" First God Almighty comes with a Thump on the Head. Then Jesus Christ comes with a balm to heal it.

The Last Judgment is an Overwhelming of Bad Art & Science. Mental Things are alone Real; what is calld Corporeal, Nobody Knows of its Dwelling Place: it is in Fallacy, & its Existence an Imposture. Where is the Existence Out of Mind or Thought? Where is it but in the Mind of a Fool! Some People flatter themselves that there will be No Last Judgment & that Bad Art will be adopted & mixed with Good Art, That Error or Experiment will make a Part of Truth, & they Boast that it is its Foundation. These People flatter themselves. I will not Flatter them! Error is Created. Truth is Eternal. Error, or Creation, will be Burned up, & then, & not till Then, Truth or Eternity will appear. It is Burnt up the Moment Men cease to behold it.

I assert for My Self that I do not behold the outward Creation & that to me it is hindrance & not Action; it is as the Dirt upon my feet, No part of Me. "What," it will be Questiond, "When the Sun rises, do you not see a round disk of fire somewhat like a Guinea?" O no, no, I see an Innumerable company of the Heavenly host crying "Holy, Holy, Holy is the Lord God Almighty."[1] I question not my Corporeal or Vegetative Eye any more than I would Question a Window concerning a Sight: I look thro it & not with it.[2]

A Public Address to the Chalcographic Society

In 1809–10 Blake wrote in his Notebook an untitled series of prose drafts of an apologia for his work as an artist, ostensibly to be given as a speech to "The Chalcographic [i.e., copper-engraving] Society." These passages frequently allude to Blake's *Canterbury Pilgrims* in its form as an engraved

1. Cf. the visions of angels in Isaiah 6:3, Luke 2:13, and Revelation 4:8; also near the end of the first part of Bunyan's *Pilgrim Progress.*
2. Cf. Keynes, pp. 615–17, and Erdman, pp. 553–55.

work; evidently Blake imagined an occasion for his address on which he would hand around prints of the work as evidence of his mastery of the art. Or it would have been possible for Blake to maintain in an illustrated pamphlet the rhetorical posture of an ideal speech, as Milton does in the *Areopagitica*. Since there seems to have been no actual group calling itself "The Chalcographic Society," it is perhaps most reasonable to assume that Blake intended his address to be a printed oration. The passages constituting the Public Address are intermingled in the Notebook with similar prose fragments on his painting, *A Vision of the Last Judgment*. The hostility or indifference accorded to his 1809 exhibition probably discouraged Blake from making the effort to work up his drafts for either project into finished essays, but he revised them heavily, and both contain powerful formulations of some of Blake's most deeply held ideas.

This selection, which draws on editorial work done by both Keynes and Erdman, with further rearrangements, is an attempt to feature the universal aspects of Blake's thought and to free up the *Address* from what appears in the Notebook as Blake's excessive preoccupation with his own neglect by the public and the success of rival schools of painting and inferior artists. Since his Notebook served partly as a diary, Blake could use it to indulge his feelings of justified resentment; his revisions, however, indicate that he would have given a less personal slant to his material if he had finished revising it; in the text of the *Address* he makes a statement to the same effect: "Resentment for Personal Injuries has had some share in this Public Address, But Love to my Art & Zeal for my Country a much Greater." He was capable of restraint even in his younger and perhaps more passionate years: in an anecdote contained in his Annotations to Reynolds's *Discourses* he exclaims, "How I did secretly Rage!" But he adds, "I also spoke my mind . . ." (p. 440). All in all, Blake's primary concern in his Notebook was with his artistic work rather than with the exploration of his own ego and the venting of his frustrations. The example of Rousseau had shown him what the extreme Romantic impulse to public confession could lead to: he saw in such works of self-justification the marks of the Antichrist. Blake would not pay that price for fame.

We have not interrupted the flow of Blake's oratory to insert references to the widely scattered passages in his Notebook, but we refer in footnotes to the standard editions to assist readers in comparing our omissions and rearrangements with the texts established by Keynes and modified by Erdman. We have silently supplied missing letters when the context makes Blake's intention clear.

A Public Address to the Chalcographic Society

If Men of weak capacities have alone the Power of Execution in Art, Mr B. has now put to the test. If to Invent & to draw well hinders the Executive Power in Art, & his strokes are still to be Condemnd because they are unlike those of Artists who are Unacquainted with Drawing is now to be Decided by The Public. Mr B.'s Inventive Powers & his Scientific Knowledge of Drawing is on all hands acknowledged; it only remains to be Çertified whether Physiognomic Strength & Power is to give Place to Imbecillity.[1] * * *

Raphael—Sublime, Majestic, Graceful, Wise—
His Executive Power must I despise?
Rubens—Low, Vulgar, Stupid, Ignorant—
His power of Execution I must grant![2]

In a work of Art it is not fine tints that are required, but Fine Forms. Fine Tints without Fine Forms are always the Subterfuge of the Blockhead.

I account it a Public Duty respectfully to address myself to The Chalcographic Society & to Express to them my opinion (the result of the incessant Practice & Experience of Many Years) That Engraving as an art is Lost in England owing to an artfully propagated opinion that Drawing spoils an Engraver. I request the Society to inspect my Print,[3] of which drawing is the Foundation & indeed the Superstructure: it is drawing on copper, as Painting ought to be drawing on canvas or any other surface, & nothing Else. I request likewise that the Society will compare the Prints of Bartolozzi, Woolett, Strange &c. with the old English Portraits, that is, compare the Modern Art with the Art as it Existed Previous to the Enterance of Vandyke & Rubens into this Country, since which English Engraving is Lost, & I am sure the Result of the comparison will be that the Society must be of my Opinion that Engraving, by Losing drawing, has Lost all the character & all Expression, without which The Art is Lost.

In this Plate M^r^ B has resumed the style with which he set out in life, of which Heath & Stothard[4] were the awkward imitators at that time; it is the style of Alb. Durer's Histories & the old Engravers, which cannot be imitated by any one who does not understand drawing. * * *[5]

Commerce is so far from being beneficial to Arts or to Empire

1. Cf. *The Complete Writings of William Blake*, ed. Geoffrey Keynes (London and New York: Oxford, 1974), p. 591; and *The Poetry and Prose of William Blake*, ed. David V. Erdman (Garden City, N. Y.: Doubleday, 1970), p. 560.
2. Cf. Keynes, p. 547; and Erdman, p. 560. Blake's notes on page 11 of his Notebook indicate that the "Raphael Sublime" lines were to come in after "Imbecillity."
3. Evidently an impression of Blake's *Canterbury Pilgrims* (1810).
4. Stothard's *Canterbury Pilgrims*, which was based on Blake's idea for the picture (though Stothard may not have been aware of this) appeared before Blake's and won considerable acclaim. The other engravers attacked were not important to Blake personally; all engraved in the softer stipple and dot-and-lozenge methods which Blake deplored, following his master Basire in a preference for clean, sharp lines.
5. Cf. Keynes, pp. 591–92; and Erdman, pp. 560–61.

that it is destructive of both, as all their History shows, for the * * * Reason of Individual Merit being its Great hatred. Empires flourish till they become Commercial, & then they are scatterd abroad to the four winds.[6]

* * *

Englishmen, rouze yourselves from the fatal Slumber into which Booksellers & Trading Dealers have thrown you, Under the artfully propagated pretence that a Translation or a Copy of any kind can be as honourable to a Nation as An Original, Be-lying the English Character in that well known Saying, "Englishmen Improve what others Invent." This Even Hogarth's Works Prove a detestable Falshood. No Man Can Improve An Original Invention. Nor can an Original Invention Exist without Execution, Organized & minutely delineated and Articulated, Either by God or Man. I do not mean smoothd up & Niggled & Poco-Piu'd[7] and all the beauties pickd out & blurrd & blotted, but Drawn with a firm & decided hand at once like Fuseli & Michael Angelo, Shakespeare & Milton.[8]

Dryden in Rhyme cries, "Milton only Planned."
Every Fool shook his bells throughout the Land.
Tom Cooke cut Hogarth down with his clean Graving.
Thousands of Connoisseurs with joy ran raving!
Some blush at what others can see no crime in,
But Nobody sees any harm in Rhyming.
Thus Hayley on his Toilette seeing the Sope
Says, "Homer is very much improvd by Pope."
While I looking up to my Umbrella,
Resolvd to be a very Contrary Fellow
Cry, looking up from skumference to Center:
"No one can finish so high as the original inventor."[9]

I have heard many People say, "Give me the Ideas. It is no matter what Words you put them into," & others say, "Give me the Design, it is no matter for the Execution." These People know Enough of Artifice, but Nothing Of Art. Ideas cannot be Given but in their minutely Appropriate Words, nor Can a Design be made without its minutely Appropriate Execution. The unorganized Blots & Blurs of Rubens & Titian are not Art, nor can their Method ever express Ideas or Imaginations any more than Pope's Metaphysical Jargon of Rhyming. Unappropriate Execution is the Most nauseous of all affectation & foppery. He who copies does not Execute; he only Imitates what is already Executed. Execution is only the result of Invention.

6. Cf. Keynes, pp. 593–94, and Erdman, pp. 562–63.

7. *Poco più* is Italian eighteenth-century connoisseurs' slang for "a little bit more." See Jean H. Hagstrum, *Philological Quarterly* 53 (1974), 643–45.

8. See Keynes, p. 595, and Erdman, p. 565.

9. See Erdman, p. 496; the passage in Keynes, p. 595, includes this poem in the text.

Whoever looks at any of the Great & Expensive Works of Engraving that have been Publishd by English Traders must feel a Loathing & disgust, & accordingly most Englishmen have a Contempt for Art, which is the Greatest Curse that can fall upon a Nation.

He who could represent Christ uniformly like a Drayman must have Queer Conceptions; consequently his Execution must have been as Queer, & those must be Queer fellows who give great sums for such nonsense & think it fine Art.

The Modern Chalcographic Connoisseurs & Amateurs admire only the work of the journeyman, Picking out of whites & blacks in what is calld Tints; they despise drawing, which despises them in return. They see only whether every thing is toned down but one spot of light.

Mr B. submits to a more severe tribunal; he invites the admirers of old English Portraits to look at his Print.[1]

* * *

It is Nonsense for Noblemen & Gentlemen to offer Premiums for the Encouragement of Art when such Pictures as these can be done without Premiums; let them Encourage what Exists Already, & not endeavour to counteract by tricks. Let it no more be said that Empires Encourage Arts, for it is Arts that Encourage Empires. Arts & Artists are Spiritual & laugh at Mortal Contingencies. It is in their Power to hinder Instruction but not to Instruct, just as it is in their Power to Murder a Man but not to make a Man.

Let us teach Buonaparte, & whomsoever else it may concern, That it is not Arts that follow & attend upon Empire, but Empire that attends upon & follows The Arts.[1]

* * *

The English Artist may be assured that he is doing an injury & injustice to his Country while he studies & imitates the Effects of Nature. England will never rival Italy while we servilely copy what the Wise Italians, Rafael & Michael Angelo, scorned, nay abhorred, as Vasari tells us.

> Call that the Public Voice which is their Error,
> Like as a Monkey peeping in a Mirror
> Admires all his colours brown & warm
> And never once percieves his ugly form.

What kind of Intellects must he have who sees only the Colours of things & not the Forms of Things?

A Jockey that is anything of a Jockey will never buy a Horse by

1. See Keynes, p. 595, and Erdman, pp. 565–66.

2. See Keynes, pp. 596–97, and Erdman, p. 566.

the Colour, & a Man who has got any brains will never buy a Picture by the Colour.

When I tell any Truth it is not for the sake of Convincing those who do not know it, but for the sake of defending those who do.[3]

* * *

I wonder who can say, Speak no Ill of the dead when it is asserted in the Bible that the name of the Wicked shall Rot.[4] It is Deistical Virtue, I suppose, but as I have none of this I will pour Aqua Fortis on the Name of the Wicked & turn it into an Ornament & an Example to be Avoided by Some and Imitated by Others if they Please.

Columbus discoverd America, but Americus Vesputius finished & smoothd it over like an English Engraver or Corregio or Titian.

* * *

There is not, because there cannot be, any difference of Effect in the Pictures of Rubens & Rembrandt: when you have seen one of their Pictures you have seen all. It is not so with Rafael, Julio Romano, Alb. Durer, Mich. Ang. Every Picture of theirs has a different & appropriate Effect.

Yet I do not shrink from the comparison, in Either Relief or Strength of Colour, with either Rembrandt or Rubens; on the contrary, I court the Comparison & fear not the Result, but not in a dark Corner; their Effects are in Every Picture the same. Mine are in every Picture different.

I hope my Countrymen will Excuse me if I tell them a Wholesome truth. Most Englishmen, when they look at a Picture, immediately set about searching for Points of Light & clap the Picture into a dark corner. This, when done by Grand Works, is like looking for Epigrams in Homer. A point of light is a Witticism; many are destructive of all Art. One is an Epigram only & no Grand Work can have them: they Produce System & Monotony.

Rafael, Mich. Ang., Alb. D., Jul. Rom. are accounted ignorant of that Epigrammatic Wit in Art because they avoid it as a destructive Machine, as it is. * * *[5]

Gentlemen of Fortune who give Great Prices for Pictures should consider the following: Rubens's Luxembourg Gallery is Confessed on all hands to be the work of a Blockhead: it bears this Evidence in its face; how can its Execution be any other than the Work of a Blockhead? Bloated Gods: Mercury, Juno, Venus, & the rattle traps of Mythology & the lumber of an awkward French Palace are thrown together around Clumsy & Ricketty Princes & Princesses

3. See Keynes, p. 597, and Erdman, pp. 566–67.
4. Proverbs 10:7.
5. See Keynes, pp. 598–99, and Erdman p. 568.

higgledy piggledy. On the Contrary, Julio Romano's Palace of T at Mantua is allowd on all hands to be the Product of a Man of the Most Profound sense & Genius, & yet his Execution is pronouncd by English Connoisseurs & Reynolds, their doll, to be unfit for the Study of the Painter! Can I speak with too great Contempt of such Contemptible fellows? If all the Princes in Europe, like Louis XIV & Charles the first, were to Patronize such Blockheads, I, William Blake, a Mental Prince, should decollate & Hang their Souls as Guilty of Mental High Treason. * * *[6]

I am really sorry to see my Countrymen trouble themselves about Politics. If Men were Wise, the Most arbitrary Princes could not hurt them. If they are not wise, the Freest Government is compelld to be a Tyranny. Princes appear to me to be Fools. Houses of Commons & Houses of Lords appear to me to be fools; they seem to me to be something Else besides Human Life.

The wretched State of the Arts in this Country & in Europe, originating in the wretched State of Political Science, which is the Science of Sciences, Demands a firm & determinate conduct on the part of Artists to Resist the Contemptible Counter Arts established by such contemptible Politicians as Louis XIV & originally set on foot by Venetian Picture traders, Music traders, & Rhime traders, to the destruction of all true art as it is this Day.

To recover Art has been the business of my life to the Florentine Original & if possible to go beyond the Original; this I thought the only pursuit worthy of a Man. To Imitate I abhor. I obstinately adhere to the true Style of Art such as Michael Angelo, Rafael, Jul. Rom., Alb. Durer left it. I demand therefore of the Amateurs of art the Encouragement which is my due; if they continue to refuse, theirs is the loss, not mine, & theirs is the Contempt of Posterity. I have Enough in the Approbation of fellow labourers; this is my glory & exceeding great reward. I go on & nothing can hinder my course:

And in Melodious Accents, I
Will sit me down & Cry, I, I.[7]

* * *

The Painters of England are unemployd in Public Works, while the Sculptors have continual & superabundant employment. Our Churches & Abbeys are treasures of their producing for ages back, While Painting is excluded. Painting, the Principal Art, has no place among our almost only public works. Yet it is more adapted to solemn ornament than Marble can be, as it is capable of being Placed on any heighth & indeed would make a Noble finish Placed above the Great Public Monuments in Westminster, St Paul's &

6. See Keynes, p. 599, and Erdman, pp. 568–69.

7. See Keynes, p. 600, and Erdman, p. 569.

other Cathedrals. To the Society for Encouragement of Arts I address myself with Respectful duty, requesting their Consideration of my Plan as a Great Public means of advancing Fine Art in Protestant Communities. Monuments to the dead Painted by Historical & Poetical Artists, like Barry & Mortimer[8] (I forbear to name living Artists, tho equally worthy)—I say Monuments so Painted must make England What Italy is, an Envied Storehouse of Intellectual Riches.[9]

* * *

I do not condemn Rubens, Rembrandt or Titian because they did not understand drawing, but because they did not Understand Colouring. How long shall I be forced to beat this into Men's Ears? I do not condemn Strange or Woolett because they did not understand drawing, but because they did not understand Graving. I do not condemn Pope or Dryden because they did not understand Imagination, but because they did not understand Verse.[1]

He walks & stumbles as if he crept,
And how high labourd is every step.[2]

Their Colouring, Graving & Verse can never be applied to Art—That is not either Colouring, Graving or Verse which is Unappropriate to the Subject.

He who makes a design must know the Effect & Colouring Proper to be put to that design & will never take that of Rubens, Rembrandt or Titian to turn that which is Soul & Life into a Mill or Machine.[3]

They say there is no Strait Line in Nature; this Is a Lie, like all that they say. For there is Every Line in Nature. But I will tell them what is Not in Nature: An Even Tint is not in Nature; it produces Heaviness. Nature's Shadows are Ever varying, & a Ruled Sky that is quite Even never can Produce a Natural Sky; the same with every Object in a Picture, its Spots are its beauties. Now, Gentle-

8. James Barry (1741–1806), Irish history painter in the Grand Manner, the academic style of the late eighteenth century, is best known for his murals for the Society of Arts, *The Progress of Human Culture* (1783). He became professor of painting at the Royal Academy in 1783 but was expelled in 1799 because of his *Letter to the Dilettanti Society*, expressing contempt for his fellow Academicians. He also resented their reception of his *Death of General Wolfe*. He was the subject of Blake's lost or projected work, *Barry: A Poem*, possibly a companion piece to *Milton*, mentioned in a private memorandum. *Barry, The Book of Moonlight* and *For Children: The Gates of Hell* are presumed to be lost writings by Blake; possibly they were among the works said to have been destroyed for religious reasons by Tatham (see p. 496).

John Hamilton Mortimer (ca. 1741–79) was an English Romantic painter of conversation pieces, anecdotal pictures, and (especially important for Blake) dramatic moments in British history. He was a free-spending dandy, whereas Barry was ill-kempt, ill-tempered, and miserly. Though in general their works could hardly be more dissimilar, Blake admired paintings of the sublime by both.

9. Cf. Keynes, p. 601, and Erdman, p. 570.

1. Cf. Keynes, p. 602, and Erdman, p. 564.

2. Cf. Keynes, p. 548, and Erdman, p. 504.

3. Cf. Keynes, pp. 602–3, and Erdman, p. 564.

men Critics, how do you like this? You may rage, but what I say, I will prove by Such Practise & have already done, so that you will rage to your own destruction. A Machine is not a Man nor a Work of Art; it is destructive of Humanity & of Art. * * *

Every Line is the Line of Beauty; it is only fumble & Bungle which cannot draw a Line; this only is Ugliness. That is not a Line which doubts & Hesitates in the Midst of its Course.[4]

* * *

In a Commercial Nation Impostors are abroad in all Professions; these are the greatest Enemies of Genius. In the Art of Painting these Impostors sedulously propagate an Opinion that Great Inventors Cannot Execute. This Opinion is as destructive of the true Artist as it is false by all Experience. Even Hogarth cannot be either Copied or Improved. Can Anglus never Discern Perfection but in the Journeyman's Labour?

I know my Execution is not like Any Body Else. I do not intend it should be so; none but Blockheads Copy one another. My Conception & Invention are on all hands allowd to be Superior. My Execution will be found so too. To what is it that Gentleman of the first Rank both in Genius & Fortune have subscribed their Names? To My Inventions: the Executive part they never disputed; the Lavish praise I have recieved from all Quarters for Invention & drawing has Generally been accompanied by this: "He can concieve but he cannot Execute"; this Absurd assertion has done me, & may still do me, the greatest mischief. I call for Public protection against these Villains. I am, like others, Just Equal in Invention & in Execution as my works shew. I, in my own defence, Challenge a Competition with the finest Engravings & defy the most critical judge to make the Comparison Honestly, asserting in my own Defence that This Print is the Finest that has been done or is likely to be done in England, where drawing, its foundation, is Contemnd, and absurd Nonsense about dots & Lozenges & Clean Strokes made to occupy the attention to the Neglect of all real Art. I defy any Man to Cut Cleaner Strokes than I do, or rougher where I please, & assert that he who thinks he can Engrave, or Paint either, without being a Master of drawing is a Fool. Painting is drawing on Canvas, & Engraving is drawing on Copper, & nothing Else. Drawing is Execution, & nothing Else, & he who draws best must be the best Artist; to this I subscribe my name as a Public Duty.[5]

William Blake

4. Cf. Keynes, p. 603, and Erdman, p. 564. Hogarth had defined the "line of beauty" as the ogee curve.

5. Cf. Keynes, pp. 601–2, and Erdman, pp. 570–71. "Anglus" in the preceding paragraph seems to be a coinage for "the English."

Late Illuminated Broadsides

Although during the last twenty years of his life Blake seems to have concentrated more on painting than poetry, he produced some illuminated works displaying new combinations of text and design as late as about 1820. *The Laocoön* is an editorial title for a group of aphorisms surrounding a picture of the classical sculpture representing the Trojan priest Laocoön and his two sons being overcome by serpents, a subject from the second book of Virgil's *Aeneid. On Homer's Poetry* and *On Virgil* are two related tractates printed on one illuminated page. The design depicts a Bard singing to the people, Blake's last treatment of a subject to which he frequently returned throughout his career. *The Laocoön* (which Blake entitled "[Jehovah] & his two Sons, Satan & Adam") and *On Virgil* epitomize Blake's art criticism; *On Homer's Poetry* is a summation of his literary criticism. All three criticisms are made with special reference to the principles of classical as opposed to Christian culture, and all comprehend much wider considerations of religion and social ethics than were customary in discussions of aesthetics. See Peter F. Fisher, "Blake's Attacks on the Classical Tradition," *Philological Quarterly*, 40 (1961).

The aphorisms of *The Laocoön* flow over the whole sheet like graffiti, so that no single arrangement can represent the proper reading order. Ideally they are to be taken in simultaneously. Various arrangements will tend to bring out different significances: our ordering resembles Keynes's spatial arrangement in *The Complete Writings of William Blake* (Oxford, 1974). Our texts have been compared with the facsimiles in Geoffrey Keynes, ed., *William Blake's Laocoön: A Last Testament* with Related Works: *On Homer's Poetry* and *On Virgil, The Ghost of Abel*. London: Trianon, 1976.

The Laocoön

יה[1] & his two Sons Satan & Adam as they were copied from the Cherubim of Solomon's Temple by three Rhodians & applied to Natural Fact or History of Ilium.

Art Degraded, Imagination Denied; War Governed the Nations.
If Morality was Christianity Socrates was the Saviour.

1. This Hebrew lettering is the first syllable in God's ineffable name Yahweh, anglicized as Jehovah. The Hebrew word after "The Divine Body" is Jesus' Hebrew name, translated Joshua in the Old Testament. On the theory that classical art was copied from Hebrew originals, Blake claims that the statue of the Trojan priest Laocoön (*Aeneid* II, 41–53, and 201–31) really represents Jehovah and that his two sons are Satan and Adam (the limits of opacity and contraction in, for example, *Milton* 13:20 and *Jerusalem* 35:1). Laocoön-Jehovah is also labeled in Hebrew and English "The Angel of the Divine Presence" and in Greek "Serpent-holder." The head of the serpent in his left hand is labeled "Good" (with the Hebrew word for Lilith, Adam's legendary first wife, under a coil of its body), and the head of the serpent biting the son on his right is labelled "Evil." The pediment of the sculptural group is inscribed "Drawn & Engraved by William Blake." On Blake's spotty Hebrew, see Arnold Cheskin, "The Echoing Greenhorn," *Blake*, 12 (1978–79).

Spiritual War: Israel deliver'd from Egypt, is Art deliver'd from Nature & Imitation.

A Poet, a Painter, a Musician, an Architect: the Man Or Woman who is not one of these is not a Christian.

You must leave Fathers & Mothers & Houses & Lands if they stand in the way of Art.

Prayer is the Study of Art.

Praise is the Practise of Art.

Fasting &c., all relate to Art.

The outward Ceremony is Antichrist.

The Eternal Body of Man is The **Imagination**, that is,
God himself } ישוע, Jesus: we are his Members.
The Divine Body }

It manifests itself in his Works of Art (In Eternity All is Vision).

The True Christian Charity not dependent on Money (the life's blood of Poor Families), that is, on Caesar or Empire or Natural Religion: Money, which is The Great Satan or Reason, the Root of Good & Evil, In The Accusation of Sin.

Where any view of Money exists, Art cannot be carried on, but War only (Read Matthew, c. x: 9 & 10 v.) by pretences to the Two Impossibilities, Chastity & Abstinence, Gods of the Heathen.

He repented that he had made Adam (of the Female, the Adamah) & it grieved him at his heart.

What can be Created Can be Destroyed.

Adam is only The Natural Man & not the Soul or Imagination.

Art can never exist without Naked Beauty displayed.

The Gods of Greece & Egypt were Mathematical Diagrams—See Plato's Works.

Divine Union Deriding, And Denying Immediate Communion with God, The Spoilers say, "Where are his Works That he did in the Wilderness? Lo, what are these? Whence came they?" These are not the Works Of Egypt nor Babylon, Whose Gods are the Powers Of this World, Goddess Nature, Who first spoil & then destroy Imaginative Art; For their Glory is War and Dominion.

Empire against Art. See Virgil's Eneid, Lib. VI, v. 848.

For every Pleasure Money Is Useless.

There are States in which all Visionary Men are accounted Mad Men; such are Greece & Rome: Such is Empire or Tax. See Luke, Ch. 2, v. 1.

Good & Evil are Riches & Poverty, a Tree of Misery, propagating Generation & Death.

The Gods of Priam are the Cherubim of Moses & Solomon, The Hosts of Heaven.

Without Unceasing Practise nothing can be done. Practise is Art. If you leave off you are Lost.

Satan's Wife, The Goddess Nature, is War & Misery, & Heroism a Miser.

Hebrew Art is called Sin by the Deist Science.

All that we See is Vision, from Generated Organs gone as soon as come, Permanent in The Imagination, Consider'd as Nothing by the Natural Man.

Jesus & his Apostles & Disciples were all Artists. Their Works were destroy'd by the Seven Angels of the Seven Churches in Asia, Antichrist Science.

The unproductive Man is not a Christian, much less the Destroyer.

Christianity is Art & not Money. Money is its Curse.

The Old & New Testaments are the Great Code of Art.

Art is the Tree of Life. GOD is Jesus.

Science is the Tree of Death.

The Whole Business of Man Is The Arts, & All Things Common. No Secresy in Art.

What we call Antique Gems are the Gems of Aaron's Breast Plate.

Is not every Vice possible to Man described in the Bible openly?

All is not Sin that Satan calls so: all the Loves & Graces of Eternity.

On Homer's Poetry

Every Poem must necessarily be a perfect Unity, but why Homer's is peculiarly so, I cannot tell: he has told the story of Bellerophon & omitted the Judgment of Paris which is not only a part, but a principal part of Homer's subject.

But when a Work has Unity, it is as much in a Part as in the Whole; the Torso[2] is as much a Unity as the Laocoön.

As Unity is the cloke of folly so Goodness is the cloke of knavery. Those who will have Unity exclusively in Homer come out with a Moral like a sting in the tail. Aristotle says Characters are either Good or Bad: now Goodness or Badness has nothing to do with Character. An Apple tree, a Pear tree, a Horse, a Lion, are Characters; but a Good Apple tree or a Bad, is an Apple tree still: a Horse is not more a Lion for being a Bad Horse. That is its Character: its Goodness or Badness is another consideration.

It is the same with the Moral of a whole Poem as with the Moral Goodness of its parts. Unity & Morality, are secondary considerations & belong to Philosophy & not to Poetry, to Exception & not to Rule, to Accident & not to Substance. The Ancients calld it eating of the tree of good & evil.

The Classics, it is the Classics! & not Goths nor Monks, that Desolate Europe with Wars.

On Virgil

Sacred Truth has pronounced that Greece & Rome, as Babylon & Egypt, so far from being parents of Arts & Sciences as they pretend, were destroyers of all Art. Homer, Virgil & Ovid confirm this opinion & make us reverence The Word of God, the only light of antiquity that remains unperverted by War. Virgil in the Eneid Book VI, line 848 says, "Let others study Art: Rome has somewhat better to do, namely War & Dominion."[3]

Rome & Greece swept Art into their maw & destroyd it. A Warlike State never can produce Art. It will Rob & Plunder & accumulate into one place, & Translate & Copy & Buy & Sell & Criticise, but not Make. Grecian is Mathematic Form. Gothic is Living Form.

Mathematic Form is Eternal in the Reasoning Memory. Living Form is Eternal Existence.

2. The Belvedere Torso, Greek relic of a muscular male nude which influenced Michelangelo. Like the Laocoön, the Torso is in the Vatican Museum; it was known to English artists through engravings and plaster casts. Various efforts were made at reconstructing the missing parts, but in the nineteenth century it began to be appreciated as a fragment.

3. Cited also in *The Laocoön*.

Blake's Marginalia

The annotations Blake wrote in the margins of books and on the title pages, endpapers, or wherever he could find a blank space, are among the most extraordinary of his writings. Of English writers only Coleridge can begin to rival Blake as an annotator. Though Blake perhaps lent books he had annotated to a few friends, thus keeping his annotations from being purely private, it is remarkable that he deployed such energies in work never intended for publication. His most famous annotations, those on *Watson's Apology for the Bible* (1797–98) and Reynolds's *Discourses* (ca. 1798–1809), show a wonderful indignation against the ideas in these books and even a detestation of their authors as well. On the other hand, Lavater's *Aphorisms on Man* (1789) inspired some of Blake's most memorable positive formulations. For example, in response to Lavater's aphorism 407, "Whatever is the vessel or veil of the invisible past, present, future—as man penetrates to this more, or perceives it less, he raises or depresses his dignity of being," Blake wrote, "A vision of the Eternal Now." Indeed, Lavater may be given credit for Blake's lifelong habit of annotating books, for Blake noted that he was following the instructions in Lavater's final aphorism: "If you mean to know yourself, interline such of these aphorisms as affect you agreeably in reading, and set a mark to such as left a sense of uneasiness with you; and then show your copy to whom you please." For the *Aphorisms* as a body of work, Blake felt an admiration so deep that he added his own name to the author's on the title page and enclosed both in an outline of a heart.

Many misapprehensions about Blake can be corrected simply by a reading of his annotations: that he was mad, that he was unlearned, that he was characteristically obscure, or sweet-tempered, or long-winded. One sees instead how often Blake was stimulated—or triggered—by his reading to write out some of his basic ideas. Least of all does one observe in this inveterate annotator a hedgehog who went his own way indifferent to what others were saying. If he had chosen to be so, Blake could have been a masterful controversialist, or even a heckler.

There is no ideal way to present Blake's Marginalia. The collected editions do their best to give the immediate passages to which Blake is responding but are unable to convey a wholly satisfactory impression of how by marginal marks, or underlinings, or even cartoons, Blake was building up a head of steam that exploded when he had had enough or could find a large enough space to mount a counterattack. Moreover, because some of the authors were given to long sentences it is often necessary in the standard editions to present many lines of uninspired thought in order to show that Blake, in one word, agreed or disagreed. The percentage of pure gold on many pages is not high and thus it is easy to overlook some of Blake's best aphorisms. For this reason we have chosen to represent (with some minor exceptions) only selections of what Blake wrote, though we would have liked to show the give and take of the original annotated books. As is evident in the "Proverbs of Hell," "Auguries of Innocence," and *The Laocoön*, Blake was a splendid aphorist; consequently, the force of many of his annotations is scarcely diminished when they are quoted out of context, and some of his longer annotations amount to miniature essays which outclass the texts that provoked them and are improved by being allowed to stand alone.

On John Casper Lavater, *Aphorisms on Man*, translated by J. H. Fuseli (ca. 1789)

Severity of judgment is a great virtue.

I hate scarce smiles: I love laughing.

To hell till he[1] behaves better! mark that I do not believe there is such a thing litterally, but hell is the being shut up in the possession of corporeal desires which shortly weary the man, *for* ALL LIFE IS HOLY.

Mark! Active Evil is better than Passive Good.

Man is a twofold being, one part capable of evil & the other capable of good; that which is capable of good is not also capable of evil, but that which is capable of evil is also capable of good. This aphorism[2] seems to consider man as simple & yet capable of evil: now both evil & good cannot exist in a simple being, for thus 2 contraries would spring from one essence, which is impossible; but if man is consider'd as only evil & god only good, how then is regeneration effected which turns the evil to good? by casting out the evil by the good? See Matthew xii Ch., 26, 27, 28, 29 v.

Man is bad or good as he unites himself with bad or good spirits: tell me with whom you go & I'll tell you what you do.

As we cannot experience pleasure but by means of others who experience either pleasure or pain thro us, And as all of us on earth are united in thought, for it is impossible to think without images of somewhat on earth—So it is impossible to know God or heavenly things without conjunction with those who know God & heavenly things; therefore all who converse in the spirit, converse with spirits.

There is a strong objection to Lavater's principles (as I understand them) & that is He makes every thing originate in its accident; he makes the vicious propensity not only a leading feature of the man, but the Stamina on which all his virtues grow. But as I understand Vice it is a Negative. It does not signify what the laws of Kings & Priests have call'd Vice; we who are philosophers ought not to call the Staminal Virtues of Humanity by the same name that we call the omissions of intellect springing from poverty.

1. A carper.

2. Aphorism 489.

Every man's leading propensity ought to be calld his leading Virtue & his good Angel. But the Philosophy of Causes & Consequences misled Lavater as it has all his Cotemporaries. Each thing is its own cause & its own effect. Accident is the omission of act in self & the hindering of act in another; This is Vice, but all Act is Virtue. To hinder another is not an act; it is the contrary; it is a restraint on action both in ourselves & in the person hinderd, for he who hinders another omits his own duty at the [same] time.

Murder is Hindering Another.

Theft is Hindering Another.

Backbiting, Undermining, Circumventing, & whatever is Negative is Vice.

But the origin of this mistake in Lavater & his cotemporaries is, They suppose that Woman's Love is Sin; in consequence all the Loves & Graces with them are Sin.

On Emanuel Swedenborg, *The Wisdom of Angels, Concerning Divine Love and Divine Wisdom*, translated by N. Tucker (1788)

There can be no Good-Will. Will is always Evil; it is pernicious to others or selfish. If God is anything he is Understanding. He is the Influx from that into the Will. This Good to others or benevolent Understanding can Work Harm ignorantly but never can the Truth be evil because Man is only Evil when he wills an untruth.

Understanding or Thought is not natural to Man; it is acquired by means of Suffering & Distress, i.e. Experience. Will, Desire, Love, Rage, Envy, & all other affections are Natural, but Understanding is Acquired. But Observe: without these is to be less than man.

Man can have no idea of any thing greater than Man, as a cup cannot contain more than its capaciousness. But God is a man, not because he is so percievd by man, but because he is the creator of man.

Think of a white cloud as being holy, you cannot love it; but think of a holy man within the cloud, love springs up in your thoughts, for to think of holiness distinct from man is impossible to the affections. Thought alone can make monsters, but the affections cannot.

Study Sciences till you are blind, Study intellectuals till you are cold, Yet science cannot teach intellect. Much less can intellect teach Affection.

On R. Watson, Bishop of Llandaff, *An Apology for The Bible * * * addressed to Thomas Paine* (1797)

To defend the Bible in this year 1798 would cost a man his life.

The Beast & the Whore rule without control.

It is an easy matter for a Bishop to triumph over Paine's attack, but it is not so easy for one who loves the Bible.

The Perversions of Christ's words & acts are attackd by Paine & also the perversions of the Bible; Who dare defend either the Acts of Christ or the Bible Unperverted?

But to him who sees this mortal pilgrimage in the light that I see it, Duty to his country is the first consideration & safety the last.

Read patiently: take not up this Book in an idle hour: the consideration of these things is the whole duty of man & the affairs of life & death trifles, sports of time. But these considerations [are the] business of Eternity.

I have been commanded from Hell not to print this, as it is what our Enemies wish.

Paine has not attacked Christianity. Watson has defended Antichrist.

Read the xxiii Chap. of Matthew & then condemn Paine's hatred of Priests if you dare.

God made Man happy & Rich, but the Subtil made the innocent Poor.

This must be a most wicked & blasphemous book.

If this first Letter is written without Railing & Illiberality I have never read one that is. To me it is all Daggers & Poison; the sting of the serpent is in every Sentence as well as the glittering Dissimulation. Achilles' wrath is blunt abuse, Thersites' sly insinuation: such is the Bishop's. If such is the characteristic of a modern polite gentleman we may hope to see Christ's discourses Expung'd.

I have not the Charity for the Bishop that he pretends to have for Paine. I believe him to be a State trickster.

Presumptuous Murderer! Dost thou, O Priest, wish thy brother's death when God has preserved him?

Mr. Paine has not extinguishd, & cannot Extinguish, Moral rectitude; he has Extinguishd Superstition, which took the Place of Moral Rectitude. What has Moral Rectitude to do with Opinions concerning historical fact?

To what does the Bishop attribute the English Crusade against France? Is it not to State Religion? Blush for shame.

Folly & Impudence. Does the thorough belief of Popery hinder crimes, or can the man who writes the latter sentiment be in the good humour the bishop Pretends to be? If we are to expect crimes from Paine & his followers, are we to believe that Bishops do not Rail? I should Expect that the man who wrote this sneaking sentence would be as good an inquisitor as any other Priest.

Conscience in those that have it is unequivocal. It is the voice of God. Our judgment of right & wrong is Reason. I believe that the Bishop laught at the Bible in his slieve & so did Locke.

Virtue & honesty or the dictates of Conscience are of no doubtful Signification to anyone.

Opinion is one Thing. Principle another. No Man can change his Principles. Every Man changes his opinions. He who supposes that his Principles are to be changed is a Dissembler, who Disguises his Principles & calls that change.

Paine is either a Devil or an Inspired man. Men who give themselves to their Energetic Genius in the manner that Paine does are no Examiners. If they are not determinately wrong they must be Right or the Bible is false; as to Examiners in these points they will be spewed out.

The Man who pretends to be a modest enquirer into the truth of a self evident thing is a Knave. The truth & certainty of Virtue & Honesty, i.e. Inspiration, needs no one to prove it; it is Evident as the Sun & Moon. He who stands doubting of what he intends, whether it is Virtuous or Vicious, knows not what Virtue means. No man can do a Vicious action & think it to be Virtuous. No man can take darkness for light. He may pretend to do so & may pretend to be a modest Enquirer, but he is a Knave.

To me, who believe the Bible & profess myself a Christian, a defence of the Wickedness of the Israelites in murdering so many thousands under pretence of a command from God is altogether Abominable & Blasphemous. Why did Christ come? Was it not to abolish the Jewish Imposture? Was not Christ murderd because he taught that God loved all Men & was their father & forbad all contention for Worldly prosperity in opposition to the Jewish Scriptures, which are only an Example of the wickedness & deceit of the Jews & were written as an Example of the possibility of Human Beastliness in all its branches? Christ died as an Unbeliever & if the Bishops had their will so would Paine, but he who speaks a word against the Son of man shall be forgiven. Let the Bishop prove that he has not spoken against the Holy Ghost, who in Paine strives with Christendom as in Christ he strove with the Jews.

The Bible says that God formed Nature perfect, but that Man perverted the order of Nature, since which time the Elements are filld with the Prince of Evil, who has the power of the air.

Natural Religion is the voice of God & not the result of reasoning on the Powers of Satan.

Horrible! The Bishop is an Inquisitor. God never makes one man murder another, nor one nation.

There is a vast difference between an accident brought on by a man's own carelessness & destruction from the designs of another. The Earthquakes at Lisbon &c. were the Natural result of Sin, but the destruction of the Canaanites by Joshua was the unnatural design of wicked men. To Extirpate a nation by means of another is as wicked as to destroy an individual by means of another individual, which God considers (in the Bible) as Murder & commands that it shall not be done.

Therefore the Bishop has not answered Paine.

Read the Edda of Iceland, the Songs of Fingal, the accounts of North American Savages (as they are calld). Likewise read Homer's Iliad; he was certainly a Savage in the Bishop's sense. He knew nothing of God in the Bishop's sense of the word & yet he was no fool.

The Bible or Peculiar Word of God, Exclusive of Conscience or the Word of God Universal, is that Abomination which like the Jewish ceremonies is for ever removed & henceforth every man may converse with God & be a King & Priest in his own house.

It is strange that God should speak to man formerly & not now, because it is not true; but the Strangeness of Sun, Moon, or Stars is Strange on a contrary account.

The trifles which the Bishop has combated in the following Letters are such as do nothing against Paine's Arguments, none of which the Bishop has dared to Consider. One, for instance, which is That the books of the Bible were never believd willingly by any nation & that none but designing Villains ever pretended to believe —That the Bible is all a State Trick thro which, tho' the People at all times could see, they never had the power to throw off. Another Argument is that all the Commentators on the Bible are Dishonest Designing Knaves, who in hopes of a good living adopt the State religion; this he has shewn with great force, which calls upon His Opponent loudly for an answer. I could name an hundred such.

He who writes things for true which none would write but the actor (such are most of the acts of Moses) must either be the actor or a fable writer or a liar. If Moses did not write the history of his acts, it takes away the authority altogether; it ceases to be history & becomes a Poem of probable impossibilities, fabricated for pleasure, as moderns say, but I say by Inspiration.

Jesus could not do miracles where unbelief hinderd; hence we must conclude that the man who holds miracles to be ceased puts it out of his own power to ever witness one. The manner of a miracle being performed is in modern times considerd as an arbitrary command of the agent upon the patient, but this is an impossibility, not a miracle, neither did Jesus ever do such a miracle. Is it a greater miracle to feed five thousand men with five loaves than to overthrow all the armies of Europe with a small pamphlet? Look over the events of your own life & if you do not find that you have both done such miracles & lived by such you do not see as I do. True, I cannot do a miracle thro experiment & to domineer over & prove to others my superior power, as neither could Christ. But I can & do work such as both astonish & comfort me & mine. How can Paine, the worker of miracles, ever doubt Christ's in the above sense of the word miracle? But how can Watson ever believe the above sense of a miracle, who considers it as an arbitrary act of the agent upon an unbelieving patient, whereas the Gospel says that Christ could not do a miracle because of Unbelief?

If Christ could not do miracles because of Unbelief, the reason alledged by Priests for miracles is false, for those who believe want not to be confounded by miracles. Christ & his Prophets & Apostles were not Ambitious miracle mongers.

Prophets, in the modern sense of the word, have never existed. Jonah was no prophet in the modern sense, for his prophecy of Nineveh failed. Every honest man is a Prophet; he utters his opinion both of private & public matters, Thus: If you go on So, the result is So. He never says, such a thing shall happen let you do what you will. A Prophet is a Seer, not an Arbitary Dictator. It is man's fault if God is not able to do him good, for he gives to the just & to the unjust, but the unjust reject his gift.

Nothing can be more contemptible than to suppose Public RECORDS to be True. Read them & Judge, if you are not a Fool.

Of what consequence is it whether Moses wrote the Pentateuch or no? If Paine trifles in some of his objections it is folly to confute him so seriously in them & leave his more material ones unanswered. PUBLIC RECORDS! As if Public Records were True! Impossible—for the facts are such as none but the actor could tell. If it is

True, Moses & none but he could write it, unless we allow it to be Poetry & that poetry inspired.

If historical facts can be written by inspiration, Milton's Paradise Lost is as true as Genesis or Exodus; but the Evidence is nothing, for how can he who writes what he has neither seen nor heard of be an Evidence of The Truth of his history?

I cannot concieve the Divinity of the books in the Bible to consist either in who they were written by, or at what time, or in the historical evidence, which may be all false in the eyes of one man & true in the eyes of another, but in the Sentiments & Examples, which, whether true or Parabolic, are Equally useful as Examples given to us of the perverseness of some & its consequent evil & the honesty of others & its consequent good. This sense of the Bible is equally true to all & equally plain to all. None can doubt the impression which he recieves from a book of Examples. If he is good he will abhor wickedness in David or Abraham; if he is wicked he will make their wickedness an excuse for his & so he would do by any other book.

All Penal Laws court Transgression & therefore are cruelty & Murder.

The laws of the Jews were (both ceremonial & real) the basest & most oppressive of human codes, & being like all other codes given under pretence of divine command were what Christ pronounced them, The Abomination that maketh desolate, *i.e.* State Religion, which is the source of all Cruelty.

They seem to Forget that there is a God of this World, A God Worshipd in this World as God & set above all that is calld God.

The Bishop never saw the Everlasting Gospel any more than Tom Paine.

Do or Act to Do Good or to do Evil: Who dare to Judge but God alone?

Who does the Bishop call Bad Men? Are they the Publicans & sinners that Christ loved to associate with? Does God Love the Righteous according to the Gospel, or does he not cast them off?

For who is really Righteous? It is all Pretension.

It appears to me Now that Tom Paine is a better Christian than the Bishop.

I have read this Book with attention & find that the Bishop has only hurt Paine's heel while Paine has broken his head. The Bishop has not answerd one of Paine's grand objections.

On Francis Bacon, *Essays Moral, Economical and Political* (1798)

Is it True or is it False that the Wisdom of this World is Foolishness with God?

This is Certain: If what Bacon says Is True, what Christ says Is False. If Caesar is Right, Christ is Wrong both in Politics & Religion, since they will divide them in Two.

Good Advice for Satan's Kingdom.

Every Body Knows that this is Epicurus and Lucretius & Yet Every Body says that it is Christian Philosophy; how is this Possible? Every Body must be a Liar & deciever. But Every Body does not do this, But The Hirelings of Kings & Courts who make themselves Every Body & Knowingly propagate Falshood.

It was a Common opinion in the Court of Queen Elizabeth that Knavery Is Wisdom. Cunning Plotters were considerd as wise Machiavels.

Self Evident Truth is one Thing and Truth the result of Reasoning is another Thing. Rational Truth is not the Truth of Christ, but of Pilate. It is the Tree of the Knowledge of Good & Evil.

Did not Jesus descend & become a Servant? The Prince of darkness is a Gentleman & not a Man: he is a Lord Chancellor.

Every Body hates a King. * * *

The Increase of a State as of a Man is from Internal Improvement or Intellectual Acquirement. Man is not Improved by the hurt of another. States are not Improved at the Expense of Foreigners.

Bacon has no notion of anything but Mammon.

What a Cursed Fool is this! Ill Shapen! Are Infants or small Plants ill shapen because they are not yet come to their maturity? What a contemptible Fool is this Bacon!

Bacon calls Intellectual Arts Unmanly. Poetry, Painting, Music are in his opinion Useless & so they are for Kings & Wars & shall in the End Annihilate them.

King James was Bacon's Primum Mobile.

On Henry Boyd, *A Translation of "The Inferno" in English Verse, with Historical Notes* * * * (1785)

If Homer's merit was only in these Historical combinations & Moral sentiments, he would be no better than Clarissa.

Every body naturally hates a perfect character because they are all greater Villains than the imperfect, as Eneas is here shewn as worse man than Achilles in leaving Dido.

The grandest Poetry is Immoral, the Grandest characters Wicked, Very Satan: Capanius, Othello a murderer, Prometheus, Jupiter, Jehovah, Jesus a wine bibber.

Cunning & Morality are not Poetry but Philosophy: the Poet is Independent & Wicked; the Philosopher is Dependent & Good.

Poetry is to excuse Vice & shew its reason & necessary purgation.

Dante was a Fool or his Translator was not: That is, Dante was Hired or Tr. was Not. It appears to Me that Men are hired to Run down Men of Genius under the Mask of Translators, but Dante gives too much [to] Caesar: he is not a Republican.

Dante was an Emperor's, a Caesar's Man; Luther also left the Priest & joind the Soldier.

What is Liberty without Universal Toleration?

If it is thus,[3] the extreme of black is white, & of sweet sower, & of good Evil, & of Nothing Something.

On *The Works of Sir Joshua Reynolds, Knight* * * * edited by Edmund Malone, 3 volumes (1798)

This Man was Hired to Depress Art: This is the Opinion of Will Blake. My Proofs of this Opinion are given in the following Notes.

Advice of the Popes who succeeded the Age of Rafael:

> Degrade first the Arts if you'd Mankind Degrade.
> Hire Idiots to Paint with cold light & hot shade:
> Give high Price for the worst, leave the best in disgrace,
> And with Labours of Ignorance fill every place.

Having spent the Vigour of my Youth & Genius under the Opression of Sr Joshua & his Gang of Cunning Hired Knaves With-

3. I.e., that there are certain bounds, even to liberty.

out Employment & as much as could possibly be Without Bread, The Reader must Expect to Read in all my Remarks on these Books Nothing but Indignation & Resentment. While Sr Joshua was rolling in Riches, Barry was Poor & Unemployd except by his own Energy; Mortimer was calld a Madman, & only Portrait Painting applauded & rewarded by the Rich & Great. Reynolds & Gainsborough Blotted & Blurred one against the other & Divided all the English World between them. Fuseli, Indignant, almost hid himself. I am hid.

The Arts & Sciences are the Destruction of Tyrannies or Bad Governments. Why should A Good Government endeavour to Depress what is its Chief & only Support?

The Foundation of Empire is Art & Science. Remove them or Degrade them, & the Empire is No More. Empire follows Art & Not Vice versa, as Englishmen suppose.

To learn the Language of Art, "Copy for Ever" is My Rule.

The Bible says That Cultivated Life Existed First—Uncultivated Life comes afterwards from Satan's Hirelings. Necessaries, Accommodations & Ornaments are the whole of Life. First were created Wine & Happiness, Good Looks & Fortune.[4] Satan took away Ornament First. Next he took away Accomodations, & Then he became Lord & Master of Necessaries.

Liberality! We want not Liberality. We want a Fair Price & Proportionate Value & a General Demand for Art.

Let not that Nation where Less than Nobility is the Reward, Pretend that Art is Encouraged by that Nation. Art is First in Intellectuals & Ought to be First in Nations.

Invention depends Altogether upon Execution or Organization; as that is right or wrong so is the Invention perfect or imperfect. Whoever is set to Undermine the Execution of Art is set to Destroy Art. Michael Angelo's Art depends on Michael Angelo's Execution Altogether.

I am happy I cannot say that Rafael Ever was, from my Earliest Childhood, hidden from Me. I Saw & I Knew immediately the difference between Rafael & Rubens.

Some look to see the sweet Outlines
And beauteous Forms that Love does wear.
Some look to find out Patches, Paint,
Bracelets & Stays & Powderd Hair.

4. This sentence was deleted by Blake.

I was once looking over the Prints from Rafael & Michel Angelo in the Library of the Royal Academy. Moser[5] came to me & said, "You should not Study these old Hard, Stiff & Dry Unfinishd Works of Art; Stay a little & I will shew you what you should Study." He then want & took down LeBruns' & Rubens's Galleries.[6] How I did secretly Rage! I also spoke my Mind.

I said to Moser, "These things that you call Finishd are not Even Begun; how can they then be Finishd? The man who does not know The Beginning never can know the End of Art."

To Generalize is to be an Idiot. To Particularize is the Alone Distinction of Merit. General Knowledges are those Knowledges that Idiots possess.

I consider Reynolds's Discourses to the Royal Academy as the Simulations of the Hypocrite who smiles particularly where he means to Betray. His Praise of Rafael is like the Hysteric Smile of Revenge. His Softness & Candour, the hidden trap & the poisoned feast. He praises Michel Angelo for Qualities which Michel Angelo abhorrd; & He blames Rafael for the only Qualities which Rafael Valued. Whether Reynolds knew what he was doing is nothing to me; the Mischief is just the same whether a Man does it Ignorantly or Knowingly. I always consider'd True Art & True Artists to be particularly Insulted & Degraded by the Reputation of these Discourses, As much as they were Degraded by the Reputation of Reynolds's Paintings, & that Such Artists as Reynolds are at all times Hired by the Satans for the Depression of Art—A pretence of Art, To destroy Art.

The Neglect of Fuseli's Milton in a Country pretending to the Encouragement of Art is a Sufficient Apology for my Vigorous Indignation, if indeed the Neglect of My own Powers had not been. Ought not the Employers of Fools to be Execrated in future Ages? They Will and Shall! Foolish Men, your own real Greatness depends on your Encouragement of the Arts, & your Fall will depend on their Neglect & Depression. What you Fear is your true Interest. Leo X was advised not to Encourage the Arts; he was too Wise to take this Advice.

The Rich Men of England form themselves into a Society to sell & Not to Buy Pictures. The Artist who does not throw his Con-

5. George Michael Moser (1704–83), German goldsmith, enameller, and medallist, Keeper of Prints and Drawings at the Royal Academy.

6. Charles Le Bruns (1619–90), court painter for Louis XIV, held that all art is reducible to rule; Sir Peter Paul Rubens (1577–1640), Flemish master of the Baroque style, worked in many European courts, including that of Charles I. Blake thought neither of these artists placed enough emphasis on outline.

tempt on such Trading Exhibitions, does not know either his own Interest or his Duty.

When Nations grow Old, The Arts grow Cold
And Commerce settles on every Tree,
And the Poor & the Old can live upon Gold,
For all are Born Poor, Aged Sixty three.

Reynolds's Opinion was that Genius May be Taught & that all Pretence to Inspiration is a Lie & a Deceit, to say the least of it. For if it is a Deceit, the whole Bible is Madness. This Opinion originates in the Greeks' Calling the Muses Daughters of Memory.

The Enquiry in England is not whether a Man has Talents & Genius, But whether he is Passive & Polite & a Virtuous Ass & obedient to Noblemen's Opinions in Art & Science. If he is, he is a Good Man; If Not, he must be Starved.

I do not believe that Rafael taught Mich. Angelo, or that Mich. Angelo taught Rafael, any more than I believe that the Rose teaches the Lilly how to grow, or the Apple tree teaches the Pear tree how to bear Fruit. I do not believe the tales of Anecdote writers when they militate against Individual Character.

Minute Discrimination is Not Accidental. All Sublimity is founded on Minute Discrimination.

Execution is the Chariot of Genius.

The Lives of Painters say that Rafael Died of Dissipation. Idleness is one Thing & Dissipation Another. He who has Nothing to Dissipate Cannot Dissipate; the Weak Man may be virtuous Enough, but will Never be an Artist.

Painters are noted for being Dissipated & Wild.

* * * No one can ever Design till he has learn'd the Language of Art by making many Finishd Copies both of Nature & Art & of whatever comes in his way from Earliest Childhood.

The difference between a bad Artist & a Good One Is, the Bad Artist Seems to Copy a Great deal; The Good one Really Does Copy a Great deal.

Servile Copying is the Great Merit of Copying.

Every Eye Sees differently. As the Eye, Such the Object.

The Man who asserts that there is no Such Thing as Softness in Art & that every thing in Art is Definite & Determinate has not been told this by Practise, but by Inspiration & Vision, because Vision is Determinate & Perfect, & he Copies That without Fatigue,

Every thing being Definite & determinate. Softness is Produced alone by Comparative Strength & Weakness in the Marking out of the Forms.

I say These Principles could never be found out by the Study of Nature without Con—or Innate—Science.

A work of Genius is a Work "Not to be obtaind by the Invocation of Memory & her Syren Daughters, but by Devout prayer to that Eternal Spirit, who can enrich with all utterance & knowledge & sends out his Seraphim with the hallowed fire of his Altar to touch & purify the lips of whom he pleases." MILTON.

The following Discourse[7] is particularly Interesting to Block heads, as it Endeavours to prove That there is No such thing as Inspiration & that any Man of a plain Understanding may by Thieving from Others become a Mich. Angelo.

Without Minute Neatness of Execution The Sublime cannot Exist! Grandeur of Ideas is founded on Precision of Ideas.

Knowledge of Ideal Beauty is Not to be Acquired. It is Born with us. Innate Ideas are in Every Man, Born with him; they are truly Himself. The Man who says that we have No Innate Ideas must be a Fool & Knave, Having No Con-Science or Innate Science.

One Central Form composed of all other Forms Being Granted, it does not therefore follow that all other Forms are Deformity.

All Forms are Perfect in the Poet's Mind, but these are not Abstracted nor Compounded from Nature, but are from Imagination.

The Great Bacon (he is Calld—I call him the Little Bacon) says that Every thing must be done by Experiment; his first principle is Unbelief, and yet here he says that Art must be producd Without such Method. He is like Sr Joshua, full of Self-Contradiction & Knavery.

What is General Nature? is there Such a Thing? what is General Knowledge? is there such a thing? All Knowledge is Particular.

What does this mean, "*Would have been*" *one of the first Painters of his Age?* Albert Durer *Is*! Not would have been! Besides, let them look at Gothic Figures & Gothic Buildings & not talk of Dark Ages or of any Age. Ages are all Equal. But Genius is Always Above The Age.

Gainsborough told a Gentleman of Rank & Fortune that the Worst Painters always chose the Grandest Subjects. I desired the Gentleman to Set Gainsborough about one of Rafael's Grandest

7. I.e., *Discourse* III.

Subjects, Namely Christ delivering the Keys to St Peter, & he would find that in Gainsborough's hands it would be a Vulgar Subject of Poor Fishermen & a Journeyman Carpenter.

The following Discourse[8] is written with the same End in View that Gainsborough had in making the Above assertion: Namely, To Represent Vulgar Artists as the Models of Executive Merit.

To My Eye Rubens's Colouring is most Contemptible. His Shadows are of a Filthy Brown somewhat of the Colour of Excrement; these are filld with tints & messes of yellow & red. His lights are all the Colours of the Rainbow, laid on Indiscriminately & broken one into another. Altogether his Colouring is Contrary to The Colouring of Real Art & Science.

Reynolds Thinks that Man Learns all that he knows. I say on the Contrary that Man Brings All that he has or Can have Into the World with him. Man is Born like a Garden ready Planted & Sown. This World is too poor to produce one Seed.

The mind that could have produced this Sentence must have been Pitiful, a Pitiable Imbecility. I always thought that the Human Mind was the most prolific of All Things & Inexhaustible. I certainly do Thank God that I am not like Reynolds.

The Purpose of the following discourse[9] is to Prove That Taste & Genius are not of Heavenly Origin & that all who have supposed that they Are so, are to be Considerd as Weak headed Fanatics.

The Obligations Reynolds has laid on Bad Artists of all Classes will at all times make them his Admirers, but most especially for this discourse, in which it is proved that the Stupid are born with Faculties Equal to other Men, Only they have not Cultivated them because they thought it not worth the trouble.

Obscurity is Neither the Source of the Sublime nor of any Thing Else.

The Ancients did not mean to Impose when they affirmd their belief in Vision & Revelation. Plato was in Earnest; Milton was in Earnest. They believd that God did Visit Man Really & Truly & not as Reynolds pretends.

Burke's Treatise on the Sublime & Beautiful is founded on the Opinions of Newton & Locke; on this Treatise Reynolds has grounded many of his assertions in all his Discourses. I read Burke's Treatise when very Young; at the same time I read Locke on Human Understanding & Bacon's Advancement of Learning; on Every one of these Books I wrote my Opinions, & on looking them over find that my Notes on Reynolds in this Book are exactly Similar. I felt the Same Contempt & Abhorrence then that I do now. They mock

8. I.e., *Discourse* V.

9. I.e., *Discourse* VII.

Inspiration & Vision. Inspiration & Vision was then & now is & I hope will always Remain my Element, my Eternal Dwelling place; how can I then hear it Contemnd without returning Scorn for Scorn?

On George Berkeley, *Siris: a Chain of Philosophical Reflections* * * * (1744)

Imagination or the Human Eternal Body in Every Man.

Imagination or the Divine Body in Every Man.

The All in Man: The Divine Image or Imagination.

The Four Senses are the Four Faces of Man & the Four Rivers of the Water of Life.

[Plato and Aristotle] considerd God as abstracted or distinct from the Imaginative World, but Jesus, as also Abraham & David, considered God as a Man in the Spiritual or Imaginative Vision.

Jesus considered Imagination to be the Real Man & says "I will not leave you Orphanned and I will manifest myself to you"; he says also, "the Spiritual Body or Angel (as little Children always) behold[s] the Face of the Heavenly Father."

Harmony [and] Proportion are Qualities & Not Things. The Harmony & Proportion of a Horse are not the same with those of a Bull. Every Thing has its own Harmony & Proportion, Two Inferior Qualities in it. For its Reality is Its Imaginative Form.

Knowledge is not by deduction, but Immediate by Perception or Sense at once. Christ addresses himself to the Man, not to his Reason. Plato did not bring Life & Immortality to Light. Jesus only did this.

Jesus supposes every Thing to be Evident to the Child & to the Poor & Unlearned. Such is the Gospel.

The Whole Bible is filld with Imagination & Visions from End to End & not with Moral Virtues; that is the business of Plato & the Greeks & all Warriors. The Moral Virtues are continual Accusers of Sin & promote Eternal Wars & Dominency over others.

God is not a Mathematical Diagram.

The Natural Body is an Obstruction to the Soul or Spiritual Body.

* * * Forms must be apprehended by Sense or the Eye of Imagination. Man is All Imagination. God is Man & exists in us & we in him.

What Jesus came to Remove was the Heathen or Platonic Philosophy, which blinds the Eye of Imagination, The Real Man.

On William Wordsworth, Preface to *The Excursion, Being a Portion of the Recluse, a Poem* (1814)[1]

All strength—all terror, single or in bands,
That ever was put forth in personal Form;
Jehovah—with his thunder, and the choir
Of shouting Angels, & the empyreal thrones,
I pass them, unalarmed . . .[2]

Solomon, when he Married Pharoh's daughter & became a Convert to the Heathen Mythology, Talked exactly in this way of Jehovah as a Very inferior object of Man's Contemplation; he also passed him by unalarmd & was permitted. Jehovah dropped a tear & followd him by his Spirit into the Abstract Void; it is called the Divine Mercy. Satan dwells in it, but Mercy does not dwell in him; he knows not to Forgive.

How exquisitely the individual Mind
(And the progressive powers perhaps no less
Of the whole species) to the external World
Is fitted:—& how exquisitely, too,
Theme this but little heard of among Men,
The external World is fitted to the Mind.[3]

You shall not bring me down to believe such fitting & fitted. I know better & please your Lordship.

—Such grateful haunts foregoing, if I oft
Must turn elsewhere—to travel near the tribes
And fellowships of Men, & see ill sights
Of madding passions mutually inflamed;
Must hear *Humanity in fields & groves*
Pipe solitary anguish; or must hang
Brooding above the fierce confederate storm
Of Sorrow, barricadoed evermore
Within the walls of cities; may these sounds
Have their authentic comment,—that, even these
Hearing, I be not downcast or forlorn![4]

Does not this Fit, & is it not Fitting most Exquisitely too, but to what?—not to Mind, but to the Vile Body only & to its Laws of Good & Evil & its Enmities against Mind.

1. Relevant passages from Wordsworth appear in reduced type, italicized to indicate Blake's underscoring. Blake's comments, written in 1826, appear in larger type.
2. Lines 31–35 of the poem in Wordsworth's Preface to *The Excursion*. According to Wordsworth's suggestion in the Preface, this poem has come to be known as the Prospectus to *The Excursion*.
3. Lines 63–68 of Wordsworth's Prospectus.
4. Lines 72–82 of Wordsworth's Prospectus. For Blake's further comments on Wordsworth, see H. C. Robinson, p. 499, below.

On William Wordsworth, *Poems: Including Lyrical Ballads*, Volume I (1815)

One Power alone make a Poet—Imagination, The Divine Vision.

I see in Wordsworth the Natural Man rising up against the Spiritual Man Continually, & then he is No Poet but a Heathen Philosopher at Enmity against all true Poetry or Inspiration.

There is no such Thing as Natural Piety Because The Natural Man is at Enmity with God.

* * * I cannot think that Real Poets have any competition. None are greatest in the Kingdom of Heaven; it is so in Poetry.

Natural Objects always did & now do weaken, deaden & obliterate Imagination in Me. Wordsworth must know that what he Writes Valuable is Not to be found in Nature.

I do not know who wrote these Prefaces: they are very mischievous & direct contrary to Wordsworth's own Practise.

It appears to me as if the last Paragraph beginning "Is it the result" Was writ by another hand & mind from the rest of these Prefaces. Perhaps they are the opinions of a Portrait or Landscape painter. Imagination is the Divine Vision not of The World, or of Man, nor from Man as he is a Natural Man, but only as he is a Spiritual Man. Imagination has nothing to do with Memory.

On Robert John Thornton, *The Lord's Prayer, Newly Translated* (1827)[5]

I look upon this as a Most Malignant & Artful attack upon the Kingdom of Jesus By the Classical Learned, thro the Instrumentality of Dr Thornton. The Greek & Roman Classics is the Antichrist. I say Is & not Are as most expressive & correct too.

THE LORD'S PRAYER
Translated from the Greek, by Dr. Thornton.

Come let us worship, and bow down, and kneel, before the Lord, our Maker. Psalm xcv.

O Father of Mankind, Thou, who dwellest in the highest of the Heavens, Reverenc'd be Thy Name!

May Thy Reign be, every where, proclaim'd so that Thy Will may be done upon the Earth, as it is in the Mansions of Heaven:

5. Passages from Thornton appear in reduced type.

Grant unto me, and the whole world, day by day, an abundant supply of spiritual and corporeal Food:
Forgive us our transgressions against Thee, as we extend our Kindness, and Forgiveness, to all:
O God! abandon us not, when surrounded, by trials;
But preserve us from the Dominion of Satan: For Thine only, is the Sovereignty, the power, and the glory, throughout Eternity!!!
Amen.

Lawful Bread, Bought with Lawful Money, & a Lawful Heaven, seen thro a Lawful Telescope, by means of Lawful Window Light! The Holy Ghost & whatever cannot be Taxed is Unlawful & Witchcraft.

Spirits are Lawful, but not Ghosts; especially Royal Gin is Lawful Spirit. No Smuggling real British Spirit & Truth!

Give us the Bread that is our due & Right, by taking away Money, or a Price, or Tax upon what is Common to all in thy Kingdom.

Jesus, our Father, who are in thy Heavens call'd by thy Name, the Holy Ghost, Thy Kingdom on Earth is Not, nor thy Will done, but Satan's will, who is God of this World, the Accuser: His Judgment shall be Forgiveness that he may be consumed in his own shame.

Give us This Eternal Day our own right Bread, & take away Money or debt or Tax (a Value or Price) as we have all things common among us. Every Thing has as much right to Eternal Life as God, who is the Servant of Man.

Leave us not in Parsimony, Satan's Kingdom; liberate us from the Natural Man & want, or Job's Kingdom.

For thine is the Kingdom & the Power & the Glory—& not Caesar's or Satan's. Amen.

This is Saying the Lord's Prayer Backwards, which they say Raises the Devil.

Doctor Thornton's Tory Translation, Translated out of its disguise in the Classical & Scotch languages into the vulgar English:

Our Father, Augustus Ceasar, who are in these thy Substantial Astronomical Telescopic Heavens, Holiness to thy Name or Title, & reverence to thy Shadow. Thy Kingship come upon Earth first & thence in Heaven. Give us day by day our Real Taxed Substantial Money-bought Bread; deliver from the Holy Ghost (so we call Nature) whatever cannot be Taxed; for all is debts & Taxes between Caesar & us & one another. Lead us not to read the Bible, but let our Bible be Virgil & Shakspeare, & deliver us from Poverty in Jesus, that Evil One. For thine is the Kingship, or Allegoric Godship, & the Power, or War, & the Glory, or Law, Ages after Ages, in thy Descendants; for God is only an Allegory of Kings & nothing Else. Amen.

Blake's Letters

To the Reverend John Trusler,[1] August 23, 1799

Revd Sir,

I really am sorry that you are falln out with the Spiritual World, Especially if I should have to answer for it. I feel very sorry that your Ideas & Mine on Moral Painting differ so much as to have made you angry with my method of Study. If I am wrong, I am wrong in good company. I had hoped your plan comprehended All Species of this Art, & Especially that you would not regret that Species which gives Existence to Every other, namely, Visions of Eternity. You say that I want somebody to Elucidate my Ideas. But you ought to know that What is Grand is necessarily obscure to Weak men. That which can be made Explicit to the Idiot is not worth my care. The wisest of the Ancients considerd what is not too Explicit as the fittest for Instruction, because it rouzes the faculties to act. I name Moses, Solomon, Esop, Homer, Plato.

But as you have favord me with your remarks on my Design, permit me in return to defend it against a mistaken one, which is, That I have supposed Malevolence without a Cause. Is not Merit in one a Cause of Envy in another, & Serenity & Happiness & Beauty a Cause of Malevolence? But Want of Money & the Distress of A Thief can never be alledged as the Cause of his Thieving, for many honest people endure greater hardships with Fortitude. We must therefore seek the Cause elsewhere than in want of Money, for that is the Miser's passion, not the Thief's.

I have therefore proved your Reasonings Ill proportiond, which you can never prove my figures to be; they are those of Michael Angelo, Rafael & the Antique, & of the best living Models. I percieve that your Eye is perverted by Caricature Prints, which ought not to abound so much as they do. Fun I love, but too much Fun is of all things the most loathsom. Mirth is better than Fun, & Happiness is better than Mirth. I feel that a Man may be happy in This World. And I know that This World Is a World of imagination & Vision. I see Every thing I paint In This World, but Every body does not see alike. To the Eyes of a Miser a Guinea is more beautiful than the Sun, & a bag worn with the use of Money has more beautiful proportions than a Vine filled with Grapes. The tree which moves some to tears of joy is in the Eyes of others only a Green thing that stands in the way. Some See Nature all Ridicule &

1. The Reverend Dr. John Trusler (1735–1820) was the author of *Hogarth Moralized, The Way to be Rich and Respectable, The Honours of the Table, The Principles of Politeness . . .*, and *A Sure Way to Lengthen Life*. He marked this letter: "Blake, dim'd with superstition." The "Design" mentioned by Blake is a watercolor drawing, *Malevolence*, now in the Philadelphia Museum of Art.

Deformity, & by these I shall not regulate my proportions; & Some Scarce see Nature at all. But to the Eyes of the Man of Imagination, Nature is Imagination itself. As a man is, So he Sees. As the Eye is formed, such are its Powers. You certainly Mistake, when you say that the Visions of Fancy are not to be found in This World. To Me This World is all One continued Vision of Fancy or Imagination, & I feel Flatterd when I am told so. What is it sets Homer, Virgil & Milton in so high a rank of Art? Why is the Bible more Entertaining & Instructive than any other book? Is it not because they are addressed to the Imagination, which is Spiritual Sensation, & but mediately to the Understanding or Reason? Such is True Painting, and such was alone valued by the Greeks & the best modern Artists. Consider what Lord Bacon says: "Sense sends over to Imagination before Reason have judged, & Reason sends over to Imagination before the Decree can be acted." See Advancem^{t} of Learning, Part 2, P. 47 of first Edition.

But I am happy to find a Great Majority of Fellow Mortals who can Elucidate My Visions, & Particularly they have been Elucidated by Children, who have taken a greater delight in contemplating my Pictures than I even hoped. Neither Youth nor Childhood is Folly or Incapacity. Some Children are Fools & so are some Old Men. But There is a vast Majority on the side of Imagination or Spiritual Sensation.

To Engrave after another Painter is infinitely more laborious than to Engrave one's own Inventions. And of the size you require my price has been Thirty Guineas, & I cannot afford to do it for less. I had Twelve for the Head I sent you as a Specimen; but after my own designs I could do at least Six times the quantity of labour in the same time, which will account for the difference of price as also that Chalk Engraving is at least six times as laborious as Aqua tinta. I have no objection to Engraving after another Artist. Engraving is the profession I was apprenticed to, & should never have attempted to live by any thing else, If orders had not come in for my Designs & Paintings, which I have the pleasure to tell you are Increasing Every Day. Thus If I am a Painter, it is not attributed to Seeking after. But I am contented whether I live by Painting or Engraving.

I am, Revd Sir, your very obedient servant,

William Blake

To William Hayley,[2] May 6, 1800

Dear Sir,

I am very sorry for your immense loss, which is a repetition of

2. William Hayley (1745–1820), a poet and man of letters who acted as a patron and invited the Blakes to Felpham, near his residence at Eartham, Sussex (see map). His illegitimate son, Thomas Alphonso, died May 2, 1800; Blake had engraved his portrait.

what all feel in this valley of misery & happiness mixed. I send the Shadow of the departed Angel: hope the likeness is improved. The lip I have again lessened as you advised & done a good many other softenings to the whole. I know that our deceased friends are more really with us than when they were apparent to our mortal part. Thirteen years ago I lost a brother & with his spirit I converse daily & hourly in the Spirit & See him in my remembrance in the regions of my Imagination. I hear his advice & even now write from his Dictate. Forgive me for Expressing to you my Enthusiasm which I wish all to partake of Since it is to me a Source of Immortal Joy: even in this world by it I am the companion of Angels. May you continue to be so more & more & to be more & more perswaded that every Mortal loss is an Immortal Gain. The Ruins of Time builds Mansions in Eternity.—I have also sent A Proof of Pericles for your Remarks, thanking you for the Kindness with which you Express them & feeling heartily your Grief with a brother's Sympathy.

I remain, Dear Sir, Your humble Servant

William Blake

To George Cumberland,[3] July 2, 1800

Dear Cumberland,

I have to congratulate you on your plan for a National Gallery being put into Execution. All your wishes shall in due time be fulfilled; the immense flood of Grecian light & glory which is coming on Europe will more than realize our warmest wishes. Your honours will be unbounded when your plan shall be carried into Execution as it must be if England continues a Nation. I hear that it is now in the hands of Ministers, That the King shews it great Countenance & Encouragement, that it will soon be before Parliament, & that it *must* be extended & enlarged to take in Originals both of Painting & Sculpture by considering every valuable original that is brought into England or can be purchasd Abroad as its objects of Acquisition. Such is the Plan as I am told & such must be the plan if England wishes to continue at all worth notice; as you have yourself observd only now, we must possess Originals as well as France or be Nothing.

Excuse, I intreat you, my not returning Thanks at the proper moment for your kind present. No perswasion could make my stupid head believe that it was proper for me to trouble you with a letter of meer compliment & Expression of thanks. I begin to Emerge from a Deep pit of Melancholy, Melancholy without any

3. George Cumberland (1754–1848), an amateur artist and engraver, author of *Thoughts on Outline;* instrumental in the founding of the National Gallery; Blake's friend for more than thirty years. For him Blake made a number of illuminated books as well as his last engraving, a small allegorical calling card.

real reason for it, a Disease which God keep you from & all good men. Our artists of all ranks praise your outlines & wish for more. Flaxman is very warm in your commendation & more and more of A Grecian. Mr Hayley has lately mentioned your Work on outline in Notes to an Essay on Sculpture in Six Epistles to John Flaxman. I have been too little among friends which I fear they will not Excuse & I know not how to apologize for. Poor Fuseli, sore from the lash of Envious tongues, praises you & dispraises with the same breath; he is not naturally good natured, but he is artificially very ill natured, yet even from him I learn the Estimation you are held in among artists & connoisseurs.

I am still Employd in making Designs & little Pictures with now & then an Engraving & find that in future to live will not be so difficult as it has been. It is very extraordinary that London in so few years from a City of meer Necessaries or at least a commerce of the lowest order of luxuries should have become a City of Elegance in some degree & that its once stupid inhabitants should enter into an Emulation of Grecian manners. There are now, I believe, as many Booksellers as there are Butchers & as many Printshops as of any other trade. We remember when a Print shop was rare bird in London & I myself remember when I thought my pursuits of Art a kind of criminal dissipation & neglect of the main chance, which I hid my face for not being able to abandon as a Passion which is forbidden by Law & Religion, but now it appears to be Law & Gospel too, at least I hear so from the few friends I have dared to visit in my stupid Melancholy. Excuse this communication of sentiments which I felt necessary to my repose at this time. I feel very strongly that I neglect my Duty to my Friends, but It is not want of Gratitude or Friendship but perhaps an Excess of both.

Let me hear of your welfare. Remember My & My Wife's Respectful Compliments to Mrs Cumberland & Family & believe me to be for Ever

Yours

William Blake

To John Flaxman,[4] September 12, 1800

My Dearest Friend,

It is to you I owe All my present Happiness. It is to you I owe perhaps the Principal Happiness of my life. I have presum'd on your friendship in staying so long away & not calling to know of

4. John Flaxman (1755–1826), a sculptor and author who for a time had an international reputation because of his neoclassical illustrations to Homer, Aeschylus, and Dante. In 1817 his designs for Hesiod, which were engraved by Blake, were published. The "Inclosed" mentioned in the postscript to this letter was a letter to Mrs. Anna Flaxman by Catherine Blake which included another poem by William addressed to Anna.

your welfare, but hope now every thing is nearly completed for our removal to Felpham, that I shall see you on Sunday, as we have appointed Sunday afternoon to call on Mrs Flaxman at Hampstead. I send you a few lines, which I hope you will Excuse. And As the time is arriv'd when Men shall again converse in Heaven & walk with Angels, I know you will be pleased with the Intention, & hope you will forgive the Poetry.

To My Dearest Friend, John Flaxman, these lines:

I bless thee, O Father of Heaven & Earth, that ever I saw Flax-
 man's face.
Angels stand round my Spirit in Heaven, the blessed of Heaven are
 my friends upon Earth.
When Flaxman was taken to Italy, Fuseli was given to me for a
 season,
And now Flaxman hath given me Hayley his friend to be mine,
 such my lot upon Earth.
Now my lot in the Heavens is this, Milton lov'd me in childhood &
 shew'd me his face.
Ezra came with Isaiah the Prophet, but Shakespeare in riper years
 gave me his hand;
Paracelsus & Behmen appear'd to me, terrors appear'd in the
 Heavens above
And in Hell beneath, & a mighty & awful change threatened the
 Earth.
The American War began. All its dark horrors passed before my
 face
Across the Atlantic to France. Then the French Revolution
 commenc'd in thick clouds,
And My Angels have told me that seeing such visions I could not
 subsist on the Earth,
But by my conjunction with Flaxman, who knows to forgive
 Nervous Fear.

I remain, for Ever Yours,
William Blake

Be so kind as to Read & then seal the Inclosed & send it on its much beloved Mission.

To William Hayley, September 16, 1800

Leader of My Angels,

My Dear & too careful & over joyous Woman has Exhausted her strength to such a degree with expectation & gladness added to labour in our removal that I fear it will be Thursday before we can get away from this ——— City. I shall not be able to avail myself of the assistance of Bruno's fairies. But I Invoke the Good Genii that Surround Miss Poole's[5] Villa to shine upon my journey thro the Petworth road which by your fortunate advice I mean to take, but whether I come on Wednesday or Thursday That Day shall be marked on my calendar with a Star of the first magnitude.

Eartham will be my first temple & altar. My wife is like a flame of many colours of precious jewels whenever she hears it named. Excuse my haste & recieve my hearty Love & Respect.

I am, dear Sir,
Your Sincere
William Blake

My fingers Emit sparks of fire with Expectation of my future labours.

To Thomas Butts,[6] September 23, 1800

Dear Friend of My Angels,

We are safe arrived at our Cottage without accident or hindrance, tho it was between Eleven & Twelve O'Clock at night before we could get home, owing to the necessary shifting of our boxes & portfolios from one Chaise to another. We had Seven different Chaises & as many different drivers. All upon the road was chearfulness & welcome; tho our luggage was very heavy there was no grumbling at all. We traveld thro a most beautiful country on a most glorious day. Our Cottage is more beautiful than I thought it, & also more convenient, for tho small it is well proportiond, & if I should ever build a Palace it would be only My Cottage Enlarged. Please to tell Mrs Butts that we have dedicated a Chamber for her service, & that it has a very fine view of the Sea. Mr Hayley receivd me with his usual brotherly affection. My Wife & Sister are both very well, & courting Neptune for an Embrace, whose terrors this morning made them afraid, but whose mildness is often Equal to his terrors. The Villagers of Felpham are not meer Rustics; they are polite & modest. Meat is cheaper than in London, but the sweet air

5. Miss Henrietta, or Harriet, Poole, also known as Lady Paulina of Lavant (the name of her village); a close friend of Hayley. The reference to "Bruno's fairies" is explained by G. E. Bentley, Jr., ed., *William Blake's Writings* (Oxford: Clarendon, 1978) II, 1539, as a reference to a horse Blake rode in Felpham.

6. Thomas Butts (1757–1845), chief clerk in the office of the Muster Master General (in charge of military records), was Blake's most loyal patron for at least twenty years. He owned about 200 pictures and 10 illuminated books. Among his commissions were two series of Biblical paintings and illustrations to Milton's works. Eventually his Blake collection outgrew his home and filled his greenhouse. At times he spent over fifteen percent of his annual income on his Blake purchases; he also hired Blake to give drawing and engraving lessons to his son Tommy.

& the voices of winds, trees & birds, & the odours of the happy ground, makes it a dwelling for immortals. Work will go on here with God speed.—A roller & two harrows lie before my window. I met a plow on my first going out at my gate the first morning after my arrival, & the Plowboy said to the Plowman, "Father, The Gate is Open."—I have begun to Work, & find that I can work with greater pleasure than ever. Hope soon to give you a proof that Felpham is propitious to the Arts.

God bless you! I shall wish for you on Tuesday Evening as usual. Pray give My & My wife & sister's love & respects to Mrs Butts; accept them yourself, & believe me forever

Your affectionate & obliged Friend,
William Blake

My Sister will be in town in a week, & bringing with her your account & whatever else I can finish.

Direct to Me:

Blake, Felpham, near Chichester, Sussex.

To Thomas Butts, October 2, 1800

Friend of Religion & Order,

I thank you for your very beautiful & encouraging Verses, which I account a Crown of Laurels, & I also thank you for your reprehension of follies by me fosterd. Your prediction will, I hope, be fulfilled in me, & in future I am the determined advocate of Religion & Humility, the two bands of Society. Having been so full of the Business of Settling the sticks & feathers of my nest, I have not got any forwarder with the three Marys or with any other of your commissions; but hope, now I have commenced a new life of industry, to do credit to that new life by Improved Works. Recieve from me a return of verses such as Felpham produces by me, tho not such as she produces by her Eldest Son; however, such as they are, I cannot resist the temptation to send them to you.

To my Friend Butts I write
My first Vision of Light.
On yellow sands sitting
The Sun was Emitting
His Glorious beams
From Heaven's high Streams.
Over Sea, over Land
My Eyes did Expand
Into regions of air
Away from all Care,
Into regions of fire

Remote from Desire.
The Light of the Morning
Heaven's Mountains adorning
In particles bright
The jewels of Light
Distinct shone & clear.
Amazd & in fear
I each particle gazed,
Astonishd, Amazed;
For each was a Man
Human-formd. Swift I ran,
For they beckond to me
Remote by the Sea,
Saying: "Each grain of Sand,
Every Stone on the Land,
Each rock & each hill,
Each fountain & rill,
Each herb & each tree,
Mountain, hill, earth & sea,
Cloud, Meteor & Star,
Are Men Seen Afar."
I stood in the Streams
Of Heaven's bright beams
And Saw Felpham sweet
Beneath my bright feet
In soft Female charms,
And in her fair arms
My Shadow I knew
And my wife's shadow too
And My Sister & Friend.
We like Infants descend
In our Shadows on Earth,
Like a weak mortal birth.
My Eyes more & more
Like a Sea without shore
Continue Expanding,
The Heavens commanding,
Till the Jewels of Light,
Heavenly Men beaming bright,
Appeard as One Man
Who Complacent began
My limbs to infold
In his beams of bright gold;
Like dross purgd away
All my mire & my clay.
Soft consumd in delight
In his bosom Sun bright
I remaind. Soft he smild,
And I heard his voice Mild
Saying: "This is My Fold,

O thou Ram hornd with gold,
Who awakest from Sleep
On the Sides of the Deep.
On the Mountains around
The roarings resound
Of the lion & wolf,
The loud Sea & deep gulf.
These are guards of My Fold,
O thou Ram horn'd with gold."
And the voice faded mild.
I remaind as a Child;
All I ever had known
Before me bright Shone.
I saw you & your wife
By the fountains of Life.
Such the Vision to me
Appeard on the Sea.

Mrs Butts will, I hope, Excuse my not having finishd the Portrait. I wait for less hurried moments. Our Cottage looks more & more beautiful. And tho the weather is wet, the Air is very Mild, much Milder than it was in London when we came away. Chichester is a very handsome City, Seven miles from us; we can get most Conveniences there. The Country is not so destitute of accomodations to our wants as I expected it would be. We have had but little time for viewing the Country, but what we have seen is Most Beautiful, & the People are Genuine Saxons, handsomer than the people about London. Mrs Butts will Excuse the following lines:

To Mrs Butts

Wife of the Friend of those I most revere,
Recieve this tribute from a Harp sincere:
Go on in Virtuous Seed sowing on Mold
Of Human Vegetation, & Behold
Your Harvest Springing to Eternal life,
Parent of Youthful Minds, & happy Wife!

W B—

I am for Ever Yours,
William Blake

To Thomas Butts, January 10, 1802

Dear Sir,

Your very kind & affectionate Letter, & the many kind things you have said in it, calld upon me for an immediate answer; but it found My Wife & Myself so Ill, & My wife so very ill, that till now I have not been able to do this duty. The Ague & Rheumatism have been almost her constant Enemies, which she has combated in vain ever since we have been here, & her sickness is always my sorrow, of course. But what you tell me about your sight afflicted me not a little, & that about your health, in another part of your letter, makes me intreat you to take due care of both; it is a part of our duty to God & man to take due care of his Gifts; & tho' we ought not think *more* highly of ourselves, yet we ought to think *As* highly of ourselves as immortals ought to think.

When I came down here, I was more sanguine than I am at present, but it was because I was ignorant of many things which have since occurred, & chiefly the unhealthiness of the place. Yet I do not repent of coming on a thousand accounts; & Mr H., I doubt not, will do ultimately all that both he & I wish—that is, to lift me out of difficulty—but this is no easy matter to a man who, having Spiritual Enemies of such formidable magnitude, cannot expect to want natural hidden ones.

Your approbation of my pictures is a Multitude to Me, & I doubt not that all your kind wishes in my behalf shall in due time be fulfilled. Your kind offer of pecuniary assistance I can only thank you for at present, because I have enough to serve my present purpose here; our expenses are small, & our income, from our incessant labour, fully adequate to them at present. I am now engaged in Engraving 6 small plates for a New Edition of Mr Hayley's Triumphs of Temper,[7] from drawings by Maria Flaxman, sister to my friend the Sculptor, and it seems that other things will follow in course, if I do but Copy these well; but Patience! if Great things do not turn out, it is because such things depend on the Spiritual & not on the Natural World; & if it was fit for me, I doubt not that I should be Employd in Greater things; & when it is proper, my Talents shall be properly exercised in Public, as I hope they are now in private; for, till then, I leave no stone unturnd & no path unexplord that tends to improvement in my beloved Arts. One thing of real consequence I have accomplishd by coming into the country, which is to me consolation enough: namely, I have recollected all my scatterd thoughts on Art & resumed my primitive & original ways of Execution in both painting & engraving, which in the confusion of London I had very much lost & obliterated from my mind. But whatever becomes of my labours, I would rather that they should be preservd in your Green House (not, as you mistakenly call it, dung hill) than in the cold gallery of fashion.—The Sun may yet shine, & then they will be brought into open air.

But you have so generously & openly desired that I will divide my griefs with you, that I cannot hide what it is now become my duty to explain.—My unhappiness has arisen from a source which, if

7. *The Triumphs of Temper.* **A Poem: In Six Cantos, 12th ed., London, 1803.**

explord too narrowly, might hurt my pecuniary circumstances, As my dependence is on Engraving at present, & particularly on the Engravings I have in hand for Mr H., & I find on all hands great objections to my doing any thing but the meer drudgery of business, & intimations that if I do not confine myself to this, I shall not live; this has always pursud me. You will understand by this the source of all my uneasiness. This from Johnson & Fuseli brought me down here, & this from Mr H. will bring me back again; for that I cannot live without doing my duty to lay up treasures in heaven is Certain & Determined, & to this I have long made up my mind, & why this should be made an objection to Me, while Drunkenness, Lewdness, Gluttony & even Idleness itself, does not hurt other men, let Satan himself Explain. The Thing I have most at Heart—more than life, or all that seems to make life comfortable without—Is the Interest of True Religion & Science, & whenever any thing appears to affect that Interest (Especially if I myself omit any duty to my Station as a Soldier of Christ), It gives me the greatest of torments. I am not ashamed, afraid, or averse to tell you what Ought to be Told: That I am under the direction of Messengers from Heaven, Daily & Nightly; but the nature of such things is not, as some suppose, without trouble or care. Temptations are on the right hand & left; behind, the sea of time & space roars & follows swiftly; he who keeps not right onward is lost, & if our footsteps slide in clay, how can we do otherwise than fear & tremble? but I should not have troubled You with this account of my spiritual state, unless it had been necessary in explaining the actual cause of my uneasiness, into which you are so kind as to Enquire, for I never obtrude such things on others unless question'd, & then I never disguise the truth.—But if we fear to do the dictates of our Angels & tremble at the Tasks set before us, if we refuse to do Spiritual Acts because of Natural Fears or Natural Desires! Who can describe the dismal torments of such a state!—I too well remember the Threats I heard!—If you, who are organised by Divine Providence for Spiritual communion, Refuse, & bury your Talent in the Earth, even tho you should want Natural Bread, Sorrow & Desperation pursues you thro life, & after death shame & confusion of face to eternity. Every one in Eternity will leave you, aghast at the Man who was crownd with glory & honour by his brethren, & betrayd their cause to their enemies. You will be calld the base Judas who betrayd his Friend! —Such words would make any stout man tremble, & how then could I be at ease? But I am now no longer in That State, & now go on again with my Task, Fearless, and tho my path is difficult, I have no fear of stumbling while I keep it.

My wife desires her kindest Love to Mrs Butts, & I have permitted her to send it to you also; we often wish that we could unite again in Society, & hope that the time is not distant when we shall do so, being determind not to remain another winter here, but to return to London.

I hear a voice you cannot hear, that says I must not stay,
I see a hand you cannot see, that beckons me away.[8]

Naked we came here, naked of Natural things, & naked we shall return; but while clothd with the Divine Mercy, we are richly clothd in Spiritual & suffer all the rest gladly. Pray give my Love to Mrs Butts & your family. I am, Yours Sincerely,

William Blake

P.S. Your Obliging proposal of Exhibiting my two Pictures likewise calls for my thanks; I will finish the other, & then we shall judge of the matter with certainty.

To Thomas Butts, November 22, 1802

* * *

But You will Justly enquire why I have not written All this time to you? I answer I have been very Unhappy, & could not think of troubling you about it, or any of my real Friends. (I have written many letters to you which I burnd & did not send) & why I have not before now finishd the Miniature I promissd to Mrs Butts? I answer I have not till now in any degree pleased myself, & now I must intreat you to Excuse faults, for Portrait Painting is the direct contrary to Designing & Historical Painting in every respect—if you have not Nature before you for Every Touch, you cannot Paint Portrait, & if you have Nature before you at all, you cannot Paint History. It was Michael Angelo's opinion & is Mine. Pray Give My Wife's love with mine to Mrs Butts; assure her that it cannot be long before I have the pleasure of Painting from you in Person, & then that She may Expect a likeness, but now I have done All I could, & know she will forgive any failure in consideration of the Endeavour.

And now let me finish with assuring you that, Tho I have been very unhappy, I am so no longer. I am again Emerged into the light of day. I still & shall to Eternity Embrace Christianity and Adore him who is the Express image of God, but I have traveld thro Perils & Darkness not unlike a Champion. I have Conquerd, and shall still Go on Conquering. Nothing can withstand the fury of my Course among the Stars of God & in the Abysses of the Accuser. My Enthusiasm is still what it was, only Enlarged and confirmd.

8. Four lines, written as two, from Thomas Tickell's "Lucy and Colin," in Percy's *Reliques of Ancient English Poetry*, London, 1765, III, 308. [Keynes.]

I now Send Two Pictures & hope you will approve of them. I have inclosed the Account of Money recievd & Work done, which I ought long ago to have sent you; pray forgive Errors in omissions of this kind. I am incapable of many attentions which it is my Duty to observe towards you, thro multitude of employment & thro hope of soon seeing you again. I often omit to Enquire of you. But pray let me now hear how you do & of the welfare of your family.

Accept my Sincere love & respect.

I remain Yours Sincerely,
Willm Blake

A Piece of Sea Weed serves for a Barometer; it gets wet & dry as the weather gets so.

To Thomas Butts, November 22, 1802

Dear Sir,

After I had finishd my Letter, I found that I had not said half what I intended to say, & in particular I wish to ask you what subject you choose to be painted on the remaining Canvas which I brought down with me (for there were three), and to tell you that several of the Drawings were in great forwardness. You will see by the Inclosed Account that the remaining Number of Drawings which you gave me orders for is Eighteen. I will finish these with all possible Expedition, if indeed I have not tired you, or, as it is politely calld, Bored you too much already, or if you would rather cry out Enough, Off, Off! tell me in a Letter of forgiveness if you were offended, & of accustomd friendship if you were not. But I will bore you more with some Verses which My Wife desires me to Copy out & send you with her kind love & Respect. They were composed above a twelve-month ago, while walking from Felpham to Lavant to meet my Sister:

With happiness stretchd across the hills
In a cloud that dewy sweetness distills,
With a blue sky spread over with wings
And a mild sun that mounts & sings,
With trees & fields full of Fairy elves
And little devils who fight for themselves—
Remembring the Verses that Hayley sung
When my heart knockd against the root of my tongue—[9]
With Angels planted in Hawthorn bowers
And God himself in the passing hours,
With Silver Angels across my way
And Golden Demons that none can stay,

9. Probably about 200 lines of blank verse written in Blake's hand, entitled *Genesis, the Seven Days of the Created World,* a translation of the opening lines of Tasso's *Le Sette Giornale del Mondo Creato.* [Keynes.]

With my Father hovering upon the wind
And my Brother Robert just behind
And my Brother John the evil one
In a black cloud making his mone–
Tho dead, they appear upon my path,
Notwithstanding my terrible wrath.
They beg, they intreat, they drop their tears,
Filld full of hopes, filld full of fears–
With a thousand Angels upon the Wind
Pouring disconsolate from behind
To drive them off, & before my way
A frowning Thistle implores my stay.
What to others a trifle appears
Fills me full of smiles or tears,
For double the vision my Eyes do see
And a double vision is always with me:
With my inward Eye 'tis an old Man grey;
With my outward, a Thistle across my way.
"If thou goest back," the thistle said,
"Thou art to endless woe betrayd;
For here does Theotormon lower
And here is Enitharmon's bower
And Los the terrible thus hath sworn:
Because thou backward dost return,
Poverty, Envy, old age & fear
Shall bring thy Wife upon a bier,
And Butts shall give what Fuseli gave,
A dark black Rock & a gloomy Cave."

I struck the Thistle with my foot,
And broke him up from his delving root:
"Must the duties of life each other cross?
Must every joy be dung & dross?
Must my dear Butts feel cold neglect
Because I give Hayley his due respect?
Must Flaxman look upon me as wild,
And all my friends be with doubts beguild?
Must my Wife live in my Sister's bane,
Or my Sister survive on my Love's pain?
The curses of Los the terrible shade
And his dismal terrors make me afraid."

So I spoke & struck in my wrath
The old man weltering upon my path.
Then Los appeard in all his power;
In the Sun he appeard, descending before
My face in fierce flames. In my double sight
Twas outward a Sun: inward Los in his might.

"My hands are labourd day & night,
And Ease comes never in my sight.

My Wife had no indulgence given
Except what comes to her from heaven.
We eat little, we drink less;
This Earth breeds not our happiness.
Another Sun feeds our life's streams,
We are not warmed with thy beams;
Thou measurest not the Time to me,
Nor yet the Space that I do see;
My Mind is not with thy light arrayd.
Thy terror shall not make me afraid."

When I had my Defiance given,
The Sun stood trembling in heaven;
The Moon that glowd remote below,
Became leprous & white as snow;
And every soul of men on the Earth
Felt affliction & sorrow & sickness & dearth.
Los flamd in my path, & the Sun was hot
With the bows of my Mind & the Arrows of Thought—
My bowstring fierce with Ardour breathes,
My arrows glow in their golden sheaves;
My brothers & father march before;
The heavens drop with human gore.

Now I a fourfold vision see,
And a fourfold vision is given to me;
Tis fourfold in my supreme delight,
And threefold in soft Beulah's night,
And twofold Always. May God us keep
From Single vision & Newton's sleep!

I also inclose you some Ballads by Mr Hayley, with prints to them by Your H^ble^ Servt. I should have sent them before now, but could not get any thing done for You to please myself, for I do assure you that I have truly studied the two little pictures I now send & do not repent of the time I have spent upon them.

God bless you.

Yours,
W B

P.S. I have taken the liberty to trouble you with a letter to my Brother, which you will be so kind as to send or give him, & oblige yours, WB

To James Blake, January 30, 1803

Dear Brother,

Your Letter mentioning Mr Butts' account of my Ague surprized me because I have no Ague, but have had a Cold this Winter. You know that it is my way to make the best of every thing. I never make myself nor my friends uneasy if I can help it. My Wife has had Agues & Rheumatisms almost ever since she has been here, but our time is almost out that we took the Cottage for. I did not mention our Sickness to you & should not to Mr Butts but for a determination which we have lately made, namely To leave This Place, because I am now certain of what I have long doubted, Viz that H. is jealous as Stothard was & will be no further My friend than he is compelld by circumstances. The truth is, As a Poet he is frightend at me & as a Painter his views & mine are opposite; he thinks to turn me into a Portrait Painter as he did Poor Romney, but this he nor all the devils in hell will never do. I must own that seeing H. like S. Envious (& that he is I am now certain) made me very uneasy, but it is over & I now defy the worst & fear not while I am true to myself which I will be. This is the uneasiness I spoke of to Mr Butts, but I did not tell him so plain & wish you to keep it a secret & to burn this letter because it speaks so plain. I told Mr Butts that I did not wish to Explore too much the cause of our determination to leave Felpham because of pecuniary connexions between H. & me—Be not then uneasy on any account & tell my Sister not to be uneasy, for I am fully Employd & Well Paid. I have made it so much H's interest to employ me that he can no longer treat me with indifference & now it is in my power to stay or return or remove to any other place that I choose, because I am getting before hand in money matters. The Profits arising from Publications are immense, & I now have it in my power to commence publication with many very formidable works, which I have finishd & ready. A Book price half a guinea may be got out at the Expense of Ten pounds & its almost certain profits are 500 G. I am sorry that I did not know the methods of publishing years ago & this is one of the numerous benefits I have obtaind by coming here, for I should never have known the nature of Publication unless I had known H. & his connexions & his method of managing. It now would be folly not to venture publishing. I am now Engraving Six little plates for a little work of Mr H's, for which I am to have 10 Guineas each, & the certain profits of that work are a fortune such as would make me independent, supposing that I could substantiate such a one of my own & I mean to try many. But I again say as I said before, We are very Happy sitting at tea by a wood fire in our Cottage, the wind singing above our roof & the sea roaring at a distance, but if sickness comes all is unpleasant.

But my letter to Mr Butts appears to me not to be so explicit as that to you, for I told you that I should come to London in the Spring to commence Publisher & he has offerd me every assistance in his power without knowing my intention. But since I wrote yours we had made the resolution of which we informed him, viz to leave Felpham entirely. I also told you what I was about & that I was not ignorant of what was doing in London in works of art. But I did not mention Illness because I hoped to get better (for I was really very ill when I wrote to him the last time) & was not then perswaded as I am now that the air tho warm is unhealthy.

However, this I know will set you at Ease. I am now so full of work that I have had no time to go on with the Ballads, & my prospects for more & more work continually are certain. My Heads of Cowper for Mr H's life of Cowper have pleased his Relations exceedingly & in Particular Lady Hesketh & Lord Cowper. To please Lady H. was a doubtful chance, who almost adord her Cousin the poet & thought him all perfection, & she writes that she is quite satisfied with the portraits & charmd by the great Head in particular, tho she never could bear the original Picture.

But I ought to mention to you that our present idea is To take a house in some village further from the Sea, Perhaps Lavant, & in or near the road to London for the sake of convenience. I also ought to inform you that I read your letter to Mr H. & that he is very afraid of losing me & also very afraid that my Friends in London should have a bad opinion of the reception he has given to me. But My Wife has undertaken to Print the whole number of the Plates for Cowper's work, which She does to admiration, & being under my own eye the prints are as fine as the French prints & please every one. In short I have Got every thing so under my thumb that it is more profitable that things should be as they are than any other way, tho not so agreeable because we wish naturally for friendship in preference to interest.—The Publishers are already indebted to My Wife Twenty Guineas for work deliverd; this is a small specimen of how we go on. Then fear nothing & let my Sister fear nothing because it appears to me that I am now too old & have had too much experience to be any longer imposed upon; only illness makes all uncomfortable & this we must prevent by every means in our power.

I send with this 5 Copies of N4 of the Ballads for Mrs Flaxman & Five more, two of which you will be so good as to give to Mrs Chetwynd if she should call or send for them. These Ballads are likely to be Profitable, for we have Sold all that we have had time to print. Evans the Bookseller in Pallmall says they go off very well, & why should we repent of having done them? It is doing Nothing that is to be repented of & not doing such things as these.

Pray remember us both to Mr Hall when you see him.

I write in great haste & with a head full of botheration about various projected works & particularly a work now Proposed to the Public at the End of Cowper's Life, which will very likely be of great consequence: it is Cowper's Milton, the same that Fuseli's Milton Gallery was painted for, & if we succeed in our intentions the prints to this work will be very profitable to me & not only profitable, but honourable at any rate.[1] The Project pleases Lord Cowper's family, & I am now labouring in my thoughts Designs for this & other works equally creditable. These are works to be boasted of, & therefore I cannot feel depress'd, tho I know that as far as Designing & Poetry are concernd I am Envied in many Quarters, but I will cram the Dogs, for I know that the Public are my friends & love my works & will embrace them whenever they see them. My only Difficulty is to produce fast enough.

I go on Merrily with my Greek & Latin; am very sorry that I did not begin to learn languages early in life as I find it very Easy; am now learning my Hebrew אבג . I read Greek as fluently as an Oxford scholar & the Testament is my chief master; astonishing indeed is the English Translation, it is almost word for word, & if the Hebrew Bible is as well translated, which I do not doubt it is, we need not doubt of its having been translated as well as written by the Holy Ghost.

My wife joins me in Love to you both.

I am Sincerely yours,
W Blake

To Thomas Butts, April 25, 1803

My Dear Sir,

I write in haste, having recievd a pressing Letter from my Brother. I intended to have sent the Picture of the Riposo, which is nearly finishd much to my satisfaction, but not quite; you shall have it soon. I now send the 4 Numbers for Mr Birch, with best Respects to him. The Reason the Ballads have been suspended is the pressure of other business, but they will go on again Soon.

Accept of my thanks for your kind & heartening Letter. You have Faith in the Endeavours of Me, your weak brother & fellow Disciple; how great must be your faith in our Divine Master! You are to me a Lesson of Humility, while you Exalt me by such distinguishing commendations. I know that you see certain merits in me, which by God's Grace shall be made fully apparent & perfect in Eternity. In the mean time I must not bury the Talents in the Earth, but do my endeavour to live to the Glory of our Lord & Saviour; & I am also grateful to the kind hand that endeavours to lift me out of despondency, even if it lifts me too high.—

And now, My Dear Sir, Congratulate me on my return to London, with the full approbation of Mr Hayley & with Promise —But, Alas!

Now I may say to you, what perhaps I should not dare to say to any one else: That I can alone carry on my visionary studies in

1. This project was never carried out.

London unannoyd, & that I may converse with my friends in Eternity, See Visions, Dream Dreams, & prophecy & speak Parables unobserv'd & at liberty from the Doubts of other Mortals; perhaps Doubts proceeding from Kindness, but Doubts are always pernicious, Especially when we Doubt our Friends. Christ is very decided on this Point: "He who is Not With Me is Against Me." There is no Medium or Middle state, & if a Man is the Enemy of my Spiritual Life while he pretends to be the Friend of my Corporeal, he is a Real Enemy—but the Man may be the friend of my Spiritual Life while he seems the Enemy of my Corporeal, but Not Vice Versa.

What is very pleasant, Every one who hears of my going to London again Applauds it as the only course for the interest of all concernd in My Works, Observing that I ought not to be away from the opportunities London affords of seeing fine Pictures and the various improvements in Works of Art going on in London.

But none can know the Spiritual Acts of my three years' Slumber on the banks of the Ocean unless he has seen them in the Spirit or unless he should read My long Poem descriptive of those Acts, for I have in these three years composed an immense number of verses on One Grand Theme, Similar to Homer's Iliad or Milton's Paradise Lost, the Persons & Machinery intirely new to the Inhabitants of Earth (some of the Persons Excepted). I have written this Poem from immediate Dictation, twelve or sometimes twenty or thirty lines at a time, without Premeditation & even against my Will; the Time it has taken in writing was thus renderd Non Existent, & an immense Poem Exists which seems to be the Labour of a long Life, all producd without Labour or Study. I mention this to shew you what I think the Grand Reason of my being brought down here.

I have a thousand & ten thousand things to say to you. My heart is full of futurity. I percieve that the sore travel which has been given me these three years leads to Glory & Honour. I rejoice & I tremble: "I am fearfully & wonderfully made." I had been reading the cxxxix Psalm a little before your Letter arrived. I take your advice. I see the face of my Heavenly Father; he lays his Hand upon my Head & gives a blessing to all my works: why should I be troubled? why should my heart & flesh cry out? I will go on in the Strength of the Lord; through Hell will I sing forth his Praises, that the Dragons of the Deep may praise him & that those who dwell in darkness & in the Sea coasts may be gatherd into his Kingdom. Excuse my perhaps too great Enthusiasm. Please to accept of & give our Loves to M[rs] Butts & your amiable Family, & believe me to be—

Ever Yours Affectionately,
Will. Blake

To Thomas Butts, August 16, 1803

Dear Sir,

I send 7 Drawings which I hope will please you; this, I believe, about balances our account—Our return to London draws on apace; our Expectation of meeting again with you is one of our greatest pleasures. Pray tell me how your Eyes do. I never sit down to work but I think of you & feel anxious for the sight of that friend whose Eyes have done me so much good. I omitted (very unaccountably) to copy out in my last Letter that passage in my rough sketch which related to your kindness in offering to Exhibit my 2 last Pictures in the Galley in Berners Street; it was in these Words: "I sincerely thank you for your kind offer of Exhibiting my 2 Pictures; the trouble you take on my account I trust will be recompensed to you by him who seeth in secret; if you should find it convenient to do so, it will be gratefully rememberd by me among the other numerous kindness I have recievd from you."

I go on with the remaining Subjects which you gave me commission to Execute for you, but shall not be able to send any more before my return, tho perhaps I may bring some with me finishd. I am at Present in a Bustle to defend myself against a very unwarrantable warrant from a Justice of Peace in Chichester, which was taken out against me by a Private[2] in Captn Leathes's troop of 1st or Royal Dragoons, for an assault & Seditious words. The wretched Man has terribly Perjurd himself, as has his Comrade, for as to Sedition not one Word relating to the King or Government was spoken by either him or me. His Enmity arises from my having turned him out of my Garden, into which he was invited as an assistant by a Gardener at work therein, without my knowledge that he was so invited. I desired him as politely as was possible to go out of the Garden; he made me an impertinent answer. I insisted on his leaving the Garden; he refused. I still persisted in desiring his departure; he then threatend to knock out my Eyes, with many abominable imprecations & with some contempt for my Person; it affronted my foolish Pride. I therefore took him by the Elbows & pushed him before me till I had got him out; there I intended to have left him, but he, turning about, put himself into a Posture of Defiance, threatening & swearing at me. I, perhaps foolishly & perhaps not, stepped out at the Gate, &, putting aside his blows, took him again by the Elbows, &, keeping his back to me, pushed him forwards down the road about fifty yards—he all the while endeavouring to turn round & strike me, & raging & cursing, which drew out several

2. Private John Scofield, Scholfield, or Scolfield. His "Comrade" was Private Cock.

neighbours; at length, when I had got him to where he was Quarterd, which was very quickly done, we were met at the Gate by the Master of the house, The Fox Inn (who is the proprietor of my Cottage), & his Wife & Daughter & the Man's Comrade & several other people. My Landlord compelld the Soldiers to go in doors, after many abusive threats against me & my wife from the two Soldiers, but not one word of threat on account of Sedition was utterd at that time. This method of Revenge was Plann'd between them after they had got together into the Stable. This is the whole outline. I have for witnesses: The Gardener, who is Hostler at the Fox & who Evidences that to his knowledge no word of the remotest tendency to Government or Sedition was utter'd; Our next door Neighbour, a Miller's wife, who saw me turn him before me down the road & saw & heard all that happend at the Gate of the Inn, who Evidences that no Expression of threatening on account of Sedition was utterd in the heat of their fury by either of the Dragoons. This was the woman's own remark, & does high honour to her good sense, as she observes that whenever a quarrel happens the offence is always repeated. The Landlord of the Inn & His Wife & Daughter will Evidence the Same, & will evidently prove the Comrade perjurd, who swore that he heard me, while at the Gate, utter Seditious words & D—— the K——, without which perjury I could not have been committed, & I had no witness with me before the Justices who could combat his assertion, as the Gardener remaind in my Garden all the while, & he was the only person I thought necessary to take with me. I have been before a Bench of justices at Chichester this morning; but they, as the Lawyer who wrote down the Accusation told me in private, are compelld by the Military to suffer a prosecution to be enterd into: altho they must know, & it is manifest, that the whole is a Fabricated Perjury. I have been forced to find Bail. Mr Hayley was kind enough to come forwards, & Mr Seagrave,[3] Printer at Chichester; Mr H. in 100£, & Mr S. in 50£ & myself am bound in 100£ for my appearance at the Quarter Sessions, which is after Michaelmass. So I shall have the satisfaction to see my friends in Town before this Contemptible business comes on. I say Contemptible, for it must be manifest to every one that the whole accusation is a willful Perjury. Thus you see my dear Friend that I cannot leave this place without some adventure; it has struck a consternation thro all the Villages round. Every Man is now afraid of speaking to, or looking at, a Soldier, for the peaceable Villagers have always been forward in expressing their kindness for us & they express their sorrow at our departure as soon as they hear of it. Every one here is my Evidence for Peace & Good Neigh-

3. Hayley's publisher.

bourhood, & yet such is the present state of things this foolish accusation must be tried in Public. Well, I am content; I murmur not & doubt not that I shall recieve Justice & am only sorry for the trouble & expense. I have heard that my Accuser is a disgraced Sergeant; his name is John Scholfield. Perhaps it will be in your power to learn somewhat about the Man. I am very ignorant of what I am requesting of you; I only suggest what I know you will be kind enough to Excuse if you can learn nothing about him, & what, I as well know, if it is possible you will be kind enough to do in this matter.

Dear Sir, This perhaps was sufferd to Clear up some doubts & to give opportunity to those whom I doubted to clear themselves of all imputation. If a Man offends me ignorantly & not designedly, surely I ought to consider him with favour & affection. Perhaps the simplicity of myself is the origin of all offences committed against me. If I have found this, I shall have learned a most valuable thing, well worth three years' perseverance. I have found it! It is certain that a too passive manner, inconsistent with my active physiognomy, had done me much mischief. I must now express to you my conviction that all is come from the spiritual World for Good & not for Evil.

Give me your advice in my perilous adventure. Burn what I have peevishly written about any friend. I have been very much degraded & injuriously treated; but if it all arise from my own fault, I ought to blame myself.

O why was I born with a different face?
Why was I not born like the rest of my race?
When I look, each one starts! when I speak, I offend;
Then I'm silent & passive & lose every Friend.

Then my verse I dishonour, My pictures despise,
My person degrade & my temper chastise;
And the pen is my terror, the pencil my shame;
All my Talents I bury, and dead is my Fame.

I am either too low or too highly prizd;
When Elate I am Envy'd, When Meek I'm despis'd.

This is but too just a Picture of my Present state. I pray God to keep you & all men from it & to deliver me in his own good time. Pray write to me & tell me how you & your family enjoy health. My much terrified Wife joins me in love to you & M[rs] Butts & all your family. I again take the liberty to beg of you to cause the Enclosd Letter to be deliverd to my Brother, & remain Sincerely & Affectionately Yours,

William Blake

Blake's Memorandum

[*August* 1803]

Blake's Memorandum in Refutation of the Information and Complaint of John Scholfield, a private Soldier, &c.

The Soldier has been heard to say repeatedly, that he did not know how the Quarrel began, which he would not say if such seditious words were spoken.—

Mrs. Haynes Evidences, that she saw me turn him down the Road, & all the while we were at the Stable Door, and that not one word of charge against me was uttered, either relating to Sedition or any thing else; all he did was swearing and threatening.—

Mr. Hosier heard him say that he would be revenged, and would have me hanged if he could! He spoke this the Day after my turning him out of the Garden. Hosier says he is ready to give Evidence of this, if necessary.—

The Soldier's Comrade swore before the Magistrates, while I was present, that he heard me utter seditious words, at the Stable Door, and in particular, said, that he heard me D——n the K——g. Now I have all the Persons who were present at the Stable Door to witness that no Word relating to Seditious Subjects was uttered, either by one party or the other, and they are ready, on their Oaths, to say that I did not utter such Words.—

Mrs. Haynes says very sensibly, that she never heard People quarrel, but they always charged each other with the Offence, and repeated it to those around; therefore as the Soldier charged not me with Seditious Words at that Time, neither did his Comrade, the whole Charge must have been fabricated in the Stable afterwards.—

If we prove the Comrade perjured who swore that he heard me D——n the K——g, I believe the whole Charge falls to the Ground.

Mr. Cosens, owner of the Mill at Felpham, was passing by in the Road, and saw me and the Soldier and William standing near each other; he heard nothing, but says we certainly were not quarrelling.—

The whole Distance that William could be at any Time of the Conversation between me and the Soldier (supposing such Conversation to have existed) is only 12 Yards, & W—— says that he was backwards and forwards in the Garden. It was a still Day, there was no Wind stirring.

William says on his Oath, that the first Words that he heard me speak to the Soldier were ordering him out of the Garden; the truth is, I did not speak to the Soldier till then, & my ordering him out of the Garden was occasioned by his saying something that I thought insulting.

The Time that I & the Soldier were together in the Garden was not sufficient for me to have uttered the Things that he alledged.

The Soldier said to Mrs. Grinder, that it would be right to have my House searched, as I might have plans for the Country which I intended to send to the Enemy; he called me a Military Painter; I suppose mistaking the Words Miniature Painter, which he might have heard me called. I think that this proves, his having come into the Garden with some bad Intention, or at least with a prejudiced Mind.

It is necessary to learn the Names of all that were present at the Stable Door, that we may not have any Witnesses brought against us, that were not there.

All the Persons present at the Stable Door were, Mrs. Grinder and her Daughter, all the Time; Mrs. Haynes & her Daughter all the Time; Mr. Grinder, part of the Time;—Mr. Hayley's Gardener part of the Time.—Mrs. Haynes was present from my turning him out at my Gate, all the rest of the Time.—What passed in the Garden, there is no Person but William & the Soldier, & myself can know.

There was not anybody in Grinder's Tap-room, but an Old Man, named Jones, who (Mrs. Grinder says) did not come out. He is the same Man who lately hurt his Hand, & wears it in a sling.—

The Soldier after he and his Comrade came together into the Tap-room, threatened to knock William's Eyes out (this was his often repeated Threat to me and to my Wife) because W—— refused to go with him to Chichester, and swear against me. William said that he would not take a false Oath, for that he heard me say nothing of the Kind (i.e., Sedition). Mr. Grinder then reproved the Soldier for threatening William, and Mr. Grinder said, that W—— should not go, because of those Threats, especially as he was sure that no seditious Words were spoken.

William's timidity in giving his Evidence before the Magistrates, and his fear of uttering a Falsehood upon Oath, proves him to be an honest Man, & is to me an host of Strength. I am certain that if I had not turned the Soldier out of my Garden, I never should have been free from his Impertinence & Intrusion.

Mr. Hayley's Gardener came past at the Time of the Contention at the Stable Door, & going to the Comrade said to him, Is your Comrade drunk?—a Proof that he thought the Soldier abusive, & in an Intoxication of Mind.

If such a Perjury as this can take effect, any Villain in future may come & drag me and my Wife out of our House, & beat us in the Garden, or use us as he please, or is able, & afterwards go and swear our Lives away.

Is it not in the Power of any Thief who enters a Man's Dwelling,

& robs him, or misuses his Wife or Children, to go & swear as this Man has sworn.

To William Hayley, October 7, 1803

London, October 7, 1803

Dear Sir,

Your generous & tender solicitude about your devoted rebel makes it absolutely necessary that he should trouble you with an account of his safe arrival, which will excuse his begging the favor of a few lines to inform him how you escaped the contagion of the Court of Justice—I fear that you have & must suffer more on my account than I shall ever be worth—Arrived safe in London, my wife in very poor health; still I resolve not to lose hope of seeing better days.

Art in London flourishes. Engravers in particular are wanted. Every Engraver turns away work that he cannot execute from his superabundant Employment. Yet no one brings work to me. I am content that it shall be so as long as God pleases. I know that many works of a lucrative nature are in want of hands; other Engravers are courted. I suppose that I must go a Courting, which I shall do awkwardly; in the mean time I lose no moment to complete Romney to satisfaction.[4]

How is it possible that a Man almost 50 Years of Age, who has not lost any of his life since he was five years old without incessant labour & study, how is it possible that such a one with ordinary common sense can be inferior to a boy of twenty, who scarcely has taken or deigns to take a pencil in hand, but who rides about the Parks or Saunters about the Playhouses, who Eats & drinks for business not for need, how is it possible that such a fop can be superior to the studious lover of Art can scarcely be imagind. Yet such is somewhat like my fate & such it is likely to remain. Yet I laugh & sing, for if on Earth neglected I am in heaven a Prince among Princes, & even on Earth beloved by the Good as a Good Man; this I should be perfectly contented with, but a certain periods a blaze of reputation arises round me in which I am considerd as one distinguishd by some mental perfection, but the flame soon dies again & I am left stupified and astonish'd. O that I could live as others do in a regular succession of Employment; this wish I fear is not to be accomplish'd to me—Forgive this Dirge-like lamentation over a dead horse, & now I have lamented over the dead horse let me laugh & be merry with my friends till Christmas, for as Man liveth not by bread alone, I shall live altho' I should want bread—nothing is necessary to me but to do my Duty & to rejoice in the

4. Blake engraved a head of Romney for Hayley's *Life*, but it was not used [Keynes].

exceeding joy that is always poured out on my Spirit, to pray that my friends & you above the rest may be made partakers of the joy that the world cannot concieve, that you may still be replenish'd with the same & be as you always have been, a glorious & triumphant Dweller in immortality. Please to pay for me my best thanks to Miss Poole: tell her that I wish her a continued Excess of Happiness—some say that Happiness is not Good for Mortals, & they ought to be answer'd that Sorrow is not fit for Immortals & is utterly useless to any one; a blight never does good to a tree, & if a blight kill not a tree but it still bear fruit, let none say that the fruit was in consequence of the blight. When this Soldier-like danger is over I will do double the work I do now, for it will hang heavy on my Devil who terribly resents it; but I soothe him to peace, & indeed he is a good natur'd Devil after all & certainly does not lead me into scrapes—he is not in the least to be blamed for the present scrape, as he was out of the way all the time on other employment seeking amusement in making verses. To which he constantly leads me very much to my hurt & sometimes to the annoyance of my friends; as I percieve he is now doing the same work by my letter, I will finish it, wishing you health & joy in God our Saviour.

To Eternity yours,
Will[m] Blake

To William Hayley, October 23, 1804

Dear Sir,

I received your kind letter with the note to Mr. Payne, and have had the cash from him. I should have returned my thanks immediately on receipt of it, but hoped to be able to send, before now, proofs of the two plates, the *Head of Romney* and the *Shipwreck*, which you shall soon see in a much more perfect state. I write immediately because you wish I should do so, to satisfy you that I have received your kind favour.

I take the extreme pleasure of expressing my joy at our good Lady of Lavant's continued recovery: but with a mixture of sincere sorrow on account of the beloved Councillor.[5] My wife returns her heartfelt thanks for your kind inquiry concerning her health. She is surprisingly recovered. Electricity is the wonderful cause; the swelling of her legs and knees is entirely reduced. She is very near as free from rheumatism as she was five years ago, and we have the greatest confidence in her perfect recovery.

The pleasure of seeing another poem from your hands has truly set me longing (my wife says I ought to have said us) with desire and curiosity; but, however, "Christmas is a-coming."

5. Samuel Rose, Blake's defense lawyer, died of tuberculosis soon after the trial.

Our good and kind friend Hawkins[6] is not yet in town—hope soon to have the pleasure of seeing him, with the courage of conscious industry, worthy of his former kindness to me. For now! O Glory! and O Delight! I have entirely reduced that spectrous Fiend to his station, whose annoyance has been the ruin of my labours for the last passed twenty years of my life. He is the enemy of conjugal love and is the Jupiter of the Greeks, an iron-hearted tyrant, the ruiner of ancient Greece. I speak with perfect confidence and certainty of the fact which has passed upon me. Nebuchadnezzar had seven times passed over him; I have had twenty; thank God I was not altogether a beast as he was; but I was a slave bound in a mill among beasts and devils; these beasts and these devils are now, together with myself, become children of light and liberty, and my feet and my wife's feet are free from fetters. O lovely Felpham, parent of Immortal Friendship, to thee I am eternally indebted for my three years' rest from perturbation and the strength I now enjoy. Suddenly, on the day after visiting the Truchsessian Gallery[7] of pictures, I was again enlightened with the light I enjoyed in my youth, and which has for exactly twenty years been closed from me as by a door and by window-shutters. Consequently I can, with confidence, promise you ocular demonstration of my altered state on the plates I am now engraving after Romney, whose spiritual aid has not a little conduced to my restoration to the light of Art. O the distress I have undergone, and my poor wife with me: incessantly labouring and incessantly spoiling what I had done well. Every one of my friends was astonished at my faults, and could not assign a reason; they knew my industry and abstinence from every pleasure for the sake of study, and yet—and yet—and yet there wanted the proofs of industry in my works. I thank God with entire confidence that it shall be so no longer—he is become my servant who domineered over me, he is even as a brother who was my enemy. Dear Sir, excuse my enthusiasm or rather madness, for I am really drunk with intellectual vision whenever I take a pencil or graver into my hand, even as I used to be in my youth, and as I have not been for twenty dark, but very profitable years. I thank God that I courageously pursued my course through darkness. In a short time I shall make my assertion good that I am become suddenly as I was at first, by producing the *Head of Romney* and the *Shipwreck* quite another thing from what you or I ever expected them to be. In short, I am now satisfied and proud of my work, which I have not been for the above long period.

If our excellent and manly friend Meyer is yet with you, please

6. John Hawkins (1758–1841) had wished to send Blake to the Continent to study the Old Masters.

7. This gallery was a collection of pictures brought to England by Joseph, Count Truchess, and exhibited in London in August 1803. See Ruthven Todd, *Blake Newsletter* Number 19 (1971) and Morton D. Paley, *Studies in Romanticism* 16 (1977).

to make my wife's and my own most respectful and affectionate compliments to him, also to our kind friend at Lavant.

I remain, with my wife's joint affection,

Your sincere and obliged servant,

Will Blake

To William Hayley, December 11, 1805

Dear Sir,

I cannot omit to Return you my sincere & Grateful Acknowledgments for the kind Reception you have given my New Projected Work. It bids fair to set me above the difficulties I have hitherto encounter'd. But my Fate has been so uncommon that I expect Nothing. I was alive & in health & with the same Talents I now have all the time of Boydell's, Macklin's, Bowyer's, & other Great Works. I was known by them & was look'd upon by them as Incapable of Employment in those Works; it may turn out so again, notwithstanding appearances. I am prepared for it, but at the same time sincerely Grateful to Those whose Kindness & Good opinion has supported me thro' all hitherto. You, Dear Sir, are one who has my Particular Gratitude, having conducted me thro' Three that would have been the Darkest Years that ever Mortal Suffer'd, which were render'd thro' your means a Mild & Pleasant Slumber. I speak of Spiritual Things, Not of Natural; Of Things known only to Myself & to Spirits Good & Evil, but Not known to Men on Earth. It is the passage thro' these Three Years that has brought me into my Present State, & *I Know* that if I had not been with you I must have Perish'd. Those Dangers are now Passed & I can see them beneath my feet. It will not be long before I shall be able to present the full history of my Spiritual Sufferings to the Dwellers upon Earth & of the Spiritual Victories obtain'd for me by my Friends. Excuse this Effusion of the Spirit from One who cares little for this World, which passes away, whose Happiness is Secure in Jesus our Lord, & who looks for Suffering all the time of complete deliverance. In the mean While I am kept Happy, as I used to be, because I throw Myself & all that I have on our Saviour's Divine Providence. O What Wonders are the Children of Men! Would to God that they would consider it, That they would consider their Spiritual Life, Regardless of that faint Shadow call'd Natural Life, & that they would Promote Each other's Spiritual Labours, Each according to its Rank, & that they would know that Recieving a Prophet As a Prophet is a Duty which If omitted is more Severely Avenged than Every Sin & Wickedness beside. It is the Greatest of Crimes to Depress True Art & Science. I know that those who are dead from the Earth, & who mock'd & Despised the Meekness of True Art (and such, I find, have been the situations of our Beautiful, Affectionate Ballads), I know that such Mockers are Most Severely Punish'd in Eternity. I know it, for I see it & dare not help. The Mocker of Art is the Mocker of Jesus. Let us go on, Dear Sir, following his Cross: let us take it up daily, Persisting in Spiritual Labours & the Use of that Talent which it is Death to Bury, & of that Spirit to which we are called.

Pray Present My Sincerest Thanks to our Good Paulina, whose kindness to Me shall recieve recompense in the Presence of Jesus. Present also my Thanks to the Generous Seagrave, In whose debt I have been too long, but percieve that I shall be able to settle with him soon what is between us. I have deliver'd to Mr Sanders the 3 Works of Romney, as Mrs Lambert told me you wished to have them—a very few touches will finish the Shipwreck. Those few I have added upon a Proof before I parted with the Picture. It is a Print that I feel proud of, on a New inspection. Wishing you & All Friends in Sussex a Merry & a Happy Christmas.

I remain, ever Your Affectionate,
Will Blake & his Wife Catherine Blake

To Dawson Turner,[8] June 9, 1818

Sir,

I send you a List of the different Works you have done me the honour to enquire after—unprofitable enough to me, tho' Expensive to the Buyer. Those I Printed for Mr Humphrey[9] are a selection from the different Books of such as could be Printed without the Writing,[1] tho' to the Loss of some of the best things. For they when Printed perfect accompany Poetical Personifications & Acts, without which Poems they never could have been Executed.

				£.	s.	d.
America	18	Prints	folio	5	5	0
Europe	17	do.	folio	5	5	0
Visions &c	8	do.	folio	3	3	0
Thel	6	do.	Quarto	2	2	0
Songs of Innocence	28	do.	Octavo	3	3	0
Songs of Experience	26	do.	Octavo	3	3	0
Urizen	28	Prints	Quarto	5	5	0
Milton	50	do.	Quarto	10	10	0
12 Large Prints,[2] Size of Each about 2 feet by 1 & ½ Historical & Poetical, Printed in Colours			Each	5	5	0

8. Dawson Turner (1775–1858), a banker, botanist, and antiquarian of Yarmouth.
9. Ozias Humphrey (1742–1810), a miniaturist.
1. This probably refers to the two series of color-printed designs known as the *Large* and *Small Book of Designs*, now in the Department of Prints and Drawings of the British Museum, consisting for the most part of designs printed from plates of illuminated books, but without the texts.
2. These are the series of large color-printed "monotypes," ten of which are now in the Tate Gallery; despite the terminology more than one version of each subject is known. This series is fully discussed by Martin Butlin in *William Blake: Essays for S. Foster Damon*, ed. Alvin Rosenfeld (1969).

These last 12 Prints are unaccompanied by any writing.

The few I have Printed & Sold are sufficient to have gained me great reputation as an Artist, which was the chief thing Intended. But I have never been able to produce a Sufficient number for a general Sale by means of a regular Publisher. It is therefore necessary to me that any Person wishing to have any or all of them should send me their Order to Print them on the above terms, & I will take care that they shall be done at least as well as any I have yet Produced.

I am, Sir, with many thanks for your very polite approbation of my works.

Your most obedient Servant,
William Blake

To George Cumberland, April 12, 1827

Dear Cumberland,

I have been very near the Gates of Death & have returned very weak & an Old Man feeble & tottering, but not in Spirit & Life, not in The Real Man, The Imagination which Liveth for Ever. In that, I am stronger & stronger as this Foolish Body decays. I thank you for the Pains you have taken with Poor Job. I know too well that a great majority of Englishmen are fond of The Indefinite which they Measure by Newton's Doctrine of the Fluxions of an Atom, A Thing that does not Exist. These are Politicians & think that Republican Art is Inimical to their Atom. For a Line or Lineament is not formed by Chance: a Line is a Line in its Minutest Subdivisions: Strait or Crooked, It is Itself & Not Intermeasurable with or by any Thing Else. Such is Job, but since the French Revolution Englishmen are all Intermeasurable One by Another, Certainly a Happy state of Agreement to which I for One do not Agree. God keep me from the Divinity of Yes & No too, The Yea Nay Creeping Jesus, from supposing Up & Down to be the same Thing as all Experimentalists must suppose.

You are desirous I know to dispose of some of my Works & to make them Please. I am obliged to you & to all who do so. But having none remaining of all that I had Printed I cannot Print more Except at a great loss, for at the time I printed those things I had a whole House to range in. Now I am shut up in a Corner, therefore am forced to ask a Price for them that I scarce expect to get from a Stranger. I am now Printing a Set of the Songs of Innocence & Experience for a Friend at Ten Guineas which I cannot do under Six Months consistent with my other Work, so that I have little hope of doing any more of such things. The Last Work I produced is a Poem Entitled Jerusalem the Emanation of the Giant Albion, but find that to Print it will Cost my Time the amount of

Twenty Guineas. One I have Finished: It contains 100 Plates but it is not likely that I shall get a Customer for it.[3]

As you wish me to send you a list with the Prices of these things they are as follows:

	£,	s	d
America	6.	6.	0
Europe	6.	6.	0
Visions &c	5.	5.	0
Thel	3.	3.	0
Songs of Inn. & Exp.	10.	10.	0
Urizen	6.	6.	0

The Little Card I will do as soon as Possible but when you Consider that I have been reduced to a Skeleton, from which I am slowly recovering, you will I hope have Patience with me.

Flaxman is Gone & we must All soon follow, everyone to his Own Eternal House, Leaving the Delusive Goddess Nature & her Laws to get into Freedom from all Law of the Members into The Mind, in which every one is King & Priest in his own House. God send it so on Earth as it is in Heaven.

I am, Dear Sir, Yours Affectionately

William Blake

3. This unique colored copy of *Jerusalem*, now in the collection of Mr. Paul Mellon, is scheduled to be kept in the Yale Center for British Art. (See color plates 24–32, made from the Blake Trust facsimile of this copy.) The copy of *Songs of Innocence and of Experience* to which Blake refers may be copy Y, now in the Metropolitan Museum (see illustration for "The Tyger," *Songs* 42.)

Criticism

Comments by Contemporaries

SAMUEL TAYLOR COLERIDGE

Letter to C. A. Tulk†

Thursday Evening
[12 February 1818]

Dear Sir,

* * * I return you Blake's poesies, metrical and graphic, with thanks. With this and the Book I have sent a rude scrawl as to the order in which I was pleased by the several poems. * * *

Blake's Poems.[1]

I begin with my Dyspathies that I may forget them: and have uninterrupted space for Loves and Sympathies. Title page and the following emblem contain all the faults of the Drawings with as few beauties as could be in the composition of a man who was capable of such faults + such beauties.—The faults—despotism in symbols, amounting in the Title page to the μισητόν, and occasionally, irregular unmodified Lines of the Inanimate, sometimes as the effect of rigidity and sometimes as exossation—like a wet tendon. So likewise the ambiguity of the Drapery. Is it a garment—or the body incised and scored out? The *Limpness* (= the effect of Vinegar on an egg) in the upper one of the two prostrate figures in the Title page, and the *eye*-likeness of the twig posteriorly on the second—and the strait line down the waistcoat of pinky gold-beater's skin in the next drawing, with the I don't know whatness of the countenance, as if the mouth had been formed by the habit of placing the tongue, not contemptuously, but stupidly, between the lower gums and the lower jaw—these are the only *repulsive* faults I

† From *Collected Letters of Samuel Taylor Coleridge*, ed. Earl Leslie Griggs, IV (Oxford: Clarendon Press, 1959), 836–38.

1. See B. R. McElderry, Jr., "Coleridge on Blake's *Songs*," *Modern Language Quarterly*, 9 (1948), 293–32; also see J. H. Wicksteed's explanation of Coleridge's word *aseity* in Geoffrey Keynes, *Blake Studies: Essays on His Life and Work*, 2nd ed. (Oxford: Clarendon, 1971), p. 84: "It is not Greek . . . but Latin, *a se*, by itself or himself, i.e., not proceding from, or created by, something more basically real or essential than itself. . . ." The Greek word μισητόν means "odious"; "exossation" means "bonelessness." Coleridge does not discuss *Songs* 4, 43, 47, though these plates were in Tulk's copy (Copy J). "P. 13" probably refers to "The Angel." For opinions of Blake by other Romantic writers, see Lamb's letter, p. 483 in this edition, and comments by Wordsworth, Southey, and Hazlitt in G. E. Bentley, Jr., ed., *Blake Records* (Oxford: Clarendon Press, 1969). [*Editors.*]

noticed. The figure, however, of the second leaf (abstracted from the *expression* of the countenance given it by something about the mouth and the interspace from the lower lip to the chin) is such as only a Master learned in his art could produce.

N.B. I signifies, It gave me pleasure, Ɨ, still greater—ƗƗ, and greater still. Θ, in the highest degree, o, in the lowest.[2]

Shepherd I. Spring I (last Stanza Ɨ). Holy Thursday ƗƗ. Laughing Song Ɨ. Nurse's Song I. The Divine Image Θ. The Lamb Ɨ. The little Black Boy Θ: yea Θ + Θ! Infant Joy ƗƗ. (N.b. for the 3 last lines I should wish—When wilt thou smile, or —O smile, O smile! I'll sing the while—For a Babe two days old does not, cannot *smile*—and innocence and the very truth of Nature must go together. Infancy is too holy a thing to be ornamented.)—Echoing Green I (the figures Ɨ, and of the second leaf ƗƗ). The Cradle Song I. The School boy ƗƗ. Night Θ. On another's Sorrow I. A Dream?—The little Boy lost I (the drawing Ɨ). The little boy found I. The Blossom o. The Chimney Sweeper o. The Voice of the ancient Bard o.

Introduction Ɨ. Earth's Answer Ɨ. Infant Sorrow I. The Clod and the Pebble I. The Garden of Love Ɨ. The Fly I. The Tyger Ɨ. A little Boy lost Ɨ. Holy Thursday I. P. 13, o. Nurse's Song o. The little girl lost and found (the ornaments most exquisite! the poem I). Chimney Sweeper in the Snow o. To Tirzah—and The Poison Tree I and yet o. A little girl lost o (I would have had it omitted —not for the want of innocence in the poem, but from the too probable want of it in many readers). London I. The sick Rose I. *The little Vagabond*—Tho' I cannot approve altogether of this last poem and have been inclined to think that the error which is most *likely* to beset the scholars of Emanuel Swedenborg is that of utterly demerging the tremendous incompatibilities with an evil will that arise out of the essential Holiness of the abysmal Aseity in the Love of the eternal *Person*—and thus giving temptation to weak minds to sink this Love itself into *good nature,* yet still I disapprove the mood of mind in this wild poem so much less than I do the servile, blind-worm, wrap-rascal scurf-coat of FEAR of the *modern Saints* (whose whole being is a Lie, to themselves as well as to their Brethren), that I should laugh with good conscience in watching a Saint of the new stamp, one of the Fixt Stars of our eleemosynary Advertisements, groaning in windpipe! and with the whites of his Eyes upraised at the *audacity* of this poem!—Any thing rather than *this* degradation[3] of Humanity, and therein of the Incarnate Divinity!

S. T. C.

2. [The character] o means that I am perplexed and have no opinion. [*Coleridge's note.*]

3. With which how can we utter "Our Father"? [*Coleridge's note.*]

CHARLES LAMB

Letter to Bernard Barton†

May 15, 1824

Dear B. B.,

* * *

* * * Blake is a real name, I assure you, and a most extraordinary man, if he be still living. He is the Robert Blake, whose wild designs accompany a splendid folio edition of the Night Thoughts, which you may have seen, in one of which he pictures the parting of soul & body by a solid mass of human form floating off, God knows how, from a lumpish mass (fac simile to itself) left behind on the dying bed. He paints in water colours, marvellous strange pictures, visions of his brain which he asserts that he has seen. They have great merit. He has *seen* the old Welch bards on Snowdon—he has seen the Beautifullest, the Strongest, & the Ugliest Man, left alone from the Massacre of the Britons by the Romans, & has painted them from memory (I have seen his paintings) and asserts them to be as good as the figures of Raphael & Angelo, but not better, as they had precisely the same retro-visions & prophetic visions with himself. The painters in Oil (which he will have it that neither of them practised) he affirms to have been the ruin of art, and affirms that all the while he was engaged in his water-paintings, Titian was disturbing him, Titian the Ill Genius of oil Painting. His Pictures, one in particular, the Canterbury Pilgrims (far above Stothard's), have great merit, but hard, dry, yet with grace. He has written a Catalogue of them, with a most spirited criticism on Chaucer, but mystical and full of Vision. His poems have been sold hitherto only in Manuscript. I never read them, but a friend at my desire procured the Sweep Song. There is one to a Tiger, which I have heard recited, beginning

> Tiger Tiger burning bright
> Thro' the deserts of the night—

† From G. E. Bentley, Jr., *Blake Records* (Oxford: Clarendon Press, 1969), pp. 284–86, with slips of the pen and obscure abbreviations normalized.

Lamb had sent Blake's "The Chimney Sweeper" of Innocence to James Montgomery as a contribution to *The Chimney-Sweeper's Friend, and Climbing Boy's Album* (1824; reprinted 1825), a project of the Society for Ameliorating the Condition of Infant Chimney-Sweepers. Barton, who had also written some verse for the volume, wanted to know whether "Blake" was a pseudonym, thinking Lamb wrote it himself. Lamb had been aware of Blake's work since 1810 when he attended Blake's exhibition with Crabb Robinson, but his remarks to Barton are characteristically inexact: mixing up his recollections of Blake's *Night Thoughts* engravings with his engravings for Blair's *Grave*, getting Blake's first name wrong, rewriting the second line of "The Tyger." Though Lamb was unable to compose a poem of his own for Montgomery's volume, his essay, "The Praise of Chimney-Sweepers" (1822), had shown an aesthetic interest in the condition of sweeps.

which is glorious. But alas! I have not the Book, for the man is flown, whither I know not, to Hades, or a Mad House—but I must look on him as one of the most extraordinary persons of the age. Montgomery's Book I have not much hopes from. The Society, with the affected name, have been labouring at it for these 20 Years & made few Converts. I think it was injudicious to mix stories avowedly colour'd by fiction with the sad true statements from the parliamentary records, &c. but I wish the little Negroes all the good that can come from it. I b*a*tter'd my brains (not butter'd them—but it is a bad *a*) for a few verses for them, but I could make nothing of it. You have been luckier. But Blake's are the flower of the set, you will I am sure agree, tho' some of Montgomery's at the end are pretty, but the Dream awkwardly paraphrased from B. * * *

Yours ever truly
C. L.

JOHN THOMAS SMITH

From Nollekens and His Times (1828) †

Much about this time,[1] Blake wrote many other songs, to which he also composed tunes. These he would occasionally sing to his friends; and though, according to his confession, he was entirely unacquainted with the science of music, his ear was so good, that his tunes were sometimes most singularly beautiful, and were noted down by musical professors. As for his later poetry, if it may be so called, attached to his plates, though it was certainly in some parts enigmatically curious as to its application, yet it was not always wholly uninteresting; and I have unspeakable pleasure in being able to state, that though I admit he did not for the last forty years attend any place of Divine worship, yet he was not a Freethinker, as some invidious detractors have thought proper to assert, nor was he ever in any degree irreligious. Through life, his Bible was every thing with him. * * *

In his choice of subjects, and in his designs in Art, perhaps no

† From *Blake Records,* ed. G. E. Bentley, Jr. (Oxford: Clarendon Press, 1969), pp. 457–58, 459–60, 464–65, 467–68, 472–73, 474–76.

As a supplement to his biography of the fashionable portrait sculptor Joseph Nollekens (1737–1823), Smith (1766–1833) published memoirs of other noted artists from Hogarth to Flaxman. Smith supplemented his own knowledge of Blake over forty years with information drawn from other friends. The best-known early biography of Blake, based on interviews with Smith, Tatham, Linnell, and others, appeared in Allan Cunningham's *Lives of the Most Eminent British Painters, Sculptors, and Architects* (1830; reprinted in G. E. Bentley, Jr., ed., *Blake Records* [Oxford: Clarendon Press, 1969], pp. 476–507).

1. About 1780. [*Editors.*]

man had higher claim to originality, nor ever drew with a closer adherence to his own conception; and from what I knew of him, and have heard related by his friends, I most firmly believe few artists have been guilty of less plagiarisms than he. It is true, I have seen him admire and heard him expatiate upon the beauties of Marc Antonio[2] and of Albert Durer; but I verily believe not with any view of borrowing an idea; neither do I consider him at any time dependent in his mode of working, which was generally with the graver only; and as to printing, he mostly took off his own impressions.

* * *

After his marriage, which took place at Battersea, and which proved a mutually happy one, he instructed his *beloved,* for so he most frequently called his Kate,[3] and allowed her, till the last moment of his practice, to take off his proof impressions and print his works, which she did most carefully, and ever delighted in the task: nay, she became a draughtswoman; and as a convincing proof that she and her husband were born for each other's comfort, she not only entered cheerfully into his views, but, what is curious, possessed a similar power of imbibing ideas, and has produced drawings equally original, and, in some respects, interesting.

Blake's peace of mind, as well as that of his Catherine, was much broken by the death of their brother Robert, who was a most amicable link in their happiness; and, as a proof how much Blake respected him, whenever he beheld him in his visions, he implicitly attended to his opinion and advice as to his future projected works. I should have stated, that Blake was supereminently endowed with the power of disuniting all other thoughts from his mind, whenever he wished to indulge in thinking of any particular subject; and so firmly did he believe, by this abstracting power, that the objects of his compositions were before him in his mind's eye, that he frequently believed them to be speaking to him. This I shall now illustrate by the following narrative.

Blake, after deeply perplexing himself as to the mode of accom-

2. Marcantonio Raimondi (ca. 1480–ca. 1534), Italian engraver; inventor of a standardized method of cross-hatching (shading by fine intersecting lines) to create a three-dimensional effect. He copied some of Dürer's woodcuts and engraved paintings by Giulio Romano and especially Raphael, all three of whom were among Blake's favorite artists. Marcantonio was the foremost practitioner of reproductive line engraving; through him and other engravers Blake and his fellow English artists—who had little access to originals—knew the Old Masters. [*Editors.*]

3. A friend has favoured me with the following anecdotes, which he received from Blake, respecting his courtship. He states that "Our Artist fell in love with a lively little girl, who allowed him to say every thing that was loving, but would not listen to his overtures on the score of matrimony. He was lamenting this in the house of a friend, when a generous-hearted lass declared that she pitied him from her heart. 'Do you pity me?' asked Blake. 'Yes; I do, most sincerely.'—'Then,' said he, 'I love you for that.'—'Well,' said the honest girl, 'and I love you.' The consequence was, they were married, and lived the happiest of lives." [*Smith's note.*]

plishing the publication of his illustrated songs, without their being subject to the expense of letter-press, his brother Robert stood before him in one of his visionary imaginations, and so decidedly directed him in the way in which he ought to proceed, that he immediately followed his advice, by writing his poetry, and drawing his marginal subjects of embellishments in outline upon the copper-plate with an impervious liquid, and then eating the plain parts or lights away with aquafortis considerably below them, so that the outlines were left as a stereotype. The plates in this state were then printed in any tint that he wished, to enable him or Mrs. Blake to colour the marginal figures up by hand in imitation of drawings.

* * *

An Engraver of the name of Cromek, a man who endeavoured to live by speculating upon the talents of others, purchased a series of drawings of Blake, illustrative of Blair's 'Grave,' which he had begun with a view of engraving and publishing. These were sold to Mr. Cromek for the insignificant sum of one guinea each, with the promise, and indeed under the express agreement, that Blake should be employed to engrave them; a task to which he looked forward with anxious delight. Instead of this negotiation being carried into effect, the drawings, to his great mortification, were put into the hands of Schiavonetti. During the time this artist was thus employed, Cromek had asked Blake what work he had in mind to execute next. The unsuspecting artist not only told him, but without the least reserve showed him the designs sketched out for a fresco picture; the subject Chaucer's 'Pilgrimage to Canterbury'; with which Mr. Cromek appeared highly delighted. Shortly after this, Blake discovered that Stothard, a brother-artist to whom he had been extremely kind in early days, had been employed to paint a picture, not only of the same subject, but in some instrances similar to the fresco sketch which he had shown to Mr. Cromek. The picture painted by Stothard became the property of Mr. Cromek, who published proposals for an engraving from it, naming Bromley as the engraver to be employed. However, in a short time, that artist's name was withdrawn, and Schiavonetti's substituted, who lived only to complete the etching; the plate being finished afterwards by at least three different hands. Blake, highly indignant at this treatment, immediately set to work, and proposed an engraving from his fresco picture, which he publicly exhibited in his brother James's shop window, at the corner of Broad-street, accompanied with an address to the public, stating what he considered to be improper conduct.[4]

* * *

4. For further discussion of this quarrel, see G. E. Bentley, Jr., *Modern Philology*, 71 (1974), 66–79. [*Editors.*]

Whatever may be the public opinion hereafter of Blake's talents, when his enemies are dead, I will not presume to predict; but this I am certain of, that on the score of industry at least, many artists must strike to him. Application was a faculty so engendered in him that he took little bodily exercise to keep up his health: he had few evening walks and little rest from labour, for his mind was ever fixed upon his art, nor did he at any time indulge in a game of chess, draughts, or backgammon; such amusements, considered as relaxation by artists in general, being to him distractions. His greatest pleasure was derived from the Bible,—a work ever in his hand, and which he often assidously consulted in several languages. Had he fortunately lived till the next year's exhibition at Somersethouse, the public would then have been astonished at his exquisite finishing of a Fresco picture of the Last Judgment, containing upwards of one thousand figures, many of them wonderfully conceived and grandly drawn. The lights of this extraordinary performance have the appearance of silver and gold; but upon Mrs. Blakes' assuring me that there was no silver used, I found, upon a closer examination, that a blue wash had been passed over those parts of the gilding which receded, and the lights of the forward objects, which were also of gold, were heightened with a warm colour, to give the appearance of the two metals.

* * *

Blake's modes of preparing his ground, and laying them over his panels for painting, mixing his colours, and manner of working, were those which he considered to have been practised by the earliest fresco-painters, whose productions still remain, in numerous instances, vivid and permanently fresh. His ground was a mixture of whiting and carpenter's glue, which he passed over several times in thin coatings: his colours he ground himself, and also united them with the same sort of glue, but in a much weaker state. He would, in the course of painting a picture, pass a very thin transparent wash of glue-water over the whole of the parts he had worked upon, and then proceed with his finishing.

This process I have tried, and find, by using my mixtures warm, that I can produce the same texture as possessed in Blake's pictures of the Last Judgment, and others of his productions, particularly in Varley's curious picture of the personified Flea. Blake preferred mixing his colours with carpenter's glue, to gum, on account of the latter cracking in the sun, and becoming humid in moist weather. The glue-mixture stands the sun, and change of atmosphere has no effect upon it. Every carpenter knows that if a broken piece of stick be joined with good glue, the stick will seldom break again in the glued parts.

That Blake had many secret modes of working, both as a colourist and an engraver, I have no doubt. His methods of eating away the plain copper, and leaving his drawn lines of his subjects and his words as stereotype, is in my mind perfectly original. Mrs. Blake is in possession of the secret, and she ought to receive something considerable for its communication, as I am quite certain it may be used to the greatest advantage both to artists and literary characters in general.

* * *

Blake and his wife were known to have lived so happily together, that they might unquestionably have been registered at Dunmow.[5] 'Their hopes and fears were to each other known,' and their days and nights were passed in each other's company, for he always painted, drew, engraved and studied, in the same room where they grilled, boiled, stewed, and slept; and so steadfastly attentive was he to his beloved tasks, that for the space of two years he had never once been out of his house; and his application was often so incessant, that in the middle of the night, he would, after thinking deeply upon a particular subject, leap from his bed and write for two hours or more; and for many years, he made a constant practice of lighting the fire, and putting on the kettle for breakfast before his Kate awoke.

During his last illness, which was occasioned by the gall mixing with his blood, he was frequently bolstered-up in his bed to complete his drawings, for his intended illustration of Dante; an author so great a favourite with him, that though he agreed with Fuseli and Flaxman, in thinking Carey's translation superior to all others, yet, at the age of sixty-three years, he learned the Italian language purposely to enjoy Dante in the highest possible way. For this intended work, he produced seven engraved plates of an imperial quarto size, and nearly one hundred finished drawings of a size considerably larger; which will do equal justice to his wonderful mind, and the liberal heart of their possessor, who engaged him upon so delightful a task at a time when few persons would venture to give him employment, and whose kindness softened, for the remainder of his life, his lingering bodily sufferings, which he was seen to support with the most Christian fortitude.[6]

On the day of his death, August 12th, 1827, he composed and uttered songs to his Maker so sweetly to the ear of his Catherine, that when she stood to hear him, he, looking upon her most affectionately, said, 'My beloved, they are not mine—no—they are not

5. An Augustinian priory in Little Dunmow, Essex, annually awarded a "flitch" (i.e., side) of bacon to any couple who could prove that they had lived in perfect harmony for the first year and a day of their marriage. In the sixteenth century the custom was secularized and a jury of six bachelors and six maids heard the cases. The same custom was followed at Wichnor, Staffordshire. [*Editors.*]

6. John Linnell, one of the young artists who befriended Blake in his later years, commissioned the Dante designs. [*Editors.*]

mine.' He expired at six in the evening, with the most cheerful serenity. Some short time before his death, Mrs. Blake asked him where he should like to be buried, and whether he would have the Dissenting Minister, or the Clergyman of the Church of England, to read the service: his answers were, that as far as his own feelings were concerned, they might bury him where she pleased, adding, that as his father, mother, aunt, and brother, were buried in Bunhill-row, perhaps it would be better to lie there, but as to service, he should wish for that of the Church of England.

* * *

FREDERICK TATHAM

From Life of Blake (1832?) †

* * *

He took infinite pains with them,[1] coloured them very highly & certainly without prejudice, either for or against, has produced as fine works, as any ancient painter. He can be excelled by none where he is successful. Like his thoughts, his paintings seem to be inspired by Fairies & his colours look as if they were the bloom dropped from the brilliant Wings of the Spirits of the Prism. This may appear too much to be said of the mad Blake, as he was called by those too grovelling & too ignorant to discern his merits. Mr Butts' collection is enough in all conscience to prove this & more & whoever does not perceive the beauties of this splendid collection ought indeed to find fault with modesty & censure with a blush.

In his 24th year he fell in love with a young woman who by his own account & according to his own knowledge was no trifler; he wanted to marry her but she refused, & was as obstinate as she was unkind. He became ill & went to Kew near Richmond for a change of air & renovation of health & spirits & as far as is possible to know lodged at the House of a market Gardener whose name was Boutcher. The Boutchers appear to have been a respectable & industrious family. He was relating to the daughter, a Girl named Catherine, the lamentable story of Polly Wood, his implacable Lass,

† From *Blake Records*, ed. G. E. Bentley, Jr. (Oxford: Clarendon Press, 1969), pp. 517–19, 519–20, 521–22, 525–26, 527–28, 529–30, with minor changes in punctuation and capitalization.

Though Tatham (1805–78), a minor sculptor remembered only for his relationship to Blake, is not considered a consistently reliable biographer, he knew the Blakes well in their last years at Fountain Court, and his unpublished memoir shows that he was very close to Catherine. After living unhappily with the Linnells as their housekeeper for the first year after William's death, Catherine moved in with the Tathams as their housekeeper, and when she died Tatham inherited Blake's unsold works, as well as his original copper plates. Since neither of the Blakes left a written will and nothing was bequeathed to Blake's impoverished sister, an unpleasant dispute arose between Linnell and Tatham over some of Blake's works. One reason Tatham wrote his memoir of Blake is that he thought it might help him sell the great colored copy of *Jerusalem*.

1. His pictures. [*Editors.*]

upon which Catherine expressed her deep sympathy, it is supposed in such a tender & affectionate manner, that it quite won him; he immediately said with the suddenness peculiar to him 'Do you pity me?' 'Yes indeed I do' answered she. 'Then I love you' said he again. Such was their courtship. He was impressed with her tenderness of mind & her answer indicated her previous feeling for him. For she has often said that upon her mother asking her who among her acquaintances she could fancy for a Husband, she replied that she had not yet seen the man & she has further been heard to say that when she first came into the Room in which Blake sat she instantly recognized (like Britomart in Merlin's wondrous glass) her future partner, & was so near fainting that she left his presence until she had recovered. After this interview, Blake left the House having recruited his health & spirits, & having determined to take Catherine Boutcher to Wife. He returned to his Lodgings, & worked incessantly that he might be able to accomplish this End, at the same time resolving that he would not see her until he succeeded. This interval, which she felt dolefully long, was one whole year, at the expiration of which, with the approbation & consent of his parents, he married this Interesting, beautiful & affectionate Girl. Nimble with joy & warm with the glow of youth, this bride was presented to her noble bridegroom. The morning of their married life was bright as the noon of their devoted love, the noon as clear as the serene Evening of their mutual equanimity. Although not handsome, he must have had a noble countenance, full of facial expression & animation. His hair was of a yellow brown, & curled with the utmost crispness & luxuriance. His locks instead of falling down stood up like a curling flame, and looked at a distance like radiations, which with his fiery Eye & expansive forehead, his dignified & cheerful physiognomy must have made his appearance truly prepossessing. After his Marriage he took lodgings in Green S[t], Leicester Square.

It is now necessary to mention somewhat concerning the fanciful representations that Blake asserted were presented to his mind's Eye: difficult as this subject is, it cannot be omitted without a sacrifice to the memory of this great man. He always asserted that he had the power of bringing his Imagination before his mind's Eye, so completely organized, & so perfectly formed & Evident, that he persisted, that while he copied the vision (as he called it) upon his plate or canvas, he could not Err; & that error & defect could only arise from the departure or inaccurate delineation of this unsubstantial scene. He said that he was the companion of spirits, who taught, rebuked, argued, & advised, with all the familiarity of personal intercourse. What appears more odd still was the power he contended he had, of calling up any personage of past days, to delineate their forms & features, & to converse upon the topic most incidental to the days of their own existence: how far this is probable must be a question, left either to the credulity or the faith of each person: it is fair however to say that what Blake produced from these characters, in delineating them, was often so curiously original, & yet so finely expressed, that it was difficult, if prejudices were cast away, to disbelieve totally this power. It is well known to all enquiring men that Blake was not the only individual who enjoyed this peculiar gift.

* * *

Although it would not be irrelevant, it would be tedious to narrate Swedenborg's opinions, or rather Swedenborg's visions, for he asserted that he only gave a detail & history of what he saw & heard; all that is necessary to prove now is that other men, other sensible men, such as scarcely could be designated as mad or stupid, did see into an immaterial life denied to most—All that is proposed here, further, is, that it is a possible thing—that it does not require either a madman to see, or an Idiot to believe, that such things are. Blake asserted from a Boy that he did see them: even when a Child his mother beat him for running in & saying that he saw the Prophet Ezekiel under a Tree in the Fields. In this incredulous age it is requisite before this possibility is admitted, even as a doubt or question, that it should be said, that he who inefficiently attempts to defend this power never has been accustomed to see them, although he has known others besides Blake, on whose veracity & sanity he could equally well rely, who have been thus favored. The Cock lane Ghost story, the old women's tales, & the young bravo, who defies the Ghost in the Tap-Room, that he shudders at in his walk home, are foolishly mixed up with Blake's visions: they are totally different: they are mental abstractions, that are not necessarily accompanied with fear, such as Ghosts & Apparitions, which either appear to be, or are, seen by the mortal Eyes, which circumstance alone horrifies. These visions of Blake seem to have been more like peopled imaginations, & personified thoughts; they only horrified where they represented any scene in which horrors were depicted as a picture or a Poem.

* * *

Again in reference to the authenticity of Blake's Visions, let any one contemplate the designs in this Book;[2] Are they not only new in their method & manner, but actually new in their class & origin? Do they look like the localities of common circumstances, or of lower Worlds? The combinations are chimerical, the forms unusual, the Inventions abstract, the poem not only abstruse but absolutely, according to common rules of criticism, as near ridiculous as it is completely heterogeneous. With all that is incomprehensible in the poem, with all that might by some be termed ridiculous in the

2. The colored copy of *Jerusalem*. [*Editors.*]

plan, the designs are possessed of some of the most sublime Ideas, some of the most lofty thoughts, some of the most noble conceptions possible to the mind of man. You may doubt however the means, & you may criticise the peculiarity of the notions, but you cannot but admire, nay 'wonder at with great admiration,' these Expressive, these sublime, these awful diagrams of an Etherial Phantasy. Michael Angelo, Julio Romano or any other great man never surpassed Plates 25, 35, 37, 46, 51, 76, 94, and many of the stupendous & awful scenes with which this laborious Work is so thickly ornamented. * * * Even supposing the poetry to be the mere Vehicle or a mere alloy for the sake of producing or combining these wonderful thoughts, it should at all events be looked upon with some respect.

* * *

It was here[3] that Flaxman used to come & see him & sit drinking Tea in the Garden, under the shadow of a Grape Vine which Mrs Blake had very carefully trained. M^r^ and Mrs Flaxman were highly delighted with Blake's Arcadian Arbour, as well indeed they might, for they all sat with ripe fruit hanging in rich clusters around their heads. These 2 great men had known each other from boyhood.[4] Flaxman was a cheerful lively young man, was very good company & sang beautifully, having an excellent & musical Voice as well as almost all of the qualities requisite for good-fellowship & innocent convivial mirth— This House & garden was adjoining the Old Astley's Theatre[5] & an anecdote showing his courage as well as his utter detestation of human slavery is too interesting & characteristic to remain untold. Blake was standing at one of his Windows, which looked into Astley's premises (the Man who established the Theatre still called by his name) & saw a Boy hobbling along with a log to his foot, such an one as is put on a Horse or Ass to prevent their straying. Blake called his Wife & asked her for what reason that log could be placed upon the boy's foot: she answered that it must be for a punishment, for some inadvertency. Blake's blood boiled & his indignation surpassed his forbearance; he sallied forth, & demanded in no very quiescent terms that the Boy should be loosed & that no Englishman should be subjected to those miseries,which he thought were inexcusable even towards a Slave. After having succeeded in obtaining the Boy's release in some way or other he returned home. Astley by this time having heard of Blake's interference, came to his House & demanded in an equally peremptory manner,

3. At Hercules Buildings, Lambeth. [*Editors.*]

4. According to J. T. Smith, Flaxman and Blake met about 1779, when they were twenty-four and twenty-two respectively. [*Editors.*]

5. According to the rate books, Astley's theatre [see map] was perhaps a quarter mile from number 13 Hercules Buildings, but Astley's own house was built in behind number 11, in the next garden but one to Blake's. [*Bentley's note.*]

by what authority he dare come athwart his method of jurisdiction; to which Blake replied with such warmth, that blows were very nearly the consequence. The debate lasted long, but like all wise men whose anger is unavoidably raised, they ended in mutual forgiveness & mutual respect. Astley saw that his punishment was too degrading & admired Blake for his humane sensibility & Blake desisted from wrath when Astley was pacified: As this is an Example truly worthy of imitation, to all those whose anger is either excited by indignation or called forth by defence, it may not be out of place to say, if all quarrels were thus settled the time would shortly come, when the Lion would lie down with the Lamb & the little child would lead them. Blake resided in Hercules Buildings in a pretty clean House of 8 or 10 Rooms & at first kept a servant, but finding (as Mrs Blake declared & as every one else knows) the more service the more Inconvenience, she like all sensible women, who are possessed of industry & health & only moderate means, relinquished this incessant Tax upon domestic comfort, did all the Work herself, kept the House clean, & herself tidy, besides printing all Blake's numerous Engravings, which was a Task alone sufficient for any industrious Woman. * * *

He was a subject of much temptation & mental suffering & required sometimes much soothing— He has frequently had recourse to the following stratagem to calm the turbulence of his thoughts: His wife being to him a very patient Woman, he fancied that while she looked on at him, as he worked, her sitting quite still by his side, doing nothing, soothed his impetuous mind, & he has many a time when a strong desire presented itself to overcome any difficulty in his Plates or Drawings, has in the middle of the night, risen, & requested her to get up with him & sit by his side, in which she as cheerfully acquiesced.[6]

When roused or annoyed he was possessed of a Violent Temper, but in his Passions there was some method, for while he was engraving a large Portrait of Lavater, not being able to obtain what he wanted, he threw the plate completely across the Room. Upon his relating this he was asked whether he did not injure it, to which he replied with his usual fun 'O I took good care of that.' He was a subject often of much internal perturbation & over anxiety, for he has spoilt as much work (which every Artist knows is not only easy but common) by over-labour, as would take some a whole life of ordinary industry to accomplish. Mrs Blake has been heard to say that she never saw him, except when in conversation or reading,

6. Cf. Tatham's account in Gilchrist (1863; 1945, p. 315): "She would get up in the night, when he was under his very fierce inspirations, which were as if they would tear him asunder, while he was yielding himself to the Muse, or whatever else it could be called, sketching and writing. And so terrible a task did this seem to be, that she had to sit motionless and silent; only to stay him mentally, without moving hand or foot: this for hours, and night after night." [*Editors.*]

with his hands idle; he scarcely ever mused upon what he had done. Some men muse & call it thinking, but Blake was a hard worker; his thought was only for action, as a man plans a House, or a General, consults his Map, & arranges his forces for a Battle. His mental acquirements were incredible: he had read almost every thing in whatsoever language, which language he always taught himself.[7] His conversation therefore was highly interesting & never could one converse on any subject with him, but they would gain something quite as new, as noble from his eccentric & Elastic mind. It is a remarkable fact, that among the Volumes bequeathed by Mrs Blake to the Author of this Sketch, the most thumbed from use are his Bible & those books in other languages. He was very fond of Ovid, especially the *Fasti*. He read Dante when he was past 60, altho' before he never knew a word of Italian & he drew from it a hundred such designs, as have never been done by any Englishman at any period or by any foreigner since the 15th Century, & then his only competitor was Michael Angelo.[8]

It has been supposed his Excessive labour, without the exercise he used formerly to take (having relinquished the habit of taking very long Walks), brought on the complaint which afterwards consumed him. In his youth he and his Wife would start in the Morning early, & walk out 20 miles & dine at some pretty & sequestered Inn & would return the same day home having travelled 40 miles. Mrs Blake would do this without excessive fatigue. Blake has been known to walk 50 Miles in the day, but being told by some Physician, that such long walks were injurious, he discontinued them, & went so far to the other extreme, that it has been said he remained in the House, so long that it was considered far from extraordinary his days were shortened. About a year before he died he was seized with a species of Ague (as it was then termed), of which he was alternately better & worse. He was at times very ill but rallied & all had hopes of him, indeed such was his energy that even then, tho' sometimes confined to his Bed, he sat up Drawing his most stupendous Works. In August he gradually grew worse & required much more of his Wife's attention, indeed he was decaying fast; his patience during his agonies of pain is described to have been exemplary.

Life however like a dying flame flashed once more, gave one more burst of animation, during which he was cheerful, & free from the tortures of his approaching end. He thought he was better, and as he was sure to do, asked to look at the Work over which he was occupied when seized with his last attack: it was a coloured print of the Ancient of Days, striking the first circle of the Earth, done

7. Blake learned Latin, Greek, and Hebrew about 1803, quoted Voltaire in French about 1808, and taught himself Italian about 1824. [*Editors.*]

8. Although Michelangelo did not illustrate the *Divine Comedy,* most of Botticelli's great illustrations (ca. 1490) were in the Hamilton Palace collection during Blake's lifetime, and Tatham may have had these in mind. [*Editors.*]

expressly by commission for the writer of this. After he had worked upon it he exclaimed 'There I have done all I can; it is the best I have ever finished. I hope Mr Tatham will like it'. He threw it suddenly down & said 'Kate you have been a good Wife, I will draw your portrait'. She sat near his Bed & he made a Drawing, which though not a likeness is finely touched & expressed. He then threw that down, after having drawn for an hour & began to sing Hallelujahs & songs of joy & Triumph, which Mrs Blake described as being truly sublime in music & in Verse. He sang loudly & with true extatic energy and seemed too happy that he had finished his course, that he had ran his race, & that he was shortly to arrive at the Goal, to receive the prize of his high & eternal calling. After having answered a few questions concerning his Wife's means of living after his decease, & after having spoken of the writer of this, as a likely person to become the manager of her affairs, his spirit departed like the sighing of a gentle breeze, & he slept in company with the mighty ancestors he had formerly depicted. * * * [9]

William Blake, in stature was short, but well made, & very well proportioned, so much so that West, the great History Painter, admired much the form of his limbs. He had a large head & wide shoulders. Elasticity & promptitude of action were the characteristics of his Contour. His motions were rapid & energetic, betokening a mind filled with elevated Enthusiasm. His forehead was very high & prominent over the Frontals. His Eye most unusually large & glassy, with which he appeared to look into some other World.

* * *

In youth he surprized every one with his Vigour & activity. In age he impressed all with his unfading ardour & unabated Energy. His beautiful grey locks, hung upon his Shoulders; & dressing as he always did in later years, in Black, he looked even in person, although, without any effort towards Eccentricity, to be of no ordinary character. In Youth he was nimble, in old age Venerable. His disposition was cheerful & lively, & was never depressed by any cares, but those springing out of his Art. He was the attached friend of all who knew him & a favourite with every one but those who oppressed him & against such his noble & impetuous Spirit boiled & fell upon the aggressor like a Water spout from the troubled deep. Yet like Moses he was one of the meekest of Men; his patience was almost incredible: he could be the Lamb, he could plod as a Camel, he could roar as a Lion. He was every thing but subtle, the serpent had no share in his nature. Secresy was unknown to him. He would relate those things of himself that others make it their utmost endeavour to conceal. He was possessed of a peculiar obstinacy that

9. Ruthven Todd learned from George Richmond's grandson that the young artist, present at Blake's death, closed Blake's eyes "to keep the vision in" (*Blake Newsletter*, no. 21 [1972]). [*Editors.*]

always bristled up when he was either unnecessarily opposed or invited out to show like a lion or a bear. Many anecdotes could be related in which there is sufficient evidence to prove that many of his Eccentric speeches, were thrown forth more as a piece of sarcasm, upon the Enquirer, than from his real opinion. If he thought a question were put merely from a desire to learn, no man could give advice more seasonably & more kindly but if that same question were put for idle Curiosity, he retaliated by such an Eccentric answer, as left the Enquirer more afield than Ever. He then made an Enigma of a plain question. Hence arose many vague reports of his oddities. He was particularly so upon religion. His writings abounded with these sallies of independent opinion. He detested priestcraft & religious Cant. He wrote much upon controversial subjects, & like all controversies these writings are inspired by doubt & made up of vain conceits & whimsical Extravagancies. * * * Irritated by hypocrisy & the unequivocal yielding of weak & interested men, he said & wrote unwarrantable arguments, but unalloyed & unencumbered by opposition, he was in all essential points orthodox in his belief,[1] but he put forth ramifications of doubt, that by his vigorous & creative mind, were watered into the empty enormities of Extravagant & rebellious thoughts.

HENRY CRABB ROBINSON

From Reminiscences (1852) †

* * *

—I had heard of him from Flaxman and for the first time[1] dined

1. As Bentley observes, it is difficult to know what Tatham may have meant by orthodoxy: according to Anne Gilchrist and others, Tatham destroyed hundreds of manuscript poems (but no designs) because influential Irvingites—members of the Catholic Apostolic Church founded in 1835 on the teachings of Edward Irving—convinced him that Blake's inspiration came from Satan. [*Editors.*]

† From *Blake Records*, ed. G. E. Bentley, Jr. (Oxford: Clarendon Press, 1969), pp. 538–40, 542–43, 544–45, 547–48, with minor changes in spelling and punctuation.

As early as 1810, Robinson (1775–1869), a diarist and man of letters who assiduously cultivated the acquaintance of literary and artistic celebrities and kept a journal of their sayings, had attended Blake's exhibition twice, the second time with Charles and Mary Lamb in tow. That year he wrote the first essay-length account of Blake's work, a German piece in *Vaterländisches Museum*, January 1811 (reprinted by Bentley). His account of Blake in his *Reminiscences* is based on diary entries made after Robinson finally met Blake in 1825. While being interviewed by this inveterate reporter, Blake may have deliberately exaggerated the strangeness of his beliefs; cf. Tatham's opinion that "many of his Eccentric speeches, were thrown forth more as a piece of sarcasm, upon the Enquirer, than from his real opinion" (above); also John Linnell's comment, "I never saw anything the least like madness for I never opposed him spitefully as many did but being really anxious to fathom if possible the amount of truth which might be in his most startling assertions I generally met with a sufficiently rational explanation in the most really friendly & conciliatory tone" (Bentley, p. 257), and Samuel Palmer's observation that he would answer a materialist "according to his folly, by putting forth his own views in their most extravagant and startling aspect" (p. 505).

1. In 1825. [*Editors.*]

in his company at the Aders'. *Linnell* the painter was there also—an artist of considerable talent, and who professed to take a deep interest in Blake, and his works, whether of a perfectly disinterested character may be doubtful, as will hereafter appear. This was on the 10th of December.—I was aware of his idosyncracies and therefore to a great degree prepared for the sort of conversation which took place at and after dinner, an altogether unmethodical rhapsody on art, religion—He Saying the most strange things in the most unemphatic manner, speaking of his *visions* as any man would of the most ordinary occurrence. He was then 68 Years of Age. He had a broad pale face, a large full eye with a benignant expression—at the same time a look of languor except when excited, and then he had an air of inspiration—but not such, as without a previous acquaintance with him, or attending to *what* he said, would suggest the notion that he was insane. There was nothing *wild* about his look—and tho' very ready to be drawn out to the assertion of his favorite ideas, Yet with no warmth as if he wanted to make proselytes—Indeed one of the peculiar features of his scheme as far as it was consistent, was indifference And a very extraordinary degree of tolerance and satisfaction with what had taken place—A sort of pious & humble Optimism—not the scornful Optimism of Candide.—But at the same time that he was very ready to praise he seemed incapable of envy, as he was of discontent.—

* * *—As I had for many years been familiar with the idea that an eternity *a parte post* was inconceivable without an eternity *a parte ante* I was naturally led to express that thought on this occasion.—His eye brightened on my saying this—He eagerly assented. 'To be sure—We are all coexistent with God—Members of the Divine Body—And partakers of the divine nature'—Blake's having adopted this Platonic idea led me on in our tete à tete walk home at night to put the popular question to him—Concerning the imputed Divinity of Jesus Christ. He answered—'He is the only God,'—but then he added—'And so am I and So are you.'—Yet he had before said—And that led me to put the question—That 'Christ ought not to have suffered himself to be crucified & He should not have attacked the government. He had no business with such matters.'—On my representing this to be inconsistent with the sanctity & divine qualities, he said Christ was not yet become the father.—It is hard on bringing together these fragmentary recollections to fix Blake's position in relation to Christianity Platonism & Spinosaism.

I put in my journal the following insulated remarks.—*Jacob Boehmen* was placed among the divinely inspired men.—He praised also the designs to *Law's* Translation of Boehmen.—'Michael Angelo could not have surpassed them'. '*Bacon, Locke & Newton* are the three great teachers of Atheism or Satan's Doctrine'—he asserted.—*Irving*[2] is a highly gifted man—'He is a sent man. But they who are sent sometimes go further than they ought.' *Calvin* —'I saw nothing but good in *Calvin's* house.—In *Luther's* there were *Harlots.*'—He declared his opinion that the Earth is flat not round and just as I had objected the circumnavigation dinner was announced.—But objections were seldom of any use.—The wildest of his assertions was made with the veriest indifference of tone as if altogether insignificant.—It respected the natural & spiritual worlds.—By way of example of the difference between them he said—'You never saw the spiritual Sun—I have.—I saw him on Primrose Hill.'—He said " 'Do you take me for the Greek Apollo?' " " 'No!' " I said. '*That*' (pointing to the Sky) 'That is the Greek Apollo—He is Satan.' "

* * *

* * * In the sweetness of his countenance & gentility of his manner he added an indescribable grace to his conversation.

* * *

On the 17th I called on him in his house in Fountain's Court in the Strand. The interview was a short one and what I saw was more remarkable than what I heard.—He was at work engraving in a small bedroom, light and looking out on a mean yard—Everything in the room squalid and indicating poverty except himself, and there was a natural gentility about and an insensibility to the seeming poverty which quite removed the impression.—Besides, his linen was clean, his hand white and his air quite unembarrassed when he begged me to sit down, as if he were in a palace.—There was but one chair in the room besides that on which he sat.—On my putting my hand to it, I found that it would have fallen to pieces if I had lifted it, So, as if I had been a Sybarite, I said with a smile, 'Will you let me indulge myself?' And I sat on the bed—and near him, And during my short stay there was nothing in him that betrayed that he was aware of what to other persons might have been even offensive not in his person, but in all about him.

His wife I saw at this time—And she seemed to be the very woman to make him happy. She had been formed by him. Indeed, otherwise she could not have lived with him. Notwithstanding her dress, which was poor, and dirty, she had a good expression in her countenance—And with a dark eye had remains of beauty in her youth. She had that virtue of virtues in a wife, an implicit reverence of her husband. It is quite certain that she believed in all his

2. Edward Irving (1792–1834), preacher ousted from the Church of Scotland for heresy; his followers founded the charismatic Catholic Apostolic Church, to which Blake's executor Frederick Tatham was converted. [*Editors.*]

visions. And on one occasion, not this day, speaking of his Visions she said—'You know, dear, the first time you saw God was when You were four years old And he put his head to the window and set you ascreaming.'—In a word—She was formed on the Miltonic model—And like the first Wife Eve worshipped God in her Husband—He being to her what God was to him. Vide Milton's *Paradise Lost—passim*.

* * *

He was making designs or engraving, I forget which.—Cary's Dante was before him—He shewed me some of his Designs from Dante, of which I do not presume to speak.—They were too much above me.—But Götzenberger,[3] whom I afterwards took to see them, expressed the highest admiration of them. They are in the hands of Linnell—the painter And it has been suggested, are reserved by him for publication when Blake may have become an object of interest to a greater number than he can be at this age.—

* * *

1826 On the 24th [December 1825] I called a second time on him—And on this occasion it was that I read to him *Wordsworth's Ode* on the supposed preexistent State. And the subject of Wordsworth's religious character was discussed when we met on the 18th of Feb. and the 12th of May.—I will here bring together W. Blake's declarations concerning Wordsworth—And set down his marginalia in the 8vo: Edit. A.D. 1815—Vol i:—I had been in the habit when reading this marvellous Ode to friends, to omit one or two passages—especially that beginning

But there's a tree of many one,

lest I should be rendered ridiculous, being unable to explain precisely *what* I admired.—Not that I acknowledged this to be a fair test. But with Blake I could fear nothing of the Kind, And it was this very Stanza which threw him almost into an hysterical rapture. —His delight in Wordsworth's poetry was intense nor did it seem less notwithstanding by the reproaches he continually cast on W. for his imputed worship of nature—which in the mind of Blake constituted Atheism.

The combination of the warmest praise with imputations which from another would assume the most serious character and the liberty he took to interpret as he pleased, rendered it as difficult to be offended as to reason with him.—The eloquent descriptions of Nature in Wordsworth's poems were conclusive proof of Atheism, for whoever believes in Nature, said B: disbelieves in God—For Nature is the work of the Devil. On my obtaining from him the declaration that the Bible was the work of God, I referred to the

3. Jakob Götzenberger (1800–1866), German history painter. [*Editors.*]

commencement of Genesis—In the beginning God created the Heaven & the Earth.—But I gained nothing by this for I was triumphantly told that this God was not Jehovah, but the Elohim, and the doctrine of the Gnostics repeated with sufficient consistency to silence one so unlearned as myself.—

The Preface to the *Excursion*, especially the Verses quoted from book 1. of the *Recluse*, so troubled him as to bring on a fit of illness.—These lines he singled out—

> Jehovah with his thunder And the Choir
> Of Shouting Angels And the Empyreal throne
> I pass them unalarmed.

'Does M^r W think he can surpass—Jehovah?' * * *

1826 —19th Feb: It was this day in connection with the assertion that the Bible is the word of God And all truth is to be found in it —he using language concerning man's reason being opposed to Grace very like that used by the Orthodox Christian, that he qualified—And as the same Orthodox would say wholly nullified—all he said by declaring that he understood the Bible in a Spiritual Sense. As to the natural Sense he said '*Voltaire* was commissioned by God to expose that.—'I have had,' he said, 'much intercourse with Voltaire—And he said to me "I blasphemed the Son of Man And it shall be forgiven me—but they" (the enemies of Voltaire) "blasphemed the Holy Ghost in me, and it shall not be forgiven to them." ' I asked him in what language Voltaire spoke.—His answer was ingenious and gave no encouragement to cross questioning: 'To my Sensations it was English. It was like the touch of a musical Key—he touched it probably French, but to my ear it became English.' I also enquired as I had before about the form of the persons who appeared to him And asked Why he did not *draw* them.—'It is not worth while,' he said, 'Besides there are so many that the labour would be too great—And there would be no use in it.'—In answer to an enquiry about Shakespeare: 'he is exactly like the *old* Engraving—Which is said to be a bad one.—I think it very good.' I inquired about his own writings: 'I have written,' he answered, 'more than Rousseau or Voltaire—Six or Seven Epic poems as long as Homer, And 20 Tragedies as long as *Macbeth*.' He shewed me his Version of Genesis, for so it may be called, 'As understood by a Christian Visionary'. He read a wild passage in a sort of Bible Style. 'I shall print no more—he said.— 'When I am commanded by the Spirits, then I write; And the moment I have written, I see the Words fly about the room in all directions. It is then published.—The Spirits can read and my MS: is of no further use.—I have been tempted to burn my MS, but my wife won't let me.'—'She is right,' I answered; 'You wrote not from yourself but from higher order.—The MSS are their property not yours.—You cannot tell what purpose they may answer.'—This was addressed ad hominem—And indeed amounted only to a deduction from his own premises. He incidentally denied *causation,* Every thing being the work of God or Devil: 'Every Man has a Devil in himself And the conflict between his *Self* and God is perpetually carrying on.' I orderd of him to day a copy of his *Songs* for 5 Guineas.—My manner of receiving his mention of price pleased him.—He spoke of his horror of money and of turning pale when it was offerd him—And this was certainly unfeigned.—In the No. of the Gents Magazine for last Jan: there is a letter by *Cromek* to Blake printed in order to convict B. of selfishness.—It cannot possibly be substantially true—

13th June: I saw him again in June—He was as wild as ever, says my journal, but he was led today to make assertions more palpably mischievous, if capable of influencing other minds, & immoral, supposing them to express the will of a responsible agent, than anything he had said before—As for instance, that he had learned from the Bible that wives should be in common. And when I objected that marriage was a Divine institution he referred to the Bible 'that from the beginning it was not so.'—He affirmed that he had committed many murders, And repeated his doctrine, that reason is the only Sin. And that careless gay people are better than those who think &c &c.

It was I believe on the 7th of December that I saw him last. I had just heard of the death of Flaxman, a man whom he professed to admire And was curious how he would receive the intelligence. It was as I expected. He had been ill during the Summer; And he said with a Smile 'I thought I should have gone first.'—He then said, 'I cannot think of Death as more than the going out of one room into another.'—And Flaxman was no longer thought of. He relapsed into his ordinary train of thinking. Indeed I had by this time learned that there was nothing to be gained by frequent intercourse—And therefore it was that after this interview I was not anxious to be frequent in my visits. This day he said 'Men are born with an Angel & a Devil.'—This he himself interpreted as Soul & Body—And as I have long since said of the strange sayings of a man who enjoys a high reputation—It is more in the language than the thoughts that the singularity is to be looked for.—And this day he spoke of the Old Testament as if it were the evil element:—'Christ, he said, took much after his Mother And in so far he was one of the worst of men.'—On my asking him for an instance—He referred to his turning the money changers out of the Temple:—'He had no right to do that.'—He digressed into a condemnation of those who sit in judgment on others: 'I have never known a very bad man who had not something very good about him.'

Speaking of the Atonement in the ordinary Calvinistic Sense, he said 'It is a horrible doctrine; If another pay your debt, I do not forgive it.'

* * *

SAMUEL PALMER

Letter to Alexander Gilchrist†

Kensington, Aug. 23rd, 1855.

My Dear Sir,

I regret that the lapse of time has made it difficult to recall many interesting particulars respecting Mr. Blake, of whom I can give you no connected account; nothing more, in fact, than the fragments of memory; but the general impression of what is great remains with us, although its details may be confined; and Blake, once known, could never be forgotten.

His knowledge was various and extensive, and his conversation so nervous and brilliant, that, if recorded at the time, it would now have thrown much light upon his character, and in no way lessened him in the estimation of those who know him only by his works.

In him you saw at once the Maker, the Inventor; one of the few in any age: a fitting companion for Dante. He was energy itself, and shed around him a kindling influence; an atmosphere of life, full of the ideal. To walk with him in the country was to perceive the soul of beauty through the forms of matter; and the high, gloomy buildings between which, from his study window, a glimpse was caught of the Thames and the Surrey shore, assumed a kind of grandeur

† From Alexander Gilchrist, *Life of William Blake: Pictor Ignotus* (1863); reprint edition, Ruthven Todd, ed. [London: J. M. Dent, 1945], pp. 301–4.

In May 1824, when Palmer (1805–81) was nineteen years old, he was introduced to Blake by John Linnell (1792–1882), a landscape and miniature painter, patron of Blake, and later Palmer's father-in-law. Palmer was the most distinguished of a group of young painters which included Edward Calvert (1799–1883) and George Richmond (1809–96) who became Blake's disciples during his late years. They referred to Blake as "The Interpreter" and to themselves as "The Ancients," and they particularly admired Blake's series of eighteen small woodcuts for Thornton's translation of Virgil's *Pastorals* (1821). Shortly after Blake's death Palmer moved to Shoreham, Kent, and for several years painted superb visionary landscapes (see Laurence Binyon, *The Followers of William Blake*, 1925; reprint edition, New York: Benjamin Blom, 1968). Linnell, Palmer, and Holman Hunt studied watercolor painting under Blake's visionary friend John Varley (1778–1842), astrologer and author of the influential manual *Landscape Design* (1815). Through Hunt and D. G. Rossetti, Blake influenced the Pre-Raphaelite Brotherhood (fl. 1849–53) and through them the international movement of Art Nouveau (fl. 1884–1914). Among painters in recent years, Blake's most ardent disciple was Paul Nash (1889–1946).

from the man dwelling near them. Those may laugh at this who never knew such an one as Blake; but of him it is the simple truth.

He was a man without a mask; his aim single, his path straightforwards, and his wants few; so he was free, noble, and happy.

His voice and manner were quiet, yet all awake with intellect. Above the tricks of littleness, or the least taint of affectation, with a natural dignity which few would have dared to affront, he was gentle and affectionate, loving to be with little children, and to talk about them. 'That is heaven,' he said to a friend, leading him to the window, and pointing to a group of them at play.

Declining, like Socrates, whom in many respects he resembled, the common objects of ambition, and pitying the scuffle to obtain them, he thought that no one could be truly great who had not humbled himself 'even as a little child.' This was a subject he loved to dwell upon, and to illustrate.

His eye was the finest I ever saw: brilliant, but not roving, clear and intent, yet susceptible; it flashed with genius, or melted in tenderness. It could also be terrible. Cunning and falsehood quailed under it, but it was never busy with them. It pierced them, and turned away. Nor was the mouth less expressive; the lips flexible and quivering with feeling. I can yet recall it when, on one occasion, swelling upon the exquisite beauty of the parable of the Prodigal, he began to repeat a part of it; but at the words, 'When he was yet a great way off, his father saw him,' could go no further; his voice faltered, and he was in tears.

I can never forget the evening when Mr. Linnell took me to Blake's house, nor the quiet hours passed with him in the examination of antique gems, choice pictures, and Italian prints of the sixteenth century. Those who may have read some strange passages in his *Catalogue*, written in irritation, and probably in haste, will be surprised to hear, that in conversation he was anything but sectarian or exclusive, finding sources of delight throughout the whole range of art; while, as a critic, he was judicious and discriminating.

No man more admired Albrecht Dürer, yet, after looking over a number of his designs, he would become a little angry with some of the draperies, as not governed by the forms of the limbs, nor assisting to express their action; contrasting them in this respect with the shaped antique, in which it was hard to tell whether he was more delighted with the general design, or with the exquisite finish and the depth of the chiselling; in works of the highest class, no mere adjuncts, but the last development of the design itself.

He united freedom of judgment with reverence for all that is great. He did not look out for the works of the purest ages, but for the purest works of every age and country—Athens or Rhodes, Tuscany or Britain; but no authority or popular consent could influence him against his deliberate judgment. Thus he thought with Fuseli and Flaxman that the Elgin Theseus, however full of antique savour, could not, as ideal form, rank with the very finest relics of antiquity. Nor, on the other hand, did the universal neglect of Fuseli in any degree lessen his admiration of his best works.

He fervently loved the early Christian art, and dwelt with peculiar affection on the memory of Fra Angelico, often speaking of him as an inspired inventor and as a saint; but when he approached Michael Angelo, the Last Supper of Da Vinci, the Torso Belvedere, and some of the inventions preserved in the Antique Gems, all his powers were concentrated in admiration.

When looking at the heads of the apostles in the copy of the *Last Supper* at the Royal Academy, he remarked of all but Judas: 'Every one looks as if he had conquered the natural man.' He was equally ready to admire a contemporary and a rival. Fuseli's picture of *Satan building the Bridge over Chaos* he ranked with the grandest efforts of imaginative art, and said that we were two centuries behind the civilization which would enable us to estimate his *Aegisthus*.

He was fond of the works of St. Theresa, and often quoted them with other writers on the interior life. Among his eccentricities will, no doubt, be numbered his preference for ecclesiastical governments. He used to ask how it was that we heard so much of priestcraft and so little of soldier-craft and lawyer-craft. The Bible, he said, was the book of liberty, and Christianity the sole regenerator of nations. In politics a Platonist, he put no trust in demagogues. His ideal home was with Fra Angelico: a little later he might have been a reformer, but after the fashion of Savonarola.

He loved to speak of the years spent by Michael Angelo, without earthly reward, and solely for the love of God, in the building of St. Peter's, and of the wondrous architects of our cathedrals. In Westminster Abbey were his earliest and most sacred recollections. I asked him how he would like to paint on glass, for the great west window, his *Sons of God shouting for Joy*, from his design in the *Job*. He said, after a pause, 'I could do it!' kindling at the thought.

Centuries could not separate him in spirit from the artists who went about our land, pitching their tents by the morass or the forest side, to build those sanctuaries that now lie ruined amidst the fertility which they called into being.

His mind was large enough to contain, along with these things, stores of classic imagery. He delighted in Ovid, and, as a labour of love, had executed a finished picture from the *Metamorphoses*, after Giulio Romano. This design hung in his room, and, close by his engraving table, Albert Dürer's *Melancholy the Mother of Invention*, memorable as probably having been seen by Milton, and used in his *Penseroso*. There are living a few artists, then boys, who may remember the smile of welcome with which he used to rise from that table to receive them.

His poems were variously estimated. They tested rather severely the imaginative capacity of their readers. Flaxman said they were as grand as his designs, and Wordsworth delighted in his *Songs of Innocence*. To the multitude they were unintelligible. In many parts full of pastoral sweetness, and often flashing with noble thoughts or terrible imagery, we must regret that he should sometimes have suffered fancy to trespass within sacred precincts.

Thrown early among the authors who resorted to Johnson, the bookseller, he rebuked the profanity of Paine, and was no disciple of Priestly; but, too undisciplined and cast upon times and circumstances which yielded him neither guidance nor sympathy, he wanted that balance of the faculties which might have assisted him in matters extraneous to his profession. He saw everything through art, and, in matters beyond its range, exalted it from a witness into a judge.

He had great powers of argument, and on general subjects was a very patient and good-tempered disputant; but materialism was his abhorrence: and if some unhappy man called in question the world of spirits, he would answer him 'according to his folly,' by putting forth his own views in their most extravagant and startling aspect. This might amuse those who were in the secret, but it left his opponent angry and bewildered.

Such was Blake, as I remember him. He was one of the few to be met with in our passage through life, who are not in some way or other, 'double-minded' and inconsistent with themselves; one of the very few who cannot be depressed by neglect, and to whose name rank and station could add no lustre. Moving apart, in a sphere above the attraction of worldly honours, he did not accept greatness, but confer it. He ennobled poverty, and, by his conversation and the influence of his genius, made two small rooms in Fountain Court more attractive than the threshold of princes.

I remain, my dear Sir,

Yours very faithfully,

Samuel Palmer,

Twentieth-Century Criticism

T. S. ELIOT

William Blake†

If one follows Blake's mind through the several stages of his poetic development it is impossible to regard him as a naïf, a wild man, a wild pet for the supercultivated. The strangeness is evaporated, the peculiarity is seen to be the peculiarity of all great poetry: something which is found (not everywhere) in Homer and Aeschylus and Dante and Villon, and profound and concealed in the work of Shakespeare—and also in another form in Montaigne and in Spinoza. It is merely a peculiar honesty, which, in a world too frightened to be honest, is peculiarly terrifying. It is an honesty against which the whole world conspires because it is unpleasant. Blake's poetry has the unpleasantness of great poetry. Nothing that can be called morbid or abnormal or perverse, none of the things which exemplify the sickness of an epoch or a fashion, have this quality; only those things which, by some extraordinary labour of simplification, exhibit the essential sickness or strength of the human soul. And this honesty never exists without great technical accomplishment. The question about Blake the man is the question of the circumstances that concurred to permit this honesty in his work, and what circumstances define its limitations. The favouring conditions probably include these two: that, being early apprenticed to a manual occupation, he was not compelled to acquire any other education in literature than he wanted, or to acquire it for any other reason than that he wanted it; and that, being a humble engraver, he had no journalistic-social career open to him.

There was, that is to say, nothing to distract him from his interests or to corrupt these interests: neither the ambitions of parents or wife, nor the standards of society, nor the temptations of success;

† From T. S. Eliot, *Selected Essays, 1917–1950* (New York: Harcourt Brace Jovanovich, Inc., 1964). This essay first appeared in 1920.

Of the distinguished writers who have admired or imitated Blake, Eliot is the most temperamentally remote from the subject of his essay. In contrast, D. G. Rossetti, A. C. Swinburne, W. B. Yeats, G. B. Shaw, James Joyce, Joyce Cary, Dylan Thomas, Theodore Roethke, Kenneth Patchen, and Alan Ginsberg have at times considered themselves disciples, advocates, or spiritual descendants of Blake; see especially Ginsberg's interview in *Paris Review*, 37 (1966), reprinted in *Writers at Work: The Paris Review Interviews*, 3rd series, ed. George Plimpton (New York: Viking, 1968), pp. 302–9. [*Editors.*]

nor was he exposed to imitation of himself or of any one else. These circumstances—not his supposed inspired and untaught spontaneity—are what make him innocent. His early poems show what the poems of a boy of genius ought to show, immense power of assimilation. Such early poems are not, as usually supposed, crude attempts to do something beyond the boy's capacity; they are, in the case of a boy of real promise, more likely to be quite mature and successful attempts to do something small. So with Blake, his early poems are technically admirable, and their originality is in an occasional rhythm. The verse of *Edward III* deserves study. But his affection for certain Elizabethans is not so surprising as his affinity with the very best work of his own century. He is very like Collins, he is very eighteenth century. The poem *Whether on Ida's Shady Brow* is eighteenth-century work; the movement, the weight of it, the syntax, the choice of words:

> *The* languid *strings do scarcely move!*
> *The sound is* forc'd, *the notes are few!*

this is contemporary with Gray and Collins, it is the poetry of a language which has undergone the discipline of prose. Blake up to twenty is decidedly a traditional.

Blake's beginnings as a poet, then, are as normal as the beginnings of Shakespeare. His method of composition, in his mature work, is exactly like that of other poets. He has an idea (a feeling, an image), he develops it by accretion or expansion, alters his verse often, and hesitates often over the final choice.[1] The idea, of course, simply comes, but upon arrival it is subjected to prolonged manipulation. In the first phase Blake is concerned with verbal beauty; in the second he becomes the apparent naïf, really the mature intelligence. It is only when the ideas become more automatic, come more freely and are less manipulated, that we begin to suspect their origin, to suspect that they spring from a shallower source.

The Songs of Innocence and of Experience, and the poems from the Rossetti manuscript, are the poems of a man with a profound interest in human emotions, and a profound knowledge of them. The emotions are presented in an extremely simplified, abstract form. This form is one illustration of the eternal struggle of art against education, of the literary artist against the continuous deterioration of language.

1. I do not know why M. Berger should say, without qualification, in his *William Blake: mysticisme et poésie*, that "son respect pour l'esprit qui soufflait en lui et qui dictait ses paroles l'empêchait de les corriger jamais." Dr. Sampson, in his Oxford edition of Blake, gives us to understand that Blake believed much of his writing to be automatic, but observes that Blake's "meticulous care in composition is everywhere apparent in the poems preserved in rough draft . . . alteration on alteration, rearrangement after rearrangement, deletions, additions, and inversions. . . ."

It is important that the artist should be highly educated in his own art; but his education is one that is hindered rather than helped by the ordinary processes of society which constitute education for the ordinary man. For these processes consist largely in the acquisition of impersonal ideas which obscure what we really are and feel, what we really want, and what really excites our interest. It is of course not the actual information acquired, but the conformity which the accumulation of knowledge is apt to impose, that is harmful. Tennyson is a very fair example of a poet almost wholly encrusted with opinion, almost wholly merged into his environment. Blake, on the other hand, knew what interested him, and he therefore presents only the essential, only, in fact, what can be presented, and need not be explained. And because he was not distracted, or frightened, or occupied in anything but exact statements, he understood. He was naked, and saw man naked, and from the centre of his own crystal. To him there was no more reason why Swedenborg should be absurd than Locke. He accepted Swedenborg, and eventually rejected him, for reasons of his own. He approached everything with a mind unclouded by current opinions. There was nothing of the superior person about him. This makes him terrifying.

II

But if there was nothing to distract him from sincerity there were, on the other hand, the dangers to which the naked man is exposed. His philosophy, like his visions, like his insight, like his technique, was his own. And accordingly he was inclined to attach more importance to it than an artist should; this is what makes him eccentric, and makes him inclined to formlessness.

But most through midnight streets I hear
How the youthful harlot's curse
Blasts the new-born infant's tear,
And blights with plagues the marriage hearse,

is the naked vision;

Love seeketh only self to please,
To bind another to its delight,
Joys in another's loss of ease,
And builds a Hell in Heaven's despite,

is the naked observation; and *The Marriage of Heaven and Hell* is naked philosophy, presented. But Blake's occasional marriages of poetry and philosophy are not so felicitous.

He who would do good to another must do it in Minute Particulars.
General Good is the plea of the scoundrel, hypocrite, and flatterer;
For Art and Science cannot exist but in minutely organized particulars. . . .

One feels that the form is not well chosen. The borrowed philosophy of Dante and Lucretius is perhaps not so interesting, but it injures their form less. Blake did not have that more Mediterranean gift of form which knows how to borrow as Dante borrowed his theory of the soul; he must needs create a philosophy as well as a poetry. A similar formlessness attacks his draughtsmanship. The fault is most evident, of course, in the longer poems—or rather, the poems in which structure is important. You cannot create a very large poem without introducing a more impersonal point of view, or splitting it up into various personalities. But the weakness of the long poems is certainly not that they are too visionary, too remote from the world. It is that Blake did not see enough, became too much occupied with ideas.

We have the same respect for Blake's philosophy (and perhaps for that of Samuel Butler) that we have for an ingenious piece of home-made furniture: we admire the man who has put it together out of the odds and ends about the house. England has produced a fair number of these resourceful Robinson Crusoes; but we are not really so remote from the Continent, or from our own past, as to be deprived of the advantages of culture if we wish them.

We may speculate, for amusement, whether it would not have been beneficial to the north of Europe generally, and to Britain in particular, to have had a more continuous religious history. The local divinities of Italy were not wholly exterminated by Christianity, and they were not reduced to the dwarfish fate which fell upon our trolls and pixies. The latter, with the major Saxon deities, were perhaps no great loss in themselves, but they left an empty place; and perhaps our mythology was further impoverished by the divorce from Rome. Milton's celestial and infernal regions are large but insufficiently furnished apartments filled by heavy conversation; and one remarks about the Puritan mythology its thinness. And about Blake's supernatural territories, as about the supposed ideas that dwell there, we cannot help commenting on a certain meanness of culture. They illustrate the crankiness, the eccentricity, which frequently affects writers outside of the Latin traditions, and which such a critic as Arnold should certainly have rebuked. And they are not essential to Blake's inspiration.

Blake was endowed with a capacity for considerable understanding of human nature, with a remarkable and original sense of language and the music of language, and a gift of hallucinated vision. Had these been controlled by a respect for impersonal reason, for common sense, for the objectivity of science, it would have been better for him. What his genius required, and what it sadly lacked, was a framework of accepted and traditional ideas which would have prevented him from indulging in a philosophy of his own, and concentrated his attention upon the problems of the poet. Confusion of thought, emotion, and vision is what we find in such a work as *Also Sprach Zarathustra*; it is eminently not a Latin virtue. The concentration resulting from a framework of mythology and theology and philosophy is one of the reasons why Dante is a classic, and Blake only a poet of genius. The fault is perhaps not with Blake himself, but with the environment which failed to provide what such a poet needed; perhaps the circumstances compelled him to fabricate, perhaps the poet required the philosopher and mythologist; although the conscious Blake may have been quite unconscious of the motives.

NORTHROP FRYE

Blake's Treatment of the Archetype†

The reader of Blake soon becomes familiar with the words "innocence" and "experience." The world of experience is the world that adults live in while they are awake. It is a very big world, and a lot of it seems to be dead, but still it makes its own kind of sense. When we stare at it, it stares unwinkingly back, and the changes that occur in it are, on the whole, orderly and predictable changes. This quality in the world that reassures us we call law. Sitting in the middle of the lawful world is the society of awakened adults. This society consists of individuals who apparently have agreed to put certain restraints on themselves. So we say that human society is also controlled by law. Law, then, is the basis both of reason and of society: without it there is no happiness, and our philosophers tell us that they really do not know which is more splendid, the law of the starry heavens outside us, or the moral law within. True, there was a time when we were children and took a different view of life. In childhood happiness seemed to be based, not on law and reason, but on love, protection, and peace. But we can see now that such a view of life was an illusion derived from an excess of economic security. As Isaac Watts says, in a song of innocence which is thought to have inspired Blake:

> Sleep, my babe; thy food and raiment,
> House and home, thy friends provide;
> All without thy care or payment:
> All thy wants are well supplied.

And after all, from the adult point of view, the child is not so

† From *English Institute Essays: 1950*, ed. Alan S. Downer (Columbia University Press, 1951), pp. 170–96.

innocent as he looks. He is actually a little bundle of anarchic will, whose desires take no account of either the social or the natural order. As he grows up and enters the world of law, his illegal desires can no longer be tolerated even by himself, and so they are driven underground into the world of the dream, to be joined there by new desires, mainly sexual in origin. In the dream, a blind, unreasoning, childish will is still at work revenging itself on experience and rearranging it in terms of desire. It is a great comfort to know that this world, in which we are compelled to spend about a third of our time, is unreal, and can never displace the world of experience in which reason predominates over passion, order over chaos, classical values over romantic ones, the solid over the gaseous, and the cool over the hot.

The world of law, stretching from the starry heavens to the moral conscience, is the domain of Urizen in Blake's symbolism. It sits on a volcano in which the rebellious Titan Orc, the spirit of passion, lies bound, writhing and struggling to get free. Each of these spirits is Satanic or devilish to the other. While we dream, Urizen, the principle of reality, is the censor, or, as Blake calls him, the accuser, a smug and grinning hypocrite, an impotent old man, the caricature that the child in us makes out of the adult world that thwarts him. But as long as we are awake, Orc, the lawless pleasure principle, is an evil dragon bound under the conscious world in chains, and we all hope he will stay there.

The dream world is, however, not quite securely bound: every so often it breaks loose and projects itself on society in the form of war. It seems odd that we should keep plunging with great relief into moral hoilidays of aggression in which robbery and murder become virtues instead of crimes. It almost suggests that keeping our desires in leash and seeing that others do likewise is a heavy and sooner or later an intolerable strain. On a still closer view, even the difference between war and law begins to blur. The social contract, which from a distance seems a reasonable effort of cooperation, looks closer up like an armed truce founded on passion, in which the real purpose of law is to defend by force what has been snatched in self-will. Plainly, we cannot settle the conflict of Orc and Urizen by siding with one against the other, still less by pretending that either of them is an illusion. We must look for a third factor in human life, one which neets the requirements of both the dream and the reality.

This third factor, called Los by Blake, might provisionally be called work, or constructive activity. All such work operates in the world of experience: it takes account of law and of our waking ideas of reality. Work takes the energy which is wasted in war or thwarted in dreams and sets it free to act in experience. And as work cultivates land and makes farms and gardens out of jungle and wilderness, as it domesticates animals and builds cities, it becomes increasingly obvious that work is the realization of a dream and that this dream is descended from the child's lost vision of a world where the environment is the home.

The worker, then, does not call the world of experience real because he perceives it out of a habit acquired from his ancestors: it is real to him only as the material cause of his work. And the world of dreams is not unreal, but the formal cause: it dictates the desirable human shape which the work assumes. Work, therefore, by realizing in experience the child's and the dreamer's worlds, indicates what there is about each that is genuinely innocent. When we say that a child is in the state of innocence, we do not mean that he is sinless or harmless, but that he is able to assume a coherence, a simplicity and a kindliness in the world that adults have lost and wish they could regain. When we dream, we are, whatever we put into the dream, revolting against experience and creating another world, usually one we like better. Whatever in childhood or the dream is delivered and realized by work is innocent; whatever is suppressed or distorted by experience becomes selfish or vicious. "He who desires but acts not, breeds pestilence."

Work begins by imposing a human form on nature, for "Where man is not, nature is barren." But in society work collides with the cycle of law and war. A few seize all its benefits and become idlers, the work of the rest is wasted in supporting them, and so work is perverted into drudgery. "God made Man happy & Rich, but the Subtil made the innocent, Poor." Neither idleness nor drudgery can be work: real work is the creative act of a free man, and wherever real work is going on it is humanizing society as well as nature. The work that, projected on nature, forms civilization, becomes, when projected on society, prophecy, a vision of complete human freedom and equality. Such a vision is a revolutionary force in human life, destroying all the social barriers founded on idleness and all the intellectual ones founded on ignorance.

So far we have spoken only of what seems naturally and humanly possible, of what can be accomplished by human nature. But if we confine the conception of work to what now seems possible, we are still judging the dream by the canons of waking reality. In other words, we have quite failed to distinguish work from law, Los from Urizen, and are back where we started. The real driving power of civilization and prophecy is not the mature mind's sophisticated and cautious adaptations of the child's or the dreamer's desires: it comes from the original and innocent form of those desires, with all their reckless disregard of the lessons of experience.

The creative root of civilization and prophecy can only be art, which deals not only with the possible, but with "probable impossibilities"—it is interesting to see Blake quoting Aristotle's phrase in one of his marginalia. And just as the controlling idea of civilization is the humanizing of nature, and the controlling idea of prophecy the emancipation of man, so the controlling idea of art, the source of them both, must be the simultaneous vision of both. This is apocalypse, the complete transformation of both nature and human nature into the same form. "Less than All cannot satisfy Man"; the child in us who cries for the moon will never stop crying until the moon is his plaything, until we are delivered from the tyranny of time, space, and death, from the remoteness of a gigantic nature and from our own weakness and selfishness. Man cannot be free until he is everywhere: at the center of the universe, like the child, and at the circumference of the universe, like the dreamer. Such an apocalypse is entirely impossible under the conditions of experience that we know, and could only take place in the eternal and infinite context that is given it by religion. In fact, Blake's view of art could almost be defined as the attempt to realize the religious vision in human society. Such religion has to be sharply distinguished from all forms of religion which have been kidnapped by the cycle of law and war, and have become capable only of reinforcing the social contract or of inspiring crusades.

When we say that the goal of human work can only be accomplished in eternity, many people would infer that this involves renouncing all practicable improvement of human status in favor of something which by hypothesis, remains forever out of man's reach. We make this inference because we confuse the eternal with the indefinite: we are so possessed by the categories of time and space that we can hardly think of eternity and infinity except as endless time and space, respectively. But the home of time, so to speak, the only part of time that man can live in, is now; and the home of space is here. In the world of experience there is no such time as now; the present never quite exists, but is hidden somewhere between a past that no longer exists and a future that does not yet exist. The mature man does not know where "here" is: he can draw a circle around himself and say that "here" is inside it, but he cannot locate anything except a "there." In both time and space man is being continually excluded from his own home. The dreamer, whose space is inside his mind, has a better notion of where "here" is, and the child, who is not yet fully conscious of the iron chain of memory that binds his ego to time and space, still has some capacity for living in the present. It is to this perspective that man returns when his conception of "reality" begins to acquire some human meaning.

The Sky is an immortal Tent built by the Sons of Los:

And every Space that a Man views around his dwelling-place
Standing on his own roof or in his garden on a mount
Of twenty-five cubits in height, such space is his Universe:
And on its verge the Sun rises & sets, the Clouds bow
To meet the flat Earth & the Sea in such an order'd Space:
The Starry heavens reach no further, but here bend and set
On all sides, & the two Poles turn on their valves of gold . . .[1]

If the vision of innocence is taken out of its eternal and infinite context, the real here and now, and put inside time, it becomes either a myth of a Golden Age or a Paradise lost in the past, or a hope which is yet to be attained in the future, or both. If it is put inside space, it must be somewhere else, presumably in the sky. It is only these temporal and spatial perversions of the innocent vision that really do snatch it out of man's grasp. Because the innocent vision is so deep down in human consciousness and is subject to so much distortion, repression, and censorship, we naturally tend, when we project it on the outer world, to put it as far off in time and space as we can get it. But what the artist has to reveal, as a guide for the work of civilization and prophecy, is the form of the world as it would be if we could live in it here and now.

Innocence and experience are the middle two of four possible states. The state of experience Blake calls Generation, and the state of innocence, the potentially creative world of dreams and childhood, Beulah. Beyond Beulah is Eden, the world of the apocalypse in which innocence and experience have become the same thing, and below Generation is Ulro, the world as it is when no work is being done, the world where dreams are impotent and waking life haphazard. Eden and Ulro are, respectively, Blake's heaven or unfallen world and his hell or fallen world. Eden is the world of the creator and the creature, Beulah the world of the lover and the beloved, Generation the world of the subject and the object, and Ulro the world of the ego and the enemy, or the obstacle. This is, of course, one world, looked at in four different ways. The four ways represent the four moods or states in which art is created: the apocalyptic mood of Eden, the idyllic mood of Beulah, the elegiac mood of Generation, and the satiric mood of Ulro. These four moods are the tonalities of Blake's expression; every poem of his regularly resolves on one of them.

For Blake the function of art is to reveal the human or intelligible form of the world, and it sees the other three states in relation to that form. This fact is the key to Blake's conception of imagery, the pattern of which I have tried to simplify by a table.

1. *Milton* 29:4–11. [*Editors.*]

EXPERIENCE		CATEGORY	INNOCENCE	
Individual Form	*Collective Form*		*Collective Form*	*Individual Form*
sky-god (Nobodaddy)	aristocracy of gods	(1) Divine	human powers	incarnate God (Jesus)
a) leader and high priest (Caiaphas)	tyrants and victims	(2) Human	community	*a*) one man (Albion)
b) harlot (Rahab)				*b*) bride (Jerusalem)
dragon (Covering Cherub)	beasts of prey (tiger, leviathan)	(3) Animal	flock of sheep	one lamb (Bowlahoola)
tree of mystery	forest, wilderness (Entuthon Benython)	(4) Vegetable	garden or park (Allamanda)	tree of life
a) opaque furnace or brick kilns	*a*) city of destruction (Sodom, Babylon, Egypt)	(5) Mineral	city, temple (Golgonooza)	living stone
b) "Stone of Night"	*b*) ruins, caves			
(not given)	salt lake or dead sea (Udan Adan)	(6) Chaotic	fourfold river of life	"Globule of Blood"

Let us take the word "image" in its vulgar sense, which is good enough just now, of a verbal or pictorial replica of a physical object. For Blake the real form of the object is what he calls its "human form." In Ulro, the world with no human work in it, the mineral kingdom consists mainly of shapeless rocks lying around at random. When man comes into the world, he tries to make cities, buildings, roads, and sculptures out of this mineral kingdom. Such human artifacts therefore constitute the intelligible form of the mineral world, the mineral world as human desire would like to see it. Similarly, the "natural" or unworked form of the vegetable world is a forest, a heath or a wilderness; its human and intelligible form is that of the garden, the grove, or the park, the last being the original meaning of the word Paradise. The natural form of the animal world consists of beasts of prey: its human form is a society of domesticated animals of which the flock of sheep is the most commonly employed symbol. The city, the garden and the sheepfold are thus the human forms of the mineral, vegetable, and animal kingdoms, respectively. Blake calls these archetypes Golgonooza, Allamanda and Bowlahoola, and identifies them with the head, heart, and bowels of the total human form. Below the world of solid substance is a chaotic or liquid world, and the human form of that is the river or circulating body of fresh water.

Each of these human forms has a contrasting counterpart in Ulro, the world of undeveloped nature and regressive humanity. To the city which is the home of the soul or City of God, the fallen world opposes the city of destruction which is doomed through the breakdown of work described by Ezekiel in a passage quoted by Blake as "pride, fullness of bread and abundance of idleness." Against the image of the sheep in the pasture, we have the image of the forest inhabited by menacing beasts like the famous tiger, the blasted heath or waste land full of monsters, or the desert with its fiery serpents. To the river which is the water of life the fallen world opposes the image of the devouring sea and the dragons and leviathans in its depths. Blake usually calls the fallen city Babylon, the forest Entuthon Benython, and the dead sea or salt lake Udan Adan. Labyrinths and mazes are the only patterns of Ulro; images of highways and paths made straight belong to the world informed with intelligence.

The essential principle of the fallen world appears to be discreteness or opacity. Whatever we see in it we see as a self-enclosed entity, unlike all others. When we say that two things are identical, we mean that they are very similar; in other words "identity" is a meaningless word in ordinary experience. Hence in Ulro, and even in Generation, all classes or societies are aggregates of similar but separate individuals. But when man builds houses out of stones, and cities out of houses, it becomes clear that the real or intelligible form of a thing includes its relation to its environment as well as its self-contained existence. This environment is its own larger "human form." The stones that make a city do not cease to be stones, but they cease to be separate stones: their purpose, shape, and function is identical with that of the city as a whole. In the human world, as in the work of art, the individual thing is there, and the total form which gives it meaning is there: what has vanished is the shapeless collection or mass of similar things. This is what Blake means when he says that in the apocalypse all human forms are "identified." The same is true of the effect of work on human society. In a completely human society man would not lose his individuality, but he would lose his separate and isolated ego, what Blake calls his Selfhood. The prophetic vision of freedom and equality thus cannot stop at the Generation level of a Utopia, which means an orderly molecular aggregate of individuals existing in some future time. Such a vision does not capture, though it may adumbrate, the real form of society, which can only be a larger human body. This means literally the body of one man, though not of a separate man.

Everywhere in the human world we find that the Ulro distinction between the singular and the plural has broken down. The real form of human society is the body of one man; the flock of sheep is the body of one lamb; the garden is the body of one tree, the so-called tree of life. The city is the body of one building or temple, a house of many mansions, and the building itself is the body of one stone, a glowing and fiery precious stone, the unfallen stone of alchemy which assimilates everything else to itself, Blake's grain of sand which contains the world.

The second great principle of Ulro is the principle of hierarchy or degree which produces the great chain of being. In the human world there is no chain of being: all aspects of existence are equal as well as identical. The one man is also the one lamb, and the body and blood of the animal form are the bread and wine which are the human forms of the vegetable world. The tree of life is the upright vertebrate form of man; the living stone, the glowing transparent furnace, is the furnace of heart and lungs and bowels in the animal body. The river of life is the blood that circulates within that body. Eden, which according to Blake was a city as well as a garden, had a fourfold river, but no sea, for the river remained inside Paradise, which was the body of one man. England is an island in the sea, like St. John's Patmos; the human form of England is Atlantis, the island which has replaced the sea. Again, where there is no longer any difference between society and the individual, there can hardly be any difference between society and marriage or between a home and a wife or child. Hence Jerusalem in Blake is "A City, yet a Woman," and at the same time the vision of innocent human society.

On the analogy of the chain of being, it is natural for man to invent an imaginary category of gods above him, and he usually locates them in what is above him in space, that is, the sky. The more developed society is, the more clearly man realizes that a society of gods would have to be, like the society of man, the body of one God. Eventually he realizes that the intelligible forms of man and of whatever is above man on the chain of being must be identical. The identity of God and man is for Blake the whole of Christianity: the adoration of a superhuman God he calls natural religion, because the source of it is remote and unconquered nature. In other words, the superhuman God is the deified accuser or censor of waking experience, whose function it is to discourage further work. Blake calls this God Nobodaddy, and curses and reviles him so much that some have inferred that he was inspired by an obscure psychological compulsion to attack the Fatherhood of God. Blake is doing nothing of the kind, as a glance at the last plate of *Jerusalem* will soon show: he is merely insisting that man cannot approach the superhuman aspect of God except through Christ, the God who is Man. If man attempts to approach the Father directly, as Milton, for instance, does in a few unlucky passages in *Paradise Lost,* all he will ever get is Nobodaddy. Theologically, the only unusual feature of Blake is not his attitude to the person of the Father, but his use of what is technically known as pre-existence: the doctrine that the humanity of Christ is coeternal with his divinity.

There is nothing in the Ulro world corresponding to the identity of the individual and the total form in the unfallen one. But natural religion, being a parody of real religion, often develops a set of individual symbols corresponding to the lamb, the tree of life, the glowing stone, and the rest. This consolidation of Ulro symbols Blake calls Druidism. Man progresses toward a free and equal community, and regresses toward tyranny; and as the human form of the community is Christ, the one God who is one Man, so the human form of tyranny is the isolated hero or inscrutable leader with his back to an aggregate of followers, or the priest of a veiled temple with an imaginary sky-god supposed to be behind the veil. The Biblical prototypes of this leader and priest are Moses and Aaron. Against the tree of life we have what Blake calls the tree of mystery, the barren fig tree, the dead tree of the cross, Adam's tree of knowledge, with its forbidden fruit corresponding to the fruits of healing on the tree of life. Against the fiery precious stone, the bodily form in which John saw God "like a jasper and a sardine stone," we have the furnace, the prison of heat without light which is the form of the opaque warm-blooded body in the world of frustration, or the stone of Druidical sacrifice like the one that Hardy associates with Tess. Against the animal body of the lamb, we have the figure that Blake calls, after Ezekiel, the Covering Cherub, who represents a great many things, the unreal world of gods, human tyranny and exploitation, and the remoteness of the sky, but whose animal form is that of the serpent or dragon wrapped around the forbidden tree. The dragon, being both monstrous and fictitious, is the best animal representative of the bogies inspired by human inertia: the Book of Revelation calls it "the beast that was, and is not, and yet is."

Once we have understood Blake's scheme of imagery, we have broken the back of one of the main obstacles to reading the prophecies: the difficulty in grasping their narrative structure. Narrative is normally the first thing we look for in trying to read a long poem, but Blake's poems are presented as a series of engraved plates, and the mental process of following a narrative sequence is, especially in the later poems, subordinated to a process of comprehending an interrelated pattern of images and ideas. The plate in Blake's epics has a function rather similar to that of the stanza with its final alexandrine in *The Faerie Queene*: it brings the narrative to a full stop and forces the reader to try to build up from the narrative his own reconstruction of the author's meaning. Blake thinks almost entirely in terms of two narrative structures. One of these is the narrative of history, the cycle of law and war, the conflict of Orc and Urizen, which in itself has no end and no point and may be called the tragic or historical vision of life. The other is the comic vision of the apocalypse or work of Los, the clarification of the mind which enables one to grasp the human form of the world. But the latter is not concerned with temporal sequence and is consequently not so much a real narrative as a dialectic.

The tragic narrative is the story of how the dream world escapes into experience and is gradually imprisoned by experience. This is the main theme of heroic or romantic poetry and is represented in Blake by Orc. Orc is first shown us, in the "Preludium" to *America,* as the libido of the dream, a boy lusting for a dim maternal figure and bitterly hating an old man who keeps him in chains. Then we see him as the conquering hero of romance, killing dragons and sea monsters, ridding the barren land of its impotent aged kings, freeing imprisoned women, and giving new hope to men. Finally we see him subside into the world of darkness again from whence he emerged, as the world of law slowly recovers its balance. His rise and decline has the rotary movement of the solar and seasonal cycles, and like them is a part of the legal machinery of nature.

Blake has a strong moral objection to all heroic poetry that does not see heroism in its proper tragic context, and even when it does, he is suspicious of it. For him the whole conception of *κλέα ἀνδεῶν*[2] as being in itself, without regard to the larger consequences of brave deeds, a legitimate theme for poetry, has been completely outmoded. It has been outmoded, for one thing, by Christianity, which has brought to the theme of the heroic act a radically new conception of what a hero is and what an act is. The true hero is the man who, whether as thinker, fighter, artist, martyr, or ordinary worker, helps in achieving the apocalyptic vision of art; and an act is anything that has a real relation to that achievement. Events such as the battle of Agincourt or the retreat from Moscow are not really heroic, because they are not really acts: they are part of the purposeless warfare of the state of nature and are not progressing towards a better kind of humanity. So Blake is interested in Orc only when his heroism appears to coincide with something of potentially apocalyptic importance, like the French or American revolutions.

For the rest, he keeps Orc strictly subordinated to his main

2. "Brave deeds of heroes." [*Editors.*]

theme of the progressive work of Los, the source of which is found in prophetic scriptures, especially, of course, the Bible. Comprehensive as his view of art is, Blake does not exactly say that the Bible is a work of art: he says "The Old & New Testaments are the Great Code of Art." The Bible tells the artist what the function of art is and what his creative powers are trying to accomplish. Apart from its historical and political applications, Blake's symbolism is almost entirely Biblical in origin, and the subordination of the heroic Orc theme to the apocalyptic Los theme follows the Biblical pattern.

The tragic vision of life has the rhythm of the individual's organic cycle: it rises in the middle and declines at the end. The apocalyptic theme turns the tragic vision inside out. The tragedy comes in the middle, with the eclipse of the innocent vision, and the story ends with the re-establishment of the vision. Blake's major myth thus breaks into two parts, a Genesis and an Exodus. The first part accounts for the existence of the world of experience in terms of the myths of creation and fall. Blake sees no difference between creation and fall, between establishing the Ulro world and placing man in it. How man fell out of a city and garden is told twice in Genesis, once of Adam and once of Israel—Israel, who corresponds to Albion in Blake's symbolism, being both a community and a single man. The Book of Genesis ends with Israel in Egypt, the city of destruction. In the Book of Exodus we find the state of experience described in a comprehensive body of Ulro symbols. There is the fallen civilization of Egypt, destroyed by the plagues which its own tyranny has raised, the devouring sea, the desert with its fiery serpents, the leader and the priest, the invisible sky god who confirms their despotic power, and the labyrinthine wanderings of a people who have nothing but law and are unable to work. Society has been reduced to a frightened rabble following a leader who obviously has no notion of where he is going. In front of it is the Promised Land with its milk and honey, but all the people can see are enemies, giants, and mysterious terrors. From there on the story splits in two. The histories go on with the Orc or heroic narrative of how the Israelites conquered Canaan and proceeded to run through another cycle from bondage in Egypt to bondage in Babylon. But in the prophecies, as they advance from social criticism to apocalyptic, the Promised Land is the city and garden that all human effort is trying to reach, and its conqueror can only be the Messiah or true form of man.

The New Testament has the same structure as the Old. In the life of Jesus the story of the Exodus is repeated. Jesus is carried off to Egypt by a father whose name is Joseph, Herod corresponds to Pharaoh, and the massacre of the innocents to the attempts to exterminate the Hebrew children. The organizing of Christianity around twelve disciples corresponds to the organizing of the religion of Israel among twelve tribes, the forty days wandering of Jesus in the desert to the forty years of Israel, the crucifixion to the lifting of the brazen serpent on the pole, and the resurrection to the invasion of Canaan by Joshua, who has the same name as Jesus. From there on the New Testament splits into a historical section describing the beginning of a new Christian cycle, which is reaching its Babylonian phase in Blake's own time, and a prophetic section, the Book of Revelation, which deals with what it describes, in a phrase which has fascinated so many apocalyptic thinkers from Joachim of Floris to Blake, as the "everlasting gospel," the story of Jesus told not historically as an event in the past, but visually as a real presence.

The characters of Blake's poems, Orc, Los, Urizen, Vala, and the rest, take shape in accordance with Blake's idea of the real act. No word in the language contains a greater etymological lie than the word "individual." The so-called undivided man is a battleground of conflicting forces, and the appearance of consistency in his behavior derives from the force that usually takes the lead. To get at the real elements of human character, one needs to get past the individual into the dramatis personae that make up his behavior. Blake's analysis of the individual shows a good many parallels with more recent analyses, especially those of Freud and Jung. The scheme of the Four Zoas is strikingly Freudian, and the contrast of the Orc and Los themes in Blake is very like the contrast between Jung's early book on the libido and his later study of the symbols of individuation. Jung's anima and persona are closely analogous to Blake's emanation and specter, and his counsellor and shadow seem to have some relation to Blake's Los and Spectre of Urthona.

But a therapeutic approach will still relate any such analysis primarily to the individual. In Blake anything that is a significant act of individual behavior is also a significant act of social behavior. Orc, the libido, produces revolution in society: Vala, the elusive anima, produces the social code of *Frauendienst*;[3] Urizen, the moral censor, produces the religion of the externalized God. "We who dwell on Earth can do nothing of ourselves," says Blake: everything is conducted by Spirits." Man performs no act as an individual: all his acts are determined by an inner force which is also a social and historical force, and they derive their significance from their relation to the total human act, restoration of the innocent world. John Doe does nothing as John Doe: he eats and sleeps in the spirit of Orc the Polypus: he obeys laws in the spirit of Urizen the conscience; he loses his temper in the spirit of Tharmas the destroyer; and he dies in the spirit of Satan the death-impulse.

3. "Service to women." [*Editors.*]

Furthermore, as the goal of life is the humanization of nature, there is a profound similarity between human and natural behavior, which in the apocalypse becomes identity. It is a glimmering of this fact that has produced the god, the personalized aspect of nature, and a belief in gods gradually builds the sense of an omnipotent personal community out of nature. As long as these gods remain on the other side of nature, they are merely the shadows of superstition: when they are seen to be the real elements of human life as well, we have discovered the key to all symbolism in art. Blake's Tharmas, the "id" of the individual and the stampeding mob of society, is also the god of the sea, Poseidon the earth shaker. His connection with the sea is not founded on resemblance or association, but, like the storm scene in *King Lear,* on an ultimate identity of human rage and natural tempest.

In the opening plates of *Jerusalem* Blake has left us a poignant account of one such struggle of contending forces within himself, between his creative powers and his egocentric will. He saw the Industrial Revolution and the great political and cultural changes that came with it, and he realized that something profoundly new and disquieting was coming into the world, something with unlimited possibilities for good or for evil, which it would tax all his powers to interpret. And so his natural desire to make his living as an engraver and a figure in society collided with an overwhelming impulse to tell the whole poetic truth about what he saw. The latter force won, and dictated its terms accordingly. He was not allowed to worry about his audience. He revised, but was not allowed to decorate or stylize, only to say what had to be said. He was not allowed the double talk of the sophisticated poet, who can address several levels of readers at once by using familiar conceptions ambiguously. Nothing was allowed him but a terrifying concentration of his powers of utterance.

What finally emerged, out of one of the hottest poetic crucibles of modern times, was a poetry which consisted almost entirely in the articulation of archetypes. By an archetype I mean an element in a work of literature, whether a character, an image, a narrative formula, or an idea, which can be assimilated to a larger unifying category. The existence of such a category depends on the existence of a unified conception of art. Blake began his prophecies with a powerfully integrated theory of the nature, structure, function, and meaning of art, and all the symbolic units of his poetry, his moods, his images, his narratives and his characters, form archetypes of that theory. Given his premises about art, everything he does logically follows. His premises may be wrong, but there are two things which may make us hesitate to call them absurd. One is their comprehensiveness and consistency: if the Bible is the code of art, Blake seems to provide something of a code of modern art, both in his structure of symbols and in his range of ideas. The other is their relationship to earlier traditions of criticism. Theories of poetry and of archetypes seem to belong to criticism rather than to poetry itself, and when I speak of Blake's treatment of the archetype I imply that Blake is a poet of unique interest to critics like ourselves. The Biblical origin of his symbolism and his apocalyptic theory of perception have a great deal in common with the theory of anagoge which underlies the poetry of Dante, the main structure of which survived through the Renaissance at least as late as Milton. Blake had the same creative powers as other great poets, but he made a very unusual effort to drag them up to consciousness, and to do deliberately what most poets prefer to do instinctively. It is possible that what impelled him to do this was the breakdown of a tradition of criticism which could have answered a very important question. Blake did not need the answer, but we do.

The question relates to the application of Blake's archetypes to the criticism of poetry as a whole. The papers delivered to this body of scholars are supposed to deal with general issues of criticism rather than with pure research. Now pure research is, up to a point, a coordinated and systematic form of study, and the question arises whether general criticism could also acquire a systematic form. In other words, is criticism a mere aggregate of research and comment and generalization, or is it, considered as a whole, an intelligible structure of knowledge? If the latter, there must be a quality in literature which enables it to be so, an order of words corresponding to the order of nature which makes the natural sciences intelligible. If criticism is more than aggregated commentary, literature must be somewhat more than an aggregate of poems and plays and novels: it must possess some kind of total form which criticism can in some measure grasp and expound.

It is on this question that the possibility of literary archetypes depends. If there is no total structure of literature, and no intelligible form to criticism as a whole, then there is no such thing as an archetype. The only organizing principle so far discovered in literature is chronology, and consequently all our larger critical categories are concerned with sources and direct transmission. But every student of literature has, whether consciously or not, picked up thousands of resemblances, analogies, and parallels in his reading where there is no question of direct transmission. If there are no archetypes, then these must be merely private associations, and the connections among them must be arbitrary and fanciful. But if criticism makes sense, and literature makes sense, then the mental processes of the cultivated reader may be found to make sense too.

The difficulty of a "private mythology" is not peculiar to Blake:

every poet has a private mythology, his own formation of symbols. His mythology is a cross-section of his life, and the critic, like the biographer, has the job of making sure that what was private to the poet shall be public to everyone else. But, having no theory of archetypes, we do not know how to proceed. Blake supplies us with a few leading principles which may guide us in analyzing the symbolic formation of poets and isolating the archetypal elements in them. Out of such a study the structure of literature may slowly begin to emerge, and criticism, in interpreting that structure, may take its rightful place among the major disciplines of modern thought. There is, of course, the possibility that the study of Blake is a long and tortuous blind alley, but those who are able to use Blake's symbols as a calculus for all their criticism will not be much inclined to consider it.[1]

The question that we have just tried to answer, however, is not the one that the student of Blake most frequently meets. The latter question runs in effect: you may show that Blake had one of the most powerful minds in the modern world, that his thought is staggeringly comprehensive and consistent, that his insight was profound, his mood exalted, and his usefulness to critics unlimited. But surely all this profits a poet nothing if he does not preserve the hieratic decorum of conventional poetic utterance. And how are we to evaluate an utterance which is now lucid epigram and now a mere clashing of symbols, now disciplined and lovely verse and now a rush of prosy gabble? Whatever it is, is it really poetry or really great and good poetry? Well, probably not, in terms of what criticism now knows, or thinks it knows, about the canons of beauty and the form of literary expression.

Othello was merely a bloody farce in terms of what the learned and acute Thomas Rymer knew about drama. Rymer was perfectly right in his own terms; he is like the people who say that Blake was mad. One cannot refute them; one merely loses interest in their conception of sanity. And critics may be as right about Blake as Rymer was about Shakespeare, and still be just as wrong. We do not yet know whether literature and criticism are forms or aggregates: we know almost nothing about archetypes or about any of the great critical problems connected with them. In Dante's day critics did know something about the symbols of the Bible, but we have made little effort to recover that knowledge. We do not know very much even about genres: we do not know whether Blake's "prophecy" form is a real genre or not, and we certainly do not know how to treat it if it is. I leave the question of Blake's language in more

1. In this passage Frye adumbrates ideas developed in his *Anatomy of Criticism* (Princeton: Princeton University Press, 1957). [*Editors.*]

competent hands, but after all, even the poets are only beginning to assimilate contemporary speech, and when the speech of *Jerusalem* becomes so blunt and colloquial that Blake himself calls it prosaic, do critics really know whether it is too prosaic to be poetic, or even whether such an antithesis exists at all? I may be speaking only of myself, for criticism today is full of confident value-judgments, on Blake and on everyone else, implying a complete understanding of all such mysteries. But I wonder if these are really critical judgments, or if they are merely the aberrations of the history of taste. I suspect that a long course of patient and detailed study lies ahead of us before we really know much about the critical problems which the study of Blake raises, and which have to be reckoned with in making any value-judgment on him. Then we shall understand the poets, including Blake, much better, and I am not concerned with what the results of that better understanding will be.

JEAN H. HAGSTRUM

[On Innocence and Experience]†

Innocence

Only one year separated Blake's beginning in composite art from his greatest masterpiece in that medium, the *Songs of Innocence.* This imperishable work—perhaps even more beautiful in its early simple coloring, where tender shades harmonize with the mood, than in the more lavish coloring of later issues—rests on the foundation of a dignified and coherent concept. Innocence recalls Eden and anticipates the New Jerusalem. Natural life flowers in uninhibited sexuality; and all its forms, vegetable, animal, and human, are holy to the imagination of the poet, who appears as piper and shepherd and in whose vision, at its burning core, stands Christ as child, lamb, or lion.

Of these three integrally related elements of Innocence—humble life, natural sexuality, the Poet-Christ—*humble life* is the particular province of the border, which is here lusher, richer, and more beautiful in itself than on any other of Blake's pages.

The woods of Arcady were far from dead. They had in childhood surrounded Blake and all others of his generation and all previous generations. And in the arts they constituted a rich heritage. Some

† From Jean H. Hagstrum, ***William Blake: Poet and Painter*** (Chicago and London: University of Chicago Press, 1964), pp. 78–87. Slightly revised by the author; footnotes renumbered and references adjusted by the editors.

of the suggestions that came to Blake were poetic: Milton's "gadding vine" and "twisted eglantine," for example, and the "gray-fly (who) winds her sultry horn." Others were pictorial. Among Blake's contemporaries, including Constable and Turner, the free border, with entwining branches or trunks, was a visual cliché. Blake's organic life is more emblematic than any other artist's—more certainly than in landscape where it was often aesthetically rich but philosophically imprecise, more even than in the emblem where it was, though symbolical, sparse and austere. In Blake's borders, with trees, vines, creepers, leaves, birds, and insects, life was abundant—and allusive. Even the letters of the title page vegetate into organic forms, and organic forms elsewhere resemble flames. For all that lives is holy, and tongues of living fire had immemorially been associated with Pentecost and with divine and poetic inspiration.

The second ingredient of Blake's Innocence, *uninhibited sexuality,* appears alike in word, border, and design. Lamb and ewe call to each other in the exquisite verse. Leaf and stem, as in "The Blossom" and "Infant Joy," suggests the phallus erect and in repose; the flower suggests the womb. The boy on the second page of "The Ecchoing Green" who hands grapes from a vine to a girl on the ground is an emblem of sexual awareness (*Songs* 7). Lyca's solitary experiences in the forest were sexual, as the embrace of man and woman on the first page of "The Little Girl Lost" seems to suggest.

The *Poet-Christ* of Innocence manifests himself in different ways but nowhere more fundamentally than in the equation of the Poetic and Prophetic character, of divine love and human imagination. The Poet of the frontispiece, who lowers his pipe at the vision, is entirely human; the child on a cloud just above his head is both natural and divine, as are the Lamb of the fields and the Infant born in a flower. All those who rescue the lost and the wayfaring are manifestations of the divine shepherd who seeks and finds the straying sheep: the father, who saves the little boy led astray by Blake's version of Wordsworth's "unfathered vapour that enwraps, / At once, some lonely traveller";[1] the lonely watchman of the night, who brings the wandering emmet back to her children; and the lordly lion, who protects the lost Lyca and who reconciles the grieving parents to separation from their daughter.

Blake's Innocence has a quality that makes it poignant—its capacity for being blighted by society. There passes now and then over it the shadow of Experience, a cloud that suggests the coming dark but that does not destroy the day. Blake had suggested some two years before that a man might be offended with "the innocence

1. *Prelude* vi. 595–96.

of a child . . . , because it reproaches him with the errors of acquired folly."[2] These songs do in fact rebuke the adult and the institutional enemies of Innocence who will one day destroy it.

The destruction Blake unmistakably adumbrates even in the borders. When his close friend Cumberland noted that the vine grasps "the distorted trunk with *snaky* twine,"[3] he provided the proper perspective on one of the most insistent visual motifs in the *Songs of Innocence.* For in border and design, tree twists around tree, creeper and vine embrace trunk, vine and stem rise in serpentine loops and often form round, Urizenic arches over the page. The entire tradition that Blake absorbed—from illuminated missal to Fuseli, from the Bible through Milton to his master James Basire—suggests that the twisting serpentine forms of his Edenic garden prefigure a Fall.

So solidly conceived is Blake's idea of Innocence and so richly is it supported in border, word, and design that it alone succeeds in making the *Songs of Innocence* an integrated and serious work of art. But the book succeeds also because of the incomparable excellence of many of its individual pages—successes that Blake was to repeat but never to surpass.

The pages of *Innocence* are of three kinds, not equally complex or rich but each capable of appropriate artistic distinction. The kinds may be called *illustration, decoration,* and *illumination*—terms here applied to Blake's single pages and only distantly related to their use elsewhere in the art of bookmaking.

Illustration refers to the most conventional form Blake employed, in which the design—sometimes literal, sometimes based on the metaphor of the poem, and sometimes capable of introducing persons and scenes not clearly in the poem—appears at the top, bottom, or middle of the page. The mother, the child, the chair and the cradle of the second plate reproduce the scene of "A Cradle Song." In "The Chimney Sweeper," the boys' vision of air and angels—not the work-a-day world of soot, bags, brushes, and chimneys that oppress them—is represented at the foot of the page.

Sometimes simple illustration is masterfully integrated with the total form of the page. The first of two exquisite plates devoted to "Spring" begins with a representation at the top of a child "welcoming the year" by stretching his hands out to the sheep while he is still held by his mother, who sings the first two stanzas. The second page, in a balancing tailpiece that is tied to the headpiece by simple looping borders, shows the child alone without his mother

2. "Annotations to Lavater," p. 589 in David V. Erdman, ed., *The Poetry and Prose of William Blake* (Garden City, N.Y., fourth printing 1970) and p. 87 in Geoffrey Keynes, ed., *Blake: Complete Writings with Variant Readings* (London and New York, 1974).

3. George Cumberland, *A Poem on the Landscapes of Great Britain* (London, 1793), p. 9.

fondling the lambs—an appropriate accompaniment to the last stanza in which the child speaks: "Little Lamb, / Here I am."

This kind of illustration also contributes to Blake's total concept of Innocence by reminding us of the world of children and naïve experience, where ideas are simplified by pictures and already simple word scenes are made even simpler by color and line.

Decoration uses only text and border. Border designs, usually in the same color as the engraved text, reinforce the abstract, metaphoric meaning. (Some borders have tiny angels or *putti* in the decorative motifs, but these do not destroy the essential abstractness of the design.) The exquisite borders of the "Introduction" stylize exuberant organic life, one of the basic ingredients of Innocence. "On Another's Sorrow" adds to rich natural life serpentine adumbrations of Experience and supports textual references to the crucifixion of Christ. The first page of "Night," which possesses a visual tact Blake did not always display, chooses from a rich variety of verbal images—wolves, tigers, birds, sheep, and a vision of the future—only tiny border angels descending in darkness, a border tree, and a small lion who does not walk around the fold. In "A Dream" Blake's border grows thicker around the title—on whose "A" and "D" two tiny forms sleep—and around the first lines, "Once a dream did weave a shade / O'er my Angel-guarded bed." In "A Cradle Song" the border vegetation also forms a shade that delicately repeats the shade formed by infant dreams in the opening lines.

Blake most triumphantly realizes his form in *illumination*, the kind of page that unites border and design in a single visual motif. That motif bounds the page, separates stanzas, represents figures and scenes from the texts, and both literally and metaphorically winds itself around the words. "Infant Joy,"[4] "The Divine Image," and "The Blossom" are in this sense illuminations, authentic and unsurpassed masterpieces of fully integrated composite art.[5]

"The Divine Image" (*Songs* 18) separates deity into its four component virtues—those four daughters of the voice of God: Mercy, Pity, Peace, and Love. It asserts that the God who embodies these virtues becomes man and that the man who embodies them becomes God. Such interpenetration of the divine and the human brings with it the ethical imperative that "all must love the human form / In heathen, turk, or jew." The organizing formal element in the design is a flame-plant that rises from lower right to upper left, forming borders as it rises. Embraced by a delicate flowering convolvulus that may presage the coming Fall, the plant is an organic

4. See color plate 5 of this edition. [*Editors.*]
5. I have been anticipated by Anthony Blunt (*The Art of William Blake* [New York, 1959], p. 48).

version of Jacob's ladder that unites heaven and earth. From heaven descends a robed lady, clearly a goddess, attended by a flying joy —a tiny personified aurora that precedes the dawn. As God becomes man—or woman, really—in the upper left, man becomes God in lower right, for Christ raises a figure from the ground, who with his companion will leave the cave of distress to climb the plant upward. Two tiny figures near the top represent the men of every clime who pray in their distress. In the poem mankind is called simply man and the divinity simply God. But in the elaborating design mankind is presented as a man and a woman, while God is presented at the bottom as Christ and at the top in female form. The presence of both sexes reminds us that one of the four divine attributes is Love, that Blake's Innocence is a world of natural sexuality, and that this particular poem recommends "virtues of delight."

Of equal profundity and even greater unity is "The Blossom" (*Songs* 11). The words seem to describe a merry sparrow, a happy blossom, and a grieving robin, but the designs imply sexual love. The flame-flower could be phallic; tiny cupids have taken the place of the textual sparrow, who appears nowhere in the design; a child with his mother has replaced the similarly absent robin; and one of the cupids rides, not a serpent as in *Thel*, but one of the leaves, or tongues, of the flame-plant. These love themes in the picture unlock the meaning of the words: the merry sparrow who seeks his narrow cradle with the swiftness of an arrow is an exquisite rendition of sexual experience, and the sobbing robin is an equally exquisite rendition of mother-love and child-sorrow. The blossom is, in the first stanza, wife, in the second, mother. An appropriate epigraph comes from *The Marriage of Heaven and Hell*, "Joys impregnate. Sorrows bring forth."[6]

Experience

Experience is blighted Innocence. It is not a period of horrible but healthy probation, a purgatory we must inevitably traverse en route to the heavenly kingdom. It is a congregation of social, political, psychological, and unnatural horrors, a pestilential state whose vapors sicken the soul. The one ray of light that penetrates its darkness is that of the coming judgment that will destroy it.

Blake's most obvious sign of man's perverted state appears in the borders—in the vegetation with which he surrounds text and design. In *Innocence* it was fresh, attractive, abundant; in *Experience* it recalls the earlier ripeness but is in fact dead or dying. The

6. Cf. "Song," *Poetical Sketches*, Erdman, p. 405, Keynes, p. 7, a poem about sexual and mother-love among flowers, birds, and trees.

tree of *Innocence* is healthy, its branches entwined in a natural embrace; but it anticipates the Fall in the serpentine creeper that often winds about its trunk. The tree of *Experience* is dry and dying, its withering branches form round arches or flat, inhibiting horizontals over the pages as its spiky twigs invade the text; but its shape and the few sprays that still shoot recall its primal vigor. Experience is related to Innocence as a fossil is to a living creature, as petrified wood to a thriving branch. Other natural details accompany the dying trees—thorns, cacti, prickly desert growths, scourgelike leaves, and serpents. Title-page letters, Roman and angular, remain unvegetated and are never softened into natural Gothic. The vegetated flames of *Innocence* are now destructive and symbolize the wrath that falls upon a corrupt society.

But though dead branch, scourgelike ivy, and jagged oak leaf are —or were—natural forms, Experience is not primarily a state of nature. It is psychological, political, social—a condition of man and his institutions, not of the universe. Analogous to the Fall that caused all nature to groan, capable of being symbolized by natural life in death and decay, Experience is the work of church, state, and man in society.

In *Experience*, Old Nobodaddy, his priests, and his kings have replaced Christ, the Poet, and the Child—the gods of *Innocence*. The Urizen of *Experience* is not primarily the fallen Lucifer, the mythic figure of Blake's prophecy, but a social creature, a supporter of repressive institutions. The design to the poem that reverses the "The Divine Image" of *Innocence* ("The Human Abstract" of *Experience*) presents a bearded and ensnared old man making nets that stand for established religion.

In Blake's angriest manifestations of him Urizen stands for the cruelty of an establishment that has failed to keep the peace and give the people bread and that has forced the young to work and weep in grime and suffering. In the beautiful landscapes and borders of "Holy Thursday" one can find corpses, one lying, ironically, on an oak leaf under the word "Holy," babes dead in a rich and fruitful land. The chimney sweeper's parents have gone to church to pray, leaving him to weep and work. His cry is matched by the sigh of a soldier that, surrealistically, flows as blood down a palace wall, and by a broken old man, who appears in the design but not the text of "London," heading for his grave, an image of his god, Urizen, whose victim he is.

But institutional cruelty, though hideously direct in its results, is subtle in its means. The wily Urizen has transformed natural pity and love, the lovely daughters of the voice of God in *Innocence*, to institutional pity and charity in *Experience*. In an analysis of social "virtues" worthy of Bernard Mandeville, Blake perceives that Urizenic pity arises from social poverty, Urizenic mercy from a lack of equal happiness. Underneath the feet of Urizen grows a plant called Humility, which he waters with holy tears and holy fears. Such an institutionalized virtue finds the natural selfishness of the child intolerable; for healthy egotism might destroy obedience and obsequiousness—that miasma spread by the "Creeping Jesus,"[7] himself a ghastly perversion of the golden Lion-Christ of *Innocence*. When a Urizenic priest encounters an unspoiled boy who loves the little bird as much as he loves his father and who loves himself more than he loves his brother, the priest screams "What a fiend is here" and burns the child as a heretic. In *Experience* the unselfish clod that permits itself to be trodden under the feet of the cattle may be considered Urizenic[8]—on the side of that God and priest and king who make a heaven out of the chimney sweeper's misery. The *selfish* pebble of the brook sings a song the poet calls "meet."

One might suppose that to have thickened the clear water of Innocent mercy to the ooze of Established pity was Urizen's greatest achievement. But the amount of space Blake devotes to the suppression of natural sexuality suggests that this is in fact the ultimate perversion. The borders hint at repressed desire and its evil results. A blighted tree stands for envy, a sure result of repression by the father of jealousy; briars are the metaphoric weapons of repressive priests; the thistles and thorns of the desert represent chastity. Even the prophetic voice of the Bard-Christ cannot be answered save by outcries against sexual frustration by Earth, a daughter of Albion chained by Urizenic jealousy. The nurse of Experience turns green with jealousy at the whispers of sex in the dale and laments the hypocritical disguises of adult life. The virgin either languishes and dreams of Los's sweet golden clime, or arms herself with the shield and spear of negation that drives the angel of love from her door. Sometimes the oppressor is a victim rather than an embodiment of Urizen—like the father in "A Little Girl Lost," who is not so much angered as frightened by his daughter's love. Even then the result is no less cruel—the banishment of daylight love for nighttime deceit, the repression and perversion of the young into the gray and palsied sufferings of the old.

It is always the institutional Urizen who perverts natural life. In the garden of love in *Experience* stands an altar, and priests read commands from a book on a lectern.

Blake's lament over lost love receives its most consummate

7. "The Everlasting Gospel," Draft *d*, l. 59 (Erdman p. 511, Keynes p. 751). See also Draft *c*, l. 25 (Keynes p. 750) and Letter to Cumberland, April 12, 1827 (Erdman p. 707, Keynes p. 878).

8. The Eternals call Urizen "a clod of clay" (*Urizen*, Plate 6, stanza 11, Erdman p. 73, Keynes p. 226). The Clod's philosophy that "builds a Heaven in Hell's despair" is parallel to that of the God of the Establishment and "his Priest & King, / Who make up a heaven of our misery" ("The Chimney Sweeper" *Songs of Experience*, Erdman p. 23, Keynes p. 212). For a full defense of this unorthodox interpretation, see my essay in the *Festschrift* to Alan D. McKillop (*Restoration and Eighteenth-Century Literature*, ed. Carroll Camden [Chicago, 1963]).

expression in "The Sick Rose."[9] The worm, a male blight that destroys the flower, is the merry sparrow of *Innocence* transformed. Where the worm enters the flower, a female joy flies away, as thorny stems and yellow, jagged leaves form arches that support languishing maidens. This is the land of sorrow, the grave-plot of love from which Thel flees with a shriek.

Although the reader of Blake's words alone will find much to satisfy him in the social anger and human pathos of the verse, the student of Blake's composite art must rate the *Songs of Experience* slightly below the *Songs of Innocence.* In *Experience* Blake too often depended on his most elemental form—the simple illustration, in which bottom, top, or middle designs reproduce the scene or point the moral. Of true illumination as we have defined it, we have only one authentic example, "The Sick Rose." Only there does Blake approach the triumphant mastery of his most complex form that he revealed three times in the *Songs of Innocence*—in "Infant Joy," "The Divine Image," and "The Blossom." Occasionally in *Experience* the design and scene, embellished in rich and glowing color, belie the desired effect: dead bodies lie among rich blues and purples that almost reconcile us to the social disasters. In the most famous of all the Songs, the magnificent verbal "Tyger" is unworthily illustrated by an ambiguous and uninspiring animal (*Songs* 42).

In spite of these lapses from a standard Blake himself has set, the *Songs of Experience* does rival *Innocence* as his greatest work of composite art. Experience is, like Innocence, a serious and integrated idea. It is expressed by the pervasive metaphor of the Fall and of the expulsion from Eden that is recalled vividly on the title page and with subtle indirection elsewhere. Aesthetically, the volume breaks new ground. Weak in illumination, it brings a new refinement to what we have called decoration, and even illustration is occasionally combined with decoration to form a page that approaches the integrated beauty of "The Sick Rose." In "Holy Thursday" the text is related to the top and bottom landscape by freely flowing lines formed by the dead tree and by the barren rocks. In "A Poison Tree," the bare tree of institutional mystery, the baleful landscape, the dead body disposed in a cruciform shape on the ground like a Gothic tomb effigy—all these visual details support the indictment of Urizen-land. One of its citizens represses anger in accord with the established code, nourishes it with deceit while his foe lives, and rejoices unhypocritically when the man is dead. Thus is Christ crucified afresh by the respectable frustrations and revenges of an inhibiting society.

9. See color plate 8. [*Editors.*]

ROBERT F. GLECKNER

Point of View and Context in Blake's Songs†

A flower was offered to me;
Such a flower as May never bore.
But I said I've a Pretty Rose-tree,
And I passed the sweet flower o'er.

Then I went to my Pretty Rose-tree:
To tend her by day and by night.
But my Rose turnd away with jealousy:
And her thorns were my only delight.

Joseph Wicksteed, the only critic to devote an entire book to Blake's songs, said this about Blake's poem, *My Pretty Rose Tree*: "it shows how virtue itself is rewarded only by suspicion and unkindness." And Thomas Wright, Blake's early biographer, commented on the poem as follows: " 'My Pretty Rose Tree,' Blake's nearest approach to humour, may be paraphrased thus: 'I was much taken with a charming flower (girl), but I said to myself, No, it won't do. Besides, I have an equally pretty wife at home. Then, too, what would the world say? On the whole it would be policy to behave myself.' But his wife takes umbrage all the same. The thorns of her jealousy, however, instead of wounding him give him pleasure, for they excuse his inclination for the flower. Moral: See what comes of being good!"

On the contrary, the moral is that such off-the-mark commentary is what comes of ignoring the context of Blake's songs (that is, whether the poem is a song of innocence or song of experience) and the point of view from which a given poem is written. *My Pretty Rose Tree* is not about virtue perversely rewarded, nor does it have to do with "policy" or morality in the ordinary sense of those words. Virtue by itself meant nothing to Blake unless clarified by context: in the state of innocence it is *The Divine Image*; in experience it is perverted to *A Divine Image and The Human Abstract.* Real virtue Blake defined in *The Marriage of Heaven and Hell*: "No virtue can exist without breaking these ten commandments. Jesus was all virtue, and acted from impulse, not from rules." In *My*

† From *Bulletin of The New York Public Library*, 61 (1957), pp. 531–36.

This material also appears in slightly different form in *The Piper and the Bard* by Robert F. Gleckner (Wayne State University Press, 1959). In discussing "Introduction" to *Experience* on p. 312 of *The Piper and the Bard*, Gleckner calls attention to the essay by Frye cited in our footnote to the poem, p. 40 above.

Pretty Rose Tree the speaker acts from rules when he refuses the offer of the sweet flower. For, as Blake wrote elsewhere,

> He who binds to himself a joy
> Does the winged life destroy;
> But he who kisses the joy as it flies
> Lives in eternity's sun rise.

The speaker in *My Pretty Rose Tree* not only has let the moment go, but also has bound to himself a joy. Furthermore, since this is a *Song of Experience,* about the state of experience, the flower offered the speaker is the opportunity for a joy, a love, an ascent to a higher innocence. We recall that it was not just *any* flower, but a superb one, "such a flower as May never bore." Still, the offer is refused—because the speaker already has a rose-tree. Now, conventionally, this is admirable fidelity; for Blake, however, it is enslavement by what he called the marriage ring. The speaker thus passes up the chance of a spiritual joy (sweet flower) to return to the limited joy of an earthly relationship (pretty rose-tree). He is sorely tempted—but his desire has fallen subject to an extrasensual force symbolized by the existence of, and his relationship to, the rose-tree.

The result of course, is the speaker's retreat from desire to the only substitute for desire in Urizen's world of experience, duty:

> Then I went to my Pretty Rose-tree
> To tend her by day and by night.

The last two lines of the poem are the crushing commentary on the whole affair. Virtuous in terms of conventional morality, the speaker is rewarded with disdain and jealousy, ironically the same reaction which would have been forthcoming had the speaker taken the offered flower. It is Blake's trenchant way of showing the "rules" to be inane.

How easily, then, in reading Blake's *Songs of Innocence and of Experience* we can ignore Blake's own individual method. Basically that method is simple, its roots lying in his concept of states and their symbols. Like many other artists Blake employed a central group of related symbols to form a dominant symbolic pattern; his are the child, the father, and Christ, representing the states of innocence, experience, and a higher innocence. These *major* symbols provide the context for all the "minor," contributory symbols in the songs; and my purpose here is to suggest a method of approach that is applicable to all of them—and thus to all the songs.

Each of Blake's two song series (or states or major symbols) comprises a number of smaller units (or states or symbols), so that the relationship of each unit to the series as a whole might be stated as a kind of progression: from the states of innocence and experience to the *Songs of Innocence* and *Songs of Experience,* to each individual song within the series, to the symbols within each song, to the words that give the symbols their existence. Conceivably ignorance of or indifference to one word prohibits the imaginative perception and understanding of the whole structure. As Blake wrote in the preface to *Jerusalem,* "Every word and every letter is studied and put into its fit place; the terrific numbers are reserved for the terrific parts, the mild and gentle for the mild and gentle parts, and the prosaic for inferior parts; all are necessary to each other."

For the serious reader of Blake's songs, then, a constant awareness of the context or state in which a poem appears is indispensable; and since each state is made up of many poems, the other poems in that state must be consulted to grasp the full significance of any one poem. Each song out of its context means a great deal less than Blake expected of his total invention, and occasionally it may be taken to mean something quite different from what he intended. Blake created a system of which innocence and experience are vital parts; to deny to the *Songs of Innocence,* then, the very background and basic symbology which it helps to make up is as wrong as reading *The Rape of the Lock* without reference to the epic tradition. Without the system, Blake is the simplest of lyric poets and every child may joy to hear the songs. Yet with very little study the child of innocence can be seen to be radically different from the child of experience, and the mother of innocence scarcely recognizable in experience. The states are separate, the two contrary states of the human soul, and the songs were written not merely for our enjoyment, or even for our edification, but for our salvation.

Closely related to the necessity of reading each song in terms of its state is the vital importance of point of view. Often it is unobtrusive, but many times upon a correct determination of speaker and perspective depends a faithful interpretation of the poem. Blake himself suggests this by his organization of the songs into series, *Innocence* introduced and sung by the piper, *Experience* by the Bard. Superficially there seems to be little to distinguish one from the other since the piper clearly exhibits imaginative vision and the Bard "Present, Past, & Future sees." Yet for each, the past, present, and future are different: for the piper the past can only be the primal unity, for the present is innocence and the immediate future is experience; for the Bard the past is innocence, the present experience, the future a higher innocence. It is natural, then, that the piper's point of view is prevailingly happy; he is conscious of the child's essential divinity and assured of his present protection. But into that joyous context the elements of experience constantly insinuate themselves so that the note of sorrow is never completely absent from the piper's pipe. In experience, on the other hand, the

Bard's voice is solemn and more deeply resonant, for the high-pitched joy of innocence is now only a memory. Within this gloom, though, lies the ember which can leap into flame at any moment to light the way to the highest innocence. Yet despite this difference in direction of their vision, both singers are imaginative, are what Blake called the poetic or prophetic character. And though one singer uses "mild and gentle numbers" and the other more "terrific" tones, both see the imaginative (and symbolic) significance of all the activity in the songs. The inexplicit, Blake said, "rouzes the faculties to act." The reader of Blake, then, must rouse his faculties to consider this imaginative point of view always no matter who is speaking or seeing or acting in a poem.

Both singers are of course William Blake. And since he, or they, sing all the songs, whether they are identifiable or not with a character in a poem contributes most importantly to the total meaning of the poem. To take an extreme example, in *The Little Vagabond* of *Songs of Experience* there are four points of view: that of the mother, who is now out of her element and can no longer protect her child as she did in *Songs of Innocence*; that of the parson, who is a part of the major symbol of experience, father-priest-king, that of the vagabond himself, a child of experience, not the carefree, irresponsible, thoughtless child of innocence; and that of the Bard, through whose vision each of the other points of view can be studied and evaluated. Without an awareness of this complexity in *The Little Vagabond* the poem dissipates into sentimental drivel. Another good example is *Holy Thursday* of *Songs of Innocence*.

From a conventional point of view it is thoughtful and kind of the "wise guardians of the poor" to run charity schools and to take the children occasionally to St. Paul's to give thanks for all their so-called blessings. But from the piper's point of view (and Blake's of course) the children clearly are disciplined, regimented, marched in formation to church in the uniforms of their respective schools—mainly to advertise the charitable souls of their supposed guardians. The point here (seen only through the piper's vision) is that in the state of innocence there is, or ought to be, no discipline, no regimentation, no marching, no uniforms, and no guardians—merely free, uninhibited, irresponsible, thoughtless play on the echoing green. Accordingly the children in *Holy Thursday* assert and preserve their essential innocence, not by going to church, but by freely and spontaneously, "like a mighty wind," raising to "heaven the voice of song." This simple act raises them to a level far above their supposed benefactors, who are without vision, without innocence, without love: "Beneath them sit the aged men, wise guardians of the poor." The irony is severe, but lost upon us unless we are aware of context and point of view.

As a final example consider the *Introduction* of *Songs of Experience*. The main difficulty here seems to be Blake's chaotic punctuation and the ambiguity it causes. Stanzas 1, 3, and 4 seem to be an invitation to Earth to arise from the evil darkness and reassume the light of its prelapsarian state. Such an orthodox Christian reading, however, is possible only if we forget (1) that this is a *Song of Experience*, and (2) that the singer of these songs is Bard, not God or a priest. In similar fashion, while ignoring the context or the point of view, one might quickly point out the obvious reference in stanza 1 to Genesis iii and forget that the speaker in that chapter is the old Testament God, Jehovah, the cruel law-giver and vengeful tyrant who became in Blake's cosmos the father-priest-king image. And finally, the Holy Word in Genesis walked in the garden not in the "evening dew" but in the "cool of day," not to weep and forgive but to cast out and curse his children, to bind them to the soil, and to place woman in a position of virtual servitude to man. In view of this, if the second stanza as read as a clause modifying "Holy Word," it is either hopelessly contradictory or devastatingly ironic.

Blake himself hints at the correct reading immediately by means of the ambiguity of the first stanza. There are actually two voices in the poem, the Bard's ("Hear the voice of the Bard"), and the Holy Word's ("Calling the lapsed Soul"); and the second stanza, *because* of its apparently chaotic punctuation, must be read as modifying both voices. The last two stanzas are the words of *both* voices, perfectly in context when the dual purpose of the poem is recognized. Only in this way can the poem be seen for what it is, an introduction to the state and the songs of experience, in which the Holy Word of Jehovah is hypocritical, selfish, and jealous, thinking and acting in terms of the physical phenomena of day and night and the earthly morality of rewards and punishments. The Bard, mortal but prophetically imaginative, thinks and acts by eternal time and according to eternal values.

But how does one discover the all-important point of view in Blake's songs? One way is to observe the reactions of various characters to the same symbolic act, object, or character, for both the characters and the symbols ultimately resolve themselves into aspects of the major symbol governing that particular poem. Thus the mother of *Songs of Innocence* is symbolic in that her protection of the child contributes to the over-all picture of the child as major symbol of the state of innocence. In addition, many of Blake's symbols are recurrent, so that once a symbol's basic significance is revealed in a kind of archetypal context, each successive context adds association to association within the song series. When the beadle's wand appears in the first stanza of *Holy Thursday* of

Innocence, for example, its immediate connotation is authority. But since a *beadle* wields the symbol, it is also religious authority, the organized church, institutionalized religion. It also represents an act of restraint which forces the children to act according to rule rather than impulse. The Wand is "white as snow" to suggest the frigidity of man-made moral purity as opposed to the warmth of young, energetic, exuberant innocence. And finally, it suggests the worldly, non-innocent concept of duty (and its corollary, harm), the duty of worship which clashes with all of Blake's ideas of freedom and spontaneity. But all of this, it will be said, strongly suggests the world of experience, and *Holy Thursday is* a *Song of Innocence;* the over-all point of view is the piper's. The point to be made here is simply this. If we do not read the poem as a *Song of Innocence*, about the *state* of innocence and its major symbol, the joyous child, we can read it as a rather pleasant picture of nicely dressed charity children being led to church by a gentle beadle to sing hymns; or as a terrible view of unfortunate, exploited charity children under the thumbs of their elders. And we would *not* see that despite outward appearance the children *are* innocent, essentially free and happy, as they spontaneously sing their songs. Without an awareness of context the symbols do not work as Blake intended them to, and the song becomes a fairly inconsequential bit of sentimental social comment.

Considering, then, the care Blake took with point of view, recurring symbols, and symbolic action, we can see that gradually many of Blake's characters merge. The final products of these mergers are what I have called the major symbols. Kindred points of view tend to unite the holders of these points of view; characters who are associated continually with the same or similar symbols tend to melt into one another; and a similar pattern of action reveals a fundamental affinity among the actors. In these ways the significance and value of any one character in any one song are intensified and expanded beyond the immediate context. The physical identity may shift, but the symbolic value remains constant—or better, is constantly enriched. When the beadle's wand in *Holy Thursday* is recognized as part of the basic sceptre motif, the beadle's identity, while being retained as representative of church law, merges with that of Tiriel, say, and the father—and ultimately with the "selfish father of men" in *Earth's Answer*, the pebble in *The Clod and the Pebble*, the cold and usurous hand of *Holy Thursday*, God in *The Chimney Sweeper*, the mother, parson, and "Dame Lurch" in *The Little Vagabond*, "Cruelty," "Humility," and the "Human Brain" in *The Human Abstract*, and Tirzah in *To Tirzah*. Within the identity are inherent all the other identities which combine to make up the major symbol of the context. The priests of *The Garden of*

Love may bind with briars love and desire, but they do so because they are selfish, fatherly, cold and usurous, worldly, cruel, humble, hypocritical, and so forth.

One serious question remains: how does one distinguish among all these characters, or are they all precisely alike and hence redundant? Professor Mark Schorer answers the question this way—I know of none better: "The point is," he says, "that the individuality of these creations lies not in their rich diversity but in the outline that separates them from their backgrounds." That is, each individual identity in its specific context is at once a part of the whole context and the whole of which it is a part. Both the priest of *The Garden of Love* and the flower in *My Pretty Rose Tree* are self-sufficient for some understanding of these two poems. Blake simply asked his readers to do more than merely understand: that, he said, is a "corporeal" function. He wanted them to imagine as he imagined, to see as he saw, even to recreate as he created. Only then does his method make sense, only then can one see the minor symbols as parts of a major symbol, only then can the individual song take its rightful place as a *Song of Innocence* or *Song of Experience.*

IRENE TAYLER

The Woman Scaly†

The jealous, carping, abusive, or domineering woman has been a familiar figure in literature since the Wife of Bath—as also long before her. Blake pointed the topic with the rueful wit in his notebook epigram:

> A Woman Scaly & a Man all Hairy
> Is such a Match as he who dares
> Will find the Woman's Scales scrape off the Man's Hairs
> (K559).[1]

The manner is comic, but the matter could hardly be more serious, for in Blake's work the "hairy youth" is a spirit of rejuvenating

† From *Bulletin of the Midwest Modern Language Association* 6 (Spring, 1973), pp. 74–87.

1. Passages from Blake's work are quoted from *The Complete Writings of William Blake*, ed. Geoffrey Keynes (New York, 1957), with abbreviations to indicate the work quoted, where that is not evident from my text.

[Blake works referred to by letter are *Marriage of Heaven and Hell* (MHH), *Visions of the Daughters of Albion* (VDA), *Jerusalem* (J), *For the Sexes: The Gates of Paradise* (GP), *The Four Zoas* (FZ), *Vision of the Last Judgment* (VLJ), and *There Is No Natural Religion* (NNR). Page references from Keynes are preceded by the letter K.—*Editors.*]

energy and revolution, the Esau whose dominion Blake heralds as "the return of Adam into Paradise [MHH, K149]. That a "woman scaly" should scrape off *his* hairs argues a danger not only individual (the henpecked husband) but social (an oppressed people) and spiritual (fallen humanity excluded from happiness). Then who may this powerful and dangerous scaly woman be? And how does she achieve her terrible ends?

Her scales place her in bad company—we know that other scaly fellow, the devil—but they also suggest through her fishiness that her home is in the sea: and for Blake that means the sea of time and space, this fallen world in which we pass our mortal lives.[2] One way to talk about her dangerous power might be to say that she is the spirit of adaptation, that part of us that accepts the fallen world of contracted senses and lives on its terms. Small wonder that her scales should scrape and abrade the "ruddy limbs and flourishing hair" ("To Summer," K1) of the prophet, for the adaptive impulse, so strong in most of us, is in Blake's view the mortal enemy (in every way mortal) of energetic visionary life. For to live in the terms of the fallen world is to accept the doctrine that one's entire being is contained within one's body, that all else is alien to one's self, accessible only through the five senses, to be dealt with by a death-grip struggle for power: control or be controlled, own or be owned. It is necessarily a world of jealousy and recrimination in marriage, of tyranny and warfare in nations, of spiritual death and human misery:

> Doubt Self Jealous, Wat'ry folly,
> Struggling thro' Earth's Melancholy
>
> (GP, K770).

But why, in the name of prophetic vision, did Blake see this ferocious and destructive power as female? Why does the man get to have that flourishing hair and represent creative energy, while the scales go on the woman? Blake himself explores the question in several different ways.

Of course, not all women in Blake's work are destructive, any more than all men are regenerative. One thinks at once of the restrictive Urizen, "Father of Jealousy" (VDA, K194), and on the other hand of Oothoon, Blake's pointed study of a liberated woman. But even Oothoon is powerless when it comes to the crunch: without male cooperation, her passion and moving rhetoric can effect no changes in the world of her experience, or of that of

2. For Blake's use of water and scales in this connection, and especially in their relevance to sexual relationships, see his illustrations to Thomas Gray's "Ode on the Death of a Favourite Cat," reproduced in my *Blake's Illustrations to the Poems of Thomas Gray* (Princeton, 1971).

the other "Daughters of Albion," who "echo back her sighs" (VDA, K195). Yet the males, too, need female cooperation in Blake, and the reason for this takes us to Blake's view of the whole issue of human relationships. In the beginning we were One, and the division into sexes is a type of all division: child from parent, class from class, man from God. In this state of blind separateness, one of the few ways back towards unity (and partial and temporary though it must be, it is nonetheless a requisite first step) is through desire gratified, the experience of sexual union. The time of Apocalypse will come, Blake assures us, when the Cherub with the flaming sword will leave his guard at the tree of life, and creation will be consumed and again appear infinite and holy. "This will come to pass," he concludes drily, "by an improvement of sensual enjoyment" (MHH, K154). The point is that for Blake sensual enjoyment presupposes a movement outward from self-enclosure, a tacit refutation of the notion that other is alien. Once the millennial state is achieved, sexual intercourse as we know it will be left behind with all the other tokens of division, such as established social, religious, or family structures. Conversation will occur in an idiom of "Visionary forms dramatic," where "every Word" is "Human" (J, K746); and embracings will be "Cominglings from the Head even to the Feet" (J, K708).

But meanwhile we all live in a world of "generation": of sexual division and mortal birth and death. In most mythologies this natural world is female, and so Blake sees it too. In "For the Sexes: The Gates of Paradise," he writes:

> The Door of Death I open found
> And the worm weaving in the Ground:
> Thou'rt my Mother from the Womb,
> Wife, Sister, Daughter, to the Tomb,
> Weaving to dreams the Sexual strife
> And weeping over the Web of Life.
>
> (K771)

The "I" of those lines is of course male, inasmuch as he is the poet Blake; but he has within himself a female aspect as well. Though he refers to himself as speaker in the singular, at one point in the poem (which throughout concerns the torments of generative life) he calls himself "A dark Hermaphrodite" and deletes "I" to replace it with "we," associating his own inner division with the "Cloven Fiction" that supports the binary concepts of all reasoned constructs:

> A dark Hermaphrodite We stood
> Rational Truth, Root of Evil & Good.

And then once more he defines the implications of male and female separation:

> Round me flew the Flaming Sword;
> Round her snowy Whirlwinds roar'd,
> Freezing her Veil, the Mundane Shell.
>
> (K770)

The flaming sword is of course phallic, both desirous and potentially cruel and killing. Such is the male, bereft of his female self—"male forms without female counterparts . . . / Cruel and ravening with Enmity & Hatred & War" (FZ, K328). The female, divided off, freezes and hardens in her separateness: her "veil" is sexually her maidenhead, but emotionally the state of mind that leads her to exalt virginity, chastity, modesty, the entire religion of what Blake called "moral virtue," "Satan's Labyrinth" of Good and Evil (VLJ, K613) that has done so much to make life miserable for both sexes. In its widest aspect, the Veil betokens all creation, the natural world seen as separate, chaste, or dead, coldly resistant to the force of the creative imagination that lives in every human being, male or female. The Veil is in other words a construct of the Woman Scaly who scrapes off the man's hairs by assuring him that the "real" world is this Veil world of the five senses, of material time and space, and that the way of sanity and reasonableness is to adapt and make the best of it, that only fools and madmen think otherwise. This, like other reasoned constructs, is true only if you accept the premises on which it rests: and Blake tirelessly devoted his creative powers to insisting that anyone who will consult his own inner life will renounce those premises as false to actual human experience. "Man's perceptions are not bounded by organs of perception; he perceives more than sense (tho' ever so acute) can discover" (NNR, K97). What he perceives is the reality beyond the created world—the reality of the undivided human spirit, what Blake called Eternity.

In calling "female" that portion of human wholeness that splits off and mistakenly assumes a selfhood of its own, Blake is of course reflecting a view prominent in Western mythologies that woman was first formed not from such original materials as man was, but from a part of man himself,[3] and thus has only a derivative kind of reality. Milton speaks for an entire culture in asserting that

3. Compare *The Book of Urizen,* K232:
> Eternity shudder'd when they saw
> Man begetting his likeness
> On his own divided image.

Eve stands to Adam in more or less the relationship that Adam stands to God:

> Not equal, as their sex not equal seemed;
> For contemplation he and valour formed,
> For softness she and sweet attractive grace;
> He for God only, she for God in him.[4]

And it is hard not to think that Blake had some such class distinction in mind as well, in line with which he saw it as woman's duty to return to her position as an element of man, and man's to renew, through his creative genius, the God in himself. This is how Blake sometimes talks about the matter: "In Eternity Woman is the Emanation of Man; she has No Will of her own" (VLJ, K613). It cannot be insignificant that he should consider the alien part of the self-divided human "female," and refer to the spirit of destructive self-division as "the Female Will," always an evil power.

But this is by no means his final word on the subject of woman's position. Of the three characters in *Visions of the Daughters of Albion,* it is the one female, Oothoon, who speaks with the voice of true prophecy; her joyous energy, undisguised desire, and clarity of vision are offered as ideals of female behavior. Her lover, Theotormon, is immobilized by his prudish jealousy, whereas Bromion, who had triggered that response by raping Oothoon, likewise addresses her as "harlot," adding possessively:

> Thy soft American plains are mine, and mine thy north & south:
> Stampt with my signet are the swarthy children of the sun.
> (K190)

His odd words are a key to the problem: surely we are here no longer talking about "female" in the sexual sense, or even in the sense of male manqué. The man who addresses Oothoon as harlot after having raped her is a victim and perpetrator of that cultural hoax that sees any extramarital sexual experience as a "fall" for the woman, regardless of the source or kind of her experience, because as a possession her value has dropped. Because Bromion's interest is in possessions only, he can hardly distinguish among kinds, but conflates all in a single language of purchase, in which he "claims" the American plains and "stamps" the black people with "his" signet. In short, he expresses the binary view of himself as opposed to all the rest of creation, which he can see only as a set of alien and potentially hostile objects that must necessarily be either his enemies or his property. And although obedience to the "Female Will" is at the root of such a view (as it is also at the root of Theotor-

4. *Paradise Lost,* Book IV, 296–299.

mon's immobilizing prudery), in this poem Blake lays the blame to Urizen, that is, to the habits of constrictive, legalistic thinking. In any case Oothoon as an individual female clearly bears no trace of responsibility for the working of the Female Will in her rapist or her beloved. She and that Will exist at quite different levels of femaleness. Oothoon, as a woman, is an incomplete creature like every other mortal, and for all her liberated spirit can find little happiness while her beloved remains stultified in his own wretchedness. The Female Will is that very spirit of separateness, the grudging and jealous state of mind, of which Oothoon is herself so entirely free, but from which she suffers because the two men are in its power.

Why, then, call it *Female* Will? The explanation lies partly in the social and economic position of the individual female, for whom Blake had consistently great understanding and sympathy: her position is the logical extension of the entire system of economic and spiritual slavery that taxes the productive farmer to support priests and king, that furthers the interests of established civil and ecclesiastical government by promoting systems of thought that keep the mind in bondage to abstractions such as honor, loyalty, chastity—words that have meaning only in their individual applications, and can therefore never be meaningfully incorporated into "one law for both the lion and the ox" (VDA, K192). One such logical extension, for women, is displayed in Blake's remarkable connective "Till she" in these lines from *Visions of the Daughters of Albion:*

With what sense does the parson claim the labour of the farmer?
What are his nets & gins & traps; & how does he surround him
With cold floods of abstraction, and with forests of solitude,
To build him castles and high spires, where kings & priests may
    dwell;
Till she who burns with youth, and knows no fixed lot, is bound
In spells of law to one she loathes? and must she drag the chain
Of life in weary lust?. . . / all the night
To turn the wheel of false desire.

(K193)

Now this bondage by law, this chain dragged in weary lust, is really slavery and harlotry, however piously the legal and social conventions may insist on calling it "marriage." It requires an appalling commitment to abstract thinking to give this condition the same name that is given the mutually loving and fruitful unions of willing men and women. Yet so fervently are the twin standards of chastity and submissiveness maintained—at no matter what cost in human frustration and grief—that young women are taught to be coy, dissembling, "modest," and men are taught to honor this hypocritical behavior, to permit women social status and economic security only through marriage, and to deem worthy of marriage only women who passively comply to these standards. The effectiveness of the requirements witnesses the true extent of female slavery and whoredom: but it also establishes the terms of revenge. Since women are bartered as objects in the commerce of marriage, it is no wonder that they should themselves assume the commercial ethic: *caveat emptor*. Barren and ungratifying lives make women's skins grow thick with scraping scales, because love, turned inward, festers into a perverse and envious self-love, ravenous and cruel:

> Are not these the places of religion, the rewards of continence,
> The self-enjoyings of self denial? . . .
> Can that be Love that drinks another as a sponge drinks water,
> That clouds with jealousy his nights, with weepings all the day.
> To spin a web of age around him, grey and hoary, dark,
> Till his eyes sicken at the fruit that hangs before his sight?
> Such is self-love that envies all, a creeping skeleton
> With lamplike eyes watching around the frozen marriage bed.
> (VDA, K194)

The jealousy, selfishness, and ruthless will to power that grows in the heart of the possessed object is "female" because in our culture it is especially the females who have been treated as commodities; and with that position has come a sharpened awareness of ways to achieve power without force.

Blake's great prophecy, *Milton*, can be read as a commentary on Milton's views of the proper relationship between men and women, and at the same time as one of Blake's own fullest statements on the subject. Milton had declared in *Paradise Lost* that Adam's "fair large front and eye sublime declared / Absolute rule,"[5] whereas Eve's very hair—her "wanton ringlets"—implied subjection that should be

> Yielded with coy submission, modest pride,
> And sweet, reluctant, amorous delay.[6]

Milton's emphasis on our first parents' innocent nakedness—"then was not guilty shame"—Blake most warmly approved. One of his "Proverbs of Hell" might even be a direct allusion: "The nakedness of woman is the work of God." And another proverb, "Let man wear the fell of the lion, woman the fleece of the sheep" (MHH, K151), seems to argue a view similar to Milton's on the subject of role division. But the notion that in a state of pure innocence love should be enhanced by coy reluctance, that "modesty" in that sense should be coupled with "pride," must have seemed to Blake the true snake in the garden, for it is based on the economics of withholding supply to increase demand. This is the wedge by which harlotry enters, a first faint inkling of the power of Female Will.

5. *Paradise Lost,* Book IV, 300–301.

6. *Paradise Lost,* Book IV, 310–311.

That Milton, as man and poet, was estranged from his own female self and from the six women of his family—his three wives and three daughters—is the assumption with which Blake's prophecy *Milton* begins. "Unhappy tho' in Heaven," Milton views his "Sixfold Emanation scatter'd thro' the deep" and is moved to descend "her to redeem & himself perish" (K481). He will "perish," of course, only in his own separateness: once rejoined to his Emanation—his own feminine part objectified in the women he has loved—he will in fact reach full, undivided humanity. In this great moment of choice he recognizes that he must annihilate his "Selfhood"—his own sense of willful separateness—in a plunge that feels like death, but is the only route to real life. As the prophecy progresses, Milton's emanation—collectively named Ololon—also readies herself for the reunion:

And Ololon said: Let us descend also, and let us give
Ourselves to death . . .
are these the pangs of repentance? let us enter into them.
(K504)

This move toward reunion on the part of the divided prophetic poet and his emanation has cosmic implications because it is a challenge to the entire way of mortal life in that each part is prepared to join the other not by possessing it but by actually becoming it. Therefore Blake pictures preparations for the event as preparations for "the Harvest & the Vintage," in which creation readies for Apocalypse. So ends the first of the two books of Blake's prophecy *Milton.*

The second book begins with what might be called a study of role division in Heaven. There are two levels of existence above that of mortal life: Beulah (Hebrew for marriage) and Eden, or Eternity.

[To] The Sons of Eden the moony habitations of Beulah
Are from Great Eternity a mild & pleasant Rest.

The Emanations cluster in Beulah, properly aware of their incompetence for the furious creative activity of Eternity:

But the Emanations trembled exceedingly. . . .
. . . . 'if we, who are but for a time & who pass away in winter,
Behold these wonders of Eternity we shall consume:
But you, O our Fathers & Brothers, remain in Eternity.
But grant us a Temporal Habitation, do you speak
To us; we will obey your words as you obey Jesus'.
(K519)

He for God only, she for God in him? Yes, without question: but the matter is complicated by the issue of female transience, and what appears as female dependence. In a striking exchange, the "Divine Voice" addresses Creation in the grip of Female Will, castigating her jealousy: "I thought that you would love my loves & joy in my delights," but "thou art terrible / In jealousy & unlovely in my sight" (K522). He then issues a peculiar threat: he says when Milton's female portion sees that Milton is annihilating himself, she will "relent in fear of death," and instead of being jealous, will give her maidens to her husband, "delighting in his delight," for "then & then alone begins the happy Female joy." Now the Divine Voice continues,

> thou, O Virgin Babylon, Mother of Whoredoms,
> Shalt bring Jerusalem in thine arms in the night watches, and
> No longer turning her a wandering Harlot in the streets,
> Shalt give her into the arms of God your Lord & Husband.[7]

The death to be feared by Ololon is not the reunion that Milton and she are headed towards but rather its opposite, the spiritual death that comes with jealous withdrawal. Recall that when Ololon saw Milton ready to "die" to meet her, she in turn descended to meet him; that was a challenge to the fallen ways of mortal life, and here the "Divine Voice" is explaining the implications of that challenge. Read as allegory, it is God saying that in Ololon's move toward Milton, all Creation (that hardened Veil, the "real" world of the senses, perceived and believed in and fought over by rapists and slaveowners and consequently here addressed as "Mother of Whoredoms") ceases complicity with the whoremongers and instead offers her rival "Jerusalem" freely to "God" her "Lord & Husband." Now, in Blake's mythological terms, this Jerusalem is the very state of spiritual freedom that such an act of un-jealous love presupposes: that is, in selfless behavior towards "God," the Veil drops away and Creation is liberated (becomes Jerusalem), ceasing to be that "Mother of Whoredoms" whose existence consisted in commitment to separation and jealous restriction. It is the moment when—"by an improvement of sensual enjoyment"—creation was to be consumed and appear infinite and holy.

This moment, seen in its individual form as the reunion of Milton and Ololon, is that with which Blake concludes his prophecy *Milton*, and it demonstrates the meaning of female transience and dependence by reiterating the transience and dependence of all that appears "in this Vegetable Glass of Nature" (VLJ, K605). Women as human beings are no more transient than men as human beings; but the "female," as metaphor for fallen creation, will pass. Beulah is for Emanations not because they are female, but

7. All these lines are from *Milton*, plate 33—which is of course the number of Christ's age at his "death" in self-annihilation for love of man (K522–23).

because they are sexually differentiated. The point of role division is that division in itself implies "roles." As I understand it, the figures in Eternity look like male "Fathers & Brothers" to the inhabitants of Beulah because those inhabitants share the Biblical and Miltonic assumption that the undifferentiated Human Form must be male. We lack the concept (as also the pronoun) for a human who is neither male nor female, but both, undividedly—utterly without role. Blake uses "Man" to mean human, not just male, as in this passage describing the sexual separation: "The Feminine separates from the Masculine & both from Man / . . . Life to Themselves assuming" (J, K736). The consequences of this action are, as we know, terrible:

> when Male & Female
> Appropriate Individuality they become an Eternal Death.
> Hermaphroditic worshippers of a God of cruelty & law.
> (J, K737)

The actual scene of reunion between Milton and Ololon is instructive, for Blake goes to great lengths to spell out his points. Recall that Blake's term for the sexually divided person, seen as a single character, is "Hermaphrodite":

> A dark Hermaphrodite We stood,
> Rational Truth, Root of Evil & Good.
> (GP, K770)

As the great reunion between Milton and Ololon is a prophetic vision seen by the poet Blake, the event takes place in Blake's own cottage garden; so as the prophecy draws to a close, Milton's "Shadow" descends to the garden, a hermaphroditic form "clothed in black, severe & silent" (K529). He is more or less the male equivalent of the woman scaly. But the true poet-prophet Milton, who is ready to rejoin Ololon, confronts this divided puritanical part of himself and defines its Satanic implications:

> Thy purpose & the purpose of thy Priests & of thy Churches
> Is to impress on men the fear of death, to teach
> Trembling & fear, terror, constriction, abject selfishness.
> (K530)

These are the purposes of "Natural Religion," based on belief in the supremacy of the veiled world of the five senses. "A World in which Man is by Nature the Enemy of Man, / In Pride of Selfhood" (J, K673). But the prophetic Milton voices his own counter-purpose, as poetic genius:

> Mine is to teach Men to despise death & to go on
> In fearless majesty annihilating Self, laughing to scorn
> Thy Laws & terrors.
> (K530)

Ololon, recognizing the parallel Satanic role played by her own past jealousy and division asks:

> Are those who contemn Religion & seek to annihilate it
> Become in their Feminine portions the causes & promoters
> Of these Religions? . . . O where shall I hide my face?
>
> (K532)

But Milton does not blame Ololon; he has come to join her, to rid himself of his own self-righteousness:

> To bathe in the Waters of Life, to wash off the Not Human,
> I come in Self-annihilation & the grandeur of Inspiration.
>
> (K332)

There follows a catalogue of the non-human that includes everything from "Rational Demonstration" to bad art and poets "Who pretend to Poetry that they may destroy Imagination." In the aggregate they comprise all the evils of the fallen view that has created and still sustains the hardened veil of the world of the five senses. In a burst of passionate denunciation Blake associates all this with sexual division once more, and that division, in turn, with the consolidation of evil that shall end all of history at apocalypse:

> These are the Sexual Garments, the Abomination of Desolation,
> Hiding the Human Lineaments as with an Ark & Curtains
> Which Jesus rent & now shall wholly purge away with Fire
> Till Generation is swallow'd up in Regeneration.
>
> (K533)

Ololon trembles at these words, declaring rightly—and the point is important—that "Altho' our Human Power can sustain the severe contentions / Of Friendship, our sexual cannot . . . / Hence arose all our terrors in Eternity." But she has come to meet Milton fully at last, and she does not turn back: "So saying, the Virgin divided" —that is, her sexual, "virginal" self, her counterpart of the "severe & silent" puritan Milton—divides off, and joins his non-Human part: "Away from Ololon she divided & fled into the depths / Of Milton's Shadow" (K534). With this, the true Milton and Ololon are united in total "Human Power," no longer clothed in "Sexual Garments," for those have been "swallow'd up in Regeneration." To talk now about "male" and "female" (or "hermaphrodite") in Milton is to lapse into a metaphoric language appropriate to the fallen universe, but quite inadequate to describe the realities of Eternity, in which there are no sexes, only Human Forms: this is the condition Blake names Jerusalem, that city traditionally figured as a bride, but by Blake best described as "Liberty": female by metaphor (as Creation had been), but really beyond issues of sex in being free of division and hence of all impulse to ownership or jealousy.

Part of the problem in understanding Blake's view of sex roles and sexuality results, then, from the way in which generative life provides a metaphoric language for Blake's mythology. Anatomy may not be destiny in Eternity, but on earth it is inevitably the women who are mothers, forming in their own bodies the bodies that we all inhabit as sexual beings; women generally raise the very young (wrapping them in symbolic swaddling bands), and so are often especially responsible for teaching the young more or less what they were themselves taught, including an allegiance to the world of the senses; and women have been forced by their relative physical weakness and lack of political leverage into finding other modes of strength—especially in their use of the fact that man's sexual desire makes women's bodies effective counters in an ever-bustling trade of marriage harlotry. Blake never lost sight of the fact that as individuals women are no more responsible for this state of affairs than men are, and that women suffer from it fully as much as men. His business as prophet was never to accuse (that is Satan's role), but rather to expose the conditions as they really are, showing the spiritual causes, "melting apparent surfaces away" (MHH, K154). Our fallen race worships "Maternal / Humanity, calling it Nature and Natural Religion" (J, K737), but the term "Maternal Humanity" has about as much to do with the individual human female as does the term Mother Earth. The Female Will is ultimately a product of the Urizenic state of mind, in male and female alike. Most of us who have seen any Blake pictures at all recall the frontispiece to *Europe*, in which "The Ancient of Days," usually interpreted as Urizen, bends forward with windswept hair and sets his compasses upon the expanse. In the Preludium to *Europe* Blake aligns the creative functions of Urizen here and of the human mother in a fascinating complex of suggestive language, turning on a play on "compass":

> And who shall bind the infinite with an eternal band?
> To compass it with swaddling bands?

Europe as a whole concerns the development of a female religion, based on the cruelty of woman's defensive position:

> Who shall I call? Who shall I send,
> That Woman, lovely Woman, may have dominion? . . .
> Go! tell the Human race that Woman's love is Sin; . . .
> Forbid all Joy, & from her childhood shall the little female
> Spread nets in every secret path.
>
> (K240)

The result is "The Religion of Generation, which was meant for the destruction / Of Jerusalem" (J, K626). It is of course the religion of the puritan Milton as Blake saw and criticized it: a religion of moral law, of Good and Evil, of accusation and punishment, of "Trembling & fear, terror, constriction, abject selfishness"—in short, of the entire range of evils of self-righteousness with which we are all so painfully familiar.

But the result has been that while "Woman" may have dominion in that rather theoretical sense, *women* suffer—both from isolation and from what might be called backlash. As they are human, women—like men—long for fulfilling union, for a return to completeness; the clearest impulse in this direction may be seen in the strength of sexual desire. That is why the gratification of desire is such an important step toward reintegration, the improvement of sensual enjoyment crucial to apocalypse, the use of sex for selfish ends so tragic. But a further absurdity of the Female Will, from woman's point of view, may be seen in woman's own response to herself in this role. I remember reading recently in a magazine questionnaire, "Would you respect your husband as much if his boss were a woman?" Blake foresaw the issue: if woman's love is sin, her power is shame, her pride self-reproach. He says the "Holy Reasoning Power" that divides everything into good and evil (J. K629) is gratified at the contentions between men and women, "knowing himself the author of their divisions & shrinkings," and he tells us in turn an important truth about what must be the results:

> The Man who respects Woman shall be despised by Woman,
> And deadly cunning & mean abjectness only shall enjoy them.
> For I will make their places of joy & love excrementitious,
> Continually building, continually destroying in Family feuds.
> (J, K734)

Blake saw that the attitude that exalts women's "purity" must at the same time rob them of realistic respect and of all practical force except what they can seize by cunning; he saw that accordingly the Female Will tyrannizes over women as well as men; and finally, he taught that both men and women achieve their power and humanity not in isolation from each other, but in closest relationship, in becoming One. When Blake says "In Eternity Woman is the Emanation of Man; she has no will of her own," we can best understand him by continuing to the next sentence: "There is no such thing in Eternity as a Female Will" (VLJ, K613). For the point is not that man is supreme and woman dependent, but rather that there is no longer a division between the two: they have one will. These human forms Blake calls "Men," who communicate by a radiant energy that might in the metaphors of fallen language be called their "female" emanations: "Man is adjoin'd to Man by his Emanative portion / Who is Jerusalem in every individual Man" (J, K675). But Blake does not always even call emanations female:

> When in Eternity Man converses with Man, they enter
> Into each other's Bosom (which are Universes of delight)
> In mutual interchange, and first their Emanations meet . . .
> For man cannot unite with Man but by their Emanations
> Which stand both Male and Female at the Gates of each
> Humanity.
>
> (J, K733)

As there are no barriers of shame and religion, no divisions by sex, union can be total, not merely phallic:

> Embraces are Cominglings from the Head even to the Feet,
> And not a pompous High Priest entering by a Secret Place.
>
> (J, K708)

As mortals can approximate this total "comingling" physically by sexual union, so it can be approximated spiritually by unselfish love:

> Mutual Forgiveness of each Vice,
> Such are the Gates of Paradise.
>
> (GP, K761)

But unselfish love does not mean passivity, sexual or intellectual—quite the reverse. It can be achieved only through the joyous energy of desire.

Blake's genius was to see that the spirit of modest submissiveness is no more virtuous in women than in men, indeed that it leads inevitably and ultimately to a condition of sadistic conflict in which men and women, by opposing each other, decimate all chance of happiness. In Blake's paradise there are no men and women for the same reason that there are no tyrants and slaves, no class divisions, no role divisions: only Human Forms "going forth & returning" by their Emanations, that are "named Jerusalem"—who, as female, is as far removed from the Woman Scaly as prophecy can take her. Ultimately, perhaps, she is the human form itself, the *shape* of prophetic energy, giving it body as an artist gives body to his vision.

Sex roles are thus themselves examples of class society—the two are parallel and interdependent expressions of the same fallen circumstance, the belief in a limited world of self versus other, whose adherents must wear defensive scales to survive within its terms. But total reunion consists in leaving behind the fallen circumstances themselves, no longer seeing one's self as opposed to the "other," exchanging the jealous "me and what I can own" for the affirmative "me and what I can become." Hair and scales will then pass from sight together like the shadows of Milton and Ololon: me becomes we, and both coalesce in the Aye of vision.

MARTIN K. NURMI

[On *The Marriage of Heaven and Hell*]†

I. Blake's Ideal of Expanded Sense Perception

One of the best places to see Blake the philosophical poet at work is in *The Marriage of Heaven and Hell.* This work, though in prose and written to expound directly two tenets of the philosophy that is needed to save man, is just as imaginative, and in its way just as poetic, as anything Blake ever wrote. It displays on every page the man who chooses to create instead of reason and compare, but who nevertheless has something to say to the reasoners.

The analysis of *The Marriage* given in Part II of the original version of this study is rather detailed, on the Blakean grounds that "he who wishes to see . . . a perfect Whole, / Must see it in its Minute Particulars, Organiz'd" (*J*91:21–2, K738). But I wish to consider briefly here the two conceptions which form its main themes: the idea of expanded "spiritual sensation" and the doctrine of "contraries." These two conceptions can be seen most clearly, I believe, in relation to Blake's humanism.

Blake is probably the most extreme humanist of all time. When he says "God becomes as we are, that we may be as he is" (*NNR*, series b, "Application," K98), he is not uttering a bit of vague piety; he means it quite literally. Man is not merely capable of divinity, but is, even in his fallen state, divine in essence. "The Eternal Body of Man," he wrote on his engraving of the Laocoön, "is The Imagination that is God himself / The Divine Body / Jesus: we are his Members" (*Laocoön*, K776). To him the terms "human" and "divine" are, in fact, interchangeable for in *The*

† From Martin K. Nurmi, *Blake's Marriage of Heaven and Hell: A Critical Study*, Research Series III of the *Kent State University Bulletin*, XLV, 4 (April 1957), pp. 14–23, 28–29, 59–61, reprinted with changes and omissions.

Page references to Blake's writings, which are preceded by the letter *K*, have been changed by the editors to refer to *The Complete Writings of William Blake*, ed. Geoffrey Keynes (London, and New York, 1974). The Blake works referred to by letter (followed by plate number) are *Jerusalem* (*J*), *There Is No Natural Religion* (*NNR*), *The Marriage of Heaven and Hell* (*MHH*), *A Vision of The Last Judgment* (*VLJ*), *Europe* (*E*), *Everlasting Gospel* (*EG*), *The Four Zoas* (*FZ*), and *Milton* (*M*). These designations have been added in parentheses by the editors, who also provide plate numbers for reference to *The Marriage of Heaven and Hell.*

Everlasting Gospel he has God tell Christ, "Thou art a Man, God is no more, / Thine own Humanity learn to Adore" (K750). And the Fall, as Blake conceived it, came about because man, in creating a false material philosophy, failed to perceive the divinity of his own humanity and thus strove to create abstract gods that were somehow more than human. Or, as Luvah, one of the fallen "Zoas," ruefully remarks, "Attempting to be more than Man we become less" (*FZ*, IX : 709, K376). Man's restoration to Eden, consequently, was to occur when man's now divided natures, the warring Zoas of Blake's psychological myth, were reunited by true philosophy and religion in the vital harmony of the Human state.

The full measure of Blake's humanism, however, may best be taken from his conception that the ultimate order of the cosmos, when perceived by that synoptic vision which perceives the grand order of all things at once, takes on the real or eternal form of "One Man." And the identity of man and God is reinforced when we learn that the One Man is Christ:

> Mutual in one another's love and wrath all renewing
> We live as One Man; for contracting our infinite senses
> We behold multitude, or expanding, we behold as one,
> As One Man all the Universal Family, and that One Man
> We call Jesus the Christ; and he in us, and we in him
> Live in perfect harmony in Eden, the land of life,
> Giving, recieving, and forgiving each other's trespasses.
> (*J* 38[34] : 16–22; K664-5)

Carrying to its ultimate limit the "anthropocentric conceit of romanticism," as Santayana called the Romantic metaphysic,[1] Blake makes the moral nature of man not only the center of the universe, but literally the universe itself.

This Christian-humanist cosmological idea—or perhaps it would be more accurate to call it a grand archetype—is the closest thing we have to a "first principle" in Blake's thought. All of his ideas can be related to it. Especially closely related to it is his conception of spiritual sensation, since only by spiritual sensation can we know the human character of the cosmos. Indeed, in the clearest explanation we have of either of these ideas, found in the poem in which he tried to explain four-fold vision to his faithful but un-visionary patron, Thomas Butts, Blake makes this relationship very clear by considering both ideas together.

In the first part of the poem, which records a visionary experience on the sand at Felpham, the sand appears merely as "Jewels of Light." Then, as Blake's vision becomes more intense and passes

1. George Santayana, *Three Philosophical Poets* (Cambridge, 1927), p. 208.

firmly into its "two-fold" state, the grains of sand begin to display their human quality, and appear as individual men:

> I each particle gaz'd,
> Astonish'd, Amazed;
> For each was a Man
> Human-form'd.

(K804)

Now follows the theoretical basis for this transformation. The ordinary apparent identities of things are only phenomena of perspective—or *analogous* to phenomena of perspective, since the differences between the various orders of vision are not spatial but psychic. We fail to recognize the human nature of creation because we look as if from a distance.

> "Each grain of Sand
> Every Stone on the Land,
> Each rock & each hill,
> Each fountain & rill,
> Each herb & each tree,
> Mountain, hill, earth & sea,
> Cloud, Meteor & star,
> Are Men seen Afar."

(K804–5)

This two-fold level of perception is superior to the "single vision" of the materialistic philosopher because it begins to show the imaginative form of things. But it does not yield a comprehensive view of the world. To gain this we must pass through an affective state, the "three-fold vision," in which objects undergo a transformation because the perceiver undergoes one: He begins to view all things in a state of delight somewhat akin to the sexual delight with which man looks on woman.

> I stood in the streams
> Of Heaven's bright beams,
> And Saw Felpham sweet
> Beneath my bright feet
> In soft Female charms . . .

(K805)

In this state he can begin to know directly by perception that on Earth there are only shadows, that the Real is elsewhere:

> My Shadow I knew
> And my wife's shadow too,
> And My Sister & Friend.
> We like Infants descend
> In our Shadows on Earth,
> Like a weak mortal birth.

(K805)

Having passed through this state, the perceiver is now ready to move on to the highest, or "four-fold" vision, which enables him to see all of existence synoptically as one, as "One Man":

My Eyes more and more
Like a Sea without shore
Continue Expanding,
The Heavens commanding,
Till the Jewels of Light,
Heavenly Men beaming bright,
Appear'd as One Man . . .

(K805)

And this One Man is the mild, forgiving Christ, who welcomes Blake to his fold, as one of those who have awakened from "Newton's sleep," or the single vision of materialism:

Soft he smil'd,
And I heard his voice Mild
Saying: "This is My Fold,
O thou Ram horn'd with gold,
Who awakest from Sleep
On the Sides of the Deep."

(K805)

When the vision is over and the Saviour's voice fades, Blake passes into that state of enriched "innocence" which he had portrayed in *Songs of Innocence*. Now all things have been permanently transformed, by his glimpse of the infinite, into objects of joy:

I remain'd as a Child;
All I ever had known
Before me bright Shone.

(K806)

A vision like this is not, in the usual sense of the word, otherworldly. The significance of Blake's four-fold vision does not lie merely in its enabling us to transcend the limited sphere of practical life, but in revealing the order and unity of life as a whole, so that even our practical life is transformed by the knowledge that "every thing that lives is Holy" (*MHH* 27, K160). When Blake was, in fact, accused by the materialistic Rev. Dr. Trusler of being "in the other world, or the World of Spirits" (K795) he settled quite unequivocally the question of his other-worldliness: "I feel that a man may be happy in This World. And I know that This World is a World of Imagination & Vision. I see Everything I paint In This World. . . ." But one must see aright:

To the Eyes of a Miser a Guinea is far more beautiful than the Sun, & a bag worn with the use of Money has more beautiful proportions than a Vine filled with Grapes. The tree which moves some to tears of joy is in the Eyes of others only a Green thing which stands in the way. Some see Nature all Ridicule & Deformity, & by these I will not regulate my proportions; & some scarce see Nature at all. But to the Eyes of the Man of Imagination, Nature is Imagination itself. As a man is, so he sees. As the Eye is formed, such are its Powers. You certainly Mistake, when you say that the Visions of Fancy are not to be found in this World. To Me This World is all One continued Vision of Fancy or Imagination, & I Feel Flatter'd when I am told so. (K793–94)

If everyone learned to see this way, however, "If the doors of perception were cleansed," as Blake writes in *The Marriage*, and everything appeared to man "as it is, infinite" (*MHH* 14, K154), there would not only be a general transformation of men's view of this world. There would also, as a consequence of this new view, be a literal transformation of this world itself, an apocalypse. Viewing this world as "One continued Vision or Fancy." (K793) and knowing that life is truly a divine—and human—unity in Christ, men would re-establish society on a new foundation, forming laws of freedom and love instead of repression, abolishing every kind of tyranny that prevents man from realizing his potentialities, and celebrating the divinity that is in every man.

Spiritual perception, therefore, is obviously not merely a superior kind of physical sense perception such as Locke conjectured spirits to possess, enabling them to see "secondary qualities" directly, as if with microscopic or X-ray vision.[2] Blake explicitly rejects as useless for his purpose any kind of improvement in perception like that afforded by the telescope or microscope, which merely "alter / The ratio of the Spectator's Organs, but leave Objects untouch'd" (*M* 29 : 17–18, K516). Spiritual perception transforms objects. And it does so imaginatively, making them into symbolic forms which reveal the significance of those objects to the life of man, and thus shows their "real" form. The real form of the sun to Blake, for instance, is not that of a "round disk of fire somewhat like a Guinea," but "an Innumerable company of the Heavenly host crying, 'Holy, Holy, Holy is the Lord God Almighty' " (*VLJ*, K617).

There is no use in objecting, "But surely the sun *is* more like a guinea than like a chorus of angels." To ordinary perception, yes, it appears so. But even ordinary perception departs from the abstract ideal of a noumenal sun independent of perception, for ordinary perception too is imaginative, whether we like it or not. In fact, as Blake suggests in the second "Memorable Fancy" of *The Marriage*

2. Secondary qualities are the imperceptible powers in objects; these qualities produce primary or perceptible qualities. Locke, *Essay Concerning Human Understanding*, Bk. II, ch. xxiii, sec. 13.

(*MHH* 12, K153), imagination is "the first principle" of human perception. Some imagination is necessary to any kind of perception, if only to synthesize discrete sense data into objects, synthesizing the brightness, warmth, roundness, etc. of the sun into the physical sun. (Modern psychology would agree, boggling only at the term imagination.) The chief difference between seeing the sun as a guinea and as a chorus of angels, Northrop Frye points out, is that the one requires only a limited amount of imagination, whereas the other requires a great deal. "The guinea-sun," writes Frye, "is a sensation assimilated to a general, impersonal, abstract idea. Blake can see it if he wants to, but when he sees the angels, he is not seeing more 'in' the sun but more of it."[3] He sees it, that is, not merely in relation to the growth of cabbages, but, to adapt Spinoza's famous phrase, *sub specie humanitatis,* under the aspect of a cosmic Humanity.

Such a way of seeing is philosophical, because it takes into account the order of all things and the nature of the Real. Spiritual perception is most philosophical, of course, when it apprehends the cosmic order directly, as it does in Blake's vision on the sands at Felpham. But Blake has too much common sense to insist that one should always see with a four-fold eye: Spiritual perception is flexible. He does hold, nevertheless, that if man is going to realize his potentialities for beauty and joy, individually and socially, he must keep the larger order of things in mind. Man must do so even when using the practical vision needed for everyday life, so that even his ordinary actions are at least consistent with a Human conception of life in which every man participates in the divinity of Christ, and in which "every particle of dust breathes forth its joy" (*E* iii.18, K237). When man can do this, "the whole creation," as Blake predicts in *The Marriage*," will be consumed and appear infinite and holy, whereas it now appears finite & corrupt" (*MHH* 14, K154). It will only *appear* so. To the visionary the creation appears infinite and holy now. But when all men learn to see aright, and act according to an expanded vision, life in "this" world will in fact become infinite and holy and man will return to Eden.

II. His Doctrine of Contraries

Spiritual perception will return man to Eden; the doctrine of contraries, the other main theme of *The Marriage,* explains what life will be like there. It will not be insipid. "How wide the Gulf and Unpassable," exclaims Blake in mirror writing on a title page

3. Northrop Frye, *Fearful Symmetry: A Study of William Blake* (Princeton, 1947), p. 21.

in *Milton,* "between Simplicity & Insipidity" (*M*30, K518). The simplicity of Eden is the simplicity of wisdom when combined with vision, or, in short, "innocence," in Blake's special meaning of the word. It also has a surpassing vigor: "As the breath of the Almighty such are the words of man to man / In the great Wars of Eternity" (*M*30:18–19, K519). These mighty words are spoken in war, but it is a war that is a creative enterprise "in fury of Poetic Inspiration, / To build the Universe stupendous, Mental forms Creating" (*M*30 : 19–20, K519), for the wars are "intellectual wars."

The theoretical basis for the dynamic creativeness of Edenic "Human" life is stated in essence in another distinction which appears on the same page of *Milton:* "Contraries are Positives / A Negation is not a Contrary" (*M*30, K518). Or as Blake states it in *The Marriage,* "Without Contraries is no progression. Attraction and Repulsion, Reason and Energy, Love and Hate, are necessary to Human existence" (*MHH*3, K149). That is, a Human world must be informed by opposed yet positive and complementary forces which, when allowed to interact without external restraint, impart to life a motion and a tension that make it creative.

Contraries have appeared in the speculations of many ages, in many forms, and Blake's conception has been rather loosely identified with the conceptions of many other thinkers. To see clearly what Blake had in mind, therefore, it might be well to make a few illustrative distinctions.

Blake is not a Hegelian. Though he uses the word "progression" in *The Marriage,* his contrary forces do not, like Hegel's "thesis" and "antithesis," constitute a world process of "becoming." Indeed, Blake's Human world, in which the contraries freely interact, is not one of becoming at all, for it is perfect; the only "progression" there is in it is that of continued creativeness. And, of course, Blake would have nothing to do with anything as abstractly systematic as Hegel's dialectic.[4]

Nor, on the other hand, does Blake's doctrine resemble that of Nicholas of Cusa (1401–1464), the skeptic who taught that the contraries of this world become identical in God. For though Blake's cosmos has ultimately the form of One Man, or Christ, the contrary forces of life do not become in any sense identical in the cosmic man, but remain as oppositions which give the cosmos its Human vitality. Cusanus' purpose was to make God a mystery transcending human understanding; Blake's, to reveal as clearly as possible the vital and energetic nature of God, man, and all of creation. Christ,

4. The distinction between Blake and Hegel, and other matters relating to Blake's contraries, are treated in relentless detail in my dissertation, "Blake's Doctrine of Contraries: A Study in Visionary Metaphysics," unpubl. diss. (Minnesota, 1954).

for instance, though forgiving, was to Blake not merely gentle—not, that is, "Creeping Jesus . . . humble as a Lamb or an Ass" (*EG* K750), as he described the Christ of the orthodox religious. He believed that Christ was characterized by love but also by a fierce energy. And, citing Christ's words, "I came not to send peace but a sword" (Matt. x. 34), Blake argues in *The Marriage* that "Jesus Christ did not wish to unite but to separate" the contrary classes of men upon earth.

Finally, Blake's contraries are not like "Yin" and "Yang," the cosmological principles of Tsao Yen (3rd century B.C.). For "Yin" and "Yang" function alternatively somewhat as do the alternations of electrical waves, whereas Blake's contraries interact simultaneously.

Blake's contraries neither progress, disappear, nor alternate because they polarize human life. They are cosmic forces to be seen in every "individual." Not, however, as forces external to individuals, but as immanences. Tigers and horses are contraries, but that which makes them contraries is not separable from them, for their contrariety is in everything they are and do. Everything, moreover, has an eternal "identity" in the cosmic scheme as either active or passive contrary: tigers and horses, male and female, poets and philosophers, plowmen and harrowers. And active and passive contraries exist in "every Nation & every Family," in every "Species of Earth, Metal, Tree, Fish, Bird & Beast" (*M*25 : 41, K511). The tension of opposition is in every fibre of Blake's world.

But this opposition is not mere opposition, for "Contraries are Positives / A Negation is not a Contrary" (*M*30, K 518). The contraries of Blake's world are opposed but not in such a way that they hinder or deny each other, for such an opposition would produce only destruction, or a kind of cold war, or a state of trembling impotence. Rather, they act positively in opposed but complementary directions, and their opposition is like that between expansion and contraction, between the creative imagination and the ordering reason, or between idea and form. To use the key terms of *The Marriage*, the contraries are "energy" and "reason," by which Blake means the desire for creation and the desire for order. And by "reason" here he intends an ideal reason which strives to supply the form and order which raw energy lacks.

"Negations," on the other hand, are not "contraries," because they simply deny and seek to destroy each other, as the false reason of the materialistic rationalists seeks to destroy imagination by denying it any validity as a means to knowledge, and as a tyrannical king seeks to destroy liberty by oppression and war.

The distinction between contraries and negations, in Blake's opinion, is a crucial one for the salvation of man. For to see the qualities of things as vital, necessary contraries is to live in a Human world of vision and imagination, whereas to see them as negations is to live in the fallen world of materialism and repressive social, religious, and political laws, a world in which the contraries are distorted and given the crude normative designations "good" and "evil." In *Jerusalem* Blake describes symbolically how contraries become negations. The fallen sons of Albion

. . . take the Two Contraries which are call'd Qualities, with which
Every Substance is clothed: they name them Good & Evil
From them they make an Abstract, which is a Negation
Not only of the Substance from which it is derived,
A murderer of its own Body, but also a murderer
Of every Divine Member. . . .

(*J* 10:8–13, K629)

That is, according to Blake, every individual contains the two contraries and is itself, in turn, "identified" as one of the contraries in the unity of the cosmic One Man, of whom "we are . . . Members" (*Laocoön,* K776). But materialistic thinkers, and especially those of his age, who are able to perceive things only with the corporeal eye further dimmed by rationalism, mistake the immanent contraries for separable Lockean "qualities." Moreover, acting in the repressive spirit of that narrow orthodoxy to which Blake believes materialism gives rise, these thinkers then apply to the contraries the normative moral designations "good" and "evil." This would be bad enough, but they go farther still, and "make an Abstract" of these normative "qualities" from the things in which these qualities really exist. Thus they cut even these distorted ghosts of the contraries off from substance and give them a spectral independence as moral and political laws, and even as gods. Such a god is "Nobodaddy" (i.e., nobody's father):

Why art thou silent & invisible,
Father of Jealousy?
Why dost thou hide thy self in clouds
From every searching Eye?

(K171)

Why indeed? Simply because he does not exist.

The great task, therefore, is to reverse this process (which is described again in the third expository section of *The Marriage*), and restore the abstractions which the "religious" call Good and Evil to their true and original identities as contraries. Good and evil, as the religious understand them, do not exist, says Blake. Good is simply "the passive that obeys Reason. Evil is the active springing from Energy" (*MHH*3, K149). In order that man can be truly happy in this world and realize to the fullest his divine potentialities for joy and wisdom, he must learn to see creation as a Human unity in Christ. And he must reject the divisive moral categories which now pit one half of creation against the other half in destructive conflict. Conflict there must be, but it must be the creative conflict of the contraries in "intellectual war" (*FZ IX*, K379).

Categories like good and evil may seem to have little to do with an ontological scheme of opposition which embraces even the nature of "Earth, Metal, Tree, Fish, Bird & Beast" (*M* 25:41, K511). And indeed they are quite irrelevant. That is part of Blake's point: The abstract thinkers have so mistaken the nature of the Real that they fail to recognize that everything that lives is imbued with the organic vitality of contrariety. When these thinkers do recognize opposition, it is always in normative moral terms which imply the need for one of the opposed forces to suppress the other as quickly as possible. But there is another aspect to this, which we must understand if we are to grasp the essential character of Blake's thought. His doctrine of contraries does offer a comprehensive theoretical explanation for the "dynamic organicism" with which the Romantics wished to invest their world.[5] In fact, Coleridge, the most theoretical of the Romantics, would have saved himself a great deal of philosophical groping had he known Blake. But though Blake was a philosophical poet on a grand scale, and though all of his conceptions must be viewed in the cosmological matrix of his thought, his real interest is man. Although the contraries are immanent in every minute particular of his world, his attention is not so much engaged by these minute particulars as it is by men. Men are the chief contraries—and the chief negations. The most important application of the doctrine of contraries, therefore, is the social one: The contraries Blake is most interested in are the two classes of men, the energetic creators and the rational organizers, or the "devils" and the "angels," as he calls them in *The Marriage*. Both classes are necessary, and both must strive positively and vigorously each in its own way if man is to live the Human life.

III. On the Structure of *The Marriage*

Entirely Blake's own is the structure of *The Marriage*. One of the reasons, I think, why this work has been misunderstood lies in its unorthodox structure. For though it expounds philosophical conceptions, it does not do so in any of the modes usual for such a purpose. It is developed according to no traditional logical or rhetorical plan. More than anything else, the structure of *The Marriage* seems

5. Morse Peckham, "Toward a Theory of Romanticism," *PMLA*, LXVI (March 1951), 5–23.

to resemble the A-B-A′ of the ternary form in music, in which a first theme and its development are followed by a second theme and its development, followed in turn by a return to the first section or a modification of it. If a little intermingling of themes be allowed, *The Marriage* could be thought of as a rich philosophical rondo. Indeed, even the mode of development employed by Blake here is closer to musical than to rhetorical modes. For he does not rely upon argument, but uses the discursive expository sections of the work as "variations" of his theme, as it were, alternating them with "memorable fancies" and the other symbolic sections. In general, the first or "A" section deals with the idea of contraries, the second or "B" section with spiritual perception, and the third or "A′" section with the contraries again. So that the ternary structure of the work may be kept in mind the three main sections of the explication have been labeled A, B, and A′.

The first or "A" part, comprised of the first expository section (*MHH* 3, K149), "The Voice of the Devil" (*MHH* 4), and the second expository section (*MHH* 5–6), states the theme of the doctrine of contraries and introduces as a sort of counter-subject Swedenborg, who is to be the symbol of the angels who do not perceive the necessity of the contraries to Human existence. The main theme is first stated in the first expository section. It is then developed by the dramatic commentary of the devil, who, preaching partisan doctrine, presents the arguments against the angels. In the second expository section, Blake develops further the idea of contraries by explaining how one half of existence came to try to restrain the other half: he gives the history of that restraint which obscures the contraries, and gives as well both the angels' and the devils' versions of the story.

The tone of the "A" part is rather drier than that of the rest of the work, since this part contains two expository sections and only "The Voice of the Devil" as a variation. The middle or "B" part, however, comprising the first memorable fancy (*MHH* 6–7) the "Proverbs of Hell" (*MHH* 7–10), the third expository section (*MHH* 11) the second memorable fancy (*MHH* 12–13) and the fourth expository section (*MHH* 14), relies more on symbolic development. The main theme of this part is enlarged sense perception, introduced dramatically but quite formally in the short first memorable fancy. It is developed contrapuntally, as it were, in the "Proverbs of Hell," with the general theme of energy, as it is seen by the devils. Thus the "Proverbs" are parallel in the structure of this part of the work to "The Voice of the Devil" in the first part. Now follows in the third expository section another history, this time of the growth of abstract systems through the corruption of the enlarged sense perceptions of the ancient poets. This history is also parallel to the history of restraint given in the first part, since it shows the role of abstraction in the development of restraint. Now the second memorable fancy develops the other side of the question by associating enlarged sense perception with excess and energy, in the lives of Isaiah and Ezekiel. Finally, the fourth expository section ends this part of the work in a prophetic tone by announcing that men's perceptions will be enlarged, and it also provides a kind of musical bridge passage in the figures of the cavern and printing, which are picked up in the third part of "A′" part.

The "A′" part is the richest part of *The Marriage*, comprising the third memorable fancy (*MHH* 15), the fifth expository section (*MHH* 16–17), the fourth memorable fancy (*MHH* 17–20), the sentence "Opposition is true Friendship" (*MHH* 20), the sixth expository section (*MHH* 21–22), and the climactic fifth memorable fancy (*MHH* 22–24), besides the final aphorism (*MHH* 24). In this part in general Blake returns to the doctrine of contraries and brings the work to a close by joining the angel and the devil. But he also keeps the idea of enlarged perception in mind.

The doctrine of contraries, together with the idea of enlarged sense perception, is reintroduced allegorically, in this part, in the very meaty third memorable fancy, which also shows how enlarged perception leads to the free interaction of the contraries and subsequently to the creativeness that is characteristic of Human life. In the fifth expository section, which follows, Blake employs demonstration to show that there are two classes of men and that they must remain contraries. Returning to Swedenborg, who had been a counter-subject in the "A" part of *The Marriage*, Blake then shows in the remarkable fourth memorable fancy the true character of the angelic metaphysics that endeavors through fear and monsters of the mind to prevent creative strife by suppressing imaginative energy in all spheres of life. And he follows this in the last expository section by a direct and serious attack on Swedenborg as one of the angels, which should be read against the background of the robust comedy of the preceding satirical memorable fancy as in part a transitional change of mood leading to the climactic and prophetic debate that brings *The Marriage* to a close. This debate, in which the two contraries embrace and become one in the person of the prophet Elijah, effects the apocalyptic resolution toward which *The Marriage* has moved throughout its last part and which was announced at the beginning of the work ("Now is the dominion of Edom, & the return of Adam into Paradise") and again at the end of the "B" part ("The cherub with his flaming sword is hereby commanded to leave his guard at tree of life"). By marrying the angels and devils of this world, it prophesies that Human life, which was allegorically portrayed in the "Printing house in Hell," will actually come to pass.

Though not, perhaps, at once. *The Marriage* moves, like Blake's great epics—and indeed his prophetic lyric "The Tyger"—toward an apocalyptic conclusion, but in the last part there sounds a slightly less positive note, in the shift back to ironic point of view in which anyone who embraces energy becomes a "devil." It reminds one of Beethoven's tempering the positive resolution of his song cycle, *An die Ferne Geliebte*, by a brief snatch of its plaintive first theme. Perhaps even in the exultant mood in which Blake wrote *The Marriage*, he was not quite sure that the oppositions of this world could in fact become the contraries of the mental war.

And, indeed, the great synthesis of *The Marriage* was not to be a final one. Blake found that the dialectics of his initial formulation of the doctrine of contraries, in which he would simply transform into fruitful contraries all oppositions now splitting this world, could not bring about the Eden he envisaged for man. After his initial excitement at the possibilities suggested by such a synthesis had lessened somewhat, he no doubt saw that the intellectual battles of an Edenic mental war of art and science were not to be fought as long as corporeal wars were waged by "spectres" such as George III. Evidently something very like evil did after all have a real existence, though it was still not what the religious call evil. And accordingly we find Blake becoming more uncompromisingly apocalyptic, demanding a more radical revolution in the modes of thought and life. In the next statement of his doctrine of contraries, in the so-called "Lambeth Books," we find that he has sharply distinguished the oppositions of this world and those of the Human world into negations and contraries; or rather, that he has applied to the idea of opposites the distinction between the positive virtue of "act" and its negative "hindering," which he had set forth at the end of his annotations to Lavater in 1789 (K88). Not all of the angels are capable of becoming contraries, for some of them can never do anything but hinder. There is no place for them in Eden.

MARTIN PRICE

The Standard of Energy†

In *The Book of Urizen* (1794) we find the beginnings of the myth that was to occupy Blake in his later poetry. This is the account of a fall. Like Milton, Blake sees all human existence as shot through with moments of fall and moments of redemption, and one fall provides an archetype for all others. This is the story of

† From Martin Price, *To the Palace of Wisdom: Studies in Order and Energy from Dryden to Blake* (Garden City, N.Y.: Doubleday Anchor: 1965), pp. 424–34, 436–37.

the emergence of "the primeval Priest's assum'd power," and Urizen (whose name seems to derive, as does our word "horizon," from the Greek form of "to limit") is the archetypal State of false Priesthood. We first see Urizen separating off from the rest of existence, creating a void, a "soul-shudd'ring vacuum" that keeps out the spirit and secedes, as it were, from Eternity: it is pictured as a landscape of turbulence—vast forests, mountains of ice, thunderous voices—which embodies the "tormenting passions" of a "self-contemplating shadow."

Urizen explains his divorce from life as the desire for fixity:

> I have sought for a joy without pain,
> For a solid without fluctuation.
> Why will you die, O Eternals?
> Why live in unquenchable burnings?
>
> II, 4:10–14)

Urizen cannot tolerate the openness of eternal movement, that is, the vital energy of imagination. He fights its irregular and unpredictable freedom until he produces a "wide world of solid obstruction." He has wrested from the moral conflict with the "Seven deadly Sins of the soul" (his way of conceiving the freedom of energy) a book of "eternal brass," and he has reduced all seeming disorder to law and to simple regularity:

> One command, one joy, one desire,
> One curse, one weight, one measure,
> One King, one God, one Law.
>
> (II, 4:10–14)

The effrontery of Urizen's speech is much like that of the Dunces or of Dulness' addresses.[1] Urizen is less a character than a State revealing itself in its fullness.

The Eternals seem, at least to Urizen, to rage furiously about him after this speech, separating themselves from him, although he has, of course, broken away from them. And now, in fear, he seeks a hiding-place, piling up mountains until he builds a "roof vast, petrific around / On all sides . . . like a womb" (III, 5:28–29). The Eternals send Los to watch over Urizen, and we encounter one of those poetic condensations that run through all of Blake's later poetry. Blake breaks down conventional narrative continuities by embodying relationships in constantly shifting images. As characters enter into new States, or as States enter into new relationships, the characters' natures alter, and they undergo the transformations that we recognize in the "condensation" of dream-processes. Here Los is

1. In Pope's *The Dunciad.* [*Editors.*]

sent to watch over Urizen, but Urizen is described as being rent from Los's side. If we take Los as the redeeming power of imagination, we can see Blake's desire to dramatize once more the separation of Urizen from all those other powers in man with which he should be in harmony. Urizen, wrenched apart from Los, is even more clearly a figure of pure rationality, a version of lifeless order. Tellingly, Urizen cannot generate a meaningful order even at the level he has reached. His "one law" needs some form of embodiment, and creates the senses through which he can receive awareness; for example, his eyes—"two little orbs . . . fixed in two little caves." As he takes on bodily form, Urizen's "eternal life" is "obliterated," and Los himself is dazed and paralyzed by this act. What horrifies Los is not the turbulence of life but the vacuity of "Space, undivided by existence" that now surrounds them.

When Los feels pity for Urizen's world, Pity itself grows into Enitharmon, the "first female now separate." As Urizen has fallen into a life bounded by the senses, so Los, out of more generous motives, falls into a State where he may be overcome by passivity. Enitharmon becomes a separate dominating will. The Eternals cover over the world with a great curtain they call Science; this may in turn be taken as Los's remoter view of eternal life now that he accepts a separate female partner. Los's marriage (which is, of course, like Adam's need for the Eve who will later seduce him) is an archetype of man's acceptance of a natural world about him as real as his own mind; a resignation of imaginative power. Enitharmon's first action is "perverse and cruel" coyness as she flees from his embrace. When she bears a male child, who issues howling with fierce flames, the Eternals close the tenting curtain: "No more Los beheld Eternity" (VI, 20:2). The descent has gone further: the prophet-poet is now committed to the world of his fallen self. He is absorbed into that world as a jealous father, and he becomes like Urizen.

Two actions follow, each the counterpart of the other. Los and Enitharmon chain to a rock their son, Orc, who embodies the rebellious principle of renewed and independent life. Los keeps Enitharmon protected and enclosed while she bears "an enormous race." At the same time Urizen awakes from sleep, "Stung with the odours of Nature," and explores his world. To his horror he finds his order is unworkable:

he curs'd
Both sons & daughters; for he saw
That no flesh nor spirit could keep
His iron laws one moment
For he saw that life liv'd upon death.

(VIII, 23:23–26)

Urizen wanders, pitying his creations; and his tears become a web, the Net of Religion. At this point we have Blake's savage parody of the creation of man in Genesis, as Urizen's creatures contract into earthbound humans:

3. Six days they shrunk up from existence,
And on the seventh day they rested,
And they bless'd the seventh day, in sick hope,
And forgot their eternal life.

4. And their thirty cities divided
In form of a human heart.
No more could they rise at will
In the infinite void, but bound down
To earth by their narrowing perceptions
They lived a period of years;
Then left a noisom body
To the jaws of devouring darkness.

5. And their children wept, & built
Tombs in the desolate places,
And form'd laws of prudence, and call'd them
The eternal laws of God.

(IX, 27:39–28:7)

At the close, Urizen's oldest son—a counterpart of the bound Orc—calls together the children of Urizen and leads them from "the pendulous earth": "They called it Egypt, & left it." We are at the point of an exodus of the spirit from the domination of the merely natural. The consolidation of error has brought the spirit to the point of rebellion.

The irony of Blake's poem is strongest when he describes the fall in the language of the Biblical creation. But this parody is simply the most transparent instance of the inverted order that the poem discloses. Blake's great satiric theme is the displacement of a true order by a grotesque mock order:

Such is that false
And Generating Love, a pretence of love to destroy love.
(*Jerusalem* I, 17:25–26)

A pretence of Art to destroy Art; a pretence of Liberty
To destroy Liberty; a pretence of Religion to destroy Relgion.
(*Jerusalem* II, 43:35–36)

This verbal pattern is Blake's most compressed statement of the inversion that insensibly creeps over man and his world, offering itself in the guise of what it seeks to usurp. Only the prophetic awareness of Los discerns what is taking place; others may sustain this awareness for a time and feel the wearying eclipse—as Dulness' sons lapse into sleep—but soon all is night. Like Pope, Blake presents the grandeur and terror of the usurpation:

> Loud Satan thunder'd . . .
> Coming in a Cloud with Trumpets & with Fiery Flame,
> An awful Form eastward from midst a bright Paved-work
> Of precious stones by Cherubim surrounded, so permitted
> (Lest he should fall apart in his Eternal Death) to imitate
> The Eternal Great Humanity Divine surrounded by
> His Cherubim & Seraphim in ever happy Eternity.
> (*Milton* II, 39:22–28)

In the same way, Blake's Urizen absorbs much of the traditional image of God the Father, making clearer the kind of God man must worship once he has resigned the energies that demand free movement and has contracted into the security of a closed system.

Blake's interweaving of mental states and outward structures, of political programs and philosophic doctrines, gives any moment in the later poems a formidable complexity. Characters voice the world view that underlies the moral and social errors they embody. Their frankness, like the shamelessness of Pope's dunces, shows how completely they are enclosed in their limited order; they are complacently untroubled by the claims of a rival order, or at most blusteringly defiant. When the Saviour appeals to Albion, the primal man who is now fallen mankind, he offers the vision of charity: "Lo! we are one, forgiving all Evil." But Albion's denial opens out into an opposed vision of reality:

> But the perturbed Man away turns down the valleys dark:
> Saying we are not One, we are Many, thou most simulative
> Phantom of the over heated brain! shadow of immortality!
> Seeking to keep my soul a victim to thy Love! which binds
> Man, the enemy of man, into deceitful friendship . . .
> By demonstration man alone can live, and not by faith.
> My mountains are my own, and I will keep them to myself:
> The Malvern and the Cheviot, the Wolds, Plinlimmon & Snowden
> Are mine: here will I build my Laws of Moral Virtue.
> Humanity shall be no more, but war & princedom & victory!
> (*Jerusalem* I, 4:22–32)

The fullness with which Albion reveals his error moves the passage toward ironic satire. Like the great speeches by Aristarchus or Silenus in the fourth book of *The Dunciad* it exposes itself in every assertion. The denial of Jesus becomes rabid empiricism ("most simulative Phantom"), Hobbesian politics ("Man, the enemy of man"), dogmatic rationalism ("By demonstration . . . alone"), and acquisitive materialism ("My mountains are my own"). Pascal's disjunction of orders was never more complete than this.

It is in such passages that we can best see Blake's resemblance to the Augustans. Like them he is acutely aware of how deeply all attitudes are rooted in systems of belief. A madman inhabits a mad world, where values are turned inside out, and each sane pattern of order has its reverse image. This takes us back to the problem of orders, to the view that each discrete order of experience tends to become self-subsistent in a world of its own making. The most insistent irony in Blake is the irony of the "mind-forg'd manacles," the enclosure and stultification of man's vision and the loss of the power even to discern the change.

Blake's constant effort is to give unmistakable form to error and thus rob it of vague and mysterious authority. To do this, he must become a master of satiric symbols and ironic confrontations. "Every honest man is a Prophet; he utters his opinion both of private & public matters. Thus: If you go on So, the result is So. He never says, such a thing shall happen let you do what you will. A Prophet is a Seer, not an Arbitrary Dictator. It is man's fault if God is not able to do him good, for he gives to the just & to the unjust, but the unjust reject his gift" (K 392). This is precisely the satirist's task: to appeal to men's responsibility by projecting the consequences of their action into the action themselves, as Swift dramatizes our failure of charity in the cannibalism of *A Modest Proposal.* Such satiric prophecy is uncomfortable; it is designed to disturb. "What do these Knaves mean by Virtue? Do they mean War & its horrors & its Heroic Villains?" (K 400).

It is important to make certain distinctions. Blake hates the "Accusers of Sin," the moralists who make impossible demands, rob the self of spontaneity and confidence, then punish its inevitable transgressions with a righteous show of pity. Everything that lives is holy; each man lives in the imagination. Each individual is unique, a law to itself so long as it remains truly alive and does not harden into the negation of life, the hindering of energy in itself and others. Judgments of good and evil deny this uniqueness and demand characterless passivity. For Blake, therefore, the prophet does not defend a moral code; he keeps the divine vision, and he seeks to restore life where men have chosen death. As a satirist he attacks not individuals but States. "Man Passes on, but States remain for Ever; he passes thro' them like a traveller who may as well suppose that the places he has pass'd thro' Exist no more. Every thing is Eternal" (606). States must be identified, so that man may recognize them and pass beyond those that are conditions of death. Man must be made to see:

> . . . What seems to Be, Is, To those to whom
> It seems to Be, & is productive of the most dreadful
> Consequences to those to whom it seems to Be, even of
> Torments, Despair, Eternal Death.
>
> (*Jerusalem* II, 36:51–54)

The satirist exposes the nature and thereby dissolves the solidity of those structures men build as resting places from thought. The most splendid structures may be the denial of life, either through externalization or through simple inversion of values.

The Walls of Babylon are Souls of Men, her Gates the Groans
Of Nations, her Towers are the Miseries of once happy Families,
Her Streets are paved with Destruction, her Houses built with
    Death,
Her Palaces with Hell & the Grave, her Synagogues with Torments
Of ever-hardening Despair, squar'd & polish'd with cruel skill.
(*Jerusalem* I, 24:31–35)

Blake insists upon the world man inhabits as a world of his making. Every thing is an imaginative act, and every demon is born of terror. Satan springs into monstrous proliferation,

Producing many Heads, three or seven or ten, & hands & feet
Innumerable at will of the unfortunate contemplator
Who becomes his food: such is the way of the Devouring Power.
(*Jerusalem* II, 33:22–24)

In such a situation, the prophet must become a liberator who destroys the Babylon men build around themselves and dispels the Satan they feed with their doubt or despair. To the extent that man accepts error through a failure of insight, through dishonesty or willful rejection of what he knows to be true, he may be treated with that therapeutic scorn we have seen in Pope. Blake's prophet-poet Los exclaims:

"I care not whether a Man is Good or Evil; all that I care
Is whether he is a Wise Man or a Fool. Go, put off Holiness
And put on Intellect, or my thund'rous Hammer shall drive thee
To wrath which thou condemnest, till thou obey my voice."
(*Jerusalem* IV, 91:55–58)

The prophet like the satirist must reject the saving lie, and he must commit himself with "triumphant honest pride" to the vision that strips away illusion. The power to penetrate the wishful blindness and the plausible pretext is the prophetic gift that leads to the satiric image. The prophet in his vision shares the detachment of the God he interprets, sees earthly power in its imminent frailty: "Though they dig into hell, thence shall mine hand take them; though they climb up to heaven, thence will I bring them down." It is this detachment, both in range of vision and in elevation of spirit above the fears of worldly power, that Blake portrayed in his version of Gray's Bard: "King Edward and his Queen Elenor are prostrated, with their horses, at the foot of the rock on which the Bard stands; prostrated by the terrors of his harp on the margin of the river Conway. . . ." As Blake says (576–77), "Weaving the winding sheet of Edward's race by means of sounds of spiritual music and its accompanying expressions of articulate speech is a bold, and daring, and masterly conception. . . ." If the Bard's spiritual music is bitter denunciation, we can turn to Chaucer, who "was very devout, and paid respect to true enthusiastic superstition. He has laughed at his knaves and fools. . . . But he has respected his True Pilgrims . . ." (575). The spiritual music of the Bard, the laughter of Chaucer, the "triumphant honest pride" of Jesus (750)—these go to compose the satirist's scorn and outrage at the pretensions of the corrupt.

What primarily distinguishes Blake as satirist from the Augustans is the shift from moral judgment to a standard of energy. It is not the evil man so much as the soulless and dead man that Blake disdains. In fact, of course, any standard of vitality tends to transform itself into one of morality, as death-in-life becomes a state of bondage to false gods. But the prophetic stance fits well, in its sense of inspiration and commanding power, with the scorn for the materialized, the rigid, the timorous and self-protective. The exposed grandeur of Gray's Bard, as well as his sacrifice of himself to the cause of liberty, becomes a dramatization of titanic energies confronting legal tyrants. So long as these titanic forces remain tied to a system or dogma, they seem oppressive. When they shake off all commitment to the limited and regular, they become symbols of infinity. They overleap doctrines and stand for the spirit that gives life and demands life of others. The pride of such a force is essential to its nature; itself infinite and divine, it can only mock any limited conceptions of its will or any simulation of its energy. And out of such pride scorn must naturally follow: the infinite can only shatter with its breath those mechanical representations of life that men devoutly compose. The spiritual music is nothing less than the whirlwind, the destruction of worldly order in the name of energy that cannot be ordered unless it orders itself.

The myths of Blake's later poetry are designed to show life under the aspect of energy. They show the primal unity of man sundered into the warring elements of the Four Zoas. Reason has been divided from feeling, Urizen from Luvah; the instinctual unity of the body from its imaginative direction, Tharmas from Urthona. Each of the Zoas is at war with the others, except for momentary conspiracies, and the conflict drives each to the impoverished extreme of its nature.

Again, Blake creates the cyclic myth of the four realms of man, which are also four conditions of spirit. Eden is a place of mastery, of active engagement in intellectual warfare and hunting, or what Shaw calls the creation of new mind. The condition of Eden is a limit of life as we customarily know it; it fixes in myth those moments of heightened intensity, confident achievement, and harmonious self-realization that confer a sense of transcedence. The principle of active mastery is crucial, for the pleasant state of repose that Blake calls Beulah carries the threat of inducing passivity. To move from Eden to Beulah is to descend from the battlefield or hunt to the domestic ease of simple accord, from vital conflict of contraries to unresisting acceptance by a benign world, like the arms of the delighted bride or the cradle of the mother's embrace. Like every descent from difficulty to shelter, it can become a movement toward dependence.

The next phase of passivity is the most important, for in the descent from Beulah to Ulro, man forgets that his imagination creates his world and accepts as solid reality what he has unconsciously imposed upon himself. Once he submits to this reality, he sets out giving it form and making it a self-subsistent order. He is under the domination of Urizen, and in *The Book of Urizen* we see the primal pattern of this self-enclosure. Just as Urizen fails to impose his law upon all of existence, so man remains aware of more than he can rationalize. The affective life he fails to acknowledge erupts into institutional warfare and sacrificial religion, the perversions of the feelings that have been repressed. (We may recall the emperor in Swift's A *Tale of a Tub*, whose blocked semen shoots up into his brain and fosters dreams of conquest.) The life man creates for himself in Ulro becomes unendurable; he is, like Pope's fallen men in the *Essay on Man*, forced into virtue. For Blake the pattern of recovery is the painful struggle of rebellion that marks the condition of Generation, the condition of the *Songs of Experience* or the *Visions of the Daughters of Albion.*

Finally, a third myth Blake uses is that of Spectre and Emanation. The Emanation that embodies man's aspirations and his vision of self-realization is driven away by doubt and jealous suspicion. The Emanation may be replaced, as Jerusalem is, by the temptress, at first in the benign image of pastoral nature, later as the whore of mystery and abominations. This is another way of seeing the descent into Ulro and the tyranny of a partial vision. The Spectre is Selfhood that encrusts man's spirit with opacity, diverts him from transcendent vision to rationalism. "Thou art my Pride & Self righteousness," Los declares to his Spectre. Opposed to the Spectre is the vision of selflessness and forgiveness:

> And if God dieth not for Man & giveth not himself
> Eternally for Man, Man could not exist; for Man is Love
> As God is Love.
>
> (*Jerusalem* IV, 96:25–27)

The complex interaction of these myths and others creates the pattern of Blake's later poetry. At any moment the forward narrative movement may give way to the sense of depth, or the opening out of levels of meanings that have been compressed into massive symbols. Blake encourages this process by stressing the simultaneity of actions on various levels and by moving abruptly from one level to another. The myths, as we see, can easily merge into each other and produce dreamlike fluidity of epic movement. One is reminded of Spenser's world in *The Faerie Queene*, where the extravagances of chivalric romance are only the outward surface of a spiritual movement within the heroes. Spenser's scene is a landscape of soul, embodied in sinister palaces or castles, deserts of despair, fountains of renewal; his dragons and witches are the temptations that live within the soul. Blake carries this further. The myths he superimposes upon history in the earlier works, such as *America* or *The French Revolution*, are at last wholly internalized, and the cosmic drama is played out within the mind and soul of fallen man, the sleeping Albion. Instead of characters as distinct as Milton's angels or Spenser's Archimago or Orgoglio, Blake creates States through which man passes, and the movement from one State to another may be apparent transformation of identity. There is always the need to identify in Blake's poems. Oothoon recognizes Urizen in Bromion's voice; Los and Enitharmon (in *Milton* 10:1) see "that Satan is Urizen."

This process of naming and identifying is a process of satiric reduction. The Augustan satirists dramatize the plausible power of error in elaborate ironic structures: the systems of belief in Swift's *Tale of a Tub*, the worship of Dulness in *The Dunciad*, the queenly hauteur of Dryden's Panther. Perhaps the finest brief instance is Pope's vision, in the *Epilogue to the Satires*, I, of the triumphal procession of Vice. But all of this ironic appreciation that seems to give in to pretension and to admire appearance prepares for the act of naming, as the satirist reveals the order within which this grandeur is contained. Swift's Peter and Jack prove to be two aspects of the same selfhood; Pope's Dulness is a phantom by which man enslaves himself; and Dryden's Panther, the more dangerous for a deceptively mild manner. Significantly, all of the great Augustan satires are works whose narrative structure seems to bend or halt under their weight of symbolic meaning. Narrative gives way to dialectic.

Blake's Urizen—reason grown to a deity and despot—is a counterpart to Pope's Dulness, the usurping deity who has undone true order and blinded her adherents to their former existence. Urizen is the impoverishing tyranny of reason, Dulness the paralyzing tyranny of pure matter; but these different tyrants achieve their power in similar ways. The uncreating word of Dulness grows in the human brain as surely as Urizen's tree of mystery. Pope's skill is to make of his ridiculous pedants, poetasters, grubs, and charlatans a formidable army of the Enemy. So in Blake, the tyranny or malice of each man creates the more formidable and frightful system, the world view in which man imprisons himself. Like Dulness, Urizen is a part of the human soul usurping the rule of other parts. Dulness represents the atavistic unconscious of self-gratification and self-absorption that may include overt pride, less obvious laziness, more fundamental selfhood. Blake's Urizen is selfhood in another guise: the selfhood of prostration before one's guilt and anxiety, of assertion through vindictive law and frustration before repressive fear, a cycle—in familiar modern terms—of frustration and aggression, the aggression turned against oneself as well as others and projected into an institution that gives it impersonal authority. Dulness surrounds her sons and herself with fogs, Urizen encloses man's mind in a mundane shell.

* * *

Therefore Pope suggests that the failure of mind is the failure of an energy different from, but no less important than, that of Dulness' unconscious and instinctive force. Much of the treatment of Dulness dramatizes the loss of this energy of mind. She is the mistress of the great yawn, the creator of moral inanition, the dissolver of critical effort and vigilance, the coddler of a boozy son. She may be busy and bold, but she is also heavy and blind. Her characteristic motion is the self-enclosing vortex, her characteristic form is sluggish and formless viscosity. Her followers are a "vast involuntary throng," led along by the mechanics of magnetism like steel filings or ball bearings, by "strong impulsive gravity of head." Here again heaviness represents a dehumanized lethargy of mind.

Blake, in his conception of Urizen, stresses the ongoing process of energy, which Urizen tries to block and freeze with rational structures. Yet Blake recognizes that Urizen's tyranny is not true reason. Like Wordsworth, Blake prizes "reason in her most exalted mood," when reason acts in unity with imagination and feeling. Urizen exemplifies A. O. Lovejoy's point that "rationality, when conceived as complete, as excluding all arbitrariness, becomes itself a kind of irrationality" (*The Great Chain of Being*, p. 331). As the promulgator of laws that can never be fully obeyed and the creator of excessive self-demands that can yield only neurasthenic paralysis, Urizen inevitably collapses into superstition and mystery. His rationalism produces a world more and more abstract and inhuman, ruled by a God that is a mere phantom lawgiver. What has been denied returns in a corrupt form. Urizen's temples are the scene of an erotic mystery cult, like that of the Magna Mater to whom Pope likens Dulness, and his religion is allied with war, that is, with "energy enslav'd." Just as Dulness' own energy is matched with mental languor, so Urizen's rationalism is matched with the debased emotions that Blake embodies in Rahab, the whore of Babylon: "Religion hid in War, a Dragon red & hidden Harlot" (*Jerusalem* III, 75:20).

Pope and Blake deal with the failure of both order and energy. Pope, whose concern is for order, shows Dulness foisting a mock order with the irresistible power that is freed by the mind's abdication. Blake, whose concern is for the energy that makes its own constantly renewed forms of order, shows Urizen checking all movement and renewal or forcing energy into perverse and wasteful forms. Pope shows Dulness ruling the world by corrupting institutions and inverting their original nature. Blake shows Urizen's power in the false authority of all institutions, which by their nature seek to preserve and extend the power surrendered to them. Both poets work, by means of dialectical encounters, toward the ultimate exposure and consolidation of error so that it may be thrown off. Once the orders are distinguished, the self-enclosure of each has been broken, and a choice can be made. Pope dramatizes the choice in the satires as a moral intensity that leads man beyond selfhood and makes his will one with God's. Blake, who regards moral judgment, based as it is upon universal law, as the worst form of institutional tyranny, sees Urizen finally absorbed into the restored unity of all the Zoas, as the primal man, Albion, at last accepts Jesus and His doctrine of forgiveness.

They walked
To & fro in Eternity as One Man, reflecting each in each & clearly seen
And seeing, according to fitness & order.

(*Jerusalem* IV, 98:38–40)

Blake can use the mathematical symbolism of Revelation, once it is purged of the taint of Pythagorean rationalism. Elsewhere he fuses the artifice of order with the vitality of organic life, and, like Milton, he does this through the metaphor of the dance:

Thou seest the gorgeous clothed Flies that dance & sport in summer
Upon the sunny brooks & meadows: every one the dance
Knows in its intricate mazes of delight artful to weave:
Each one to sound his instruments of music in the dance,
To touch each other & recede, to cross & change & return.

(*Milton* I, 26:2–6)

every Flower,
The Pink, the Jessamine, the Wall-flower, the Carnation,
The Jonquil, the mild Lilly, opes her heavens; every Tree
And Flower & Herb soon fill the air with an innumerable Dance,
Yet all in order Sweet & lovely.

(*Milton* II, 31:58–62)

DAVID V. ERDMAN

America: New Expanses†

Today the inquiry into the art of Blake's Illuminated Printing is moving far beyond the simple but long prevailing question whether the design on a given page illustrates or illuminates or counterpoints the text: whether poem is like picture or picture like poem. We are now, at a minimum, concerned with what the two arts are doing in harness, pictura *atque* poesis. At maximum we are concerned with much more. But allow me at this level to make a point about the interchange or sharing of pictorial imagery between picture and text. On the seventh plate of *Jerusalem* the words describe the "opake blackening" Spectre of Los as one who "panting like a frighted wolf and howling . . . stood over the Immortal . . . among the Furnaces." The etched picture (*Jerusalem* 6)[1] shows us the blacksmith with tongs, fire, hammer, anvil, bellows, and a chain that operates the bellows; but the Spectre is not standing; it has no visible feet but hovers over the smith on wings, like a bat not a wolf. A moment later, in the text, the Spectre "groaning" kneels before Los at the furnace—presumably more like a man than a wolf or a bat. The effect may be called metaphorical density, but it is more than that and not quite that. Whether the Spectre is bat, wolf, or man (we are to realize) depends on how the mind sees it or him. These are alternative or simultaneous visionary forms of one form that hint at metamorphoses to tease us *into* thought, for their one form is in turn a shadow form of the human blacksmith, who is the metaphorical heroic form of the poet-artist, William Blake of South Molton Street (as he tells us within the poem). *Because* he faints at the anvil he is haunted by his spectral self-shadows: *or* because they are in his mind, he faints at the forge. The action of the poem-picture is larger and more complex than would be indicated by the picture or the words taken separately, for these point not at each other (as in the usual picture book) but beyond themselves. The artifact only opens the sensory doors to the mental theater.

In other words, the text is not there to help us follow the pictures, nor the pictures to help us visualize the text; both lead us to an imaginative leap in the dark, a leap *beyond* the dark and the fire—from perception to Intellectual Vision, a last judgment in which fools perish.

† From "*America*: New Expanses," *Blake's Visionary Forms Dramatic*, eds. David V. Erdman and John E. Grant (Princeton: Princeton University Press, 1970), pp. 92–103, 109–11, 112. Footnotes have been renumbered and some footnotes have been omitted.

1. See color plate 26 in this edition. [*Editors.*]

We must attend to Blake's definition (*Jerusalem* 98) of true communication as practised by humans in paradise:

And they conversed together in Visionary forms dramatic which
bright
Redounded from their Tongues in thunderous majesty, in Visions
In new Expanses, creating exemplars. . . .

Their converse involves mastery of all the arts of discourse, ornamentation, dramaturgy, exploration, and moral suasion (exemplars). Using only the arts of poetry and painting (and engraving) Blake must suggest all the others. And all must serve Intellectual Vision, seen through the window of the artifact. His illuminated pages become a prompt book of suggestions for Visions, Expanses, New Songs, and Thunderous Dramatic Forms, in which he wishes us to converse. "I give you the end of a golden string," he says. "It will lead you. . . ." His text is a clue-thread. On the thread of text the emblematic etchings are mere sketches for cosmic motion-pictures, or rather color-motion-music pictures, on a four-dimensional mental screen—the cinerama of William Blake.

The man who tried "all experiments" in art and mixed art might have been delighted at the potentialities of the cinemonsters of our day—if horrified at their Satanic intellectual focus. The man who, when the sun rose, did not fixate on a "round disk of fire" but saw (and heard) "an Innumerable company of the Heavenly host crying Holy Holy . . ." abhorred the kind of realism which does not open the interior and exterior worlds.[2]

It was a sense of Blake's objective that led Northrop Frye to go on, after suggesting the (remote) analogy of "the union of musical and poetic ideas in a Wagner opera," to the proposition that Blake's work involves the building up of a unified structure of meaning as "a total image, a single visualizable picture."[3] This view is valid, at a distance from the work, but dissolves as we approach; for the visualizable picture is in motion—and is not really single. It is usually at least twofold, with a polar or antiphonal or dialectical tension between two contrary images (or image systems), each striv-

2. *DC* 9 (E539 / K583), *VLJ* (E555 / K617). For a more thoughtful consideration of the "problem in visualization that presents itself everywhere in Blake's poetry" see Harold Bloom, "The Visionary Cinema of Romantic Poetry," *Essays for Damon,* 18–35. "Blake, I think, like his master Milton (as Eisenstein hinted) wants his reader to be more of a film-script reader or even a director than a film-viewer."

[In this and subsequent notes for this essay, *E* and *K* references are to pages in David V. Erdman, ed., *The Poetry and Prose of William Blake* (Garden City, N.Y., 1970) and Geoffrey Keynes, ed., *Blake: Complete Writings with Variant Readings* (London and New York, Oxford, 1974). Blake works referred to by letter, in notes and text (followed by plate number) are *A Descriptive Catalogue* (*DC*), *A Vision of the Last Judgment* (*VLJ*), *America* (*A*), *A Public Address to the Chalcographic Society* (*PA*), and *Marriage of Heaven and Hell* (*MHH*).—*Editors.*]

3. Frye, "Poetry and Design in William Blake," *Journal of Aesthetics and Art Criticism,* X (1951), 35–42; reprinted in John E. Grant, *Discussions of William Blake,* Boston, 1961, 44–49.

ing to be determinate—as, for example, the rival cities of Jerusalem and Babylon in *Jerusalem*. Beyond that, it can be apocalyptically threefold or fourfold, as I hope to reveal in the present close look at *America, A Prophecy*, 1793.

Physically *America* is an eighteen-page folio booklet "in Illuminated Printing" consisting of a frontispiece, an illustrated title page continuing the picture of the frontispiece,[4] a Preludium of two and a Prophecy of fourteen illuminated pages. The work concerns a cycle of history that begins with the birth and rising of an Orc or human serpent of Independence, during the American War and Revolution, and concludes with the end of the war (in 1781) and that spirit's repression for "twelve years." The cycle is viewed prophetically from 1793, a time of auguries of a new cycle. That year, on January 21, the King of France was guillotined. In February, France and England went to war. In June, Blake issued an engraved print of a king hysterical, flanked by two chief warriors gripping sword and spear, above the caption *Our End is Come*. In October he offered *America* for sale, with the specific prophecy in its concluding lines that "their end should come"—the end of "Angels & weak men" who "govern o'er the strong"—"when France reciev'd the Demons light."[5]

Joel Barlow in his *Vision of Columbus*, Book Five, had rearranged the chronological and geographical materials of the historical American War into an epic pageant viewed prophetically by Christopher Columbus from a Mount of Vision in Spain.[6] Barlow's stage was the American coast, which Columbus could see from his Spanish mountain; his machinery consisted of one angel; his main stage device was a cloud that hid the scene during intermissions. Blake extended the stage to include the British coast, swelled the machinery to a large cast of angels and demons, replaced the Mount of Vision with the "vast shady hills" of an archetypal Atlantis "between America & Albions shore," and replaced Columbus as European spectator with the King of England, who, "looking westward" from Albion, trembles at a "vision" which is, largely, the relevant part of Barlow's *Vision*. But of course Blake's symbolic fusion of military and political and psychic history, heightened by apocalyptic imagery from descriptions of the Black Death, soars beyond the troubled fountains of Barlow's couplets. Blake's choreography is utterly new; action as well as communication crisscrosses the Atlantic and leaps from its depths to the zenith; and he departs fur-

4. See color plate 15 in this edition. [*Editors.*]

5. *A* 16 (E56 / K302); Prospectus of 10 October 1793 (E670 / K207); *Our End is Come / Published June 5, 1793 by W. Blake Lambeth* (E660): behind the alarmed trio is an oaken door frame; in later versions flames are added beside or behind them; in the color print the door frame has been burnt up. * * *

6. See my "William Blake's Debt to Joel Barlow," *American Literature*, XXVI (1954), 94–98; also my *Blake: Prophet Against Empire* (1969), pp. 23–27, 57, and, for the addition of Black Death imagery, pp. 58–59.

ther from the narrative form of history, epic or chronicle, in the direction of musical form and mural allegory as in paintings of the Last Judgment by the Italians or by Blake himself. *America* we might look upon as an acting version of a mural Apocalypse.

Drawing upon both text and pictures, let us examine first the music of it and then the visualizable drama—an order which will stress Blake's departure from narrative but not from progression.

Blake, working as a musician, first gives us silence, then the early emergence of articulate sound, and finally a conflagration of apocalyptic thunders and war-clarions. Silent are all the figures in the illustrations of the frontispiece and title page: slain warriors, anguished maiden (and, above, the preoccupied—yet also the alert—reading public);[7] the mother and children who seem to have been, but are not now, weeping; the chained angel in the broken wall, his face buried; the dismounted cannon and broken sword in the foreground, the brokenness suggesting an irreversible silence (though later we shall see the sword reforged). Utterance begins in the Preludium, but first (in the text) in the silence of dark air stands "dumb" the dark virgin of nature: "for never from her iron tongue could voice or sound arise." (In the illustration the first implied sound is the wailing of Eve over the chained Orc: see identifications later on) Then, as "an eagle *screaming*," a lion *raging*, or whale or serpent, the hairy youth *howls* his joy. "Silent as despairing love" (A2), he *rends his chains*, seizes the womb. Then *bursts* the virgin *cry*—the birth of articulate desire, a "first-born smile." Fire and frost mingle in the "*howling* pains" of a Behmenesque Genesis.[8]

Then in the center of the first page of "A Prophecy" is pictured a trumpet from which are blown flames undoubtedly ear-piercing as well as, according to the text, soul-piercing—indicative of the music to come, which is chiefly of flames and terrible blasts of wind and strong speeches. Here are the opening lines (with emphasis added):

The Guardian Prince of Albion *burns* in his nightly tent.
Sullen fires across the Atlantic *glow* to America's shore:
Piercing the souls of warlike men, who rise in *silent* night.
Washington, Franklin Paine & Warren, Gates, Hancock & Green:
Meet on the coast *glowing with blood* from Albions *fiery* Prince.

7. Clouds separate these two readers, and four attendant spirits, from the work itself. The alert female is reading properly; her position echoes that of Michelangelo's Delphic sibyl, as Janet Warner notes, and her feet and her attendant's fingers point to "PROPHECY." The male's reading requires redirecting.

8. * * * I am thinking of such embracings as the following from ch. 3, "Concerning the Birth of Love," Jacob Behmen, *Works*, London, 1763, vol. II: "And so when the first desire . . . is *filled* with Glance of the Light, then all the Essences (which have *laid hold* on the Light) stand in the first desiring will, and the will thereby becometh *triumphant*, and full of joy, that the child of Light is generated in it . . . and the Joy (*viz.* the source of the Fire) flieth upward, and the Center retaineth it. . . . one form embraceth the other. . . . the sourness retaineth its fierce might . . . in the sharpness of the Love; but . . . is very soft; and . . . maketh voices, tunes and sounds . . . and with the breaking through of the source, they *feel* one another" and so on. (Italics in original.)

Out of this pierced silence Washington speaks. When his "strong voice" ceases, a terrible blast sweeps over the heaving sea, and the eastern cloud curtains part, to reveal the Prince (over England) in his dragon form "clashing his scales." Whereupon arises in demon form the giant Orc of independence with a voice whose "thunders" shake the temple. Heard by a sympathetic ear, however, these thunders are a sweet and lusty hymn of resurrection: "The morning comes, the night decays, the . . . bones of death . . . breathing! awakening! / Spring like redeemed captives . . ." (plate 6).

Note that our imagination must have two ears as well as two eyes. To the Prince of Albion, rebellion is a horrid spectre with voice of thunder. To "coarse-clad honesty" it is "the soul of sweet delight" singing of "a fresher morning." The page is Blake's rendition of the Declaration of Independence; after "darkness and . . . sighing" the "inchained soul" and "his wife and children" (remember the frontispiece) burst into laughter and song, and their song is that the Sun "has left his blackness" and the "fair Moon rejoices" and those roarers "the Lion & Wolf shall cease." It is this sort of "duality in union" in Blake which Mrs. Bodkin approves of as "harmonized clash."[9]

An interchange of loud challenges between Orc and Albion's Prince—or Angel, for George III has modulated to a higher spiritual form—ends in a climactic chant of escalation delivered by the Angel (plate 9). Structurally this twenty-seven-line chant opens and closes with a two-line refrain:

Sound! sound! my loud war-trumpets & alarm my Thirteen Angels!
Loud howls the eternal Wolf! the eternal Lion lashes his tail!

The first of these lines is also repeated internally twice, making cadences at the thirteenth and twenty-first lines of this trumpet voluntary; musically as well as pictorially the page is organized as a unit.

Uttering these lines, the Angel-Prince is acting as the magician or conductor of an orchestral whirlwind of war. "Thus wept the Angel voice," we are told in a kind of stage direction, "& as he wept the terrible blasts / Of trumpets blew a loud alarm." Even the answering silence is described in orchestral terms:

> No trumpets answer; no reply of clarions or of fifes,
> Silent the Colonies remain. . . .

In the remaining pages of text, trumpeting and challenging give way to action. The fires "roaring fierce" are so often given as sound effects (and remember the flaming trumpet of the first page of "A Prophecy") that even where sound is not specified it is connoted. The fires and deep rolling thunder become less and less musical, however, and more and more evidently the fire and thunder of

9. Maude Bodkin, *Archetypal Patterns in Poetry*, London, 1934, 317.

incendiary cannonades. In the final page (plate 16) the fire is said to rage so high it melts the heavens, rousing the old man Urizen (the Prince's highest spiritual form) who damps the flames and noise with "icy magazines" of "stored snows"; and for "twelve years" the sound is of his "Weeping in dismal howlings" (the phrase repeated as a refrain). Barlow's focus on the December hailstorm which prevented the revolutionists' capture of Quebec evidently prompted these "snows poured forth, and . . . icy magazines"; perhaps we may see Niagara Falls at the right edge of the plate—see, not hear, because the bottom of the falls is not represented. Yet the reversion to silence is incomplete and temporary. In the final eight lines "shudderings" are shaking thrones and there is a crackling (though so sharp a word is not used) of "fierce flames . . . round the heavens, & round the abodes of men."

Let us now consider what we are shown and what we are told to visualize. Working as a painter, Blake begins not on a fresh canvas but on one filled with a vision he does *not* want. The scene pictured in the frontispiece[1] and on the title page[2] is taken, we discover, from his early painting, exhibited at the end of the American War: *A Breach in a City the Morning after the Battle.* We shall find out later whose shell the wall is; Orc placed in the broken wall is stopping a gap or has made a breach, but is manacled; he represents the strong governed by the weak.[3] We must understand that in Blake's view the Revolutionary War was sad not only because of the bloodshed and possibly some continuing impairment of liberty in America but also because it ended with tyranny still enthroned in Britain and the rest of Europe; at the end of the Prophecy it is Orc's chains that melt as thrones totter.[4]

But just as, musically, Blake starts with a long silence; so pictorially he starts with a static tableau before moving into the dynamic vision. In this sad scene of the frontispiece and title page, motion is still, life is at its low ebb; the warriors are horizontal, the women exhausted with weeping, the sword broken, the cannon dismounted; the Titan is chained by his wrists to the horizontal stone. Below the heavens, where hope springs, there is no motion except (in the title page) the slanting rain or sleet; no vegetation, except that imitated

1. *America* i, p. 105. [*Editors.*]
2. See color plate 15. [*Editors.*]
3. See *Blake: Prophet*, p. 75. On the three extant versions of *A Breach* see *Romantic Art in Britain,* ed. Frederick Cummings and Allen Staley, Philadelphia, 1968, 159–160. In the version called *War* and inscribed "Inv WB 1805" the Orc figure, wingless but the same naked, curly-headed youth with face buried, is added on top of the heap of bodies in the breach; the wings of the *America* title page remain on the eagle. Reproduced in Mark Schorer, *William Blake: The Politics of Vision*, New York, 1946, opp. 254.
4. John E. Grant: This is not literally the imagery Blake uses, however, but the melting of the "bolts and hinges" of the gates of the "law-built heaven." When the book swings back again to the start, we see (in the frontispiece) that the manacles are on Orc while the *gate* has been melted or blown up.

in the stone. There is silence also in the absence of text. This is not the "single visualizable picture" Blake wants us to *see* but one that is to be erased or seen through or burnt away by the dynamic vision of the Prophecy itself, announced by the flaming trumpet on its first page. Yet he does not step at once from death to life, from stone to flame, from horizontal to spiral. He supplies first the two transitional pages of the Preludium, in which silence is broken by the very fact of the introduction of text (beneath the design at first, then above it) and by various *rehearsals* of the moment of revolutionary birth. In the text a "silent" youth suddenly, as "an eagle screaming," seizes a "dumb" (and "shadowy") female, who utters the virgin cry of articulate desire, a "first-born smile," and so on. In the pictures we are shown first that the chained Promethean lies in a middle state between the cave dweller and the man standing free.

This first page of the Preludium[5] is a progressive cartoon, to be read clockwise; and then counterclockwise. Forgetting the headless worm (of six coils: sixty winters?), which is there at the start and finish of the journey only if you are committed to corporeality and intellectual death, man is, at his lowest *living* stage, the self-clutching cave dweller in the dark, though he can sit up and look about even there, and next a metamorphosing root-shoot rising to air and light. Reaching the surface, he is (1) horizontal with his eyes shut, as the title-page warrior, i.e., dead or mentally asleep, or (2) able to sit up (the Titan in the wall) but still self-clutching, eyes buried despite demonic-angelic wings, or (3) chained flat, cruciform, but with open eyes looking straight up, as in Preludium 1.[6] The picture leaps ahead to upstanding man, and woman, already Adam and Eve, *turning about*, looking backward. They are compelled to, hearing the youth's cry, seeing him crucified; yet this dangerous retrospection is apt to reverse the progression. This plate traps hope, risen from the worm, and sends it back to the worm. Even the almost leafless tree droops.

On the second Preludium page,[7] however, we are shown dynamic growing things reaching up from the earth though rooted in it—a vine shooting up taller than Adam, a sprout of wheat, hopeful metamorphoses upward in the dynamic scale, and between them chainless man crouching in a furrow, ready to spring up—a stage skipped in the first page, the good news rehearsed and announced by the youthful female on the title page. Blake has reversed the direction again, forward, and turned the angle of our vision. Seeing this burgeoning phase to be *where we are now*, we know we are out of the trap, are looking and springing up free of death—even while, in the

5. *America* 1. [*Editors.*]

6. In a pen and watercolor variant at the Tate there is horror in Orc's face: the vultures are descending just above the picture. (In Martin Butlin's Tate Gallery *William Blake*, London, 1966, pl. 5.)

7. *America* 2. [*Editors.*]

words above our eye as we crouch to spring, the virgin pathetically fearful, in joy and pain of giving birth, imagines with Sophoclean irony: "This is eternal death: and this the torment long foretold." Consider the interaction: while the text rehearses struggle and outcry and change, the pictures subdue these to the potential mode yet prepare the *release* of potentials.

A grace note of yellow light behind the crouching Orc (in copy M at least)[8] calls attention to the rising-sun position of his head against the curve of the earth, and on the next page[9] we see him aloft, soaring free of the trap—yet dangling chains. How reassuring this token: he did not bypass that stage but broke through it. In this figure the manacled Orc of the frontispiece is freed, the earth-chained crucified slave of plate 1 is risen. We have the central prophecy of the poem—that tyranny is not eternal, that freedom is worth a second try—even as we reach "A Prophecy," the very lettering of which is vibrant with flight and exuberance and fruition.

Everything Blake's mind touches grows to his purpose. Even his title lettering heralds the progression from geometry to vitality. "AMERICA" on the title page is square, static, carved in stone; "*PROPHECY*" below it begins a forward tilt and takes color. Then "*Preludium*" introduces the more curved, vital lines of italic lower case with a swash capital.[1] Finally, "A *PROPHECY*" is all swash, flowing, swirling, fruitful, flowering, with leaves and lilies and ripe heads of wheat.

And only now, in the Prophecy itself, we begin to focus on the central dynamic and apocalyptic picture of the drama. The stage areas of it are indicated in the opening lines: on the right side, Albion's cliffs, where the Prince burns in his nightly tent; on the left side, the coast of America, where Washington, Franklin, Paine, and others rise and meet and stand. The two coasts are linked by fire *or* blood "glowing" across the Atlantic. The Atlantic itself fills the center of the area; Orc is born there; and we can see from its deeps to the zenith—and beyond, for we are told that "above all heavens" resides Urizen, old Nobodaddy aloft.

Notice the link of the coasts by blood *or* fire: we need twofold vision to see that the same relationship can be vital or destructive. Words can give the twofold vision in one image: the Americans "Meet on the coast glowing with blood from Albions fiery Prince." And in one picture we can see flames as tendrils—or tendrils as flames.

8. In Copy E, reproduced on p. 109, the light is not shown. [*Editors.*]

9. Not included in this edition. [*Editors.*]

1. Copy M (used for the Blake Trust facsimile) is not representative; by the time of its printing the separate slip of copper with the word "Preludium" was lost; adding the word by brush, Blake reverted to the simpler italic capitals of the title page. [Copy E, p. 107, does show this contrast.—*Editors.*]

In the fourteen pages of the Prophecy, the main body of the work, the actions and persons of the American War and Revolution, interpreted as Armageddon and Apocalypse, are arranged choreographically on this world stage into a single Judgment Day picture—with God at the top above several cloud layers of angel-filled heavens, and the Atlantic deeps at the bottom, whence God's mocking adversary arises, mocking his stance, defying repression with naked energy. On the eastern side are Tory angels ascending and circling above Albion's cliffs, led by George the Third in his dragon form; on the western are rebel angels, led by the Angel of Boston, descending to assist the warlike patriots standing on the American shore.

For twelve of the fourteen pages the jealous wrath from Albion hurtles upon America fires, chains, insults, and a bacteriological attack of forty million of Albion's angels armed with disease. The stern Americans *stand* unconsumed, the standing representing the unity of their rushing together. In the last two pages the whirlwind recoils upon Albion and inflames Bristol and London and unhinges the gates of the senses throughout Europe.[2]

This is Blake's dynamic "single" visualizable picture—of shifting multiple perspectives. Reaction makes more noise, smoke, and mileage, but freedom in two hours makes more progress. On the last page (plate 16) the silent, static image of the "Morning after the Battle" threatens to reassert itself as the tyrant god Urizen pours down ice and snow to reduce the rebel Orc to his Atlantic deeps, and the picture subdues to quiet: Niagara Falls as hair. We think again of the rain or sleet of the title page. Yet the work concludes with a reassertion of the main image of the conflagration of the old heaven and earth.

* * *

To return to the central picture, in three further illustrations we are given glimpses of the Atlantic. Urizen in his clouds (plate 8), but with ocean waves beneath, confronts Orc on the waves, which appear as flames (plate 10). In plate 13[3] we see on the watery shore the female in Promethean state and the male sunk to sea bottom. Blake is here using his stage center for the physical-mental horror of war. All the other pictured "visionary forms" are either metaphors of textual detail not in the idiom of the main picture,

2. Here, as in *A Song of Liberty,* the poet conflates the whole revolutionary era of the tottering of thrones in "France Spain & Italy" because people defeated redcoats in America. To quote *A* 14, *MHH* 12, *PA* 18, and *A* 14–15: the "wrath" of their unity is "the voice of God," i.e., of honest men, the "Public Indignation of Men of Sense in all Professions"—"citizens . . . mariners . . . scribe . . . builder"—against war and obedience to tyranny; its infectious civic fire inspires the citizens of Albion to *stand* also, naked of "their hammered mail." * * *

3. The illustration on plate 13 is not included in this edition. [*Editors.*]

not located on its stage, or constitute emblems of persons and events quite outside the poem we have been perceiving.

By the text, too, we are supplied only a few graphic elements of the single picture, plus a wealth of metaphorical and contrary or ambivalent visionary forms to fill the canvas: so that we are able to see this single dynamic vision in motion and inside out or upside down. For example, in the view that accepts Urizen as a God above all heavens in thunders wrapped, the place of Orc is that of Satan in the abyss. But in the eyes of democrats Urizen is a god of snow and ice and is really just an arbitrary shell hardening on the outer surface of mundane life; Orc is not Satan but Christ in the fearful symmetry of his Second Coming (for this was Armageddon); and the Atlantic where he appears is not an abyss but a mountain rising above the abyss of nonentity. In this view Albion and America are not separated by a great gulf but are parts of the base of the Atlantic Mountains. There are many indications that the apparently central image of continents *divided* by an Atlantic deep is a false or temporary image. A more "eternal" image is of Atlantean hills, seen as the One Earth of true human geography: a picture of "vast shady hills between America & Albions shore . . . from [whose] bright summits you may pass to the Golden world" (plate 10). It is "Here on their magic seats" that "the thirteen Angels" sit by right, before the divisive behavior of Albion's Prince forces them to come down and side with "warlike men." * * *

But finally the central vision is dynamic because *it is going to change*, to *hatch* into a vision of Eternity beyond the flames which are referred to as giving "heat but not light." Observe that the image is global, not in the usual sense but as the inside of a mundane egg framed by the orbed concave sky and the concave deeps of the sea. Blake's single (but twofold) visualizable picture has a third "fold"—that it can be seen as the seed or egg or embryo of a change beyond the change. Orc is born in fire "o'er the Atlantic Sea" (plate 4), but observe that this world of bloody fire is embryonic: "enrag'd the Zenith grew, / As human blood shooting its veins all round the orbed heaven." What look like clouds rising from burning towns, Barlow's Falmouth, Charlestown, Bristol, Groton, Fairfield, Kingston, [New] York, and Norfolk, are really "vast wheels of blood," the veins of a vast embryo.

As the Preludium hinted, this process cannot stop short of a further and more complete metamorphosis. A further or fourfold vision must follow the breaking of the Urizenic shell or, in a cognate image, the throwing down of the spears of the old cold heavens. A new humanity, a new human form of society, is the vision Blake wants us to see *beyond* the revolutionary drama presented on this split stage of the American and British shores of the Atlantic.

Some of the pictured and verbal images of the Prophecy are there to suggest the third or generative view of the central picture, while some are glimpses of the picture beyond the Revolution. The children sleeping with a sheep (plate 7)[4] are under a tree of paradise in which sit recognizable birds of paradise.

In other words, when we wind up the thread of the illuminated poem into the golden ball of a single, dynamic, visualizable orb, we are ready to enter into new expanses, through heaven's gate, built in Jerusalem's wall—or, in this instance, through the "breach in the city . . . after the battle." It may be, as Frye says, that Blake "hardly seems to have noticed that he had perfected a radically new form of mixed art." He hardly seems to have cared, any more than he cared to question a window concerning his sight. It mattered little to him whether picture penetrated poem or poem penetrated picture, if only their human, apocalyptic meaning would penetrate our hearts and minds.

A Note on the "Orc Cycle"

As history moved on, the Orc that appeared "in the vineyards of red France" (Europe 15:2) became Napoleon; by 1804 Blake, intead of humming "ça ira," was arguing that "Resistance & war is the Tyrants gain," that the "iron hand" which "crushed the Tyrants head . . . became a Tyrant in his stead" (*The Grey Monk*). Orc *became* (not the specious Urizenic dragon but) the serpent that Urizen believed him to be. This suggests a very different kind of progression: slave-rebel-tyrant, not to be equated with the cycle in *America* and the *Marriage* of restraint-freedom-restraint-freedom, i.e., slave-rebel-slave-rebel. Northrop Frye wrote a brilliant mythopoeic chapter on the "Orc cycle," and the term is now so current that some people father it upon Blake (Frye, *Symmetry*, ch. 7, esp. pp. 206ff.). Frye ranges through the Lambeth works but with his focus on the *America* pattern. Recent criticism often focuses on the Napoleonic cycle, implying the corruption of revolutionary energy (equated with "power") into tyrannic cruelty. To call this the "Orc cycle" and then read that kind of corruption into *America* is to wander far astray.

The *prophetic* importance of the distinction makes it worth laboring. The cycle of history prophetically examined in *America* and *Europe* is not that of rebellion-vengeance-tyranny; it is of enslavement-liberation-reenslavement, the prophet's concern being how to escape the reenslavement. * * *

4. See color plate 16 of this edition. [*Editors.*]

HAROLD BLOOM

[On *Milton*]†

The title plate of *Milton* shows the poet striding into the flames of creative desire, right hand and right foot forward. Beneath is the legend "To Justify the Ways of God to Men," the twenty-sixth line of *Paradise Lost*. So *Milton*, like *Paradise Lost* and the Book of Job, is intended as a theodicy, a treatment of the problem of evil. Originally in twelve books, like *Paradise Lost*, Milton was concentrated by Blake in only two books, with the result that the poem may be overorganized.

Milton begins with the famous dedicatory hymn "And did those feet in ancient time," in which Blake sees himself as inheriting the Miltonic chariot of fire, the prophetic vehicle that first appears in Ezekiel's vision. Beneath the lyric is the outcry of Moses against Joshua: "Would to God that all the Lord's people were prophets."

John Milton died in 1674. One hundred years later the young Blake began to write the later poems in *Poetical Sketches*, and the prophetic Protestant and radical vision of Milton revived in English poetry. What moved Milton to descend again, to incarnate himself once more in an English poet?

Say first! what mov'd Milton, who walk'd about in Eternity
One hundred years, pond'ring the intricate mazes of Providence
Unhappy tho' in heav'n, he obey'd he murmur'd not; he was silent
Viewing his Sixfold Emanation scatter'd thro' the deep
In torment! To go into the deep her to redeem & himself perish?
What cause at length mov'd Milton to this unexampled deed?[1]

For one hundred years Milton has continued in error, "pond'ring the intricate mazes of Providence," even as his fallen angels sat in Hell.

and reason'd High
Of Providence, Foreknowledge, Will, and Fate,
Fixt Fate, free will, foreknowledge absolute,
And found no end, in wand'ring mazes lost.[2]

Like them, Milton has been Urizenic, but his imagination does not let him rest in that moralistic labyrinth. His Sixfold Emanation, his three wives and three daughters, is still separated from him, and so he realizes that he must perish as a selfhood to redeem it (which he had not done in his poetry). The direct cause of Milton's

† From Harold Bloom, *The Visionary Company*, 2nd ed. (Ithaca: Cornell University Press, 1971), pp. 97–99, 102–8.

1. *Milton* 2:16–31. [*Editors.*]

2. *Paradise Lost* II, 558–61. [*Editors.*]

resolve is a "Bard's Song" that he hears in Eternity. This Song, which continues throngh Plate 11, is both an extraordinary transformation of a vital part of Blake's biography and a theory of psychological types.

* * *

When the Bard ends his Song, many in Heaven condemn it, saying: "Pity and Love are too venerable for the imputation of Guilt." But Milton has heard enough. The necessity for a new Rintrah is clear to him, and the behavior of Leutha suggests that he has undervalued the female capacity for self-sacrifice, and was wrong therefore to abandon his Emanation in the deep. He states the purpose of his descent:

> I will go down to self annihilation and eternal death,
> Lest the Last Judgment come & find me unannihilate
> And I be seiz'd & giv'n into the hands of my own Selfhood.
> The Lamb of God is seen thro' mists & shadows, hov'ring
> Over the sepulchers in clouds of Jehovah & winds of Elohim
> A disk of blood, distant; & heav'ns & earth's roll dark between
> What do I here before the Judgment? without my Emanation?
> With the daughters of memory, & not with the daughters of
> inspiration?
> I in my Selfhood am that Satan: I am that Evil One!
> He is my Spectre! in my obedience to loose him from my Hells
> To claim the Hells, my Furnaces, I go to Eternal Death.[3]

In this brilliant passage Milton identifies himself with his own Satan, whom he thrust into Hell in *Paradise Lost*. Now, taking "off the robe of the promise" and ungirding himself "from the oath of God," Milton throws off the bondage of Urizenic religion and goes naked to his Hells of Eternal Death, to remake himself there into the image of Eternal Life. Heaven and Hell are to be married together, and the fires of wrath are to be the furnaces of Los, in which the human is shaped.

Milton leaves Eternity and takes on his mortal Shadow as his own again. His vision becomes that of fallen man once more as he enters a vortex, like the Mental Traveller of Blake's ballad, and so again accepts nature as his wide womb. He sees Albion in a sleep of death upon his rock, and then falls further, into the "Sea of Time & Space":

> Then first I saw him in the Zenith as a falling star,
> Descending perpendicular, swift as the swallow or swift;
> And on my left foot falling on the tarsus, enter'd there;
> But from my left foot a black cloud redounding spread
> over Europe.[4]

3. *Milton* 14:21–32. [*Editors.*]

4. *Milton* 15:47–50. [*Editors.*]

The return of Milton is signaled by the portent of a falling star, and by a cloud of prophetic menace over Europe. Milton seeks his Sixfold Emanation, which is divided in the dark Ulro, but his coming frightens not only Urizen but Los as well, who believes he is the fallen star Satan.

The crucial contest for the incarnated Milton is with Urizen, who meets the poet in a desperate wrestling match on the shores of a river of error, the Arnon. The story of wrestling Jacob finds its parody in this struggle:

> Silent they met, and silent strove among the streams, of Arnon
> Even to Mahanaim, when with cold hand Urizen stoop'd down
> And took up water from the river Jordan: pouring on
> To Milton's brain the icy fluid from his broad cold palm.
> But Milton took the red clay of Succoth, moulding it with care
> Between his palms; and filling up the furrows of many years
> Beginning at the feet of Urizen, and on the bones
> Creating new flesh on the Demon cold, and building him,
> As with new clay a Human form in the Valley of Beth Peor.[5]

Urizen is like Jehovah at Peniel, but Milton is more than a Jacob desiring a blessing. The Valley of Beth Peor is the burial ground of Moses in the land of Moab, and to build a Human form there is to replace the grave of the moral law of Urizen by a new Adam, a man of "red clay," associated with the harvest festival of booths, in which four plants represent the four classes of men who unite as one man in the cooperation of worship. Milton is renovating Urizen and defying his icy intellectual baptism even as he does so.

As Milton works on in this heroic contest, Albion's sleeping Humanity begins to turn upon his couch. Los, in despair at Milton's descent until now, remembers an old prophecy:

> That Milton of the Land of Albion should up ascend
> Forwards from Ulro from the Vale of Felpham; and set free
> Orc from his Chain of Jealousy.[6]

In the spirit of this prophecy, a great illumination comes to Blake:

> But Milton entering my Foot; I saw in the nether
> Regions of the Imagination; also all men on Earth,
> And all in Heaven, saw in the nether regions of the Imagination
> In Ulro beneath Beulah, the vast breach of Milton's descent.
> But I knew not that it was Milton, for man cannot know
> What passes in his members till periods of Space & Time
> Reveal the secrets of Eternity: for more extensive
> Than any other earthly things, are Man's earthly lineaments.

5. *Milton* 19:6–14. [*Editors.*]

6. *Milton* 20:59–61. [*Editors.*]

And all this Vegetable World appear'd on my left Foot,
As a bright sandal form'd immortal of precious stones & gold:
I stooped down & bound it on to walk forward thro' Eternity.[7]

This giant metaphor can best be read together with the other moment of vision soon after, when Los joins himself to Milton and Blake:

While Los heard indistinct in fear, what time I bound my sandals
On; to walk forward thro' Eternity, Los descended to me:
And Los behind me stood; a terrible flaming Sun: just close
Behind my back; I turned round in terror, and behold,
Los stood in that fierce glowing fire; & he also stoop'd down
And bound my sandals on in Udan-Adan; trembling I stood
Exceedingly with fear and terror, standing in the Vale
Of Lambeth: but he kissed me and wish'd me health
And I became One Man with him, arising in my strength:
'Twas too late now to recede. Los had enter'd into my soul:
His terrors now possess'd me whole; I arose in fury & strength.[8]

Both these passages are full-scale incarnations of the Poetical Character, in the tradition of Collins' *Ode*. Udan-Adan, the lake of the indefinite, symbolizes the Ulro, while the bright sandal of the Vegetable World represents Generation. Milton entering into Blake redeems Blake from Generation; Los's similar entering into him redeems him from Ulro. The errors of Experience and of Self-hood leave Blake, and he is free to write of the re-entry into Beulah which will precede the apocalyptic thrust into Eden in *Jerusalem*.

The agent of Milton's restoration into Beulah is Ololon, the Emanation who is the goal of his quest. She is already in Eden as "a sweet River of milk & liquid pearl," but she too descends, to seek her poet even as he seeks her.

The rest of Book I describes the world of Blake's own day, which is overripe for apocalypse, like the world of Night VIII of *The Four Zoas*. The function of Milton-Blake-Los is to achieve a vision of this world which is the transcending contrary of its vision of itself.

Book II begins with Blake's fullest account of Beulah as the first state into which Ololon descends. As this is the world of Thel, the exquisite rhetoric of Innocence returns:

First e'er the morning breaks joy opens in the flowery bosoms
Joy even to tears, which the Sun rising dries; first the Wild Thyme
And Meadow-sweet downy & soft, waving among the reeds
Light springing on air, lead the sweet Dance: they wake
The Honeysuckle sleeping on the Oak: the flaunting beauty
Revels along upon the wind; the Whitethorn lovely May
Opens her many lovely eyes: listening the Rose still sleeps

7. *Milton* 21:4–14. [*Editors.*]

8. *Milton* 22:4–14. [*Editors.*]

None dare to wake her: soon she bursts her crimson curtain'd bed
And comes forth in the majesty of beauty; every Flower:
The Pink, the Jessamine, the Wall-flower, the Carnation
The Jonquil, the mild Lilly opes her heavens! every Tree
And Flower & Herb soon fill the air with an innumerable Dance
Yet all in order sweet & lovely, Men are sick with Love!
Such is a Vision of the lamentation of Beulah over Ololon.[9]

Beulah is sexual, Eden human; the first is the emanation of the second. A passage like the one above is technically interesting as a vision of Beulah, but also reminds us that Blake's rejection of nature has nothing to do with any supposed blindness toward the beauty of the natural world. The human form is Blake's index of delight, as it is Wordsworth's, but where Wordsworth found that love of nature led to love of man, Blake feared that love of nature more frequently led to the sacrifice of man on a natural altar.

Yet Ololon's descent is accepted by the inhabitants of Beulah as a sign that the Female Will of nature can "pity & forgive." More than Oothoon, who desired to carry Innocence into Experience but failed for want of an imaginative male will, Ololon is the final redemption of poor Thel. From Beulah Thel descended, but fled back shrieking. Ololon goes down as multitudes, in a descent into every possible depth, like Asia's descent to the cave of Demogorgon in *Prometheus Unbound*. In a supreme Moment of renovation, "when the morning odours rise abroad / And first from the Wild Thyme," and to the music of a Lark, Ololon

> Appear'd: a Virgin of twelve years nor time nor space was
> To the perception of the Virgin Ololon but as the
> Flash of lightning but more quick the Virgin in my Garden
> Before my Cottage stood.[1]

With Blake observing, Milton and Ololon confront one another in the garden at Felpham. Milton takes the lead in the mutual purgation by annihilating his negating Selfhood, the Satan that is within him:

The Negation is the Spectre; the Reasoning Power in Man
This is a false Body: an Incrustation over my Immortal
Spirit; a Selfhood, which must be put off & annihilated alway.
To cleanse the Face of my Spirit by Self-examination,
To bathe in the Waters of Life; to wash off the Not Human
I come in Self-annihilation & the grandeur of Inspiration
To cast off Rational Demonstration by Faith in the Saviour
To cast off the rotten rags of Memory by Inspiration
To cast off Bacon, Locke & Newton from Albion's covering
To take off his filthy garments, & clothe him with Imagination
To cast aside from Poetry, all that is not Inspiration

9. *Milton* 31:50–63. [*Editors.*]

1. *Milton* 36:17–20. [*Editors.*]

That it no longer shall dare to mock with the aspersion of Madness
Cast on the Inspired by the tame high finisher of paltry Blots,
Indefinite, or paltry Rhymes; or paltry Harmonies.
Who creeps into State Government like a catterpiller to destroy
To cast off the idiot Questioner who is always questioning,
But never capable of answering.[2]

When Milton is done with this declaration, everything that hides the Human Lineaments has been purged away with fire. The Virgin Ololon, so long as she remains virgin, cannot understand Milton, and replies in despair:

> Altho' our Human Power can sustain the severe contentions
> Of Friendship, our Sexual cannot: but flies into the Ulro.
> Hence arose all our terrors in Eternity! & now remembrance
> Returns upon us! Are we Contraries O Milton, Thou & I
> O Immortal! how were we led to War the Wars of Death
> Is this the Void Outside of Existence, which if enter'd into
> Becomes a Womb? & is this the Death Couch of Albion
> Thou goest to Eternal Death & all must go with thee.[3]

The image of the vortex, which becomes nature's wide womb, dominates these lines, that are the last the separate Female Will, which is Ololon's virginity, ever speaks. With a shriek, the Shadow of Ololon separates from her and leaves her as the poet's bride. The forty-first plate, one of Blake's finest, shows the redeemed Milton tenderly comforting the repentant Ololon.[4] The Four Zoas appear in Blake's Vale of Felpham to sound the four trumpets that herald apocalypse:

> Terror struck in the Vale I stood at that immortal sound
> My bones trembled. I fell outstretch'd upon the path
> A moment, & my Soul return'd into its mortal state
> To Resurrection & Judgment in the Vegetable Body
> And my sweet Shadow of Delight stood trembling by my side[5]

With his wife Catherine by his side, and Milton and Ololon vanished, Blake is reminded of his vision's reality by the messengers of Los, the Lark's trill, and the odor of the Wild Thyme:

Immediately the Lark mounted with a loud trill from Felpham's Vale
And the Wild Thyme from Wimbleton's green & impurpled Hills
And Los & Enitharmon rose over the Hills of Surrey
Their clouds roll over London with a south wind, soft Oothoon
Pants in the Vales of Lambeth weeping o'er her Human Harvest
Los listens to the Cry of the Poor Man: his Cloud
Over London in volume terrific, low bended in anger.[6]

2. *Milton* 40:34–41:13. [*Editors.*]
3. *Milton* 41:32–42:2. [*Editors.*]
4. The sex of the figure being supported is indeterminate; commentators who think the figure being supported is male interpret Milton's action differently. [*Editors.*]
5. *Milton* 42:24–28. [*Editors.*]
6. *Milton* 42:29–35. [*Editors.*]

Oothoon, who received so little in the *Visions*, now gathers her Human Harvest. Los the prophet returns to the tradition of social justice, the line of Amos, as the Poor Man's cry comes up from the streets of the London of *Songs of Experience*. Rintrah and Palamabron, Reprobate and Redeemed, prophet of Wrath and artist of Pity, can return to their cultivation of a Human Harvest, as the poem comes to its conclusion with an image of immediate potentiality:

Rintrah & Palamabron view the Human Harvest beneath
Their Wine-presses & Barns stand open; the Ovens are prepar'd
The Waggons ready: terrific Lions & Tygers sport & play
All Animals upon the Earth, are prepar'd in all their strength

To go forth to the Great Harvest & Vintage of the Nations[7]

Milton is Blake's last *Song of Innocence*, and is incomplete without its matching contrary. To go from *Milton* to *Jerusalem* is to pass from the Divine Image to the Human Abstract, but the passage is necessary if all Human Forms are to be identified, and if we are to converse "with Eternal Realities as they Exist in the Human Imagination."

E. J. ROSE

The Symbolism of the Opened Center and Poetic Theory in Blake's *Jerusalem*†

Early in *The Four Zoas*, Blake describes metaphorically the way in which eternal time becomes historical time and, conversely, the way in which historical time becomes eternal. It is an especially important metaphor in Blake's work because it explains a great deal about the symbolic context of *Jerusalem*. It explains also his conception of the moment of poetic inspiration which is all time and which is the "Moment in each Day that Satan cannot find" (M 35:42).

Then Eno, a daughter of Beulah, took a Moment of Time
And drew it out to seven thousand years with much care & affliction

7. *Milton* 42:36–43:1. [*Editors.*]

† From E. J. Rose, "The Symbolism of the Opened Center and Poetic Theory in Blake's *Jerusalem*," *Studies in English Literature* 5 (1965), 587–92; 602–6.

Line references to Blake's works refer to Geoffrey Keynes's edition *The Complete Writings of William Blake* (London and New York, 1974); page references preceded by the letter K ("Keynes") pertain to this edition. The Blake works referred to by letter are *Milton* (*M*), *The Four Zoas* (*FZ*), *Jerusalem* (*J*), *A Vision of the Last Judgment* (*VLJ*), and *The Marriage of Heaven and Hell* (*MHH*).

And many tears, & in every year made windows into Eden.
She also took an atom of space & open'd its centre
Into Infinitude & ornamented it with wondrous art.

(*FZ* 1:222–26)

The "Moment of Time" and the "atom of space" are our world. By drawing out the eternal moment, Eno makes eternal time, the moment, linear. Every year has insights into Eden or imaginative existence, which lies before and beyond yet is parallel to the seven thousand years of fallen creation. Though Eden is outside of historical time, beyond fallen creation, it is, nevertheless, analogous to our world. The seven days of creation are analogous to seven millennia. The millennia are, therefore, the eternal "Moment of Time" or moment of creation made into duration or history from which man is able to see into Eden. By opening the atom of spacc, like an egg, and causing it to expand, like an infinite womb, Eno (an anagram, possibly, for *eon*) makes space out of infinity. The purpose of the following discussion is to suggest some solutions to the several problems in interpretation raised by the patterns of metaphor, symbol, and myth in *Jerusalem* and to show how they are related to Blake's poetic theories.

We have at the end of *Jerusalem* an extended description of the opened center, whereby man perceives that all outside himself is really inside himself. Man is identifiable simultaneously with a globule of blood and the cosmic-man-God. As the sun is in the solar system, the "Globe of Blood" is his heart and each man's heart; his brain and eye (and the eye in the sky, the sun) are each man's brain and eye. By identifying the particular with the universal, Blake's imagery describes oneness as individual form and also as the unity of the cosmos—man as soul and man as solar system. Los's light, his "globe of fire" which is identifiable with the "Globe of Blood," is in each man because it is the light of the imagination within the cosmic man, within Albion's Bosom (*J* 31:3).

The "Allegoric pomp," the "little lovely Allegoric Night" of *Jerusalem* (89:5; 88:31), is sleep without desire or life without desire. It is a nightmare from which there seems to be no waking, and it is the life of the Antichrist, a little allegoric night of pomp and ceremony. "Divine Analogy" in *Jerusalem* (85:7) becomes the means by which the allegorical is reborn as vision. It is the climax of the poem, for Los (like Eno) gives time to space and recreates a *four*-dimensional world whose creations (works of art) preserve the Divine Vision by re-establishing man's existence in "The Eternal Body of man [which] is The Imagination, that is, / God himself / The Divine Body" ("The Laocoön" engraving: K776). Through Divine *analogy* the pomp and ceremony of the little *allegoric* night is reborn or recreated by the imagination of man as the *identity* of the infinite day or moment of creation, eternally present.

Creativity or the imagination, like eternity, is *now*. Eternity is the opposite of the ruling Beast of Revelation (17:8) "that was, and is not, and yet is." The metaphor of temporal existence is the female "Falshood" or female dream which grows and grows till it becomes "a Space & an Allegory around the Winding Worm" (embryo man) (*J* 85:1). In *Jerusalem*, Gwendolen, one of the daughters of Albion, utters a falsehood by hiding the "Deceit" (metaphor or *conceit*) in her left hand, as in the illustration on plate 81. The "Falsehood is prophetic" (*J* 82:20), however, and by placing her left hand which contains the falsehood "Upon her back behind her loins" (*J* 82:21), she ironically begins the allegory that Los is to call "Divine Analogy." This world of space-time is named Canaan by the daughters of Albion (*J* 85:2). The spatial world of fixed temporal existence comes into being and is sustained by analogy. Man is enwombed in time, but his imagination turns the falsehood or "little lovely Allegoric Night" (*J* 88:31) into "Divine Analogy," by giving it "a Time & Revolution" (*J* 85:6). It is the labor of the imagination to open the center of this womb-tomb to eternity, for "the Loins" are "the place of the Last Judgment" (*J* 30:38). In *A Vision of the Last Judgment*, Blake clarifies the relationship of the last judgment to his poetic theories.

> The Last Judgment is an Overwhelming of Bad Art & Science. Mental Things are alone Real; what is call'd Corporeal, Nobody Knows of its Dwelling Place: it is in Fallacy, & its Existence an Imposture. Where is the Existence Out of Mind or Thought? . . . Whenever any Individual Rejects Error & Embraces Truth, a Last Judgment passes upon that Individual.
>
> (*VLJ* p. 95, K617; p. 84, K613)

The opened center is the destruction of the selfhood, the egoistic "white Dot" (*J* 33:29). When a center opens it dilates, expanding into infinity: the "Globe of Blood" contains the *Word* and expands to become the *human form divine*. The "Globe of Blood" is within the womb-tomb of time and space from which it is to be *delivered*. In *Milton* we see "round" Jesus's limbs

> . . . folded as a Gament dipped in blood,
> Written within & without in woven letters, & the Writing
> Is the Divine Revelation in the Litteral expression,
> A Garment of War. I heard it nam'd the Woof of Six Thousand
> Years.
>
> (*M* 42:12–15)

The literal expression and the metaphor are one, written within and without. The garment of the man, the "scarlet robe" (the body) and the "peculiar Light" of "every particular Form" (*J* 54:1) become the Divine Vision or Divine Body. The "Six Thousand Years" is "Divine Analogy," our world made analogous to Eden. Jesus walks forth *into it,* just as Los, the watchman-poet-prophet, walks up and down *in it,* and *it* is Albion. The six thousand years precede the last and seventh millennium or day, the creative moment or still point, when Jesus, Los, and Albion identify as the fourfold man, when the seven days of creation are complete and cease to be analogous to the seven millennia because they are one identity. Historical time, therefore, becomes divine because it has always been analogous to eternal time. In aesthetic terms, allegory becomes vision.

To "enter into Albion's bosom" is to enter "the bosom of death." On the seventh day, Jesus reveals that to put on the "scarlet robe" is the first act in casting it off. The "scarlet robe" is the natural body, the natural man. The real man, the imagination, is the spiritual body and it is manifested by acts of freedom that fulfill the self, recreate man. On the seventh day, creation is truly complete. The eighth day is forever, for the seven eyes of God, of which Jesus is the seventh, become the "Starry Eight"—the risen Albion, fourfold in time and fourfold in space.

When Albion awakes, he throws himself into the "Furnaces of affliction," which then become "Fountains of Living Waters flowing from the Humanity Divine" (*J* 96:27). Tharmas's chaotic seas of sorrow which mark the openings of *The Four Zoas* and *Jerusalem* become living waters. The forest of affliction burns up in the furnaces of affliction. That which has drowned the spirit of man in despair becomes the baptismal water of his rebirth. The smith (Los) drops the hammered, heated form hissing into the watery bath as the engraver dips his etched outline into the acid bath. The image of the furnace-fountain with its respective primal elements both spouting and dancing, contrary as fire and water are, emphasizes the paradoxical nature of the identity of opposites which the artist has fused. Man becomes himself when he becomes all men without ceasing to be himself.

When in Eternity Man converses with Man, they enter
Into each other's Bosom (which are Universes of delight)
In mutual interchange, and their Emanations meet
Surrounded by their Children; if they embrace & comingle
The Human Four-fold Forms mingle also in thunders of Intellect.
(*J* 88:3–7)

The "swing of my Hammer," Los proclaims, "shall measure the starry round" (*J* 88:2). Man expands infinitely by possessing his own identity through finding himself in the infinity of self. In such a state or experience, man can identify with each *and* the "All" without generalizing himself into non-entity.

The false appropriation of universality, described at great length in *Jerusalem*,[1] is the basis of the selfhood's power—abstraction. Creating separate entities ironically results in non-entity. The world becomes a heap of rocky fragments fallen from eternity. Thus, fallen man generalizes on a mistaken principle. The irony of man's fallen condition is intensified because the selfhood, male and female, then appropriate individuality (sex) in accordance with the nature of abstract categories. This is the rule of Satan who is the God of this world, the "Great Selfhood," the "Reasoning Power," and classification—his method—is a form of death, the result of living in death. Any attempted unity upon fallen principles, therefore, is necessarily hermaphroditic, since it is the yoking of the unlike upon the basis of partial likeness or upon the indefinite doubled. That is to say, two abstract and therefore indefinite or general ideas, no matter how similar they may be, can never produce one concrete, definite, or particular reality which is true unity. Bisexuality or the sexual experience itself is not, therefore, to be identified with the condition of Adam before his rib was made woman. "Without Contraries is no progression," writes Blake in *The Marriage of Heaven and Hell* (3, K 149). In the process of turning Calvinistic terminology on its head by reversing the Elect and the Reprobate, Blake ironically parodies the marriage sacrament: let no man put together what God has put asunder unless he is capable of substituting Divine Vision for his fallen Reasoning Power. In moral terms the products of hermaphroditic or mistaken unity, that is, generalization, are cruelty and law; in aesthetic terms the products are fable and allegory. Both the moral and the aesthetic products make the indefinite and the abstract or general stand for identity. Dealing with non-vital fixities (rocky fragments), law and allegory generalize the grains of sand into trackless arid deserts. The storms of the fallen intellect become dust-laden and eye-blinding siroccos of airy abstractions—the prevailing winds of the wasteland. In not being wholly just, law is cruel; in not being complete vision, allegory distorts.

The consolidation of error, "One Great Satan," is a composite of Deistic natural religion. It is the great hermaphroditic form of the indefinite—the appearance, the cruelty, and the denial of life. Los proclaims the Apocalypse in terms of this consolidation.

* * *

The rebirth or regeneration of fourfold man, of eternal identity, is

1. See especially *J* 90. Blake's criticism of Reynolds (Annotations to Sir Joshua Reynolds's "Discourses"; xcviii; 9; 61; 63 and elsewhere in Keynes, 445–479) outlines his attitude toward "General Knowledge" and the generalizing power. See also "Public Address," page 59 in particular, for another criticism of Reynolds and for Blake's conception of the imagination and his random opinions on painters and artists (in Keynes, 591–603). Cf. *VLJ* 82–84, K 611.

conceived of as the vibration of the One Word continually returning to itself, its origin.[2]

Frye has observed that the only truly effective "course open to the poet in an age of Deism is, first, to visualize the reversibility of time and space, to see the linear sequence of history as a single form; and, second, to see the tradition behind him as a single imaginative unity."[3] The state of the imagination is itself a unity. Los creates the vehicle that preserves every act of man. He makes language. He prepares the means by which the imagination passes from the inside to the outside.

(I call them by their English names: English, the rough basement.
Los built the stubborn structure of the Language, acting against
Albion's melancholy, who must else have been a Dumb despair.)
(*J* 40:58–60)

The imagination is man's expression of himself, hence the eternal forms or "bright Sculptures" in Los's Halls (*J* 16:1–2). The language of the poet preserves time and space for eternity. The "exemplars of Memory and of Intellect" are everpresent archetypal symbols identical with that which they represent.

The conceptual implications of the imagery of Part Three of *Jerusalem* are directed toward an understanding of the Deistic consolidation of error and its relationship to the Female Will of Druid-Judaism. This is further emphasized by the continual opposition of the imagination, Los.

. . . Compell the Reasoner to Demonstrate with unhewn
Demonstrations.
Let the Indefinite be explored, and let every Man be Judged
By his own Works. Let all Indefinites be thrown into
Demonstrations,
To be pounded to dust & melted in the Furnaces of Affliction.
He who would do good to another must do it in Minute
Particulars:
General Good is the plea of the scoundrel, hypocrite & flatterer,

2. The structure of *Jerusalem* is not based upon historical time. I must disagree, therefore, with the view expressed by Karl Kiralis. See his "The Theme and Structure of William Blake's *Jerusalem*" in *The Divine Vision,* ed., V. De Sola Pinto (London, 1957). His essay surveys the most important critiques of Blake's last major poem (141–143), but his own basic point is that *Jerusalem's* structure is based upon the order of the ages of man, as Blake records them in *Jerusalem* 98 : 32–33, "the Three Regions immense / Of Childhood, Manhood & Old Age" (147). (See also, *J* 14.) The structure of Blake's major poetry is always controlled by the imagery associated with the figures of the Zoas (especially in the case of the four parts of *Jerusalem*), and Blake, like other Romantic poets, often reverses the apparent temporal sequences of the fallen world. Following Genesis, Blake begins the day and, also, the history of man at the end of the previous day or prior existence—as in "it was evening and it was morning, one day" and, also, as in the expluslion from Eden. Cf. Asia's song in *Prometheus Unbound*, II.v. 98–110. See my essay, "The Structure of Blake's *Jerusalem*," *Bucknell Review,* XI (1963), 35–54.

3. *Fearful Symmetry* (Princeton, 1947), p. 320. Eno is also *one* spelled backwards. To an engraver the reverse mirror-like perspective is an everyday experience, for he must often conceive and execute in reverse so as to print the design from his plate as he would have others see it.

For Art & Science cannot exist but in minutely organized
Particulars
And not in generalizing Demonstrations of the Rational Power.
The Infinite alone resides in Definite & Determinate Identity;
Establishment of Truth depends on destruction of Falsehood
continually,
On Circumcision, not Virginity, O Reasoners of Albion!
(*J* 55:56–66)[4]

So much for *pure* reason and the *neat* mind, the unviolated, snowy-white skull of rational man.

The living are plowed in with the dead (*J* 57:14), since "no one can consummate Female bliss in Los's World without / Becoming a Generated Mortal, a Vegetating Death" (*J* 69:30–1). The smith must have crude material on which to work; he "ladles the Ore" he lifts, "pouring it into the clay ground prepar'd with art" (*J* 11:4). Thus,

. . . the Infernal Veil grows in the disobedient Female,
Which Jesus rends & the whole Druid Law removes away
From the Inner Sanctuary, a False Holiness hid within the Center.
For the Sanctuary of Eden is in the Camp, in the Outline,
In the Circumference, & every Minute Particular is Holy:
Embraces are Cominglings from the Head even to the Feet,
And not a pompous High Priest entering by a Secret Place.
(*J* 69:38–44)

Again, Blake juxtaposes and contrasts the secretive, rationalistic white-dot-center with the *revealed*, outline-circumference, the general with the particular. Also juxtaposed is the pompous, selfish, and secretive action of the jealous Elect with the open, unmysterious and complete empathy of the Redeemed. The irony of the *dot* that is indefinite and the *outline* that is definite is characteristically emphasized. The allusions to the Temple of Jerusalem, the curtained Ark, and the priesthood, accompanied by the sexual symbolism, effect a twofold summary of the symbolism of female error throughout *Jerusalem*. The geometric images epitomize the reversals of perspective.

What is Above is Within, for every-thing in Eternity is translucent:
The Circumference is Within, Without is formed the Selfish
Center,
And the Circumference still expands going forward to Eternity,
And the Center has Eternal States . . .
(*J* 71:6–9)

4. Cf. *J* 5:56–60 in Part One where Blake describes the struggle between the artist of the definite (Los, the imagination) and the philosopher of the abstract (the Spectre, the reasoning power).

. . . all within is open'd into the deeps
of Eututhon Benython,
A dark and unknown night, indefinite,
unmeasurable, without end,
Abstract Philosophy warring in enmity
against Imagination
(Which is the Divine Body of the Lord
Jesus, blessed for ever),
And there Jerusalem wanders with Vala
upon the mountains.

All that is said of the demonic fallen world is accompanied by a description of the creative state, the artist's role and the nature of art, for fallen perception is the Divine Vision upside-down and inside-out.

In searching out the minute particulars within Albion, Los (the artist or creative state) records all so that nothing will be lost.

> For Los in Six Thousand Years walks up & down continually
> That not one Moment of Time be lost, & every revolution
> Of Space he makes permanent . . .
>
> (*J* 75:7–9)[5]

From *Milton* we know that "A Moment equals a pulsation of the artery" (*M* 28:47), and that

> Every Time less than a pulsation of the artery
> Is equal in its period & value to Six Thousand Years,
> For in this Period the Poet's Work is Done, and all the Great
> Events of Time start forth & are conceiv'd in such a Period,
> Within a Moment, a pulsation of the Artery.
>
> (*M* 28:62–29:3)

It is because of such a conception that Blake can see "a World in a Grain of Sand," "a Heaven in a Wild Flower," or hold infinity in the palm of the hand, "And Eternity in an hour."[6]

The imagination acts timelessly in time to redeem the acts of man, to prevent regeneration from being swallowed by generation, and inspiration by memory or a remembrance of things past. It places the outline of identity around the eternal man.

> From every-one of the Four Regions of Human Majesty
> There is an Outside spread Without & an Outside spread Within,
> Beyond the Outline of Identity both ways, which meet in One,
> An orbed Void of doubt, despair, hunger & thirst & sorrow.
>
> (*J* 18:1–4)

The risen man cannot be woven in the looms of Enitharmon because for him appearance is no longer his conception of reality, ego no longer his identity: the "orbed Void," a "Void outside Existence, which if enter'd into / Englobes itself & becomes a Womb" (*J* 1; *M* 41:37–42:1), is opened. "Eternity is in love with the productions of time," writes Blake in the "Proverbs of Hell" (*MHH* 7, K 151): the creative man goes into eternity continually and his goings, a kind of birth-death continuum, are his works of art. For him there is only the creative present, an *opened center*—eternal and infinite.

5. Cf. *J* 31 and the illustration on plate 1. See also, *J* 16 : 61–2, where

> All things acted on Earth are seen in the bright Sculptures of
> Los's Halls, & every Age renews its powers from these Works . . .

Cf. *A Vision of the Last Judgment*, pp. 68–69 in particular: K 605.

6. "Auguries of Innocence," 1–4, K 431.

Bibliography

Because the originals and certain facsimiles of Blake's works are rare and quite valuable, the Blake materials in research libraries and museums are ordinarily accessible only to scholars, by special arrangement. The largest collections of Blake's illuminated books are in the Department of Prints and Drawings, British Museum (London), the Fitzwilliam Museum (Cambridge), the Paul Mellon Collection (in process of being given to the Yale Center for British Art), the Henry E. Huntington Library (San Marino, California), the Pierpont Morgan Library (New York), the Houghton Library, Harvard University, and—the most fully representative of all American collections—the Lessing J. Rosenwald Collection, Library of Congress (until 1979 kept in Jenkintown, Pennsylvania). The only place where many of Blake's pictures are continually on exhibition is the Tate Gallery, London; however, this great collection does not contain complete copies of any of the illuminated books.

In most college libraries the Blake materials are divided between the art and literature sections, with facsimiles and microfilms in special sections. The mass of writings by and about Blake is formidable. It is not hard to answer the question: "What are the best editions of Blake's writings?" But almost all the other basic questions about research on Blake can be answered only in essay-length statements, two of which are especially recommended: The best recent brief guides to all Blake scholarship are by G. E. Bentley, Jr., *William Blake: The Critical Heritage* (London and Boston: Routledge & Kegan Paul, 1975), and by David V. Erdman in *English Poetry: Select Bibliographical Guides*, ed. A. E. Dyson (New York: Oxford, 1971). A more thorough discussion by Northrop Frye, revised by Martin J. Nurmi, is in *The English Romantic Poets and Essayists: A Review of Research and Criticism*, eds. C. W. and L. H. Houtchens (revised edition, New York: New York University, 1966). The standard guide to writings by and about Blake (through 1973) is G. E. Bentley, Jr., *Blake Books: Annotated Catalogues of William Blake's Writings . . . , Reproductions of His Designs, Books With His Engravings, Catalogues, Books He Owned, and Scholarly and Critical Works About Him*, Oxford: Clarendon, 1977. This massive volume largely supersedes earlier, less comprehensive guides edited by Geoffrey Keynes, *A Bibliography of William Blake* (New York: Grolier Club, 1921); Geoffrey Keynes and Edwin Wolf II, *William Blake's Illuminated Books: A Census* (New York: Grolier Club, 1953)—both reprinted, New York: Kraus, 1969—and also G. E. Bentley, Jr. and Martin K. Nurmi, *A Blake Bibliography* (Minneapolis, Minn.: University of Minnesota Press, 1964). Comprehensive reviews of Blake scholarship are published each year in two bibliographies: "The Romantic Movement," which since 1965 has been issued as a supplement to *English Language Notes*, and "The Eighteenth Century," published in *Philological Quarterly*, 1928–74; for 1975 and succeeding years the latter is being issued as a separate annual volume by the American Society for Eighteenth-Century Studies. A compilation of the first thirty-five years of the former was published as *The Romantic Movement Bibliography*: 1936–1970, edited by A. C. Elkins, Jr. and L. J. Forstner, Ann Arbor, Mich.: Pierian Press and R. R. Bowker, 1973. A similar compilation of the first forty-one years of the eighteenth century bibliography was published as *The Eighteenth Century: A Current Bibliography:* 1928–1969, edited by Curt A. Zimansky, Princeton University Press, 1970. In addition, bibliographical lists without reviews have for many years been published annually by *PMLA* and more recently, and irregularly, by *Blake Newsletter*. An annual review of Romantic scholarship appears in *Studies in English Literature*.

Two illustrated journals are devoted exclusively to Blake's work: the quarterly *Blake Newsletter* (1967–77), retitled in 1977 *Blake: An Illustrated Quarterly* and numbered continuously with *Blake Newsletter*; and the biannual *Blake Studies* (1968–). *Blake Newsletter*, numbers 17–18 (1971), contains a finding list by Robert N. Essick of all published reproductions of Blake's art. *Blake Newsletter*, number 33 (1975), consists of Everett Frost's checklist of Blake slides and other reproductions, including posters and postcards, with addresses of all the major collections of Blake's art. Among the other guides published by this quarterly are number 20 (1971), a handlist of the British Museum Collection; number 35 (1975), a handlist of the Lessing J. Rosenwald

Collection of the Library of Congress; number 37 (1976), a survey of Blake materials suitable for instructional purposes, by Mary Lynn Johnson; number 44 (1978) handlists of the Henry E. Huntington Library and Art Gallery by Robert N. Essick and of the Metropolitan Museum of Art, the Boston Museum of Fine Arts, the Fogg Art Museum of Harvard University, and the Victoria and Albert Museum, London, by Morton D. Paley and Michael Davies. A complete catalogue raisonné of Blake's art by Martin Butlin is to be published in 1979 by the Trianon Press for the Blake Trust.

Many books and articles in the following checklist overlap in various ways, but we have listed, where feasible, the most comprehensive recent treatment of major subjects (these in turn refer to important earlier studies). We have tried to represent all the most important schools and movements in Blake studies, though we cannot recommend all the items with equal enthusiasm. If the separate essays in collections (section VI) were itemized, only perhaps three or four from each collection would be included in the selected essays (section VII). Anyone using this guide should remember, however, to check the collections edited by Pinto, Rosenfeld, Erdman and Grant, Curran and Wittrtich, Paley and Phillips, and Essick and Pearce, since these are volumes of original essays rather than reprints, in order not to overlook major essays which we could not cross-list in both section VI and section VII. Some articles on specialized subjects cited in our headnotes and footnotes are not listed again in the bibliography; brief citations in the notes (surname and date) are usually supplemented by a fuller listing in the bibliography.

I. LITERARY WORKS

Editions

The Complete Writings of William Blake, with Variant Readings, ed. Geoffrey Keynes. London: Oxford University Press, 1966. Fourth printing, 1974.

The Letters of William Blake, ed. Geoffrey Keynes. 1956. Revised edition, Cambridge, Mass.: Harvard University Press, 1968.

The Poetry and Prose of William Blake, ed. David V. Erdman, with a commentary by Harold Bloom. Garden City, N.Y.: Doubleday, 1965. Fourth printing, 1970; an amplified complete edition is forthcoming.

The Poems of William Blake, ed. W. H. Stevenson with a text by David V. Erdman. London: Longman, 1971; New York: Norton, 1972.

William Blake's Writings, ed. G. E. Bentley, Jr. Oxford: Clarendon Press, 1978. 2 vols., with numerous illustrations.

Facsimilies of Manuscripts

The Notebook of William Blake: A Photographic and Typographic Facsimile, ed. David V. Erdman and Donald K. Moore. Oxford: Clarendon, 1973. Revised edition, New York: Readex Books, 1977.

The Pickering Manuscript of William Blake, introd. Charles Ryskamp. New York: Pierpont Morgan Library, 1972.

Vala or The Four Zoas: A Facsimile of the Manuscript, A Transcription of The Poem, and a Study of Its Growth and Significance, by G. E. Bentley, Jr. Oxford: Clarendon, 1963.

Reproductions and Facsimiles of Illuminated Books

By far the most successful—but also the most expensive—facsimiles are the hand-colored limited editions produced by the Trianon Press, Paris, under the direction of Arnold Fawcus for the Blake Trust. All eighteen of the illuminated books were published in this series, 1950–1976, some in more than one version; each was edited by Geoffrey Keynes. Other superbly colored Trianon Press volumes of Blake illustrations have also been issued—illustrations to the Bible, 1957; designs for Gray, 1972, designs for Dante, 1978; and others are in prospect, notably the designs for Job. Blake's uncolored illuminated works in this spendid series are *Jerusalem* (1953) and *Gates of Paradise* (1968). The Trianon Press in association with Oxford has also begun to issue fine photographic reproductions in color, with commentaries by Geoffrey Keynes: *Songs of Innocence and Experience* (1967); *Marriage of Heaven and Hell* (1975); *Visions of the Daughters of Albion,* forthcoming. An earlier photographic series in color was published by Dent: *Marriage of Heaven and Hell* (1927); *Urizen* (1929); *Visions of Daughters of Albion* (1932); *Illustrations of Job* (1937). In 1971 Dover issued a colored reproduction of *Songs of Innocence* and the New York Public Library and Brown University Press a colored *Book of Thel.* The American Blake Foundation has begun a series: *America* (uncolored), 1974, *Europe* (uncolored), 1979. A related series, edited by Kay P. and Roger R. Easson, was begun in 1978 with *Milton* and

Urizen in color; six more illuminated books are scheduled for publication in 1979 (Boulder: Shambhala; New York: Random House). Earlier monochrome reproductions include *The Marriage of Heaven and Hell* (1963) and *Urizen* (1966), edited by Clark Emery, University of Miami Press; and *America* (1975) by *Blake Newsletter.*

The following volume is of enormous value for scholars, since it presents good though unexciting likenesses of all Blake's illuminated designs: David V. Erdman. *The Illuminated Blake: All of William Blake's Illuminated Works with a Plate-by-Plate Commentary.* (Garden City, N.Y.: Doubleday-Anchor, 1974; London: Oxford University Press, 1975.)

Fifteen copies of the illuminated books and some other Blake illustrations have been reproduced in color microfilms and slides by E. P. Microform, Wakefield, Yorkshire. Although these often make a splendid impression when projected on a screen, the magnified scale falsifies the impact of Blake's precise art form, which is proportioned for a book that can be held in two hands.

II. ART: COLLECTIONS AND COMMENTARIES

Baker, C. M. Collins and Wark, R. R., eds. *Catalogue of William Blake's Drawings and Engravings in the Huntington Library.* Second Edition. San Marino, Calif., 1957.

Bentley, G. E., Jr. *The Blake Collection of Mrs. Landon K. Thorne,* introduction by Charles Ryskamp. New York: Pierpont Morgan Library, 1971.

Binyon, Laurence. *The Drawings and Engravings of William Blake,* ed. Geoffrey Holme. London: Studio, 1922.

Binyon, Laurence. *The Engraved Designs of William Blake.* London: Ernest Benn, 1926, New York: Da Capo, 1967.

Bindman, David. *William Blake: Catalogue of the Works in the Fitzwilliam Museum.* Cambridge: W. Heffer, 1970.

Bindman, David, *Blake as an Artist.* Oxford: Phaidon; New York: E. P. Dutton, 1977.

Bindman, David. *The Complete Graphic Works of William Blake.* London: Thames and Hudson, 1978.

Blunt, Anthony. *The Art of William Blake.* New York: Columbia, 1959.

Butlin, Martin. *William Blake: A Complete Catalogue of the Works in the Tate Gallery,* Introduction by Anthony Blunt, Foreword by John Rothenstein. Revised edition, London, 1971.

Butlin, Martin. *William Blake.* London: The Tate Gallery, 1978. An exhibition catalogue, with an introductory essay, "The Art of William Blake."

Damon, S. Foster. *Blake's Job: William Blake's Illustrations of the Book of Job.* Providence, R.I.: Brown University Press, 1966.

Easson, Roger R., and Essick, Robert N. *William Blake: Book Illustrator: A Bibliography and Catalogue of the Commercial Engravings.* Vol. I, Normal, Ill.: The American Blake Foundation, 1972. Vol. II, Memphis, Tenn.: The American Blake Foundation, 1979; Vol. III, forthcoming.

Erdman, D. V., Grant, J. E., Rose, E. J., and Tolley, M. J., eds. *William Blake's Designs for Edward Young's Night Thoughts: A Complete Edition.* Oxford: Clarendon, 1979. 2 vols.

Essick, Robert N. and La Belle, Jenijoy, eds. *Night Thoughts or The Complaint and The Consolation.* Illustrated by William Blake. Text by Edward Young. New York: Dover, 1975.

Figgis, Darrell. *The Paintings of William Blake.* London: Ernest Benn, 1925.

Keynes, Geoffrey, ed. *Drawings of William Blake: 92 Pencil Studies.* New York: Dover, 1970. (A selection of two earlier Keynes-edited collections: 1927, 1956).

Keynes, Geoffrey, ed. *William Blake's Engravings.* London: Faber, 1950.

Keynes, Geoffrey. *Engravings by William Blake: The Separate Plates:* A Catalogue Raisonnée. Dublin: Emery Walker, 1956.

Keynes, Geoffrey. Introduction to *The Pilgrim's Progress* by John Bunyan. New York: Limited Editions, 1941.

Keynes, Geoffrey. *William Blake's Water-Colour Designs for the Poems of Thomas Gray.* Chicago: O'Hara, 1972.

Lindberg, Bo. *William Blake's Illustrations to the Book of Job.* Acta Academiae Aboenis, series A, vol. 46. Abo, Finland: Abo Akademi, 1973.

Lister, Raymond. *Infernal Methods: A Study of William Blake's Art Techniques.* London: Bell, 1975.

Paley, Morton D. *William Blake.* Oxford: Phaidon; New York: Dutton, 1978.

Preston, Kerrison, ed. *The Blake Collection of W. Graham Robertson.* London: Faber, 1952.

Roe, Albert S. *Blake's Illustrations to the Divine Comedy.* Princeton: Princeton University Press, 1953.

Tayler, Irene. *Blake's Illustrations to the Poems of Gray*. Princeton: Princeton University Press, 1971.
Todd, Ruthven. *William Blake: The Artist*. London and New York: Studio Vista/Dutton, 1971.
Vaughan, William. *William Blake*. London: Thames and Hudson, 1977.
Wick, Peter, ed. *William Blake: Water-Color Drawings*, introduction by Helen Willard. Boston: Museum of Fine Arts, 1957.

III. REFERENCE WORKS

Bentley, G. E., Jr. *Blake Books: Annotated Catalogues of William Blake's Writings* in Illuminated Printing, in Conventional Typography, and in Manuscript, and Reprints Thereof: Reproductions of his Designs: Books with his Engravings: Catalogues: Books he owned: and Scholarly and Critical Works about him. Oxford: Clarendon, 1977.
Damon, S. Foster. *A Blake Dictionary: The Ideas and Symbols of William Blake*. Second Printing, Providence, R. I.: Brown University Press, 1967.
A Concordance to the Writings of William Blake, edited by David V. Erdman et al., 2 vols. Ithaca: Cornell University Press, 1967.

IV. BIOGRAPHIES

Bentley, G. E., Jr., ed. *Blake Records*. Oxford: Clarendon, 1969
Gilchrist, Alexander. *Life of William Blake*. 1863, 1880; reprint edition, Ruthven Todd, ed., London: Dent, 1942; revised 1945.
Margoliouth, H. M. *William Blake*. London: Oxford, 1951.
Wilson, Mona. *The Life of William Blake*. 1927; revised by Geoffrey Keynes, Oxford, 1971.

V. BOOKS OF CRITICISM

Adams, Hazard. *William Blake: A Reading of the Shorter Poems*. Seattle: University of Washington Press, 1963.
Altizer, Thomas J. J. *The New Apocalypse: The Radical Christian Vision of William Blake*. East Lansing: Michigan State University Press, 1967.
Ault, Donald. *Visionary Physics: Blake's Response to Newton*. Chicago and London: University of Chicago Press, 1974.
Bloom, Harold. *Blake's Apocalypse*. 1963. Revised, Ithaca and London: Cornell University Press, 1970.
Bronowski, J. *William Blake and the Age of Revolution*. 1943. Revised, with this title, New York: Harper & Row, 1965.
Damon, S. Foster. *William Blake: His Philosophy and Symbols*. Boston: Houghton Mifflin, 1924. Reprint edition, Gloucester, Mass.: Peter Smith, 1958.
Digby, George Wingfield. *Symbol and Image in William Blake*. Oxford: Clarendon, 1957.
Erdman, David V. *Blake: Prophet Against Empire: A Poet's Interpretation of the History of His Own Times*. Princeton, N.J.: Princeton University Press, 1954. Revised edition, 1969. Third edition, 1977.
Fisher, Peter F. *The Valley of Vision: Blake as Prophet and Revolutionary*, ed. Northrop Frye. Toronto: University of Toronto Press, 1961.
Frosch, Thomas R. *The Awakening of Albion: The Renovation of the Body in the Poetry of William Blake*. Ithaca and London: Cornell University Press, 1974.
Frye, Northrop. *Fearful Symmetry: A Study of William Blake*. Princeton, N.J.: Princeton University Press, 1947, 1968.
Gleckner, Robert. *The Piper and the Bard: A Study of William Blake*. Detroit: Wayne State University Press, 1959.
Keynes, Geoffrey. *William Blake: Poet, Printer, Prophet: A Study of the Illuminated Books*. New York: Orion, 1964.
Keynes, Geoffrey. *Blake Studies: Essays on His Life and Work*. Second edition. Oxford: Clarendon, 1971.
Klonsky, Milton. *William Blake: The Seer and His Visions*. London: Orbis; New York: Harmony Books, 1977.
Mitchell, W. J. T. *Blake's Composite Art: A Study of the Illuminated Poetry*. Princeton: Princeton University Press, 1978.
Murry, John Middleton. *William Blake*. 1933; New York: McGraw-Hill, 1964.
Nurmi, Martin K. *William Blake*. London: Hutchinson, 1975.
Ostricker, Alicia. *Vision and Verse in William Blake*. Madison, Wis.; University of Wisconsin Press, 1965.
Paley, Morton D. *Energy and the Imagination: A Study of the Development of Blake's Thought*. Oxford: Clarendon, 1970.
Percival, Milton O. *William Blake's Circle of Destiny*. New York: Columbia University Press, 1938; Octagon, 1964.

Raine, Kathleen. *Blake and Tradition.* The A. W. Mellon Lectures in the Fine Arts. 1962. Bollingen Series XXV. ii. 2 vols. Princeton, N.J.: Princeton University Press, 1968.

Schorer, Mark. *William Blake: The Politics of Vision.* New York: Henry Holt, 1946. Abridged edition, New York: Anchor, 1959.

Wicksteed, Joseph H. *Blake's Innocence and Experience: A Study of the Songs and Manuscripts.* London: Dent, 1928.

Wilkie, Brian and Johnson, Mary Lynn. *Blake's "Four Zoas": The Design of a Dream.* Cambridge, Mass.: Harvard University Press, 1978.

Wittreich, Joseph Anthony Jr. *Angel of Apocalypse: Blake's Idea of Milton.* Madison, Wis.; University of Wisconsin Press, 1975.

VI. COLLECTIONS OF ESSAYS

Bentley, G. E., Jr., ed. *William Blake: The Critical Heritage.* London and Boston: Routledge and Kegan Paul, 1975.

Bottrall, Margaret, ed. *William Blake: Songs of Innocence and Experience: A Casebook.* London: Macmillan, 1970.

Curran, Stuart, and Wittreich, Joseph Anthony, Jr., eds. *Blake's Sublime Allegory: Essays on The Four Zoas, Milton, and Jerusalem.* Madison, Wis.: University of Wisconsin Press, 1973.

Erdman, David V., and Grant, John E., eds. *Blake's Visionary Forms Dramatic.* Princeton, N.J.: Princeton University Press, 1970.

Essick, Robert N., ed. *The Visionary Hand: Essays for The Study of William Blake's Art and Aesthetics.* Los Angeles: Hennessey and Ingalls, 1973.

Essick, Robert N. and Pearce, Donald, eds. *Blake in His Time.* Bloomington and London: Indiana University Press, 1978.

Frye, Northrop, ed. *Blake: A Collection of Critical Essays.* Twentieth Century Views Series. Englewood Cliffs, N.J.: Prentice-Hall, 1966.

Grant, John E., ed. *Discussions of William Blake.* Boston: Heath, 1961.

Paley, Morton D., ed. *Twentieth Century Interpretations of Songs of Innocence and of Experience.* Englewood Cliffs, N.J.: Prentice-Hall, 1969.

Paley, Morton D., and Phillips, Michael, eds. *William Blake: Essays in Honour of Sir Geoffrey Keynes.* Oxford: Clarendon, 1973.

Pinto, Vivian De Sola, ed. *The Divine Vision: Studies in the Poetry and Art of William Blake.* London: Victor Gollancz, 1957.

Rosenfeld, Alvin, ed. *William Blake: Essays for S. Foster Damon.* Providence, R.I.: Brown University Press, 1969.

Weathers, Winston, ed. *William Blake: The Tyger.* The Merrill Literary Casebook Series. Columbus, Ohio: Charles E. Merrill, 1969.

VII. SELECTED ESSAYS

Adams, Hazard. "Blake, *Jerusalem,* and Symbolic Form." *Blake Studies* 7 (1975), 143–166.

Behrendt, Stephen C. "Blake's Illustrations to Milton's *Nativity Ode.*" *Philological Quarterly* 55 (1976), 65–95.

Brisman, Leslie. "Re: Generation in Blake." In *Romantic Origins.* Ithaca and London: Cornell University Press, 1978.

Brower, Reuben Arthur. "The Beautiful Gate of Enjoyment," in *Fields of Light: An Experiment in Critical Reading.* New York: Oxford, 1951, pp. 3–16.

Eaves, Morris. "Blake and the Artistic Machine: An Essay on Decorum and Technology." *PMLA* 92 (1977), 903–927.

Essick, Robert N. "Blake's Newton." *Blake Studies* 3 (1971), 149–162.

Essick, Robert N. "Blake and the Traditions of Reproductive Engraving." *Blake Studies* 5 (1972), 59–103.

Fisher, Peter F. "Blake's Attacks on the Classical Tradition." *Philological Quarterly* 40 (1961), 1–18.

Frye, Northrop. "The Road of Excess" and "The Keys to the Gates," *The Stubborn Structure: Essays on Criticism and Society.* Ithaca: Cornell University Press, 1970, pp. 160–74; 175–99.

Gleckner, Robert F. "William Blake and the Human Abstract." *PMLA* 76 (1961), 373–79.

Gleckner, Robert F. "Blake's Seasons." *Studies in English Literature* 5 (1965), 533–51.

Gleckner, Robert F. "Blake and the Senses." *Studies in Romanticism* 5 (1965), 1–15.

Grant, John E. "Apocalypse in Blake's 'Auguries of Innocence.'" *Texas Studies in Literature and Language* 5 (1964), 489–508.

Grant, John E. "The Fate of Blake's Sun-Flower: A Forecast and Some Conclusions." *Blake Studies* 5 (1974), 7–64.

Grant, John E., and Brown, Robert E. "Blake's Vision of Spenser's *Faerie Queene:* A Report and an Anatomy." *Blake Newsletter* 31:8 (1975), 56–85.

Hagstrum, Jean H. "Blake's Blake." *Essays in History and Literature*, ed. Heinz Bluhm. Chicago: The Newberry Library, 1963, pp. 169–78.

Hagstrum, Jean H. "The Wrath of the Lamb: A Study of William Blake's Conversions." *From Sensibility to Romanticism*, eds. F. W. Hilles and H. Bloom. New York: Oxford, 1965, pp. 311–30.

Jakobson, Roman. "On the Verbal Art of William Blake and Other Poet-Painters." *Linguistic Inquiry* 1 (1970), 3–23.

Johnson, Mary Lynn. "Beulah, 'Mne Seraphim,' and Blake's *Thel.*" *JEGP* 69 (1970), 258–78.

Johnson, Mary Lynn. "Emblem and Symbol in Blake." *Huntington Library Quarterly* 37 (1974), 151–70.

Mitchell, W. J. T. "Style and Iconography in the Illustrations of Blake's *Milton.*" *Blake Studies* 6 (1973), 47–71.

Pevsner, Nikolaus. "Blake and the Flaming Line." In *The Englishness of English Art*. London: Architectural Press, 1956; Penguin, 1964, pp. 128–56.

Pointon, Marcia I. "William Blake and Milton." In *Milton and English Art*. Manchester, 1970, pp. 135–73.

Rose, Edward J. " 'Mental Forms Creating': Fourfold Vision and the Poet as Prophet in Blake's Design and Verse." *Journal of Aesthetics and Art Criticism* 23 (1964), 173–83.

Rose, Edward J. "Blake's Metaphorical States." *Blake Studies* 4 (1971), 9–31.

Rose, Edward J. "The Spirit of the Bounding Line: Blake's Los." *Criticism* 13 (1971), 54–76.

Wittreich, Joseph Anthony, Jr. "William Blake: Illustrator-Interpreter of *Paradise Regained,*" and "Appendix A: Illustrators of *Paradise Regained* and Their Subjects" (1713–1816). In *Calm of Mind: Tercentenary Essays on Paradise Regained and Samson Agonistes*, ed. Joseph Anthony Wittreich. Cleveland: Case Western Reserve Press, 1971.

Yeats, W. B. "William Blake and His Illustrations to the *Divine Comedy*" (1903), in *Essays and Introductions*. New York: Macmillan, 1961, pp. 116–45.

Index of Titles and First Lines

"A crowned king," 394
"A flower was offerd to me," 49
"A little black thing among the snow," 46
"A Wall of Canvas or Wood . . . ," 398
"A Woman Scaly & a Man all Hairy," 190
"Abstinence sows sand all over," 189
"Adam!" / "I will not hear thee more thou Spiritual Voice," 360
Advice of the Popes who succeeded the Age of Rafael, 438
Africa, 135
"After my three years' slumber . . . ," 311
Ah! Sun-flower, 51
"Ah Sun-flower! weary of time," 51
Ahania, The Book of, 160
"All Bibles or sacred codes . . . ," 87
All Religions are One, 12
"All the night in woe," 44
America: A Prophecy, 102
"An Angel came to me . . . ," 95
"An old maid early eer I knew," 193
An ancient Proverb, 185
"And did those feet in ancient time," 238
"And in Melodious Accents I," 422
The Angel, 49
"Anger & Wrath my bosom rends," 187
An answer to the parson, 182
"Are not the joys of morning sweeter," 191
"As a new heaven is begun . . . ," 86
"As I walked forth one May morning," 387
"As I was walking among the fires . . . ," 88
"As the true method of knowledge . . . ," 13
Asia, 137
Auguries of Innocence, 209
"Awake awake my little Boy," 205

Bacon's *Essays*, Marginalia on, 437
Berkeley's *Siris*, Marginalia on, 444
The Birds, 197
Blake, James, letter to, 462
Blakes apology for his Catalogue, 199
Blake's Memorandum, 470

The Blossom, 25
The Book of Ahania, 160
The Book of Los, 168
The Book of Thel, 60
The Book of Urizen, 140
Boyd's *Historical Notes on Dante*, Marginalia on, 438
Butts, Thomas, letters to, 453, 454, 456, 459, 460, 465, 467

"Call that the Public Voice which is their Error," 420
"Can I see another's woe," 36
"Children of the future Age," 57
The Chimney Sweeper (Experience), 46
The Chimney Sweeper (Innocence), 25
The Clod & the Pebble, 42
"Come hither my boy tell me what thou seest there," 187
"Come hither my sparrows," 191
A Cradle Song (Innocence), 28
A cradle song (Notebook), 194
"Cruelty has a Human Heart," 60
The Crystal Cabinet, 207
Cumberland, George, letters to, 450, 477

Dante, Marginalia on, 438
"Daughters of Beulah! Muses who inspire the Poet's Song," 239
Day, 189
"Dear Mother, dear Mother, the Church is cold," 52
"Degrade first the Arts if you'd Mankind degrade," 438
A Descriptive Catalogue, 398
A Divine Image (Experience), 60
The Divine Image (Innocence), 30
"Does the Eagle know what is in the pit?" 61
A Dream, 36
"Dryden in Rhyme cries . . . ," 419

"Each Man is in his Spectre's power," 329
"Earth rais'd up her head," 41
Earth's Answer, 41
The Ecchoing Green, 20
"England! awake! awake! awake!," 348
English Encouragement of Art, 200
"Eno, aged Mother," 168
"Enslav'd, the Daughters of Albion weep . . . ," 68
Eternity, 183
Europe: A Prophecy, 121
The Everlasting Gospel, 364
"Every Poem must necessarily be . . . ," 428
Exhibition of Paintings in Fresco . . . , 398
Experience, Songs of, 40
[Experiment], 182

"Fa ra so bo ro," 388
The Fairy, 191
"Father, father, where are you going," 26
"Five windows light the cavern'd Man . . . ," 121
Flaxman, John, letter to, 451
The Fly, 48
The Four Zoas, 214
"Fresh from the Dewy hill, the merry year," 7
"Fuzon, on a chariot iron-wing'd," 160

The Garden of Love, 51
The Ghost of Abel, 359
The Golden Net, 202
"Great Men & Fools do often me Inspire," 186
"Great things are done when Men & Mountains meet," 188
The Grey Monk, 208
"Grown old in Love from Seven till Seven times Seven," 194

"Hail Matrimony made of Love," 388
"Having given great offence by writing in Prose," 199
Hayley, William, letters to, 452, 472, 473, 475
"He never can be a Friend to the Human Race . . . ," 331
"He who binds to himself a joy," 183
"Hear the voice of the Bard!," 40
"Hear then the pride & knowledge of a Sailor," 384
"Her whole Life is an Epigram smack smooth & neatly pend," 187
Holy Thursday (Experience), 42
Holy Thursday (Innocence), 32
"Honour & Genius is all I ask," 379
"How do you know but ev'ry Bird that cuts the airy way," 88
"How sweet I roam'd from field to field," 4
"How sweet is the Shepherd's sweet lot," 20
How to know Love from Deceit, 190
The Human Abstract, 53

"I am no Homers Hero you all know," 187
"I asked a thief to steal me a peach," 193
"I bless thee, O Father of Heaven & Earth, that ever I saw Flaxman's face," 452
"I cry my matches as far as Guild hall," 387
" 'I die, I die,' the Mother said," 208
"I Dreamt a Dream! what can it mean?," 49
"I feard the fury of my wind," 192
"I give you the end of a golden string," 345
"I have no name," 35
"I heard an Angel singing," 187
"I laid me down upon a bank," 193
"I love the jocund dance," 5
"I love to rise in a summer morn," 59

"I loved Theotormon," 68
"I rose up at the dawn of day," 199
"I saw a chapel all of gold," 192
"I saw a Monk of Charlemaine," 332
"I stood among my valleys of the south," 347
"I traveld thro' a Land of Men," 202
"I walked abroad in a snowy day," 193
"I wander thro' each charter'd street," 53
"I was angry with my friend,"55
"I was in a Printing house . . . ," 94
"I washd them out & washd them in," 194
"I went to the Garden of Love," 51
"I will sing you a song of Los, the Eternal Prophet," 135
"I will tell you what Joseph of Arimathea," 185
"I wonder whether the Girls are mad," 212
"If Moral Virtue was Christianity," 364
"If it is True What the Prophets write," 184
"If Men of weak Capacities . . . ," 417
"If you have formd a Circle to go into," 183
"If you mean to Please Every body you will," 200
"If you trap the moment before its ripe," 183
"In a wife I would desire," 190
"In futurity," 43
"In Heaven the only Art," 349
"In seed time learn, in harvest teach, in winter enjoy," 89
"In the Moon, is a certain Island . . . ," 374
Infant Joy, 35
Infant Sorrow, 54
Innocence, Songs of, 19
Introduction (Experience), 40
Introduction (Innocence), 19
The Invention of a Portable Fresco, 398
"Is this a holy thing to see," 42
An Island in the Moon, 374

Jerusalem, 311
Jerusalem the Emanation of the Giant Albion!," 320
"Justice hath heaved a sword . . . ," 9

Lacedemonian Instruction, 187
The Lamb, 21
The Land of Dreams, 205
The Laocoön, 425
The Last Judgment, A Vision of, 408
Laughing Song, 27
Lavater's *Aphorisms on Man*, Marginalia on, 430
"Leave O leave me to my sorrows," 393
"Let the Brothels of Paris be opened," 186
Letters, 448ff

The Lilly, 51
The Little Black Boy, 22
The Little Boy Found, 27
A Little Boy Lost (Experience), 56
The Little Boy Lost (Innocence), 26
"Little Fly," 48
The Little Girl Found, 44
A Little Girl Lost, 57
The Little Girl Lost, 43
"Little Lamb who made thee," 21
"Little Mary Bell had a Fairy in a Nut," 212
"Little Phebus came strutting in," 378
The Little Vagabond, 52
"Lo, a shadow of horror is risen," 142
"Lo the Bat with Leathern wing," 386
London, 53
Long John Brown & Little Mary Bell, 212
Los, The Book of, 168
Los, The Song of, 134
"Love and harmony combine," 5
"Love seeketh not Itself to please," 42
"Love to faults is always blind," 190

Mad Song, 6
"Madman I have been calld Fool they call thee," 200
"Man has no notion of moral fitness . . . ," 14
"Man's perceptions are not bounded . . . ," 15
Marginalia, 429ff
The Marriage of Heaven and Hell, 81
Mary, 206
A Memorable Fancy, 88, 92, 94, 95, 99
Memorandum, Blake's, 470
"Memory, hither come," 6
The Mental Traveller, 202
Merlins prophecy, 185
"Merry Merry Sparrow," 25
Milton, 234
"Mock on Mock on Voltaire Rousseau," 184
Morning, 189
Motto to the Songs of Innocence & of Experience, 187
"My mother bore me in the southern wild," 22
"My mother groand! my father wept," 54
My Pretty Rose Tree, 50
"My silks and fine array," 4
"My Spectre around me night & day," 195

"Never pain to tell thy love," 192
Night, 33
"Nought loves another as itself," 56

"Now Art has lost its mental Charms," 197
Nurse's Song (Experience), 47
Nurse's Song (Innocence), 35

"O Autumn, laden with fruit, and stained," 2
"O father father where are you going," 392
"O For a voice like thunder, and a tongue," 9
"O holy virgin! clad in purest white," 4
"O I say you Joe," 392
"O lapwing thou fliest around the heath," 182
"O Rose thou art sick," 47
"O thou, who passest thro' our vallies in," 2
"O thou, with dewy locks, who lookest down," 2
"O why was I born with a different face," 469
"O Winter! bar thine adamantine doors," 3
"Oer my Sins Thou sit and moan," 196
Of the Measure, in which the following Poem is written, 312
"Of the primeval Priest's assum'd power," 140
"Of the Sleep of Ulro! and of the passage through," 313
On Another's Sorrow, 36
On Homer's Poetry, 428
On Virgil, 428
"Once a dream did weave a shade," 36
"Once I saw a Devil in a flame," 99

"Phebe drest like beauties Queen," 386
The Pickering Manuscript, 200
"Piping down the valleys wild," 19
"Pity would be no more," 53
Poetical Sketches, 1
A Poison Tree, 55
"Prepare, prepare, the iron helm of war," 10
Prologue . . . for . . . King Edward IV, 9
Prologue to King John, 9
Prospectus: To the Public, 395
Proverbs of Hell, 89
Public Address to the Chalcographic Society, 417

"Rafael—Sublime, Majestic, Graceful, Wise—," 418
"Reader! lover of books! lover of heaven," 312
"Remove away that blackning church," 185
Reynolds's *Works*, Marginalia on, 438
Riches, 183
"Rintrah roars & shakes his fires in the burdend air," 81

"Sacred Truth has pronounced . . . ," 428
The School Boy, 59
The Shepherd, 20
The Sick Rose, 47
"Silent Silent Night," 191

"Sleep Sleep beauty bright," 194
The Smile, 201
"Soft deceit & Idleness," 199
Soft Snow, 193
"Some look to see the sweet Outlines," 439
"Some Men created for destruction come," 184
Song, 4, 5, 6, 7, 8
Song by an Old Shepherd, 11
Song by a Shepherd, 11
A Song of Liberty, 101
The Song of Los, 134
Songs of Experience, 38
Songs of Innocence, 19
Songs of Innocence and of Experience, 15
"Sound the Flute," 34
Spring, 34
Spring, To, 1
Summer, To, 2
Swedenborg's *Wisdom of Angels*, Marginalia on, 431
"Sweet dreams form a shade," 28
"Sweet Mary the first time she ever was there," 206

"Terror in the house does roar," 188
"The Angel that presided oer my birth," 187
"The Caverns of the Grave Ive seen," 198
"The countless gold of a merry heart," 183
"The daughters of Mne Seraphim led round their sunny flocks," 60
"The deep of winter came," 126
"The Door of Death is made of Gold," 198
"The Errors of a Wise Man make your Rule," 187
"The Eternal Female groand! it was heard over all the Earth," 101
"The fields from Islington to Marybone," 321
"The Good are attracted by Mens perceptions," 187
"The Guardian Prince of Albion burns in his nightly tent," 110
"The harvest shall flourish in wintry weather," 185
"The Hebrew Nation did not write it," 184
"The Kings of Asia heard," 137
"The Labours of the Artist . . . ," 395
"The Last Judgement: when all those are Cast . . . ," 409
"The little boy lost in the lonely fen," 27
"The look of love alarms," 191
"The Maiden caught me in the Wild," 207
"The modest Rose puts forth a thorn," 51
"The nameless shadowy female rose from out the breast of Orc," 124
"The only Man that eer I knew," 200
"The Prophets Isaiah and Ezekiel . . . ," 92
"The shadowy daughter of Urthona stood before red Orc," 107
"The Song of the Aged Mother . . . ," 214

"The Stolen and Perverted Writings . . . ," 234
"The Sun arises in the East," 189
"The sun descending in the west," 33
"The Sun does arise," 20
"The sword sung on the barren heath," 185
"The Vision of Christ that thou dost see," 369
"The wild winds weep," 6
Thel, The Book of, 60
Thel's Motto, 60
There is not one moral virtue, 364
"There is a Smile of Love," 201
"There is a Void, outside of Existence, which if enterd into," 311n
There is No Natural Religion, 14, 15
"There's Doctor Clash," 393
"This city & this country has brought forth many mayors," 390
"This frog he would a wooing ride," 388
Thornton's *The Lord's Prayer*, Marginalia on, 446
"Thou fair-hair'd angel of the evening, 4
"Thou hast a lap full of seed," 182
"Three Virgins at the break of day," 202
"To a lovely mirtle bound," 194
To Autumn, 2
"To be or not to be," 374
"To find the Western path," 189
To God, 183
To Lord Byron in the Wilderness, 359
"To Mercy Pity Peace and Love," 30
To Mrs Butts, 456
To Morning, 4
To My Dearest Friend, John Flaxman, these lines, 452
"To my Friend Butts I write," 454
To my Mirtle, 194
To Nobodaddy, 183
"To see a World in a Grain of Sand," 209
To Spring, 1
To Summer, 2
To The Accuser who is The God of This World, 373
To the Deists, 331
To the Christians, 345
To the Evening Star, 4
To the Jews, 320
To the Muses, 10
To the Public (Jerusalem), 311
To the Public (Prospectus), 395
To the Queen, 198
To Tirzah, 58
To Winter, 3
"Truly My Satan thou art but a Dunce," 373

Trusler, letter to, 448
"Twas on a Holy Thursday their innocent faces clean," 42
The Tyger, 49
"Tyger Tyger, burning bright," 49

"Upon a holy thursday their innocent faces clean," 391
Urizen, The Book of, 140

Vala (The Four Zoas), 214
The Vision of Christ that thou dost see, 372
A Vision of the Last Judgment, 408
Visions of the Daughters of Albion, 68
The Voice of the Ancient Bard, 60
The voice of the Devil, 87

"Want Matches," 387
A War Song to Englishmen, 10
"Was Jesus Born of a Virgin Pure," 366
"Was Jesus Chaste or did he," 369
"Was Jesus gentle or did he," 368
"Was Jesus Humble or did he," 366
The Washer Womans Song, 194
Watson's *Apology*, Marginalia on, 432
"We are told to abstain from fleshly desires . . . ," 345
"Welcome, stranger, to this place," 11
"What can this Gospel of Jesus be?," 365
"What doest thou here Elijah?," 360
"What is it men in women do require," 189
"Whate'er is Born of Mortal Birth, 58
"When a Man has Married a Wife," 190
"When early morn walks forth in sober grey," 8
"When Klopstock England defied," 188
"When my mother died I was very young," 25
"When Nations grow Old, The Arts grow Cold," 441
"When old corruption first begun," 382
"When silver snow decks Sylvio's clothes," 11
"When the green woods laugh, with the voice of joy," 27
"When the tongues of children are heard on the green," 392
"When the voices of children are heard on the green" (Experience), 47
"When the voices of children are heard on the green" (Innocence), 35
"When this Verse was first dictated . . . ," 313
"Where thou dwellest in what Grove," 197
"Whether on Ida's shady brow," 8
"Who will exchange his own fire side," 186
"Why art thou silent & invisible," 183
"Why of the sheep do you not learn peace," 182
"Why should I be bound to thee," 194

"Why should I care for the men of thames," 185
"Why was Cupid a Boy," 190
"Wife of the Friend of those I most revere," 456
William Bond, 212
"With happiness stretchd across the hills," 460
Wordsworth's *Poems*, Marginalia on, 446
Wordsworth's Preface to *The Excursion*, Marginalia on, 445

"You dont believe I wont attempt to make ye," 184
"Youth of delight come hither," 60

NORTON CRITICAL EDITIONS

AUSTEN *Emma* edited by Stephen M. Parrish
AUSTEN *Pride and Prejudice* edited by Donald J. Gray
Beowulf (the Donaldson translation) edited by Joseph M. Tuso
Blake's Poetry and Designs selected and edited by Mary Lynn Johnson and John E. Grant
BOCCACCIO *The Decameron* selected, translated, and edited by Mark Musa and Peter E. Bondanella
BRONTË, CHARLOTTE *Jane Eyre* edited by Richard J. Dunn
BRONTË, EMILY *Wuthering Heights* edited by William M. Sale, Jr. *Second Edition*
Robert Browning's Poetry selected and edited by James F. Loucks
Byron's Poetry selected and edited by Frank D. McConnell
CARROLL *Alice in Wonderland* selected and edited by Donald J. Gray
Anton Checkhov's Plays translated and edited by Eugene K. Bristow
Anton Checkhov's Short Stories selected and edited by Ralph E. Matlaw
CHOPIN *The Awakening* edited by Margaret Culley
CLEMENS *Adventures of Huckleberry Finn* edited by Sculley Bradley, Richmond Croom Beatty, E. Hudson Long, and Thomas Cooley *Second Edition*
CONRAD *Heart of Darkness* edited by Robert Kimbrough *Revised Edition*
CONRAD *Lord Jim* edited by Thomas Moser
CONRAD *The Nigger of the "Narcissus"* edited by Robert Kimbrough
CRANE *Maggie: A Girl of the Streets* edited by Thomas A. Gullason
CRANE *The Red Badge of Courage* edited by Sculley Bradley, Richmond Croom Beatty, E. Hudson Long, and Donald Pizer *Second Edition*
Darwin edited by Philip Appleman
DEFOE *Moll Flanders* edited by Edward Kelly
DEFOE *Robinson Crusoe* edited by Michael Shinagel
DICKENS *Bleak House* edited by George Ford and Sylvère Monod
DICKENS *Hard Times* edited by George Ford and Sylvère Monod
John Donne's Poetry selected and edited by A. L. Clements
DOSTOEVSKY *Crime and Punishment* (the Coulson translation) edited by George Gibian *Second Edition*
DOSTOEVSKY *The Brothers Karamazov* (the Garnett translation revised by Ralph E. Matlaw) edited by Ralph E. Matlaw
DREISER *Sister Carrie* edited by Donald Pizer
ELIOT *Middlemarch* edited by Bert G. Hornback
FIELDING *Tom Jones* edited by Sheridan Baker
FLAUBERT *Madame Bovary* edited with a substantially new translation by Paul de Man
GOETHE *Faust* translated by Walter Arndt and edited by Cyrus Hamlin
HARDY *Jude the Obscure* edited by Norman Page
HARDY *The Mayor of Casterbridge* edited by James K. Robinson
HARDY *The Return of the Native* edited by James Gindin
HARDY *Tess of the d'Urbervilles* edited by Scott Elledge *Second Edition*
HAWTHORNE *The Blithedale Romance* edited by Seymour Gross and Rosalie Murphy
HAWTHORNE *The House of the Seven Gables* edited by Seymour Gross
HAWTHORNE *The Scarlet Letter* edited by Sculley Bradley, Richmond Croom Beatty, E. Hudson Long, and Seymour Gross *Second Edition*
George Herbert and the Seventeenth-Century Religious Poets selected and edited by Mario A. Di Cesare

HOMER *The Odyssey* translated and edited by Albert Cook
IBSEN *The Wild Duck* translated and edited by Dounia B. Christiani
JAMES *The Ambassadors* edited by S. P. Rosenbaum
JAMES *The American* edited by James A. Tuttleton
JAMES *The Portrait of a Lady* edited by Robert D. Bamberg
JAMES *The Turn of the Screw* edited by Robert Kimbrough
JAMES *The Wings of the Dove* edited by J. Donald Crowley and Richard A. Hocks
Ben Jonson and the Cavalier Poets selected and edited by Hugh Maclean
Ben Jonson's Plays and Masques selected and edited by Robert M. Adams
MACHIAVELLI *The Prince* translated and edited by Robert M. Adams
MALTHUS *An Essay on the Principle of Population* edited by Philip Appleman
MELVILLE *The Confidence-Man* edited by Hershel Parker
MELVILLE *Moby-Dick* edited by Harrison Hayford and Hershel Parker
MEREDITH *The Egoist* edited by Robert M. Adams
MILL *On Liberty* edited by David Spitz
MILTON *Paradise Lost* edited by Scott Elledge
MORE *Utopia* translated and edited by Robert M. Adams
NEWMAN *Apologia Pro Vita Sua* edited by David J. DeLaura
NORRIS *McTeague* edited by Donald Pizer
Adrienne Rich's Poetry selected and edited by Barbara Charlesworth Gelpi and Albert Gelpi
The Writings of St. Paul edited by Wayne A. Meeks
SHAKESPEARE *Hamlet* edited by Cyrus Hoy
SHAKESPEARE *Henry IV, Part I* edited by James J. Sanderson *Second Edition*
Bernard Shaw's Plays selected and edited by Warren Sylvester Smith
Shelley's Poetry and Prose edited by Donald H. Reiman and Sharon B. Powers
SOPHOCLES *Oedipus Tyrannus* translated and edited by Luci Berkowitz and Theodore F. Brunner
SPENSER *Edmund Spenser's Poetry* selected and edited by Hugh Maclean
STENDHAL *Red and Black* translated and edited by Robert M. Adams
STERNE *Tristram Shandy* edited by Howard Anderson
SWIFT *Gulliver's Travels* edited by Robert A. Greenberg *Revised Edition*
The Writings of Jonathan Swift edited by Robert A. Greenberg and William B. Piper
TENNYSON *In Memoriam* edited by Robert Ross
Tennyson's Poetry selected and edited by Robert W. Hill, Jr.
THOREAU *Walden and Civil Disobedience* edited by Owen Thomas
TOLSTOY *Anna Karenina* (the Maude translation) edited by George Gibian
TOLSTOY *War and Peace* (the Maude translation) edited by George Gibian
TURGENEV *Fathers and Sons* edited with a substantially new translation by Ralph E. Matlaw
VOLTAIRE *Candide* translated and edited by Robert M. Adams
WHITMAN *Leaves of Grass* edited by Sculley Bradley and Harold W. Blodgett
WOLLSTONECRAFT *A Vindication of the Rights of Woman* edited by Carol H. Poston
WORDSWORTH *The Prelude: 1799, 1805, 1850* edited by Jonathan Wordsworth, M. H. Abrams, and Stephen Gill
Middle English Lyrics selected and edited by Maxwell S. Luria and Richard L. Hoffman
Modern Drama edited by Anthony Caputi
Restoration and Eighteenth-Century Comedy edited by Scott McMillin